REVISED EDITION

CONSTITUTIONAL GOVERNMENT AND DEMOCRACY

Theory and Practice in Europe and America

By

CARL J. FRIEDRICH

Professor of Government, Harvard University

GINN AND COMPANY

BOSTON · NEW YORK · CHICAGO · ATLANTA · DALLAS · COLUMBUS
SAN FRANCISCO · TORONTO · LONDON

THIS BOOK IS A REVISED EDITION OF THE AUTHOR'S
CONSTITUTIONAL GOVERNMENT AND DEMOCRACY
PREVIOUSLY PUBLISHED AS
CONSTITUTIONAL GOVERNMENT AND POLITICS

To

LENORE

Preface to the Revised Edition

The Fascists have been vanquished and the capacity of constitutional democracy has been once more demonstrated in striking fashion. Yet as this revised edition of *Constitutional Government and Democracy* goes to press the future seems as uncertain as it did nine years ago, before the United States entered the Second World War. The "unnecessary war," Winston Churchill has called it. But was it unnecessary? Churchill meant that adequate precautions would have given sufficient warning to Hitler, who was encouraged by a policy of appeasement and vacillation. But how were such precautions to be secured? The failure of the United States and Great Britain to adopt any satisfactory safeguards is no doubt a serious indictment of their constitutional systems, not to speak of the systems of France and other European countries. In some ways it is perhaps as serious an indictment as that of the Weimar Republic when it allowed itself to be overthrown by Hitler. Yet is it not asking too much of a free people that they should calmly envisage the prospect of war? Is it not necessarily the chosen few of exceptional insight who will be prepared to travel so perilous a road?

There would be little need now of recalling these problems, already clearly defined in 1941, were it not for the fact of the conflict between "East and West," that sharp antagonism which has arisen between the United States, Great Britain, France, and their friends on one hand and the Soviet Union and her associates on the other. This conflict is once again a conflict of ideas concerning government, economics, and the good life, but more especially concerning constitutionalism. For while both parties to the global antithesis proclaim themselves champions of "democracy"—both making it amply clear that they do not mean what the others mean—it is only the Western powers who insist upon constitutionalism. More especially the basic rights of human beings are central to the Western position—their right to live without fear of arbitrary arrest and punishment, their right to express themselves freely in accordance with their convictions, and finally their right to work and to enjoy the fruits of their labor. But it is a position which is more easily stated in general terms than applied in concrete and actual politics. Not only are there limits beyond which no community can allow such rights and freedoms to go lest it invite anarchy, but the willingness to condone a lack of agreement on all fundamentals, except on these basic procedures of the democratic process itself, entails risks which may prove fatal in the face of a determined and totalitarian opponent.

In short, the assessment of constitutional democracy in all its ramified manifestations, theoretical and practical, has lost none of its urgency of ten years ago. Continued critical re-examination in the light of new facts and deeper insight, of broader experience and a sharpened sense of values, is indeed of the essence in the co-operative process upon which constitutional democracy depends for its success. In revising the earlier edition, an effort has been made to live up to this task of critical scholarship. While the basic approach remains, the varied experiences of the past ten years provide numerous occasions for revision of detail, as well as for some major additions. Two entirely new chapters have been added, one on problems of local government, the other on socialization and planning, and half a chapter has been added to the discussion of constitutional dictatorship to outline the hitherto neglected problems of military government. My experience in the intervening years, as well as a number of studies and inquiries, had convinced me that a consideration of constitutional democracy without attention to "grass-roots democracy" must remain incomplete. My work and studies in the field of propaganda and public opinion, and more especially of the control of radio broadcasting, as well as my experience in the teaching and practice of military government, all pointed toward this conclusion. On the other hand, no one who considers the shape of constitutional development in postwar Europe can help realizing that socialization and planning are becoming, for better or for worse, established features of constitutional democracy. And in spite of American protestations to the contrary, the United States herself is deeply involved in these trends. On the regional level, for instance, I had the pleasure of helping to shape the *Plan for Greater Boston* (1945), which was accorded first prize by a group hardly to be classified as radical. On the international level, the United States, by putting forward the Marshall Plan, urged and at times insisted upon the very planning which those Europeans who had talked loudest but had done least hesitated to put into effect. Even on the national level the efforts in Britain, France, and Sweden, to name only three, lacked the full democratic backing without which their success within the setting of constitutional democracy could not be considered even probable, as I had opportunity to learn at first hand when accompanying the Congressional Committee on Foreign Aid (Herter Committee) to Europe in 1947. But the importance of grassroots democracy as well as the vicissitudes of careless planning (involved as it was in the Level of Industry Plan) was highlighted for me during my experience in Germany in 1946, 1947, and 1948. Ever since my experience during the War as Director of the Civil Affairs Training School at Harvard University, the problem of what place to assign to military government in the constitutional order had seemed to me of vital importance. This practical experience and an examination of the bitter controversies in both Britain and the United States surrounding the conduct of military government have led me to the conclusions now embodied in this volume.

Regretfully, it was decided to eliminate the chapter dealing with methodological problems. My hope is to offer a more comprehensive treatment of these matters in a separate volume about two years hence. In the meantime, the publishers have kindly agreed to reprint the chapter as a separate brochure, to be available to those who do not possess the first edition. A revision of this chapter to bring it up to date in terms of my views as shaped by experience with area studies and continued association with sociologists, anthropologists, and social psychologists—an association which I greatly value—would have meant expanding it to several times its present length. This seemed impracticable in view of the somewhat greater scope of the new edition as it is here being offered.

Besides the acknowledgments contained in the preface to the first edition of *Constitutional Government and Democracy* (reprinted below), I wish to thank especially my friend and colleague John M. Gaus, who kindly read both of the new chapters and offered valuable help, and to Theodore S. Baer and Lester Hawkins, who gave similar help. I also feel that I ought to record my genuine appreciation of the assistance of my colleagues in the School for Overseas Administration, especially Professors Merle Fainsod, Talcott Parsons, Clyde Kluckhohn, Charles Cherington, and Douglas Haring, and to my associates in the Greater Boston Contest, who included, besides Cherington and Parsons, Professors Seymour Harris, Walter Bogner, and Al Simpson, as well as Mr. George Walker. Finally, it would be unfair not to say a word of thanks to the men whose association I was privileged to share through "thick and thin," more especially General Lucius DuB. Clay, Messrs. Henry Parkman, J. A. Panuch, and Charles M. LaFollette, and Dr. Richard S. Scammon as well as Drs. Edward H. Litchfield, Hans Simons, and Kenneth Dayton; also Colonels John Raymond and J. L. Harbaugh, and Mr. Seymour Bolten. These men all labored hard in the vineyard of constitutional democracy in Germany, barren though the ground is, beset by uncomprehending critics at home and abroad among our Allies and erstwhile enemies.

I have had as well the devoted assistance throughout of Mrs. Dorothy Smith and Mrs. Shirley Coyne, who rendered the kind of continued and cheerful aid without which such books as this one would hardly ever be written. I should also like to thank the library staffs at Harvard University and at Concord for continued friendly and unfailing courtesy.

C. J. FRIEDRICH

Concord, Massachusetts
Armistice Day, 1949

Preface to the Second Edition

This book is written for those who are puzzled about the future of constitutional government and democracy. It tries to show the present disturbances in proper perspective by setting them off against the ground swell of long-range secular trends. In these days of profound crisis when the international civil war has once more come out into the open, it is undoubtedly an act of faith, for both the writer and the publisher, to bring out a new edition of *Constitutional Government*. Four years ago, when the first edition was published, there had been no Munich, the French Republic seemed firmly entrenched behind the Maginot line, and the smaller countries of Europe, Czechoslovakia, Denmark, Norway, Holland, and Belgium, if not Poland, were joined with Sweden, Finland, and Switzerland in carrying forward the constitutional tradition. And yet, in a deeper sense, the outlook for constitutionalism was more uncertain then. The British people were in an appeasing mood and America hid her face in the sand. There was little aggressive belief in the future of democracy and free institutions. Many people who were then indifferent, if not cynical, have since rediscovered the essential of constitutionalism: a vivid appreciation of the rights of free men. In the preface to the first edition, I wrote: "Within the lifetime of this generation, the present barbarities will be abandoned, and finer, more noble conceptions of life will reassert themselves. There are great latent reservoirs of faith in a higher morality which were overgrown with the slime of nineteenth-century decadence. I do not propose to know how the creative sensibilities will manifest themselves. I will confess to a faith in their potential strength." The English people have already given proof of this prediction.

The present edition is almost a new book. Not only have revisions been made on almost every page, but a new first chapter has been added to give historical perspective to the rise of constitutionalism, and the role of executive leadership has been brought out more fully in the light of recent events, English and Dominion material has been given greater emphasis as contrasted with French and German, and many other minor changes made. It may be asked by some why anything should be retained about the ill-fated German Republic or even France. The answer would seem to be that we can learn as much from our failures as from our successes. And since the purpose of this volume is definitely to do more than summarize descriptively what various governments are like, such failures are often needed to point up the central tenets concerning the working of constitutionalism. For constitutionalism is probably the greatest achievement of modern civilization, without which little or none of the rest is conceivable. Under it, for the first time in the history of man, has a measure of freedom and well-being been achieved for the common man. There is nothing complete or final about this achievement, but it is a great achievement just the same. To understand, even partially, the conditions for the success of this system is, it seems to me, the most important task of political science. What is here offered is no final answer. But it is the best the author could do. And it is considerably changed in at least one important respect from the first edition. At that time, it was assumed, following Balfour and others, that agreement on fundamentals was a necessary condition of constitutionalism. That tenet has now been abandoned. In fact, constitutionalism is about the only system of government which seems able to get along without such agreement on fundamentals. It is part of the organization of freedom that this should be so.

I have enjoyed so much help and stimulation from the discussion with friends throughout the years during which this book has reached its present scope that I am utterly incapable of setting a suitable memorial for each of them individually. Wherever I could, I have tried to emphasize in the bibliography such special debts. But some of the greatest benefits I have derived from men and women who have not written anything, and their share in shaping my thoughts must remain obscure.

It may be permissible to mention, however, those who have taken part in the arduous and trying task of reading the manuscript and the proof. In the first edition, Jane Barbour, William Yandell Elliott, Rupert Emerson, H. Schuyler Foster, William P. Maddox, George Pettee, David Riesman, Jr., Frederick M. Watkins, Harold Winkler, and the whimsical person to whom this volume is dedicated, have all lent a helping hand. Since then, so many more have come to my aid that it seems impossible to list them. I have particularly appreciated those friendly critics who have called my attention to flaws in the presentation and argument. It is hoped that they will find the new edition improved in the right direction. Besides these scholars, Emily Whitman, Helen Parsons, and Miriam Berry have rendered great assistance in preparing the new manuscript and bringing the bibliography up to date.

C. J. FRIEDRICH

Beechwood Hill Farm
Brattleboro, Vermont
July 4, 1941

Contents

PART III

THE FUNCTIONING PROCESSES OF CONSTITUTIONAL GOVERNMENT

XIV

CONSTITUTIONAL GOVERNMENT
AND DEMOCRACY

PART I

MODERN GOVERNMENT:

NATURE

AND DEVELOPMENT

I

A Historical Sketch of Modern Constitutionalism in Theory and Practice

Introduction · Aristotle and modern political science · Mind versus matter · National unification · Material factors of unification · Nonmaterial factors of unification · The Roman law as a formative force · The state · Sovereignty · Reason of state and the problem of responsibility · The nature of power · The core of the power system: bureaucracy · The essence of constitutionalism · England's leadership in constitutionalism · The spread of constitutionalism · Democratization of constitutionalism · Socialism and constitutionalism · Conclusion.

Introduction · Democracy has become the battle cry of our day. Everyone is for democracy as he understands it. In the United States it is the existing scheme of things, or some idealized version of it, or else what the men of Philadelphia intended their constitution to be. In Britain it is what the Labour Party has been doing since it came into power. In the Soviet Union they have been laughing at such reactionary views; according to them "true" democracy can only come after capitalism has been destroyed and the dictatorship of the proletariat has been organized. Since the end of the Second World War, these differences have grown increasingly acute.

Is all this pure madness? Shall we assume that words have no meaning, and that propaganda is in complete charge? What is the ascertainable difference between the Western Powers and the Soviet Union as far as their political systems are concerned? If the question is put in that form, it is found that the answer will be: in America and England political power is divided among many, whereas in Russia it is concentrated in one group headed by one man. This concentration does not mean that many others do not participate in the exercise of this power, but it does mean that their participation takes place at the pleasure of the ultimate, absolute controller, that is, only as long as the despot pleases.[1]

Division of power is the basis of civilized government. It is what is meant by constitutionalism. Constitutionalism can be monarchical, or it can be democratic, and it has been both. When we in America say "democracy," we usually mean constitutional democracy. Of course, there are

5

those who would define democracy simply as the rule of the majority, without any constitutional pattern within which such majority decisions are set. But they are utopian theorists or partisans of a particular majority, a party they happen to agree with.

Constitutionalism is an achievement of the modern world. It is a very recent achievement, and it has by no means become stabilized. Indeed, it is a complex system of providing for orderly change, and there is no reason for assuming that the need for change will come to an end in the immediate future. Both nationally and internationally, we are confronted with gigantic tasks. Changes are taking place which rival in magnitude any the world has seen. Constitutionalism has provided a setting for these changes in some cases, and it has failed to do so in others. Both the promoters and the opponents of change have been dissatisfied. They have declared constitutionalism bankrupt, and have proceeded to erect governments of an absolutist type. Their systems, marking a return to older methods of government, have brought many men to a fuller appreciation of the importance of constitutionalism. Much more than appeared to be challenged at first, is actually at stake. Science and art and religion, the whole realm of free creative effort, are in fact threatened. It is clear, at last, that there can be no more important study than the study of the conditions of the rise of constitutionalism in general and constitutional democracy in particular. The crisis has revealed the poignancy of Aristotle's claim that the study of politics, of the working of government, is the most important study of all. Without an understanding of politics, man's other works are in danger of being destroyed.

Aristotle and modern political science · Aristotle's philosophy has probably exercised a deeper influence upon the Western mind than any other source except the teachings of Christianity. Nowhere has this influence been more all-pervading than in the field of politics. Monarchists and Republicans, aristocrats and democrats, idealists and realists—all have drawn upon *the* philosopher for inspiration and authority. And yet, the realities of Western development have made Aristotle's analysis more and more inadequate, until today a student of imagination, sent to consider contemporary politics in terms of Aristotelian theory, might well report that the Republic of Andorra would be the place of greatest interest.[2]

There are a number of reasons for this divergence of modern politics from Aristotle, but two stand out as of greatest importance. Philosophically, it is probably not too much to say that the concept of the *state* crystallized during the Renaissance. It was the mainstay of political theory in the age of absolutism, as developed by writers like Hobbes and Pufendorf.

It received its final apotheosis in Hegel; Hegel and his followers have inspired both conservative and radical thinking throughout the West during the last hundred years. The state, modeled upon the Greek concept of the polis, was deified by them as the concrete embodiment of all value as represented by man's culture. The rise of key words in politics, of symbols, is usually associated with the rise of new forces in political society. The word *state* crystallized in the sixteenth and seventeenth centuries, because secular rulers who wanted to achieve absolute power needed a symbol that they could set against the church, something that would be awe-inspiring and clothed with an abstract corporate halo. Hobbes typically concludes the *Leviathan* with a violent denunciation of the church. The prophet of the totalitarian monster, of the state as the guardian of all value, revealed the mainspring of the new mythology in the final book of the *Leviathan*.

This deification of the state, that is, the government, was, of course, a gross misrepresentation of the Greek and Aristotelian concept of the polis. The Greek Olympus with its many gods had permitted each polis to share in the deity through a special local favorite, such as Athens' Athene. Governmental offices were closely related to priestly ones, and in many cases overlapped. Thus the polis was really a church as well as a "state," and the two were so closely intermingled that a man's religious as well as his political allegiance was bound up in such a polity. By associating the general ideas rooted in this reality with the bare government of monarchical administrators, the mythmakers of state and sovereignty not only distorted the Aristotelian political philosophy, but they saddled our culture with a heritage of which the totalitarian states of our time are the penultimate sequel. These totalitarian states have once again come to claim the whole man; yet on account of the vast masses they include this claim is abstract and impersonal. In any case, little of what Aristotle has to say concerning the polis can be rightly said of modern *government*. The word *state* has been the vehicle for confusing the issue.

Not only was the reality with which Aristotle dealt different from modern government, but his approach was dominated by a logic which is as outworn in politics as it is in physics. Aristotle, as well as Plato, was concerned with static problems of classification. Classification is important in scientific work, but if the principle used in classifying is irrelevant, classification obstructs rather than forwards the analysis. The Greeks classified governments according to two principles, (*a*) the number of rulers, and (*b*) fixed moral judgments concerning the objectives of government. Moreover, these judgments were couched in vague and highly abstract terms, so that the word *good* could be applied to an institution like slavery, and the moral implications of poverty could be neglected. The two principles of classification were combined with an unexplained major premise: all change is intrinsically bad. It was held, therefore, that all change should be resisted. The radical changes which an existing polis would have to undergo, if it were to be "reformed" in the light of such value judgments, were held to be unique events, without precedent or sequel. It should be obvious that such a view forms the very antithesis of our modern approach. Our emphasis upon *becoming*, upon the history of institutions and their development, makes our outlook dynamic. We are preoccupied with processes and functions. In our moral judgments we seek to be specific; we do not care so much whether George III was a good man in vague abstract terms, but whether in pursuing the policy he did concerning the colonies he violated detailed standards of free government or not. Thus monarchy, the very word which for Aristotle essentially meant rule by one man when directed to good purposes, has for the modern mind become a historical term.[3] Broadly speaking, it designates a peculiar type of political legitimacy founded upon the divine calling of the monarch, who, no matter how limited may be the extent of his governing functions, is thereby enabled to represent the people. The monarch is the symbol of the living growth of a unified culture pattern of which the political order is but an aspect. What made France a monarchy in the time of Richelieu was not the rule of one man— Richelieu—but the fact that there existed by divine grace a hereditary king from whom Richelieu derived his authority and legitimate powers. The modern scientific approach is interested in questions of historical fitness, in evolutionary patterns. From such historical considerations there results a very different attitude toward change. Change is looked upon as intrinsically necessary and unavoidable. The question is, therefore, how to turn such change to good account, how to adapt political life to the changing social context in order to secure the greatest satisfaction for the people.

Mind versus matter · The Christian tradition emphasizes ideas and ideals. Western man's interest in history and evolution has therefore often taken the road of exploring the rise of ideas and ideologies. Constitutionalism has been traced in its relation to liberalism, to rationalism, to individualism. Each one of these general philosophies has indeed contributed its fair share to the making of constitutionalism. But a different perspective results, depending upon which one of these isms is emphasized. Liberalism, the most recent of the three, seems at variance with the rising socialism; hence if constitutionalism is linked with liberalism, it seems reasonable to conclude that it is about to pass away. Rationalism is the most ancient and is associated with many different forms of culture; if constitutionalism is the political outgrowth of rationalism, it acquires a more universal significance. But rationalism has been dominant in societies the constitutional order of which did not much resemble modern constitutionalism. Again, individualism crystallized in the period when modern constitutionalism began to take shape. To this individualism, constitutionalism owes the development of the doctrine of individual rights, which in some ways is the distinguishing feature of modern, in contrast to ancient and medieval, constitutionalism. Any sequence of ideas is difficult to trace, because the interrelations are so numerous. Political science, though vividly cognizant of the role of ideas, has been inclined in recent years to turn to more material aspects of political institutions. In this it has followed the change in outlook among historians. The economic interpretation of history has produced an economic interpretation of politics.

Inquiries into the economic setting of modern constitutionalism have led to the assertion that it is associated with capitalism and imperialism.[4] This is not merely a coincidence in time, it is held, but the more thoroughly constitutionalized countries are also those who have advanced farthest in the direction of either capitalism or imperialism or both. Great Britain would, of course, furnish the outstanding example. Behind both capitalism and imperialism, modern industrialism appears as the basic material setting from such a standpoint. It is important to call attention to this underlying basis, because capitalism and imperialism may be transitional phases of a technology which persists. In other words, industrialism and constitutionalism appear to be linked and may persist together even after the industrial economy has become socialized. Whether this will happen or not, nobody knows. The student should beware of the conflicting claims of propagandists; they all, as was said a moment ago, favor democracy, some claiming that democracy (meaning constitutionalism) cannot be fulfilled without complete socialization, others insisting that only a system of free enterprise is compatible with democracy.

A comparative analysis of constitutionalism and its developments has to take all these sociological and ideological elements into account. There is no good reason (metaphysics aside) for saying that it is either all mind, or all matter, or more one rather than the other.[5] A certain number of determinants or factors seem to be operative in human society, and a careful analysis will comprise all, in order to be realistic. There are the ideological factors, foremost among them the religious factor, there is the economic factor, there is the military factor, and finally there is the geographical factor. To these should probably be added the factor of nationalism, which contains elements of several of the others, but which has, in recent times, come to play a role comparable to religion; it is a substitute for religion and has contributed considerably to a reappearance of the kind of tribal allegiance which animated the Mediterranean world in the days of the Greek city "state."

National unification · Constitutionalism, wherever it appears, is a refinement of ordinary government. In any society, there is practically always some sort of government, no matter how inadequate, but only a firmly established government is capable of being constitutionalized. In the evolution of our Western world, this meant that national unification had to precede constitutionalism. It is here that the great difference may be seen between Germany and Italy, as contrasted with England and France. Some small countries, like Sweden and Holland, offer interesting parallels. England became unified at an early date, when Italy was completely divided; hence constitutionalism could make substantial headway in England in the seventeenth century, but not in Italy. The only real exception is provided by Switzerland, and Switzerland, throughout the earlier period, was not so much a constitutional order as a league of small-town and rural cantons for the defense of the kind of local autonomy which national unification destroyed in the large territorial realms. It thus came to pass that a communal sentiment of political loyalty, based upon the common enterprise of joint defense against their feudal overlords, came into existence among the Swiss people which surpassed the national-cultural feelings of its German-, French-, and Italian-speaking components. This powerful, yet distinctive, group feeling had become so well-rooted by the time nationalism triumphed throughout Europe that it could act as the basis of an effective constitutionalism in 1848 (whether one calls the Swiss a nation or not is a terminological quarrel). However, nationalism itself is not a necessary or even a desirable basis of constitutionalism.[6] About this, more will be said presently.

National unification was carried out by medieval and early modern kings. Feudalism, though providing some national and even international unity, rested upon the autonomy of local lords, with towns acquiring a species of constitutionalism under royal or imperial charter. In a struggle raging for many centuries, certain kings succeeded in extending their centrally controlled rule. It is quite arbitrary to single out a particular ruler, such as Henry VIII of England or Louis XI of France, as the "founder." These long-drawn-out conflicts had many ups and downs. Their course is marked by decided upswings of royal power and of the services which the kings controlled, only to be followed by retrogressions accompanied by the inevitable dispersion of power. Nor was this process by any means a uniform one in the several countries. Thus in England, under the Norman and early Plantagenet kings, remarkable strides were made toward centralization, but the period of Magna Charta is marked by the ascendancy of the local lords. The consolidation which followed was almost entirely lost during the Wars of the Roses, which in turn paved the way for Tudor absolutism. In France the development was no less turbulent, yet it resembled the English case in that it steadily progressed toward greater consolidation of the nation. In Germany and Italy, on the other hand, the forces of disintegration gained the ascendancy. This is, at any rate, true for the nation as a whole; but within the more limited areas of city states and principalities, centralizing forces were, in turn, victorious. The histories of Florence and Venice, no less than those of Bavaria and Brandenburg-Prussia, bear witness to this trend.

In all these countries, the late Middle Ages witnessed the rise of a medieval constitutionalism which rested upon the dualism of king or crown and estates (see below, pp. 126, 262). The persistence of certain elements of this medieval constitutionalism in England has tended to obscure the fact that there, as elsewhere, modern constitutionalism is a distinctive development which was possible only after national unification had provided an effective central government. The disappearance of the universal church as an everpresent counterpoise to the national monarchies was probably also important. Practically a century was consumed in the process of stabilizing the Anglican (National) Church in England; only when that process was completed, and the king-pope James I set forth his claim to totalitarian authority, had the moment come for modern constitutionalism. Thus it can be seen that developments followed a different path in each country, and hence no single time schedule can be made out for the history of constitutionalism. But nowhere do we find modern constitutionalism until an effective central government has been brought into existence.

Material factors of unification · Various causes, military, economic, geographic, religious, and nationalist, have been offered to explain this progress of national unification. We shall treat of these several important factors as conditions of unification, centralization, and bureaucracy.[2] These factors may conveniently be divided into the material and the nonmaterial. Both are important. Among the material factors, the economic factor has received much attention.[7] Writers on mercantilism, like Schmoller, have dealt extensively with the economic side of unification. In the early period the expansion of trade played a decisive role. It created a need for better police protection and security in transportation and communication. The story of these activities is a long and complicated one, but there is little disagreement concerning the fundamental facts as revealed in the mounting trade figures in Venice, Florence, Antwerp, London, Frankfurt, and many other centers of urban progress. The citizenry of London and Paris, as well as the imperial cities of Germany, were, on the whole, willing supporters of the princely overlord against local feudal barons, regarding him as the likeliest guarantor of the public peace. But in Italy, where the development of trade was perhaps most marked, the cities did not support such a central head; these cities, in fact, offered the most violent opposition to imperial as well as papal pretensions. Here traders preferred to rely upon the growing power of their own city. This led to incessant warfare between the cities, which eventually, in the age of Machiavelli, brought foreign intervention and subjugation. It was the success of Northern monarchs in integrating and pacifying their kingdoms which in part inspired Machiavelli's ardent concern with Italian unification.[8] In the Europe north of the Alps, by increasing the security of commercial intercourse, these political developments provided a fertile field for the expansion of trade activities.

During the later phase of the evolution of modern government, when differentiated bureaucracies were being established all over Europe, the industrial revolution with its growing number of manufacturing establishments is said to have "caused" the expansion of governmental services. There can be no doubt that the growth of these industries provided an important concomitant condition of governmental expansion; still, it is more nearly true that the governments grew the industries. In fact, the term mercantilism, generally used for characterizing this age, suggests just that type of governmental participation and stimulation in the economic realm.

Another factor making for unification was the military. The military cause or determinant is most clearly seen when we consider the development of various weapons and techniques of warfare during these centuries.[9] If we compare the military establishments of early modern times with those prevalent in the Middle Ages, we discover three important technical differences: (1) they are very much larger, (2) their main force consists of infantry, (3) they are equipped with firearms and guns. Besides these three technical differences, there are three important administrative contrasts: (1) the military establishments are permanent (standing armies), (2) they are mercenary, or at least regularly paid, (3) they possess a central command, entrusted to a professional officer corps. The story of how all these changes came about differs considerably for the various countries. Even more important, in England the military establishment was predominantly naval, while on the Continent the army occupied the center of attention. Army and navy exercised a similar effect upon the growth of central administration; but a navy proved less dangerous to constitutionalism than an army (see below, ch. III, p. 61). In the first place, as irregular forces become standing mercenary armies, expensively equipped, they require ever increasing sums for their sustenance and thereby oblige the prince to perfect his tax-gathering machinery. Officials must be hired and organized, not only to collect the taxes, but to break down local resistance, and to give assistance to those groups in the community which promise larger tax returns through the development of industry and manufacture. Again, the large size of the armies presupposes the organization of offices for collecting the food for men and horses as well as for distributing it. Finally, the development of a professional officer corps suggests a similar hierarchy for the administrative services. Obviously, if one starts from this military development as a fact, he could undertake to explain the entire evolution of modern government from that viewpoint. Actually this military development itself is as much caused by the evolution and growth of modern government; for in the struggle with local lords, as well as in the conflicts which arose between the several kingdoms, we recognize the most powerful stimulants to this military progress. Modern infantry first appeared in Switzerland, where peasants on foot defeated the Austrian duke's cavalry; it appeared again in the Hundred Years' War when the newly organized archers gave the victory to England, until Charles VII of France succeeded in establishing his regular infantry. In short, we find that military and governmental development stimulate each other as concomitant aspects of the same process.

Attempts have been made from time to time to explain the evolution of modern government largely in terms of geography.[10] The distinctive evolution of government in England has provided seemingly convincing proof of such arguments. England's island position obviously facilitated her subordination to one government and the accompanying centralization by making foreign assistance to the weaker party relatively difficult, if not impossible. On the other hand, England has always been an island. The difficulty under which any geographic explanation labors is the static character of all geographic conditions. Growth is change, and cannot be explained by what has always been. Consequently, we find that those who would make us believe that geography was the final cause always slip in an unexplained, but firmly asserted, "natural" tendency of the "state" to grow. This natural tendency toward growth once accepted, it is easy to show how the governments of England, France, and Switzerland, for example, grew the way they did, because mountains, rivers, plains, and other such "facts" conditioned the particular form of their growth. There is little in the geography of Burgundy, to pick an example at random, which would lead us to conclude affirmatively that it was to become part of France rather than of Germany. Nor can the general assertions about the relation of climate to national character, first expounded by Aristotle, be considered adequately tested scientific hypotheses. Of the three causes or conditions which we have considered so far, the geographic, though from the point of view of the natural scientist the most "natural," would appear to be the least likely to explain satisfactorily unification of the national governments.

Nonmaterial factors of unification · The determinants or conditions which we have so far discussed have been of the material sort. But there are other determinants which condition men's behavior through their minds without reference to a material factor.[11] The broadest and most inclusive interpretation of this type is that which sees modern governments essentially as attempts at a realization of the social teachings of the Christian churches. In medieval political life all moral and legal restraints of governmental authorities were reinforced by ecclesiastical sanctions, including pressure upon individual rulers. The Reformation disrupted the unity of faith which lent to such ecclesiastical restraint its essential legitimacy. It greatly intensified the older doctrine of a right of resistance, and in turn reinforced the monarch's efforts to surround his office with the halo of a "divine right." The Protestant inclination to make the prince the head of the church as well as the state became important in that it gave the state a new kind of ecclesiastical sanction by allowing it to participate in the symbolism of a mystical body, a divinely ordained superentity. Naturally, the Catholic rulers of the Counter Reformation, more especially Philip II of Spain, strove to achieve a comparable status. The sanctification of such worldly offices in turn permitted the idea to spread that the office, and not the office-holder, was entitled to such profound veneration, and that the office-holder must display a corresponding regard for the duties and responsibilities of his office. The life-stories of individual leaders, such as Cromwell and Coke, the Great Elector and Henry IV, Gustavus Adolphus and the princes of Orange, reveal the force of these ideas in shaping their own conduct as well as the standards which they set for their officials. Such religious ideas were therefore a concomitant condition of the evolution of modern government.

Another important explanatory "cause" of modern governments is the nation, or the national spirit. This factor is closely linked to religion, for if nationalism is not a religion, as has been pretended, it certainly has been a secular substitute for religion since the French revolution. Both in England and France this nationalist explanation of a national unification has found many advocates, on account of the strength of the national tradition in these countries. Fundamentally, it is held under this theory that modern constitutional government (England) or modern centralized governmental machinery (France) is the work of a "national genius," a collective group spirit, as it were, which created the government as we know it. Letters and statements of politicians and officials abound with more or less unctuous references to their devotion to the national cause, and there can be no question that the development of a public, as compared to a royal, service was greatly aided by the emergence of national consciousness. The nation as the sum total of the cultural environment offered a welcome substitute for the person of the king. Cromwell and Richelieu are alike in their allegiance to their country, their nation. The French revolution immensely intensified these sentiments, and carried them into lands, like Germany, where they had previously not taken root. But it is easy to exaggerate the causative importance of this factor. Some modern states arose where there was no nation, nor any national spirit. Countries like Prussia and the Hapsburg domains rivaled England and France in the perfection of modern governmental machinery.

The Roman law as a formative force · There is one nonmaterial factor which deserves special emphasis, on account of its formative importance, and that is the Roman law.[12] For law is essentially the embodiment of the established forms of recurrent social behavior patterns. This is the reason why all political, economic, and sociological studies are impossible without an adequate analysis of the legal forms within which a particular activity or process has been clothed. The political scientist is interested in the system of law as a whole, the political function it serves, because of the formal elements it happens to contain. Roman law greatly aided unification and centralization, because royal judges everywhere (imitating the papal legates) tended to employ the Roman law during the later Middle Ages and early modern times. It was long believed that this was not so in England, but more recent investigations have shown that the impact of the Roman law is merely more obscure, because it lay farther back in time in England. Why should the royal judges have used the Roman law? Until the idea of man-made law, of legislation, was definitely established, the greatest obstacle to the king's or prince's efforts toward centralization and expansion of the royal jurisdiction was the multitude of local laws, embodied in eternal custom. As against this obstacle, the Roman law offered an ideal weapon. It was a more ancient and therefore almost divine system of law, this law of the Roman Empire as embodied in the Institutes, the Digests, and the Code of Justinian. Emperor and Pope alike sought in its provisions weapons against traditional local customs; the several national kings soon followed their example. French lawyers developed the famous

15

doctrine that the French king is *imperator* (emperor) in his own kingdom. He can, therefore, draw upon the Roman law in which were presumably embodied the principles of a *common* law of the whole kingdom. With the help of this doctrine, the jurists, called *Legists*, slowly succeeded in breaking down the feudal organization.

It is perfectly obvious that in the process of interpretation and application the Roman law was twisted, and arbitrary selections from its tenets gave it a wholly different flavor from the one it had possessed when it regulated the social life of the Eastern Roman Empire. Yet, it so happened that the Roman law, being the law of a highly developed commercial community, contained many principles which were better adapted to the needs of the emerging commercial classes than the local customs of a cruder agricultural society. Its urbanity, you might say, strengthened its position and insured it the support of the rising townsfolk everywhere.

The essentially *political* significance of the impact of Roman law has at times been overlooked, because it came much earlier in England and France than in Germany. The dreamlike aspirations of the medieval German emperors had prevented "nationalization" of the Roman law. Therefore the true "reception" of the Roman law, as the process was baptized by German scholars, came only when ultimate political authority passed to the several territorial princes in the sixteenth and seventeenth centuries. Then suddenly these princes commenced to put the Roman law to the same use to which it had earlier been put by the kings of France, England, and Spain; for they no longer needed the local law for combating imperial pretensions. But here, as there, it served the purpose of consolidating and centralizing scattered feudal realms, facilitating commerce, and last, but not least, rendering abstract and impersonal the relation of official and prince, as well as that of prince and people, by the Roman doctrine of magistracy.

The state · The Roman law itself did not develop a state concept in the modern sense. However, the Roman *civitas* or *res publica* comes closer to the modern idea of the state than any Greek notions regarding the polis or city. Similarly, the Roman practices of government in the republican period more nearly resembled modern constitutionalism than anything else in the world of antiquity. Indeed, they have often been equated, but mistakenly. For the modern state concept—and that of the constitution associated with it, though by way of juxtaposition—was born of the Western church concept. The state as a concept was forged by political theorists as a tool of propaganda for absolute monarchy. Jean Bodin and those who followed him wished to give the king's government a corporate halo roughly equivalent to that of the church. The "state" was the "estate" of the king;

in France, where the idea was first most sharply stated, the word *État* to this day covers both estate and state. In setting off the state against church and empire, Jean Bodin provided an effective rationalization for the centrifugal and particularistic forces which eventually led to the modern nation state.[13]

A very large gloss has in the course of centuries covered the groundwork which Bodin first laid. Yet, fundamentally all definitions of sovereignty still revolve around Bodin's original ideas, including the recent notions of the state as a "sovereign juristic association" or "person" or what have you. Every state, said Bodin, is an association of families, and in order to be well ordered it requires a single sovereign, that is to say, a person or group of persons who possess supreme legislative power; a sovereign, therefore, can change any existing law.[14] It is clear that the state and the sovereign are here linked in such a way as to be in effect Siamese twins; these artificial twins became one when the state itself was proclaimed sovereign, first by Hugo Grotius and more commonly in recent years.

As an ideology for monarchical absolutism, this concept of state and sovereignty was perfect. It provided the absolute rulers with a conceptual tool for establishing unrestrained control over all lesser associations, including the church. Seventeenth-century writers, especially Thomas Hobbes and Baruch Spinoza, further radicalized the doctrine by founding it upon natural law, thus eliminating the possibility, still recognized by Bodin, that natural law might be pleaded as a ground for limiting state authority. Only in Britain, where the idea of modern constitutionalism was developed in antithesis to the "state" concept in the course of the revolutionary struggles of the seventeenth century, did the doctrine fail. When Sir Edward Coke snorted that sovereignty and the common law were not suitable bedfellows, he may have been echoing medieval ideas, but these medieval ideas of a government effectively restrained were soon converted into a more explicit constitutional structure in the *Instrument of Government* (see below, p. 133). Only in the nineteenth century, through Jeremy Bentham and John Austin, did the notions of state and sovereign gain an entering wedge into English legal thought, but legal practitioners have remained troubled by its implications. It is all very well to claim that parliament or the majority of the people is "sovereign," but the moment one does so it becomes impossible to maintain the idea of a constitutional system, with its protection for the individual and the minority against arbitrary action of the majority in parliament or out. Absolutism in its various forms provides for a concentration of power, while constitutionalism provides for a divided exercise of power. This is the ancient idea of a mixed system of government, and hence arguments about democracy do not properly apply; by definition, a constitutional democracy is one which does not grant *all* power to the majority. This issue dramatically presented itself again in Europe after the Second World War, when in France, Italy, and Germany the Communists came to plead for unrestrained and absolute majority rule in the name of democracy.

The "state" concept in association with sovereignty is based upon the fallacious idea that you can comprehend under one concept the antithetical systems of absolutism and constitutionalism. This is sometimes done, allegedly from a sociological (that is, scientific) standpoint, by asserting that the state exercises a "monopoly of force." This emphasis on coercion does not fit the co-operative community. If persuasion, or, more broadly speaking, consent, is given the place which it in fact occupies from time to time in the management of political communities by providing a basis for power and authority, the antithesis between the sovereign state and the self-governing community becomes clear.[15]

A political community is governed in one of two ways. Either a constituent group (see below, ch. VIII) has organized a pattern providing for the expression of consent by a substantial body of *citizens* (the common man) or a conquering group has set up a system of controls providing for effective constraint of the *subjects*. The antithesis is an abstract and theoretical one and there are many communities which fall into intermediary patterns. But the basic difference is of great importance in assessing even these communities. It was to idealize a government based on constraint that the concepts of "state" and "sovereignty" were developed. Any close analysis reveals that the central bureaucracies, supported by growing military establishments, conquered the medieval constitutional systems from within, and established the monarch as the symbolical figurehead of a system in which they became the final arbiter of what should be done.

Sovereignty · A very important corollary politically of the idea of state and sovereignty, however, was the depersonalizing of governmental relationships. To put this another way, against feudalism the trend toward legislative unification and centralization found its most challenging expression in the doctrine of sovereignty. It was the theoretical culmination of a long secular trend in France and elsewhere. Sovereignty rendered impersonal the relation of the king to his subjects. Under feudalism, all such relationships were patterned upon the personal fealty of lord and vassal. That is to say, the principle of the relation between the lord (*dominus*) and the vassal was personal "mutuality." Such personal relationship must needs be limited in extent, and was therefore ill-adapted to wide territorial realms. The hierarchy of the mutual relationships which feudal society had

18

tried to evolve in the effort to bridge the gap had shown a dismal tendency toward disintegration and anarchy. This tendency had resulted from the growth of complex intermediary authorities which opposed the prince's rule. To escape from this confusion it was then asserted that no true government existed unless there was somewhere an authority for making laws binding upon all the inhabitants of a given territory. The true achievement which lay in this recognition of the need for a central government has been obscured by the struggle over the control of such a government. It was forgotten that it was necessary first to create a government before the question of its control could even arise. And it was furthermore forgotten that this question of control could arise earlier in England than in France, because Tudor absolutism had consolidated previous efforts to establish an effectively centralized bureaucracy at a time when France was in the grip of an extended civil war. From this civil war the crown emerged with a considerable army at its command, which made it possible to crush the *Fronde*, while Cromwell's Model Army triumphed over the weak royal forces in England. This military ascendancy of the French crown, stimulated as it was by the possibilities of foreign invasion, delayed the outbreak of the struggle over the control of the government for one hundred and forty years. But the usefulness of the concept of sovereignty in providing a symbol for national unification and for the monarchical governments which destroyed feudal localism did not outlast its time. It was in the pre-constitutional period that "sovereignty" was destined to play its most significant role. The word itself served as a symbol for concentrated power, deriving from the word "sovereign," connoting the holder of such power. Since under constitutionalism there is not supposed to exist any such concentrated power, sovereignty as a conception is incompatible with constitutionalism,[16] and all constitutional regimes have shown a marked tendency to resist its use. Even under a constitutional democracy this is true. The notion of "popular sovereignty"—a confused expression at best—needs to be supplanted by that of the "constitutional group." For this group is not the holder of concentrated power, but exercises the revolutionary, residuary, constituent power of establishing a new constitution. Most of the time other groups exercise intermediary powers of decision, such as amending the constitution, legislating, and so forth.

Reason of state and the problem of responsibility · As long as rulers were effectively influenced in their conduct by the moral teachings of the church—a united church with universal claims of obedience—the problem of responsibility could remain obscure. Our modern secularized methods of securing responsibility through electoral controls and the like (see below, chs. XIV, XV) has tended to make us forget that through long ages responsible conduct had to be brought about by other means, and that even today much remains of these ancient ways. Historically speaking, we find that responsible conduct of power-holders has been enforced not only through secular, political, administrative, or judicial sanctions, but through religious sanctions as well.[17] In fact, such religious responsibility has bulked larger than any of the others. Medieval constitutionalism (see ch. VII, p. 126) was largely built upon that sanction. When a religious ethic prevails in a community (and it does not inherently matter what particular religion it is), the possibilities of producing responsible conduct in terms of that religious spirit are on the whole more promising than any of the secular devices. Since responsibility presupposes logically a set of norms or standards in terms of which conduct can be evaluated, the actual prevalence of a believed-in set of such norms makes responsibility of conduct almost automatic, as long as the faith lasts. It would be instructive to show the workings of Chinese bureaucracy in these terms, but even our own civilization has relied upon religious sanctions for long periods. As might be expected, there exist two primary forms corresponding to the two primary patterns of Christian ethics, the Catholic and the Protestant. Yet they have much in common. Under both creeds, the person who is supposed to be made responsible for his acts is made responsible for his acts to God. In practice this means, of course, responsibility to the clergy who legitimately interpret the will of God. Luther's frank and often angry letters to the Elector of Saxony and other German princes are a striking case in point. The only thing a prince can do to escape clerical censure as long as he accepts the faith is to conform as nearly as possible to the religious ethic. Luther's notion that the prince himself could function as the head of the church, if spiritually guided by an ecclesiastically unencumbered clergy, made the clergy sufficiently subservient to the government to make it increasingly ineffective as an instrument for securing responsible conduct. The result was either civil war, as in England, or absolutism, as in the various German principalities. The career of Archbishop Laud stands as an example of the unmistakable tendency within the clergy to extol the princely position for the sake of ecclesiastical support.

Basically, the position and approach of the Catholic Church was not dissimilar. Throughout the Middle Ages, the increasingly independent and highly effective administrative organization of the Catholic Church had run into bitter conflicts with the secular authorities. In these conflicts the secular authorities gradually gained the upper hand. The appearance of the concepts of "state" and of "sovereignty" marked the ascendancy of the secular authorities. At the same time, the secular authorities now became

themselves "clericalized" in the sense that their offices were being surrounded with a quasi-religious halo and sanction. It proved impossible
in the sequel for the ecclesiastical authorities to recapture the medieval
position in the Counter Reformation. Like the Protestant clergy, the
Catholic authorities were obliged to concentrate on maintaining the loyalty
and support of individual princes by every available means.

But as soon as the compelling standards of a divinely ordained faith
faltered, a prince and his administrative following were able to emancipate
themselves from the restraints which a religious conviction had imposed on
them. Just as responsible conduct had almost completely disappeared from
the republics of Renaissance Italy, so it now tended to disappear from the
Northern kingdoms. The doctrines of the agnostic pagans for whom
Machiavelli had spoken spread throughout Europe. The clash of his doctrines with the earlier religious notions of responsible government produced the doctrine of "reason of state."

Since religious responsibility means responsibility to transcendent
ethical norms, it involves peculiar pitfalls for the official who seeks to be
guided by it. There are bound to occur situations in which the ethical
norm conflicts with the exigencies of the conduct of government. The
government which follows the norm may succumb to its rival who disregarded it. To have observed and described this fact with corrosive frankness is the achievement of Machiavelli. His attempt to escape from the
dilemma by idealizing power (the state) has earned him the condemnation
of all Christian people. It is no accident that a Catholic priest, Giovanni
Botero, attempted to fit this view into the Christian pattern of thought by
constructing the idea of a *ratio status*, a special governmental rationality
which is at the bottom of the doctrine of the two moralities.[18] Reason of
state has not been recognized in Anglo-American political thought. But
the fundamental category of purposive rationality in political behavior, of
efficiency in the strictly military and technical sense, has been playing an
increasing role in American thought. There has been, however, a studied
soft-pedaling of the underlying issue which Machiavelli faced, and which
he answered in favor of standards of expediency pure and simple. Even
though we reject his answer as wrong, we are hardly justified in not facing
the issue of a conflict between vital needs and a prevailing ethical norm.
"Responsible" conduct of government is a phrase without precise meaning, until a decision is made between the ultimately valid ethical norms on
the one hand and practical exigencies on the other. Toleration is liable to
carry with it a weakening of the absolute standards which a religious sanction presupposes. Modern constitutionalism is essentially an effort to produce responsible conduct of public affairs without religious sanctions.[19] In

the place of religious standards mutually accepted interests (public interests, so-called) are taken as guideposts for official action. But until constitutional methods were discovered and perfected, the issue remained open. Reason of state then, indicates the attempt of human minds, the Christian mind, to grasp the meaning of deviations from an ethical standard, and concludes that the only way in which it could be done was to make government itself a divine institution. It was thus that government by divine law became the divine right of kings in the seventeenth century. Out of these efforts to deify government came the concept of "state," the Leviathan, the great one who could neither be seen nor heard nor communicated with, but who was all-powerful, all-wise, and in every other way a secular form of the deity. But seeing that governments were conducted by human beings with human weaknesses, the deification of the State failed to convince the more critical. Hence the problem of the relative importance of the ethical norm as contrasted with political necessity remained unresolved. Machiavelli and his followers tried to cope with the issue by glorifying power. If that approach is unacceptable, it must be possible to show that the Machiavellian approach to power is in error.

The nature of power · The national unification which successful kings accomplished at the beginning of the modern era was accompanied, then, by a sanctification of power politics which is symbolized by the words "state" and "sovereignty." They were invented by the apologists of absolute power, by men like Bodin, Hobbes, Grotius, and Spinoza, the object being to provide a universal value and appeal for the prince's efforts to extend and consolidate his realm.

This hallowing of political *power* makes it important to face the question of what *power* is. In recent years, this question has received a good deal of theoretical attention. In the age of Hobbes it was of all-absorbing interest. Hobbes, inspired by the passion of his time for geometry, described power as "the present means to secure some future apparent good." Such a definition is much too broad; for what is wealth but a "present means to secure some future apparent good"? Wealth and power are, of course, interrelated, but a definition which fails to bring out the difference between them is not much good. It is very revealing that the age which saw the creation of modern government should have favored such a concept. In order to get a fuller view, some elementary points need to be made. Power, though often spoken of as if it were a thing, is actually nothing of the kind. It is, as the Hobbesian definition suggests, oriented toward things, and anything can become the basis of power. A house, a love affair, an idea, can all become instruments in the hand of one seeking

22

power. But in order to convert them into power, the power-seeker must find human beings who value one of these things sufficiently to follow his leadership in acquiring them. Power, therefore, always presupposes several human beings who are joined together in pursuing a common objective. Without common objectives there can be no power. Enduring common objectives engender organization. All more stable power is therefore based on organization and the control of organization.[20]

The nature of the human relationship which we call power must even today be considered controversial. That it is a human relationship has not always been accepted as axiomatic by political thinkers. Two aspects of the power relationship may be reasonably well distinguished: it may be either *substantive* or *relational*. That is to say, power may be considered a substance, or a relation. Hobbes and the entire school of thinkers following him, from Spinoza and the natural-law writers through the utilitarians and Hegelians down to our various totalitarians of the present day, have variously written of power as if it were a *thing had*, a substance possessed by some human beings and employed by them in an effort to control others. A diagram might indicate more clearly the structure of this "corporeal" or "substantive" view of power:

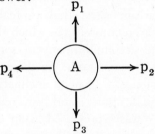

A = agent possessing power
p_1, p_2, p_3, p_4 = powers possessed by agent

Other thinkers have been inclined to stress the mutual interdependence of human beings in a political situation. They have emphasized primarily the fact that there must be people *over* whom to have power. Power, when taken in this sense, is a bond between people simultaneously embracing the leader and the led, the ruler and the ruled. Such a "relational" concept of power is found in John Locke's philosophical writings, though his political tracts follow the other terminology.[21] It has been more fully explored only in recent times, aided by our increasing knowledge of human psychology. This view of power also might be represented by a simple diagram:

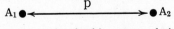

A_1, A_2 = agents involved in power relationship
p = relationship containing power

Although stress is laid at various points upon this mutual aspect of the power situation in the analysis of constitutionalism which follows, each of the two interpretations covers *part* of the facts as we know them. Actual power situations, in other words, contain both the mutual relationship between leader and led, and the corporeal possession of an ability to exact obedience by the leader. It is to some extent a matter of long-run and short-run analysis, or, to put it more abstractly, it is a matter of neglecting or including the time factor.[22] The relational conception makes allowance for the time factor, and thus provides the basis for a long-run analysis.

The two approaches to power are reflected in two distinct views concerning the importance of consent and constraint. The corporeal concept of power inclines toward a neglect of the phenomena of *consent*, interpreting them as propaganda, symbols, myth, and so forth. Marxist and Fascist writers have a good deal in common with Hobbes in this respect. Thinkers who emphasize the relational concept of power tend to neglect the phenomena of conquest and government through force or constraint. Both consent and constraint are something real, they both *do* something, accomplish something. It is wrong to look upon consent merely as nonconstraint, or upon constraint as nonconsent. Consent and constraint are something more than the negation of their opposites; they are realities generating power.

Power, then, is a human relationship in which the leader and the led are banded together for the accomplishment of some common objectives, partly by consent, partly by constraint. In the age in which modern government came into existence, a general inclination prevailed to hallow power for its own sake. The "state" and "sovereignty" were the symbols in terms of which power was represented as an end itself, rather than a means toward accomplishing ends which it would be the task of government to ascertain through consultation with the governed. It may well be that such an exaggeration of the role of power was inevitable to bring into existence the unified national governments which were later constitutionalized.

The core of the power system: bureaucracy · In the age of absolutism, we suggested, public policy was dominated by *mercantilism*—a body of thought which its ablest expositor has called a "system of power."[23] Mercantilism, though usually associated with the idea of protectionism, was committed to freedom of trade. Internally, it was an economic corollary of the monarchical policy of centralization and unification. "Domestic tolls, local privileges, and inequalities in the system of coinage, weights and measures, the absence of unity in legislation, administration and taxation, it was against these that the mercantilist statesmen struggled. They therefore opposed everything that . . . obstructed trade within the boundaries of the state." Thus Eli F. Heckscher has characterized the mercantilist position. It was a particular branch of mercantilism, which the so-called "cameralists" expounded.[24] They developed the practical implications of mercantilism in terms of government action. They thus became the expositors and theorists of administration. For no matter how keen the statesmen of mercantilism, men like the Cecils in England and Colbert in France, might be about *freedom of* trade, they found themselves confronted with innumerable existing restrictions *in* trade which had to be removed. Willy-nilly they had to undertake governmental intervention; in other words, they had to interfere with interferences.

It was the intention of the mercantilists, then, to enhance—along with the wealth of the nation—the *power* of the government, that is to say, its strength and resources, regardless of the effect upon individuals. To put it another way, they believed in government and in administration. They looked upon the "state" as a creative agency. In this outlook they differed completely from the times preceding and following theirs. When Thomas Jefferson said that that government is best which governs least, he formulated a political outlook diametrically opposed to that of the mercantilist admirers of the "creative state." On the other side, many mercantilists had little else than scorn for the medieval constitutionalism which their centralized administrative systems supplanted. They believed in centralization and in administrative action, none more so than Francis Bacon, whose thinking was really a theoretical projection of Tudor absolutism. As we have already remarked, English developments were more than a century ahead of Continental ones, so that we find thinkers like John Locke combining constitutionalist and mercantilist views. This fact has tended to veil the parallelism between the two; from the standpoint of economic and constitutional development, Cecil, Colbert, and Frederick William I are "contemporaries." Although one worked in the sixteenth, one in the seventeenth, and one in the eighteenth century, they were each responsible for consolidating one of the modern power systems. They were each responsible likewise for consolidating an administrative service, a bureaucracy, which a succeeding generation could then subject to controls and thus convert into a constitutional system (see below, ch. II and elsewhere).

The essence of constitutionalism · At various points in the preceding discussion, constitutionalism has been mentioned as if it were well-defined and thoroughly understood. At the outset, constitutionalism was described as divided power. It is high time that the essence of this central concept be more fully stated. For even though a complete analysis cannot be given until later (chs. VII ff.), a sketch of constitutionalism's historical evolution presupposes a general grasp of what it is, or is taken to mean here. Constitutionalism by dividing power provides a system of effective restraints upon governmental action. In studying it, one has to explore the methods and techniques by which such restraints are established and maintained. Putting it in another, more familiar, but less exact way, it is a body of rules ensuring fair play, thus rendering the government "responsible." There exist a considerable number of such techniques or methods, and they will receive fuller treatment at the appropriate place.

In this general historical sketch, the question confronts us: how did the idea of restraints arise? And who provided the support which made the idea victorious in many countries?[25] There are two important roots to the idea of restraints. One is the medieval heritage of natural-law doctrine. For while the royal bureaucrats gained the upper hand in fact, the other classes in the community who had upheld the medieval constitutionalism, the barons and the free towns and above all the church, developed secularized versions of natural law. At the same time, they clung to residual institutions, such as the *parlements* in France. After the task of unification had been accomplished, and the despotic methods of absolutism could no longer be justified, these elements came forward with the idea of a separation of power. Both the English and the French revolutions served to dramatize these trends.

But why did the same not happen in Germany and Italy? Remembering that the centers of medieval universalism were Empire and Papacy, we can readily understand that they would stay intact much longer, both institutionally and ideologically, in the countries which constituted their core, that is to say, in Germany and Italy. Political organizations and systems of government disintegrate at the periphery first; hence Sweden and Britain were among the first to evolve national unification and emancipation from the medieval system. Indeed, both countries never fully belonged to the universal structure of medieval Europe. They developed their own *imperium in imperio*, and hence their transition from medieval to modern constitutionalism was interrupted by only a comparatively short period of absolutism. This English absolutism, moreover, never went so far as it did in the countries nearer the center of medieval universalism.

The other root of the idea of restraints is shared by medieval and modern constitutionalism, and is peculiar to some extent to Western culture. It is Christianity, and more specifically the Christian doctrine of personality. The insistence upon the individual personality as the final value, the emphasis upon the transcendental importance of each man's soul, creates an insoluble conflict with any sort of absolutism. Here lies the core of the objection to all political conceptions derived from Aristotelian and other Greek sources. Since there exists a vital need for government, just the same, this faith in the worth of each human being is bound to seek a balance of the two needs in some system of restraints which protects the individual, or at least minorities, against any despotic exercise of political authority. It is quite in keeping with this conflict that the apologists of unrestrained power have in all ages of Western civilization felt the necessity of *justifying* the exercise of such power, a necessity which was not felt elsewhere. Bacon and Hobbes, Bodin and Spinoza, and even Machiavelli insisted that some sort of inanimate force, reason, natural law, or enlightened self-interest would bring about what their constitutionalist opponents would embody in effective institutions: restraints upon the arbitrary exercise of governmental power.

Turning to the question of who provided the effective support which made the idea of restraints victorious in various countries, the answer must be that it was essentially the mercantile middle class who did. The bourgeoisie, as it has come to be called, furnished everywhere the mainstay of political support for constitutionalism. This fact is noteworthy, but should not be overemphasized. In recent times, organized labor has stepped into the role of the bourgeoisie in many countries, for the simple reason that it, above all other classes in the community, is an exposed minority. To be sure, the class-war doctrine of orthodox Marxism took exactly the opposite line, but two things should be kept in mind: First, in the countries most deeply permeated by constitutionalism the Marxist doctrine never gained a substantial following, except amongst intellectuals. Second, the terrible persecution of the labor class in countries which have lost constitutionalism in our generation has produced a "crisis" of Marxism[26] amongst its most ardent upholders. It is undeniable that the economic problems of our industrial society have generated strains which are taxing established constitutional systems to the breaking point. But the evils of despotism have so rapidly become manifest that the most diverse groups, classes, and nations throughout the world are seen banding together for the reconstruction of constitutionalism on a new social and international basis.

Since the Second World War, perhaps the most striking development is the growth of a European Union which in the course of 1948–49 made the first halting steps at achieving actual institutional form. The common base of the nations of Western and Middle Europe is their attachment to constitutional, as contrasted with Soviet, democracy. Prevailing opinion is socialist, but the gradualist approach is prevalent.[27] (See below, ch. XI, for further analysis.) The idea of uniting Europe in defense of her traditions has a long history; for a brief period in the thirties it looked as if it might save the peace, but the forces of nationalism were still too strong.

England's leadership in constitutionalism · Although the idea is firmly rejected that constitutionalism is somehow the result of a mysterious English national character which has more recently been expanded into Anglo-Saxon or even Anglo-American tribal character to placate the Americans, it is nevertheless true that the English-speaking peoples have developed their political traditions more steadily in a constitutional direction and have thereby become the leaders of modern constitutionalism.[28] Why? We do not know. But the fact is incontrovertible. Probably many different factors combined to make possible this steady deepening and expansion of political culture among the English-speaking people. Some features have already been mentioned. The English revolution came so early that it practically transformed the medieval constitutionalism of king and estates, of "the king in parliament." Ever since, British constitutionalism has been more traditionalist than rationalist in its foundations. But Sir Edward Coke's partisan glorification of Magna Charta, basically a feudal charter, cannot alter the fact that he was a typical representative of the commercial middle class. This commercial middle class had been behind Tudor absolutism during the sixteenth century, because Henry VIII and Elizabeth had been engaged in breaking down the feudal privileges of barons and church; they were building what has been called by economic historians the metropolitan economy (see below, p. 93 f.). But once these feudal powers had been weakened sufficiently, the rising commercial interests felt no longer the need of royal absolutism. For two full generations, from the accession of James I to that of William and Mary, the revolutionary struggle went on, finally producing the constitutionalism that has been developing uninterruptedly in England ever since. During these two generations the whole range of political issues, from absolutism in Hobbes to anarchy in the Levellers, was explored, fought over with word and sword, and finally settled in favor of a division of power between king, lords, and commons, which, while it sounded medieval and traditionalist, was in fact modern in that the real foundation of this division was the electorate behind the Commons, rather than the ecclesiastical authorities and feudal land owners behind the Lords. It was the Commons who from now on were to restrain the exercise of the Crown's power, reinforced by the independent courts. After they, in the eighteenth century, had become the real core of the government, the division was maintained through the recognition of the opposition, the basis of the party system.

The English system of free institutions aroused a great deal of interest in other countries in the course of the eighteenth century. The eyes of all those who were disgusted with absolutism turned toward Britain. But not only theirs; the eyes of kings, too, looked at the home of liberty to be sure that things would not turn out that way in their own realms. Frederick the Great of Prussia, in one of his political testaments, advised his successors not to allow the development of the office of Prime Minister; he rightly recognized in him the leader of the popular forces. The movement of Enlightenment preached to the absolute rulers the necessity of rationally conducting their office so as to forestall constitutionalism. Even so enlightened a spirit as Voltaire would rather educate Frederick of Prussia than build a constitution. So unique appeared the British system that Montesquieu built his entire discussion of *The Spirit of the Laws* around the contrast between Britain and France, and though he was behind the time in detail, generalized effectively the importance of the separation of powers as the essence of the constitutionalism which Britain had produced.

The spread of constitutionalism · The pride which the British themselves took in their constitution must have been very general. It runs through the writings of an ardent Tory like Dr. Johnson; it was encountered by travelers, even when they were preoccupied with very different matters, such as Casanova, who tells at length about it. Bentham and Burke, though worlds apart in general outlook, share this sense of achievement. Since British wealth and power were, at the same time, continually on the increase in that period, it was natural that the old ideas about absolutism should be viewed with increasing scepticism everywhere. But what is more, in France and elsewhere the rising middle class, just as in England a century or more earlier, no longer felt the need of royal aid in combating the local power of church and nobility. The French crown had effectively destroyed the power of local authorities. The middle class, grown strong and wealthy, increasingly resented the privileges of those classes in the community which no longer served any vital function. Against these privileged groups, the idea of the equality of all men was pitched and was gaining ground steadily through the years.

But there was another side to British constitutionalism. In the Empire's North American colonies, populous settlements of white men had developed a new sense of independence.[29] Many of them were Englishmen; they claimed with insistence the rights of Englishmen for themselves. When the Commons refused to heed such voices, they finally sounded the bugle call of universal constitutionalism. In spite of the grandeur of the French revolution, it should not be forgotten that it was once again in the English tongue that this all-embracing constitutionalism was declared. "We hold these truths to be self-evident, that all men are created equal, that they are endowed by their Creator with certain inalienable rights, that among these are Life, Liberty and the Pursuit of Happiness . . ." At the time, these famous phrases seemed to most of the powerful an empty challenge of a small crowd of rebels sure to be defeated. In actual fact they heralded the irresistible forward march of constitutionalism during the nineteenth century. In America, this constitutionalism struck deeper root than almost anywhere else on earth, except England and Switzerland. The American fight for independence foreshadowed the constitutional development of the British Empire. As Lloyd George once said when speaking under a statue of Washington: "He taught us how not to run an empire." The very fact of their revolting against England protected the American constitution-makers from committing the error of copying, or rather trying to copy, the English constitution, an error which wrecked so many constitutional efforts elsewhere.

For it was and continues to be the curse, in a sense, of continental European constitutional development that it had to be carried forward in the shadow of the British success. It is hardly surprising that this should be so; numerous failures resulted in France and elsewhere from the fact that the conditions of English political life could not be reproduced in other countries. The difficulties were enhanced by the fact that the actual functioning of British institutions was never fully understood, either at home or abroad, until much later. Only Switzerland, Sweden, and to some extent Holland, where a measure of constitutionalism was native, managed to evolve steadily in a constitutional direction.

The landmarks of the spread of constitutionalism in the eighteenth and nineteenth centuries are, summarily put, the American war of independence and adoption of the constitution, 1776–87; the outbreak of the French Revolution in 1789, followed by numerous constitutional experiments in France; the reforms of Baron Stein in Prussia, 1806–09; the Restoration in France in 1814–15; the establishment of the German Union (*Bund*) in 1818; the French revolution of 1830, followed by a revolution in Belgium and elsewhere; Lord Durham's famous *Report* in 1838, which eventually led to the creation of the Dominion of Canada in 1867; and finally the revolutions of 1848, including the abortive effort of the Germans to achieve both constitutional government and national unity at the same time. It testifies to the strength of the movement that even such "Machiavellians" as Bismarck and Cavour could unify their countries only through the adoption of a constitution.

The steady spread of constitutionalism followed pretty definitely the curve of industrialization. This is only natural, since it was the commercial and professional middle class which carried forward not only the industrial revolution, but the demand for constitutional government as well. The bourgeoisie, to repeat, unquestionably furnished the minds and the men for this politico-economic revolution. But it is quite another matter whether the leadership stayed with them. Even the term middle class, quite appropriate at an early stage in the evolution of modern society, gradually loses its distinctness in the course of the nineteenth century. This broadening at the base will be dealt with presently.

Industrialization brought with it one feature peculiarly favorable to constitutionalism, and that is the progressive cheapening of the printed word. For the modern press, the channel of mass communication, was everywhere in the vanguard of advancing constitutionalism (see ch. XXIV below).

Democratization of constitutionalism · Constitutionalism, both in England and abroad, was at the outset not at all democratic, but rather aristocratic. In spite of the fact that the *Declaration of Independence*, and the *Rights of Man* of the French revolution, had proclaimed the equality of all men, dominant political practice remained sceptical. The *Federalist* has not much love for the mass of the common people; it has much to say about the "gusts of popular passion" and the like. Throughout the nineteenth century, intellectuals in England and elsewhere remained highly critical of democracy.[30] What is more important, democracy, in the sense of universal suffrage of men and women, the equal participation of all classes, especially the labor class, in political life, and the elimination of racial and religious discrimination—democracy in this sense spread slowly throughout the nineteenth century, and has not yet reached its culmination.

The milestones in the process of democratizing constitutionalism in the nineteenth century were: Jackson's presidency; the Reform Act of 1832; the revolution of 1848 in France; and the Civil War. Although none of them, obviously, realized democracy, they each contributed a significant forward step. Jackson's presidency provided the first effective frontal attack upon government by the elite; through the Reform Act of 1832, and the other great measures of reform which accompanied it, a broad breach was made in the system of government by the privileged, as exemplified in rotten boroughs and vote restrictions. The revolution of 1848 in France challenged the power of financial and industrial capital, and while its premature, radical experiments with socialism led to the Bonapartist reaction, it nevertheless heralded the coming of labor into its own. Farther east beyond the Rhine, the revolution precipitated an unsuccessful attempt to unite Germany by popular movement, after having swept away the system of Metternich. In Italy a similar initiative failed. But in spite of the fact that popular forces proved too weak to unite and free nations, the idea of self-determination took root. Finally the Civil War in the United States destroyed slavery after four formidable years of armed conflict. In the course of this struggle, the leader of the antislavery forces of the North, Abraham Lincoln, formulated some of the most hallowed tenets of democratic faith. Nowhere has the progressive spirit of democracy found more eloquent expression than in the Gettysburg address: ". . . that government of the people, by the people, for the people shall not perish from the earth." The sentiments which inspired this speech are still far from having been realized.

Every one of these milestones marks an element in the process of democratization which in spite of many setbacks is still going forward. The successive extensions of the suffrage, eventually embracing women's suffrage, as well as numerous social and governmental reforms carried on the work that the Reform Act of 1832 began. Likewise in the United States, the administrations of Theodore Roosevelt, Woodrow Wilson, and Franklin D. Roosevelt have extended and deepened the control over concentrated economic power and monopoly. France, in successive phases of the Third Republic, realized part of the program of the revolutionaries of 1848, while in Germany the Weimar Republic gave a first token of what a fully democratized and socially conscious German people might contribute to a democratic world order. For here, for the first time, *social* democracy was taken up in earnest. The Fascist reaction there and in other countries of Europe meant a desperate attempt to stem the tide of advancing democracy. By exploiting all the stresses and strains of a new social pattern, Fascism managed to install itself, and then, by the ruthless exploitation of every known method of violence, to maintain itself until the inner tensions and strains resulting from such desperate repressive efforts embroiled the Fascist dictators in foreign wars that spelled their doom. But even the dictators found it necessary to make continuous bows toward the people, thus acknowledging the fact that democracy alone offers an acceptable ground for the exercise of political power.

This increasing recognition of popular majorities as the only basis of legitimate government naturally has led to a fading of the monarchical tradition. Kings, not having been popularly elected, could rarely stand up against a leader of the people. The reign of Queen Victoria is most interesting in this respect. Time and again her monarchical sense of responsibility clashed with the parliamentary responsibility of successive prime ministers. Continental crises may have been more dramatic outwardly; they brought revolution and reaction in their train. But the deep roots which constitutionalism had struck in English thinking make the slow fading of royal prerogative worthy of detailed attention. The story of the bedchamber comedy is characteristic. Peel would not form a cabinet unless, as evidence of the Queen's confidence, he should be given the right to nominate the ladies of her household. The Queen refused. The Queen thought that she would be "supported by my country who are very enthusiastic about it and loudly cheered me on going to church Sunday." The basis of this conflict was the fact that court gossip still played a significant role in the forming of a government. That was in 1839. It was not long before the idea of the politically "sovereign" people had taken root to such an extent that only the parliamentary support of a man could determine his leadership. The kings just faded out of the picture.

Socialism and constitutionalism · The revolution of 1848 projected, as has been said, a new issue: socialism. Though there is no inherent logical reason for it, the demand for socialism became the primary goal of the rising labor class. The *Communist Manifesto* had by one year anticipated the revolution of 1848. It has remained a radical challenge ever since. It had denounced some of the very weaknesses which contributed to the failure of "utopian" socialism as represented by men like Proudhon. More particularly, the *Communist Manifesto* rejects any possibility of co-operation between the revolutionary socialist proletariat and other classes in society. Consequently, the *Manifesto* denies completely the central idea of constitutionalism. It combines an advocacy of force and violence during the revolutionary and post-revolutionary period, a ready acceptance of dictatorship, with a belief in a vague anarchical type of democracy after all classes except the labor class have been destroyed.[31] The *Communist Manifesto* and all orthodox Marxists who followed it revived the belief in the creative possibilities of violence; they expounded the concept of a totalitarian dictatorship in the name of the proletariat. This is not the place for entering upon an analysis of the Marxian view of society, to discover the underlying reasons for the Marxist rejection of constitutionalism. It seems a curious paradox in the light of the fact that the working class constituted and still constitutes a minority, since constitutionalism is designed to protect the minorities against arbitrary action by the government, even when supported by a majority. But this paradox disappears when it is remembered that Marx expected the evolution of industrialism to turn the labor class into a majority. His predictions in this respect, though striking, were basically erroneous. Quite contrary to his views, the growth of the middle class, the managerial, professional, and clerical workers, together with the inability of the Communist antiproperty view to gain a substantial number of adherents among the farmers, provided mass support for the Fascist reaction.

33

A sense of these realities and the strength of the constitutional tradition combined to keep English and American labor largely hostile to Communism and its doctrine of violence. Even in those European countries where Marxism became powerful, Socialist parties found themselves in practice obliged to soften the rigor of the doctrine. Sharp conflicts raged which led to an increasing recognition of the desirability of working within a constitutional context. After the First World War, the Socialists entered a number of governments and proceeded to apply their general policies under constitutionalism. But owing to their failure to face the issues involved in a combination of socialism and constitutionalism, very serious strains developed. Germany, Italy, Sweden, Czechoslovakia, France, all these and many others, experienced dangerous crises which in a number of cases proved fatal. The advent of the Labour Party into power in Britain in the twenties was somewhat less disturbing, but provided no real test because of its lack of a majority. In the meantime, the Dominions of New Zealand and of Australia have been governed for some time by Socialists under a constitution.[32]

It is a curious fact that the two countries with the most distinctively democratic constitutional tradition, the United States and Switzerland, have not participated in this experimentation. Some would say, of course, that Franklin D. Roosevelt's presidency was socialist in outlook. There is no need here to go into these partisan arguments; the fact is that neither Roosevelt nor many of his followers ever acknowledged a theoretical attachment to socialism, let alone Marxism. To this extent he certainly differed from the Blums, Scheidemanns, and Benešes. But while there has been no participation of professed socialists in these two democracies, the socialization of the economy, that is to say, the extension of governmental participation in the economy, has gone forward apace in both these as in all other countries. The constitutional system of the United States and Switzerland has often creaked under the load, but it has not broken down. In both Switzerland and the United States, some grave warnings have been heard.[33] Basing their analysis upon the "state" concept, which we have rejected, these writers have urged that a continuous expansion of the state was bound to destroy the individual and hence the free society of "capitalism." As a result there are quite a few today who would hold that constitutional democracy requires "capitalism" or "free enterprise" for its operation. These slogans are not often very carefully defined. A realistic view reveals that words like "free enterprise" and "free competition" refer to conditions which have never actually existed.

Since the Second World War, the social democratic movements in the leading countries of Europe have increasingly stressed constitutionalist views, and all major new constitutions, like those of France, Italy, and Germany, are more cognizant of the need for regularized restraint. To be sure, the first French constitution, rejected by the voters in 1946, was radically unrestrained in its concentration of most power in the hands of a parliamentary majority, as are indeed the German constitutions of the Soviet Zone of Occupation, as well as the draft constitution for all of Germany, published by the German Communists. But the Social Democrats of Germany, as well as the Socialists of France to some extent, are sharply opposed to such corruption of the constitutionalist position. More especially do all moderate elements now perceive the importance of a firm guarantee of fundamental human rights or civil liberties. At the same time, the British Labour government has proved at least premature those prophets of doom who freely predicted a collapse of English constitutionalism at the time the Labour Party would attempt to institute socialism.[34] The crucial point is unquestionably this: that socialism can be realized gradually enough, in the view of these Europeans, to become compatible with constitutional democracy in the process.

Without pretending to pronounce final judgment in the matter, it would seem, in the light of present evidence, to be quite probable that constitutionalism is combinable with a considerable variety of economic patterns. Constitutionalism rests upon a balance of classes in a society. But this balance is not a hard and fast one, it is not an equipoise of mechanical weights, but rather a moving equilibrium of a kaleidoscopic combination of interests. The government, through the parties, operates as the balancer of these combinations. In a wider and deeper sense, the introduction of the "state" concept distorts the outlook of constitutionalism. For, when socialism is interpreted as "state" socialism, "state" and "society" are confronted as if they were two mutually exclusive corporate entities. Constitutionalism embodies the simple proposition that the government is a set of activities organized by and operated on behalf of the people, but subject to a series of restraints which attempt to ensure that the power which is needed for such governance is not abused by those who are called upon to do the governing. There is no apparent reason why a greater or lesser amount of such governmental activities should be incompatible with effective restraints, provided the concentration of power in one group or one man is guarded against. "Social democracy," one of its ablest historians has said, "is not a miracle which comes to life at a particular moment and then continues to function automatically, but it is rather a political task upon which it is necessary to work continuously."[35] Change, as we pointed out at the beginning, is not something to be feared and avoided, as Aristotle thought, but is of the very warp and woof of modern constitutionalism.

35

Conclusion · There are two issues which confront constitutionalism today: socialism and the international or world order. In spite of the fact that internationalism and socialism are linked in many minds, the two issues are intrinsically distinct and perhaps even liable to suggest conflicting solutions. For to the extent that socialism implies planning, it impedes the progress of internationalism, since planning is more complicated on an international plane. It is a striking fact of contemporary life that convinced adherents of constitutional democracy usually split on the issue of the relative urgency of these two tasks. Fortunately, from a more comprehensive viewpoint, the conflict resolves itself. The history of the past thirty years has shown beyond a shadow of a doubt that constitutional democracy cannot function effectively on a national plane. An international pattern of constitutionalism is clearly indicated for all that part of the world which is democratically governed. The League of Nations, no matter what its faults, and they were many, nevertheless represented a first decisive effort to extend constitutionalism to the world at large. It was a projection of the aspirations of the Declaration of Independence. Whether the United Nations will prove to be more viable remains to be seen. Its greatest advantage over the League is that the United Nations really encompasses the world.

The worldwide tasks of constitutionalism should not be allowed to obscure the many unfulfilled tasks of democracy at home. Even in the most democratic countries, the process of democratization has stopped short of some of the most obvious issues, racial, social, and others. The need for a responsible government service is widely felt; yet the methods best adapted to fit such services into a constitutional democracy are as yet untried. The fear of the bureaucracy, inherited from a monarchical past and enhanced by a totalitarian present, remains a powerful factor inhibiting bold solutions. The role of public opinion and propaganda is casting a shadow over the conventional formulas of "the will of the people" and "the belief in the common man," which have been axiomatic in democratic constitutionalism.

Even more disturbing are recent trends, engendered by the concern over security, which are weakening the tradition of basic civil rights, including academic freedom. Investigatory and intelligence functions, believed necessary to cope with the enemies of constitutionalism, are dangerous activities in themselves. They are firmly rooted in "reason of state," and in the traditions of government in the preconstitutionalist period. Yet, the collapse of constitutional systems has raised the issue of how to deny the protection of constitutionalism to its avowed enemies. Any analysis of constitutionalism today would be incomplete if it did not attempt to assess recent efforts made to cope with the dangers which the rise of totalitarian dictatorship has created.

II

*The Core of Modern Government: Bureaucracy** *

Introduction · The elementary or basic aspects of bureaucracy: England · Same subject: Brandenburg-Prussia · American colonial bureaucracy · Functional and behavior aspects · The differentiation of functions · Centralization and integration · The hierarchy · Discipline and morale · Qualification for office · Training for public service and the educational system · Publicity · Objectivity · Precision and continuity · Discretion versus secrecy · Conclusion.

Introduction · In discussing constitutional development, we called the body of servants devoted to the prince a bureaucracy. We might have called it officialdom, magistracy, government service, or even civil service, as long as it is clearly understood (1) that we are talking of a group of human beings, not some mysterious superentity such as is suggested by the word "state," and (2) that these human beings perform definite functions which the community at large considers worth while. In primitive agricultural communities, these functions are directly attached to the possession of the land; they frequently become hereditary. Such was the foundation of the feudal system. Hereditary offices attached to the land offered the most promising means of securing a certain amount of law and order over widespread areas under primitive conditions of communication. It was a very inefficient system, allowing wide latitude for personal abuse and great variations from one locality to the next. To cope with the attendant evils, the royal overlords sought to extend their personal estates through marriage, escheat, and various other means which the feudal law placed at their disposal.

As the royal domains grew, it became of vital importance that a central body of direction be created to prevent new disintegration at the center, a process we find taking place in England, France, Spain, Prussia, Austria, and other realms. The only serious competitor to the princes in their determined efforts to concentrate power in their own hands was the church. In

*Besides this broad sketch, important aspects of bureaucracy are dealt with later; the general functions of the developing administrative services of modern government are treated in chs. III–VI, while ch. XVIII takes up executive leadership, and ch. XIX the modern governmental service with particular reference to the question of responsibility.

many ways the church became the example of secular rulers. In no respect was this more true than in that of the techniques of administration. More amply provided with literate personnel, the church developed, during the Middle Ages, the rationalized techniques of administration which the princes were quick to follow, at the suggestion of clerical advisers. These central bodies of royal servants are the beginnings of our modern administrative systems.

The elementary or basic aspects of bureaucracy: England · Conventional English and American history-writing has so exaggerated the role of Magna Charta and Parliament that the administrative core of British institutions of government has been obscured. Out of a justifiable pride in later developments, constitutionalism and democracy, the myth has grown up that the origins of modern government in Britain and America were different from those in continental Europe, that constitutionalism came first and the administrative services afterwards. Such a view is not only contrary to the facts, but it obstructs a real understanding of the strength of constitutionalism itself. Constitutionalism comes as a restraining, civilizing improvement; there must, in other words, first be government before it can be constitutionalized. That is why we suggest the study of administrative government, of bureaucracy, as the necessary preliminary of a full grasp of constitutional government. A comparison between the English and Prussian development, one very early and the other very late, will be instructive, though other countries, such as France and Spain, could serve equally well, since the development in the early phases is very similar throughout Western civilization, notwithstanding the great divergencies in the coming of constitutionalism.

A number of English historians, outstanding among them T. F. Tout,[1] have in recent decades brought to light the main outlines of early administrative history. The great Stubbs already had shown that the administrative system was set up in the days of the later Norman kings and found its first full development in the reign of Henry II (1154–1189). But to him "the Angevin administrative system was important, not so much in itself, as because he regarded it as the source of the parliamentary organizations of later times." His main interest "was in the origins of our modern constitution." It is the more striking that he should have stressed the early administrative system. But of course the great administrative departments kept on developing, and it is not too much to say that without that continuous development the government could not have succeeded in uniting the nation, which enabled it to undertake the task of constitutionalizing the centralized system. In the Middle Ages, Tout has rightly observed, when legislation was small in amount and largely declaratory in character (see below, ch. V, pp. 92 ff.), the administrative side of history bulked immensely larger. To be sure, administrative, legislative, and judicial functions greatly overlapped, and not until the fourteenth century was the differentiation of these functions begun in earnest.

The administrative system of the Norman and Angevin kings, while set within a strictly feudal pattern of society, nevertheless showed the decisive elements of modern rationalized administration. Its most important task being the centralization of the realm, we find a corresponding centralization of supervision and control. Under Henry II this was carried out through the king's council, the *curia regis*, and the exchequer. In the course of time, the law courts and the chancery were separated from the council, while the exchequer's control of financial business was divided between the exchequer, the wardrobe, and the machinery for the collection of parliamentary grants. Among these several bodies, the council was the over-all controlling and co-ordinating body. But it was not administrative in the strict sense. According to Tout, the central administration of England centered around the exchequer, the chancery, and the household offices. This pattern we find in all the developing European governments: household offices become transformed into public functions as the king's rule expands and takes root.

Records and files have become so much a matter of course today that we tend to forget that a great deal of determined effort went into their development. If the administrators in England had not on the whole been so conscientious in keeping these records and files, we could not know what we do know about the establishment and execution of their task. Even a cursory survey of the sources which a study of the medieval administrative system calls for reveals the astounding mass of carefully preserved records. There are striking differences between the household offices, and the chancery and exchequer. The officials of the former often took their archives away with them, considering them strictly secret. Time and again regulations were directed toward working out the details of this keeping of records, and official keepers were appointed at an early date.

Space does not permit even the sketchiest outline of the development of the several functions and departments of administration. Throughout the twelfth, thirteenth, and fourteenth centuries we can observe a continuous process of differentiation of functions, with various aspects of financial business becoming distinct, as the exchequer, the wardrobe, and other offices struggle for their respective spheres of influence. Though only detailed study can offer convincing proof, all evidence points toward the conclusion that the differentiation of functions resulted largely from such struggles for power of the different departments in the administration, and from the need for defining their respective competencies. After the granting of Magna Charta, this interdepartmental conflict was broadened through the efforts of the barons to control at least part of the administration. Yet "it would be rash to maintain that constitutional and political considerations played an important part in bringing about the division of the task of ruling England between a national administration, controlled by the chancellor, and a court executive, controlled by the clerks of the wardrobe."[2] It was primarily a matter of expediency, as the government became more complex and more modern, that produced the "imperative necessity" for greater differentiation of functions.

Qualification for office is another aspect of rationalized administration which progressed slowly throughout these centuries, as trained clerks took the place of nobles. The king's interest in freeing himself from baronial pressure aided mightily in making him seek for acceptable personnel elsewhere. Clerics were, of course, the most obvious source for such personnel throughout the Middle Ages, apart from legally trained men to staff the courts. Elsewhere in this volume, the particular and highly significant development of the legal profession in England is briefly outlined. Eventually, with the coming of humanism, inroads into the clerical monopoly on higher education were made by men trained in the humanities. The role of humanism in strengthening Tudor absolutism has never been thoroughly investigated. Some brilliant men, like Bacon and the Cecils, are associated with this movement. It is characteristic of England, no less than of other countries, that royal absolutism, in its desire to free itself from the influence of the feudal constitutionalism of the estates, especially of the barons and the church, found a mighty ally in these *literati* educated to admire the spirit of classical antiquity. The development of such a central bureaucracy was checked in England by the Puritan revolution and the subsequent ascendancy of parliament. The price Britain paid for the uninterrupted retention and effective transformation of important elements of medieval constitutionalism was a corrupt administrative service. British administration at the beginning of the nineteenth century was honeycombed with nepotism and political patronage to an extent which contrasted painfully with the bureaucracies of absolutist governments. The thoroughgoing reforms of the fifties recaptured, however, all that had been lost and more, and gave Britain an administrative service superior in integrity and ability to that of any of the bureaucratic continental governments. The qualification for office could, by that time, be determined in a truly modern scientific spirit by a system of competitive examinations based on professional training.

Same subject: Brandenburg-Prussia · Since Brandenburg-Prussia forms in many respects a complete antithesis to British institutional history, the parallels in her evolution, as far as the administrative establishment are concerned, are the more striking. Since Brandenburg worked out a centralized government almost five hundred years later than England, developments are telescoped into a few decades.[3] We are well supplied with documentary evidence. In 1598, when Joachim Friedrich became Elector of Brandenburg, absolutism was unknown in his lands. Under his predecessor, Brandenburg was ruled by the Estates (Parliament). But Joachim Friedrich wanted to create a rule by officials (*Beamtenregiment*), a bureaucracy. Most educated people siding with the Estates, he resolved to draw upon foreigners, men brought to Brandenburg from other territories (they were, of course, Germans) and made into a Council by the order of 1604. This document, together with one amending it in 1651, shows again, in embryo, the vital constituent elements of a government service, or bureaucracy. Admitting openly that he was motivated in this step by the example of other states (presumably France), this order sought to centralize control, where a great confusion of councils had prevailed before. In general it made the following provisions: The councilors should be allowed to speak and vote freely, and, for the sake of order, the votes should be counted. So that the transactions might be remembered, the prince's private secretary should keep records, and produce them when needed. (This practice of keeping records, characteristic of an effective government service, did not prevail in the English cabinet until recently (see below, ch. XVIII), though all the lower offices in Britain as elsewhere keep careful records of all transactions.) All these records should, however, be kept strictly secret. In accord with this secrecy was a further provision regarding the mails. The prince's chamber secretary was to bring all the letters unopened to the prince, who would read them and decide upon the answer either with or without consulting the councilors. The provision that every councilor who was given a letter for answering should make out a receipt for it points to the fact that many letters were lost by being taken away from the office. We have here, then, full confirmation of four elementary constituents of a bureaucracy: (1) centralization of control and supervision, (2) safeguards for the independence of judgment of each member of the organization, (3) maintenance of records and files, and (4) secrecy.

In the succeeding decades, certain difficulties appeared which had to be dealt with if the bureaucracy was to triumph over the Estates (Parliament). These arose from the acquisition of additional territories, which in turn caused a multiplication of functions. The unification of a number of territories and provinces under one princely house was for Prussia, as it was for

Austria, the most powerful impulse toward the development of an efficient bureaucracy (as it had been in France and England before). The aim was to make Brandenburg-Prussia strong, to win respect for her abroad, and to make her prosperous and progressive. By the ordinance of 1651, the authority of the privy council was extended to all the different parts of the realm. Moreover, each councilor was assigned certain definite and specific functions which he must perform in the name of the prince. In accordance with this differentiation of functions, each councilor was to receive the mail which referred to his functions, read it, make comments, and then submit it to the prince and the other councilors. When the business at hand was familiar to all, council was to be held. In the council, the councilor especially in charge had the first vote and the votes were registered; but the ultimate decision was reserved for the prince. When we inspect the list of duties or functions, we also find a beginning made in the direction of distributing functions according to the qualification of the several councilors; court work was assigned to lawyers, diplomatic work to high nobles having experience therein, and so forth. We note, therefore, (1) the differentiation of functions, and (2) qualification for office. This document clearly marks the appearance of two more aspects of a rationalized government service which were also noted in the British case. The parallelism with the much earlier English development is therefore striking. All the later documents merely reaffirm and expand these elementary aspects, and all these factors or aspects could be as readily shown to have appeared in other governments—France, Spain, Sweden, Austria; they all went through a parallel development.

American colonial bureaucracy · In spite of the fact that the American revolution was explicitly waged against the royal bureaucracy, or perhaps because of it, the view is often expressed that "bureaucracy," that is, the administrative services, is not the core of modern government in the United States. "The Mayflower compact men, the framers of the constitution, and others, could start from scratch, creating their new institutions with an awareness of other countries' experience . . . having little need to accommodate their new ideas to a continuing institution like bureaucracy."[4] Such a view, though persuasive, is nonetheless untenable. One might be satisfied with pointing toward the bitter denunciations of federal bureaucracy in the period of the Jeffersonian and Jacksonian assault upon the Federalist knee-breechers. But it was not merely a partisan matter. The colonial governor, who in the course of the 150 years of colonial development emerged as the key official in American government, reveals clearly the inescapable fact that the organization of the executive power

42

must inevitably precede the constitutionalizing process. Until there was a rationalized and co-ordinated government, there could not be any efforts at restraining it and subjecting it to popular influence, if not control.

The American administrative system crystallized, of course, still later than that of Prussia. Nor did it achieve the rationalized forms which Prussia's absolutist rulers could give it. Indeed, the colonial governor found himself hamstrung by the inadequacies of British administration. Colonial offices were treated as plums to be handed out to deserving party followers, many of whom preferred to stay at home and let their office be administered by an agent. The resulting inadequacies were admittedly an important factor in creating that sense of dissatisfaction in the North American colonies which eventually led to revolt. This experience created a permanent suspicion of executive power which has stood in the way of responsible government service ever since. It gave color to the facile contrast between democracy and bureaucracy which still would try to tell us that a government can give satisfaction without adequate administrative staff work. Carl Russell Fish, in tracing the evolution of the civil service, commenced his searching study by pointing out the extent to which George Washington had emphasized qualification for office. This remained the major bone of contention throughout; for the differentiation of functions was so well recognized by the time Washington's administration was organized that there was no need for him to grope for such elementary distinctions as administrators had done in the days of Henry II. This shows us more clearly than anything else that American constitutionalism *presupposes*, as does all constitutionalism, that the core of modern government, a functioning bureaucracy, has already been brought into existence. The rich experience of British administrative genius had already been at work in creating the framework of a government service into which the constitutionalizing forces merely had to put new men to carry on. All the elements which we have noted and which had been discovered by trial and error and the survival of the most suitable techniques were thus made readily available. At times some of these insights were lost, as when central supervision and control by the governor was dissipated in the wake of democratic enthusiasm; but after some unhappy experiences, a later generation readily returned to a recognition of their worth.

More recently, Leonard D. White, in his searching study of the establishment of the federal government service, has shown how inadequate is[5] the view, which imagines a society governed only by economic laws, readily overlooking the extent to which modern business and corporate organizations had themselves learned the lessons of a rationalized bureaucracy. People looking at America through such spectacles failed to see that the rationalized methods of modern business administration are merely elaborations of techniques which the governmental bureaucracy had first developed. Rightly did Carl Russell Fish observe that "as long as the controlling element in the country (namely, business) manage their private affairs in a careful systematic manner, we may expect the government to conduct its business on approximately the same principles."

Functional and behavior aspects · The six elements of a bureaucracy brought out by this analysis fall naturally into two groups. Three of them order the relations of the members of the organization to each other, namely, centralization of control and supervision, differentiation of functions, and qualification for office (entry and career aspects), while three embody rules defining desirable habit or behavior patterns of all the members of such an organization, namely, objectivity, precision and consistency, and discretion. All these elements are familiar enough to the modern science of administration. But it is sometimes forgotten that they were originated by men of extraordinary inventiveness who were laying the basis of a rationalized society by these inventions.[6]

Turning first to the relations of the members of an organization, we find that they are elaborated and defined with reference to the functions to be performed. We may therefore call this group of elementary aspects functional criteria. These simple functional criteria, while underlying elaborate modern rules and regulations, as far as governments are concerned, still are far from being fully carried out. Practically all modern governments have struggled time and again to revamp their administrative pattern in terms of these basic functional relationships, but whether it be the *Report of the Hoover Commission* (1949), the *Report on Administrative Management* (1937), or the *Machinery of Government Report* (1918), there are always many vested interests ready to resist such simplification and reform.

When we come to the second group of criteria, dealing with behavior, we find a similar situation. In fact, these criteria contain normative elements which are puzzling. They are really striking instances of the intimate connection between fact and norm which is characteristic of social-science concepts. As in other cases, the normative aspect is dominant when individual conduct is examined in the light of the concept. An official who is indiscreet is immoral. But these criteria are rules of expediency founded on experience when an organization is examined in relation to the concept; organizations which fail to maintain discretion among their staffs usually fail. A more detailed analysis of the functional aspects must next be undertaken.

The differentiation of functions · The first two functional aspects, namely, centralization of control and supervision, and differentiation of functions, are in a sense related; for the centralization of control and supervision is itself a kind of differentiation of a particular function, viz., the function of control and co-ordination. Central supervision is necessary only when a differentiation has previously existed. This is why centralization stands in close relation to integration. They both co-ordinate diffuse functions. But while centralization co-ordinates spatially diffused functions, such as the feudal age bestowed upon early modern times, integration co-ordinates technically differentiated functions, such as arose from the early differentiation of functions at the center.[7] The differentiation of functions means that offices or functions are distributed carefully and rationally among the members of a given organization, like a government service, and are then arranged into an integrated whole, thus producing a more or less elaborate system of competencies or jurisdictions. This differentiation seems such an obvious prerequisite of an administrative task of any magnitude that it is frequently given only the most cursory attention. And yet, literally hundreds of years of the history of modern government were consumed in evolving even the most elementary distinctions, and in discovering by trial and error that, all things considered, functional differentiation is superior to regional differentiation, though a certain amount of both are always necessary. Furthermore, the process of differentiation is a continuing one. To be sure, every modern government has a separate ministry (department) of foreign affairs, of finance, of commerce, of labor, and so forth, and what cannot be readily classified is thrown into the ministry of the interior. But here the simplicity ends. There are the greatest variations between the several governments when we go into further detail. Students of administration are wont to consider the problems which arise under this heading as those of departmentalization. In reality the problem is intimately related to the broader questions of constitutional framework. In the United States, for example, tariff problems occupy not only the Department of Commerce and the State Department (handling foreign affairs), but also a special Tariff Commission which owes its existence to the separation of powers. In European countries where the separation of powers has not developed along the same lines, we do not find such a body. Brief reflection upon this and many other similar items will show that a rule embodying the principle of differentiated functions is more frequently pronounced in general terms than put into practical effect. Constant experimentation and change are necessary in order to keep the differentiation of functions of a government service abreast of developing communal needs. For example, every government in recent years has had to

45

struggle with the problem of a distinct air force. In every case, the established services have strenuously resisted the differentiation of that function. Everywhere they have yielded in the end. In the United States the issue was resolved only partially in the face of the war, in 1941. Even the establishment of the Department of the Air Force after the war has not wholly settled the matter. Likewise, the vast problems of the public-welfare field have raised very difficult differentiation issues. Welfare occupies a central place in recent reorganization plans in the United States.

Centralization and integration · The technical differentiation of functions, as we have pointed out, may be complicated by a regional differentiation. Under such regional differentiation, which is often spoken of as decentralization, all kinds of governmental functions are assigned to an individual or to a body having jurisdiction over a territorial subdivision, such as a province, a department, a county, a town, and so forth. The functions of such local authorities will invariably overlap to some extent the functions of technically differentiated central authorities. For this reason, some supervision and control are invariably found necessary, and are usually vested in ministries of the interior (France, Italy, and so forth), but may be lodged elsewhere for historical reasons (England: Board of Health). This central authority then acts as an intermediary seeking to integrate technically and regionally differentiated functions. This often causes a great deal of red tape when the central authorities themselves have widely scattered local representatives. It might be very much easier for the local assessors to deal with the field staff of the Treasury, but apart from personal contacts they are dependent upon some central authority, like a ministry of the Interior, for effective co-ordination. This shows vividly the close relationship between functional differentiation and central supervision and control. For when we pass from the top level of offices in a large organization, say the Treasury, to the next lower one, the differentiation must be carried forward into the regulation of activities of individual officials on that level. Each official's sphere of competency is smaller, and comprised within a higher official's competency along with that of several other officials. There is, then, a double differentiation, namely (1) a technical differentiation on each level, and (2) a differentiation between more routine and more discretionary activities, as we go up and down the line in each organization (or chain of command, as the armed services like to call it). Because of its peculiar significance for the development and rationalization of a government service, we must isolate this type of differentiation as a distinct process. Historically speaking, functional differentiation commences at the top, and gradually is extended downward, limiting in its course the sphere of regional differentiation, or, as it is usually called, local self-government (home rule). But as it proceeds downward, such differentiation raises problems of integration with regard to differentiated functions, and problems of centralization with regard to functions not yet technically differentiated, but regionally dispersed. These problems of integration and of centralization, of supervision and control, may be lumped together under the heading "hierarchy."

The hierarchy · Nowhere is the impact of ecclesiastical experience upon administration more apparent than in the term hierarchy. Indeed, the word has such definite associations with the Catholic church that it might be well if we had another term. But since none is readily available, we will say that hierarchy is the pattern of subordination by which the several levels of command and obedience are defined. The hierarchy is a concomitant of the rational distribution of functions. As soon as an organization grows to any size the large number of officials who exercise partly conflicting functions stand in constant need of integrating and co-ordinating leadership. This seems obvious enough, and yet the implications of administrative leadership have received rather inadequate attention, except in connection with private business management. The urgency of such administrative leadership springs from two related and recurrent problems. On the one hand, the detailed and specific functions of the lower-downs need constant reinterpretation in terms of the larger objectives which they presumably serve. On the other hand, the obstacles and difficulties encountered in the exercise of these detailed and specific functions require consideration with a view to the possible improvement or alteration of these larger objectives or purposes. Even so general a statement shows that the semimilitary, authoritarian nature of a government service is by no means a gratuitous invention of petty autocrats, but is inherent in the very nature of the processes which form the essence of all administrative services. This point hardly requires emphasizing in an age which exhibits examples of such authoritarian, hierarchical control on all sides, since large-scale business corporations, trade unions, and many other organizations are conducted on precisely this pattern.[8]

The need for administrative leadership explains to some extent why monarchies have been so successful in developing a high-class government service. If the powers of control and coercion connected with the various offices and functions are arranged in more or less concentric circles which become smaller as we ascend to the higher levels, a single individual or bureau acting as a unit would presumably have ultimate control and power. Moreover, such an individual or group must be himself a part of the hierarchy, though not necessarily chosen from among it. This unitary central control characteristic of a fully developed hierarchy may, of course, be quite effectively exercised by elective officials, provided there is a sufficient amount of continuity and agreement between successive office holders as to the conduct of governmental activities. The English cabinet in the latter half of the nineteenth century succeeded in building up a remarkable public service corps; it may be well, however, to keep in mind that the English Prime Minister has often been called a practical dictator once he has entered No. 10 Downing Street with a safe majority in the House of Commons (see below, ch. XVIII, p. 363).

Even though a trend toward unitary leadership be inherent in the hierarchical aspect of bureaucracy, or of effective government service, it seems undesirable to overemphasize this point. Hierarchy in our opinion should describe more generally any determinate system of distributing the powers of control and coercion. Hierarchy subordinates officials performing very specific and tangible functions to other superior officials, who supervise and direct a determinate number of these subordinates; the superior officials in turn may be supervised and directed by a still more limited number of "higher-ups." Nor need this scale of subordination and control be restricted to individual officials. A hierarchy may subordinate one group of officials to another group of officials acting together as a unit. Or individual officials lower down may be subordinated to a group superior higher up. The Swiss (Executive) Council, American administrative commissions, and practically all judicial systems are of this structure. In Anglo-Saxon countries, although the power of specific coercion of the higher courts to determine the decisions of lower ones is limited, the power of reversing decisions produces a similar effect crystallized in the rule of *stare decisis.* This rule limits narrowly the discretion of lower courts. An element of discretion remains, however, and this fact has led some writers to overemphasize the difference between courts and administrative bodies. In terms of actual conduct, the difference is quite small; for although the hierarchical principle seems to imply flawless subordination, the extent to which any given hierarchy conforms to that standard is limited by other competing principles which are essential for its life, such as the principle of differentiating and distributing functions. A higher official will hesitate to reverse the decision of a lower official when he feels, as is often the case, that the lower official has a better knowledge of the facts in detail. The question of whether judicial or administrative action should be provided for is only to be answered in respect of the purposes or objectives to be achieved. There is nothing inherently beautiful in either. Both are techniques for accomplishing certain purposes, as we shall show further on. And both are comprehended within the governmental services or the bureaucracy, as that term is here understood. These processes can be fully grasped only if the rule of anticipated reactions is taken into account.

Discipline and morale · Almost all administrative hierarchies have well-defined rules of discipline, according to which acts of alleged insubordination are judged. Some rudimentary discipline is inherent in any hierarchy.[9] The rigor of the discipline should be studied by the political scientist in relation to the purpose for which the administrative setup has come into existence. Moralizing should at all costs be avoided. If the purpose of the particular hierarchy is kept in mind, a better understanding will result. A purpose which is likely to be defeated by delay in execution will produce a more rigorous discipline than one which is not imperiled by being postponed. An army at war and business enterprises in highly competitive fields offer good examples of rigorous discipline, while much ordinary government service, in peace time, and business enterprises in distinctly monopolistic fields offer examples of rather relaxed discipline. Sometimes the operations are intrinsically fraught with danger, as they are in the railroad business. Then even a monopolistic business may show high disciplinary standards. A further condition making for variation is the general state of public morale. The student of the history of administration is struck with the extent to which discipline is initially very severe, but is gradually relaxed. As the service becomes well established, organizations with poor discipline are likely to be outdone by their rivals, whether in business or government. The comparatively static condition of most governmental activities during peace time has made it possible to subject all disciplinary action to fairly elaborate judicial procedure; its main purpose is to protect the official against arbitrary exercise of the disciplinary power. His punishment and removal cannot take place until he has been accused, indicted, examined, and pronounced guilty, either by a regular court, or by a court composed of his peers (see below, ch. XIX, pp. 405 f.).

The discipline of an administrative organization is intimately related to its morale. Where morale is high, the problems of discipline are reduced considerably; they stand in inverse relation to each other. The task of maintaining morale has always been of central concern to military men and they have developed an elaborate set of techniques for maintaining it. It is obvious that morale enhances the chance for effective co-operation. It may be defined as "group persistence in the pursuit of collective purposes" (Lasswell). Evidently it depends upon the sharing of purposes or ends, and therefore everything that assists in securing loyalty to common purposes or ends is relevant to him who would deal with morale, either theoretically or practically.[10] A potential danger to good morale lurks in excessive discipline. The annals of warfare are full of it. The techniques suitable for peace time may be disastrous when applied to troops shaped in the crucible of war. Likewise, every administrator worth his pay knows that disciplining his subordinates can never be an effective substitute for securing voluntary co-operation, which is the equivalent of good morale. Hence modern students of administration have given increasing attention to co-operative techniques of administration. This is largely a matter of making sure that the subordinates understand the reasons for taking certain actions or for making certain policy decisions. The effective management of morale here impinges upon the problem of communication. Successful administration under democratic, that is to say, co-operative, conditions will seek to broaden the range of participation on the part of all members of the organization.

Qualification for office · Our third functional criterion, the qualification for office, has received so much attention from students of public administration in the United States that the problem of government personnel is treated by many people as identical with that of qualification for office. The great movement for the establishment of the merit system was focused upon qualification for office. Nor can there be any question that the rationalization of the bureaucracy finds its most significant expression in provisions for such qualifications. There have been marked national differences in the past (see ch. XIX, pp. 389 f.), but at present they are gradually being supplanted by a universal drift toward "technical" qualifications in the strict sense. What is meant by that is the tendency, particularly in this country, to select men in the light of their training for some technical specialty, such as civil engineering, banking, or animal husbandry. Speaking very broadly, such requirements may be called a unique expression of our technological civilization. Altogether the emphasis upon special intellectual achievement and promise in technical fields, as contrasted with literary skill (China) or with other personal aptitudes and character traits, is a peculiarity of the modern age. Only very recently has the perfecting of psychological tests opened up new avenues to the problem of how to select the person best qualified for a particular office.

Training for public service and the educational system · In view of the preoccupation in the United States with the problem of qualification, it is curious that the cognate problem of training for the service has, until recently, received only cursory examination. Yet the system of public schools and universities traditional in Europe originated to a considerable extent in the requirements of the government for well-trained officials.

Speaking broadly, such a system of public schools and universities fulfills the function of co-ordinating educational facilities with the differentiated hierarchy of official functions through an elaborate system of standardized examinations. If such co-ordination is effective it becomes possible to consider the degrees from the several educational institutions as constituting, at least in part, satisfactory evidence that the person passing such examinations and holding the corresponding degree is qualified for a certain function in the hierarchy. Civil Service Commissions, as we find them in the United States, could possibly be an effective substitute for such a system of co-ordinated schooling if they made a persistent effort to bring about a mutual adaptation of the required qualifications for service and of the training which is given to acquire them. Unfortunately, the opposite is the case (ch. XIX, p. 395). European governments in days gone by could not rely upon such a co-ordinator, because there were few schools to co-ordinate, and so they undertook to organize schools and universities themselves. Schools and universities in this country are being increasingly influenced in their programs by the requirements of the government services. The numerous governmentally financed training programs, such as the Army Specialized Training Program (ASTP), sharply increased these trends. In England, not to speak of Continental countries, there has been worked out a close correspondence between service training needs and school programs. Not only the so-called administrative class of higher officials, but also the lower ranks, are recruited in accordance with their schooling. Thus the clerical class is recruited through an examination "framed with reference to the standard of development reached at the end of the intermediate stage of a secondary school course."[11] In the United States there is a marked contrast in the upper range of the service. In this field, where the requirements for qualifications are in Europe most rigorous, the spoils system continues to hold sway, while in the subordinate positions an approximation to the standards of a developed bureaucracy is found to prevail.

Publicity · The foregoing analysis of the functional aspects of a developed bureaucracy would be incomplete if we did not discuss briefly a feature which these several aspects gradually acquire to an ever increasing extent. This is the feature of determinateness and publicity.

It will be recalled that we found all the elementary aspects present in the embryonic bureaucracy of the Brandenburg councils of the seventeenth century. What they then lacked was determinateness and publicity. In a sense, it is possible to assess the stage of development of a given bureaucracy by examining the extent to which its functional aspects are determinate and publicly known. We must link determinateness with publicity, because determinateness is never insured unless full publicity enables any reasonably intelligent and interested person to judge for himself whether equality of treatment is safeguarded and favoritism, nepotism, arbitrariness, and so on are excluded. Under a popular government, the governmental services will attract that high caliber of personnel which is an essential prerequisite for its ultimate success only if public scrutiny enables the citizenry to have confidence in its public service. Publicity is very difficult to achieve because it is the natural tendency of officials to be secretive. Indeed, even in relatively democratic countries, the public is not able to find out important facts. Questions in parliament and investigations are heavy tools to bring into play. Perhaps the most advanced system among all modern governments is that of Sweden, where a long tradition of making official files available to the interested citizen has provided full publicity for the transactions of most of the services (foreign affairs is, of course, excluded). In some ways, however, the United States has been a pathfinder in this field, especially through the development of the regular press conference of high officials where they answer relatively freely questions put to them by duly accredited correspondents.[12] One branch of the government's work, however, has been conducted in most countries within public view for a long time, and that is judicial business. In this field the need for rationalized procedure is particularly urgent.[13]

Objectivity · Having examined the functional aspects of bureaucracy, we may comment briefly on the three behavior aspects of bureaucracy; that is, traits of the administrators. It is not possible to examine them in detail.

What was called "objectivity" in the administrator is both an ideal and, within limits, a distinguishing trait. It is closely related to *expertise*, and is usually found in persons who possess such *expertise*. No one can be a good craftsman, nor indeed a craftsman at all, who does not acquire the capacity and inclination to think in terms of objective needs, in terms, that is, of what the particular job in hand requires. Thus an administrator, if he needs to hire a secretary or any other subordinate, will ask: How good is she? What experience has she had? and so forth. A politician, on the other hand, will be more inclined to give consideration to who recommended her, whom she knows, etc. There is something to be said for both points of view, but obviously the relative weight to be assigned to each will depend upon how difficult and technical the tasks, how much depends upon them, and how expensive are the services. The same difference in viewpoint permeates all other fields of action and decision. Evidently, an administrator will be successful to the extent to which he is capable of that sort of objectivity; taking the word success in the sense of real achievement, of course, not in that of "making a career." For it is unfortunately a fact that subserviency to the views of a superior, and hence lack of objectivity, often helps an official to advance. Much of the most searching thought on administrative management has gone into discovering methods for preventing that sort of deterioration in the service. Some of these methods will be discussed in a later chapter (see ch. XIX below).

Objectivity has often been belittled in English-speaking countries. Behind it there seemed to lurk the danger of autocratic disregard of public opinion. And yet the British civil service today yields to none in its attachment to the needs of the service. Some American federal agencies also have achieved an enviable tradition of objectivity. It is true, of course, that the expert inclines toward dogmatism. The very fact that he knows more than most others with regard to a certain matter induces him to be satisfied with his particular views. He is likely to disregard the "broader" considerations, that is to say, those points at which his particular problem links up with others concerning which he is no expert at all. Since we have to work with finite minds, this issue has become increasingly aggravated as the complexity of our industrial society has increased. Government public relations officials have battled with this problem for some time now. The final integration of will and understanding, of decision and knowledge, of man's laws and of nature's laws (which are always enforced), cannot be accomplished once and for all. It is a continuing process, and the administrator's penchant for objectivity plays a vital role in bringing about a sound balance. His craftsmanlike pride in actual achievement, as contrasted with make-believe, derives its satisfaction from the admiration it arouses in fellow craftsmen rather than in the public at large. It is unlikely without long training in the social sciences (including the law); for only such knowledge enables a man to develop objective standards and an awareness of the limits of his knowledge.[14]

Precision and continuity · The effective administrator usually is precise in what he says and steady in what he does. This is generally recognized and perfectly sound. Imprecision in speech and writing leads to faulty communication, with the result that the subordinate does not understand what he is being asked to do, while the superior does not understand what has been reported to him. Vacillating action obviously is undesirable; it bewilders subordinates, irritates associates, and endangers the achievement of lasting results. Both precision and continuity are so evidently desirable that the observations concerning them might be considered trite, were it not for the fact that much public indignation over red tape and other rigidities in the behavior of administrators results from precisely these two traits. An intimate knowledge of a certain field of public policy or governmental activity is a prerequisite to rendering an informed judgment concerning administrative actions. The routine which seems annoyingly rigid to the occasional citizen may be the result of long efforts and repeated trials of alternative procedures. Private organizations of any size are bound to develop the same rigidities in dealing with outsiders that governmental organizations do. It is only too often forgotten by all of us that a large organization is an amazing achievement of human co-operativeness, and that it is possible only through the making of *rules*. Exceptions to such rules require decisions by higher-ups who cannot always be readily consulted. The good administrator must abide by his rules in most instances. If he makes exceptions too readily, particularly to rules which have been made with regard to other rules over which he has no control, he is likely to throw the whole organization into confusion. It is somewhat like the difference between driving an ox-cart and an express train. The ox-cart driver can stop to chat with a friend; the engineer of the express train cannot. It is, of course, easy and only too common among administrators to fall into the opposite error of refusing to adjust the rule, even when its application is evidently unreasonable. It is the great merit of constitutionalism that it provides machinery for the airing of any complaints that may arise. In discussing the use of questions in the British parliament (below, pp. 326 f.), an attempt is made to suggest the operation of that corrective. Such a forum for venting complaints has the added advantage of offering an opportunity to the skillful administrator to explain necessary rules and regulations to a wider public, and thus to gain support and understanding of the need for precision and continuity as essential features of a functioning administration.

Discretion versus secrecy · Many writers on government and administration might object to including secrecy as a main behavior aspect of a functioning bureaucracy. The word, like bureaucracy itself, has a derogatory connotation. But a realistic view of the facts obliges one to recognize the undeniable importance which rules and regulations looking toward secrecy have played in the history of administrative organizations. The documents concerning Brandenburg and Britain are apt illustrations of what could be documented down to this very day as a major concern of administrators, both governmental and private. There is no use in closing our eyes to the facts; the determined efforts of all organizations to secrete their more important evidence in controversial and competitive matters show vividly that "power hides." In thus insisting upon the importance of secrecy, are we not contradicting ourselves and what we said in our discussion of publicity? The apparent contradiction resolves itself when we recall that publicity has come with the growth of constitutionalism. The range of what is to be kept secret has been more narrowly circumscribed, different services showing marked variations. Thus foreign and military affairs, even in the most highly developed democracies, have been much more widely recognized as entitled to a broad measure of official secrecy. However, the progressive inclusion of more and more aspects of industrial production under the term "military affairs" has once again extended the area of required secrecy. In a crisis this has led to a very broad definition of "official secrets" in the *Official Secrets Act* (1939) passed in Britain just prior to the outbreak of the Nazi war. In the United States, too, the problem of "security," after being highlighted during the Second World War, has been further aggravated by the problem of atomic and other weapons. Fear of the Fifth Column of Soviet spies, heightened by the presence of Communists, has not only led to the exclusion of members of this party and its sympathizers from government work, but to more and more elaborate policing by highly secretive organizations, such as the Federal Bureau of Investigation. *The Espionage Act* (1917) and the *Alien Registration Act* (1940) highlight this development, but the situation has been further aggravated by Soviet espionage and the atomic-war problems.

As a trait of the administrator, this aspect of secrecy is appropriately spoken of as "discretion." Though an essential trait of administrators of all kinds, it has not received much attention, except where its excesses have been attacked. The secrecy of the bureaucracy under monarchical absolutism was a source of continuous irritation to the liberal forces contending against them. It also served as a convenient target. In the discussion of the press and censorship below (ch. XXIV) these issues are more fully developed. The sympathy which most of us feel with that outlook, the revival of complete secretiveness in the totalitarian regimes, and the general human dislike of secrets which we cannot share, all combine to make difficult a recognition of discretion; that is, the ability to keep a secret. Disgusted at the secrecy which shrouded governmental transactions, reformers in the past have tended to assume that anything which is secret is *ipso facto* bad.[15] They too easily overlooked the practices of their own organizations, or assumed that their own secrecy was merely the result of having to deal with opponents who practiced secrecy. While this is understandable enough, it bars a realistic insight into the requirements of a well-functioning bureaucracy. For while discretion can be abused, its ubiquity is due to the real needs which it serves.

There are many details of human relationship which, if bandied about, would make such relationships more difficult. A supervisor reporting on his men should be able to speak with complete frankness; but if his views are not kept confidential, he will not be able to do so, since he has to continue satisfactory working relationships with the men. An administrator engaged in tracking down some violations of rules and regulations would be likely to find such investigation impossible if what he was doing were publicized and thus brought to the attention of the violators. Occasions of this sort are numerous; they occur wherever conflicts arise in the work of government and administration. Of course the most noted instances, often emphasized to the exclusion of the mass of minor cases, are found in the field of foreign affairs; the conflict between nations adds drama to the issue of secrecy as the "secret services" of the several governments carry on their efforts to wrench from a hostile power the information which is being guarded by diplomats and staff officers.

While the public and its representatives incline to frown upon secrecy (although the secrecy of Congressional committee proceedings makes American Congressmen more willing to defend a measure of secrecy, see below, ch. XVII, pp. 349 f.), administrators often incline in the opposite direction. They consider matters secret which are or could be known to everyone. A well-known scholar and adviser of the State Department used to tell a story, the gist of which involved a vigorous protest to him from the Department concerning a confidential matter he had mentioned in a public address. In his reply he dryly remarked: "I do not blame you for considering matters secret which have been published in the Congressional Record." This secretiveness of certain officials and departments often is quite innocuous, but when it takes the form of forbidding high officials of the government to express in print their views on matters of grave public concern, it is unequivocally contrary to the public interest in a constitutional democracy. Since these officials are, or ought to be, the leading experts in their respective fields, the public is clearly entitled to share their knowledge. This is not the place to enter into all the arguments brought forward on both sides of this issue (see below, pp. 349 f., and the references given there). But it is the place to say that this tendency among officials to broaden the sphere of "official secrets" to include matters of *public* policy is both common and harmful. Perhaps the most famous case is that of the late Admiral Sims, who boldly incurred the displeasure of his superiors by airing certain highly detrimental naval practices. But he succeeded, where many others have failed. The case of the civil engineer whose sound analysis of the consequences of governmental land-grant policies lay buried in the files for fifty years, while the country went the predicted road toward destruction of its soil, is even more poignant.

The foregoing discussion shows, it is hoped, two things: (1) secrecy is an inherent feature of all governmental administration, and discretion a carefully cultivated trait of administrators, and (2) the sphere of applicability of both is dependent upon the nature of the tasks in hand, the conditions under which the task must be executed, and the governmental framework' whether democratic or authoritarian. We know too little about the probable limits of discretion and secrecy to formulate precise hypotheses concerning the sphere of applicability. But this fact should not mislead us into denying the great importance of secrecy and discretion as parts of bureaucratic behavior, regardless of whether we like what the particular bureaucracy is doing.

Conclusion · We have sketched the nature of a government service or bureaucracy in broad outline. All realistic study of government has to start with an understanding of bureaucracy (or whatever else one prefers to call it), because no government can function without it. The popular antithesis between bureaucracy and democracy is an oratorical slogan which endangers the future of democracy. For a constitutional system which cannot function effectively, which cannot act with dispatch and strength, cannot live. Fortunately, both the Swiss and the British have shown that an effective, responsible bureaucracy is quite compatible with vigorous constitutionalism (see below, ch. XIX). British constitutionalism, like all constitutionalism, developed as a system of controls imposed upon a vigorous bureaucracy. The early unification of England made her one of the pioneers in developing administrative techniques for modern government. But the trend is universal throughout the Western world. In the course of this analysis, six primary criteria of such bureaucracies have been identified: (1) the differentiation of functions, (2) qualification for office, (3) centralization and integration of control and supervision, (4) objectivity, (5) precision and consistency or continuity, and (6) discretion. They are found in a small administrative council at the beginning of Norman England, and they pervade a vast administrative machine such as the British Empire. As administrative organization unfolded, an increasing amount of publicity could and had to be given to governmental activity. Such publicity, though often bitterly resented and opposed by the bureaucracy, really contributed powerfully to its development by making it more determinate and institutionally stable. The effective working of such responsibility and publicity depends upon a viable constitutional system. Therefore constitutionalism, though historically opposed to monarchical "bureaucracies," actually reinforced and aided the full development of bureaucracy—a process which is still going forward.[16]

III

Territorial Expansion, Security, and the Military Establishment

Introduction · Outside attacks · British navy and continental armies · Size of armies · The development of arms · The evolution of arms and science · Government control of universities · The provisioning of armies · The problem of revenue · The situation of Estates on the Continent · Commissioners and the emergency power · Civil and foreign war · The military aspect of the totalitarian rise to power · Disarmament · Conclusion

Introduction · The conditions which form the background of modern government are closely related to its central objectives. In fact, if they were not related to such objectives, they could not form conditions for the development of these governments. For such is the nature of human and social, as compared to subhuman and inorganic life, that many of its most essential conditioning factors must and do pass through the forge of human consciousness where they are wrought into swords of willful purpose.[1] Thus the geographic factor exerts its most powerful influence where a determinate will for territorial expansion exists. This desire for territorial expansion is deeply rooted in human history; for long periods the control of land was the primary basis of all power. Feudalism had been altogether built on it. As has been remarked, the process of territorial unification was at first almost exclusively directed toward the extension of the royal domain. The great kings of Europe who built modern governments were in a sense land-hungry farmers.

When several such "farmers" live in close proximity, the question of security at once arises. Everyone has heard the ancient tales about the peasant who in the depth of night goes out to his field to shift the stone which divides his field from that of his neighbor. The peasants can go to court. But not the "sovereign" princes. Where there are no courts to decide the quarrel, armed conflict will be the only method of settling the dispute. Thus the idea of security arises as a corollary to the will for territorial expansion; the dread of foreign invasion haunts those who dream of territorial acquisitions.

Rare are the occasions when a government has admitted blatantly its intentions of territorial conquest, except in the colonial sphere, even in the stark days of the seventeenth century. Louis XIV, Frederick the Great, and Napoleon are among the few who have dared to speak out frankly and admit the brutal facts. And even they sought support for their aggressive schemes in the records of the past, like Louis XIV citing Cæsar and Charlemagne. Usually each government insisted upon its own pacific intentions and its need for security, as they do to this day. But when the scientific observer places the various declarations side by side and compares them with the actual behavior of their authors, he clearly perceives that armed conflicts, and hence insecurity, result from the policy of territorial expansion. Each of the contestants seeks to increase his armed strength. Thus an expansion of the military establishment became the obvious corollary objective of those who sought territorial expansion and talked of security.

Outside attacks · It would be incorrect to attribute the evolution toward vast military establishments alone to the passion for territorial conquest innate in the land-hungry kings. The tendency toward ever-increasing armaments also received a tremendous impetus from the onslaught of the conquering Turk. After the Reformation had swept away the halo of a united religion which had sanctioned the medieval empire, the Hapsburgs found in their struggle against the huge armies of the Moslem a new justification for asking the united support of the German princes.[2] Nor can we deny that military and administrative methods were deeply affected by them. The extraordinary military successes of the Ottoman Turks hastened the abandonment of feudal, and the adoption of modern, bureaucratic methods; the standing armies of the Sultans forced the organization of similar troops in the Hapsburg realms. Once such an army had been raised, and a central bureaucracy had consolidated the scattered Hapsburg dominions and organized them for the support of a large standing army, it did not take long to destroy the Turkish power, at the beginning of the eighteenth century. A similar, though slower, evolution can be traced in the rise of Spain against the Arabs, and in that of Russia against the Tartars. It is noteworthy that the military establishments of each of these powers became of decisive importance.[3]

British navy and continental armies · There has been a tendency to overlook the parallelism of the English development and that on the Continent. As far as the evolution of modern governmental methods is concerned, England was at least as aggressively expansionist as other European governments. Finding her road to European conquest blocked by the consolidation of the French kingdom, she limited herself on the Continent to balance-of-power diplomacy (see next chapter), and turned her attention to conquest overseas. For this reason her military development is predominantly naval.[4] But the needs of this royal navy engendered, as was remarked before, the same administrative problems as did those of the army in other European countries. The decisive turn came, as might be expected, during the reign of Henry VIII—a natural sequel to his policy of expansion and rivalry with the Hapsburg and Bourbon princes. In 1546 he established the Navy Board as a central administrative body. Naval development continued unchecked through the reign of Elizabeth, but under the Stuarts the increasing hostility of Parliament made it impossible for the kings to get the necessary funds. The rapid development of naval organization during the Commonwealth period strikingly illuminates the dependence of modern military development upon unimpeded executive leadership, such as the dictatorship of Cromwell afforded. It is well known that the decisive defeat of the Dutch in 1653–1654 was of crucial importance to nascent British imperial aspirations. The victory would have been impossible without the rapid expansion of the naval forces under the administrative leadership of the Cromwellian Navy Commissioners. Ever after the navy remained the mainstay of English centralized administration, just as the army did in France. Hence, the search for territorial expansion overseas led to the typical military establishment of Britain, as elsewhere.

At the same time, it was a most important circumstance for the growth of constitutionalism that this should have been so. For a navy is very much less dangerous to the freedom of the citizen than an army. G. M. Trevelyan has stressed this point. "The possession of a royal navy does not enable the monarch to hold down his subjects as a royal army may do. In England, there was no royal army, and in the Civil War of Charles I, the royal navy actually took the side of Parliament." Trevelyan even ventures to suggest that had the British fought the Spanish Armada as an army carried by a fleet, "in all probability the character of such a military effort would have diverted English society and politics in a martial and monarchical direction." Perhaps this is going a bit far. A remarkable Swiss writer of the eighteenth century, J. L. de Lolme, argued in his book on *The Constitution of England* (1775) that "the crown, in England, does not rely for its support, nor ever has relied, upon the army of which it has command. From the earliest times,—that is, long before the invention of standing armies among European princes,—the kings of England possessed an authority certainly as full and extensive as that which they now enjoy . . . they began to derive from the civil branch of their regal office that secure power which no other monarchs had ever possessed, except through the assistance of legions and praetorian guards. . . ." The truth is that there is to be noted an interdependence between the growth of constitutional liberty and the absence of a standing army which decisively influenced the British development.[5]

Size of armies · Nothing shows more vividly the trend of the development than the bare figures of the size of the several armies.[6] In medieval days armies were small—people were astounded at the French army of 32,000 men at Crécy in 1346. Four hundred years later, in 1750, Austria, France, and Prussia had armies of 297,000, 182,000, and 190,000 men respectively. Nor were these armies collected temporarily and for a specific purpose as was the French army at Crécy; they were permanent standing armies which had to be fed, clothed and sheltered all the year round. Soon this matter of provisions became the touchstone of victory. To revert once more to the Hapsburg victory over the Turks, it is interesting to find that Prince Eugene of Savoy has been described as "a provider and husbander of resources, as well as a leader of armies," and that "he set to work with a firm hand to organize the finances which he found in the worst possible condition with debts of enormous proportions. . . ." Similarly, the attention of the Great Elector and his Prussian successors was concentrated to a considerable extent on building up an effective administrative machine to safeguard once and for all the financial and provisional rear of their big armies. Toward this aim, the French and later the English Treasury contributed on a large scale; indeed, it would have been utterly impossible for Brandenburg-Prussia to maintain such a large army on its own resources. In a sense, the Prussian army of the eighteenth century gave Britain a mercenary standing army on the continent.

The development of arms · Along with the constant growth of the size of the armies, there took place a constant improvement in the effectiveness of the arms which these armies employed. If the Middle Ages were on the whole an epoch in which defensive weapons were stronger than aggressive ones, that relative superiority was now reversed. To be sure, fortresses continued to play a decisive role in the East, where the Turkish onslaught broke under the walls of Vienna, though even here only after outside reinforcements under a Polish king made a successful counterattack against the beleaguering forces. But usually the force of attack was strengthened more by the new weapons of firearms than was the force of defense. The trench warfare of the First World War seemed momentarily to give supremacy to defensive techniques—only to be broken once more by the advent of the tank and poison gas. The history of the Second World War is one of striking superiority of the means of attack, especially of the airplane; once air supremacy was achieved on a battlefield, all defenses caved in.

The relative strength of defensive and aggressive weapons is of great importance in shaping government and politics. The superiority of defensive weapons strengthens the chances of local resistance, and therefore entails a dispersion of political authority. Aggressive weapons, conversely, strengthen the chances of successful attack by growing units, and therefore help the concentration and centralization of political authority. This has been true since the dawn of civilization, when tribes of horsemen, equipped for successful attack by their greater swiftness, first succeeded in building large territorial dominions. But while these horsemen, and later similar conquerors down to the bombarding battleships and aircraft of modern imperialism, fell upon alien civilizations, the curious and striking aspect of modern army development in Europe was a constant parallel forward march of a group of competing countries, each at once ready to adopt a new device introduced by one of its opponents, and by its civilization fully equipped to do so. This is as true of the spread of Swiss compact infantry technique in the fifteenth century as it is of the firearm and the gun in the sixteenth, of rapid troop movements in the seventeenth, of the goose step and sudden cavalry attacks in the eighteenth, of the loose infantry technique evolved by the *levée en masse* of the French revolution and its attendant compulsory military service (the nation in arms), of the ironclad, the machine gun, the airplane, poison gas, the atomic bomb, and so on in more recent years. Here is a long list of some of the most remarkable achievements in the development of modern weapons and military techniques, each of them signifying a new impetus to potential aggression.[7] During the Second World War one small country after another was vanquished by the Germans, until the technical superiority of the United States eventually triumphed over them in turn. But the decisive blow came with the atomic bomb released over Japan. Until that event occurred, there was still some lingering doubt as to whether an island might not provide adequate defensive support under modern conditions. Since then, the terrifying aggressive potential of this new weapon has led to a protracted struggle for achieving international control of its use. It has at once greatly enhanced the need for and the willingness to accept world-wide government and the difficulty of achieving it under present conditions. A sharp conflict has developed between the two dominant powers, the United States and the Soviet Union, over the methods of control to be employed, each naturally insisting upon the adoption of a plan in accordance with its own governmental and political pattern of organization and thought.[8]

The evolution of arms and science · If we consider this evolution in retrospect, we see at once that it is intimately linked to modern science, and thereby to the whole context of modern industrial civilization. Every great discovery, we find, has its counterpart and concomitant effect in new engines of destruction.[9] So intimately are the two related to each other

that if governments and peoples should resolve tomorrow to abandon armaments, they would face a major economic crisis. If they wished to mitigate
it, they would have to place orders on a large scale for peace-time products
to be made by the armament factories. The close link between bathtubs
and mortars, between the progress of civilization and science and the intensification of warfare, has received inadequate attention.[10] A German professor's invention of synthetic nitrogen during the First World War solved
a raw-material problem which otherwise might have led to the defeat of the
German government at a much earlier date. Synthetic gasoline and rubber
played a similar role in the Second World War. This and many similar
"achievements" illustrate the close connection between man's struggle
with nature and with his fellow men. Is it too much to hope that a time
will come when science can progress without giving new tools to the
warmakers? Does science need this stimulant? Now that our industrial
society has reached maturity, may not science carry forward on its own
momentum?

It is the hope of those who are seeking to establish world government
that the time has come for science to progress without the continued stimulus of war and its requirements. Now that modern industrial technology
has reached so advanced a stage, this disappearance of war as a stimulus to
the progress of science might conceivably slow down this progress. It has
been argued that such a slow-down may be even desirable. For scientific
advance has been so rapid that social and governmental institutions and
policies have failed to keep up with it and controls tend to become antiquated. But these are but hopes, whereas the present situation is characterized by a fierce armaments race, especially in terms of atomic and air
weapons.

Government control of universities · As long as a strong connection exists between science and the engines of war, governments are bound
to take a decisive interest not only in science but in the institutions where
it is developed and taught. That is one of the reasons why war-minded
European governments have always controlled universities and other institutions of higher learning. Harold Nicolson, in a popular novel, undertook to picture the intense excitement which surrounds any new invention
affecting the course of a future war;[11] cabinets fall, and the whole politics
of a large country like England are shown to revolve around questions
raised by the discovery of a new metal-alloy with the help of which more
formidable airplanes can be built. Naturally, the greatest importance must
be attached by the government concerned to insuring the loyalty of the
inventor. This is much easier when the inventor is an official of the govern-

ment, as all state university professors are. The chances of winning a war are of such decisive importance to expansionist governments that large amounts of purely "academic" work might well be supported with a view to the gambling prospect of a major discovery of that kind. For this reason, research work is closely associated with the military techniques evolved by governments seeking expansion and security. This link has vastly and characteristically expanded in the United States during and since the Second World War.

Other associated techniques, such as taxgathering and the stimulation of trade and industry, will be treated in a separate chapter (see ch. V). Their development also serves modern government's second major objective, namely, the fostering of prosperity, and their importance and ramifications are so considerable that the thread of our argument would be lost if we were to consider them at this point. But we must briefly discuss one aspect, namely, the provisioning of the armies.

The provisioning of armies · Arming, feeding, and clothing soldiers acquired only slowly the prominence which it occupies in the military program of modern governments. In medieval days every soldier, knight as well as hired mercenary, had to bring his own arms and clothes, had to buy his own food.[12] Heavy guns made a first dent in this system; cities and princes commenced to set up armories from which to supply their troops. Soon it was discovered that other arms, too, might be secured on advantageous terms and rented out to the mercenaries, deducting fees from their pay. Similarly, the purchase of clothes wholesale made possible considerable savings; standardization of these clothes into *uni-forms* readily suggested itself as the next step. Regarding food, a mixed system prevailed for a long time. But as armies grew, troop commanders found themselves shouldered with the task of providing canteens where the soldiery might secure food at reasonable prices. Graft and corruption were difficult to avoid. Therefore it seemed imperative, particularly to princes with a sense for economy, to take over entirely the feeding of troops, particularly after the general draft got under way. Perhaps the early beginnings of this system of governmental provisioning must be sought in countries with a considerable navy. It was palpably impossible to let sailors do their own buying of food. Therefore in maritime nations like the English, governments entered at a very early date into the "detail business" of feeding their navies.

During the Second World War, the United States military establishment took full measure of the importance of food for morale, and succeeded in making its army and navy the best-fed in the world. Scientific insight into dietary problems is brought to bear upon this problem; at the same time the advantages of centralized purchasing are carried to the point where "rations" are determined in the Pentagon for all armed forces scattered over the globe, so that for months ahead the menus of hundreds of thousands of military personnel are "planned" day by day.

The problem of revenue · It is apparent that for all these activities of organizing and keeping intact arsenals and armories, of collecting, storing, and distributing foodstuffs and drinks, and of purchasing, storing, and handling uniforms, considerable administrative organizations had to be set up.[13] For a time, attempts were made to handle these problems within the context of the medieval constitutional order by multiplying councils and boards, partly under royal, partly under parliamentary direction. Incredible confusion resulted. Where a strong and capable administrator-king attempted to cut the Gordian knot by independent measures, his activities encountered very serious difficulties from a constitutional viewpoint. Since the levying of additional taxes was in varying degrees subject to the consent of the Estates (Parliament), the princes had great difficulty in securing the necessary revenue. Debasing the currency was a temporary expedient often resorted to. The chartering of colonial trading companies helped some governments, but the returns were much less considerable than was commonly hoped for. The seizure of church lands helped the Protestant princes. Both transactions were obviously of a predatory nature. It has never been determined how much the government of Holland or the king of England gained from their chartered companies, because these princes were not regular stockholders. Whatever they were able to extract from organizations like the East India Company they received in the form of charter fees, loans, and so forth. What benefit kings derived from the confiscation of church lands, and the like, is almost as difficult to determine. But a very rough estimate, based on extant sources, and probably representing a minimum, suggests that these confiscations yielded Henry VIII £1,890,500 between 1524 and 1547. The military significance of such loot can roughly be gauged by comparing it with the cost of a medium-sized man-of-war, such as the *Ark Royal*, the flagship for which Queen Elizabeth paid £5000. Had these sums been used by the English kings to organize and equip a sizable army, as Charles V and his Hapsburg successors in Spain and Austria did with their American gold, they might well have triumphed over the parliamentary forces. But since the road to territorial expansion lay overseas, they concentrated on the navy, and as colonial revenue was slow in coming into the royal treasury, they had to wrangle with a Parliament which was quite aware of the dangers of allowing the king to build up military support.

The situation of Estates on the Continent · Estates' assemblies on the Continent were, of course, no less alive to the threat which any rapid expansion in royal military forces contained for their own position. But the immediacy of dangers from abroad made it difficult, if not impossible, for them to refuse to grant the revenues which the prince demanded, and, what was worse, proceeded to collect anyway, if the Estates were slow in making the grant. In other words, the continual imminence of foreign invasion gave to Continental monarchs the entering wedge for expanding their revenues.[14] They could appeal to the "emergency power," a power always recognized even in England as part of the royal prerogative. This royal prerogative appears to have been a decisive factor which might explain why Continental Estates did not proceed to develop parliamentary armies along the lines of Cromwell's Model Army. For strange as it may seem today, it was quite common in the sixteenth and the first half of the seventeenth centuries for representative assemblies to maintain their own military establishments, a situation which is so contrary to our unitary conception of modern government. But they were seldom as ably led as the Model Army, and if they attempted to take the field against an oppressive prince, as happened in Bohemia after 1618, the civil war at once embroiled them in foreign complications and actual invasion. In the course of such intervention the monarchical cause could more surely count upon support from foreign princes than the Estates. Thus the battle on the White Hill (near Prague, 1620) was lost because the Bohemian Estates and their elected king could not secure adequate foreign support. Would the Parliaments of Cromwell and William III have fared better if they had needed such aid?

Commissioners and the emergency power · Estates and princes alike were dependent upon a host of intermediary officials, commissioners or commissaries, as they were called, but the princes could much more effectively employ such agents on account of their claim to "emergency power" under the prerogative.[15] Such commissaries often appeared with the armies in the field and collected money, grain, horses, and what not from the unfortunate local populace, claiming simply that it was needed. Thus constant deprivations of the civilian population, particularly of the peasantry, but also of the cities, took place because of an alleged impending threat to peace and security. Such commissions varied greatly in scope; some commissioners, as in the cases just cited, were merely sent to do one particular errand, others had more or less plenary powers to accomplish a certain result, such as quelling disturbances and re-establishing the authority of the prince. But in all these cases, the decisive point was a specific need requiring immediate or, as it is nowadays often called, "direct" action. It is an interesting and striking fact, and one well illustrating the persistence of political techniques within a given culture pattern, that with the advent of the dictatorship of the proletariat in Russia and the innumerable occasions for direct action (the legal order having practically vanished), the commissary instantaneously appeared on the scene as the People's Commissar—an agent of the revolutionary leaders and the mass behind them. The same thing had happened during the French Revolution, and there can be little doubt that the word came from there into Russia, though the technique itself is inherent in the very situation requiring direct action. Thus we may say in conclusion that direct or emergency action is an important concomitant technique of modern military evolution (see ch. XXVI and below).

Civil and foreign war · There is a kinship between civil and foreign warfare, between internal and external armed conflict, which is of broad significance.[16] The unrealistic quality of much nineteenth-century political thought is revealed in the fact that it failed to perceive this close kinship. In fact, in recent times the group which has shown a distinct propensity toward foreign war is the modern nation and the princes under whose leadership it arose. Religious and class interests are more likely to get embroiled in civil war. Thus the "pacifism" of revolutionary socialists preaching the doctrine of class warfare turns out to be little more pacific than the pacifism of a government which keeps its peace with one adversary to concentrate all its force upon crushing the other.

The bellicose spirit of militant socialism and communism raises not only the specter of civil war, but difficult questions regarding the prospects of lasting peace in a fully socialized world. Self-contained empires such as Russia might in such a world be pacific since they possess all they need. But recent events, especially the Soviets' harsh policy toward its satellites, raise serious doubts on this score. Furthermore, the very exclusiveness of socialist governments with their trade and production monopolies augurs ill for international co-operation. New causes for war seem to be lurking in the struggle for raw materials and markets; the attitude of British labor, or at least sections of it, toward Egypt and India has at times in the past been rather imperialistic. There is, then, no certainty that a family of socialist nations might not become engaged in armed conflicts as fierce as those fought between expansionist monarchies. The mere adoption of socialism will not abolish or even minimize the danger of war. No matter how considerable might be the solidarity of the labor class when confronting their employers, this solidarity weakens when the labor classes of various countries confront each other. The Soviet Union has in fact been playing the Communist parties of the several countries against each other.

The military aspect of the totalitarian rise to power · We have seen how the exigencies of external pressure facilitated the monarchs' military ascendancy. We have seen how the prince in times of release from external pressure could broaden his military ascendancy into a general political ascendancy. He became a monocrat, almost a despot. When, in the course of events after the French Revolution, this central control was wrested from the princes and appropriated by the "people" through its representatives, the control of the military establishment passed into the latter's hands. Maintenance of this control has always seemed of vital importance to those who reflected upon the conditions of successful constitutional government, from Cromwell to Gambetta. It is a striking confirmation of their views that the collapse of constitutional orders in postwar Europe has occurred where that monopoly of control over military techniques (violence) was not or could not be maintained. Germany, Austria, Russia, and Italy all suggest the trend of development in countries where the government surrenders this monopoly of military power which the autocratic governments of seventeenth and eighteenth century Europe labored so persistently to establish.[17] In Russia, the Kerenski government allowed itself to be so misled by the wiles of Entente diplomacy and the liberal doctrinaire's indifference to the vital condition of effective control over the military forces that it continued an increasingly unpopular war, and thus hastened the disintegration of the regular army. Trotsky expressed it well: "The mass of the soldiers shaken by the revolution was looked upon by Kerenski as clay with which he could do as he pleased. . . . He ordered a new offensive (in June). . . . It soon was clear that no 'democratic army' stood behind Kerenski; . . ." Lenin and Trotsky knew that they must strike while the army was defunct. Foreign observers have agreed with reactionary generals in making the same point.[18] In Germany, the Communists were unable to employ similar tactics, because the moderate Socialists immediately made peace. A sufficient body of the army and police remained loyal to cope with the situation. But owing to these services the army was able to entrench itself sufficiently to escape from all serious efforts at effective democratization. In this endeavor it was greatly helped by the provisions of the Treaty of Versailles which forced Germany to reduce her army to a small professional force; a liberalist indifference toward military problems of government common among the new leaders of the democracy did the rest. As a result, the democratic leaders later were placed at the mercy of generals who were admittedly quite indifferent to the fate of the new regime. "Private" armies, both Communist and National Socialist, scheming for the overthrow of the "system," were allowed to grow up alongside the rather puny army of defenders of the new constitution. For a time, each of these "armies" numbered about 100,000 men, red fighters, brown shirts, Steel Helmets, and National Banner men. They balanced each other, with the official army and the police endeavoring to keep the "peace." But when the Steel Helmets made common cause with the brown shirts, and the official army was won over, too, the democratic and constitutional forces found themselves cornered and without even a superiority of armed force, let alone a "monopoly" such as the maintenance of government is claimed by many to require.[19] In Italy, where the situation was somewhat obscured by the gradual emergence of Mussolini's power, the "humiliations" of the peace treaty had undermined the position of the parliamentary leaders in the popular mind. The army was profoundly affected. It is significant that the proclamation of the Fascists after their March on Rome stated, first of all, that the march was not made against the army. What is more, the government's intention to declare a state of siege was thwarted by the king's refusal to sign such a declaration and this refusal was motivated by urgent advice given the king that "the army would not fight." These situations suggest that a constitutional government's loss of superiority in military force heralds its imminent collapse. Lenin in Russia, Hitler in Germany, Mussolini in Italy have all shown by their later actions that they were most anxious to remove the weakness which had given them success. They may not, in Hitler's and Mussolini's cases, have been successful, but their military policies showed a clear realization of the dangers to which a government is exposed which does not rest upon a firm basis of military support. On the other hand, the remarkable resiliency shown by the United States upon the occasion of both the First and the Second World War in putting very large armed forces and vast equipment into the field in a relatively short time is striking evidence of the dormant reservoirs of military strength which a co-operative society contains.[20] But it must not be forgotten that these reservoirs could only be activated because the United States was given two full years in which to mobilize its resources and manpower. It is a key task of effective strategic planning and the foreign policy resulting from it to keep this advantage of time until effective world organization can be achieved.

Disarmament[21] · As part of the struggle against militarism carried on by the democratic and pacific nations, the idea of disarming the aggressor has come to be generally accepted. It has more especially been adopted as a policy toward those countries dominated by the Fascists which were held responsible for the Second World War. Such "demilitarization" is, of course, hopefully viewed as the beginning of a general disarmament. There is, however, an unresolved paradox involved in disarming the German democrats, leaving them in the difficult position of facing totalitarianism.

The paradox of this situation has recently been made apparent by the repeated Soviet proposal for the withdrawal of all occupation troops; these forces constitute, until a German army is permitted, the only legitimate military support for the democratic government. What this special situation clearly reveals is that "disarmament" can only mean a pooling of armed forces and military establishments. This may indeed mean a reduction of the total contingents required, but it is a transfer of arms, rather than their abolition. It means an international or supernational army (or police force, as it is often euphemistically called).

Armaments do not "cause" wars; military establishments are the governmental techniques for realizing the territorial objectives: expansion, security, defense. As long as these objectives remain, the close connection between the progress of civilization, science, culture, and military undertakings will make it inevitable that disarmament turn into a change of armaments. Nor, in a world-wide industrial society, can the abolition or limitation of certain types of weapon in use at present ban the specter of wholly new weapons. It is, in other words, not the possession of arms, but the disposition to use them for nationalist and aggressive purposes which must be uprooted. Such a change in outlook and purpose can only come about gradually, as territorial questions recede in importance. In 1866 the several German states, Prussia, Bavaria, and the rest, were fighting each other, and the victorious Prussians appropriated large amounts of territory, including the entire kingdom of Hanover. Fifty years later such a proceeding seemed to most Germans hard to imagine. The problem of the country's territorial divisions had largely become a question of administrative expediency. If a civil-war situation flared up between Bavaria and the Reich in 1923, it was not over territorial questions, but concerned the political organization of the whole country, the problems of monarchy, socialism, and so forth. The territorial objectives had been minimized, if not eliminated, by creating a government comprising the several German states. This does not mean that the conflict over boundaries may not be a bitter one—attempts to change state boundaries in the United States show that; but they can be settled within an international framework by decision of the people affected. Modern military techniques, with their predominantly aggressive potentialities, afford the most persuasive argument for supernational government as the only effective guaranty for lasting peace between nations, because only such government will reduce the passions engendered by territorial issues and make them arbitrable. Even the chances of civil war would be somewhat decreased in such a larger context. Size reduces the possibility of frictions developing into fighting because of the pressure from the remainder of the community which is not involved in the controversy. These considerations apply to supernational government, even if such a government does not comprise the entire globe. This is one of the key arguments behind the emerging Union of Europe, and more especially the idea that only such a Union provides a secure basis for a solution of the German problem.

The increasing determination of people the world over to be rid of war has raised for many the problem of how to discover a "moral equivalent for war," as William James put it in a celebrated essay. Proceeding from the assumption that the sacrifices required by fighting and dying for a cause bring out some of the finest qualities in man, various ideas for comparable joint efforts have been advanced. André Maurois has imaginatively depicted mankind united against the people of the moon. Another poetical soul has seen the world brought together in the effort to build a building as high as Mont Blanc, presumably engaging the attention of mankind for more than a hundred years. Still others have urged the war against microbes as a sufficiently powerful unifying objective—the health work begun by the League of Nations and continued by the United Nations representing a first vanguard engagement. Economic crisis may also call forth supernational organization of a government type. It too had its beginnings in the League and is now being developed by the Economic Commission of the UN. But all things considered, these promising seedlings are likely to be crushed if the existing territorial rivalries continue to engender a feeling of violent insecurity and a consequent determination to remain armed. When, as at present, these territorial rivalries are embittered by ideological conflicts, the "spheres of influence" become more rigid, and symbolized in phrases like the "iron curtain."

Conclusion · From a careful consideration of the facts of military force in relation to government, political science is justified in concluding that the military establishment is a necessary concomitant of all government, that it transcends territorial objectives and ultimately is rooted in the general objective of security. Its basic paradox, so baffling to Hobbes and other political philosophers, that man, seeking peace, makes war, is rooted in one of life's basic aspects: where there is life, there is death. When man feels that his life is threatened, he gets ready to kill. "Death is so permanent," reads a warning to reckless drivers posted throughout United States Army installations. Hobbes was wrong in making the search for security from fear of violent death the only, or at least the dominant, objective of man. He was right in stressing its persistence. Especially in revolutionary periods fraught with civil war potentialities, this fear and this search reassert themselves. For group dissensions within a community also can reach the point where violence flares more readily than more stable periods are willing to allow. The people of the United States whose most dangerous wars have, like the Civil War and the Second World War, involved revolutionary situations may be expected to be alert to the lessons which this experience implies. But neither should the United States become oblivious to the tremendous risks to a constitutional order which a large military establishment may become if its leadership loses confidence in the viability of the constitution. The military, like other experts, should be on tap, but not on top, as a popular phrase has it. One way to keep them there is to make sure that the military remain dedicated to freedom. It is one of the toughest problems of contemporary constitutionalism.

IV

Peace and Diplomacy

Introduction · Diplomacy and war · The art of negotiating · Foreign and domestic affairs · The language of diplomacy · The system of ambassadors · The "social" functions of the professional diplomatist · Technical experts abroad · The Foreign Service as an organized administrative service · The international civil servant · The balance of power · Peace and foreign policy · Conclusion

Introduction · The living together of modern nations seems to be a continuous warfare, interrupted by brief periods of relaxation caused by utter exhaustion. Contemplating the history of Europe during the last four hundred years a gloomy philosopher would certainly be tempted to reiterate Heraclitus' sinister phrase that war is the father of all things. Still, most of the time the inevitable friction resulting from territorial and other maladjustments has been successfully reduced by the methods of diplomacy. Diplomacy, the textbooks tell one, is (or at least was) "the application of intelligence and tact to the conduct of official relations between the governments of independent states" (Satow). Napoleon's mocking sally to Talleyrand that "treaties might be signed by diplomats, but they are made by soldiers" notwithstanding, war would thus appear as the breakdown of diplomacy, since it is the application of brute force. Appearances to the contrary, diplomacy, by reducing the friction which is inevitable between governments striving toward conflicting objectives, such as territorial acquisitions, tries to avoid war, while yet realizing a maximum of a government's purposes. Contested territories, like Alsace-Lorraine, are the classic source of international conflict. But the expanding industrialism of the modern age has added many others, such as raw materials. Whenever a government reaches beyond its boundaries, diplomacy comes into play.

Diplomacy and war · The proposition that diplomacy strives to avoid war is often questioned on the supposedly realistic ground that the diplomacy of a Louis XIV, a Napoleon, or a Bismarck was more concerned with preparing for war than with avoiding it. This is undoubtedly true, and if it had been asserted that it was the objective of diplomacy to avoid *all* war, the objection would be well taken. But when the diplomacy of certain aggressive statesmen was employed to isolate a particular enemy so as to facilitate his defeat, the diplomat's task in effecting such isolation consisted in an effort to maintain peace with the enemy's potential allies. The failure of Louis XIV's diplomacy is generally admitted; his inability to prevent the great alliance which was formed by England, the Netherlands, and the House of Hapsburg resulted in his being checked by the series of wars which ended in the peace of Utrecht (1713–1714). Likewise Frederick the Great was almost crushed beneath the combination of Russia, France, and Austria which Maria Theresa succeeded in bringing together against him; a brilliant strategist and army leader, this extraordinary Prussian king was handicapped by his ineffective diplomacy. Napoleon Bonaparte, another remarkable soldier, also affords a striking illustration of how superior military strength will suffer defeat if not aided by skillful diplomacy. The alliance of almost all of Europe, led by England, Russia, Austria, and Prussia, proved too strong even for Napoleon's military and administrative genius; diplomacy, such as Talleyrand had advocated, would have anticipated this alliance and tried to prevent it. The success of Bismarck's diplomacy, on the other hand, lay precisely in his careful elimination of potential allies of whoever happened to be his particular opponent. In Prussia's war with Austria he succeeded in keeping out France, England, and Russia (1866), while in Germany's war with France he similarly kept peace with Austria, Russia, and England. It is small wonder that after the brilliant victories which his diplomacy had prepared, he spent the rest of his days haunted by the specter of coalitions which might be brought together against Germany. It was in an effort to prevent such coalitions that Bismarck became so interested in maintaining peace throughout Europe; the catastrophic consequences of the failure of later German governments to follow his lead are well known. Throughout all these great cycles of recent history a tendency can be observed: the dominant objective of successful diplomacy is the reducing of friction between governments, and, if possible, the maintaining of peace. These efforts at eliminating the friction necessarily engendered by the conflicting interests of the various countries must be continuous. Diplomacy would be perfect if through mere art in negotiation it could realize the maintenance of peace, while at the same time securing such advantages as are demanded by the people, a prince, big business, or whoever happens to determine the policy of the particular government.

The art of negotiating · Unfortunately, the so-called "sovereigns," whether princes, peoples, or interest groups, are and have been in the habit of demanding things which no diplomat, no matter how skillful, could secure without the ultimate use of armed force. We have here confronting us a paradox which has puzzled the students of diplomacy, both of democratic and of autocratic governments. There is the desire for peace, and the concurrent insistence upon things which cannot be had without recourse to war, because someone else's vital interests are involved. This suggests the need for differentiating between goals of foreign policy and the negotiations involved in realizing them.[1] Apparently, when talking of diplomacy as a method of government, one considers it mainly in terms of the art of negotiation. The goals, and their realization through negotiation, however, are often fused in reality. One of the goals of British foreign policy, in the days of Palmerston and Gladstone, was "free trade." The prevailing trend in Continental Europe and the United States was to resist British commercial supremacy by protective tariffs designed to shield infant industries and achieve a measure of equality. No art of negotiation could hope to eliminate the basic conflict of interests, as conceived by the several powers. Indeed, in the course of negotiating trade policies, British goals themselves gradually changed, until eventually "imperial preference" emerged as an alternative policy, or goal. Many similar examples could be cited, especially in recent American diplomacy, for example, the Marshall Plan and the Atlantic Pact. There is a tendency at present to conceive of foreign policy as some kind of fixed and static pattern, similar to the pattern of agricultural or labor policy. But what John Locke in a rather picturesque phrase called "the design of foreigners" provides an ever-shifting need for alternative solutions. Hence the cases just cited show that the distinction between goals of policy and the negotiations required to realize them is a rather difficult one to maintain. A closer analysis of reality reveals that the actual negotiation generates a policy, and a given policy imposes certain and peculiar methods of negotiation. To say, therefore, that we wish to consider diplomacy largely as the art of negotiation means defining our standpoint and method of approach; foreign affairs consist of an undifferentiated complex context which is compounded of policies and negotiations.

The interrelation between objectives and techniques, between goals and the negotiations directed toward achieving them, constitutes the quintessence of what goes under the title of "foreign policy." Recurrent panaceas are offered under this head, as "shields of the republic" and other such ingratiating phrases, which pretend to be "solutions," to the problem of a "sound" foreign policy for a particular country. Actually, such plans never explain how acceptance is to be gained from a divided and confused public, nor how the "design of foreigners" is to be dealt with. It stands to reason that any particular "foreign policy," if firmly stated as such, will elicit adjustments on the part of other powers with divergent interests, which would in turn necessitate readjustments, and so forth indefinitely. What these disquisitions usually boil down to is either a series of goals for a given country; or vague and unquestionable "principles" such as the one that a country should not try to "overextend" itself; or, finally, critical comments upon the particular conduct of foreign affairs, either in terms of the persons responsible for foreign policy, or of institutional arrangements, such as legislative control. These are all important issues, but they do not, in the nature of things, yield to general solutions. In any event, such arguments as whether a country like the United States should or should not make "peace" its major goal are not scientific problems, but preachments presumably addressed to the general electorate in the hope of persuading it to the writer's view. A coherent "foreign policy" is probably a marginal case, occurring only at rare intervals under unique conditions and exceptional leadership. The rest of the time, and especially in democratic countries, it is more "realistic" to speak of "foreign affairs" rather than foreign policy. Foreign affairs may be understood as the complex manifold of policies, relationships, and negotiations which in retrospect yield to the analyst some coherent pattern as a result of the emergent realities.[2]

Foreign and domestic affairs · To define the term foreign affairs is not as easy as the constant use of the phrase would lead one to believe. The various human activities involved in carrying on the relations between nations are fairly clearly discernible by examples: Poincaré making a speech on the war debt; the German Parliament ratifying the Locarno Treaty; Lord Halifax, the British ambassador, calling upon President Roosevelt; a conference held at The Hague; a clerk in the State Department deciphering a message from one of the embassies; these and many similar situations suggest themselves. Perhaps the phrase "foreign relations" would be more indicative of the true nature of these activities; together they constitute the relationship through which nations and their governments are bound together. Nations at any rate are not truly independent in any factual sense, even though governments may be. But legally their relations are treated *as if* they were independent of each other. This leads to many difficulties, both in learned analysis and in popular views. The United States is a particularly happy hunting ground for those who have been and are inclined to treat foreign relations as if nations were in fact independent of each other, thus making the fatal mistake of treating as a fact what is a legal fiction. Even to treat foreign relations as a separate thing amounts to committing a similar mistake; for the distinction between foreign and domestic affairs is a fiction also.[3] Particularly under modern industrial conditions, is there any such thing as a purely domestic concern when speaking of major policies? Law may treat the tariff, the restriction of immigration, the regulation of various fields of production, governmental subsidies, and all such measures of governmental policy as strictly domestic, but are they in fact? Matters of governmental organization likewise are anything but domestic, unless they concern minor details. Were the coming of the Nazis, of the Fascists, of the Communists, purely domestic matters? How could Wilson have insisted upon the disappearance of monarchy in Germany if governmental organization had no bearing upon foreign relations? Similarly, did not the question of maintaining monarchy inject itself into the League of the Three Emperors and the Holy Alliance? Searching students of foreign relations and diplomacy have always known that foreign and domestic affairs constitute a whole which one is bound to discover, if one digs deep enough. One of the great turning points of European diplomacy before 1914 was the conclusion of the Franco-Russian alliance (1894);[4] historians have shown how powerful a role Russia's need of large loans played in her shift from Germany to France. A comparably important shift occurred in 1933 when the emergence of the Hitler government led to a realignment of the powers, and to the accession of the Soviet Union to the League of Nations. From this vantage point one perceives the difficulty of maintaining the time-honored principle of the "primacy [priority] of foreign over domestic policy"; the two are so much part of one pattern or web that the meaning of the principle is obscure.

The language of diplomacy · The supposed failure of diplomacy to eliminate war has made people forget what a great advance over earlier conditions its carefully worked-out and subtle methods represent. The oft-quoted wisecrack that ambassadors are honest men sent abroad to lie for the good of their country is less than a half-truth. Many statements which to the average lay reader of diplomatic documents would seem to be "lies" or pretenses are in fact conventional phrases which carry to the informed recipient precisely the meaning they possess in the mind of the person who uttered them.[5] When the President of the United States, in his letter of credence for the American ambassador to Mexico, speaks of "the desire to cultivate to the fullest extent the friendship which has so long subsisted between the two governments," he obviously is not "lying," and when the ambassador on suitable occasions repeats such phrases, his candor cannot on that account be questioned. Formally amicable relations between two governments constitute a "friendship" in the soothing language of diplomacy. It was, therefore, an extraordinary breach of diplomatic tradition when the government of the Soviet Union announced that it would teach unfriendly powers "to keep their swinish snouts out of our potato patch." Such language is very dangerous in the intercourse between powerful nations. It has been the purpose of diplomatic etiquette to avoid these dangers by carefully prescribed traditional restraints in conduct and language. The British Foreign Office "was aghast," we are told, at the breach of diplomatic etiquette which Lord Curzon committed, when, in 1923, he "proceeded to quote the text of messages and instructions exchanged between the Soviet government and their representatives in Persia and India which had been intercepted" by the British Intelligence Service. The Foreign Office was aghast, not because the statements were untrue, but because "never, even in the most embittered diplomatic controversy, had information thus obtained been cited as evidence." In other words, governments maintain a secret service to spy upon their "friends," but they will never, never admit it. Yet labeling as deceit this failure to admit such a generally recognized practice would be little short of absurd.

The development of diplomacy, that civilized form of intercourse, parallels, therefore, the general development of constitutionalism. The recurrent breaches of diplomatic etiquette, indeed the wholesale abandonment of the methods of diplomacy by the totalitarian governments, is the manifestation abroad of their nonconstitutional conduct of government at home. But this decline in manners cannot be blamed entirely on totalitarian dictatorships. A democratic age is given to rougher language, and the elected representatives of the people the world over have committed breaches of etiquette. It pervades the meetings of international bodies, too, when the rival conceptions of government clash.

The system of ambassadors · The elaborate system of ambassadors and other plenipotentiaries which one is inclined to take for granted today is a major achievement of the evolution of modern diplomacy. The practice of sending such representatives originated with the medieval church and from it spread first to the city states of Renaissance Italy.[6] From there it was taken over and developed, as were so many other practices, by the monarchical governments north of the Alps. Yet regularized practices developed very slowly. Ambassadors were often given a discourteous reception, if they were not actually maltreated. Many protracted struggles arose over questions of etiquette, and the prestige connected with them. How imperfect the arrangements still were at the end of the Thirty Years' War, toward the middle of the seventeenth century, can be seen from the fact that almost four years were consumed in clearing up innumerable questions of etiquette before the peace conference could commence to sit at Muenster and Osnabrück in 1645. Nor were the succeeding negotiations easy: they lasted for fully three years. The slow development of tradition in the subsequent hundred and fifty years brought into existence a pattern of diplomatic conduct which was codified by the Congress of Vienna in

1815. This was some twenty-five years after the professional diplomat had almost accidentally made his debut. That happened in France, where, after the Revolution had swept away the titled ambassadors of the old regime, the conduct of affairs had been left in the hands of their secretaries. The latter were mostly commoners who had acquired a semipermanent professional status by the force of custom and circumstance. To be sure, seasoned and quasi-professional diplomats had existed in the monarchical service wherever a man held his post for a considerable length of time, but the service as a whole was amateurish, except perhaps that of the Catholic church and the Republic of Venice. Even a casual reading of the instructions handed to French ambassadors of the period will reveal that fact. These instructions often sound like an introduction into the nature of the relations of the two governments concerned. Only during the nineteenth century did a professional bureaucracy take hold of the field of foreign affairs. It is perhaps worth passing notice that with the exception of the French service under the Third Republic and of course that of the United States, these services even in the nineteenth century were dominated by titled noblemen; the diplomatic service, like the corps of cavalry officers, was considered the exclusive province of the upper crust of society. Just the same, or perhaps as a result of this circumstance, the diplomatic corps developed certain characteristics which bear scrutiny beyond that given the officialdom which carries on the government's work at home.

The "social" functions of the professional diplomatist · Great importance is attached to social etiquette in the conduct of international negotiations. It has been shown how deeply this regard for etiquette and procedure is embedded in the intensity of the power struggle; its sensitizing effect and its heightening of the feeling for all questions of prestige has also been shown. In private life, people are apt to smile about someone who makes a great fuss over who should go first to the dinner table. But where each person is a public person, representing a nation jealous of its prestige, this is no small matter, and the salutary effects of etiquette are seen in the rule of seniority, which ranks each representative according to the length of time he has been accredited to the particular government (with the papal *nuncio*, however, ranking ahead of all others). This custom attests to the fiction of equality between all the states, great and small: no balance of power intrudes itself into the dinner parties. This is more important than may be thought at first glance. Countless memoirs, written by distinguished diplomats such as Sir Cecil Spring-Rice and Walter Hines Page, attest to the fact that much of their most important information is gathered at social functions of one sort or another. Since the seventeenth century, the houses of distinguished diplomats have been the center of a brilliant social life. It is the glamour of this past which often draws young men into the foreign service. They forget that it, too, has been sullied by the smoke of the machine age. Most members of the foreign service spend a large proportion of their lives in relatively small and remote cities, often not even capitals of unimportant countries. But even in the great metropolitan centers of London, Paris, and Berlin, it is not today a matter of court intrigues and cabals of the high aristocracy, but rather dull dinner parties for press magnates and industrial tycoons with an occasional journalist or parliamentarian to brighten up the atmosphere. But of course it is social life just the same.[7] Consequently, no person can make a success in the foreign service unless he is able to handle social relations effectively. This fact, too, differentiates the professional diplomat from other officials. Since social grace is acquired more easily by those who grow up with silver spoons in their mouths, the monopoly of the nobility, later shared with the wealthy upper-middle class, is quite understandable, though not necessarily beneficial for the service.

Technical experts abroad · What has so far been said concerning qualifications remained very largely true until the First World War. But since that time, considerable change has come about. The creation of the League of Nations, and constant international conferences widely participated in by governmental officials outside the foreign service proper, set the stage for intergovernmental relationships of a technical sort in the many fields which require international action, such as communications, transportation, and health. Such technical contacts have multiplied since the Second World War and fiscal, agricultural, cultural, labor, and many other issues are the concern of specialized agencies. In these fields, the old "secret" diplomacy is no longer the acknowledged method of handling business. The administrative technique of bureaucracies within federal systems has taken its place. This technique is characterized by solicitude for the opinion of every member of the group. Since it is impracticable to coerce a recalcitrant member of the co-operating group, every effort has to be made to avoid the possibility that any member may become recalcitrant. Naturally, such co-operative efforts are rendered considerably more difficult when the members belong to different nations proud of different cultures. Yet the fact that such co-operative undertakings were commenced long before the First World War in specific fields, such as that of the Universal Postal Union, shows conclusively that their rapid development after the First World War and under the aegis of the League was by no means gratuitous; the UN, as the League before it, merely affords a convenient administrative device for co-ordinating the various activities.

In view of the central importance which the bureaucracy has had for the growth and development of modern government, this expansion of administrative services into the international field is very important. The more advanced industrial countries consequently undertook to send more and more permanent experts abroad whose task it was to follow the developments in their particular fields.[8] They are attached to the legation, and hence are called *attachés*. As these activities grew, diplomats found themselves surrounded by commercial, agricultural, and labor experts who were in direct communication with their corresponding ministries at home. The presence of such experts frequently has been the cause of considerable friction in the foreign legations. Independent and often conflicting points of view are at times held and expressed by these experts on issues of international significance, particularly within their own bailiwicks. Thus a commercial attaché may favor the lowering of tariff rates at a time when the representative of the foreign office considers such a plea very inopportune. From the point of view of integration, the complaints of the professional diplomat are undeniably justified. But from the point of view of governmental growth, the lack of co-ordination may open up new avenues of international progress, just as in centuries past expanding technical services served, we have seen, as the vanguards of national unification.[9]

The Foreign Service as an organized administrative service · If we apply our analysis of bureaucracy we find that the three functional criteria, namely, differentiation of functions, centralization and integration of control (hierarchy), and finally qualification for office (professionalization), are found in all modern diplomatic services. The differentiation is partly along geographical and partly along functional lines. It varies from government to government, as one country or another looms large in importance. Thus Germany appears of greater significance to France than to the United States, South American countries more important to the United States than to the Soviet Union. Sometimes policy trends are discernible in these arrangements, as when the United States State Department sets up a separate office for Germany and Austria outside its European Division. Functional differentiation appears when such sections as the legal, the commercial, and the cultural are organized as separate units in the foreign office, as is now generally the case. As far as the commercial work is concerned, foreign services have for a long time recognized a distinction between the consular and the "diplomatic" service, though the tendency to separate these two services as careers is now generally criticized as unsound. In reorganizing their foreign service, the British have recently abolished the distinction, as has the United States. Field services, in turn, are sometimes distinguished from the work in the central foreign office (Department of State in the United States), but again without differentiating the career. Even in the arrangements for these field services, policy trends can be shown. After the Franco-Prussian War, the French abandoned a number of consulates in Germany. After the First World War, Great Britain, France, and Germany changed their missions in the ABC states to embassies, thus recognizing the enhanced power of the new world.

As far as integration and centralization of control are concerned, the foreign services present problems distinct from other services. The great distance between the central directing office and the field offices necessitates a large measure of autonomy, even under modern communication conditions. Not only ambassadors, but consuls as well, are still their own masters in all matters not specifically directed from the central office. While the embassy in a large country, like the United States, may have general direction of affairs, it is not definitely the hierarchical superior of the various consulates in its territory; they may and often do communicate directly with the home office.

Within the last fifty years, clearly defined professional requirements have become established in all the major countries, with the United States following suit by the Rogers Act (1924). Each country, in its own way and in keeping with its peculiar traditions of preparing and testing for the administrative services of the government, has set up its own system. It is unnecessary to describe the detailed provisions here. Suffice it to say that the higher ranks of the service (except for political appointments in the top rank of the United States service) are, in all the leading countries, manned by men and women possessing some type of academic university training.

Besides these functional criteria, we have seen that certain behavior patterns are essential to effective administrative services. Objectivity, continuity, and precision, as well as discretion—these, of course, are also essential aspects of a good diplomatic service. Therefore, a good diplomatist is, in the words of one of them, "indifferent to public applause, has devoted some thirty years to the study of foreign psychology, is unaffected by vanity, dislikes controversy, eschews all forms of publicity, and is not subject to acute time pressure or overwork. In addition, as a trained expert in a common science working with other experts, he is intent upon producing a piece of work which will satisfy his own professional standards." According to the same author, "a man who has spent some thirty years in the diplomatic service acquires, inevitably, an international frame of mind." He comes to have a kind of masonic feeling for other diplomatists and to feel that parliamentary and public opinion is foolish and ill-informed. While the latter attitude is often found among professional administrative officials in national services as well, it seldom is held with as much show of good reason. There are always citizens who know as much as any government officials about particular governmental tasks (though most citizens do not), but there are rarely, if ever, citizens who have a full grasp of all the implications of a given decision in the field of foreign affairs. (See below, pp. 345 ff., for a discussion of parliamentary control.) This "international frame of mind" is subtly adjusted to a rapid, though careful, calculation of the effects which a given move will have throughout the network of international relationships. This chess-player's attitude often results in a neglect of underlying trends of long-range significance, particularly of social and economic forces. But the diplomatist is, on the other hand, acutely aware of the balance of power at any particular moment, and highly sensitized to the prestige connected with certain developments.[10]

The international civil servant · As international organizations develop, the officials employed by them become more numerous. Their relations with the foreign services of the several governments represented in these organizations constitute a problem of great complexity. Ideally, the international civil servant should be completely devoted to the organization he serves and quite neutral with regard to the wishes and preferences of the national government which speaks for the nation to which he belongs. Actually, the United Nations, like the League of Nations, administers an oath of office which embodies this ideal. Nevertheless, human beings vary in their ability to rise to so unusual a challenge. What is more, governments vary in the extent to which they will permit their nationals to serve without "instructions." It is hard to believe that the Soviet Union, to take an extreme example, would readily condone a Soviet citizen's stepping far away from the party line; anyhow the official's self interest tends to combine with various other factors to keep the official linked to his homeland.

In spite of the aforementioned drawbacks, the international civil service is constantly expanding and gaining in prestige and influence. Generally speaking, the secretariat of the United Nations is a stronger, more active body than its predecessor, the League secretariat, though splendid work was done by it. But the emphasis in the League was on research and informational activities, whereas under the United Nations and associated international bodies, such as the World Bank, the International Monetary Fund, and the International Children's Emergency Fund, a high degree of executive and administrative skill is required. The same is true of the several technical branches of the United Nations which call for and command a highly specialized and technically trained personnel, whether it be in aviation, communications, or shipping. The continued expansion and consolidation of these specialized services means, of course, that once again the process of establishing a responsible bureaucracy is building the core of a governmental system, this time of world-wide scope. There is undoubtedly coming into being a devoted corps of international civil servants whose loyalty and devotion transcend national and cultural boundaries. This does not mean a loss of national identity, for it is generally agreed that a person without deep roots in his national community is apt to be handicapped in negotiating the compromises which the international community involves. But they do not think in terms of the struggle for power all the time, as the professional diplomat is trained to do. Though many come from the diplomatic service, and may even return to it, they are becoming allergic to the allurements of the game of the balance of power which Woodrow Wilson hopefully proclaimed to be "forever discredited" in 1917.[11]

The balance of power · The phrase balance of power since the sixteenth century, when it was first used by Guicciardini and other Florentine historians, has been a euphemistic description of any particular distribution of the power among nations which happened to be acceptable to the person using the phrase. The French, after 1871, said they wished to *restore* the balance of power in Europe which the unification of Germany had disturbed. The Germans held that they must *maintain* the balance of power which the French desire for revenge threatened. These observations were reversed after the First World War. Thus it can be seen that the balance of power does not necessarily refer to the maintenance of the *status quo*; it may also be the basis for arguing that this status be changed. Since the phrase describes any kind of distribution of power, the history of the balance of power is obviously identical with the history of foreign relations.[12]

Whatever the actual balance or distribution of power may happen to be, the idea affords a ready argument in international negotiation, and presumably even a foundation for international law. As such, it has always had its greatest vogue when it was a question of checking the tendency toward concentration of power in the hands of a single government. The desirability of "redressing the balance of power" was thus invoked against the Hapsburg world empire by Francis I during the first half of the sixteenth century. It was, in turn, brought forth against Louis XIV by William III. Maria Theresa used it against Frederick the Great, the tottering French monarchy against the British Empire under George III and Pitt, everybody against Napoleon I. In the course of the nineteenth century, the scope of its application was widened. The United States, by the Monroe Doctrine, forbade the extension of balance-of-power politics to the American continents, and thereby maintained its own supremacy with considerable success. But we begin to hear of a balance of power in the Balkans, in the Near East, and in the Far East. More recently, the most decisive balance of power is said to be grouped around the Pacific.

There has been a *balancer* behind each balance. The power equilibrium has never worked when it was merely looked upon as a dead, material equipoise of power taken in the corporeal sense (see above, p. 23). Henry VIII of England once said: *"Cui adhaereo, praeest."* It was a boast rather than a fact, but the claim is characteristic. It shows that the *balancer* is playing one power against another in order to prevail himself. Hence, the balance of power carries us beyond diplomacy in the strict sense. It is foreign *policy*. Peace, or at least the avoidance of war, may be the immediate objective, but security and national aggrandizement are behind it. The balancer is substituting the balance for military methods.

The Fourteen Points enunciated by President Woodrow Wilson in 1918 undertook to banish the balance of power from the world. No longer were people to be bartered about from sovereignty to sovereignty, as the balance-of-power diplomats had done; instead all nations were to determine their own status under an all-embracing League of Nations. But even had the League become truly all-embracing, and even had the treaties terminating the First World War been negotiated on the basis of the Fourteen Points, it is doubtful whether the balance-of-power argument would have disappeared. The problem of the distribution of power is almost as pressing in a federation as it is in a family of nations. How could Wilson, an American and a Southerner, have failed to perceive this? Had he forgotten the lesson of the Civil War? Was not the whole story of the genesis of that baneful conflict a tale of balancing power of state against state, till the final rupture occurred? Had not the same happened under the Swiss Confederation (see chap. XI), and under the German Union almost at the same time? The failure to reckon with the continuance of balance-of-power politics within the League contributed its share to the League's difficulties. At the same time, we should not forget that both the League and the balance are mechanisms for conducting internal negotiations. Who would question that the League or some similar organization offered the superior technique if for no other reason than that it contains whatever is useful of the balance of power within itself? For it became apparent soon after the First World War that there was much need for considering the balance of power within the League, and successive international crises brought out the importance of careful attention to that problem. The problem forced itself to the fore much more rapidly after the Second World War in the United Nations.

Every problem faced by the UN is affected by the shifting balance of power between the USSR and the Western powers. Whatever the future of international organization, the problem of the distribution (balance) of power will remain a matter of prime concern to all professional diplomats, and we shall very probably continue to use the concept as a convenient standard or idea in terms of which to discuss the shifting scene of international power relationships. On the other hand, the recognition of a continuing effort at maintaining a balance of power within the UN must not blind us to the fact that this organization possesses distinct advantages. It constitutes a framework, and it thereby eliminates the need for a "balancer." All those members who are "neutral," relatively speaking, in a given controversy tend to operate as "balancers." This fact was clearly apparent in the role Argentina played in the Security Council regarding the issues raised by the blockade of Berlin in 1948. The substitution of such an international *organization* for an intermittent balancer is, in a sense, merely a specific instance of the general feature of all constitutions; any constitutional system seeks to balance various governmental powers and organizes a balance of interests, including classes, in the community (see below, ch. VII).

Peace and foreign policy · In a recent study, Walter Lippmann wrote mockingly that we must ask ourselves "whether peace, as so many say, is the supreme end of foreign policy." And he answered this question with an emphatic "no," alleging that survival is, or should be, the supreme end, and that "the logic of peace as the supreme national idea leads to absurdity."[13] This view, or some version of it, has impressed many Americans who are in search of a "realistic" foreign policy. It is argued persuasively by Lippmann in terms of his conception of power politics relative to national states and to the notion that any such states must conduct their foreign policy on the basis of their actual power resources. There is, he feels, a tendency for the United States to over-extend itself in regard to ideological concerns, and more especially in the search of peace. As a critique of the kind of foreign relations the United States conducted in the 1930's— a kind of mumbo-jumbo compromise between isolationism and interventionism, resulting from the almost even balance of forces behind either of these alternatives—Lippmann's argument has great force. But its weakness is revealed by its treatment of the Soviet Union, for he is not inspired by any vivid sense of the revolutionary issues involved. Although he argues that the United States cannot permit the rise of a predominant power in Europe, showing how persistently this policy was pursued by American statesmen, he yet states that Russia (not the Soviet Union) will "emerge from this war the great military power of Europe, . . ." and that "the Russians (not the Communists) will almost certainly have an overwhelming preponderance of military force . . ." Yet he somehow seems to pitch his hope on the "Russians" not engaging in a policy of aggrandizement, on their readiness to respect the freedom of their neighbors, and in the light of this hope advocates a "nuclear alliance" of Great Britain, Russia, and the United States. After even a five-year perspective, these hopes and expectations and policy recommendations reveal where the supposedly "realistic" analysis in terms of "power resources" led. The measure of present difficulties is directly proportional to this analysis and advice. "We should not have learned the lesson of our failures in the past . . . if in our projects for organizing world peace we did not fix our attention first of all upon the *powers capable of organizing it*." (Italics mine.) And therefore we need not "shrink from insisting that the precondition of a better world order is a nuclear alliance of the three powerful military states which will emerge victorious from the present war." "Combined action by America, Britain, and Russia is the irreducible minimum guarantee of security of each of them [sic] and the only condition under which it is possible even to begin to establish any wider order of security." These statements reveal that Lippmann (and many others following him) have failed to understand the true reality of military establishments in their relation to security. He never asked from what quarter danger would threaten the security of the United States, or of the USSR for that matter. Stalin, in his famous speech announcing the Five-Year Plan in the election of February, 1946, gave the clear and unmistakable answer pointing to the capitalist powers, especially America. The United States has reluctantly come to the corresponding conclusion. If one were to accept Lippmann's criteria of "survival" as the supreme test of foreign policy in the light of these developments, the obvious conclusion would be to wage a preventive war to destroy the Soviet Union while it can be done with military superiority in the hands of the United States. But the government and the people of the United States continue the "absurd" logic of peace as the supreme national ideal, partly because too many Americans fear that they might not be the ones to survive as individuals. American diplomacy has been engaged in a tough program of containing the Soviet Union and the revolutionary forces which it sponsors throughout the world without war. It is a calculated risk, but, in terms of constitutional democracy, it is a lesser risk than that of becoming an aggressor in the name of "national survival." Recent experience in no wise invalidates the established theory, based upon long observation, that security is primarily the objective of military establishments (even international police forces), while the objective of diplomacy and foreign policy is peace.

Conclusion · In the long run, friction between governments is unquestionably reduced by administrative internationalism; for each participant becomes in time a bit more internationally minded. He perceives that the most diverse cultural backgrounds and personal habit patterns may be combined with high achievement in a given specialty. This is true to such an extent that the resulting situation has given rise to the query whether the regular, old-fashioned diplomatic service is needed any longer at all. The answer is that the regular old-fashioned diplomatic service is not at all old-fashioned, if it is good. The modern diplomat will look upon himself as a liaison officer who will promote co-operation and understanding on all sides. He will induct experts into the general setup of a foreign country, will furnish them introductions as well as an adequate meeting ground, will smooth out difficulties wherever he can; in short, he will act according to the first paragraph of the general instructions of the American Department of State to foreign service officers: "He creates good will and common understanding, and, with restrained and critical leadership born of mature experience and profound knowledge of men and affairs, he uses these as instruments for enhancing international confidence and co-operation among governments and people." A man of this type is a far cry from the honest fellow sent abroad to lie for the good of his country.

In keeping with this outlook, the foreign policy of all constitutional governments, but more especially constitutional democracies, will be directed toward peace as its primary objective and chief end. For it is the quintessence of political wisdom that the moral imperative that "there shall be no war" is reinforced by the "realism" of the basic objectives of human beings in politics.[14] Two insights, (1) that constitutionalism needs peace for its survival, and (2) that only a world-wide constitutionalism will provide an eventual guarantee of lasting peace under law, are the culmination of constitutional theory and practice in Europe and America.

V

Prosperity, the Police, and Legislation

Introduction · The organismic fallacy · Prosperity and government expenditure · Police or administrative action · Early legislation · The ordinance · Increase in wealth the central goal · The trade balance and tariffs · The stimulation of trade and industry through monopolies · Enforcement · Stable money · Paper money · Colonial policy · Conclusion ·

Introduction · When considering expansion as an objective of modern government, the stimulation of trade and industry was discussed briefly. But while the governmental activities were related to the tax resources and hence to the provisioning of armies, they were undertaken also in pursuit of a distinct, though related, objective: general prosperity. It has been claimed that prosperity was wanted solely because it facilitated the maintenance of armies and navies, and therefore territorial expansion. May it not reversely be claimed that territorial expansion was sought because of the added opportunities for insuring prosperity, particularly in the case of colonies? As has been suggested before, all the objectives are interrelated. But prosperity was sought by many governments as an end quite in itself. Indeed, mercantilism was, in the first place, a doctrine concerned with how this might be accomplished. The marvel of the Dutch wealth in the seventeenth century was, in a way, the cause of all the speculation about commerce which mercantilism comprises.

Growth of the community would seem to be the drive behind territorial expansion and prosperity. At certain times, communities undeniably tend to grow. The ultimate whys and wherefores of such growth are rather obscure. All growth is mysterious, in the last analysis. But what the mercantilists sought to discover were the causes of making a country grow rich and powerful, on the assumption that that is what they all wanted to do. Governments, they believed, can do a lot to bring such growth about.[1]

The organismic fallacy · The recognition that countries grow in wealth, power, population, culture, and so forth gave rise to the organismic fallacy.[2] The mercantilists were amoral in the sense that they did not interest themselves in the moral issues that might be involved in such governmental action. Many of the medieval restrictions were the result of such moral considerations; the new outlook on power discouraged them. The mercantilists extended to all society what the doctrine of "reason of state" had claimed specifically for governments (see above, pp. 21 f.): that whatever was necessary was justified by that necessity. This organismic view of society and its government (the "state") survived mercantilism and became a major ideological weapon in the hands of those who desired to oppose *laissez-faire*. Seeley in England and Treitschke in Germany are leading examples of European thought on this subject, while the manifest-destiny school of historians provided America with similar notions. In order to buttress their view that governments do tend to grow, they have gone farther and asserted that governments, or rather states, are organisms. From the time of John of Salisbury in the twelfth century, writers have reveled in relating various parts of the government to various parts of the human body. The prince was said to be the head, his councilors the nerves, the army the hands and feet, and so forth. Even to this day, these analogies survive in speaking of the president of a country as its head. It is easy to ridicule this "organic" concept, particularly in its more extravagant forms, and to point out that governments are composed of human beings, each with his own will and consciousness. Since nobody has ever seen the entity apart from these separate human beings, it is indeed doubtful whether it exists in the same way as the body of an animal exists apart from the cells composing it. Yet, on the other hand, these human beings composing the government are living human beings, and there is no very tangible reason why we should not assume that the government and the nation live too. If they do, they will tend to grow for a certain length of time, as all living things do. The whole controversy over the "organic" nature of governments, communities, "states," comes down in the last analysis to an argument over what meaning should be attached to the word *organism*. The reason that it has aroused such a furor ever since the eighteenth century is probably that throughout these two hundred years it has been taken for granted that anything was justified if it was "natural." The cult of nature made this assumption possible. There is nothing inherently evident about it. But as long as it prevails, it will always be possible to argue that statesmen are justified in whatever measures they adopt to insure such "natural" growth.

Prosperity and government expenditure · Prosperity appeared to be an intrinsically desirable state of affairs to all those princes who looked upon their countries in the same way in which a proprietor looks upon his estate. This desire for good husbandry may be motivated by a love of lavish expenditure, as we find it in France, in Austria, or during the Restoration in England. Nor ought we merely to scoff at these extravagant masters;

for much of the enjoyment of later generations is derived from the master-pieces of art, architecture, and music which the prodigal expenditures of these courts called forth. As the cathedrals of the medieval church were lifted skyward upon the backs of serfs, so the castles and picture galleries of Europe were born of the extortions of vainglorious princes. Mozart and Beethoven were made possible by the autocratic Austrian government, no less than Raphael and Leonardo by the tyrants of Renaissance Italy.[3]

But, of course, this desire for lavish display was really a minor *motif*, though a very palpable one. The incessant labor of a Cecil, a Colbert, a Frederick the Great, was dictated by no such considerations. Prosperity was clearly an objective of primary importance in making the country more powerful. Hence much revenue was expended by the government to pro-vide capital for new industries, to develop trading companies, and to build up shipping, mining, roads, and forests. They thought of the economy as an enterprise to be planned and promoted for the betterment of all. The word paternalism was quite appropriate. But it is not true that this pater-nalism was primarily restrictive. Indeed, the liberty of commerce was one of the main slogans of Colbert.

Police or administrative action · A whole welter, then, of different "policies" was initiated by these incipient modern governments for the purpose of fostering prosperity at home. These policies were carried into execution by administrative officials who took a strong hand in enforcing them.[4] Again this enforcement must not be considered primarily a matter of restrictions, but rather of instigating private initiative. It is no accident that the word policy is so intimately related to that of police. Both derive from the old French *policie*. The Oxford Dictionary tells us that the general connotation of police is "civil administration," which is charged, of course, with the several courses of action adopted by the government (policies). The second connotation of police is "public order" and that of course is to be maintained by these several policies. It is, therefore, hardly surprising to find early modern governments preoccupied with the problem of police. After our modern industrial society had gotten well under way, and we had begun to reap the profits of the manufactures and the commerce which these governments had initiated, it became the fashion to decry their attitudes and techniques as paternalistic. It was easy to forget what governments had done and to assume that the entire industrial revolution had been a work of "nature." It was an easy step from such an assumption to the belief that any organized effort of the community or its government to take a hand in industrial development would be an "interference." But if we use a homely analogy, the interference appears to be no greater than that of a gardener who, having sown vegetables, proceeds to pull up those which he finds too thickly grown. It is by no means an accident, but a revival of ancient precedents, if today in the United States the "police power" is so often called upon to interfere in the industrial sphere.

Early legislation · Administrative action, however, was not enough. A great many ancient customs stood in the way of the desired development of manufacturing industries. Under time-honored charters given to cities in a period when urban handicraft was predominant, craft guilds had entrenched themselves as exclusive and monopolistic associations. To break their resistance, new rules had to be worked out and established. Both general and special legislation, in other words, were needed to clear the way for infant industries. It was this need, more than anything else perhaps, which contributed to the appeal of Bodin's famous doctrine of sovereignty.[5] For this sovereignty consisted of all but constitutionally limited legislative power; in other words, the power to make laws without regard to any previous laws already existing. Without such a power, Bodin and his contemporaries argued, there was no real government at all. In medieval times, by and large, the oldest law was considered the best law; and when popes, emperors, and kings sought to overcome the confusion of local customs, they had recourse to the Roman law, as we have seen before. Certainly in so far as the government was there to work out and apply *policies* which would enhance the *general* welfare, the power to make general rules was essential. We are thus compelled to recognize legislation, or the purposeful making of new rules, as a second method of modern government in its pursuit of prosperity. This association of the legislative with the police power seems startling nowadays, for we have come to look upon the police as administrative action, and under the separation-of-powers doctrine it is customary to differentiate sharply between administrative and legislative activities. It has been pointed out that the division of powers is the essence of constitutionalism. It will be seen later that this differentiation could not take place until power had been concentrated in the hands of autocratic princes: under the Tudors in England, under Henry IV and Louis XIV in France, under Frederick William I and Frederick the Great in Prussia. All these autocrats were, economically speaking, "progressive." They pushed mercantile progress through legislation. When their successors slipped into "unprogressiveness," they were overthrown, through either revolution, or war, or both.

The ordinance · The formal method of police action and legislative reform, its legal instrument, was often the same, at least on the Continent of Europe. It was the royal ordinance. The ordinance was not only employed for specific action, but for broad legislation as well. In fact, much of the most important early legislation of France is found in the *Ordonnances du Roi*, and the same is true in other countries. Even in England, under the Tudors and Stuarts, much actual legislation of paramount significance is embodied in royal ordinances and decrees. But here the subservience of Parliaments under Henry VIII and Elizabeth often made it easy and advisable for the prince to "pass the buck" to the representatives of the "people." This policy had the great advantage of keeping Parliament "in the picture." The mercantilist reforms of Elizabeth, such as the *Statute of Artificers*, were carried through as regular statutes.[6] On the Continent, by contrast, the Estates' assemblies became, in the course of the sixteenth and seventeenth centuries, economically reactionary bodies. They represented too definitely those classes in the community whose interest lay in preventing industrial progress. The royal emissary or intendant, carrying an ordinance to accomplish some definite purpose, was resisted by these estates, which in France and other countries had remained on a local basis. Thus the ordinance was also an instrument of centralization.

There are some curious parallels between those ordinances of early modern times and the recent emergence of rule-making activities on the part of executive or administrative authorities in America. In continental countries, where monarchical government is less remote, such law-making ordinances have continued to be recognized as part of the executive's work. But in America they have come as instrumentalities of federal centralization and legislation. To describe them as "quasi-legislative" disguises only thinly the true nature of these instrumentalities of central government intervention. They are, as they were then, accepted as instruments to produce desired economic change.

Increase in wealth the central goal · Turning now from the forms of government activity again to their specific content: What things did these governments do in order to bring about what they conceived to be prosperity? The various undertakings of centralizing governments were all directed toward increasing the wealth of the country. They believed that wealth could be increased in a number of different ways. They were primarily concerned with two closely interrelated economic problems: commodities and money.

In view of their policy of stimulating the growth of industry, the governments inclined toward a protectionist policy. Their attitude toward goods or commodities was that of producers: they "feared" goods and wanted to protect their countries against wasting their wealth by buying goods abroad.

But what was this wealth they were wasting? It was essentially money, in their view. Montchrétien, a French exponent of this school, wrote in 1615: "We live not so much from trade in raw materials as from gold and silver." And in *The British Merchant* (1713) it was said that all countries with whom England traded "contribute to the Prosperity and Happiness of this nation" in proportion as England's trade with them yielded a balance of gold and silver.[7] Just as a simple farmer measures his wealth by the number of coins he has stowed away in his chest, so the princes of those days and the governments which they directed looked upon the actual gold and silver in their treasuries as the only reliable measure of prosperity. Their entire policy was aimed at increasing these treasures, or at least preventing their decrease. During this period various devices were worked out to satisfy this craving for money, in the most primitive sense of "coin." Apart from simply prohibiting the export of precious metals, a device which goes back to the Middle Ages, we find that governments groped their way toward a well-defined monetary policy calculated to assist their struggle to attract as much precious metal into their coffers as possible.

The trade balance and tariffs · The governmental activities which were directed toward promoting industry and commerce could be divided into the granting of privileges and monopolies and the attendant regulation on the one hand, and into measures affecting the trade balance on the other. It is from this preoccupation with the trade balance that the whole system derived its name: mercantilism.[8] The fact that England first abandoned mercantilism has led to our forgetting that she also probably first consciously embraced it. At any rate, England practiced mercantilism like all other European governments. For mercantilism was not merely an economic theory (and a wrong one at that), it was a very powerful formative force in the growth of modern government. In fact, there are those who would claim it as the cradle of modern government (Sombart). Now, the effort to interfere directly with the flow of trade took, as we said, the form of impeding or prohibiting certain imports and exports. This policy was carried out by means of general legislation, as in the Navigation Acts, and tariffs were employed on a very considerable scale. It is impossible to say at what point commercial tariffs commenced to develop out of the older fiscal tariffs. It seems that they emerged more or less gradually as people found that the manufacture of goods subject to a fiscal tariff, that is, a tariff for revenue purposes only, offered a margin of protection against foreign competition. Certain it is that at the time of Colbert these ideas were fully worked out and that the greatness of this remarkable minister of Louis XIV lay rather in the zest with which he pursued the policy than in his discovery of it. The French tariff of 1581 was certainly a protective tariff. Protective tariffs dominated throughout the seventeenth and eighteenth centuries, and the commercial treaty negotiated in 1786 between France and England made the first real breach in the system. This tariff policy consisted in placing high duties upon the export of raw materials and unfinished products, and high duties upon the import of finished products, while at the same time facilitating the export of finished products, and the import of raw materials. It is easy to see why the contemporary trend of economic nationalism is sometimes called neomercantilism.

The stimulation of trade and industry through monopolies · This direct method of affecting the balance of trade favorably was complemented by the policy of stimulating industry and commerce through the granting of more or less extensive monopolies. Such grants were usually in the form of specific action, rather than of general legislation. Every American knows that the Massachusetts Bay Company received a charter from the king of England. Few have stopped to consider what this meant with regard to the growth of modern government. The granting of charters was a device carried over from medieval days, when it was the legal method for bringing municipal corporations within the context of a feudal order.[9] In the period when modern governments emerged from the medieval context, such charters were turned to the rather different use of licensing corporations for diverse commercial purposes. These were the regulated companies of the England of the seventeenth and eighteenth centuries. The device of creating such corporations and granting such privileges was employed on so vast a scale as to revolutionize the whole economic life of the several peoples. Naturally, administrative authorities had to be developed to supervise and regulate these undertakings, at home and abroad. The multiplication of central authorities in England, France, Austria, and other states is directly related to the rapid expansion of trade and manufacture under governmental guidance and supervision. Ministries of commerce and boards of trade developed everywhere, and local commissioners were sent out to break down the resistance of old-fashioned craft guilds. The development of such industries would keep the money at home. The arts and manufactures must be promoted, according to the preamble of the Edict of Henry IV of 1603, "for they are . . . the only means of preventing the taking of gold and silver out of the kingdom and thus enriching our neighbors." Therefore he sent out his intendants to discover what industries might be started and where, and to find persons interested and able to undertake such efforts.

Enforcement · It is obvious that this policy of stimulating trade and commerce entailed regulation and supervision of industrial and business life on a large scale.[10] There was no point in decreeing tariffs unless the border control was made effective for dealing with smugglers. Nor was it worth while to grant a manufacturing monopoly to a particular enterpriser unless an effort was made at the same time to set up authorities to enforce that privilege. The English government, which granted many trading monopolies to colonizing companies, solved the problems of enforcement by delegating governmental authority to the commercial corporations themselves. This transfer of governmental authority was the basic premise of Edmund Burke's fight against the practices of the East India Company. Adam Smith protested against this transfer of governmental authority to the Company. For by this policy the government really allowed the establishment of a separate government which in course of time might elect to declare itself independent, as the American colonies did. After this experience, the British changed their policy and commenced to reabsorb the great commercial corporations into the government. At home, governmental authority was more readily retained and central administrative bodies continued to regulate and supervise until the full-grown industrial society swept away most of these restrictions.[11]

The process on the Continent was quite similar, except that it lagged behind England by several generations. In fact, in the countries east of the Rhine the governments never quite released their grip on industry and commerce; or, to put it another way, industry and commerce could never quite get along without the support of the government, English competition being too powerful. Consequently, all these countries inclined to look with greater equanimity upon governmental restrictions, and even acquiesced in collectivism on a comprehensive scale. As the breakdowns of industrial society have made men eager for remedial action, this once more predisposes opinion in continental European countries toward some variety of socialism, or *étatisme* as the French put it; that is, of governmental direction of the economy. But the trend is world-wide.[12]

Stable money · The amassing of gold and silver being, as we saw, closely related to the central goal of mercantilist governments, it was only natural that they should also attempt to affect the flow of precious metals by a suitable monetary policy. Perhaps it is a travesty to call the activities in which early modern governments engaged a monetary policy.[13] Certainly they had little in common with the subtle and complicated operations which are today comprehended under that term. Nor can they be said to have been very successful at the outset. During the entire Middle Ages, the purchasing power of the monetary units created by Charlemagne (pound, shilling, penny) had declined along with a constant decrease in their metallic weight. For example, in England a silver-penny's weight in troy grains fell from 22 to 12 between 1300 and 1464. This fall continued during the sixteenth and seventeenth centuries. The utter confusion into which such handling of the monetary units plunged trade and commerce caused the city of Florence, the forerunner of so much that is significant in modern government, to establish as early as 1252 a stable monetary unit, the florin, later adopted by Edward III for England, but not maintained stable by his successors. Not until the eighteenth century did England get a monetary unit with a fairly stable metallic content. This followed upon the rapid deterioration of silver coins during the "clipper period" at the end of the previous century (from 1672 to 1696, when all silver was re-coined). In other European countries, the decline continued all during the eighteenth century. Yet there can be little question that an ordered fiscal economy was impossible as long as such uncertainty as to the monetary units prevailed. With rising prices, tax returns were bound to fall below the requirements, even though the salaries of the officials were not ad-justed to the rising price level. This consideration alone would show that a modern government with its extensive purchasing of materials and supplies must seek to maintain a stable monetary system. Yet for the longest time the temptation of getting something for nothing by making the coins smaller was irresistible. Fundamentally it was inflation, of course. Conse-quently, inflation cropped up time and again as a "policy" (see next para-graph). All inflation aids the debtor class, and that meant it aided industry wherever industrial establishments had been newly set up with capital from either the government or others. But the effects monetary policy had in this direction were certainly quite unintentional. Nor was all of the weight decrease intentional, as a matter of fact. Certain scholars, at least, have argued that technical inefficiency in the coining of money had a good deal to do with it.

Minting coins was a very complicated process which made certain varia-tions in weight difficult to avoid. This fact was seized upon by shrewd men who discerned a chance of making money by sorting the coins. In the language of an Englishman of the late seventeenth century: "But tho' all the pieces together might come near the pound weight or be within remedy; yet diverse of 'em compared one with the other were very disproportion-able; as was too well known to many persons who pick'd out the heavy pieces and threw 'em into the Melting pott, to fitt 'em for exportation or to supply the Silver Smiths. And 'twas a thing at last so notorious, that it 'scap'd the observation of very few."[14] Once all the heavier pieces had been withdrawn from circulation, the inducement to coin at the lower level was obviously great. Since, according to Gresham's Law this poorer coin forth-with commenced to invade adjoining countries and to drive the better coin off the market (by making the latter desirable for hoarding), the governments of those countries would willy-nilly be driven to debase their coins also. This was particularly true as long as money consisted of metallic coins, and the governments looked upon wealth in terms of the amassing of precious metals. They were not in the happy position of the American government after the war, which could cheerfully let Europeans hoard American dollar bills, since they were nothing but paper representing the credit of the government. On the other hand, the peculiar dangers of that situation in case the government's credit collapsed were much less pronounced under the earlier conditions.

Paper money · On the whole, governments were pretty helpless in dealing with monetary conditions. The more extravagant courts, like those of the Hapsburgs and the Bourbons, were almost always heavily in debt, and they often had recourse to quite dubious practices in order to escape the burden. The most notorious of these was the huge stock swindle into which the French government allowed itself to be persuaded around 1720 by the Scotch adventurer John Law. This man had the notion that the government's debt might be taken care of by forming a colonial corporation and selling its stock to the public. When the ensuing speculative boom collapsed, the idea of paper money, implicit in it, was utterly discredited, though with sound handling it might have made history. About the same time, the English government made the first very tentative steps in that direction through the organization of the Bank of England, which issued notes to the amount of its capital (£2,000,000). These notes were at first issued in very large denominations (£20), and constituted hardly more than two per cent of the total currency. Even in 1796–1797 there were only approximately £10,000,000 available, or about ten per cent. Yet a significant beginning had been made here, soon to be followed by other governments. The Bank of France was established by Napoleon in 1800 and followed the English example. In the meantime, methods of coining had been steadily improving, and by the beginning of the nineteenth century governments were already on the road toward effective management and control of this difficult technique, so vitally important for real prosperity.

Colonial policy · Though colonial policy is usually treated as a part of foreign policy, it exerted the profoundest influence upon the growth of modern economy and its government, and it formed an absolutely essential part of its mercantilist scheme. As we have said before, colonies made it possible to safeguard markets for a country's industrial products and, what was even more important at first, to control sources of raw material supply.[15] Gold, around which mercantilist policy has been found to revolve, was brought back from America in large quantities by the Spanish *Conquistadores*, and its impact upon government was so decisive that one writer has gone so far as to say that "modern government emerged from the silver mines of Mexico and Peru and from the gold mines of Brazil" (Sombart). This is of course meant only as a necessary, not as a sufficient condition: without such an abundant production of precious metals modern government could not have blossomed forth as it did. For one thing, the arms of Hapsburg would not have been nearly as potent against the popular forces in Germany without American gold. Likewise, it is quite imaginable that the Stuarts might have triumphed in England, if the North American trading companies which they had chartered had discovered gold, instead of land for colonists. It is interesting that Charles I tried to capture part of the rich India trade, but he only succeeded in throwing the East India Company's rich traders behind the Puritans and Pym. The wealth of the traders thus reinforced constitutionalism, and England was forced to travel the slower road of converting an agricultural society into an industrial one. This gave superior strength to the great commercial families (Whigs), and strengthened the aristocratic rather than the monarchical forces. But as American gold was claimed by the *Conquistadores* for the royal chest of Spain, so the agricultural produce of the colonies was restricted to London merchants. The Navigation Act of 1660 (i. Charles II, c. 18) well expresses in its Article XIII the prevailing temper of the time: "No sugar, tobacco, cotton-wool, indigo, ginger, fustic, and other dying woods, of the growth or manufacture of our Asian, African, or American colonies shall be shipped from the said colonies to any place but to England, Ireland, or to some other of His Majestys said plantations, there to be landed." 64660

Much of this tale is very familiar to Americans, since these policies stand at the threshold of their national history. Yet it seems desirable to recall the facts here, in order to show how profound a relation they bore to the early growth of modern government. Besides the policies already mentioned, colonial mercantilism prohibited colonies from manufacturing those products which the mother country produced, claimed a monopoly of transportation to and from the colonies for the mother country, and imposed duties between the several colonies and between the colonies and the mother country. This entailed a vast amount of additional governmental activity, and ministries for the colonies became a settled part of the great colonizing nations. Since these colonies consisted almost invariably of conquests beyond the seas and were hotly contested, they required very considerable military forces, both land and naval, but particularly the latter. Here, then, is another vital point of contact between the mercantilist policy of furthering prosperity by governmental action, and the absolutist policy of territorial expansion, the one involving administrative and the other military efforts on an unprecedented scale.

These colonial policies constitute "the old colonial system."[16] This system was justified in terms of mercantilism, but was of primary advantage to the merchants. This student feels that there is little exaggeration in the judgment of Adam Smith when he declared: "Of the greater part of the regulations concerning the colony trade, the merchants who carry it on, it must be observed, have been the principal advisers. We must not wonder, therefore, if, in the greater part of them, their interest has been more considered than either that of the colonies or that of the mother country." This writer seems to agree with the basic conception of our approach here, namely, that the colonial policies grow out of the objective of prosperity, rather than of territorial expansion in this period. "What England primarily looked for in the colonies," he says, "was neither extension of territory per se, nor overseas aggregations of Englishmen, but goods and markets." It was the belief that commodities could be secured without loss of precious metals which underlay the "old colonial system." In this outlook, it is markedly different from later colonial imperialism.[17]

Conclusion · In conclusion, the question may be raised as to whether the mercantilist economic policies were basically economic or governmental in origin. In one view, they were definitely governmental. Much effective support came from those classes in society which were benefiting from the policies. But as Eli Heckscher has so rightly said: "Economics means the adaptation to given noneconomic ends." It was the primary fallacy of the *laissez-faire* outlook to assume that the economy is a system of nature rather than a pattern of methods used by men in the pursuit of whatever ends they have in view. Mercantilism was a system for unifying the country and increasing its power as well as for increasing its wealth. The increase in wealth was sought through manipulating both commodities and money. The builders of modern administrative government believed in the ability of government to do all these things, and they believed this in England no less than on the continent. But the industrial revolution which they set in motion proved too much for government to handle. The social classes which rose with it, the commercial and professional middle class, eventually recognized that greater prosperity could be achieved through limiting governmental, i.e. administrative, participation. But this historical limitation should not blind us to the achievement of the governmental administrators who built the modern "state." This is the more true since recent breakdowns of free enterprise have brought a new development of governmental administrative participation in the economy (ch. XXIII).

VI

Justice and the Judicial Function

Introduction: justice and government · Rival conceptions of law · "Artificial reason" of the law · The judicial process · The rule of precedent and the judicial process · Judicial organization in continental Europe · Bench and Bar and the Act of Settlement · The judiciary and the rule of law in Prussia: a contrast · Judicial restraint as the beginning of constitutional government · Administrative law · The *Conseil d'État* · French administrative justice and American problems · Conclusion.

Introduction: justice and government · "Justice is the end of government," *The Federalist* noted. "It ever has been and ever will be pursued until it be obtained, or until liberty be lost in the pursuit." Justice has often been expounded as the primary, or even the only "ideal" purpose of government. This is the view of Plato, especially as stated in *The Republic*. That marvellous dialogue, perhaps Plato's greatest, bears the subtitle: "or about the just." But do Plato and *The Federalist* mean the same "justice"? Plato himself makes it quite clear that he is not talking about "states as they actually are," but about an ideal commonwealth, perhaps realizable with great good luck, but certainly not then in existence. Careful reading soon shows that what Plato meant by "justice" includes a large part of morals. That government should be conceived and carried on with the objective of making its citizens "good men" is an idea which many may laugh at, but as an ideal it seems to modern man questionable primarily because of the totalitarian implications of employing the force of governmental power for such spiritual purposes. In any case, justice as an objective of modern government, in the sense in which objectives are treated here, is a more limited concept. It is neither identical with law, nor entirely transcending law; nor is it the subjective quality in the individual which makes him try to achieve justice. The ancient Aristotelian conception of justice as related to equality distinguished between corrective and distributive justice. Corrective justice is concerned with equal distribution of goods between persons, distributive justice with the relative equality of persons in accordance with their differences. Distributive justice is the more important of these. But justice as a primary objective of modern government is concerned with two things: to insure that all persons are put in a position to get what they are entitled to under the law, and to insure that no one is punished, that is to say, suffers injury to life or limb, as the old phrase goes, unless he has infringed the law. But the phrase "the law" must not be taken to mean merely the positive enactments of legislative authorities; it encompasses standards of fairness, reasonableness, and the like which the judge must bring into play at certain points.[1]

A large part of the task of settling the problems connected with this objective of justice arises in disputes between private parties. From the governmental standpoint, this means that the maintenance of justice is closely related to the task of maintaining internal peace. Unless people could be reasonably certain of securing their "rights" through a process of adjudication, violence would often flare up. Hence one of the most ancient governmental functions is unquestionably that of settling disputes between members of the group. Among the great variety of methods and techniques developed to fulfill this function, the most permanent are judicial. Far back in prehistoric times, verdicts were pronounced and punishment meted out to the evildoer in accordance with traditional customs.[2] The legendary Germanic chieftain, with a long beard, sitting under an oak tree and performing this crucial function, is not peculiar to one racial group, as the Romantics once imagined; he could be duplicated in practically every other land. This tribal chieftain, if successful, eventually emerged as a king surrounded by a group of elder statesmen, a council of wise men, the Witenagemot of Anglo-Saxon times. Its members were counselors of the king, the bishops, the ealdormen, and the thegns. Besides exercising many other functions of government, this great council sat as a high court of justice over all persons and causes. The function of a high court was later inherited by Parliament, or rather by the king in Parliament, as the ancient phrase goes. Throughout the Middle Ages this judicial work was the central function of Parliament. It is one of the most significant developments under modern government that this function was ultimately differentiated from the lawmaking, the legislative function, and allocated in large part to separate organs and officials. Indeed, from the legal point of view, the most significant feature of modern government is this differentiation of the judicial process. This was clearly stated by Montesquieu who, generalizing from English practice, considered an independent judiciary the essence of constitutional government. In the *Spirit of the Laws* he observes: "There is no liberty yet, if the power to judge is not separated from the legislative and executive power. . . . In the majority of the kingdoms of Europe, the government is moderated, because the prince leaves the exercise of the judicial power to his subjects." Montesquieu's idea of a moderated government corresponds, in general, to the notion of a constitutional government. (See below, Part II.)

Rival conceptions of law · Differentiation of the judicial function could not commence, of course, until the idea of "making" laws had become distinct. In the Middle Ages there existed, broadly speaking, no such idea. Law was assumed to be something already in existence, fixed and immutable. All that was thought necessary was to find out what this law was, to interpret and determine it (*jus dicere*). Custom was supposed to be the fountain of this law. But custom is local, and the inconveniences which resulted from the great variety of rules seriously troubled medieval governments. As we have already pointed out, one ideal weapon, the Roman law, was available against this multiplicity of local laws. It fitted in with the prevailing notion that law is something immutable, but had the advantage of stemming from a single source. What was more, the Roman law was patterned on the needs of a highly civilized society, built on commerce and industry. It was, to that extent, a welcome instrument to the commercial and industrial classes in their conflicts with the feudal landowning classes. Emperor, pope, and king alike sought refuge and relief in its provisions. However, the struggle between royal and papal authority, which was so significant an aspect of the later Middle Ages, made national kings turn away from the Roman law. More particularly in England, a common law, expounded by the king's judges, rapidly amalgamated the more useful ideas of the Roman law with the broader principles of Germanic customs. This development is most strikingly illustrated by the work of Bracton (1216–1272). As a result, England already possessed a substantial body of common national law at the time when elsewhere the Reformation, by eliminating most of the ecclesiastical jurisdictions, for the first time made possible the consolidation of national systems of law. On this law judges could base their decisions in opposing the royal claims to supremacy in the field of lawmaking, which Bodin's sovereignty had so ingeniously vindicated for the royal authority. Coke's famous claim that the king is *under* the law assumed a significance which it could not have had when no national law was extant.[3] In the course of the century from 1520 to 1620 (the Reformation), it became increasingly clear that in England parliamentary statutes were laws made by the king in Parliament. Legislation became an acknowledged fact; but it took quite some time until it was generally recognized. To be sure, Sir Thomas Smith in his *English Commonwealth*[4] distinctly speaks of a legislative function apart from the judicial function of Parliament. Francis Bacon's entire work on the common law is also permeated by this distinction, which is implied in his celebrated dictum that "the common law is more worthy than the statute law." Yet it is not easy to fix with any exactness the beginnings of the legislative activity which has become one of the main characteristics of modern Parliaments, or to assign the causes of its growth (McIlwain).[5] Probably the many statutes consequent upon the Reformation and involved in the separation of the Church of England from the Catholic Church represent a first genuine outburst of legislation in the modern sense. Here was a genuine rupture in the community, and whatever was done in the form of parliamentary enactment could not but appear in the light of man-made law to those opposed to it. Sir Thomas More was executed because he would not take an oath established by parliamentary "legislation." And when, under Mary, the opposing faction gained the upper hand, and repealed a good many statutes, only a blind man could have failed to perceive that laws were made and unmade by human beings. Yet the older idea constantly recurs. "King Henry VIII," Bacon recalls, in suggesting the making of a Digest of English Law to James I, "was authorized by Parliament to nominate thirty-two commissioners to purge the canon law, and to make it agreeable to the law of God, and the law of the land." This idea that all laws should be related to the "fundamental law" of the land gained ground constantly. In Dr. Bonham's case, Sir Edward Coke, then Chief Justice of the Court of Common Pleas, claimed "that in many cases the common law will control acts of Parliament and sometimes adjudge them to be utterly void." The difficulty in extracting the true meaning of this statement lies in the fact that "acts" of Parliament could, in that period, refer to judicial decisions as well as to legislative enactments. At the trial of the Earl of Strafford, in 1641, a member of Parliament declared that if any question arises concerning either a custom or an act of Parliament, "the Common Law of England, the First, the Primitive and the General Law, that's the Rule and Expositor of them, and of their several extents," must be decisive. In other words, the common law was supposed to contain within itself broad basic principles regarding the procedure and limitation of governmental organs which no one of them could undertake to change. To this day, the "common law" tradition has retained something of the older notion in the emphasis placed upon court decisions.

Bacon's attempt to supersede this idea of a fundamental law (which he recognized as judge-made law) by resuscitating the Roman doctrine of a law of nature as the rule of right reason failed utterly. This is striking and significant, since natural-law doctrines were so very successful on the Continent as pathmakers for monarchical absolutism. Bacon wanted to place the law of nature above both common law and statute law. By the "law of nature" he meant, of course, the rule of right natural reason. This encountered the fierce opposition of Sir Edward Coke, who in answer evolved the doctrine of the "artificial reason of the law." This peculiar notion has been of decisive significance in the development of the judicial process.

"Artificial reason" of the law · The doctrine of the "artificial reason," then, grew out of an argument as to whether the king was or was not above the law. Sir Edward Coke had been restricting the jurisdiction of the ecclesiastical Court of High Commission. He was asked to discuss the matter with the clergy in the presence of King James November 13, 1608, and he roundly asserted that he would not be able to accept the Romanist interpretation of the clergy. James, taking exception to this dogmatic view, declared that he was the supreme judge, and that under him were all the courts. To this Coke replied: "The common law protecteth the King." "That is a traitorous speech," King James shouted back at him in great anger; "the King protecteth the law, not the law the King. The King maketh judges and bishops." He then proceeded to denounce Coke so vehemently, shaking his fists at him, that Coke "fell flat on all fower" before the King, and humbly begged his pardon.[6] But the matter did not long rest there. In 1616, a similar quarrel ensued over whether the king could stay a court proceeding which he considered contrary to his prerogative. Under the leadership of Coke, then Lord Chief Justice of King's Bench, the judges had claimed such a proceeding to be contrary to law. To this claim James answered that although he never studied the common law of England, yet he was not ignorant of any points which belong to a king to know.[7] Thereupon his idea that "natural reason" unrelated to a knowledge of the law of the land could be employed in interpreting statutes was rejected by Coke in the most explicit form. "Reason is the life of the law, nay the common law itself is nothing else but reason; which is to be understood as an artificial perfection of reason, gotten by long study, observation and experience, and not as every man's natural reason . . . by many successions of ages [the law of England] has been fined and refined by an infinite number of grave and learned men, and by long experience grown to such a perfection, for the government of this realm, as the old rule may be justly verified of it, that no man out of his private reason ought to be wiser than the law, which is the perfection of reason." Thus reason is clearly not a standard, philosophical or otherwise, brought to the law from outside, but the essence of the law itself, acquired in the process of learning the law. This notion is not only historically significant, but has a certain general validity. For it is only when general rules, embodied in legislative enactments, are transformed into detailed statements applicable to everyday life that they become part of the living law.

The judicial process · To the judicial function corresponds a distinctive process. This process is typically that of deciding what is just in a controversy between two or more contending parties. The decision may be rendered by one man or by several men acting as a body. Characteristically it offers the contending parties an opportunity to state their case to the best of their ability, either stating it themselves or through a representative (counsel); such statement may be cast in terms of more or less formalized law, but the judicial process when fully developed presupposes some kind of rational basis (law) in terms of which all arguments, including the decision of the judge, is cast.

This basic pattern of the judicial process can be elaborated and refined in many different ways; each system of law is apt to have some features that are distinctive. The knowledge of these is vital to anyone who wishes to "practice law" under that system. This fact may raise very difficult problems if an attempt is made to constitute a court composed of judges trained in different systems of law, as happened at Nuremberg in connection with the International War Crimes Trials. But such difficulties can be composed, provided there is agreement on the basic aspects of the judicial process. [8]

Increasing sophistication concerning all rationalizations and the emphasis on semantics as a "tyranny of words" have tended to produce a facile cynicism concerning the judicial process. Wisecracks about the judge at the breakfast table are all right, for they call attention to the human failings of judges. But we can yet appreciate the significance and value of this process, even though we are no longer able to consider the tentative "hypotheses" or generalizations contained in legal judgments as eternal truths. Such generalizations may be as important and influential as absolute and immutable laws once were. And even though we appreciate the irrational forces which affect judicial conduct, "the traditional beliefs, acquired convictions, and the deep-rooted prejudices" which mold the judge's interpretations of the law, we continue to realize the essential service which is rendered by the man who struggles to find the just decision in the light of all the available facts and rules. For even if the fabric of the law be considered a huge web of effective make-believe, the life of the community and the maintenance of government are dependent upon it.

The rule of precedent and the judicial process · The artificial reason which permeates the judicial process is, in turn, so firmly grounded in the tradition of *stare decisis*, [9] that is, the idea that the courts must abide by rules set up in previous decisions, that some consideration must now be given to this important technique of the judicial process. Rules set up by previous decisions are called *precedents*. That judges are guided by such precedents is hardly surprising. "It takes effort and time to solve problems. Once you have solved one it seems foolish to reopen it.... Both inertia and convenience speak for building further on what you have already built; for incorporating the decision once made, the solution once worked out, into your operating technique without re-examination of what earlier went into your reaching your solution." In other words, the following of precedent is firmly rooted in human experience, and characteristic of all human activity. It is the governmental equivalent of what, in the community at large, we know as folkways, and of what, in the individual, we know as habit. As Justice Cardozo once put it, "the power of precedent . . . is the power of the beaten track." And even if the judges were willing to discard their previous decisions, the lawyers at the bar pleading their cases are constantly reminding the judges of these former decisions, and thus keep the courts conscious of such precedents. What is more, the precedents not only stabilize and unify governmental practices, but they make available to the inexperienced newcomer the accumulated experience of the past. Perhaps they also heighten the sense of responsibility of the judge who confronts an unprecedented situation, since he knows that the precedent which he sets may become the guiding star of many judges following him. It would, however, be foolish to assume that all cases can be decided by precedent. As a matter of fact, precedent makes for change as well as stability. How? Essentially through the use of two rather contradictory views of precedent which one might call the strict and the loose view (Llewellyn). According to the strict view, the judge must make certain just what it was that the precedent decided, he must confine the case to its particular facts. This view is applied to unwelcome precedents. It is the technique for freeing the lawyer and the judge of precedents. The loose view, on the other hand, maintains that the court has decided any or all points on which it chose to rest a case, no matter how broad the statement. This loose view accordingly provides lawyer and judge alike with a technique for capitalizing welcome precedents. The doctrine of precedent is therefore two-faced, and if applied to the same precedent at the same time, it yields contradictory results. It is apparent how this equivocal "rule" provides for both stability and change, by offering a technique for getting rid of previous rules, as well as for bringing in previous rules. Broadly considered, it is a most extraordinary make-believe calculated to maintain the continuity of the legal system and to bind the new judge to the experience of the past.

Judicial organization in Continental Europe · On the European Continent, the ingenious make-believe of the rule of precedent does not prevail.[10] Do Continental judges then fail to follow precedent? Of course not. Precedent, we saw, is so much a reflection of general human experience with law that we find it wherever human beings pursue the same tasks for any length of time. But European judges call their following of precedent by a different name, namely *usus fori*, that is to say, the "usage of the Court." Continental practice focuses attention on the corporate activity of the courts rather than on individual pronouncements. There are no "dissenting opinions." The decisions themselves are much less elaborate in most jurisdictions. The judges are, in fact, considered a species of government officials. Organized into a distinctive group, quite separate from the practicing lawyers, or "members of the bar," the judges are members of a hierarchically organized bureaucracy. Into this bureaucracy men enter after appropriate training and remain in it for the rest of their lives. Until recently, at the top of the system there was a ministry of justice which supervised the system, attended to promotions, and in general acted as a directing force in making judicial experience available to the legislature. As a consequence, ministries of justice have been the spearhead in promoting the recurrent great codifications of Continental law, of which the French *Code Civil* is perhaps the most striking instance, although the Prussian and Austrian codes preceded it. A prime motive for the individual judge in following the precedents in the interpretation of these codes is the ministry's influence upon promotions. This ministerial system has now been sharply altered in France by the establishment of the Superior Council of the Judiciary (arts. 83–4). This Council, presided over by the President of the Republic, is a body composed in part of judges, in part of lawyers, and of some others. It submits nominations for judicial appointments to the President, and it is enjoined to "ensure the discipline of these judges, their independence and the administration of the courts." The Germans, unfortunately, have not followed this example, but have retained the system of ministerial control, restricting only the removal of judges, and proclaiming them "independent and subject only to the law" (art. 97). Thus we find that the two most important practical objectives of the doctrine of precedent, (1) to bridge the gap between experience and inexperience, (2) to maintain relative continuity of the legal system, are here achieved through administrative devices, to wit, an adequate apprentice training and a judicial career leading to the higher judicial positions. The dangerous potentialities of this method of bureaucratizing the judiciary were revealed in the extent to which judges in Germany and Italy betrayed their judicial office under Fascist influence.[11]

The contrast in judicial organization and precedent between the European continent and common-law countries is in keeping with the general lines of differentiation between the political traditions of England (and America) as compared with those of the Continent. In England (and America), reliance is placed upon believed-in traditional groupways resting upon common consent as compared to authoritarian, administrative devices. In order to understand better the cleavage which underlies this differentiation in the judicial process, it will be helpful to describe the particular group with whose ways we are here concerned. In England and America judges usually are appointed from among the practicing lawyers, so that there does not exist any distinct judicial profession. Instead, judges are included in the lawyers' guild.

Bench and Bar and the Act of Settlement · The lawyers' guild in English-speaking lands is one of the most ancient and honorable professions. It goes back to the thirteenth century.[12] As we have seen, England had acquired centralized institutions and was in the process of acquiring a national common law as well. This common law was being developed by royal judges and drew extensively on custom for its sources. Since the universities (under ecclesiastical guidance) taught Roman and Canon law, the practice grew up of teaching the common law in fraternal organizations, of which the four so-called Inns of Court were the most important. The education given at these Inns was primarily of a practical nature; it was an education which trained students for their work both at the bar and on the bench. In connection with this development, the custom grew up that the judges must be taken from among the practicing lawyers, rather than from the universities where the Roman and Canon law was taught. Eventually these Inns of Court acquired the exclusive right to call men to the bar, through calling them to the so-called bar of the Inn. Thus legal education became a monopoly of the professional class itself, uniting as it did in one body both judges and advocates. This development of an all-inclusive professional guild was of the greatest political consequence. At first, and well into the sixteenth century, the common lawyers constituted a force strengthening the monarchical position in its struggle with the Catholic Church and the local feudal lords. But their allegiance shifted gradually as the apologists for royal power and prerogative in the field of government, such as Bacon and King James, began to expound truly Romanist pretensions, as far as the law and its adjudication were concerned. Thus the position taken by Sir Edward Coke that the king is under the law is a consistent expression of the traditional groupways which the legal guild had developed in the preceding age.

It is only against this background of a consolidated legal profession, priding itself upon its mastery of the "artificial reason" of the law, that the emergence of judicial "independence" can be evaluated. Truly communal control effected through the lawyers' guild had become so well established and "independence" from authoritarian governmental control served the dominant interests of the community so well that it was not challenged until the Reform movement of Bentham and the Utilitarians began to press the neglected interest of the town laborer. The role of the judiciary in protecting exploitation and injustice was mercilessly portrayed in the novels of Charles Dickens. But the reformers sought the remedy in changed legislation, rather than in making the judiciary dependent upon political pressure, as was done in the United States. Here, in many local jurisdictions, the election of judges was the "democratic" answer to an excess of conservatism on the bench. In England, it would seem wisely, reliance has been placed upon the control which professional standards and judgments tend to exert. The same is true, of course, for the higher judicial positions in America. Without adequate consideration of this collegiate control, judicial independence would indeed spell judicial "tyranny." The irresponsibility of such a tyranny is avoided by the fraternal community of bench and bar. It continues to make the English and the American judge highly sensitive to the criticism of his brethren off the bench. As long as judges held office during royal pleasure, they were in some difficulty whenever "the royal pleasure" ran contrary to predominant lawyers' sentiment. Coke made the common law, as we have seen, the basis of his attacks upon James' conception of the prerogative as of divine right. Is it surprising that James' instinctive feeling toward lawyers should have been hostile? Bacon tells us that the king realized that "ever since his coming to the crown, the popular sort of lawyers have been the men, that most affrontedly in all Parliaments have trodden upon his prerogative." On the other hand, it was rather natural that the legal brotherhood should have felt that the royal displeasure should only be displeasure with the conduct of judicial business, according to the established law of the land. Hence, the demand arose that judges should hold office during good behavior, or, as the ancient phrase goes, *quamdiu se bene gesserint.* This aspiration was realized in the Act of Settlement, which thereby supplemented the Bill of Rights in a very important regard. But what does good behavior mean? The standard of conduct implied by that phrase is set by the collegial and fraternal organization of bench and bar. The compelling force of professional ethics was thus given governmental recognition.

The judiciary and the rule of law in Prussia: a contrast · The utterly different situation on the Continent is strikingly illustrated by the famous case of the miller Arnold which occurred under Frederick the Great in Prussia, in 1779–80.[13] A technically correct, but substantially unjust, decision led to the summary dismissal and imprisonment of six judges. They had incurred the royal displeasure, because they did *not* employ the rule of right reason, but followed the artificial reason of the law, and rendered a judgment which favored the wealthy landowners to the detriment of a simple peasant-miller. Frederick's despotic, yet popular, action was widely acclaimed throughout Europe; yet in Prussia it had the unhappy consequence that direct complaints to the king were pouring in from all sides. The king himself was profoundly worried, lest he had punished an innocent man. It was so affirmed after the king's death. Perhaps the most striking result of this case was the king's resolution to have a general code prepared. This code was to be based upon reason and the Prussian common law. It was, in other words, conceived in the same terms as Francis Bacon's celebrated proposal for the codification of the laws of England. But whereas Bacon's plan foundered upon the solid rock of opposition of the lawyers' guild, the Prussian code was completed in 1794, and thus became the first of a long series of codifications which characterize the law of European constitutional governments in the nineteenth century. These codes mark, broadly speaking, the passing from the arbitrary government of absolutist monarchy to the "government according to law" which followed it. But the codes are, at the same time, striking expressions of the authoritarian conception of government, which subjects the judicial process to general rules.

In disposing of the case of the miller as he did, Frederick the Great followed his father, Frederick William I, who had been filled with a deep distrust of the courts. He looked upon them as the last refuge of feudal privilege and patrician intrigue. The upper classes were so strongly entrenched in these local courts that Frederick William saw no other escape than to develop separate jurisdictions where judicial functions would be exercised by his own administrative officials. His endeavors in this direction stand in close parallel to the development of the Court of Star Chamber and the Court of High Commission under the Tudors in England. But whereas England was already a united realm with a strongly developed judicial system expounding a national common law, the kingdom of Prussia consisted of scattered fragments in each of which the established courts attempted to maintain a local law. They consequently lost ground constantly to administrative officials. This conflict led to the demand for a common law. The consequent return to a system of strictly judicial procedure was the prime object of the reforms of Samuel von Cocceji[14]. Under his influence Frederick the Great decided to submit himself and all his administrative officials to the law. Thus, in 1748, he decreed that "the judicial boards should decide the case according to the written law." And even though later certain cases were excepted from this general instruction, and were declared suable before administrative tribunals, it was provided that in all these cases the same procedure should be used as that employed in the ordinary courts; in other words a measure of due process of law was guaranteed. We have here, together with the recognition of some kind of "rule of law," the emergence of the idea of administrative law. The idea of administrative law is rooted in the continental notion of a royal or public domain, of the public needs in military, tax, and police matters, and of a code of behavior for the official hierarchy itself.

Judicial restraint as the beginning of constitutional government · A generation ago, administrative law was the occasion of a heated controversy in which Dicey maintained that such law was utterly alien to English and American legal traditions, and that any growth of it must be viewed with profound alarm. In his statement of the problem he harked back to the time-honored argument that law when administered by administrative agencies becomes arbitrary and bureaucratic. We are facing here the fundamental problem of how to enforce responsibility. It is unquestionably desirable to have a king cherish the noble sentiment that he is the first servant of his state, but it is not enough if he is left to himself in determining whether he has lived up to this standard. Now the least objectionable method, from the point of view of monarchy, appears historically to have been the proposition that the king is bound by the law. We have seen how this rule was insisted upon by Sir Edward Coke in his struggle with James I, and how it underlay the judicial reforms of Cocceji. But the question immediately arises as to who is to say what the law is. In other words, the problem of who determines the personnel of the courts is politically the decisive question. Just as the control of many courts by the Catholic Church had seemed an unbearable situation from the point of view of national monarchies in the late Middle Ages, so the control of the courts by the patrician classes represented in Parliaments and Diets had carried with it economic and social implications which aroused bitter struggles. Since the patrician classes were quite prepared to interpret the law in their own favor, their control of the courts was resented not only by the king, but by the common people as well. This issue is related, therefore, to the conflict of various groups in the community, each attempting to secure supremacy.[15] The common man cannot be said to have been on the side of judicial supremacy at a time when courts were closely linked to the patrician class. And yet, the era of modern constitutional government commences with the establishment of judicial restraints upon the executive branch of the government. This is due to the fact that such judicial restraints mark the beginning of a division of power in the community which the advocates and builders of absolute monarchy had denied. They, like their modern brethren advocating dictatorial forms of government, were persuaded that nothing but a complete concentration of power could hope to overcome the grave disorders which religious disunity had produced.

Administrative law · From this point of view, administrative law, that is, the administration of certain bodies of law by administrative agencies, is undoubtedly a step in the direction of the concentration of powers.[16] It is, therefore, bound to be welcomed by all those who have a leaning in the direction of dictatorial methods, provided it is employed in support of objectives which they approve. Since, broadly speaking, the expansion of governmental activities is the goal of reformers or "progressives," we find these groups actively supporting the expansion of administrative jurisdiction. But it should be apparent that efficiency, expediency, and utility are formulas which can be diverted to various ends, as nothing is inherently and ultimately efficient, expedient, or useful. It all depends finally upon what you want to do or have. On the other hand, it cannot with any show of factual evidence be claimed that the existence of administrative law, that is, the exercise of judicial functions by administrative agencies in limited fields, heralds the disappearance of the "supremacy of law" or of constitutional government (*Rechtsstaat*). On the contrary, the development of administrative law in France and elsewhere is a definite achievement of the constitutional era. For it does not signify the supremacy of administrative officials over the law, but its exact opposite, namely, the standardization of all administrative conduct in terms of legal rules. The central concern of administrative law has been the legal limitation of administrative "discretion." Thus the first principle of administrative law is that no administrative measure which imposes a burden upon anyone can be taken without legal authorization. Through this principle, "discretion" is enclosed within the narrowest possible limits. It may be claimed, in fact, that the exercise of judicial functions by administrative officials, which so thoroughly frightened Dicey, is, when seen in historical perspective, an indication of the fact that large areas of formally administrative activity are actually judicial in nature, or are in the process of being judicialized. The failure to develop truly judicial bodies and techniques in England and America has occasioned criticism, and at times violent criticism. It is difficult, however, to arrive at a balanced judgment. Such a judgment is well expressed by Harold Laski: "If administrative tribunals are to command public confidence it may be suggested that their membership must satisfy certain historic canons on which public confidence appears to depend. Their composition must be stable in character. The minister or department head must not be able to change their membership at his discretion or to overrule their findings on issues of fact. . . . The men appointed to such tribunals must be known and chosen for their competence in the theme of their particular jurisdiction. Such tribunals should moreover always contain a legal element. These canons are in fact satisfied by the French and German systems; it cannot be said that they have yet been satisfied in the tribunals which the necessities of the modern state have led Great Britain and the United States to erect."

The *Conseil d'État* · It may be well to examine a bit more closely the apex of the French system, the *Conseil d'État*.[17] It is a common mistake to describe the French Council of State as primarily, if not exclusively, a judicial body. In fact, this council combines its judicial activities with very important administrative functions, particularly in the field of ordinance-making (*réglements* and *décrets*). The judicial functions constitute the work of merely one section of the council. The regular members of the council, thirty-five regular councilors, thirty-seven masters of petitions, and eighteen auditors, are the only ones to participate in the work of this judicial branch of the council. The majority of these members are career men who have entered the council as assistant auditors (*auditeurs de seconde classe*) on the basis of a competitive examination, and have been promoted on merit. Councilors and masters of petitions taken from outside the council are not spoilsmen without preparation; usually they are career officials and university professors who, the French believe, add a valuable element of flexibility to the council's work. To the extent that the *Conseil* is a court, it is objectionable that even the regular members of the council hold office at the pleasure of the government. It is argued that since the council is engaged in administrative as well as judicial work, tenure during good behavior is rather impracticable. It is, as in the case of administrative commissions in the United States, a question of the right balance of advantages and disadvantages; for the loss of administrative experience may not be sufficiently balanced by the gain of complete judicial independence. Certainly thorough familiarity with many branches of administration (the regular members are rotated from section to section at from one to three year intervals) is no mean gain to men who are called upon to settle judicially contentions or disputes (*contentieux*) which arise over administrative activity. Though many such disputes are raised and settled in ordinary courts, even in France, the bulk is brought before the Council of State. Administrative law, therefore, cannot be defined in terms of the jurisdiction of the Council of State—a tendency which is ever-present in common-law countries. It is much more comprehensive, and includes, in the language of Professor Hauriou, that branch of public law which regulates (1) the organization of public administration and of the several administrative officers; (2) the powers and privileges which these administrative officers possess in order that they may operate the public services; and (3) the exercise of these powers and privileges through the prerogative, specially through the procedure of official action (*action d'office*), and the disputes which result therefrom. In considering these questions of administrative adjudication under the Council of State, we must keep in mind, then, that administrative law comprises a broader sphere, and that the council has administrative functions other than those of adjudication.

French administrative justice and American problems · Perhaps the greatest difficulty which arises in connection with a separate set of administrative courts is that of a conflict of jurisdiction between such courts and the ordinary judicial courts. In France that problem is settled by the organization of a separate court of conflicts (*Cour de Conflits*). This *Cour de Conflits* is, as M. Hauriou has pointed out, essentially a court interpreting the constitution, since the whole separation of administrative adjudication rests upon the French doctrine of the separation of powers (see below, ch. X). There is no reason why in the United States this sort of problem could not be settled by the Supreme Court, which is the interpreter of the Constitution, anyway. A case concerning an alleged conflict of jurisdiction can only be raised by an administrative court, because according to the French conception it is a matter of protecting matters involving the government against interference by the ordinary courts. In the United States, it would undoubtedly be more in keeping with constitutional traditions if that question could be raised by ordinary courts as well. But there is another side to the development of truly judicial bodies in the administrative field, which is equally fundamental, and which seems to stand in the way of building up a high administrative court on the French model, as has been suggested. The French administrative courts have grown out of what is known in France as consultative, as contrasted with active, bodies of administration. This idea of consultative, advisory bodies goes back to the *Ancien Régime*, was retained during and after the revolution, and remains a significant feature of French as well as of other European administrative systems. The personnel of these consultative bodies is considered a sort of passive administrator. In the United States, consultative bodies are of very minor significance, though the Governor's Council in Massachusetts shows the persistence of these older (monarchical) forms. What is more, these consultative bodies have not been active in usurping the growing amount of judicial work which modern administration entails. In keeping with the tendencies of the federal government, many administrative boards and commissions with quasi-judicial as well as quasi-legislative functions have

115

been created. Their work is quite un-co-ordinated. In France, where such a consultative body existed at the center of the government, it offered a personnel which was at once conversant with administration and yet not actively involved in the administrative decisions. It could, therefore, lay claim to a position of neutrality and impartiality such as a judicial body must possess if its decisions are to be accepted. French writers are correct in emphasizing the fact that the Council of State and the lower administrative courts are *public* bodies, and thus clearly distinguished from the secret working of any kind of appeal to active administrators. Even though the latter device through long periods of history has proved a satisfactory instrument for the maintenance of political order (Catholic Church), there can be no question of comparing such an appeal with any sort of appeal to an independent administrative judiciary. The procedure before the Council of State is essentially that of an investigating commission; that is, the case is conducted by the judges themselves. This is the final point of real difficulty in applying the remarkable experience of the French Council of State to American problems; for this kind of procedure does not satisfy the standards of the American constitutional tradition. But "administrative law," whether we like it or not, is on the march. Casting aside the outworn legal rule that "the king can do no wrong," we can see and describe the growth of administrative law as an application of the judicial methods to the work of the government. This is necessary in order to keep abreast of the ever-widening sphere of administrative activities entailed by the expansion of our industrial civilization. In the eloquent phrases of William A. Robson, the ablest expositor of administrative law in England, we may conclude: "The judicial power which has been given to administrative bodies will be exercised wisely, and the results are likely to be good. . . . I am convinced that Administrative Tribunals have accomplished, and are accomplishing, ends which are beyond the competence of our courts of law as at present constituted. Furthermore, those ends seem to me socially desirable ones which compare favorably with the selfish individual claims based on absolute legal rights to which the formal courts are so often compelled to lend ear. I believe that administrative law as it has developed in modern England is filling an urgent social need which is not met by any other branch of the law; and that there is no inherent reason, if due care and foresight are exercised, why it should be unfitted to take its place side by side with the common law and equity and statute law in the constitutional firmament of the English governmental system."[18]

Conclusion · In conclusion, it may be said once again that the judicial function is one of the most ancient, most persistent functions of government. The methods employed to fulfill that function are of central importance in any political system. A full appreciation of the contrast of Anglo-American and Continental political development is impossible without taking into account the great differences in the position assigned to judicial bodies and the techniques employed by them.

The extension of judicial methods is a concomitant of civilized government. Judicial methods, especially in the matter of taking of evidence, are, or at any rate ought to be, akin to the spirit of science and the search for objectivity characteristic of science in the broad sense. That, basically, is the meaning of the rationalized procedures of a modern judiciary.

The view, often heard at present, that the judicial function is at variance with the requirements of democracy is unsound. Only an unrestrained democracy and an arbitrary judiciary conflict with each other. A constitutional democracy finds one of its important institutional expressions in a judiciary *under the law.*

Existing courts usually resist the extension of judicial methods, and hence at present seem hostile to administrative justice. This must not deceive us; administrative justice represents another step in the evolution of modern government. Constitutionalism is the application of judicial methods to basic problems of government; administrative justice, extending this application, attempts to extend the judicial methods to the wider sphere of activities which government is handling today. It is, therefore, an extension of constitutionalism itself.

PART II

THE PATTERN

OF CONSTITUTIONAL

GOVERNMENT

VII

The Making of a Constitution as a Political Process

Introduction · Five concepts defined · The constitution as effective regularized restraint · Non-uniformly constitutional development of Anglo-American government · Restraint a question of degree · The medieval constitutionalism · The dilemma of Cromwell · The constitution as the decision regarding the organization of the government · Free speech and free assembly · The constituent power and the right of revolution · Locke's view restated scientifically · Conclusion.

Introduction · A certain Senator from the South, when told that a measure he defended was unconstitutional, expostulated in reply: "When the Constitution comes between me and the virtue of the white women of South Carolina, I say: To hell with the Constitution." Autocrats and revolutionaries of all ages have always spoken in a like vein. By doing so they have revealed their common opposition to restraints placed upon political and governmental action. As a political process, the constitution can be described as analogous to the rules of a game insuring fair play. This is the meaning of the word "constitution" in its functional sense, as distinguished from its meaning in law, in history, and in medicine. The political scientist inquiring into the process of constitutionalizing a government must study the technique of establishing and maintaining effective restraints on political and governmental action. How do such restraints function? He must not allow himself to be side-tracked by the many senses in which the word "constitution" is used.

We may recognize as outstanding *three* nonpolitical concepts of a "constitution," the philosophical, the legal, and the historical. The first of these is a generic concept, the other two specific. What I mean by specific is that the historian may speak of the Constitution of Athens, the Constitution of Medieval England, and the Constitution of the United States, and by each mean something particular or specific, found only at the time and place with which he is concerned. Similarly, the constitutional lawyer of America, England, or France is talking about *the* constitution when he discusses the particular constitution with the legal connotation with which he is familiar in terms of a whole "system of law." Philosophical concepts of the con-

121

stitution, on the other hand, are usually generalizations from the several such historical or legal constitutions with which the author happened to be acquainted. In the case of European philosophers their concepts of a constitution are usually derived by contrasting the meaning commonly attached to the word constitution (*constitution, Verfassung*) in their own country at the time of their writing with what the Roman law and Aristotle presumably suggested as being the meaning of constitution in classical antiquity.

Five concepts defined · Long lists of such "meanings," historical, legal, and philosophical, can easily be compiled. It seems more profitable to summarize such an inventory in terms of a few dominant concepts. Aristotle's concept of a constitution—or rather his concept of *politeia*, which is commonly translated as constitution—refers to the whole order of things in a city. Hegel, who so profoundly influenced the nineteenth century, entertained a very similar idea. Akin to this conception is the notion that the constitution describes the actual organization of the government in broad outline, so that we can speak of a monarchical constitution, a democratic constitution, and so forth. Finally there is found the idea, current among lawyers with a philosophical bent of mind, like Coke, that the constitution embodies the basic legal conceptions of the community, their outlook on life or *Weltanschauung*, in so far as it can be embodied in general legal rules. A similar conception is found in Jean Jacques Rousseau. It is obvious that these three descriptive, general concepts of what a constitution is apply to all political communities, to a Fascist and Communist dictatorship just as much as to the United States or England.

Besides these general descriptive concepts of a constitution we find two concepts which are based upon specific formal aspects. Of these, one maintains that a constitution must be *written*, in order to be a constitution, that it must be embodied in a document.[1] Superficial though this view may seem to us today, it was widely held during the age of constitution-makers in the past century and a half. This may be called the documentarian concept. It was bound to be challenged by students of the English political system like Lord Bryce; for English law makes considerable use of the concept of a constitution without having a written document to argue from. The other concept of a constitution stresses the need for a democratic or popular mode of amendment. In other words, it is the procedure of constitutional change which the procedural concept highlights. Such a concept is elusive because of the uncertainties surrounding the word democratic. What are we to think of the need of assent by the House of Lords, required in England until 1911? It does not appear very satisfactory to exclude such arrangements as out of keeping with constitutional principles. On the other hand, the Soviet constitution of 1936 has amending-power provisions.

The constitution as effective regularized restraint · For the sake of convenience, the five basic concepts which we have so far enumerated may be labeled philosophical, structural, legal, documentarian, and procedural. They are all valuable within their respective contexts, but none of these concepts is concerned with the *function* of a constitution and what it is supposed to accomplish. Function is intimately related to process; it is in terms of function that a process is molded. Hence the functional concept here used must be clearly understood. The definition given at the outset of this chapter said that to render a government constitutional required the establishment and maintenance of effective restraints upon political and more especially upon governmental action. Why should we insist that the restraints must be effective? What is this standard of effectiveness? It should be evident that the existence of formally legal restraints is in no wise an indication of the existence of a constitutional order in the political sense. All the cumbersome formalism of the Roman republican constitution cannot alter the fact that Rome in the first century before Christ had become an aristocratic absolutism, with power concentrated in the hands of the senate. Similarly, the legal separation of powers under the British constitution as expounded by Blackstone during the second half of the eighteenth century cannot blind us to the fact that power in England was largely concentrated in the hands of the aristocracy whose political will found expression in Parliament. On the other hand, a restraint might be very effective and thoroughly regularized, without necessarily being embodied in positive law unless law is very broadly defined as including all custom. Thus, what is perhaps the most important restraint of the English constitution, namely, the alternation of government between two or three parties, is quite effective. From what has been said it can be seen that the problem of effectiveness involves a factual situation and an evaluation and existential judgment of that situation. If no one has "absolute" power, if in actual fact there exists no sovereign who holds unrestrained power in a given community, then the restraints may be said to be effective.[2]

At this point it becomes necessary to introduce another important qualification. Unless such restraints are regularized, they cannot be said to have value as constitutionalizing factors. Madame Pompadour scolding the king at her bedside, or a Brown Shirt rebellion against Hitler, while possibly very effective checks upon the arbitrary whims of an unconstitutional ruler, cannot be classed as even rudimentary constitutional devices.

123

The restraint which they produce is wholly irregular; it is also entirely un-predictable. Obviously, it is not always easy to determine what is a regu-larized procedure. A practice which at one time is wholly irregular, and at another fully regularized, will, for a certain period, be hard to classify. But it is enough that we can readily determine when a procedure is fully regularized. In the United States, a decision of the Supreme Court ordi-narily marks the point of ultimate regularization, as happened not long ago with the presidential pocket veto.

Non-uniformly constitutional development of Anglo-American government · To this broad functional concept of a constitution it may be objected that it is a generalization derived from English and American political development. But while it is true that English and American constitutional development afford some admirable illustrations for the ab-stract concept, actual developments in England have at times largely veered toward a scheme of powers concentrated in the hands of a landed aristocracy, aided by other big property owners.[3] When Sir Edward Coke waged his historic battle with James I, he did it, to be sure, in the name of the constitution. He took the constitution to mean the basic legal notions accepted by the community. He alleged that only the acceptance of this constitution provided the "rule of law" to which England had been accus-tomed since time immemorial. The king's claim that the royal prerogative was beyond the law was flatly denied. Coke would, however, allow Parlia-ment to exercise the power which he withheld from the king in the name of the law. Thus the particular importance of his struggle lay, admittedly, in his insistence "upon the exclusive right of Parliament to change the laws of England, his vigorous opposition to the claim of any right, even by the king himself, to change the law of the land." Thus the Constitution, the fundamental law, restrained all but the organized people speaking through parliament. But while Coke still meant by "Parliament" the "king in Parliament," or "the ancient body politic composed of kings, Lords and Commons," a decade or two later that medieval aspect of Coke's thought was forgotten. Parliament emerged clothed with unrestrained power. Once parliamentary supremacy was established, it was not long before a new opposition developed to restrain parliamentary absolutism, ending in the dictatorship of Cromwell. After this collapsed, a return to the former constitution based upon a separation of powers between king and parliament provided an unstable equilibrium. This equilibrium was only temporarily disrupted by the civil war issuing in the Glorious Revolution. During these decades of conflict, the constitutional issues exposed the shifting bal-ance of political power between the two classes in the community struggling for supremacy: the land-owning squirearchy allied with the church, and the mercantile classes. In the course of the eighteenth century the latter gained increasing ascendancy as the formal constitution of divided powers was superseded by a new concentration in the hands of parliamentary leaders. This emergency of "parliamentary government" under Walpole eventually brought on the American revolution and the Reform Bill (1832). Both were fought by new classes in the community who sought to establish an effective and regularized restraint. From this sketch it can be seen that what appears to the legalist or the historian as an unbroken period of constitutionalism (simply because men in authority called it so), must appear from the standpoint of political science and its functional concept of a constitution as oscillating between constitutional and unconstitutional periods. It also makes it easier to recognize basic rights or civil liberties as patterns of restraint. This means that they are variable in correspondence with the shifting class structure of society, rather than God-given or nature-given absolutes. Thus the personal rights recognized in eighteenth-century England differ markedly from those adopted later in America. They were the rights which mattered most to the landed gentry and the mercantile aristocracy ruling the land. They represented an "area of agreement" beyond the class conflict upon which most people agreed. In short, such restraints depend for their maintenance upon a balance of classes in the society to which they apply.[4]

Restraint a question of degree · Upon further reflection, it will be apparent that no government, in the light of the preceding discussion, can be described as strictly constitutional. Nor will a completely unconstitutional order be discovered amongst the governments, known to us. Like all true functional concepts, the notion of constitutional government is essentially descriptive of two poles: very strong restraint and very weak restraint. Between these two poles, all actual governments can be ranged. The unreal limits are "complete restraint" and "no restraint," thus:

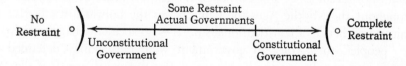

For rough descriptive purposes, governments near the no-restraint pole could be classed as unconstitutional; governments near the complete-restraint pole as constitutional. In the middle there would remain an area of uncertainty. Thus the Soviet Union today would be in the first class, the United States in the second; Prussia in 1860 (before Bismarck's usurpations) might be put into the third along with England before 1832. As we have seen, the maintenance of all restraints depends in the end upon a balance of groups and classes in the community to whose government they apply. But whatever the classes, there are certain recurrent forms.

The functional and qualitative analysis of the constitution as the process by which governmental action is effectively restrained can be pushed much farther. In the first place, it is possible to describe the several restraints which have actually proved effective in the historical experience of mankind. This task will be undertaken with some care in three later chapters (X, XI, XII). There is also the problem of who decides what restraints shall be employed and under what conditions; finally, there is the question of how such a system of restraints is generally related to various forms of government. Each particular form of government has its particular tendency toward concentration of power, and the so-called "pure" forms of Aristotle are all characterized by such a concentration of power in the hands of one, a few, or the many, as the ancient formula goes. No actual government ever conformed to these pure types, though a good many of the Greek city-states seem to have come perilously close to being completely unrestrained and hence unconstitutional in the functional sense.

The medieval constitutionalism · Even in the Middle Ages, the governments of Western civilization tended toward the constitutional pattern.[5] This tendency may justly be attributed to the *Christian* concern for the individual and his personal salvation. Attempts by nationalist historians to claim that Germanic folk traditions or English national character are responsible for it are unconvincing. For the tendency is universal throughout Christian lands, though continually under pressure from one quarter or another. Newly emerging classes and vested interests have each in turn clamored for restraints to prevent the abuse of power by their opponents. Hence the development of political institutions in our civilization has been continuously concerned with discovering effective restraints. The authoritarian aspects of Catholicism must not blind us to the fact that throughout the Middle Ages the Church was the bulwark of effective restraints, and hence of constitutionalism. It is no accident that the rights of the "people" to a voice in government were persistently defended by Church writers. It was in the course of the thirteenth century that the earlier military feudalism became transformed into the government by estates (see above, p. 66) which is epitomized in the phrase "the King in parliament." The curious dualism of this *Ständestaat* underwent many transformations and shows marked differences in different countries. But from England to Hungary, from Spain to Poland and Sweden, we find charters, resembling Magna Charta, which provide for restraints upon the princes and a division of governmental power between the several states, i.e. groups or classes, in the community. The story of Magna Charta shows as clearly as any of the charters that the Church officials, the bishops, prelates, abbots, and others, played a vital part in developing these systems. In most countries the rise of the burgher class, of merchants and professions and craft guilds, also played an important role. But the Church's role was vital. Hence, the eclipse of the ecclesiastical power during the later Middle Ages and upon the advent of the Reformation paved the way for absolutism, first in England, later in France and other Continental countries. The efforts made and the techniques employed in restraining it often brought on revolutionary upheavals. While France, Germany, and other lands went through the religious wars, only England, of the large countries, saw these revolutionary efforts succeed.

The dilemma of Cromwell · In England the problem of a constitution had to be squarely faced in the age of Cromwell. It is well known that the *Instrument of Government* which the more radical followers of Cromwell in his Model Army submitted to him in 1649 was not accepted. But even though this prophetic document with its strongly democratic bias failed to become the first English "constitution," Cromwell was haunted by a sense that his arbitrary exercise of power needed a sanction.[6] This sanction he sought to obtain from several Parliaments which were elected in rapid succession. Yet, since they endeavored to restrain him as well as to sanction his rule, they were dissolved one after the other. The long-drawn-out story of Cromwell's conflicts with his several Parliaments serves, therefore, as an admirable illustration of the fact that once the *de facto* government, controlling power by force of arms, seeks to secure the approval of the community, it will find itself confronted by demands for effective restraint. This statement is subject to one exception. If a purely formal plebiscite (see below, ch. XXV) is employed for the purpose, "the ayes will have it." There is probably a simple psychological reason for this result in that the majority of human beings dislike the futile gesture of pure negation.

The constitution as the decision regarding the organization of the government · To some, there may appear to be a close similarity between defining the constitution as a political process invariably concerned with the technique of establishing effective restraints and the seemingly broader definition of a constitution as the fundamental decision about the form of government. However, this latter definition is rather misleading.[7] Often there is no conscious decision, nor can the resolution of an all-powerful tyrant to maintain his tyranny be called a constitution without rendering

127

the meaning of the term absurd. However, the establishing of such restraints does invariably *imply* the choosing of some form of government. We may therefore say that every constitution implies such a decision, but not that every such decision necessarily implies a constitution. Thus if it be clearly understood that unconstitutional government is excluded, we can speak of the constitution as the basic decision about the organization of the government.

Who, it may now be asked, will make such a basic decision? It used to be customary to answer: the people. Yet, did the electorate which stood back of the Commons in England during the seventeenth century constitute more than a fraction of the people? It did not; and still in common parlance we speak of the Glorious Revolution as one seeking to set up a constitutional government, and the stricter language of political science cannot deny that a constitution in our functional sense was in the making in Britain at that time. To be sure, the Act of Settlement's guarantee of judicial independence was another very essential step. But the Glorious Revolution certainly aimed at setting up restraints on governmental action, and therefore at constitutionalizing the government. That only a fraction of the governed participated in the fray does not alter this fact. Therefore all that we can say in answer to the question: By whom is the decision made? is "By not too few." "Not too few" is a less ambiguous if vaguer statement of the actual facts. But this numerical description is not all that we can offer regarding the makers of constitutions. To make the constitutional decision genuine it is also necessary that it be participated in by some of those who are being governed as contrasted with those who do the governing. This differentiates such a constituent act from the *coup d'état*. The participation by some of those who are being governed, that is, the politically passive members of the community, does not necessarily mean democracy. It does mean, however, that an effort will be made to restrain governmental action. Therein lies the importance of the participation of these passive members. Any decision arrived at solely by the governing bodies is not likely to be directed toward defining methods of restraining governmental action. Cromwell realized this vaguely, and therefore persisted in his efforts to secure parliamentary and popular approval. But since he was unwilling to allow restraints on his power in concrete instances, he found himself obliged to scrap one constitution after another. He could not shake off the idea, so characteristic of all absolutist governments, that opposition was rebellion.

Free speech and free assembly · There is, however, another important condition which must be fulfilled, in order to render the constitutional decision genuine: the decision must be reached after the mature deliberation of those who participate in the decision. Confusing *opposition* with *rebellion* prevents the mature deliberation of those who participate in the decision. Thus no genuine decision results. Neither free speech nor free assembly are "natural rights," but they are necessary concomitants of constitutional decisions. For mature deliberation of an issue by any number of people who are to act collectively presupposes an exchange of views on the issues involved in the decision. If that opportunity is not available, nothing can be decided. This is the fundamental reason why plebiscites, so popular with dictators from Cromwell to the present day, fail to have the legitimizing effect which their initiators always hope for. Though they seem to offer an opportunity for collective approval of a government, their effectiveness in accomplishing that purpose is quite small. They carry little persuasive force in the community, because few of the participants feel any responsibility for the action taken.

The constituent power and the right of revolution · We are now ready to designate the group of human beings which we have broadly characterized in the last two paragraphs. No matter how large or small, it is a very decisive group which it is here proposed to call the constituent group wielding constituent power. Political thinkers during the seventeenth and eighteenth century were deeply concerned with this power, and we owe to them a great deal of our elementary insight. A thorough discussion of their views belongs to a history of political theory, where it is commonly discussed under the heading "the right of revolution." These early thinkers were preoccupied with the question of rights. A descriptive political science has no such concern; it does not ask whether people have a right to make a revolution, but rather what are the conditions under which they do make it. Those early writers, however, in their efforts to vindicate a right of revolution, brought out with much learning what the conditions of revolutions were. The traditional doctrine of the "right of revolution" contains at least this kernel of scientifically valid generalization. Thus Calvinist theorists, like Althusius and Rutherford, pointed to the many revolutions recorded in the Old Testament as proof of the fact that God permitted and even commanded revolutions, provided such revolutions were directed toward restraining the government in accordance with the command of God as interpreted by the priests. This argument the church had already used extensively in the Middle Ages. Still others, like Hotman and Buchanan, had likewise emphasized the historical fact of revolution as a valid part of their national history, whether French or Scotch. This earlier scientific interest in revolutions as manifestations of constituent power was obscured by the moralist turn which this problem was given by Locke, and more emphatically by Rousseau. But the more realistic analysis back of it continues to be the mainstay of the argument.

Locke's view restated scientifically · In his *Second Treatise of Civil Government* (¶ 149), the great English myth-maker remarks: "For no man, or society of men, having a power to deliver up their preservation, . . . to the absolute will and arbitrary dominion of another; whenever anyone shall go about to bring them into such a slavish condition, they will always have a right to preserve what they have not a power to part with; . . . And thus the community may be said in this respect to be always the supreme power, but not as considered under any form of government, because this power of the people can never take place till the government is dissolved." On the basis of our previous discussion, we should rewrite this statement, as follows, in order to fit it into the hypothetical form of scientific thought: "For a considerable number of men (who constitute the more intelligent and vital part of the community at large) have a tendency to maintain their freedom (of decision) . . . against the unrestrained and arbitrary decision of others; whenever anyone shall go about to bring them into a constrained and dependent condition, the presumption is that they will try to escape from it even at considerable sacrifice; . . . and through this (more intelligent and vital) part of the community what may be called 'the constituent group' manifests itself, but not as considered *under* any government, because their power can never come into play except to dissolve the established government and set up a new constitution." This transcription shows that Locke's juridical statement contains the kernel of two important scientific generalizations: (1) there tends to exist a residuary and unorganized power of resistance in the community which seeks to restrain the government, and (2) this constituent power can only come into play when the government fails to function. This second proposition is important in differentiating the constituent power from the constitutional amending power, for which provision is made in most modern constitutions (see below, ch. VIII). To be sure, the amending power is set up in the hope of anticipating a revolution by legal change, and, therefore, as an additional restraint upon the existing government. But should the amending power fail to work, the constituent power may emerge at the critical point. It was part of the optimism of these rationalists to assume that the revolutionary group necessarily and always employed its power to *establish* a constitution. This is not the case. Events in our time, as well as Cromwell and the Napoleons, have shown that such revolutionary groups may set up an autocratic system. Such groups therefore are not a "constituent power."

Conclusion · The word "constitution" has, then, for modern political science, a very distinct meaning, namely, as the process by which governmental action is effectively restrained. In spite of the fact that the word "constitution" has a variety of other meanings, biological, legal, philosophical, and what not, it seemed best to retain it in this traditional sense. Perhaps it would be less ambiguous not to speak of this process as the constitution at all. But as long as the word "constitution" is understood to refer to this process, the possible ambiguity may be excused so as to retain the superior suggestive value of the word "constitution." There is another reason for this way of putting the matter. The total complex of effective restraints which makes up the "constitution" of a given community will necessarily crystallize into more or less familiar word patterns, such as "legislative, executive, and judicial power," "states' rights," "due process," "freedom of speech," and so forth. These word patterns gradually become symbols of order, and thus the constitution becomes itself a political force (see below, ch. IX).

VIII

The Constituent Power, the Amending Power, and Revolution

Introduction: the plebiscite · Cromwell and the Puritan revolution · Napoleonic plebiscites · Constituent and amending powers · Constitutional change without amendment · Flexible versus rigid constitution · The American federal amending process · Conditions for formal amendment · Holland, England, and France · Limitations on the amending power · Nonfundamental constitutional provisions · Limited and unlimited revolutions · The pattern of great revolutions · Difficulty of anticipating unlimited revolution through amending process · Hypotheses derived from Hitler's coming into power · Negative revolutions · Aristotle's theory of revolution · Conclusion.

Introduction: the plebiscite · Revolutions are successful rebellions. If they have failed, their makers have with rare exceptions been executed for treason. Treason is commonly understood to be an attempt to overthrow the established order. The constituent power bears an intimate relation to revolution. To be sure, not all revolutions are made by a constituent group, as Locke and Rousseau tended to assume. For the constituent group wields the power through which it seeks to establish a constitution. Many revolutions do nothing of the kind. We have been witnesses in our own day of a whole series of revolutions which sought to destroy a constitution rather than establish one. But every time the constituent group becomes active, a revolution (or at least a rebellion) will take place.

This constituent power, as we have seen, is exercised by a group of persons. They must be not too few and they must include some of the governed. After the existing order has been overthrown, a measure of free speech and free assembly is established so that the constituent group can work. The suppression of free speech and free assembly thwarted the constituent group in Cromwell's time as well as in our own. National Socialist, Fascist, and Communist revolutionaries are united in their opposition to free speech. It is but natural, therefore, that no constitution should have been established in countries ruled by these groups. But since the need for popular approval is still felt, these parties tend to employ the plebiscite as a substitute.[1] They act as if they felt that a constituent group should have brought them into power, as its leaders; they do not appear satisfied with merely having usurped the absolute power of government. Therefore they seek the plebiscitary semblance of wide popular acclaim. Cromwell, the two Napoleons, Mussolini, Hitler—they all have employed this technique.

Cromwell and the Puritan revolution · Cromwell's *Instrument of Government* of 1653 provided in its Article XII that the officers supervising the elections to Parliament under this instrument should obtain from the electors a written acknowledgment "that the persons elected shall not have the power to alter the government as it is hereby settled in one single person and a Parliament."[2] This provision contains the notion of an implied consent of the electorate, and a characteristic device for escaping the need for an effective constituent group. Yet, no sooner had this Parliament assembled than it commenced an extensive debate on the constitution. This provoked Cromwell (after locking up Parliament) into making a speech to justify his demand that each member of Parliament sign a statement similar to the one just cited. In the course of this speech, the Lord Protector made it quite clear that he perceived a constitution to be a fundamental decision, and basically concerned with restraining arbitrariness. During the Long Parliament there had been, in his opinion, a definite drift toward parliamentary absolutism. "And so the liberties and interests and lives of people not judged by any certain known Laws and Power, but by an arbitrary Power; which is incident and necessary to Parliaments. By an arbitrary Power, I say: to make men's estates liable to confiscation, and their persons to imprisonment,—sometimes even by laws made after the fact committed; often by the Parliament's assuming to itself to give judgment both in capital and in criminal things, which in former times was not known to exercise such a judicature. . . ." For that reason he claimed the dissolution of the Long Parliament had been necessary. But Cromwell did not wish to take over the absolute power thus revoked. In bringing together the Little Parliament, popularly dubbed Barebones Parliament, he had another end in view which he himself claimed to be his greatest end, namely, "to lay down the power" which was in his hands "in which unlimited condition" he "did not desire to live a day." In other words, he wished them to draft a constitution. But they despaired of the task and decided "to deliver up unto the Lord-General (Cromwell) the powers we received from him." Upon the failure of these representatives to exercise the constituent power, the *Instrument of Government* was drawn up by some of Cromwell's supporters in the army and elections were called with the *proviso* cited in the beginning of this paragraph. After Cromwell's exhortation, most of the members signed the pledge not to propose or give their consent "to alter the Government as it is settled in a Single Person and Parliament"; yet immediately upon reconvening they returned to constitutional controversies. Cromwell's admission that in every governmental charter "there must be something Fundamental, something like a Magna Charta, which should be standing, should be unalterable," and therefore in this "establishment there are some things which are Fundamental," others which "are Circumstantial," had left an avenue open for such a discussion of constitutional issues. To be sure, Cromwell had himself outlined three fundamentals of the *Instrument*: (1) "that Parliaments should not make themselves perpetual," (2) that there should be "Liberty of Conscience in Religion," and (3) that the army "should be placed so equally that no one party neither in Parliament nor out of Parliament have the power of ordering it." Each one of these will readily be recognized to be a measure of restraining the government and dividing its power between the executive and the legislative power. When Parliament kept on debating about the constitution, instead of attending to its constitutionally appointed task, Cromwell dissolved it, and thereafter governed as a military dictator,—a constituent group had not emerged in England, and Cromwell's rule collapsed with his death. The implied consent of the plebiscite of 1653 had remained a futile gesture.

Napoleonic plebiscites · Cromwell's failure by no means deterred the two Napoleons from seeking to sanction their rule by a similar device. After the first Napoleon had staged his *coup d'état* (November, 1799), he proceeded to draft a constitution which centered all power in the first consul and submitted it to a plebiscite. Here, then, the consent was not implied, but explicitly asked for—and overwhelmingly given. The same thing happened again in 1802 when the consulate was bestowed upon Bonaparte for life. It is, however, important to realize that these "constitutions" contained no provisions for the restraint of the government, and were therefore not constitutions in the functional sense which we have here employed. It is noteworthy that Louis Napoleon should also have had recourse to the plebiscite. After his *coup d'état* of December 2, 1851, the third Napoleon demanded from the people that they sanction his authority and that they delegate to him the necessary powers for making a constitution along the general lines of a proclamation he had issued. Again, the plebiscite was accepted by an immense majority, which is hardly surprising, in view of the wording of the plebiscite: "The French People wants to maintain the authority of Louis-Napoleon Bonaparte and delegates to him the necessary powers for making a constitution. . . ." The voter could either accept or reject this proposal, but was not given any positive alternative. Practically the same tactics prevailed about a year later when the imperial office was re-established under a plebiscite modeled on the precedent of the first Empire. The restraints established by these charters were quite weak, and even the more liberal Constitution of 1870, also submitted to popular plebiscite, was definitely monarchical. That no effective constituent power came into play through their adoption was emphasized by a speaker who wished to see the constitutional laws of 1875 submitted to popular approval. On the 28th of January, 1875, M. Naquet said in the Assembly: "I believe that a constitution must be ratified by the whole people. By affirming that, I merely return to the tradition of our great (revolutionary) assemblies; for the Constitution of 1793 and the Constitution of the Year III were submitted to direct ratification of the people. . . . We do not have to abandon this right merely because the Empire has abused the plebiscite, the right derived from an appeal to the people. . . . There is an immense difference between the imperial plebiscites which posed the question *a priori* (*ex post facto*) and made it one between some solution and pure negation, and an appeal to the people destined to ratify the charter voted by a national assembly after long and serious deliberations."[3] In this concluding sentence, we find a clear recognition of the necessary conditions of the functioning of a constituent group, as we have here depicted it: not only participation of some of the governed, but also free speech and free assembly.

When seen in this perspective, the plebiscites of Napoleon were hollow gestures. The same is true of present-day despots (see below, ch. XXV). Wholly different were the circumstances of the adoption of the Constitution of the United States. Here wide popular discussion, even heated controversy, preceded a vote on the Constitution. Likewise the Constitution of Switzerland of 1848 owes its existence to the work of a genuine constituent group. The parallel is interesting in that both these constitutions established a federal government in place of a federation of governments.

Constituent and amending powers · The rather orderly procedure which led to the adoption of the Constitution of the United States must not mislead us into thinking, however, that the constituent power can itself be brought "within the four corners of the constitution."[4] To be sure, since a constitution is by definition a technique (or a set of techniques) for the restraining of the government, acts of arbitrary and tyrannical violence are much less likely to occur under a constitutional government. Moreover, a well-drawn constitution will provide for its own amendment in such a way as to forestall, as far as is humanly possible, revolutionary upheavals. That being the case, the provisions for amendment form a vital part of most modern constitutions. The value of such provisions was, however, by no means realized at the outset. The several Cromwellian constitutions did not contain any adequate provisions for their own amendment. During the French Revolution people came around to a realization of the importance of amending provisions with much delay. Thereafter, in the nineteenth century constitutions were rarely made without some thought being given to this problem. But no matter how elaborate the provisions for amendment may be, they must never, from a political viewpoint, be assumed to have superseded the constituent power. The inner relation and the difference between the amending power and the constituent power is brought out with particular vividness by the constitutional history of Switzerland. In 1848 a new federal constitution superseded the federation of cantons which had broken down and given rise to a civil war in 1847. This federal constitution was adopted by a constituent assembly and submitted to the people of the several cantons for ratification, being accepted by a considerable majority. In 1874, this conservatively liberal constitution was entirely overhauled and democratized, but the draft failed to secure the necessary majority of cantonal ratifications as provided in the amending provisions of the constitution. Thereupon the draft was remodeled and adopted in accordance with regular amending procedure in the same year. The constitutional amending authority proved sufficient to make the necessary changes. The potential constituent group worked through the amending power. But that does not mean it is identical with it. For the constituent group in the exact sense is to be understood as that part of the community which is capable of wielding the *de facto* residuary power of changing or replacing an established order by a new constitution.

Constitutional change without amendment · The constitutional history of England is less simple. Formally speaking, her constitution dates back to the Glorious Revolution of 1688. That constitution was enacted by a genuine constituent power. But since that time the English constitution has gone through a number of profound changes without there being any explicit decision on the part of anybody.[5] The English love to talk about that process as "muddling through." Actually, it is part of their astute political realism. These constitutional conventions—for that is what they are called in England—have grown up from precedents. Thus Walpole's way of conducting the government created a series of precedents which became the basis and form of parliamentary government. In turn, the nineteenth century saw that same parliamentary government transformed into a cabinet government by a similar slow evolution. The masterly analyses of writers like Bagehot and Jennings come at the end; it all happens without any but the men who are "insiders" quite understanding what is going on. The English constitutional development is more informal anyway, on account of the fact that the amending power is vested in a parliamentary majority. This arrangement is reinforced, however, by the convention which calls for a new election in case the opposition should stress the importance of the issue. But the fact remains that the basic changes have been quite gradual. They have been accretions or growths rather than decisions. All this merely goes to confirm our earlier statement that revolutions often take place without any constituent group coming into play. The seemingly unrestrained power of Parliament, or of the oligarchy whose interests and ideas it voiced, was restrained by the evolution of the two large parties. This constitutional device, generally recognized today to have been of fundamental importance during the nineteenth century, is not based upon any explicit decision. By some it may be considered only a rather weak restraint. But such weakness, if any, in the English constitution as a political process is offset by the strong traditionalism in England.

The British case, however, raises a very general problem. When one talks of a constitution as the basic decision regarding the political organization of a community, the impression is conveyed that all is settled once this decision has been made. The constitution is represented as absolute. But we know already that all restraints are matters of degree (see ch. VII, pp. 125 f.). What is more, even a carefully considered and widely discussed decision is subject to certain inherent limitations. Human language is anything but unequivocal. The working out of human relationships is difficult to forecast. The actual conditions of human society change. These three inherent limitations of all human decisions affect constitutions profoundly. Some of the subsequent changes may be made by using a supple amending power. But others will be made by those who govern, and they usually will be acquiesced in by those who are governed. They very often take the form of constitutional interpretation, not only by the courts, but by all departments of the government. The relative importance of such constitutional interpretations depends upon a number of factors, including the clarity of the constitutional document itself and the nature of the formal amending process. If the process of formal amendment does not respond readily to any widely felt need for change, the change will be accomplished through interpretation. In the United States, where the formal process is rather cumbersome, many constitutional adjustments have taken place through such interpretation, and constitutional usages or conventions are numerous. Under the First German Republic, which merely required a two-thirds majority of the two chambers of the legislature, constitutional amendments were frequent, and usages of the constitution were few and of minor importance. Again, the Swiss procedure of amending the constitution by popular referendum has lent itself rather readily to formal changes. In the period from 1893 to 1924 the referendum was used twenty-three times; eighteen of the proposed amendments were passed. In some of the American states where the amending process functions more smoothly than legislation (or, to put it another way, where determined minorities can more readily gather a popular than a legislative following), the constitutional amendment is employed for a great deal of legislation (see below, p. 144).

The other important factor is the relative simplicity or complexity of a constitution. The American Constitution is more complex than the constitution of the Third French Republic; for it contains a federal system and a bill of rights. The German republican constitution of 1919 was even more complex than the American Constitution; for its bill of rights was based upon conflicting political and social philosophies, liberal, Catholic, and socialist, and was therefore in many respects quite equivocal. If one provision of the constitution seemed to set up a separation of church and state, another forthwith denied it by implication (Articles 135, 136, 137, and 146). Which of the two interpretations was a court to enforce if a controversy came before it in which one of the litigants based his case upon one interpretation, the other upon its opposite? The development of the due-process interpretation by the American courts since the adoption of Amendment XIV offers another striking illustration of the opportunity which equivocal provisions of a constitution provide for constitutional interpretation. Even more significant is the role of interpretation in connection with the whole welter of complex provisions through which the American Constitution attempts to settle the relation between the federal government and the states. Undoubtedly a certain measure of such difficulties and complexities are inherent in any constitution embodied in written documents.

Flexible versus rigid constitution · These two factors, easy process of amendment and inherent complexity, together constitute what is often discussed as the relative flexibility or rigidity of a constitution.[6] The argument is usually extended to include the English system of government, where no distinction is made between the legislative and the amending power, or, to put it another way, where no fundamental distinction is admitted between constitutional and other law. Such a system seems more flexible than any other. But we have already seen that the traditional device of a two-party system embodies an effective restraint, the more so when, as in Britain, the government in power feels obliged to appeal to the electorate on any major issue. Such fundamental changes as would involve a repeal, let us say, of a principle established and set down in the Act of Settlement, like the tenure of judges during good behavior, could not, it is held, be enacted by a government, unless it had fought and won an election on it. (But see below, p. 143 for illustrations to the contrary.) When in 1911 the Liberals wished to curtail the powers of the House of Lords, they had to carry the issue to the voters. From a political point of view, therefore, the amending power is recognized in Britain as belonging to the electorate. Only a referendum will sanction constitutional change. But that means a bare majority of the electoral districts, which may not be a majority of the people (see below, ch. XV). The discussion of the relative advantages and disadvantages of rigid and flexible constitutions is equally inconclusive.

The great and outstanding advantage of a flexible constitution is the smoothness with which it can be adapted to new conditions and altered conceptions in the community. This advantage is particularly apparent, of course, in times of rapid change. An oft-cited example is afforded by legislation regulating the conditions of labor under modern industrial conditions. In England the introduction of new rules prohibiting child labor proceeded apace and unincumbered by constitutional provisions regarding freedom of contract, and the same is, of course, true in France. It is, however, obvious that such flexibility presupposes a nation steeped in traditions and by nature opposed to change, or the whole political structure will easily become the object of attack from restless and irresponsible groups. A most formidable illustration of the great dangers inherent in an easy amending process was brought out by the events of March 1933 in Germany. Here a bare majority of Nationalist and National Socialist deputies abused its legislative power to bar part of the opposition (the Communists) and then proceeded to "amend" the constitution by giving the government absolute power to change it. This "Enabling Act" was a procedure which had never been sanctioned by a majority of the electorate.[7]

The overthrow of the German constitution "from within" brings to light the great advantage of a rigid constitution. In fact, it would be better to call such a constitution firm, because the epithet "rigid" intentionally or accidentally prejudices the case. A firm constitution seeks to provide effective safeguards against what one might, with de Tocqueville, term majority tyranny. It seems for that reason better adapted to a community which is not firmly rooted in tradition, or one in which the people are deeply divided by religious, racial, or class conflicts. If, moreover, the form of government is new and untried, a firm constitution lifts it somewhat above the party struggle, while a soft and pliable charter would be tossed about by the shifting currents of party strife. A firm constitution, by making constitutional amendments more difficult, obliges advocates of such changes to concentrate upon the essentials and to build up solid popular sentiments behind them. If such support has been secured, however, the changes will be swift and decisive. This conclusion is amply supported by the history of constitutional amendments in the United States. Accordingly, American policy, in promoting democratic constitutionalism in Germany, has stressed the need for a constitution protected against too easy changes.

The American federal amending process · The American federal amending process, while cumbersome, has turned out to be less of an impediment to change than was at one time assumed. In spite of the great impact of "interpretative" customs and usages, this American procedure deserves attention. Its drafters had clearly grasped the conclusion that certain amendments to a constitutional document are unlikely if the power of amending the document is vested in an official or a group of officials whose own power might conceivably be curtailed by such an amendment. Article V provides four methods for amending the constitutional document, thus making it impossible for either Congress or the state legislatures to block a constitutional amendment. In keeping with this idea it has been decided by the Supreme Court that neither the President nor state governors have any veto power over amendments. In practice only one of the methods has, however, been used so far, namely, that which requires the collaboration of Congress and the state legislatures. Amendments have originated in Congress, on the approval of two thirds of both houses, and have been ratified by the legislatures in three fourths of the states. But if Congress wished to avoid calling upon the state legislatures, it could insist upon special conventions in the states. If, on the other hand, a widespread movement for amending the Constitution got under way, and Congress would not respond to it, the legislatures of two thirds of the states could demand that a national convention be called. Such a move was contemplated before the repeal of the eighteenth amendment; it has recently been advocated in connection with broad programs of constitutional reform. It will be noted that the American Constitution does not admit an initiative on the part of the "people," as does the Swiss constitution. (Since no amendment has been added to the Swiss constitution by that process, it may be doubted whether the loss is serious.) At any rate, no governmental authority has a monopoly of the amending power, as is the case wherever the power of amending a constitution is vested in a legislature alone. It may, however, be asked whether the process need be as elaborate as it is in the United

States; the provisions of the United States Constitution have been subjected to serious criticism. It was estimated at one time that some 3000 amendments have been proposed in Congress. In 1912 Senator LaFollette and others gave vent to the resulting indignation by suggesting an amendment to the amending process permitting future amendments by a majority of both houses of Congress, to be ratified by a majority of the voters in a majority of the states. This suggestion failed. Since that time, several amendments have been passed. Particularly the repeal of Amendment XVIII has inclined people to feel that the constitutional amending process is probably sufficiently responsive to popular demands for change as well as for progress.[8]

Conditions for formal amendment · Interpretation and formal amendment of a constitutional document are not, however, simple alternatives. In spite of the great changes which interpretation and practice may produce, certain specific changes may be quite impossible without a formal amendment. This is sometimes forgotten by those who would have us rely entirely upon informal change. The American federal structure, the division of the country into states, could not be altered without a formal amendment, nor could the explicit distribution of functions. Still, it is extraordinary how far interpretation and practice may go under favorable conditions. Thus intrastate commerce, which for a long time was held to be a matter which the federal government could not regulate, has now been interpreted as subject to federal regulation if it affects interstate commerce. In view of the close interdependence of all economic factors it seems almost impossible to draw a line between *intra*state commerce which *does* affect and *intra*state commerce which does *not* affect *inter*state commerce. It all seems to depend upon how imperative the need for federal regulation is. Where the pressure of need is small, and the formal and human obstacles are great, changes are not likely to be brought about by interpretation, particularly if gradual measures are out of the question. Thus the equal representation of the states in the United States Senate seems rather unlikely to be interpreted away. Similarly the coequal power of the House of Lords in matters of taxation was effected by formal abolition. A further reduction in the power of the House of Lords has been on the Agenda of the Labour Party. In other words, matters about which the written law itself is reasonably explicit usually are explicitly changed too. If the formal process is too elaborate, the constitutional structure may in the course of time be very seriously warped. As long as limitations of time and resources are not important, such warpings may be endured. The years of effort and the millions of revenue lost in the struggle to put through the amendment

141

allowing the American federal government to levy graduated income taxes may fail to arouse the wealthy American nation; the Germans were not equally patient with the difficulties arising from their federal system after the First World War. When the amending provisions fail to work in adjusting the constitutional document to altered needs, revolution may result. This is quite generally admitted at present. But in addition, it is now realized by many that even a process of amendment which responds to the need for widely felt change cannot completely protect the constitution against revolution. For revolution may be made by others than those who would constitute a constituent group. Just the same, the fact that all men must die does not dispose of arguments in favor of a doctor.

Holland, England, and France · An interesting combination of the English procedure of constitutional amendment by simple legislative enactment, and the American emphasis upon the more basic importance of constitutional changes, is found in the Dutch constitution.[9] This constitutional kingdom requires first a dissolution of the chamber and a new election, and then a new vote by a two-thirds majority. Through such a provision the amending power is vested in the representative legislature, and the new election insures the truly representative nature of the Parliament enacting the change. In making this arrangement, the Dutch have put into practice what Dicey wished to see adopted in England. The principle he advocated was "that no far-reaching changes in the governmental system should be made until the voters have had a chance to pass judgment upon the proposed amendment, at a general election" (Ogg). This has, indeed, at times been the case. Thus in 1832 the Liberal majority secured a mandate from the electorate to carry out electoral reform; but lacking a majority before, it could not have done otherwise. More significant is the instance when in 1910 the Liberal government, possessing a stout majority in the Commons, went to the electorate with a plan for reform of the House of Lords. But in contrast to this move, the enfranchisement of women and other changes in the electoral system were adopted in 1918 by a Parliament elected eight years before; similarly the Irish Free State was created in 1922 without consulting the voters. In the French Third Republic, no appeal to the people was required for enacting a constitutional amendment. In keeping with traditional conceptions of parliamentary government (see below, ch. XVIII) the two chambers, after separately accepting the proposal of a constitutional amendment from the cabinet, would go to Versailles, where in a joint meeting of the two chambers they would proceed to ratify the amendment, thus marking the solemnity of the proceeding. This arrangement was a clever device for combining the recognition of a distinct amending power with the parliamentary system—a system under which the electorate has acquiesced in the complete exercise by the Parliament of the amending power. Under the new constitution, of 1946, the French have gone considerably farther in recognizing a distinct amending power. It is provided that constitutional amendments have to be submitted to popular referendum, unless the National Assembly has adopted the amendment by a three-fourths majority, or unless the Assembly and the Council of the Republic (Senate) have adopted it by a three-fifths majority of each. The process is further complicated by a delaying device: a resolution has to be taken first on two successive votes, three months apart. To ensure that this more cumbersome procedure is actually followed, a Constitutional Committee has been established. It must be remembered that the constitution of 1946, in contrast to that of 1875, was itself adopted by referendum; in other words, its popular, democratic sanction is substantially greater than was that of the "organic law" of the Third Republic.

Limitations on the amending power · Where the constitutional amending power is vested in the legislature, limitations are usually imposed upon it. In France, an amendment of 1884 provided that the republican form of government should never be made the subject of a proposed revision.[10] English constitutional lawyers have argued that Parliament cannot abolish itself, for that would mean binding its successors irrevocably. Even in the United States, the states are not supposed to be deprived of their equal representation in the Senate without their own consent. Whatever the ultimate validity of such provisions and arguments, they make violent revolution more likely by limiting the chance of effecting "revolutionary" changes gradually. For example, Poincaré, in arguing the binding character of the French inhibition just cited, insisted that "any revision which would have for its object the substitution of the monarchical system for the republic would be illegal and *revolutionary*." By thus forcing those who might constitute an emerging constituent power to have recourse to a violent revolution, such inhibitions would have the political effect of depriving the amending power of some part of what is its essential function, viz., to forestall the revolutionary emergence of the constituent power. That is the sound kernel of the objections raised to such provisions by those who insist that they are merely declaratory and cannot bind the "will of the people"—a remark repeatedly made in the French Chamber. But the "will of the people" is too broad a term. It has often been a cloak for revolutionary gangs endeavoring to destroy the constitution and the constituent power. Therefore, such limitations also have the effect of inhibiting revolutionary upheavals which are admittedly or secretly opposed to the

143

continued existence of any constitution or constituent group. For as we have seen, revolutionary movements opposed to free speech and free assembly are quite frequent. They are politically possible in communities where the constituent group is atrophied for diverse reasons. A determined gang is then able to seize power and reorganize the government in its own interests and without consultation with the governed.

Nonfundamental constitutional provisions · Some things in a constitution are "fundamental," Oliver Cromwell used to insist, while others are "circumstantial."[11] A provision in the *Instrument of Government* had set aside £200,000 for the civil offices, that is the administration, with which to pay the judges and other officials, to defray the charges of the council in sending their embassies, to support the governor-in-chief, and so forth. This provision Cromwell called a circumstantial thing, "to be 'regulated' as occasion shall offer." He freely admitted that there were many such circumstantial things in the *Instrument* "which are not like the laws of the Medes and Persians" but a "matter of consideration between you and me." Many modern "constitutions," that is, documents containing a real constitutional system of restraints, will, along with this system of restraints, contain such "circumstantial" provisions. Ordinary legislation within the confines of a "constitution" is particularly notorious in the state constitutions of the United States. The constitution of Oklahoma, Professor Holcombe tells us, contains eleven pages of legislation relating to the subject of corporations alone, besides much more ordinary legislation relating to homesteads and exemptions, banks and banking, insurance, the employment of children, and education. It forbids plural marriages, fixes the maximum rate of interest, abolishes the so-called fellow-servant doctrine and regulates the use of the contributory-negligence and assumption-of-risk doctrines as defenses in certain suits for damages, establishes the eight-hour day on public works and coal mines, and determines the test for the purity of kerosene oil. The constitution of Oklahoma is an extreme instance, but the tendency is manifest elsewhere. The German constitution of 1919 abounded with constitutional legislation about railroads, schools, and other phases of community life. Now it is clearly unreasonable to place a provision like the one that Germany is a republic, or that all power emanates from the people (Article 1), on the same footing as the provision that all children graduating from normal school shall receive a copy of the constitution (Article 148). Similar contrasts, though perhaps not quite as extreme, can be found in the Constitution of the United States. Yet nowhere have the amending provisions been organized in such a way as to take account of this difference. The simplest technique for coping with the difficulty would seem to be a provision that parts of the same constitutional document might be amended by different methods. A process requiring much deliberation and delay might be provided for the fundamental parts of the document, while constitutional provisions of a legislative nature could be amended by a simpler and more rapid mode. From the standpoint of considering the constitution a political process for restraining the government, this would seem a sound plan; the "fundamental" parts of the document would thereby be marked as the basic constitution. Oklahoma and Virginia have attempted something of this order. It must be considered doubtful, however, whether their example will be widely emulated; the reasons for this difficulty result from the constitution also being a political force (see next chapter). Under the alternative scheme of leaving the amendment of the constitution to the legislature, as in England, reliance is placed upon public opinion for maintaining the "fundamentals." The idea is that since revolutions turn upon these "fundamentals," their emergence cannot be prevented by a constitution anyway.

Limited and unlimited revolutions · In our own day, Trotsky proclaimed that revolutions are the mad inspirations of history.[12] Earlier times saw them, with Cromwell, as the work of God. Both views bear testimony to the fact that the great revolutions of our civilization touch the foundations of a way of life, and that their source is inspirational. Revolutionary leaders have conceived of themselves as instruments either of God or of nature. Eugen Rosenstock-Hüssy has developed the brilliant thesis that each of the great European revolutions has been made by one of the great nations of Europe which in the course of its revolution has found its own basic form of life. This view is easily substantiated for the French and English Revolutions; it is more difficult to follow the argument in the case of the Reformation for Germany, and still more so in the case of the Papal Revolution through which the Italian people are alleged to have expressed themselves. Rosenstock-Hüssy has also undertaken to show that each of these "totalitarian" revolutions has claimed in spite of its national aspect to be a "world revolution" of which the authors expected that it would become the pattern of life for all of Europe. This phase of Rosenstock-Hüssy's theory is least apparent in the English Revolution; it would be hard to deny it of any of the others. Rosenstock-Hüssy has finally called attention to the widening group of active political "leaders" from the one pope, to the 100 princes of the Reformation, to the 3000–5000 gentry of England, to the 90,000 members of the bourgeoisie in France, to the million or more "proletarians" of the Russian Soviets. This widening of the revolutionary group is related to the changing class structure of society. Hence, each of these comprehensive "revolutions" was in a measure directed against the immediately preceding revolution, because it had been made by the class whose rule it was now proposed should be overthrown. This brilliant and engaging synthesis of Hegelian, Comtian, and Marxist elements in terms of an autonomous group life is admittedly not a political theory of revolution—revolution taken in the limited sense of a change of government. Neither Rosenstock-Hüssy's, Cromwell's, nor Trotsky's language is applicable to Bolivia, which has had sixty-eight revolutions in the sixty-five years of her existence. Aristotle drew a distinction between revolutions which aimed at a change of government, and others which merely substituted one person or group for another but left the form of government intact. A survey of modern history makes it seem more imperative to distinguish between revolutions affecting a change in a whole way of life, including religion, economics, and manners, as well as politics, and revolutions changing the form of government. Curiously enough, a revolution of this latter sort was going on right in the very lifetime of Aristotle without his ever noticing it as such.

In France, a keen feeling for the difference between the Revolution of 1789 and the many revolutions which followed during the nineteenth century has crystallized into the expression *la grande revolution* as an appropriate designation for the earlier event. The "great" revolution had a spiritual significance which the others lacked. Though Cromwell listed freedom of conscience along with strictly governmental restraints upon parliamentary absolutism as a fundamental aspect of the *Instrument of Government*, this freedom of conscience in matters of religion, while operating as a restraint on the government, also represented a new spiritual conception which grew out of the Reformation. Likewise the Bill of Rights of man which appears in the American and French revolutionary constitutions represents a new spiritual departure in that it secularized and expanded the freedom of conscience. It thus gave political form to ideas which had germinated in the period of Enlightenment. Finally, the socialist constitutions of postwar Europe, in setting forth the right to work, or even basing citizenship upon this quality of being a worker, as the constitution of the Soviet Union does, provided expression for the ideas which had taken root in the labor movement of the preceding generations. What these broad elements mean politically will be shown in the next chapter, when we take up the constitution as a political force. For the present, it is enough to conclude that revolutions may be limited to the political, governmental sphere, or they may be not so limited, and thus be unfathomable, incalculable, and incomprehensible to all but those who have been "seized by the spirit."

The pattern of great revolutions · While the deeper impulses remain unfathomable, except to the initiated, the pattern of these revolutions seems to be rather uniform. Crane Brinton, taking the English, French, American, and Russian revolutions as the material for a comparative analysis, has sketched a convincing set of generalizations. To be sure, they are strictly inductive, and it is quite possible that the pattern is limited to our culture and to that type of revolution. But within these limits, it is an enlightening analysis.

So far as the signs of an approaching revolution are concerned, they are not very distinctive. They seem largely to be intensification of the sort of strains and stresses that are always found in modern society. Nor is there anything very definite to be said about the work of revolutions; they leave society changed, but there seems no distinctive pattern to the change, except a measure of exhaustion. But there is a definite succession of stages, a rhythm, to revolutionary upheavals of this "unlimited" variety. In the first stage the revolutionaries, full of the "new spirit," engage in an orgy of revolutionary perfectionism. They set to work in the conviction that the millennium is at hand. But this honeymoon does not last very long. The practical tasks of carrying on the government have to be faced, and a split develops between the moderates and the radicals. (By the way, Brinton brings forward plenty of evidence that "revolutionaries" are no particular kind of people, that "it takes almost as many kinds of men and women to make a revolution as to make a world.") The conflict between radicals and moderates ends in the failure of the moderates, the rise of the extremists, and the *concentration of all power* in their hands. This concentration of power then is followed by the terror. It is a desperate attempt to make earnest with the revolutionary purposes by force and violence, and it is soon followed by a strong reaction. This is the *Thermidor*, to use an expression the French revolution coined. "Thermidor comes as naturally to societies in revolution as an ebbing tide, as calm after a storm, as convalescence after fever, as the snapping-back of a stretched elastic band." *Thermidor* brings a tyrant or dictator, a man who speaks the revolutionary language but refuses to act upon it, who is preoccupied with practical problems of how to restore "order" and organize administration. Old habits of daily life reappear, though restricted by the dictatorship. The revolutionary symbols, now become devoid of psychic appeal, loose their hold; as time goes on the dictatorial power appears increasingly naked; and the road is paved for a "restoration" which seeks to re-establish the old regime. But the changes wrought in the society by the revolution are too profound, and a new pattern emerges.[13]

While the features just outlined, following Brinton to a considerable extent, are clearly discernible in the case of the English, French, and Russian revolutions, it is not possible to discover more than faint resemblances to them in the case of the American revolution. For the moderates, not the extremists, won out; there was no terror, no concentration of power, etc. Nor does the pattern fit the Glorious Revolution of 1688, nor the German revolution of 1918, nor yet the numerous limited revolutions which have produced a change of government time and again. Indeed, it may be doubted whether these three revolutions are not a very special brand, intimately related to the dynamics of Western Christian culture. Rosenstock-Hüssy has suggested that they are, and has brought forward much striking evidence to support his thesis. One characteristic of these great cultural upheavals in the Western world is certainly that they were associated with the idea of a "constitution." The revolutionary groups were seeking a constitution. They thought of themselves as fighting against absolutism. Hence the concentration of powers in the hands of a dictator involved the revolution in a self-contradiction. Cromwell, as we saw, more than any other revolutionary leader struggled with this paradox, but in vain.

The distinctive and uniquely Western problems resulting from the relationship between revolution and constitutionalism, which the English and French revolutions reveal, become obscured if the process of revolution is linked to that of the "state," as George Pettee attempted to do when he defined revolution as the "reconstitution of the state." The state itself he describes as an association, and later adds that this is "nearly the same as the ordinary condition of an organized society." The difficulty with all such "definitions," as I have argued in *The New Belief in the Common Man* (1942), is that they are based upon the belief that *one* theory of *the* state can cover the governmental practice of absolutism as well as constitutionalism. Actually, the concept "state" remains too vague if used in so comprehensive a fashion; it hides radical differences in the organization of power, if so used. Realistically and substantively, a revolution carried forward by a "constituent group" and directed toward the establishment of a true constitution is a process of an entirely different nature than a revolution carried forward by an anticonstitutional group of self-appointed elitists. Once this difference is understood, it becomes clear why the course of the Russian revolution differed in very important respects from that of the French and English revolutions.[14]

Difficulty of anticipating unlimited revolution through amending process · The distinction between limited and unlimited revolutions has important consequences. Limited revolutions afford a safer field for scientific inquiry. At the same time, the transcendental, metaconstitutional nature of the constituent power is nowhere so clearly seen as in the great spiritual upheavals. A wisely drawn constitution can anticipate the revolutionary potentialities of the constituent power by so constructing the amending process that sustained pressure would be able to produce sweeping changes in the system of governmental restraints. But even the most supple provisions for amending the constitution may fail when wholly different ideas or a basically altered economy make their appearance. Assuming, then, a more resistant amending process, the forces opposed to the "new spirit" are bound to appeal to the fundamentals of the "constitution" in their struggle to stem the rising tide of impending change. By doing so, they force this new spirit to attack and often to destroy the constitution. Sometimes, as in Germany after 1918, a new constitution will be built to take the place of the old. At other times, no constitution results, but a government without restraint will attempt to realize the new spirit by force. An amending process broad enough completely to revamp as well as to amend the existing constitution is an extremely difficult thing to construct. The Swiss, as we have already shown, accomplished a change approaching a fundamental one in 1874. The English did it in 1832. Walter Lippmann has argued, in his *Method of Freedom*,[15] that England and the Dominions, America, Switzerland, Holland, and the Scandinavian countries are in the process of revamping their governments so as to make room for the "socialist" right to work. It may well happen. Much undoubtedly depends upon the rapidity with which the demand for these changes develops and culminates. Much also depends upon the prevalence of that intelligent view which looks upon the constitution as a human creation subject to change, rather than as a divinely ordained thing of primordial perfection.

Hypotheses derived from Hitler's coming into power · It is easy to exaggerate the dangers which spring from an amending process facilitating change. While it is undeniable that such a process might be used for destroying the constitution as a system of restraints altogether, it is not as likely as some writers would have us believe. There are people who might be tempted to cite the overthrow of the German republic as evidence to the contrary. Did not the German parliament abdicate its own powers and hand them over to a dictator?[16] Might not Congress do likewise, if the amending power were vested in it? The answer is that the German parliament did not abdicate. In order to get parliament to do this, the Hitler government first purged it of many Socialists and all Communists. This purge terrorized many of the remaining deputies. It is significant that constitutional lawyers apologizing for the National Socialist government have themselves shown convincingly that the constitution of the Republic was not only violated but actually abolished when a considerable group of deputies was excluded from parliament. These opposition leaders were prevented from participating in the session of March 21, 1933, which voted to invest Hitler with absolute power. It was by revolutionary force, by a *coup d'état*, that Hitler came into power. But why should the Nazis first go through this "constitutional" ceremonial, and then have their crown jurists claim it to be unconstitutional? Their reason for arguing thus, once the transition had been achieved, was to prove that the government was no longer bound by the constitution at all; no provision of the constitution of 1919 could be cited against any measures or decrees of the government, no matter how arbitrary. On the strength of this "revolution," the constitution of 1919 had become "mere legislation." But basically the conflict was a concrete expression of the unnatural alliance between the revolutionary Nazi masses under Hitler and the conservative Nationalist group headed by Hindenburg. The "legitimacy" of the National "revolution" had to be proven to the old field-marshal at the very moment when illegal violence was sweeping away the remnants of a much older constitutional order than that embodied in the Weimar Constitution.

While it would be an exaggeration to describe the Weimar Republic's situation as one of parliamentary absolutism, it rather closely approached the radical democracy which Rousseau had envisaged, with very extreme powers vested in a popular majority. The makers of the Weimar Constitution were filled with Rousseauistic ideas. The full portent of this setup was hidden for a while by the multiple-party system. But the latent arbitrary powers of a popular majority were bound to appear as soon as such a majority could be built up. Governmental powers were unrestrained. The constitutionally decisive reason for the failure of the Republic in Germany appears, therefore, to have been the weakness of the political constitution itself. Without an adequate system of restraints on governmental action, dictatorship supplanted parliamentary absolutism through the simple device of reducing the membership of parliament sufficiently to give the partisans of change a safe majority.

There is a famous historical analogy for these developments. The events of the 21st of March, 1933, were a close parallel of Pride's Purge, of December 6th, 1648. When the detained Presbyterian M.P.'s demanded of the officers: "By what Law, by what Law?" Hugh Peters, Cromwell's secretary, had to admit: "It is by the Law of Necessity; truly, by the Power of the Sword." We shall return to this question of necessity in our chapter on dictatorship (ch. XXIV). As far as the amending process and revolution are concerned, these historical cases show three things. First, even the most flexible amending process cannot guarantee the constitution against revolution by those wishing to destroy not only the particular system of restraints, but all restraints. Second, a flexible amending process in fact facilitates a *coup d'état* (revolution from within) by a group desirous of destroying the constitution as a system of restraints upon governmental power. Third, a concentration of the amending power in a central legislature invites the application of violence in an effort to coerce such a body into exercising the amending power for the destruction of the constitution. It would follow from these propositions as a maxim of practical politics that constitutional limitations upon the amending power should not take the form of absolute prohibitions, but should provide for a greater diffusion of this power both by making it work slowly, and in separate localities. The federal Constitution of the United States provides accordingly.

Negative revolutions · The peculiar conditions of Europe after the Second World War have produced a series of quasi-revolutionary upheavals which may be called *negative* in character. By this we mean to suggest that they were motivated not so much by any positive enthusiasm for a presumably splendid future as by a negative distaste for a sordid past. The French constitution of 1946, the Italian constitution of 1947, and the (West) German constitution of 1949 are all of this negative type. In the case of France, the driving force came from the resistance groups which were radically antagonistic to the Third Republic, as well as to the Vichy (Fascist) regime, and repeated efforts of the Radical Socialist Party (see below, ch. XXI) to have the Third Republic revived were roundly rejected. Yet, as the preamble of the new constitution clearly shows, the draftsmen of this document were looking back to the glorious traditions of the great French Revolution and its philosophy as expressed in the rights of man (see next chapter, pp. 156–163). The resistance clearly constituted a constituent power in the sense of this analysis, but its constitutional ideal was conservative; the earlier draft, rejected by the electorate, was somewhat more radical, though far from being a Soviet constitution.[17]

The Italian constitution bears the same hallmark of the negations associated with the violent overthrow of the Fascist government. In the case of Italy, too, the first draft was more radically Rousseauistic and "democratic" than the constitution finally adopted. But while it is quite true, as Einaudi has said, that "the new republican constitution represents the first deliberate effort by the Italian people as a whole to guarantee their freedom and common welfare within a constitutional framework," it is equally true that the Italian people only received this opportunity at the hands of conquering armies of the United States and Great Britain. The Anglo-Saxon democrats considered themselves liberators of the Italians, and were eager to see the Italians undertake the task of giving themselves a constitution. Many of them were pleased when the Italian people by referendum abolished the monarchy so unhappily associated with the Fascist regime. A constituent group undoubtedly came into being in the course of the three years between 1944 and 1947. That there were relatively only a few who participated in the group, as Einaudi notes, is not decisive. But it is important to be clear about the "negative" aspect of the revolution which begot the "constituent power." It was the victory of foreigners over an unconstitutional system which cleared the road for the reassertion of constitutionalism. It is a lukewarm revolution at best.[18]

Even more extreme is the situation in Germany. Here no pretense was made at liberation; foreign conquerors imposed "democratization" as the essential condition of their own security. In using this term, the Western powers meant, as events were to prove, democratic constitutionalism of one kind or another, while the Soviet Union meant as much proletarian dictatorship as could be achieved in "co-operation" with the West. In their own zone, the Soviet Union eventually developed "constitutions" which look as innocuous on paper as her own "constitution" of 1936. They are actually modeled on the pattern of the French constitution of 1946 and rejected by the French voters; this constitution placed a complete concentration of all power in the hands of a majority of parliament. Such a constitution is, of course, very workable as a camouflage for one-party control, if the realities of politics are handled with the support of a secret police and an occupying army determined to suppress any divergent political activities. But just how free and democratic, how genuinely "constitutional," are the developments in the Western zones? This anxious question has been a source of persistent worry to genuine constitutionalists and "democrats" among the Western occupying powers. In the first place, and at the start, the "negation" was that of the occupying powers; they were unequivocally determined to destroy the Fascist dictatorship in Germany. Denazification was the concrete policy directed toward this end, and an elaborate system of eliminating former Nazis from all positions of influence was inaugurated[18] and at least partially carried out. This "cold revolution" had, of course, its parallel in the "epuration" procedures, by which Fascists and collaborators in both France and Italy were criminally prosecuted. But unlike these processes, which were highly selective and focused attention upon the most responsible individuals, denazification, especially in the American zone, took the form of a very broad sweep, and unfortunately concentrated upon the little party member. The results of this process are now hotly contested, and it will be some time before a fair assessment can be made.

But in spite of this cold revolution imposed from above—some writers have now commenced to argue that a real revolution from among the people was thereby prevented, without giving any very convincing evidence in support of its prospects—there are many signs that a constituent power did develop from among the Germans themselves. The parties, quite clearly linked to the parties of the Weimar Republic (see below, ch. XXI), soon entered upon vigorous discussions of the constitutional issues and organized special commissions to prepare drafts. By the time the Western Allies, in June 1948, reached agreement on what kind of constitution to ask the Germans to prepare, their agreement resembled in very broad terms the probable compromise between the several positions the parties had taken. Although the drafting process proved very difficult, due to the determination of the constitutional assembly (parliamentary council) at Bonn to find viable compromises between the Christian and the Social Democrats, eventually 80 per cent of the constitutional assembly voted for the basic law, thus giving it the approval of a majority of the German people.* Thus a broad constituent group did in fact crystallize, but it was not so much animated by any enthusiasm for democracy and constitutionalism as it was prepared to reject the totalitarianism of right and left. The Basic Law is a negation of dictatorship. One would like to think that General Clay was right when he reported to the Congress of the United States on his return, in May 1949, that the siege of Berlin, its blockade, and the airlift had lighted "a flame of freedom." He said he saw in Berlin "the spirit and soul of a people reborn." And he expressed the belief that some of that spirit had "spread throughout Germany," and that "the German people have responded. The Germans have cast their die for a government which stands for the dignity of man as an individual." And as the general spoke, the Germans in the Eastern zone under the Soviet terror rejected the Soviet and Communist solution of German unity in sufficiently large numbers (over 35 per cent) to reinforce his belief that Germany may be part "of a new European concept devoted to common economic effort and to a common love of freedom."[19]

There has always been a degree of negativism associated with the rise of constitutionalism. Human beings are more alert to the "blessings of liberty" after they have had a good dose of authoritarian abuse of power, of despotism. But in the seventeenth, eighteenth, and nineteenth centuries revolution spelled great hopes for the future. This is not entirely true, though, for the most lasting constitutions, especially the American constitution, were made by men who entertained much doubt about their

---

*80 per cent of the Western zones constitute about 55 per cent of all of Germany, leaving Berlin out of account, which would actually somewhat swell the percentage.

lasting importance. Perhaps the scepticism accompanying the new constitutions in Europe augurs well for their lasting value.

Aristotle's theory of revolution · The modern mind is and has been preoccupied with making suitable arrangements for change in a constitutional order. Change is viewed in an evolutionary sense, and is assumed to be moving in a definite direction which may be considered optimistically as progress or pessimistically as decline. In any event, change is taken for granted and revolution is deprecated, when it is deprecated, not because it is change, but because it is violent change. *Natura non facit saltum.* Revolution, but not change is unnatural. Very different was the view of Aristotle.[20] Motion in modern physics is the natural state. Modern political science also is kinetic. However, Aristotle's theory of revolutions is still the only fully developed theory. Aristotle described revolutions in terms of his fourfold method of stating a case ($αἴτιον$), namely, to use modern expressions, the material and energetic conditions, the conceptual framework, and the end or objective. Stated simply, the material conditions of revolutions are found by Aristotle to root in the economic class structure, and more particularly in the division of the community between the poor and the rich. The energetic conditions are provided by the restless scheming of potential leaders who are seeking ascendancy. Certain indications are offered concerning their psychology. The conceptual framework for revolutions persists in the form of ever-conflicting ideas concerning the just share of each individual and group in the community. The end or objective of all revolutions is the complete seizure of power by the revolutionaries. This remarkably lucid and comprehensive theory of revolutions may have been adequate for the Greek city-states, though no serious attempt has been made at verification. But the theory may not be adequate when we consider the great revolutionary upheavals of modern times, such as the French Revolution. For while the Aristotelian elements are present, spiritual elements have also loomed large. Modern theories of revolutions in their turn have been attempting to focus attention upon these elements. Accepting change not only as the "natural" state of affairs, but as intrinsically necessary and desirable, they have often viewed revolutions as approaches to a progressively realizable millennium. And if not that, they have taken periodic adaptations of the political order to underlying social change as a necessary "adjustment." Aristotle, on the other hand, while admitting the fatal persistence of revolutions, viewed them as substituting one kind of maladjustment for another. He therefore tried to find the least unbalanced political order (in which the conceptual framework of revolutions would have smallest scope) and then to maintain the *status quo*. But in many passages he seems to lean toward the skeptical view that any political order persistently maintained is better than change. He was at least sufficiently interested in such a view to study the methods of maintaining various types of political order and thus prevent change.

Conclusion · In conclusion it may be said that the phenomena of revolution, though vitally related to the making of constitutions, and therefore of decisive importance for an empirical theory of constitutions and constitutional government, have so far been only partially analyzed. We know something, though far too little, about the working of plebiscites and amending processes. We have large-scale metaphysical interpretations of history asserting generalities concerning the implied political change. We have Aristotle's presumably empirical theory of revolutions in the Greek polis. But a welter of more or less detailed questions and facts present themselves with which we have not as yet effectively coped. Even after we discard "causes" and limit ourselves to the more modest inquiry into concomitant variations of interdependent variables, we are at the present moment only able to advance certain very tentative hypotheses, such as those stated on pages 147 ff. Some further light will be thrown on the subject of revolutions in the course of chapter XXVI. One deviation from the Aristotelian view is fairly certain: when the revolution is carried out by a constituent group in the modern sense, the end is not the seizure of complete power by the revolutionaries. The end being the making of a constitution, such a revolution aims at a separation of powers.

IX

The Constitution as a Political Force

Introduction · Bills of rights · Such rights not natural but political · Recent restrictive tendencies · Conflicts of principle · Preambles · Parties and public opinion · Two basic cleavages: cultural and economic divisions · Autocratic imposition of unity · Cultural disunity overcome: Switzerland · Contrast between Germany and Great Britain · Symbols and stereotypes · Conclusion.

Introduction · According to Rousseau, the most important of all laws "which is not graven on tablets of marble or brass, but on the hearts of the citizens" is embodied in what he calls "the real constitution." It "takes on every day new powers, when other laws decay or die out, restores or takes their place, keeps a whole people in the ways in which it was meant to go, and insensibly replaces authority by the force of habit."[1] In this curious passage, reminiscent of Burke and other traditionalists, the great Swiss revolutionary is, according to his own words, "speaking of morality, of custom, above all of public opinion; a power unknown to political thinkers, on which none the less success in everything else depends." Since the days of Rousseau, political scientists have, however, been much occupied with this important power, although not infrequently neglecting its relation to custom and to the constitution. On the other hand, Professor Holcombe stressed the connection when he said: "The fundamentals of state government are predetermined outside of the conventions by public opinion. . . . In so far as this is true, and written constitutional charters set forth the accepted moral standards, customs and public opinion, they themselves constitute a political force of great influence. In a sense this is obvious; for were it not so, there would be little sense in making constitutional charters."

Bills of rights · The political force of the Constitution is particularly apparent in connection with whatever restraints a bill of rights imposes upon governmental action. Clearly, such bills of rights differ materially from institutional safeguards such as a separation of powers.[2] If the President is given power to veto a bill passed by Congress, he is thereby enabled to restrain the action of Congress. This type of restraint, entrusted to a living human being, will be attended to by that trustee. It is a procedural restraint. But if it is provided that no person shall be deprived of his property without due process of law, that restraint depends directly upon the political force which the Constitution itself possesses. It may be converted into a procedural restraint by giving the injured party the right of appealing to a court, but primarily it is a substantive restraint. These substantive restraints embody a people's way of life.

The way of life thus safeguarded by the restraints of a bill of rights constitutes a specific pattern of freedoms. As everyone knows, the American pattern is sketched in the Constitution. A few comments may be in order. The freedom which seems to be most crucial, although it was not so when it first emerged, is what is commonly referred to as *habeas corpus*,— the freedom to one's own corporeal liberty. Very elaborate rules are prescribed in the United States for the conditions under which a man can be seized by the authorities. The American people have enjoyed this freedom for so long without any material interference that they are inclined to think very little of it. People living under the totalitarian regimes feel the loss of this particular freedom more bitterly than the loss of any other. By way of contrast, the people of Europe are vitally aware of these rights, and the new constitutions of Europe are much more emphatic in protecting this freedom and its corollaries, the freedom from searches and seizures. The French constitution of 1946, in its preamble, reaffirmed the revolutionary Declaration of the Rights of Man of 1789 which had been quite forceful on this point. Since arbitrary arrests, searches, and seizures had been central to the agitation against the *Ancien Regime*, the Declaration did away with them as definitely as the amendment to the American constitution which was patterned upon it. The German Basic Law of 1949 goes further and devotes its first nineteen articles to "basic rights" which it derives from the "dignity of man."[3] These basic rights are headed by (*a*) free development of the personality, and (*b*) the right to life and physical inviolability (art. 2). Nora Waln vividly portrays the terror of the average human being, when subject to arbitrary seizure, in her moving book *Reaching for the Stars*. More recently, Kravchenko in *I Chose Freedom* has described the life in the secret-police state. Such books serve to show us what *habeas corpus* means.

The second freedom, that of bearing arms, is related to the first, but it is not so widely recognized for two reasons. In the first place, people do not ordinarily make a practice of attacking their fellow men, and in the second place, the greatly increased superiority on the part of organized force, whether it be that of the United States government or of gangsters, mitigates against the successful use of arms by an individual. Yet the founders of the Republic attached considerable importance to it. As Charles Beard has reminded us, Jefferson understood the ancient truth that where military power is highly centralized and separated from the masses of the people, the latter are in peril of losing their liberties. It is remarkable how small a role this once-prized right has played in the discussions over universal military service although one should have thought that the American people, like the Swiss, possessing this right would have wanted to exercise it in face of mortal peril. The right to bear arms has its value, though, for instance in strikes, for it gives organized labor a measure of protection against the abuse of military force by their opponents, self-appointed vigilantes, and the like. It is a right which has always been highly esteemed by the Swiss, whose deep-seated democratic instincts recognize in the armed citizenry the true safeguard of liberty. Not so in the more recent constitutions: no such right is stated in either the French or the Italian constitutions, and of course not in the German Basic Law. Instead, these constitutions are prepared to limit sovereignty in the interest of peace.

The third freedom is the right to worship as one chooses. This particular liberty was of great importance at the time of the English Revolution. Jellinek undertook to show that the freedom of religion constituted the first basic right to be recognized. Interest in this right has been revived in recent years by the religious persecutions of the totalitarian dictatorships. There is now a tendency for the constitutional protection to extend to every kind of conviction. Thus the German Basic Law (art. 4 (1)) prescribes that "freedom of faith and conscience and freedom of religious and ideological conviction shall be inviolable." The scope of religious freedom has posed very special problems in cases involving a refusal to obey the law, more especially laws connected with universal military service. While the treatment of the "conscientious objector" has been by no means ideal, there was a fairly general recognition of his position in England and the United States. In keeping with these trends, the German Basic Law now states it as part of religious freedom that "no one may be compelled against his conscience to perform war service as a combatant."

The fourth freedom, the one most frequently highlighted when people talk about civil liberties, is the freedom of speech. This freedom is, of course, vital in its most obvious manifestations to the operation of a free society, and is fundamentally related to the pattern of democracy. It is essential to keep in mind the fact that a menace to this freedom may arise from group pressure just as easily as it may from the government, especially in time of crisis. The development of radio broadcasting has also raised serious issues concerning freedom of speech through the use of radio; the charge of monopoly control is frequently heard and great difficulties have been encountered in apportioning time for presenting both sides of controversial matters (see below, pp. 531, 533). Academic freedom, the freedom of the teacher to say what he wishes, is another facet of the same problem.

Closely related to the freedom of speech is (fifth) the freedom of the press. "Press" here means the printed word, books and magazines as well as the newspapers, now usually referred to as "the press"; but, as in the case of arms, the modern technology has produced factual limitations. This liberty no longer necessarily means the freedom to use the press to expound any particular view. Today the freedom of the press often means the protection of large business concerns in their use of the printed word for the purpose of making money, regardless of the moral, social, or other effects of that printed word, and regardless of who writes those printed words. The anxious question has been raised: "Is not the freedom of the press becoming an instrument for preventing views from being expressed, instead of making it possible for views to be expressed?" (See below, ch. XXIV, esp. pp. 520, 525 ff.).

The sixth freedom, that of assembly, the right to hold peaceful meetings, is nowadays often broadened to include the freedom of association, though the latter is not expressly guaranteed in the American Constitution. Like the other freedoms of expression, freedom of assembly cannot be exercised unless protection of peaceful group meetings against interference on the part of hostile groups of citizens is undertaken by the government (see next section). These freedoms can be taken together as primarily concerned with a citizen's right to political self-expression,—effective participation in political life, and hence constitutive of democracy itself. The new European constitutions all safeguard the right of association; it is of primary concern to the labor unions. Associated with this right is the right to strike. Thus the preamble of the French constitution of 1946 says that "the right to strike may be exercised within the framework of the laws"; the German Basic Law does not go as far, but explicitly recognizes the right of such associations "to safeguard and improve working and economic conditions" (art. 9 (3)). The Italian constitution, like the French, recognizes this right within the framework of the laws.

A seventh freedom has in recent decades been much discussed, a new freedom which is not included in the Bill of Rights of the American Constitution. This is the freedom to work, which is essential to the free citizen. It is impossible for a responsible person to maintain his self-respect and therefore to develop sanely, soundly, and completely, without the opportunity of putting his hands to something that is definitely worth-while in terms of appreciation by the community, expressed in pay. This is one of the most important freedoms at the present time, and needs to receive a good deal of serious consideration if constitutional government is to continue. Totalitarian dictatorship, both in Russia and Germany, has perverted this emerging freedom to mean that every man is part of the chain gang working for the state. Their much-advertised abolition of unemployment is actually the re-introduction of serfdom. Such serfdom may be preferred by people if they are too long deprived of employment and the opportunity to participate usefully in communal life. For this, like all the freedoms, has a social as well as an individual value. All the rights, so-called, express points of significant mutual service between the individual and the community.

This right to work has two aspects, a positive and a negative one. The preamble of the French constitution of 1946 states that "everyone has the duty to work and the right to obtain employment." A similar provision was contained in the Weimar constitution, and is now embodied in the Italian constitution. The German Basic Law, on the other hand, is more concerned with "forced labor," also outlawed by the American constitution. Such labor is permitted only as part of a criminal penalty. In the same article (12) Germans are given "the right freely to choose their occupation, place of work, and training." It is doubtful, however, whether such a "right" can be vindicated in face of a general depression, except in the form of an unemployment insurance.

Such rights not natural but political · It is customary to look upon the bill of rights in any constitution as the instrumentality through which the arbitrary expansion of government is limited, and a sphere of "natural" rights of each individual is thus safeguarded against political interference. The idea that certain rights are natural rights has a long history. It produces the impression that certain things, like private property, or freedom of assembly, have an existence and meaning quite apart from any government. Yet, in fact, all of them presuppose a government. It would therefore be more appropriate to call these rights social, or political.[4] Although they are not necessarily limited to citizens, they require a government for their enforcement. They are rooted in deep conviction. Bills of rights express the dominant ideas concerning the relations between the individual citizen and the government. Take, as an example, the right of free peaceable assembly. The struggle against the authoritarian governments of the eighteenth century created the impression that interference with the free exercise of this right proceeded necessarily from the government. Closer scrutiny reveals that this impression is not tenable in the light of historical experience. If the community happens to be rent asunder by profound conflicts touching its customs and ways of life, such as are engendered by religious and social dissensions, serious handicaps to freedom of assembly (and freedom of speech) arise from the interference of opposing groups with each other. Communists and Fascists, in this country and abroad, have repeatedly sought to break up the meetings of their opponents. Throughout American history, self-appointed guardians of the public weal have undertaken to interfere with assemblies, no matter how peaceful, of dissident minorities. At all such occasions, the presence of large numbers of police demonstrates very strikingly the need for governmental protection of these supposedly "natural" rights. A further striking proof is the British *Public Order Act* of 1936. It was the purpose of this act "to prohibit the wearing of uniforms and the maintenance by private persons of associations of military or similar character, and to make further provision for the preservation of public order on the occasion of public processions and meetings in public places." It was the view of chiefs of police that the wearing of political uniforms was the source of special provocation. Section 2 of the Act prohibited organizations from training and equipping men for the purpose of enabling them to usurp the functions of the police or of the armed forces. Other sections gave the police power to control processions, dealt with the use of abusive or insulting language or behavior, and the interrupting of meetings. Although the Act was hotly debated in Parliament, it was the general opinion back of this Act that all were willing to recognize the need for protection of their liberties against antidemocratic influences, and thus to protect the democratic system itself. All were agreed that the *government* must proceed to check action calculated to destroy existing liberties.

Recent restrictive tendencies · In all Western countries, including the United States, novel problems have arisen in connection with the activities of anticonstitutional, subversive groups and movements. The crucial question is this: to what extent can a constitutional democracy afford to grant the protection of its civil liberties to those who employ them for the purpose of undermining and eventually destroying the constitutional order? The annals of the Nazi movement prior to seizure of power are strewn with incidents where Hitler and his lieutenants made the greatest possible use of freedom of speech, of the press, and of assembly and association for the furtherance of their subversive activities and purposes. Similar things happened in France and Italy. The German Basic Law is rather explicit in seeking to prevent a repetition of such use; it contains provisions which are of course also directed against the Communists. Thus article 18 states that "whoever abuses the freedom of expression of opinion, in particular the freedom of the press, the freedom of teaching, the freedom of assembly, the freedom of association, the secrecy of mail, post and telecommunications, property, or the right of asylum, in order to attack the free democratic basic order, shall forfeit these basic rights. The forfeiture and its extent shall be pronounced by the federal constitutional court." These provisions obviously suggest various dangerous potentialities; it is a hopeful sign that a judicial interpretation may prevent police action of an arbitrary sort. No similar provision is found in the French constitution. But in the United States, restrictive legislation of various sorts has been adopted from time to time. Some of the most radical provisions of this kind were included in the Alien Registration Act (1940). At the time, because of its title, most people believed that it was a statute concerned with the fingerprinting of foreigners and similar matters. Zechariah Chafee, Jr., wrote a little later: "Not until months later did I for one realize that this statute contains the most drastic restrictions on freedom of speech ever enacted in the United States during peace. . . . The act gives us a sedition law for everybody, especially citizens of the United States." Like the German provisions, the law is directed against those who seek the overthrow of the government of the United States, but it restricts itself a great deal by including only the *forcible* overthrow. However, the American method of making a particular kind of conduct punishable is certainly sounder than the German one of permitting the "suspension" of "inalienable rights" in case of such conduct.[5] But that the Germans, in light of their experience, should be particularly concerned with the problem of subversive activities is not surprising. Actually, the Germans also provided constitutional sanctions against subversive elements, and in article 143 made it as near a serious crime as they could (having abolished capital punishment) to incite, attempt, or threaten to change, or to actually change by force the constitutional order—in fact they provided penal servitude for life.

Conflicts of principle · If bills of rights express the ideas dominant in the community regarding the desirable relations between the government and individual citizens, such bills of rights must necessarily undergo considerable alterations when these dominant ideas change. For as new interests arise in the community they will clamor for recognition as soon as they become sufficiently weighty to arouse a sizable group of people to rally to their support.[6] The resulting need for adjustment creates sharp tensions. The threat of revolution arises and calls for compromise. And since compromises are well-nigh impossible between mutually conflicting fundamental positions, such compromises often assume a very peculiar form. Two mutually exclusive, conflicting clauses or formulæ may be inserted into the constitutional charter, each expressing the outlook of one group.

The American federal Constitution contained very few if any such clauses until the enactment of Amendment XVIII. The courts could settle the conflicts with older rights which arose out of the enforcement of this amendment by maintaining the ancient principle that the later rule of law supersedes the earlier. There are, however, indications that Amendment XVIII was approved by an electorate which was only dimly aware of the implications of its principle and their effect upon the older rights, and that the movement for the repeal of this amendment gained momentum as these implications became apparent. But what would be the attitude of a court or other official when the original constitutional charter embodied such compromises in the form of contradictory clauses? The German constitution of 1919 was drafted and enacted by what later became known as the Weimar Coalition, a conjunction of Liberals, Catholics, and Socialists. These parties had been united in their opposition to the monarchical government of Germany. But had they enough in common to draw up a constitutional bill of rights? Even a casual inspection of the second part of the Constitution of the German Republic would incline one to reply with an emphatic: No. These "Rights and Duties of Germans" contained liberal, Catholic, and socialist principles in a motley assortment. Such questions as church and state, the schools, and economic life reveal the indecision of the makers. Private property rights are declared to be inviolable, except where laws provide otherwise—which means that private property rights are not inviolable. The church was excluded from control of the schools, but a majority of the parents were given decisive influence—which meant that the Catholic Church would nevertheless control the schools wherever it predominated, and so forth. Nor is the German constitution singular in this respect. Many of the postwar European constitutions contain a mixture of liberal and socialist principles. It was the comparative unanimity of the American Constitutional Fathers in matters of general principle, all of them being more or less liberal in their outlook, which gave the American Constitution its great inner coherence. The new German Basic Law and the French constitution are much more satisfactory than the previous form in these respects. Their statements of basic rights are forthright and on the whole they avoid the artificial compromises of the Weimar constitution. In fact, the Basic Law tries specifically to prevent the destruction of such basic rights by legislation, where such legislation may under the constitution restrict it (as is the case with property, for example). Such restrictions may in no case affect the core of such a basic right (art. 19 (2)).

Preambles · Preambles of constitutional charters are of considerable weight as an indication of the public opinion to which a particular constitution owes its force.[7] The well-known American preamble is characteristic: "We, the people of the United States, in order to form a more perfect union, establish justice, insure domestic tranquillity, provide for the common defense, promote the general welfare, and secure the blessings of liberty to ourselves and our posterity, do ordain and establish this Constitution for the United States of America." It may be contrasted with the preamble of the French constitution of 1946 and of the German Basic Law, both of which stress peace and social progress; the French, in fact, goes so far as to proclaim that the French Republic "accepts the limitations of sovereignty necessary to the organization and defense of peace." The Germans provide similarly in their article 24. As previously noted, the French preamble contains the entire bill of rights; after solemnly reaffirming the traditional rights of man as stated in the epochal revolutionary Declaration of the Rights of Man, it recites the more recent rights: equality of women, health and old age protection, child care and education, as well as those rights noted in preceding paragraphs. Interestingly enough, it couples with these rights the community's right to control any "national public service or monopoly." In many ways, the French preamble is a legal anomaly; for such a preamble must needs have more than declaratory force. The stress laid upon peace and social progress is indicative of a new spirit, and one which would doubtless express itself forcefully in the preamble of any American Constitution written today. It is, therefore, often maintained that the *real* Constitution of the American people is no longer fully expressed in the written document. On the other hand, the preamble of the constitution of the Soviet Union sets forth ideas which are as yet quite generally rejected in the United States.

Parties and public opinion · The first change in insight concerning the power of public opinion since the time of Rousseau has turned upon the discovery of the political party (see below, chs. XX, XXI). More recently the role of interest groups has been added. The division of the people into more or less lasting groups which carry on the process of creating a public opinion has been found to be an essential feature of popular government. Rousseau obviously assumed popular opinion to be one and indivisible, but we incline to view it as divided. And yet, Rousseau remains in the right as far as the constitution is concerned. There must be some binding elements of unity in outlook which constitute the *real* constitution. If a people should be fundamentally at odds, it would be difficult for a constitution to exist. It was superficial, yet characteristic, of much nineteenth-century political thought to assume that constitutional government could be long maintained without regard to this sentiment. However,

Burke, Bagehot, and Balfour inclined to make the opposite error of speaking too generally and vaguely about "agreement on fundamentals" as an essential condition for constitutional government. There can be much disagreement on fundamentals, as even a casual glance at English, American, and Swiss history shows. Indeed, the only agreement which is essential is the agreement on the elements of constitutionalism.[8]

Lowell, Lippmann, and other writers on public opinion have been concerned mainly with tracing the psychological and other aspects of divisions in opinion. Lippmann finally came to the conclusion that the "public" is a phantom. This view is an exaggeration and due to an overemphasis upon consciously expressed opinion. Burke, de Maistre, and other writers reacting to and reflecting upon the fundamental challenge of the French Revolution were more concerned with the processes by which a certain measure of common agreement is reached and maintained. Thus even wholly irrational factors of tradition found a place in their view. Marx and the Marxists, who expound the economic interpretation of history and institutions, have been preoccupied with the forces which prevent any common agreement. Seeing the community basically divided into classes, they had no use for constitutionalism. Indeed, if parties are formed which embody such class divisions and hence are opposed to each other all along the line, civil war is imminent. Harold Laski, in his pessimistic analysis of *Parliamentary Government in England* (1938), insisted that traditional constitutional principles would break down under such conditions. Ivor Jennings, however, has argued, in *Cabinet Government* (1936), that the Labour and Conservative parties do not embody such diametrically opposed class interests, and, on the whole, the development to date seems to support his contention.

Two basic cleavages: cultural and economic divisions · The two most formidable cleavages which divide modern nations are the cultural and the social or economic groupings.[9] People are willing to go to war and to die for a national culture or for the working class. If we accept this willingness to die as the final test of effective allegiance, any citizenship which is divided by such loyalties would seem to be distinctly heterogeneous. The relative size of these heterodox groups is of great importance. The significance of heterogeneity would be small if the ratio were nine to one; it would be very great if it were one to one. Countries like old Austria or contemporary Czechoslovakia and Poland, which include large numbers of people who are sentimentally attached to other national cultures than that of the majority, or who even strive for complete independence, would seem to be so constituted that constitutional popular government can at best maintain no more than a very precarious existence. However, as the case of Switzerland shows, such heterogeneity can be resolved in a higher unity: the real attachment to the basic principles of constitutional democracy can overcome national cultural divisions, as it has overcome religious and other cleavages in the past. The case is different when the disagreement turns upon the basic institutions of constitutional democracy itself. Countries which, like Weimar Germany, had a large, organized Communist or Fascist party were equally or perhaps even less likely to maintain such a system of government. This was simply the result of there being anticonstitutional forces which not only were ready to destroy the existing constitutional order but were opposed to establishing a new one. In short: an effective constituent power was nonexistent and the constitution was not real enough to become a political force.

Autocratic imposition of unity · The making of culturally united nations has been a long and arduous process wherever it has been carried through, as in England, France, Holland, Denmark, Sweden, and Norway.[10] In these countries, unification was accomplished before the rise of the international labor movement added a new element of dissension and disunity. However, the leaders of the labor movement in these countries were imbued with a sense of national loyalty even after they had begun to admit a higher allegiance to the international labor community. In Italy and Germany, where national unity was achieved only with difficulty and *after* the rise of the international labor community had already commenced to take hold of their working class, the conflict remained unresolved. The intensification of nationalist emotionalism during and after the First World War led to a violent reaction against all popular constitutional government. Fascism here, National Socialism there, proceeded to attack ruthlessly the flourishing internationalist labor movement. Determined to achieve national unity at all costs, these movements went far beyond the methods which were in vogue in the sixteenth and seventeenth centuries under the autocratic monarchies of England and France, and which had started those countries on the road toward their unitary national culture. Once united, the British and French nations in two bloody revolutions had long since asserted their right to rule themselves. There was something strangely atavistic about the Fascist position, and yet there was good reason for placing Mussolini and Hitler in parallel to Cromwell and Napoleon. All these men radically completed national unity in an autocratic fashion after a period of confusion attendant upon a revolutionary upheaval. Is it conceivable that Germany, like France after the collapse of Napoleonic imperialism, will purge itself and evolve a popular constitutional government?

Doubts may be entertained on account of the persistence of the international class conflict. Furthermore, economic and technological factors point toward an international rather than a national order. The European unification (see below, ch. XI) offers, according to its protagonists, the "only solution" to the German problem.

Cultural disunity overcome: Switzerland · Those who object that such a multinational constitutional system is inconceivable should examine the case of Switzerland.[11] Here popular constitutional government has achieved great stability, though it rests upon three very distinct national cultural groups. To aggravate the difficulty, each of these constituent elements of the Swiss people belongs to one of three most powerful national cultures on the Continent; French, German, and Italian are the three official languages of the little mountain republic. Nor are the Swiss linked by a common religion. But these three distinct cultural groups are united by a long tradition of common political customs which through centuries separated them from the surrounding monarchical governments. The partly democratic, partly aristocratic member states, today called cantons, were uniformly republican and very proud of it. Protected to some extent by natural geographic conditions, and long surrounded by the halo of their startling victories over much more powerful princes (see ch. XI, p. 192), the Swiss Confederation profited by peace and afforded an asylum to victims of the religious persecutions. Though each of its cultural groups stuck with tenacity to its own language, customs, and habits, none went far in attempting to proselytize the others. The leading French Swiss canton, Geneva, was kept away from France politically by its stern protestantism, and neither Germany nor Italy possessed a united national government to which their Swiss brethren could have rallied on the basis of common national sentiment. Thus a tradition of common political destiny welded the culturally divided cantons into a united whole.

In important respects, the sentiment of nationality in Switzerland resembles that in the United States and in Canada. The racial and cultural elements which play the decisive role in England and France are supplanted by a kind of secular religion: the free political traditions common to different and distinct racial and cultural groups. The shared experience of fighting for these traditions, both spiritually and materially, builds up a common store of memories which finds poetic expression in symbolic paintings and in holidays such as Columbus Day which emphasize the distinctive contributions. As far as the United States is concerned, there is no more vivid epic depicting the saga of such joint endeavor than Stephen Vincent Benét's *John Brown's Body*, with its panoramic view of races and peoples.

Switzerland most strikingly illustrates the weight of a common tradition rising from a joint past as the procreator of that *real* constitution which transforms a written charter into a political force of lasting importance. Burke has well stated the need for real unity in favor of a common government as a necessary prerequisite. In his *Appeal from the New to the Old Whigs* he said: "The power of acting by a majority . . . must be grounded on two assumptions; first, that of an incorporation produced by unanimity; and secondly, an unanimous agreement that the act of a mere majority . . . shall pass with them and with others as the act of the whole." Now this unanimity at the start of an association or a group (what Burke calls an incorporation) must, in the case of so extensive and complex a group as that which constitutes the citizenship of a modern country, be built upon a fairly long period of living together or upon an overwhelming sense of the need for association, such as existed at the start of the American federal union.

Contrast between Germany and Great Britain · It was not pusillanimity, as the radicals charged, when Friedrich Ebert sought to retain the monarchy, but a sound sense of the fragile foundation of German political tradition. Germany having been united under one government for less than fifty years, the time was not ripe, according to Ebert, for overthrowing it without jeopardizing the underlying sentiment of unanimity and cohesion. That sense for the need of continuity found expression in the curious phrase of the preamble of the Weimar Constitution ". . . to renew and strengthen *their* Reich . . . ," as well as in a lengthy debate over the retention of the word *Reich* itself. There is a great contrast between the use of the word *Reich* in this preamble and the meaning given to it in the preamble of the imperial constitution of 1871. There it was said that "His Majesty the King of Prussia, . . . His Majesty the King of Bavaria, His Majesty . . . and so forth, [enumerating all the ruling German princes and the governments of the free cities of Hamburg, Bremen, and Lübeck] . . . do conclude an everlasting union for the protection of the federal territory and of the rights valid therein, as well as for the furtherance of the welfare of the German people. This union shall bear the name of the German Reich and shall have the German constitution." In this preamble, then, the term *Reich* is nothing but the name for the union of monarchs ruling in Germany, who even insisted that the emperor be merely German Emperor and not Emperor of Germany. Those members of the republican constitutional convention were doubtless right who maintained that the term *Reich* referred to the monarchical past.[12] But when they contended that the term *Reich* should be eliminated in favor of the term German Republic,

Friedrich Naumann and others urged that the word *Reich* was a symbol of German national unity, that it embodied much more than the Bismarckian preamble allowed one to infer, and that it should be retained. The contrary conclusion was reached by the Western Allies and by the Germans who drafted the Basic Law of 1949. The word federation or *Bund* has replaced the *Reich* of Weimar days. Whether this is the last word remains to be seen. Britain and the United States are more fortunate. Their slow evolution has enabled them to handle their symbols of national unity more effectively. Recent disruptive tendencies in Britain's far-flung Empire, however, have caused novel problems. It was a stroke of genius when Lord Balfour, in search for a symbolic formula around which sentiments of underlying traditional unanimity could rally within the British Empire, hit upon the expression "British Commonwealth of Nations." For in the days of Cromwell too, several nations had been united under a common weal.

Symbols and stereotypes · The traditionalism of the British in matters of politics has always manifested itself in a strong sense of the importance of symbols. Skillful handling of symbols is as important for constitutionalism as for other forms of government. The symbols can be of many different types. Picturesque customs, such as surround the conduct of judicial business in Britain, have a definite symbolic value. Special celebrations greatly aid in strengthening the sense of community; practically all modern nations have special holidays of their own, none more so than the Americans. These patriotic occasions, while often irritating to the more sophisticated (note such deprecatory expressions as "fourth-of-July oratory"), symbolize allegiance to the community, whether local or national, or perhaps soon supranational. The ritual of the flag, so consistently observed in the United States, is an everyday illustration of how the symbols of communal unity are instinctively hallowed in a democracy. In recent years, the problem of symbols has received more general attention from political scientists than it used to. Professor Hayes's searching inquiries into the nature of nationalism have focused attention upon the important role which flags, national anthems, and the like play in rallying mass sentiment.[13] Walter Lippmann has shown that the actions of the mass-man are largely determined by certain fixed notions which Lippmann has called stereotypes. These stereotypes elicit more or less predictable responses, and it is obvious that distinct appeals to the senses can be produced by certain combinations of colors, shapes, or sounds. All this is by no means new; for unless shrewd practical men had been aware of these effects, such symbols would not have been created. But what is new is a clear recognition of the bearing these psychological factors have upon the government of men. It is, however, quite

169

easy to exaggerate the manipulative side. Thurman Arnold, in his *Symbols of Government* (1935) and his *Folklore of Capitalism* (1937), has advanced the extreme proposition that most scientific word usages constitute folk-loristic ceremonials. In thus making light of all the analytic elements contained in modern economics, jurisprudence, and political science, he finds himself without any coherent analytic terminology. As a result, both his books end on a note of plaintive preaching. Harold Lasswell, in his *Politics: Who Gets What, When, How* (1936), has stated a similar view, but without the factual case material which reveals Thurman Arnold as a lawyer impatient with the make-believe of his symbol-laden trade. The charge has been made against such opinions that they represent a new Machiavellianism. Maybe they do. But the more important question seems to be: Are these analyses accurate, are they realistic, as they certainly pride themselves on being? For if they are, no highfalutin name-calling will dispose of them. Unfortunately, the answer to such questions leads beyond arguable evidence; certainly their underlying assumptions are different from those of the present study. They are, we believe, also different from those underlying the Western constitutionalist tradition. For their metaphysics is deterministic; it is the metaphysics underlying Freud and the psychoanalytic approach. The human being is seen as motivated largely by drives beyond his control. Charles Merriam has called these aspects the "credenda" and the "miranda" of power. There is a great deal of make-believe in social intercourse, and especially in politics. The "constitution" tends to become a symbol, and its provisions become so many symbols in turn. It is this symbolic function of *words* which makes the constitution a political *force*. It is no longer possible for us to look upon traditions and customs as God-given or natural, as was done by Burke and many of his contemporaries and predecessors. We know that even the most hoary tradition has been created by men, that all such traditions can be manipulated, and, in short, that propaganda permeates our existence on every side.

It is readily apparent how this "disenchantment" of ideas and sentiments through exposure to the glaring searchlight of modern psychology, how this "debunking" of ideals once held to be sacrosanct as "natural rights," shatters the foundations of the unanimity which has been held to be an essential prerequisite of a constitutional order. If all ideas and ideals are merely shrewdly designed veils hiding special interests in their sparring for position, where is that underlying unanimity to come from which can give a constitution lasting force? Are modern communities bound to dissolve into a free-for-all in which the most ruthless will eventually win out by imposing their will, trampling popular constitutional government underfoot? Or are there traditions and customs which, though admittedly created by men, yet do represent habitual preferences and patterns of behavior in certain communities? These questions are more easily raised than answered at this stage of our inquiry. (See below, ch. XXII.)

In the meantime, it may be worth while to cite one of Burke's most telling arguments in favor of English traditionalism. In his *Reflections on the Revolution in France*, he argues as follows:[14] ". . . from Magna Charta to the declaration of right, it has been the uniform policy of our constitution to claim and assert our liberties, as an *entailed inheritance* derived to us from our forefathers, and to be transmitted to our posterity; as an estate especially belonging to the people of this kingdom, without any reference whatever to any other more general or prior right. By this means our constitution preserves an unity in so great a diversity of its parts. We have an inheritable crown; an inheritable peerage; and a house of commons and a people inheriting privileges, franchises, and liberties, from a long line of ancestors." This view was expressed by a man who was by no means unaware of the power of propaganda. For in the same essay he speaks of the matter at length, particularly when discussing the alliance which in his opinion the commercial wealth and the masses in France had concluded for the overthrow of the landed aristocracy. "Writers, especially when they act in a body, and with one direction, have great influence on the public mind; the alliance therefore of these writers with the monied interest (their connection with Turgot and almost all the peoples of the finance), had no small effect in removing the popular odium and envy which attended that species of wealth. These writers, like the propagators of all novelties, pretended to a great zeal for the poor, and the lower orders, whilst in their satires they rendered hateful, by every exaggeration, the faults of courts, of nobility, and of priesthood. They became sort of demagogues. They served as a link to unite, in favor of one object, obnoxious wealth to restless and desperate poverty." There is clear realization here of willful influence upon public opinion, the clothing of interests by effective stereotypes, as far as the enemies of traditionalism are concerned. But Burke does not similarly note the propagandistic aspect of the symbols of traditionalism itself. What is the "entailed inheritance" but a skillful analogy to a species of private property and special privilege? Surely, the bitter comment of Thomas Paine that Burke proposed to enslave the living to the dead was not without justification. "The vanity and presumption of governing beyond the grave, is the most ridiculous and insolent of all tyrannies," Paine exclaimed in *Rights of Man*; what he failed to realize is that these rights of man themselves depend upon a working constitutionalism with its attendant symbols, myths, and make-beliefs. Rights are constitutional, not natural.

Conclusion · The constitution, then, which *is* the process by which governmental action is effectively restrained, *functions* also as the most effective symbol of the unifying forces operative in a community. Our insight into social motivation owing to modern research enables us to distinguish fairly well between the system of institutional safeguards, patterned in many different ways but always designed to prevent the concentration of power, and the congeries of symbols expressive of communal traditions and general agreements. Through recognizing this, we should avoid the cynicism which springs from a naïve rational search for close correspondence between such symbols and the things they refer to. It is equally important to recognize the need for continual change. An appreciation of the symbolic value of the "constitution" need not obscure the dynamic, changing nature of the traditions and agreements which it symbolizes. That is the meaning behind Lincoln's famous remark that "Any people anywhere being inclined and having the power, have the right to rise up and shake off the existing government, and form a new one that suits them better. This is a most valuable, a most sacred right . . . More than this, a majority of any portion of such people may revolutionize, putting down a minority . . . It is a quality of revolutions not to go by old ideas or old laws. . . ."[15]

X

The Separation of Powers

Introduction · Europeans are even today little inclined to adopt constitutions which closely resemble the American structure. Among the aspects they object to, perhaps the most important is the separation of powers doctrine. In the last fifty years many critical voices have likewise been raised in the United States. And yet the entire history of government shows that substantive restraints embodying the opinion and customs of the community, its way of life, rest upon a tenuous foundation unless reinforced and backed up by procedural restraints of one sort or another. True constitutional government does not exist unless procedural restraints are established and effectively operating. Such restraints involve some division of power; for evidently some considerable power must be vested in those who are expected to do the restraining. Such a division of governmental power under a constitution has largely taken two forms: the functional division such as that into legislative, executive, and judicial, and the spatial (territorial) division of federalism. Though federalism and the separation of powers have been thus intimately related, their theoretical and practical connection has often been overlooked. Leaving federalism to the following chapter, we shall be primarily concerned in this one with the modern, rational theory of separated powers which is only a late and more scientific statement of views well established in classical antiquity. This contention can be verified, in a sense, by the fact that the totalitarian theory and practice are solidly opposed to any institutional division of power. Efficiency and planning seem indeed to call for a concentration rather than a division of power. A line of argument that runs back through Marx and Bentham to Hobbes makes the practitioners of concentrated power and their theoretical apologists contemptuous of any separation of powers. Perhaps the view of Bentham and his friends is: "If the power is being used for good, why divide it; if it is being used for evil, why have it?" The Constitutionalists' reply ought to be: "Who is the judge of what is 'power for good' and what 'power for evil'?"

The theory of mixed government · The Roman Republican constitution affords a particularly striking example of carefully divided powers. When Polybius came to analyze the Roman constitution in terms of the classification of forms of government evolved by Plato and Aristotle, he must have been baffled by the discovery that several forms were mixed together. He thereupon constructed his theory of mixed government, which exerted a considerable influence down to modern times.[1] Political theorists in the seventeenth century evolved from it the theory of the "separation of powers." Particularly, English theorists, during the civil wars, tended to generalize from the experience and the institutional pattern developed by medieval constitutionalism (see ch. VII, pp. 126 f.). It is too little realized that we owe to this approach the theory of the separation of powers which forms so vital a part of modern constitutionalism. Political thinkers undertook to analyze political processes from a functional point of view and thus they discovered the distinctive features of certain basic functions or "powers." This pattern of thought found its clearest theoretical expression in James Harrington's *Oceana* (1656). Reverting to thoughts on Roman constitutionalism, Harrington undertook to answer the question of how a commonwealth comes to be an empire of laws and not of men. Harrington candidly recognized that men are predominantly governed in their decisions by interest rather than reason, and he therefore felt that unless one can show how different men can be restrained—"constrained to shake off this or that inclination," Harrington says in the language of the seventeenth century—one will not achieve a government of laws. The crucial point, according to Harrington, is that of achieving a balance between various orders. There are two main orders, the "natural aristocracy" and the common people. These must concur in order to make a law, and together constitute the legislative power. Of necessity there must be a third "to be executive of the laws made, and this is the magistracy." Once this balance is achieved, you have a commonwealth, or government of laws: the commonwealth consists of "the senate proposing, the people resolving, and the magistracy executing."[2]

Importance of institutional background · In the definitive form which Locke gave the theory of the separation of powers,[3] it was an attempt to generalize the results of the struggle of the English Parliament for an equality of status with the Crown. As is usual in political theory, it was the product of a long evolution of political organization, and by looking primarily to theoretical precursors we mistake the theory for something largely divorced from practice. Nothing is further from the truth. English political thinkers would never have evolved the theory of the separation of powers from that of mixed government if the institutional evolution in England had not pointed in that direction. Here the function of interpreting the law in a high court of Parliament was transformed by a very gradual process into the function of making the law. Early statutes were conceived of as stating what the old law was rather than as creating new law. From the time of Fortescue, who in the fifteenth century praised the rule of law as the outstanding feature of English government, this function of creating the law became increasingly important. Through that function, the position and power of parliament were necessarily increased. Not content with the skillful manipulation of M.P.'s as practiced by Henry VIII and Elizabeth, James I undertook to challenge explicitly the supremacy of the law. He claimed this as reasonable, because the law was rapidly becoming manmade legislation instead of eternal custom. But his efforts caused violent opposition. Sir Edward Coke, though often medieval in his outlook on law and highly partisan in his guild-spirit as a lawyer, came to claim absolute parliamentary supremacy. The rapid succession of royal and parliamentary absolutism, Cromwellian dictatorship, and a return to royal absolutism, which marks the several phases] of this struggle, impressed upon English minds the need for some harmonious balance between those who make the law and those who execute it. This harmony the Glorious Revolution of 1688 tried to achieve, and in the fashion of the age Locke's essay gave it the halo of general and eternal truth.

Cromwell's *Instrument of Government* · Cromwell's *Instrument of Government* (1653) made a first attempt to distinguish and separate the executive and the legislative power.[4] In Article XXIV it provided "that all Bills agreed unto by parliament, shall be presented to the Lord Protector for his consent; and in case he shall not give his consent thereto within twenty days . . . that then . . . such Bills shall pass into and become laws, although he shall not have given his consent . . . ; provided such Bills contain nothing in them contrary to the matters contained in these presents" (the constitution). Again, in Article XXX it was provided "that the raising of money . . . shall be by consent of parliament, and not otherwise. . . ." The great importance which Cromwell himself attached to these separate legislative powers can be gleaned from his speech on dissolving the Parliament elected under the *Instrument*. Cromwell, deeply disgusted at their debating constitutional issues instead of making laws and granting money, told them that they had wasted their time instead of attending to their duty, which was to make "those good and wholesome laws which the people expected" of them. His opening speech, in which he had outlined the necessary legislation much as the American chief executive does in his Inaugural Address, he had concluded by saying: "I have not spoken these things as one who assumes dominion over you; but as one who doth resolve to be a fellow-servant with you to the interest of these great affairs, and of the people of these Nations." When he finally dismissed them, after their injudicious palaver, he told them more explicitly that the government was limited and divided between a single person as chief executive and a Parliament. "This was thought most agreeable to the general sense of the Nation;—having had experience enough, by trial, of other conclusions; judging this most likely to avoid the extremes of Monarchy on the one hand, and of Democracy on the other; . . ." he exclaimed, thus showing the connection between the separation of powers and mixed government in the minds of practical politicians of the day. It never did, however, seem acceptable to Cromwell to provide for his own popular election, and so English constitutional development drifted back to hereditary monarchy as the safest method for securing the chief executive.

Locke's view · Locke's view of the system is briefly this. He distinguishes the legislative power, that is, the power which makes general rules, from the executive and federative power. The latter is concerned with foreign affairs and security. But he does not at all attribute the legislative power to Parliament, and the executive and federative power to the king, as is often supposed. Rather he divided the legislative power itself, attributing it to the king in Parliament, as orthodox English constitutional law provided. This is also the system which we have just found to underlie the Cromwellian *Instrument of Government*. The difference lies solely in how the chief executive is created, a point not germane to the theory of the separation of powers proper. The division of authority between the king and Parliament with respect to the legislative power is not, however, balanced by an analogous division of authority in the executive and federative power. These are solely attributed to the king and his council. An explanation for such concentration of power is given only in the case of the federative power. The conduct of foreign affairs requires expedition and cannot be bound by general rules because it depends too much upon the changing international situation. This division of authority and the separation of the executive and legislative powers is justified and explained by Locke as by Harrington before him on the well-known ground that it is necessary for the maintenance of liberty; liberty suffers when the same human beings make the laws and apply them. This view was canonized by Blackstone in his *Commentaries on the Laws of England* (1765): "In all tyrannical governments, the supreme magistracy, or the right both of *making* and *enforcing* the laws is vested in one and the same man, or one and the same body of men; and wherever these two powers are united together, there can be no public liberty."[5]

Montesquieu's reinterpretation · When Montesquieu came to rewrite Locke's doctrine, the Act of Settlement of 1701 had already, in paragraph three, undertaken to guarantee to English judges tenure during good behavior. Montesquieu was, of course, equally concerned with liberty. Granting that as a starting point, he was next primarily interested, as a result of the contemporary situation in France, in the problem of how to secure or rather to maintain an independent status to judges (see above, ch. VI, p. 112). What could be more natural for him, therefore, than to rename Locke's executive power and to call it the judicial power?[6] The executive's function, as described by Locke, had been to execute the laws, in any case. This transformation of Locke's executive power in the analysis of Montesquieu was accompanied by another equally significant though bewildering change in terminology, whereby Locke's federative power became the executive power in Montesquieu. By emphasizing the importance of maintaining internal as compared to external peace, and by thus assimilating the police functions to the functions of defense and foreign policy, Montesquieu constructed the modern executive power. This executive power included also the prerogative which English lawyers had always carefully kept apart for special purposes. It will be seen that through these changes Montesquieu assimilated the core of modern government, bureaucracy, as it had developed on the Continent, to the English doctrine, which had emphasized legislation or the power to make general rules. It is therefore not surprising that the theory had much wider appeal in the form which Montesquieu gave it. Men of affairs throughout Europe recognized in Montesquieu's executive power the type of government with which they had been familiar.

American problems · It was of the greatest moment that these constructions happened also to fit the political experiences of most of the American colonies, where a governor, a distinct colonial legislature, and a fairly independent judiciary had come to constitute the essential organs of government.[7] After the Declaration of Independence had severed the bonds with the mother country, a brief experiment with legislative supremacy in some of the states had led to what seemed to many majority tyranny, and had thus made people ripe for an application of the celebrated theme.

177

Nevertheless, in many of the state constitutions which contain an express statement of the doctrine, the older English emphasis upon the importance of general laws remains intact. The most famous and perhaps the most succinct statement of that doctrine is contained in the constitution of Massachusetts, which declares that the reason for the separation of powers into a legislative, executive, and judicial branch is to make sure that this will be "a government of laws and not of men." The federal Constitution, too, though abstaining from stating the doctrine, puts the legislative power first and therefore by implication foremost. In spite of the silence of the Constitution regarding the doctrine, the Supreme Court has repeatedly called it a "fundamental tenet." Many who in recent discussions have belittled the separation of powers seem unaware of the fact that their clamor for efficiency and expediency may easily lead to dictatorship (see below, ch. XXVI). Fortunately, the one-party dictatorships in many countries have gradually awakened a realization of where the fusion of power leads. "The flexible scope of the Constitution and the qualities of statesmanship demanded for its construction are illustrated by what is often alleged to be the greatest defect of the Constitution, namely, the doctrine of the separation of powers. That doctrine embodies cautions against tyranny in government through undue concentration of power. The environment of the Constitution, the debates at Philadelphia and in support of the adoption of the Constitution, unite in proof that the purpose was, not to avoid friction, but by means of the inevitable friction incident to the distribution of the governmental powers among the three departments, to save the people from autocracy. As a principle of statesmanship, the practical demands of government preclude its doctrinaire application. The latitude with which the doctrine must be observed in a work-a-day world was insisted upon by those shrewd men of the world who framed the Constitution." The most important argument advanced against this point of view is derived from what is alleged to be the nature of parliamentary government in England. There an increasing fusion of executive and legislative powers does not seem to have destroyed the foundations of free government.

Fusion of powers in England · Though the problems of parliamentary government will receive more careful treatment later on (see below, ch. XVIII), it is necessary to deal here in a general way with the fusion of the legislative and executive branches in England. The relative absolutism which this fusion appears to have created has been endurable because of a constitutional safeguard which no one clearly envisaged until after Montesquieu's time: the regular alternation of two large parties in controlling this broad power.[8] These parties represented a slow growth, for in most cases they went back to the "town and country" divisions prior to and after the Glorious Revolution when political groups, growing out of the earlier conflicts of the civil wars, had formed in each local district. It is this traditionalism which accounted for a good deal of the aristocratic, gentlemanly character of British politics throughout the nineteenth century. To this day the remnants of aristocratic organization retained by English society exert a profound influence upon the political life of the nation. The absence of this traditional aristocratic basis of the English parliamentary government has had a good deal to do with the failure of European systems presumably modeled after the English pattern. The confusion of small parties fails to respond to the recurrent popular demand for clearly recognizable leadership. In some countries this confusion contributed to the development of one-party systems. Under the pressure of threats of a communist dictatorship which is so freely advocated by the adepts of a proletarian revolution, the public at large accepted a complete fusion and concentration of powers without the constitutional custom of a recognized opposition as we know it in England. In any case, the growth of parliamentary and eventually of cabinet government as a system of consolidated power as it occurred between 1740 and 1940 certainly seems to have obliterated the separation of powers, as envisaged by eighteenth-century doctrine. This change must be seen, however, against the background of party development. If, as happened in England, there is a genuine development of a constitutional custom of party alternation, if there is fairly general recognition that, leaving aside the judiciary, the elected representatives debate and "propose," in Harrington's phrase, while the people resolve through general elections, then that basic conception of a balance and counterpoise is effectively preserved. It is important to realize that there are many ways of arranging regularized restraint. What appears, then, as a fusion of powers in modern England is really a different and more subtle division of powers. Still another pattern is represented by the "constitutional monarchies" of nineteenth-century Europe.

The French _Charte Constitutionnelle_ of 1814 · It is often forgotten that the constitutions of nineteenth-century monarchies in Europe were in fact almost as much built upon a separation of powers as was the American Constitution.[9] These constitutions were at the same time dictated by a deep-seated mistrust of the theory itself, which was supposed to be inextricably related to the rights of man and of popular government. This had actually been the case in the ill-fated constitution of 1791, in which the principle had made its debut in continental constitutional law. In Title III, which deals with the "Public Powers," it is provided that the

179

legislative power is delegated to one national assembly, that the judicial power is delegated to judges, and that the executive power is delegated to the king in order to be exercised under his authority by ministers and other agents. But all these powers were said to be ultimately derived from the people. On the other hand, the *Charte Constitutionnelle* of Louis XVIII (1814) is built upon a separation of powers in fact and a denial of the separation of powers in theory. To quote the relevant passage: ". . . although all authority in France resides in the person of the king, our predecessors have not hesitated to alter the exercise thereof in accordance with the change of times . . . that only the supreme authority can give to institutions which it establishes the strength, permanence, and majesty with which it is itself invested; . . ." In these words the preamble of the Restoration Charter reasserts the doctrine of monarchical absolutism. But it should not be overlooked that the preamble speaks of authority rather than power. In the same spirit the charter is granted: "We have voluntarily and by the free exercise of our royal authority, accorded and do accord, grant and concede to our subjects, as well for us as for our ancestors forever, the constitutional charter which follows . . ." But when we come to the actual organization of the government, we find that the separation of powers—though not of authority—is recognized. Like the American Constitution, the *Charte* implied the separation of powers; it does not enunciate the doctrine. Its articles reveal a close analogy with the pattern of government in England after the Act of Settlement, and before the evolution of parliamentary cabinet government had commenced. Nor was it long before a similar evolution commenced in France, gradually reducing the king to a neutral and moderating role. The provisions of this charter soon became the model for a considerable number of other constitutions, such as those of Holland and Bavaria.

German constitutions · In central Europe, however, the actual separation of powers was carried even further, while general declarations which seemed to maintain the absolute authority of the monarch were rigidly maintained.[10] For here the separation of powers became in time the bulwark behind which the executive establishment, directed or presided over by the monarch, entrenched itself against the rising tide of legislative pretensions. Thus the constitution of Bavaria (1818) states in the preamble: "Maximilian Joseph, by God's Grace king of Bavaria . . . the present constitution is the work of our *free* and firm will, drawn up after mature and extensive consultation." Similarly, Title II, 1 provides that the king is the head of the government (state), unites in himself all rights of government (state power), and exercises these powers according to the provisions of this constitutional document *given by himself*. What is here asserted, namely, a concentration and fusion of powers in the person of the king, is not borne out by the later provisions of the constitution, which confer the essential legislative and financial power upon the Estates' Assembly (Diet), set up a relatively independent judiciary with jurisdiction even in constitutional matters, and finally bind the king by a solemn oath upon this constitution. It will be noted that this document has nothing to say regarding the responsibility of ministers, a matter which was only regulated formally after the uprising in 1848 in Bavaria as in other German states and in the Netherlands. We have here, then, a rather strict separation of powers between king, Estates, and judiciary. It is a characteristic of these Germanic countries that they continued to use the expression "Estates" for parliament. The word is symbolically reminiscent of medieval constitutionalism. Already in the fourteenth and fifteenth centuries the governments of some of the great and almost independent cities, like Strasbourg, had evolved a fair separation of powers between three councils, each charged with more or less distinct functions. But since the territorial governments which superseded these free cities concentrated the powers in the prince and his council (see above, ch. II), continental theorists adopted the theory as doctrine only when it came to them from England. The examples of France and Bavaria are indicative of the general pattern of monarchical constitutionalism on the continent. It is important to recall this phase of European development, because the later struggles for a republican and democratic system have obscured the essential features of these constitutions.

Weakness of monarchical executive · Constitutional monarchies proved weak and unstable. They encountered great difficulty in maintaining a separation of powers intact; in spite of the grandiloquent proclamations of their preambles, the king usually lost control over the ministers as the result of a gradual broadening of the power of elected parliaments. Though at first glance the French king under the *Charte Constitutionnelle* seems to be considerably stronger than the President of the United States, he did not prove so in practice. That he shared in the legislative power to a larger extent tended to weaken his position rather than strengthen it. What is more important, tenure based upon heredity proved inadequate when pitched against the popularly elected parliament. The American President as leader of his party possesses resources of reserve strength which were utterly lacking to these constitutional monarchs. If they did not wish to submit to the dictation of their parliaments, they had to assume absolute power and by a *coup d'état* break the constitution. This happened in Prussia under Bismarck in the period of conflict, 1861 and the years following. When, at that juncture, the Prussian parliament sought to maintain its position and extend its authority, Bismarck retorted: "Prussia's kings have not yet fulfilled their mission. Prussian kingship is not yet ripe enough to form a purely ornamental trimming of the constitutional system, it is not yet ready to become a dead piece of machinery in the mechanism of parliamentary rule."* For more than fifty years after, Germany, under the leadership of Prussia, held out against parliamentary government under a constitution which separated the powers much as they had been separated under the *Charte Constitutionnelle* and other monarchical constitutions. During this period the same drift toward parliamentary supremacy which had transformed the English and the French constitutions manifested itself in Germany, but before it could culminate, the First World War broke loose, Germany was defeated, and her constitutional evolution was revolutionized after 1918.

Sweden's unusual separation · A unique development occurred in Sweden. Here parliamentary as well as royal absolutism was tried during the seventeenth and eighteenth centuries. This experience led to the elaboration in 1809 of a constitutional system based upon a unique dualism of king and representative assembly; even the coming of cabinet responsibility to parliament did not supersede this unusual system. In a sense, administrative power became separated from the executive power.[11] While the executive power of the crown is conducted according to the system of parliamentary responsibility, the great public services, like the post office, are conducted with considerable independence, "according to law." Their responsibility is enforced through judicial boards especially concerned with complaints against administrative action, and these complaints are facilitated by throwing all the files open to public inspection. In other words, if a Swedish citizen believes that he has been arbitrarily mistreated by an official, he can and frequently does request permission to look over the files which deal with that particular matter. To buttress further the responsibility of these very independent administrative services, a solicitor-general, elected every year by Parliament, has the right to prosecute any employee who has failed to discharge his official functions properly. Since the duties, competence, and organization of these boards and offices have been outlined by permanent instructions, issued by the executive, no considerable difficulties are encountered. Without any theoretical recognition of the fact, the American federal government tends in the same direction of differentiating between strictly executive and purely administrative functions.

---

*Today, what strikes one most in this remark of Bismarck's is the unquestioned assumption that parliamentary constitutionalism is coming.

A modern theory of divided powers · Differentiating between executive and administrative functions brings us once more to a discussion of the theory of separated powers. However, we shall not consider it any longer from the historical point of view, but shall ask ourselves instead what truth it contains from the scientific point of view here expounded.[12] The general doctrine has an implicit double meaning. On the one hand it contains a generalization, theory, or hypothesis; on the other hand it contains a practical suggestion, a proposal for the organization of government in the interest of individual liberty. For the doctrine declares that governmental powers can be separated into three categories: executive, legislative, and judicial. Is this generalization concerning the division of power valid? What are the grounds for it? On the other hand, the doctrine also holds that the exercise of these same powers should be entrusted to three separate bodies or persons. Is it essential, is it feasible, is it expedient that these powers be attributed to different bodies for attaining the purpose?

The idea that there are three major types of governmental power would seem to be a valid generalization and one in accord with the operations of the human mind. Immanuel Kant was the first to observe that this distinction of powers corresponds to the pattern of a practical syllogism, divided as a syllogism is into the major premise, the minor premise, and the consequent. The separation of powers doctrine, unique to Western culture, is thus linked to Aristotelian logic. The resemblance of the distinctions underlying the separation of powers and the pattern of a syllogism is due to the fact that commands imply decisions, and decisions in turn imply judgments.[13]

Political theorists when speaking of power mean, among other things, that a person or group possesses the ability to command. This ability to command involves the ability to decide, whenever there is a choice between several alternatives. Such decisions are of two elementary types, which might be illustrated by the following examples. A man seeing a hat lying about may say to himself: "I will pick up that hat," a decision which is directed toward one particular instance. On doing so, he may continue by resolving: "I shall never allow hats to lie about," a decision which involves an indefinite number of instances. What has just been said regarding decisions holds equally true regarding commands, of course. It is evident that if two basic types of deciding and of commanding can be distinguished, powers admit of a corresponding classification. Specific decisions and commands are the realm of the executive power, general decisions and commands the sphere of the legislative power. The latter is for that reason often called the rule-making power. Analogously, the executive power may be called measure-taking. As to the judicial power, it will now be apparent that it stands between the two; for it transforms a general into a specific decision. When a general command has been given, or a general decision made, that is, a rule has been established, there still remains the further decision involved in applying the rule. If I have resolved never to let any hat lie about, I may be obliged to decide whether a particular object, for example, a cap, is a hat and therefore falls under my general rule, or whether a hat placed on an anteroom table is "lying about." This kind of decision is related to the general decision in that it cannot arise without a rule having previously been established; it is related to the specific decision in that it is itself a specific decision. Evidently this kind of decision, and the judicial power which makes it, is more intellectual, less active than the other two. It does not involve a command, and that is why the courts' activities are described as decisions. This analysis also shows that most of the time we are our own judges; for whenever we decide to do or not to do something because the law demands or forbids it, we are applying that law by subsuming the particular situation with which we are confronted under the established legal rules. Ordinarily, it is only the doubtful and controversial points of law which are brought up before the courts. It is indicative of the truth of this typology of decisions that the so-called "independent" commissions, like the Interstate Commerce Commission, have developed the same differentiation of powers or functions. Although combining legislative, executive, and judicial functions, they have been organizing the exercise of these functions according to the established pattern, providing distinct procedures for each. Thus in the I.C.C. administrative decisions are made by one Commissioner, quasi-judicial decisions by three, and quasi-legislative decisions by the entire Commission. Clearly, then, the "separation of powers" reappears at a lower plane,[14] differentiating the functions according to the nature of the decision. Those who incline to criticize the doctrine of the separation of powers have rarely shown any appreciation of these sound underlying observations. The reason for this lack of discrimination is that the theoretical aspect is seldom clearly distinguished from the practical proposal of attributing these several powers to different bodies. But while the distinction contained in the classical doctrine is sound, there is nothing sacrosanct about it. There are other ways of distinguishing powers or functions, for example, by reference to their technological content. Thus the power over commerce or that over coinage may be distinguished; they have been so distinguished in the American Constitution, of course.

Practical aspects: checks and balances · The classical doctrine, we said, held that these powers, as distinguished, should be allocated to distinct bodies. But let us correct a false impression. It was never proposed that the exercise of all of each power be entrusted to one person or body.

On the contrary, the doctrine of checks and balances requires that after the main exercise has been allocated to one person or body, care should be taken to set up a minor participation of other persons or bodies.[15] Budget and impeachment, judicial review and pardon, are examples of this sort of check. Moreover, we have already seen that everywhere in Europe the separation of powers was in practice always and foremost a separation or division of the legislative power between the king and parliament, and that this separation was clearly demanded by Locke, if not by Montesquieu. When seen in this light, there is nothing peculiarly impracticable about the proposal contained in the doctrine. It makes no sense to fulminate against it on the ground that a complete separation is not expedient or practicable. Whether such division of power, however, will effectively restrain governmental action, as the doctrine maintains, depends upon other considerations as well.

It is often said that the reason the separation of powers has worked in the United States is due to the party leadership of the President.[16] The party bosses of both executive and legislative power are said to have re-integrated them and brought them together for fruitful action. Of course, whenever either house of Congress has a majority belonging to another party than the President's, this argument does not hold. Yet unquestionably the emergence of the modern mass party has introduced a new factor. It does not obliterate the separation of powers, but it certainly softens it. At the same time, as has been shown already, the alternation of two parties itself constitutes a regularized restraint which consequently reduces the need for a rigid separation. In any case, there is a danger here of getting involved in the following contradiction. Writers like Woodrow Wilson in his *Congressional Government* and W. Y. Elliott in his *Need for Constitutional Reform* have emphasized and deplored the extent to which the Congressional majority and the president are working at cross purposes. The cases in which one has blocked the other are too numerous to mention. But if we thus insist that the separation of powers does incalculable damage, we can not then turn around and argue that it does no longer operate, as a result of the growth of our party system. The fact is that the majority party, usually led by the President, controls its own members of Congress only very partially, that most of them give primary consideration to their own constituencies, while the President must look toward his own larger constituency, that is, the nation. This has so often been a fact that it is hardly possible to treat it as an exception. An established two-party system helps in maintaining a constitutional separation of powers intact. Wherever one-party rule establishes itself with any degree of permanence, as it did in England during the better part of the eighteenth century, and as it now prevails in some of the American states, the separation of powers is weakened too. It may actually fail to operate as an effective restraint upon governmental action. As a result, the government may drift in the direction of parliamentary supremacy, as it did in England. Or it may lead to one-man rule and dictatorship, as was the case in Louisiana. A single party at times contains sufficiently powerful factions to prevent such an outcome, as it has done in Wisconsin. The Wisconsin case reveals with great clarity the interrelation between party and class structure and the deeper significance of dividing powers. Such division is a method for making it difficult for any one class or group in the community to seize all the power and then exercise such concentrated power for the complete subjugation of other classes or groups. Even though class lines are fluid in America, this is an important objective in any "free" society. If we consider the history of the institutional development of divided powers, it is very clear that such division has facilitated the maintenance of an equilibrium between various rival groups and claims, not a stable equilibrium, but a moving one which continuously adjusts itself to the shifting balance of these groups as they evolve (see below, ch. XVIII).

The need for a guardian or neutral power · Such entrenchment, however, will never afford real protection to the weaker of the two opponents, unless there is somewhere a fairly neutral arbiter. John Adams's view that a balance of powers in the constitution itself will be able to control the parties and thus keep them in check can no longer be accepted.[17] To be sure, a carefully worked-out balance of separated powers is a first step in the direction of controlling party ascendancy, but a mere mechanism can never defend itself against the lust for power of organized human beings. John Adams himself would consider the only alternative to be a monarchy and a standing army. But might it not be possible to combine the two devices and to make the monarch the neutral arbiter over and above a balance of separated powers? Benjamin Constant, in his famous *Reflections on Constitutions and Their Guarantees* (1814) proposed to do just that. If the three powers of Montesquieu interfere with each other, disturb each other, or impede each other, it is necessary to have a power which puts them back in their place. This conception of the royal as the neutral power is closely akin to the English prerogative which, in the words of Dicey, is "the residue of discretionary or arbitrary authority which at any time is legally left in the hands of the Crown." It is, therefore, the final security of the subject against abuse by ministers, politicians, and pressure groups. While it was difficult for the king to maintain this prerogative against a prime minister backed by a compact parliamentary majority, it remains in the background to be used in an emergency. When, in 1931, the weak Labor Cabinet fell apart the king stepped into the breach by authorizing Mr. Ramsay MacDonald to form a coalition cabinet, after his Labour cabinet had resigned. Harold Laski has expressly claimed a breach of the constitution by the king on this occasion, but the course of succeeding events seems to have vindicated the exercise of royal authority in this instance. In imperial affairs, likewise, the royal prerogative has emerged anew as the effective link between the parliaments at home and in the Dominions. It would, however, be contrary to fact to call the English king a guardian of the constitution. Whether he could, for example, effectively oppose an onslaught against the independence of judges may be doubted.

Under the Weimar constitution of Germany, it was hoped by some that the president might become such a neutral arbiter and guardian of the constitution. His powers were typically those of a constitutional monarch.[18] In the exercise of these powers, he was bound to the countersignature of a minister responsible to parliament. But owing to the confusion of parties, and to the state of emergency which arose, the German president inclined toward assuming wider and wider powers of actual government. From a representative head of the government, he became its executive center. Thereupon he lost the neutrality which would have been essential for a guardian of the constitution. Under their new constitution, the Germans have tried to take advantage of this experience by (a) stripping the president of the excessive emergency powers which he had under article 48 of the Weimar constitution, and (b) by establishing a constitutional court with broad powers to interpret the constitution and review legislation. In short, the new German constitution is turning toward the American system of a high court as the neutral power and umpire.[19]

The Supreme Court of the United States · More than a hundred years before the German Republic was established, the drafters of the American Constitution had clearly perceived that it is highly improbable, if not impossible, that a neutral guardian will be secured by election. Hamilton therefore urged that the courts appeared to be the most promising escape from this dilemma. In the *Federalist*, we are told: "the judiciary, from the nature of its functions, will always be the least dangerous to the political rights of the constitution; because it will be least in a capacity to annoy or injure them. . . . Limitations can be preserved in no other way than through the medium of the courts of justice whose duty it must be to declare all acts contrary to the manifest tenor of the constitution void. . . ." John Marshall, in *Marbury v. Madison*, declared this doctrine to be part of the "manifest tenor" of the Constitution. The problems raised by this doctrine are too intricate to pass over without further consideration, so another chapter will be entirely devoted to them. Here it may suffice to call attention to the fact that the Supreme Court[20] has hardly been neutral in the great controversies which have divided the nation. The reason that the courts appealed to Hamilton and Marshall as the final arbiter was obviously that a court is likely to be on the conservative side. That the Supreme Court bases its decisions upon "the law" means, politically speaking, that its decisions are related to accepted viewpoints. For the same reason judicial review still appeals to all conservatives. This fact is actually due to the Court's neutralizing function. No power is absolutely neutral, or it would not be any power at all.

Conclusion · In short, the doctrine that the making of rules and their application and the adjudication of controversies regarding the applicability of such rules in the main should be entrusted to different bodies is still valid. We have shown that it rests upon a broad logical and psychological foundation. At any rate, governmental powers in a constitutional system should be divided between several relatively independent bodies or persons. It may be wise to modify the three-fold scheme by charging a separate body or person with the representative function and therefore with foreign relations as well. If so, the distinction between the executive and the administrative functions will have to be clarified and perhaps broadened. The recognition of a governmental (executive) function exercised in common by the legislative and the administrative branches would insure the degree of integration which must be maintained for the safety of the political order as a whole. Anyway, against the advocates of a dictatorial concentration of power in one leader, the case for a separation of powers may be allowed to rest upon much broader grounds than are suggested by the limited doctrines of Locke and Montesquieu. Lack of historical sense prevents the prophets of absolutism from perceiving that their allegedly *new* form is a very ancient and primitive form: the tribe at war led by its chieftain amid the shouts of the multitude. The difficulties resulting from divided powers are great. But the consequences of concentrating power are disastrous. Hence, it seems of paramount importance that an effective system of divided powers should continue to operate; a scheme suitable, on the whole, to the needs of an industrialized society.

XI

Federalism and the Territorial Division
of Power

Introduction · Federalism as a pattern of objectives · Federations and leagues, a comparative view · The common objective of many federations: resistance · Nationalism and economic forces · Organizational aspects of federation: (1) Participation through a representative assembly · (2) The common executive · (3) Judicial or arbitral setup · A pragmatic view of federal governments · Federal representative assemblies: the United States and Switzerland · Same subject: Germany and Austria · The distribution of legislative functions: a matter of expediency · Participation of the component units in the amending process · Federal executives · The constitutional judiciary · The British Dominions · The Commonwealth of Nations · The French Union · The Union of Europe · The "new" federalism · Decentralization · Conclusion: strength and weakness of federal structures of government.

Introduction · The rise of modern constitutional government has been accompanied by the establishment of an increasing number of federal schemes. The parallel is so striking that federalism must be considered one of the most important aspects of constitutionalism. Federalism, when spoken of in general discussions, is used rather vaguely to mean any kind of association of autonomous units. The word may therefore refer to a league or federation of states, as well as to a federal system, such as the United States. Not only this country, but Switzerland, Germany, Canada, Australia, the Union of South Africa, Brazil, Austria, and finally the British Commonwealth of Nations have evolved a governmental structure of this federal type. It was prescribed for the Germans by the London Agreement in June 1948 as an essential aspect of the Allies' policy of establishing constitutional democracy. The organization of the world at large into the United Nations points in the same direction. So does a united Europe which is now in the making, though both are at present loose leagues or federations of states. It must be remembered that many of the more close-knit federal systems developed their structure out of a preceding league. The realistic study of the political nature of these federal schemes has been handicapped by an exceptional amount of formalistic, juristic argument. Having first posited that all "states" possess an indivisible "sovereign," jurists have strained human ingenuity to discover such a "sovereign" in a federal "state." But, as a critic remarked, even the incredible learning of a German scholar could not find something which was not there. The following discussion will not be concerned with these controversies about "sovereignty" and the "state." Instead, it will discuss federalism as the territorial form of dividing political powers under a constitution.

Federalism as a pattern of objectives · From a pragmatic viewpoint, an effectively centralized government, a decentralized government, a federal government, a federation, confederation or league of governments, an alliance, an alignment, a system of "independent" governments, and finally completely "independent" governments (such as those of Rome and China in the time of Caesar), all these could be represented as differences of degree in the relation of government to the territory affected by it, between two extremes, complete unity and complete separateness. An inordinate amount of interest has centered upon the point at which we pass from a federal government to a federation or league of governments, for it seems at this point that we pass from unity (no matter how organized) to multiplicity. But this is an illusion; for a federal government is as hard to distinguish clearly from a federation of governments as it is to distinguish it, at times, from a thoroughly decentralized government. Federal schemes, generally speaking, seek to combine a measure of unity with a measure of diversity; usually the diversity follows a territorial pattern, such as French spoken in Western Switzerland, German in Eastern Switzerland. Federalism is the form of political organization suited to communities where this territorially diversified pattern of objectives, interests, and traditions can be effectively implemented by joint efforts in the pursuit of common objectives and interests and the cultivation of common traditions. Whether the particular federal structure is best described as a single federal government, or as a federation of several governments, may sometimes be difficult to determine. The distinction should be drawn in accordance with the balance of these patterns of objectives.[1] The same observation holds true for all territorial divisions of government power. When the particularistic local objectives are sufficiently strong and compact to hold together the territorial subdivisions of the more comprehensive group, sustaining them as or molding them into autonomous groups, then the adequate political pattern is federational. On the other hand, the federal organization comes into existence when conflicting objectives (interests, traditions, purposes) are not as yet, or are no longer, sufficiently strong to sustain autonomous units. The contrast between the federal and the federational type of organization must not blind us, therefore, to the great similarities between them. Communities pass readily from one into the other. For, to repeat, they are both organizational patterns evolved in response to a (varying) combination of common and particular objectives. This is most clearly seen when we do not limit either conception to governmental organizations. In fact, both federations of groups and federally organized groups are found in all fields of human activity. The American Federation of Labor, the Federal Council of Churches of Christ in America, the International Federation of Cities, or the Second International, all these and many others represent such federally structured groups, held together by common objectives, but composed of distinct and often autonomous entities. A truly comprehensive analysis of federalism should undoubtedly comprehend all these groups. But since we are concerned in these pages with modern constitutional government, we will limit ourselves to federal structures formed by and among governments.

Federations and leagues, a comparative view · Historically speaking, federal governments often evolved out of leagues or confederations. It was so in the United States. It had been so in Switzerland and in the Netherlands. In view of this, it seems reasonable to inspect the organizational features of federations if we wish to progress along pragmatic lines in our analysis of federalism. If we study the early city leagues, like the Achaean League, the Hanse, and the Suabian City League, or if we study the Swiss Union and the Dutch Union, or if we study the American Confederation, the German Confederation, and finally the League of Nations, the United Nations and the Union of Europe, we always find a charter or agreement, embodying three elements of organization: (1) an assembly of representatives of the constituent members making and maintaining the charter (treaty = [Latin] *foedus*); (2) an executive organ of some sort, set up by the members, carrying out the decisions of the assembly of representatives; (3) an arbitral or judicial body interpreting the charter in its bearings upon the relation between particular members of the federation and the federation itself, as well as upon the relation between two or more particular members of the federation; such arbitral procedure is ordinarily supposed to eliminate the recourse to arms between members. Now what were the common objectives of these federations? They were different for different federations, but there was always (with the possible exception of the United Nations) the objective of resisting some outside pressure to which all the members were alike exposed. This rule is again at work, it seems, in the newly established European Union, which clearly seeks to unite the many

European peoples with a common culture and common economic and social interests in the face of the Soviet Union's overpowering position—with some thought also of defense against the pressures emanating from the United States. However, the position of the United States is peculiar in that she herself has been promoting the European Union.

The common objective of many federations: resistance · This common desire to resist outside pressure is well-documented in the case of the city leagues. The Swiss Union was formed in order to resist the feudalizing and later the centralizing efforts of the Dukes of Austria and those of Burgundy.[2] From the thirteenth to the sixteenth century these tendencies were dominant. From then on, outside pressure tended to disappear, and the Union tended to disintegrate, though the neighboring monarchical and absolutist governments remained sufficiently threatening to prevent a final dissolution. The invasion by revolutionary French forces, and the forcible establishment of a centralized Helvetian Republic (1798), served to remind the Swiss of the precariousness of their existence, and the federation set up at the end of the Napoleonic wars was not as loose as the preceding federation. Ultimately, after the forces of dissension had once more sought to reassert the complete autonomy of the constituent cantons in the abortive War of Secession (*Sonderbundskrieg*, 1847), the federational system was abandoned in favor of a federal government under the constitution of 1848. Perhaps even more striking, and certainly as dramatic, is the case of the United Dutch Provinces which for decades after 1555 waged an apparently hopeless war against the most powerful government of the day, the Spanish monarchy, because that government attempted to force Catholicism upon them. But unlike the Swiss cantons, the Dutch Provinces eventually merged under a unitary government, although the Dutch upper chamber preserves to this day the remnants of the country's federational past. It is hardly necessary to elaborate upon the outside pressure in response to which the American Confederation was formed. Here, however, common (economic) objectives so completely overshadowed other considerations that the federational structure soon gave way to a federal government. Not so in Germany. Though the economic forces might have been expected to produce a similar result, the several principalities with their well-integrated administrative organizations under monarchical leadership proved themselves more stubborn preservers of local autonomy; they provided conflicting objectives of more enduring tenacity than the newly formed state governments in the United States. But eventually they, too, were welded into a federal whole. The common objective here was not only to resist the recurrent pressure of neighboring nations, but to attain the entire complex of cultural aspirations which modern nationalism has proclaimed as the objective of a people having a common speech.

Nationalism and economic forces · Though resistance to a common enemy has continued to play its role, nationalism has in modern times been a powerful factor in providing common objectives for a group of autonomous units. To it was added the increasing pressure for a widening market of mass-production goods. Indeed, the latter tended to transcend national boundaries, but has, up to the present, proved insufficient as a basis for a federal system when unsupported by national considerations.[3] It is well known that many people pinned their hope for the success of a League of Nations upon the binding force of world economic interests which, it was felt, would balance the nationalistic forces of regional antagonism. But only as long as the countries united in the League of Nations shared the two common enemies, Germany and the Soviet Union, did the League possess sufficient community of interest. Germany's entry into the League in 1926 revealed certain hitherto concealed antagonisms, and her presence added new ones besides. In *Foreign Policy in the Making*, I showed that a balance-of-power system had appeared within the League. These disruptive forces were important in wrecking the League though it had grave structural defects. A federation of democratic governments alone would presumably not encounter this difficulty in the same aggravated form: antidemocratic governments would provide the pressure which the members were united in resisting, while strengthening each other through a broadened economy. Such, at any rate, has been the history of the United States and Switzerland. In both these countries a federation merged into a federal union with a common government for the whole. Perhaps this accounts for their modern development, which contrasts so markedly with earlier federations, such as the city leagues; it was the latter's history and the application of it to these emerging federal unions which misled Freeman into his mistaken generalizations about federalism as such. The outbreak of the Civil War certainly offered him a convincing point of departure.

Organizational aspects of federation: (1) participation through a representative assembly · We shall now sketch briefly the historical experience of federations or leagues, as far as their three elements of organization, namely, an assembly, an executive, and a judicial body, are concerned. It will be best to begin this analysis with a study of the representative assembly, its nature and its functions. All the federations of which we know have had some kind of representative assembly. The Achaean League as well as the Hanse, the Swiss Confederation, and the United Provinces, all held periodic gatherings of one or more days duration, in the course of which they settled broad questions of policy involving war and peace.[4] There was, however, often a curious lack of formal regularity about these assemblies. The gatherings of the Hanse contained, so Gierke tells us, now the representatives of some towns, and now those of some others. The leading cities, Lübeck and Hamburg, seem always to have been on hand; but whatever the attendance, the decisions of the gathering bound the whole federation. Altogether, the organization of the Hanse League seems to have been very loose; the exchequer arrangements were quite indefinite; the executive leadership of Lübeck was just "muddling through." The Rhenish City League, on the other hand, sprang into life in 1254 with a well-worked-out organization; but it did not last. Is there some deeper meaning in this curious contrast? It is certainly striking that the Swiss Federation—which of all the territorial conglomerations is the one which endured—also is distinguished by a vague setup which only very gradually reached a distinctive federational pattern. However, even the earliest agreement, the Perpetual League of the three forest cantons, concluded in 1291 that they might "better defend themselves and their own," provided for recurrent consultation, and the settlement of dissension by an arbitral body of representatives. After 1353, there were fairly regular meetings or diets composed of representatives from the several members of the league, but no real executive was established during the entire lifetime of the old federation, down to 1798. Civil war occurred repeatedly, for example, 1442–1450 and again in 1531; the latter was engendered by the religious dissensions of the Reformation period, and even afterward Switzerland remained internally divided by these fundamental antagonisms. Nevertheless, the federation lasted, and in the course of the nineteenth century the rising forces of integration produced a federal union in 1848. All federations have organized similar representative assemblies, and it would be tedious to describe them one by one.

All these assemblies have one provision in common, the equal representation of the members of the league. To be sure, there are occasional slight exceptions to this rule, as when the very powerful city of Ulm is given two votes in the Suabian City League. But even such deviations do not alter the fundamental truth that equality of the federated units is one of the keys to federational organization. It is certainly interesting that the same had been true, as far as we know, of the Achaean and the Aetolian Leagues in ancient Greece. The minimum effect of such equality is that each member has at least one vote. But often it goes much farther. The rational foundation for such an arrangement is easy to perceive as long as the actual differences between the federated units are not too great. The explanation for this equality is that if the smaller units had not been given equality, they would have been likely to break away. This had been the experience of the Hellenic League, in which the smaller cities felt themselves to be discriminated against and consequently tended to rebel. In contrast, the Achaean and the Aetolian Leagues hoped to create a centripetal force on the part of all the cities by basing their federations squarely on the cities as units. The reason underlying this decision is probably of general validity. But there is another reason. These leagues were mainly the result of external pressure; the federal movement resulted from a generally felt need. The Hellenic League, on the other hand, was created by the superior strength and leadership of Macedon; the dominant government therefore sought to preserve its position, as did Prussia in our own day. Such organizations should, perhaps, be distinguished altogether from real federations as cryptoleagues. It is interesting how this problem reappeared in the League of Nations and once more in the United Nations, since the East-West conflict developed.

(2) **The common executive** · Besides the federative assembly, there is the common executive. In federations whose sole objective is defense against common enemies, this executive will be of a military type. The military establishments themselves, however, remain local. The military executive is a co-ordinator, strictly speaking. It was so in the Achaean and Aetolian Leagues, but the military commander was supported by a treasurer and general secretary. In early modern times, many different arrangements prevailed. In the Swiss federation, arrangements for even rudimentary military co-operation were made in terms of rules binding upon the member communities, rather than by setting up a unified command. Such unity as the recurrent warfare of the fourteenth and fifteenth centuries made necessary was brought about by *ad hoc* arrangements under the leadership of individual member governments; it is truly extraordinary how much action, not only defensive, but soon distinctly offensive in nature, was possible on the part of so vaguely organized a body. The Hanseatic League was almost as haphazard in providing for unity at the center. Here the common objectives were not only military, but commercial; yet skillful and unpretentious leadership on the part of Lübeck seems to have provided for the federation's need of executive direction. There was, however, a common treasury kept by Lübeck, and one gains the impression that Lübeck's leadership was to some extent justified in the eyes of the lesser confederates by her willingness to make up the deficits. The United Provinces, on the other hand, set up a distinct federal executive at the outset. Although the consecutive members of the house of Nassau and Orange were formally called to office by the representative Estates General, their able

and skillful management of common affairs soon gave their governorship a halo resembling that of the other European monarchs. Well into the seventeenth century, however, their position was that of a federal executive, a highest magistrate. Under such a system, the executive is expected to carry out the decisions of the representatives of the federated governments, particularly in the field of foreign affairs, to maintain an effective military organization with the fiscal resources placed at his disposal, and in general to safeguard the common objectives of the federation.

(3) **Judicial or arbitral setup** · The final, and in some respects perhaps the most crucial, feature of all genuine federations is the erection of some kind of arbitral machinery to forestall the outbreak of internal dissension. This was an important aspect of the work of the League of Nations.[5] If we go back to earlier and less comprehensive federations, we find that some kind of judicial or arbitral body is always provided for the settlement of (a) disputes between the federated members, (b) disputes between a member and the federation. We find a great variety of specific arrangements. The means of coercion, though often in the form of fines, range all the way from diplomatic pressure to actual war; in the Hanseatic League the extreme measure seems to have been exclusion from the League, a measure which carried with it a boycott by all the members of the League. In view of the fact that the League comprised a very large portion of the trading towns of Northern Europe, such a boycott spelled disaster. At first it was largely used to enforce compliance with the decisions of the representative assemblies; later on it was used for the conservative purpose of maintaining an aristocratic constitutional order in the cities; in the fourteenth century the League thus forced the city of Brunswick to abolish its craft-guild government. After the maintenance of existing constitutions had been made a fundamental principle of the federation, in 1418, any internal change within the member-cities was liable to develop into a dispute between the member and the federation. Yet, while it is always formally possible to turn the arbitral powers of a federation toward the enforcement of such "constitutional uniformity," it is not in keeping with the facts to claim that such uniformity, or homogeneity, is a necessary concomitant of a federation, as has sometimes been done. The Swiss Federation contained all sorts of governments, ranging from the extreme democracies of the forest cantons to the arbitrary oligarchy of the city of Bern. The Achaean League also abstained from going beyond the prohibition of tyranny. "This [prohibition of tyranny] was doubtless," says Ferguson, "a requirement of the federal laws, which, consisting of treaties . . . and of general enactments . . . bound the citizens of the individual cities no less

than the local laws which they themselves passed. Otherwise the city-states were at liberty to adopt whatever form of government they chose." Turning the inherently necessary arbitral function to the task of enforcing "constitutional uniformity" may well be, as Gierke claims for the Hanse, an indication of coming collapse. At the same time, the constitutional provision of such homogeneity as we know it in the United States un-doubtedly removes many aggravating problems with which arbitral bodies of a federation might not otherwise be able to deal. No attentive student of the League of Nations can fail to appreciate the cogency of that con-clusion which was expounded by Immanuel Kant when he maintained that such a league presupposed that all government would become republican, that is, popular.

While in earlier days arbitral functions were often exercised by the federal assembly or by the federal executive (in minor disputes), even then there often appeared a distinct judicial organization. Thus the Rhenish City League of 1254 had an elaborate judicial setup. The same was true of the United Provinces later. But these arbitral bodies usually recognized the autonomy of the members by providing that a representative from each of the contestants should participate in the arbitration of the dispute. Disputes between a particular member and the federation as a whole were even here settled by action of the representative assembly. It was, in other words, never so much a question of protecting the member against the whole, as of holding the whole federation together and overcoming the unwillingness of the members to conform.

A pragmatic view of federal governments · If we now turn from true federations, or leagues, to federal governments, or states (sometimes rather confusingly also called federations), that is, if we turn to countries where the constitutional order divides power between a central and various local governments, we find that such a government is characterized simply by the fact that it resembles a confederation or league in respect to one or more of its organizational features; that is all. Nor is this very surprising in the case of those federal structures which have supplanted a preceding league or federation, as was the case in the United States, in Switzerland, and in Germany. The fact that such constitutional charters declare the local units "sovereign" does not need to disturb the political scientist; we have in such declarations simply a verbal concession to those who might oppose the establishment of the union—a concession to which nothing real corresponds. In reality, once "we, the people . . ." or some equivalent group has constituted itself the constituent power and made a constitution for the whole, from which the territorial subdivisions can no longer secede, we do not have a league or federation of governments, but one single government, even if it is federative in pattern, and its powers consequently divided between a central (national or federal) government and local (state) governments. This fact may be contested by legalists, but it will actually manifest itself in coercive measures preventing secession, such as occurred in the *Sonderbundskrieg* in Switzerland, the Civil War in the United States, or the executions against Bavaria and Saxony under the Weimar Republic. The contrast with, let us say, the League of Nations or the Pan-American Union is obvious.

(The United Nations Charter does not explicitly recognize a right of withdrawal; however, no sanctions against it are provided either.) To show the way in which organizational features of a federation may be embedded in a constitutional order constitutes the pragmatic "theory" of federalism. It is of sufficient interest to warrant analysis of a few of the leading examples in the following paragraphs. For the purpose of this analysis we shall concentrate upon experience in the United States, Switzerland, and Germany. All three have had "independent" federal governments for a long time. To round out the results, we shall then throw a quick glance at the Dominions and the Commonwealth of Nations. No doubt the federal experience of these governments is of the greatest long-range significance, but until recently it was affected by the peculiar circumstance that the Dominions were nonsovereign countries, without a foreign policy or a military establishment of their own. In each case we shall have to inquire: (1) Is there a representative assembly legislating (and amending the constitution, if the latter is recognized as distinct) in which the local governments are represented as if they were equal, or nearly so; (2) do the local units as such have a part in selecting the executive or in conducting the executive work for the whole; (3) is there a judicial body or bodies for the settlement of disputes between local government units and the central government? Let us first take up the representative assembly in the United States and Switzerland, and in Germany under the Empire, the Weimar Republic, and the Basic Law.

Federal representative assemblies: the United States and Switzerland · All three, the United States, Switzerland, and Germany, provided for participation of the component units in the formation of general policy and legislation for the whole commonwealth. Each organized a scheme of representation for the whole which is a compromise between a federational scheme, in which the representative assembly is exclusively composed of representatives of the component units, and a unitary scheme, in which national representation is based upon legislatively determined subdivisions of the whole.[6] Thus in the Congress of the United States the Senate represents equally the people of each State, while the House of Representatives represents the people in the districts as determined by Congress. Traditionally, this difference finds expression in the claim that the Senate represents the States, the House the people. Actually (see below, ch. XIV), the Congress as a whole represents the people as a whole and each individual member his constituency. Similarly, the Swiss Council of Estates, representing the cantons, contrasts with the National Council, representing the several districts on a numerical basis. This sort of compromise, dividing as it does the legislative power, provides a rather effective constitutional restraint, and one which appears reasonable. It is, however, important to keep in mind the mounting criticism which has in recent years been leveled at the American Senate as "unrepresentative" of the people. What this means is that the federational equality of the component units within a federal structure conflicts with the "democratic" equality of the citizens within the federal whole. The Senate, it is claimed, distorts the popular "will." Each voter of Nevada has one hundred and twenty-two times as much voting strength in the Senate as has each voter of New York, because Nevada has 110,247 inhabitants, and New York has 13,479,-142.* Similarly, there are fifteen states with less than 1,000,000 inhabitants giving them (with a total population of a little over $7\frac{1}{2}$ million inhabitants) thirty senators, as compared with two senators for each of four states having nearly as great or a greater population than these fifteen states combined, namely, California 6,907,387, Illinois 7,897,241, New York 13,479,142, and Pennsylvania 9,900,180. In certain matters over which the Senate has a large measure of control, such as foreign or agricultural policy, this difference may be of considerable consequence, because region is often arrayed against region. During the thirties, the prevalence of isolationist sentiment in rural unpopulous states probably forced upon the country a more cautious course than might otherwise have been necessary. Certain writers, like W. Y. Elliott, have therefore argued that a maintenance of a federal scheme in the United States will require a consolidating and regrouping of the component units. "The states as at present geographically constituted have lost all reality as economic units. Even as rough boundaries of cultural unity and traditional loyalties, there are few of them that possess enough vitality to resist the inevitable march toward federal centralization." This view is hotly contested by some people, and not only states' righters; those strongly in favor of centralization feel, too, that such larger component

*These figures are based on the Census of 1940. The voting ratio as calculated on the basis of inhabitants is slightly distorted in favor of Nevada, since the families are smaller in Nevada, 3.5 as against 4 persons per family in New York.

units would be objectionable, because they would throw greater obstacles in the path of the central authorities. Whatever the merits or demerits of such a change, the United States would still retain a federational represent-ative assembly composed in part of representatives of the component units. In view of this fact, it may be well to consider whether the divergencies are not being exaggerated when we compare Nevada with New York. After all, Nevada and New York together contain less than ten per cent of the population of the United States. While the differences between the next two members, at both ends, Wyoming with 250,742 and Pennsylvania with 9,900,180, are still great, each voter in Wyoming has only thirty-nine times the voting strength of the voter in Pennsylvania. If we list all the states in order of their population, we find that, with the exception of Nevada on one end and Pennsylvania and New York on the other, they constitute a series, few elements of which are more than 20 per cent apart, and the mean difference between them is roughly 12 per cent. In other words, they approximate a statistical continuum. (See the table in first edition (1941), p. 199.) In any case, the regional groupings average up, as is shown by the regional groupings in the Statistical Abstract of the United States. The same would be true of the regions which Professor Elliott wishes to consolidate into regional commonwealths. When taken as such groups, they already have a voting strength in the Senate much more nearly equal than the individual votes by states. In 1930, the division called "Mountain," with eight states and therefore sixteen votes, had 3,702,000 inhabitants, whereas New England, with 8,166,000 inhabitants, contained six states, giving her twelve votes. Similar differences, none too serious, exist between the other "regions." These regions are, of course, not too well or too surely delimited. Still, when all factors are considered, equal representation in the Senate is not so absurd as is claimed at times.

The Swiss have likewise provided strict equality of the component units, called cantons, in their Council of Estates. Further concessions are made to their federational past by leaving the election and tenure of these representatives (two for each canton, and one for each half-canton) to the cantons themselves. As Professor Brooks remarks, the Council of Estates, or States, as he prefers to say, "was designed in a peculiar sense to represent the cantons. Consequently it was felt that the latter should be left to decide everything possible regarding the make-up of this body." Unlike the Senate of the United States, the Swiss States' Council is on an even keel with the popular National Council, as far as functions are concerned; it has neither more nor fewer. Once the members are elected, they are, however, no longer dependent upon the cantons; legally, they cannot be instructed regarding their vote. Actually, there is between them and their electors the usual interplay. In most cantons today, the members of the States' Council are elected by the people; but in some of them election is still by the cantonal representative assembly. In recent years, the principle of equal representation has been attacked, and efforts have been made from time to time to introduce a system which would take account of the differences in population. For in Switzerland, too, the differences between the weight of votes are quite striking. A citizen in the canton of Uri with 23,000 inhabitants has thirty times as much influence upon federal legislation through the States' Council as has a citizen of the canton of Bern with 690,249. However, no such efforts have thus far been successful. In spite of these divergencies, Swiss cantons are roughly like American states in that they can be arranged in a series in which no two consecutive elements differ excessively from each other. Their population figures, too, form a fair statistical continuum.

Same subject: Germany and Austria · The setup in Germany was different. Due perhaps to the strength of bureaucratic authoritarianism in the monarchies which Bismarck united into a federal Germany in 1871, the federal representative assembly was structured as a "council" of administrative officials rather than as a representative senate. The very great difference in the size of the component states also may have had something to do with it. The state of Prussia contained, according to the 1925 census, roughly three fifths of the population of the whole country, with the next largest state, Bavaria, containing less than one fifth of the population of Prussia, and the smallest state, Schaumburg-Lippe, 24,000, or one sixteen-hundredth of that of Prussia.[7] Under such conditions, a mechanical application of the principle of equal representation was entirely out of the question. As a result, following the imperial constitution, the Republican constitution of 1919 contained provisions for a council designated *Reichsrat* (*Reich* Council). Representation was unequal, though the constitution recognized the minimum of equality among the component units by giving each state at least one vote. It also recognized equality by arbitrarily reducing the difference between Prussia and the other states, limiting her to two fifths of all the votes.

We may now ask (1) who appointed these representatives, and (2) how did they vote? The *Reich* Council never became the chamber type of assembly which the American Senate typifies. It remained a "Congress of ambassadors." We find that state governments were represented by members of their cabinets, who in turn appointed deputy delegates. They were usually permanent officials of the respective ministries who handled certain

Council business as part of their regular routine. How did delegates in the Council vote? They always voted *en bloc*, the delegation of each state casting its vote as a whole, as they do in the electoral college in the United States. This was possible because the delegations were definitely instructed and ready to act on their instructions, since they were composed of members of the administrative hierarchy in the several states. Most of the business of the Council was transacted in its standing committees. A group of administrative officials had no desire to avail themselves of plenary debates; a more intimate discussion, in committees composed of "experts" like themselves, was more in keeping with their methods of work. This fact promoted the practice of sending officials who were specialists in particular fields of legislation and administration to attend meetings of particular committees when certain bills were pending. This kind of council, then, appears to have been essentially modeled after the pattern of an international congress, or a federational assembly: the delegates voted by states, they acted according to instructions, they were members of the administrative branch of the several governments. Seen in the large, it appears to have been an endeavor to integrate the several administrative centers which the member governments had built up in the centuries before Germany had a national government. The Weimar Republic made a determined effort to reform this system, and the goal was in sight when the Hitler party took over in 1933.[8]

The persistence of this "German" tradition was again demonstrated at Bonn. Although a strong movement for the establishment of a true second chamber of the Senate type made itself felt, especially among the Social Democrats, the Basic Law of 1949 resuscitates the *Bundesrat* or Federal Council. To make doubly sure that this council would not evolve in the direction of a Senate, that is to say, to make sure that votes by party would be excluded, article 51 provides in paragraph (3) that the votes of each *Land* may be given only uniformly (*einheitlich*). In other words, the *Länder* are obliged to vote as such. Due to the breakup of Prussia and to the relatively similar size of the eleven *Länder*, it would have been easy at least to provide for equality of representation by giving each *Land* one vote (since it must be cast as one anyhow). Instead, each *Land* is given three votes, but those with more than two million inhabitants are given four (Hesse, Schleswig-Holstein, and Württemberg-Baden), and those with more than six million are given five votes (Bavaria, Lower Saxony, and North Rhine–Westphalia). This is significant from a political and party standpoint, because five states with definite Christian Democratic majorities will have an absolute majority in this body in the foreseeable future. The same would not be true if each *Land* had one vote. This perhaps explains why the Christian Democrats, in spite of their federalistic leanings, should have favored this kind of body, and why the Social Democrats, in spite of their centralist preferences, a true Senate; for the decision to have the states represented in a nonpopular body, such as this council, weakens its prospects in Germany. The functions of this Council are limited, but they pertain to both legislation and administration. Members may introduce bills in the Federal Diet (*Bundestag*) through the government, and in turn the government's bills must pass through the Federal Council. What this means, even though a limit of three weeks is set, is that all federal government bills, before being introduced, come to the attention of *Land* governments which thus secure the valuable opportunity to object. Without going into details, it should be noted that the Council also has considerable powers of delay, through veto and otherwise, but can be overruled. What is more, constitutional amendments require approval by two thirds of the Council. The Council also participates in the making of administrative ordinances and has an important part in the fiscal procedures and powers of the federal government.

The retention of the council type was probably a mistake. The chamber type of federal representative assembly seems to be better adapted to popular governments, because it responds more readily to the party system without which popular government cannot be successfully operated. As we pointed out before, the council system of German federalism is a distinctive device for integrating autonomous administrative systems. The Senate of the United States evolved into its modern form through a slow process of gradual adaptation; the lack of any elaborate administrative setup in the states and the parallel emergence of a system of the same two parties in Congress and the state legislatures no doubt greatly aided this process.

Austria, by contrast, adopted the senate principle in its original American form, but without admitting equality of the *Länder*. The complicated compromise between strict equality and strict proportionality produced (in 1945) the following numbers of representatives: Vienna 12, Lower Austria 10, Styria 7, Upper Austria 6, Carinthia, Tyrol, Burgenland, Salzburg, and Vorarlberg each 3, or a total of 50 members of this second chamber, also called *Bundesrat* (Federal Council)*. The election is by the *Landtage*, or the parliaments of the several *Länder*, on the basis of proportional representation, with some exceptions, and these representatives lose their mandate when the mandate of the parliament which elected them ends. The Austrian representative assembly is relatively weak, as is its German

---

*To increase the confusion, the Swiss executive is also called *Bundesrat* or Federal Council, while the Swiss federal representative assembly is, as noted above, called Estates Council (*Ständerat*).

counterpart. It may initiate laws, it ordinarily has the right to object to proposed laws, and sometimes its consent to such laws is required; a third of this council may force a referendum on a proposed constitutional amendment.[9]

The distribution of legislative functions: a matter of expediency · Owing to the variety of possible origins, every federalism is likely to be different from every other. The composition of federal representative assemblies may well startle the student by a wealth of heterogeneous forms. The distribution of their legislative functions is even more complex.[10] Many federal constitutions contain long catalogues of what the federal legislature may do; the American Constitution is relatively simple as compared to the German Basic Law. It goes without saying that such divisions of the "competencies," that is, the sphere within which each may operate, must and will vary according to time and space. Economic and social life, the military and geographical factors, all will play their role in determining the particular arrangement. From a political standpoint, no distinctive generalization or principle can be derived. It is a question of more or of less, with a general implication that if the functions of the central government are increasing at the expense of those of the local governments, the federal government is being transformed into a unitary government. Legalists have made a great deal of the difference between a central government with powers specifically delegated to it, such as that of the United States, Switzerland, and Germany, and one in which the powers are specifically delegated to the provinces, as in the case of Canada. The existence of residuary powers has even been held to constitute the decisive test of "statehood" for the component units. In reality, such residuary powers are an illusion, if the powers or functions delegated to the central government are practically all-embracing, as they were in Weimar Germany; broad delegated powers would mean more "local government" in actual practice than such a "residue" of "genuine self-determination." In either case, the only guaranty for whatever distribution of functions there is, delegated or residuary, is the constitution which determines the governmental structure as a whole.

Allied policy regarding the re-establishment of federalism got caught in this difficulty. Policy pronouncements to the Germans, including the London Agreement of 1948, stressed the fact that the federal government was to be one of "delegated" powers only. When the drafters of the Basic Law made this delegation very broad, a sharp conflict was precipitated in March 1949 endangering the entire Western position. The result, inevitable once the Allies had decided to find a compromise, is too extensive a delegation of legislative powers and a failure to draw reasonably accurate lines of demarcation.

In sum, a comparison of the several federal constitutions shows that certain matters, such as foreign affairs, customs, money and currency, posts and national defense, are invariably attributed to the federal authorities. On the other hand, certain matters, such as education and cultural affairs, the police, and local government, are very usually left to the component units. But the focal point of modern life, namely, the economy in all its ramifications of technology, welfare, and taxation, is handled with the widest variation. Whether by judicial interpretation of the commerce clause, or by amendments broadening the scope of federal jurisdiction, we find that the United States, Switzerland, and all the other federal systems display the most varied distribution of functions and competencies.

Participation of the component units in the amending process· A more important question as far as functions are concerned is this: Do the local units, states, cantons, *Länder*, provinces, dominions, or whatever one calls them, actually participate as such in the process of amending and altering the constitution, either through their representatives in the federal representative assembly, or directly, or both? Every federal system of government we have examined provides for the participation of the local units in the amending power. The particular provisions in the American and Swiss Constitutions we described in an earlier chapter when we discussed the general problems of this power and its relation to the constituent power. In America, as in Switzerland, the provisions for a constitutional amendment developed quite organically from those of a preceding federational compact. In fact, we probably could trace the importance attached to the amending process and the practical procedure for it to the federational origin of these constitutions. Certainly before the adoption of the Constitution of the United States the need for adequate amending provisions was not distinctly perceived.[11] On the other hand, the various federations of an earlier time all had to face this issue of changing their charters, usually through the action of instructed delegates. The United States and Switzerland, it will be recalled, both provided for participation of the local units as such in the amending process. In both countries the component states' representatives in the federal representative assembly as well as the component states themselves assent by qualified majorities. In the United States (in the process usually employed) the local legislatures or special conventions have to "ratify" the amendment as proposed by the Congress; in Switzerland amendments proposed by the federal legislature (or by a popular initiative) must, like ordinary laws, be ratified by a majority of the cantons as well as by a majority of the voters at large. To be sure, disagreements sufficiently wide to make the national majority and cantonal majorities vote opposite are rare (among the thirty-two amendments noted by Brooks there was only one such disagreement), but this is hardly surprising, since the upper house already represents the cantons.

In Germany, under the Empire, under the Republic, and now under the Basic Law of 1949, no direct participation of the territories (*Länder*) or their electorates in amendments was required. Though natural enough under the Empire, under the Republic this omission was another indication that federalism was on the way out. A weak remnant was the provision that two thirds of the *Reich* Council's votes had to be cast in favor of constitutional amendments. If it refused thus to "ratify" the amendments proposed by the *Reichstag*, they were to be submitted to a popular referendum. Though never actually invoked, this provision shows that constitutional amendments could be put through without the consent of even an ordinary simple majority of the states. The amending power under the Weimar constitution was certainly not very federalistically organized. Strangely enough, the Western Allies failed to maintain their position in this crucial respect, and accepted an amending process very similar to that under the Weimar constitution (the Basic Law eliminates the referendum).

In contrast to German federalism, the emergent federal structure of the British Commonwealth shows this typically federal participation of the component units, England and the Dominions, in the determination of the constitutional order through the Imperial Conference, whose acts must be implemented by acts of the several Parliaments. This method is quite in keeping with the British tradition of drawing no clear distinction between constitutional and other legal rules. If the British constitution proper was allowed to evolve as a congeries of rules, regulations, and customs, it is natural that the Commonwealth should follow in these footsteps. Yet attentive students of this development have been able to point out a distinctive pattern of Commonwealth-Empire relationships which partake of the "constitutional" order. It will be interesting to watch, however, whether the British will not gradually be diverted from their older tradition of treating constitutional rules on a par with ordinary legislation. For the rise of constitutions embodied in a single document has had one of its most powerful stimulants in the needs of federal governmental structures. In setting up fairly permanent adjustments between the central and the local governments, such documents have served a most useful purpose in the political life of peoples as closely akin to the English as the Americans and the Swiss, not to speak of several Dominions which themselves are part of the Commonwealth.

Federal executives · Our second organizational feature of a federation was found, it will be remembered, in the executive-administrative sphere. The local units as such either have a part in selecting the federal executive or in conducting the executive work for the whole or both. The federal structures in the United States, Switzerland, Germany, and the Dominions all satisfy this criterion. To be sure, in none of them (except the German Empire) have the local units more than fragments of the power of selecting the federal executive. Thus, in the United States we may say that voting by states in the electoral college is a partial recognition of the states; for the President is not elected by a majority of the whole people (as under the German Republic) but by a majority of state majorities. Another fragment of state participation is the constitutional right of the Senate to advise on and consent to presidential appointments. Out of this has grown the rather important tradition of "senatorial courtesy." It is a kind of *liberum veto*, and means no more than this: that while the Senate will not suggest particular nominations, it expects that the President, in naming certain local office-holders, will choose persons satisfactory to the Senator or Senators of the President's political party from the state in which the offices are located, or from which the appointees come. "The strength of the pack is the wolf, and the strength of the wolf is the pack."[12] In recent years, the President has been inclined to disregard this rule in the case of senators who, though formally of his party, did not acknowledge his leadership. However, the President's desire to hold certain states in line for renomination affects his policies, as well as his appointments, and the Senate's regional sensibilities insure to the citizens of all the states a certain measure of "opportunity." Another more formal recognition of the same type is the civil-service rule according to which each state is given a certain quota of appointments to the service. It is difficult to assess the relative advantages and disadvantages of these practices.

In Switzerland, the president and the executive council are elected by the two houses of the legislature; hence the cantons have a decisive voice. The strength of local autonomy is recognized in certain customs: Bern and Zürich are always represented on the Council, and Council seats are evenly distributed among the other cantons. This means primarily that the French and Italian cantons get at least one or two members.

A much less satisfactory arrangement prevailed in Germany. Under the Weimar Republic the states in Germany had a large part in conducting the executive and administrative work for and on behalf of the federal government. The member "states" were administering a good part of federal legislation. The existence of a large and highly efficient administrative organization in Prussia, covering three fifths of the *Reich's* population and centered at Berlin, undoubtedly had a good deal to do with it. The states were supposed to do this under federal supervision. Here was a fruitful source of conflicts. Under a controversial, constitutional grant of power (article 15) the central government could and did send delegates to the states to investigate the execution of *Reich* law. These delegates or commissioners did not have executive or administrative authority themselves; they merely could ask questions, look into files, hear testimony. If they found something wrong, it was up to the central government to address a complaint to the government of the state. But what if the government of the state paid no attention? In such cases, the central government was given the authority to enforce its view, under article 48, though the state government could appeal the matter to the Court of State. This "execution" was by no means a paper rule but came into play time and again against Saxony, Thuringia, and finally against Prussia in the summer of 1932. But the arrangement cannot, on the whole, be judged very satisfactory. A detailed examination of the several conflicts to which it gave rise shows that they invariably occurred when different parties controlled the central and local governments. In the cases of Saxony and Thuringia, the central government was opposed to the radicalism of the local governments, and these provisions provided a convenient pretext for proceeding against them. Later on, in the case of Bavaria, reactionary tendencies provoked the conflict. The complications between Thuringia and the central government in 1931 were engendered by the Nazis' entry into the Thuringian government. Finally, and most seriously, the conflict between Prussia and the *Reich*, which led to the overthrow of the Prussian government in July 1932, was brought about by the resistance, weak though it was, which the Prussian government offered to the reaction brought on by von Papen in the central government. The Prussian government appealed the case to the Court of State. This Court held that Prussia had not violated any of its obligations or duties. Still, the Commissioner who had displaced the Prussian government remained in office; the German federal structure collapsed. The central government had displaced the state government in all but name.

In light of the dramatic impact of these events at the time, it is strange that the legend could grow up later that it was the centralization of Germany which favored Hitler when, as a matter of fact, it was the relative autonomy of Bavaria which provided the seed bed for Hitlerism before and after the Beer Hall *Putsch* in Munich in 1923. It was likewise the autonomy of the *Länder* under the Weimar constitution which enabled Thuringia, after she had gone National Socialist, to confer German citizenship upon Hitler without which he could not have become either a candidate for the presidency or chancellor. By analogy, any sharply federalistic structure will provide a foothold and jumping board for an emergent totalitarianism, whether of the right or the left. In fact, the Basic Law is so constructed that the German government would probably be unable to handle such a situation as was handled by the Weimar Republic when the Stresemann government in 1923 suppressed first a Communist seizure of power in Saxony and then a Fascist attempt in Bavaria. These experiences certainly do not support the contention that a federalistic scheme protects either the weak German democracy or other countries against totalitarian adventures. One cannot help suspecting that the argument associated with the Allies' policy of "decentralization," that is, insistence upon an extremely federalistic structure, is associated basically not so much with the problem of how to cope with totalitarian movements as with the notion that "dividing" Germany would be an aid to peace.

The constitutional judiciary · We find a judicial body for the settlement of disputes between the central and local authorities in all federal systems.[13] In the United States the Supreme Court, of course, is charged with this duty. Though on the whole favoring the federal government, it has not followed a consistent course as between the central and the local governments. The Court was nationally minded under Marshall, and several of his most famous decisions, like *McCulloch v. Maryland* and *Gibbons v. Ogden*, asserted doctrines which favored the central government. Later on, the Court, in the course of the slavery controversy, shifted toward a states' rights position which culminated in the ill-starred *Dred Scott* decision. After the Civil War, the Court returned to its earlier outlook. There was prevalent a feeling that the war had settled all questions in favor of the central government. The doubtful logic of this sentiment has recently become manifest by the court's swing back to a states' rights viewpoint. But whatever the merits of detailed issues under dispute, the notion of judicial settlement of such disputes between local and central authorities remains as a clear indication of the federal nature of the American governmental structure.

This is likewise the case in Switzerland, and it is noteworthy that provisions about the administration of federal legislation by the cantons have not resulted in complications similar to those which arose in Germany under the Weimar Republic. This is probably owing to the fact that not a single canton is large in relation to the federation as a whole, that the cantons have been less sharply divided by partisan issues (neither Communism nor Fascism assuming serious proportions), and that the central government has practiced marked moderation in employing force, relying rather upon persuasion and other kinds of pressure. Under their new Basic Law the Germans will have to follow similar methods; whether they will be equally successful may be doubted in view of the different conditions.

The British Dominions · Besides providing a new pattern for imperial relationships, federalism has played a significant role in the development of those colonies of Great Britain which were predominantly settled by white men. In all these vast territories, a demand for self-government arose in time. Thus effectiveness in dealing with the mother country rather than resistance to outside pressure became the common objective, along with the economic and national considerations in the federating of groups of colonies in Canada, Australia, and South Africa.[14] India represented a separate constitutional problem.

These federal structures, while self-generated in the colonies, received encouragement from Britain. Each one of these constitutions is embodied in an Act of Parliament. Canada was the first to enter upon this development. Out of the Union of Upper and Lower Canada (1840), which was inspired by the far-sighted report of the Earl of Durham (1838), grew a broader federalism which eventually comprised all of British North America. The original federal union, established through the British North America Act of July 1, 1867, comprised only Upper Canada (Ontario) and Lower Canada (Quebec), New Brunswick, and Nova Scotia. But soon after, the Western territories were added. It was at once a matter of uniting in the face of the rapidly growing United States and of overcoming the cultural cleavage which divided English and French Canadians. Lord Durham had felt that the cultural division was threatening Canada's future; the united provinces would, he believed, show more homogeneity through the dominance of the British element. His expectations have been in a measure fulfilled, though the double division of race and religion produces at times serious strains.

Australia's federal union, though obvious in view of her insular unity, did not come into existence until 1901, after more than ten years of trial and error and intense agitation. Australia's original impulse was in some measure national defense. After the withdrawal of British troops in 1870, it soon became apparent that some measures for the common defense would have to be adopted. As early as 1889, Australia's defense problem had been analyzed by a military expert who suggested a federal setup. It was in keeping with this background that Australia was the first English-speaking country to adopt universal military service in peacetime, in 1911. The Australian Federal Commonwealth, composed of the six provinces, called States, of New South Wales, Victoria, Queensland, South Australia, Western

Australia, and Tasmania, and one territory, the Northern Territory, operates under a rather rigid constitution, which is a blend of English and American elements. It is patterned on the Constitution of the United States in its provisions for equal representation of the component units in a Senate, its requirement of state participation in constitutional amendments, and its judicial power of constitutional interpretation. On the other hand, it vests executive power in the Governor-General, representing the Crown, and in an Executive Council, presided over by the leader of the majority party. This prime minister, dependent upon parliamentary majority, is of course the real executive, and hence we have a parliamentary system of government. This system is ill-adapted to a federal parliament with two houses; difficult conflicts arise when the majorities in the two houses differ from each other, as has happened repeatedly in Australia. The legislative power is formally vested in parliament, consisting (according to the time-honored formula) of the King (represented by the Governor-General, in turn represented by the prime minister and his cabinet), the Senate, and the House. In fact, the tendency toward cabinet government (see below, ch. XVIII) has rendered obsolete the distinction between legislative and executive power in this traditional sense.

The Canadian system follows a somewhat more centralized pattern, since the national government possesses all the residuary powers not specifically assigned to the provinces. In point of real issues, this difference has not proved important. But the problem of executive power, as between the Governor-General and the prime minister, issued in a constitutional crisis in 1926. Mr. Mackenzie King, having suffered defeat in parliament, wanted to dissolve that body and hold an election. The Governor-General insisted upon appointing the leader of the opposition; but when an election became necessary, a few weeks later, Mr. King was returned. It was assumed that this result established the principle that the Governor-General, like the king in England, is bound by the advice of the prime minister.

The Union of South Africa, finally, created as a sequel to the bitter Boer War on May 31, 1910, out of the four self-governing provinces of Cape, Transvaal, Natal, and the Orange River Colony, plus Rhodesia, has been called a "unitary state." It is, however, still something of a federalism. Though it operates essentially under a unitary parliamentary government, its parliament is divided into two houses, the upper house or Senate being composed of an equal number of representatives from each province. But the provinces possess only such powers as are given to them by the parliament. South Africa, like Canada, has a difficult cultural cleavage to cope with: both Dutch and English are recognized as official languages. Besides, the native issue is a bitter one. The colored aborigines have no vote, nor are they otherwise treated as the equals of the white settlers. Although South Africa, like Canada and Australia, joined Great Britain in the Second World War, support for this policy was lacking in enthusiasm and vigor. A very substantial minority desired South Africa to remain neutral, and any less closely knit federalism than that prevailing in the Union might have been split apart by this issue, since the Dutch and English settlers are unequally represented in the several provinces.

All these Dominions are novel experiments in government through their effective combination of federalism with parliamentarism. Whether that combination could be successfully worked without the benevolent neutralizing influence of a distant "crown," remains undetermined.

The Commonwealth of Nations · Up to the present time, the United States and Switzerland have developed an ever-increasing centralization. The British Empire, or rather that part of it referred to as the Commonwealth of Nations and composed of the United Kingdom and the self-governing Dominions, is on the contrary evolving in the opposite direction. While before the First World War it might have been argued[15] that the Commonwealth was still a federal structure of government, the conduct of Eire (and to a certain extent South Africa) in refusing to make common cause with the Commonwealth in its life-and-death struggle against Hitlerism reveals the Commonwealth as remaining scarcely a federation today.[16] It has in fact been described as a "League of Nations." The Dominions have separate military establishments and they possess separate diplomatic representatives. On the whole, the situation is somewhat clarified by the secession of Eire (1947) and the granting of independence to India. Until that happened Eire's insistence upon remaining neutral does not seem to have been interpreted as tantamount to secession. The difference between the Commonwealth and a federal setup such as the American one is striking. In the light of what has been said above, there is not much point in laboring the distinction between a federal and a federational pattern except as an indication of the general direction of the evolution. If the possibility of secession be accepted as *one* pragmatic test of a loose federational structure, then the Commonwealth is today in an uncertain position. The League of Nations, the Swiss Federation, and the Hanse, as well as many other historic leagues or confederations of actually separate governments, have recognized the right of members of the league to withdraw from membership. Hence it might be said pragmatically that the Commonwealth became a League when the Irish claimed this "right." John Calhoun and his friends, when claiming the same right of secession in the United States for the States, threatened the dissolution of the American Union.

212

The Commonwealth occupies some kind of intermediary position be-tween a federal system and a loose confederation. There is no functioning common government, although Britain provides a part of it, and there are various meetings of officials high and low, from the Prime Ministers on down. In a way, the Commonwealth has a representative assembly in its Imperial Conferences in which the local governments, Great Britain, and the Dominions are recognized as equal in law. This representative assembly is evolving the constitution for the whole Empire, as noted, and is col-laborating with certain offices, like the Foreign Office, which are being conducted by Great Britain for the whole, just as Prussia conducted the foreign policy for the German Empire. This collaboration takes the form of "consultation," which is acclaimed as the magic formula for strengthening the bonds between the several Dominions and Great Britain. Ireland re-fused, by formal enactment of a law in 1948, to be so represented. Yet the British government served notice that it will "not regard the enactment of this legislation by Eire as placing Eire in the category of foreign countries."[17] But the meetings of these Imperial Conferences, now called Prime Min-isters' Conferences, are too infrequent.

Returning to the executive branch, we find that to some extent the local units share in its conduct. From 1904 until the Second World War an Imperial Defense Committee united in a rather informal way various cabi-net members in Great Britain and the Dominions, as well as other officials, around a permanent secretariat; this Committee takes a definite hand in military questions, though in a purely advisory way. During the First World War its functions were greatly expanded, and it became a "War Council," co-ordinating the war machine of Great Britain and keeping elaborate records. In the words of Lord Balfour, the Committee of Im-perial Defense provided "a continuing instrument of consultation within and without the Government Departments, the ministers responsible to the British Parliament, and, when they desire it, the ministers responsible to the Dominion Parliaments. But nowhere and under no conditions can it modify or limit parliamentary control or ministerial responsibility." It was not re-established after the Second World War.

To provide some common bond, the British have developed the same device which was so popular with seventeenth-century monarchs in central Europe: a common crown dealing with each local parliament separately. Of course, the impersonal nature of the "crown" and its complete depend-ence upon the several parliaments through parliamentary responsibility of its ministers makes such "personal union" much more precarious than it was in the past. Federal governmental structures, however, are always somewhat precarious. The greatest measure of local autonomy does not transform a common government—the confederate crown, as it has been called for the British Empire—into a federation of governments.

To come to our third organizational element of a federal system, there is finally a judicial body, the Commonwealth Tribunal (as well as the Judicial Committee of the Privy Council). Of these, the former interprets the several Dominion constitutions in relation to the law of the mother country, the latter settles justiciable disputes between the governments of the British Commonwealth. It is not a permanent court, but rather it provides the framework for the arbitral settlement of each dispute; its use is discretionary with the disputants, and membership is determined anew in each case. Students of the British Commonwealth are inclined to consider this setup another step in the direction of organizing a confederate Crown for the whole Commonwealth, because it keeps the Dominions from appealing to the Permanent Court of International Justice.

The whole situation adds up to a strange conglomeration of conflicting currents. There is clearly to be observed the emergence of institutional patterns of federalism in a governmental structure subject to marked forces of decentralization and local autonomy in certain areas. This process is of considerable interest because it contradicts an assumption often made in nineteenth-century discussions about federalism, namely, that the federal "state" is nothing but a half-way house toward a unitary "state" with an orthodox "sovereign." This assumption is owing perhaps to the unquestioning acceptance of nationalism as a permanent factor. Actually, even in these terms the manifest trend in Austria-Hungary might have cautioned a realistic observer. At any rate, it may be seriously doubted today whether the emergence of such incomplete institutional patterns of a federal structure justifies us in considering the congeries of governments comprised under the term British Empire (including the Commonwealth of Nations) as together constituting an effective common government at all. Inasmuch as the Empire was at one time a unitary government, it is, at any rate, the most striking modern illustration of a government becoming federalized. Comparable trends have appeared in the French Empire since the Second World War. To the trend from federation through federalism to unity, emphasized in the nineteenth century, we must add the opposite trend from unity toward federalism, as indeed a more extended view of history should have maintained right along.

The French Union · A development comparable to the British Commonwealth has been initiated by France in relation to her Empire. The French Union, as it has been called by the constitution makers, is embodied in Title VIII of the constitution of 1946. The earlier draft contained a considerably more advanced conception of equality of the "native" populations. It is difficult to say at this writing whether the feeble pattern of this Union will suffice to develop the added loyalties required to hold the Empire together. It is, in any case, not a true federal system, but rather mute testimony to France's inability to understand federalism. The older French tradition of granting to selected groups of natives, especially in North Africa, the rights of citizenship did not prove a very strong tie when the French home country was swept by the Nazis. Hitler's agents were very successful, as a matter of fact, in taking advantage of anti-Semitic sentiment among the Arabs and in appealing to the pride and a race consciousness of these peoples. That the Union will be able to cope with comparable pressures seems more than doubtful. How can an organization, consisting of the two representative bodies of a Council and an Assembly, both restricted to consultative and advisory functions and both containing a predominant French element, hope to arouse the enthusiasm of peoples kindled by the new "national" sentiment which is stirring Asia and Africa? As one recent writer has put it: "At best, the Constitution erects a framework, within which future federalist institutions may perhaps develop." The skill and the democratic know-how for such a development are the result of long association and depend upon deep bonds of common tradition, such as united the peoples of the Dominions (except India) with Britain. Merely a paper declaration, such as that of article 60: "The French Union shall be composed on the one hand of the French Republic which comprises Metropolitan France and the overseas departments and territories and on the other hand, of the Associated Territories and States," will not create a "people federally united, but composed of autonomous parts." It is unfortunate that this initially promising approach to colonial problems should have become entangled in the East-West conflict through Communist sponsorship of colonial aspirations. Perhaps a federally united Europe will provide a way out of the present stalemate.[18]

The Union of Europe · The loosening of the ties of the British Empire has contributed positively to the developing program of a union for Europe. The idea of a United States of Europe is an old one. It has always had a certain appeal to Americans, but until recently it seemed a Utopian proposal considering the sharpness of national rivalries on the European continent and the extent of Europe's overseas empires and commitments. The late twenties brought a very tentative proposal by Aristide Briand, fashioned in the hope of saving Europe from another war.[19] But the movement did not really get under way until 1946. The most active and energetic leadership has come from Britain and France, although the British have been divided among themselves as to how far they could afford to go in light of their Empire and Commonwealth commitments.

The movement has been greatly promoted by the danger of the Soviet expansionism; this provides the "external" stimulus so vital to federalization, as noted above. It has also been considerably stimulated by United States economic aid under the European Recovery Program, and the same power's military aid, both actual and potential, under the Atlantic Pact. Both of these programs are, of course, in turn intimately linked to the first factor, Soviet expansionism. Security and prosperity, in short, the ever-recurring objectives of modern government, are once more at the center of the whole development.

On January 28, 1949, M. Schuman, French Foreign Minister, succeeded in securing agreement on the basic French proposal of establishing a representative European assembly, and an executive council to work with it. These bodies have since been in process of organization, but their functions are not yet clearly defined or delimited. The British have tried to keep the Council of Europe confined to the role of a permanent foreign ministers' conference with consultative functions. The French, on the other hand, want a European parliament with genuine legislative functions able to take cognizance of any general European problem. For the time being, a compromise has been struck which gives Europe a representative assembly, but it is restricted to consultative work, and cannot raise issues without the unanimous consent of the council of ministers. It must be borne in mind, however, that the European OEEC, or Organization for European Economic Co-operation, with its permanent secretariat provides another very important nucleus.

It is noteworthy that the demand of the movement for a constituent assembly has not so far been met by the governments in spite of a prevailing view that "the German problem can only be solved within the framework of a United Europe." Nor is there provision for any arbitral authority so far.

The "new" federalism · Federalism, with its division of powers between central and local authorities, is a mainstay of free constitutional government. But the restraint which they exercise upon each other should not blind us to the fact that all governmental units share in the common task of accomplishing the "will of the people." Miss Jane P. Clark, in her thoughtful description of federal-state relationships,[20] has remarked that "an emphasis on separateness or rivalry tends to forward the least desirable developments in American government today." To put it thus may be to belittle the constitutional importance of divided powers; yet there is great merit in her view that "the sphere of government is increasing in its relation to life and there is a growth in both federal and state functions along a wide front." In short, there has grown up a wide area of effective co-operation between the states and the federal government which is mutually advantageous and not necessarily destructive of the broader constitutional division of powers. The federal government stands in need of the more intimate contacts with local problems in such fields as social security, while on the other hand the local authorities in the poorer sections of the country may require the financial aid of the national government. The forms which such co-operation between the federal and state governments may take are many. Grants-in-aid, federal tax credits, co-operative use of personnel, as well as agreements and formal compacts have been employed. In recent years there has been an increasing amount of dovetailing of legislation, examples of which include making federal laws contingent on state activities, suggesting model statutes, and protecting through federal legislation one state against the unfair competition of another. There is, of course, forever present a fear that fiscal aids by the federal government may turn into means of compelling state action contrary to the preferences of the people's majority in the state. Even the fact that a state has sought federal aid under such conditions is no conclusive argument against the presence of compulsion. However, a measure of gentle pressure such as we find in the field of agriculture is probably a good thing. It certainly helps to keep the country's economy on an even keel.

The trend toward concentration of economic power makes such co-operation well-nigh inescapable in the United States at present. The zone of necessary regulation which the courts have withdrawn from the federal government's authority, in spite of the fact that the economic conditions make it inaccessible to the state authorities, can thus be handled by co-operative effort. The marketing of agricultural products is an outstanding example here. Although a number of objections are raised against the federal government's use of state personnel for the administration of federal legislation, the trend has been persistently forward in that direction. The defense emergency cannot but hasten that tendency. We have here an interesting parallel to Swiss and German experience. With no such large units as Prussia or Bavaria to cope with, it is to be hoped that this country can avoid the conflicts which arose over the scope of "control" and supervision when bitterly antagonistic party factions were in power.

The broadening scope of effective co-operation between state and federal agencies obscures the difference between a closely knit federal setup and an effectively decentralized government such as that of England,—so much so that Miss Clark can foresee the day "when the character of a state is changed or modified into a kind of administrative unit to carry out federal plans and policies." The pressures and exigencies of a compact and highly industrialized national economy may force us to abandon our federal pattern. While this would undoubtedly weaken our constitutional restraints in one important respect, it need not spell the end of constitutionalism. As the example of Canada (if not of England) shows, there are other methods available. A government—even a constitutional government—has to function effectively if it is to last.

The Second World War, probably the most dangerous war the United States has so far fought, brought in its train a great many additional centralized activities. The draft, price and many rationing controls, as well as many of the directed production problems immediately growing out of the requirements of procurement for the armed services, all but swamped the American federal structure. This is perhaps nowhere as clearly visible as in the weight of the federal budget as compared with that of the states. Every citizen of the United States since 1941 has had to pay a large part of his income to the federal government while state budgets have remained relatively stable. Recently the local governments have seen a rapid increase of their expenditures, but these are due to price and wage increases rather than to expanded functions. The postwar efforts to reverse this war-induced trend have been only very partially successful. It would be a mistake, however, to declare federalism in the United States dead; in some areas the states have recaptured some of their power through more vigorous insistence upon their participation in the federal administration.

Decentralization · Local self-government had throughout the nineteenth century been a battlecry of freedom in nondemocratic countries, such as Prussia, whereas the more conservative forces have been inclined to support it under democratic conditions. These political slogans should not prevent one from recognizing decentralization as part and parcel of free institutions. In England a long series of statutes, beginning with the *Poor Law Amendment Act*, has continuously enlarged both the powers and the duties of local authorities. Through these statutory reforms, local authorities have been transformed completely, until the semi-feudal justices of the peace of before 1834 have given way to what is a system of effective civic participation in numerous matters of immediate local interest, such as health, sanitation, schools, housing, and so forth. While it is not possible here to treat of these matters at the length which they deserve, let us note the large extent to which England and other countries modeled on the English parliamentary pattern have relied upon this device so as to escape from a deadening centralism in administration.

In the United States this approach is of real significance within the states. While there is great variety throughout the Union, local authorities are not so free as in England. In fact, in some states the centralizing tendency of the state government has been marked. That two towns in Massachusetts should not be able to merge without an act of the legislature seems unfortunate. That the voting on liquor regulations should be done in Vermont towns contrary to the best judgment of town officers, because of a state statute, seems hard to believe. Federal authorities have encountered all kinds of unreasonable restrictions in securing the effective co-operation of municipal authorities because the state was found watching jealously over "its" local powers. As both state and federal powers expand in response to various novel tasks, it seems important that more effective decentralization accompany the new federalism if the citizen is to retain a measure of participation in the government. If one reads the *Federalist* or Jefferson with this in view, one cannot but discover that the state a hundred and fifty years ago was to the citizen what at best the town or city can be today.

If, from this vantage point, one were to contrast federalism and decentralization, one would find the conclusion equivocal. As long as unitary government is thought of as centralized government, there is no great difficulty in distinguishing between it and a federal structure. But what if the unitary government should be decentralized, as it has been in England or Prussia? In fact, in the latter there appeared after the war a State Council organized somewhat like the United States Senate, which gave Prussia at least one element of a federal structure (thus placing her on a level with the Netherlands, which also has an upper house of that type). Are there no distinctions between such a decentralized government and a federal one, as one distinguished scholar has recently asserted? Is it merely a matter of "the territorial composition of the state"? Can "no issues different in kind" be raised in regard to one or the other? The preceding discussion ought to have shown that the answer to these questions is in the negative, and not only in terms of "the time-honored divisions of Federalism and Local Government." The difference is precisely this, that federalism affords a constitutional sanction to the territorial division of governmental powers. On account of that sanction, the change of this division is beyond the reach of the central government. Of decentralized England it has been said that "the British system is nevertheless dominated by the idea that all legislative power is presumed to lie in the first instance in the king in Parliament and all executive power in the Crown—a twofold constitutional principle which represents the very apotheosis of centralization."[21] This is rather loose language; for English traditions of local self-government are so deeply embedded in the pattern of English constitutionalism that any major attack upon it would raise a "constitutional" issue. All that is centralized is the power over the constitution and general legislation. But even if elements of decentralization should be supported by a formal constitutional sanction, as they are in many American states, we do not have federalism unless the local units are represented as such in the representative assembly which changes the constitution (and legislates), and unless these units' powers are safeguarded by adequate arrangements for a constitutional judiciary. There is no object in laboring the distinction, however.

Conclusion: strength and weakness of federal structures of government · The foregoing shows that federalism is intimately related to modern constitutionalism, as indeed is suggested by its rise alongside of it. There is nothing in the distinction between federalism and decentralization which would imply an inherent superiority of one over the other; their advantages and disadvantages can only be contrasted in terms of the peculiar conditions of the time and place under which a particular government is supposed to operate. But federalism is an integral part of modern constitutionalism. A federal governmental structure provides a spatial or territorial, as distinguished from a functional, division of powers. Such a division operates as a rather effective restraint upon the abuse of governmental powers by the central authorities. Indeed, in many situations it is more likely to be effective than a functional division, for this, as we have seen, can be more readily overcome by the extra-constitutional activities of an effective party organization. In other words, what federalism does is to mobilize firmly entrenched local powers in support of the constitution, and to offer them protection under the constitution as well. Localized groupings are treated in a manner analogous to the treatment of the individual citizen, to whom a sphere of relative independence, of civil liberties, is likewise guaranteed. Besides these constitutional considerations, there is a great advantage in providing an opportunity for limited experimentation in one or more of the component units. However, federal structures of government share with all formalized constitutionalism the difficulty of adjusting a relatively rigid scheme to the shifting exigencies of a dynamic industrial society. Under modern conditions areas of friction are bound to develop where technological change radically alters the conditions under which government has to be conducted. If competencies are divided between the central government and the local governments, as they are in the United States, governmental functions emerge which can only be performed by one of these units, and for which no constitutional provision has yet been made.[22] The particular difficulties in the United States are at present believed to be solvable by delegating specific functions to the state governments and by making the central government one of residuary powers, but it would be a mistake to assume that the problem would thereby be solved permanently. There would presently appear situations in which the local (state) governments alone could act, and yet, under the new constitutional arrangement, only the federal government, with its residuary powers, would be constitutionally able to act. In other words, the rigidities which arise from a division of powers are inherent in the federal scheme and are the price which has to be paid for the advantages set forth above. In this respect the spatial division of powers does not differ from the functional division. In both cases a measure of inefficiency is the price for the measure of freedom which such constitutional restraints afford.

XII

Judicial Review of Legislative Acts; the Guardianship of the Constitution

Introduction · The supremacy of Parliament · The impact of federalism · Constitutional interpretation and due process · Judicial review politically restated · Judges and propertied interests · Disinterestedness and representative quality · Universality versus partisanship · European constitutional tribunals · Representative quality of judiciary uncertain · Conclusion.

Introduction · Hamilton's view that a high court of justice affords the best protection of a constitutional system[1] was a political restatement of the famous dictum of Sir Edward Coke that "Magna Charta is such a fellow that he will have no sovereign." In the days of Justice Coke, to be sure, it was the king in Parliament who seemed to threaten this "supremacy of the law." But in Hamilton's time the English Commons had pretty nearly achieved parliamentary supremacy. It therefore seemed apparent to him and to many other Americans that what was needed were limitations upon the legislative authority, irrespective of whether it was being exercised by a prince or by an elective body. A "tyranny of the majority" had loomed up in some of the states, and the makers of the Constitution sought to restrain it. The development of this power of the courts to interpret the Constitution is closely related to the doctrine of the separation of powers; yet the doctrine did not originally include it.

The origins of the idea of an independent judiciary interpreting *the* law are to be found in medieval England. As we saw (in ch. VI, pp. 104 f.), Coke and other seventeenth-century expounders of the supremacy of law claimed the right of the courts to interpret acts of Parliament according to the common law.[2] Coke's most signal conflict with King James originated in his belief that the high courts of England had the right to decide whether an act of Parliament was "legal" or not. However, this view did not triumph in England. Lip service was paid to it, though, until the end of the eighteenth century, just long enough to influence American juridical thought. By combining the Constitution as the fundamental law of the land with the common law, a great deal of common law has been worked into the American legal fabric in the course of a century and a half of judicial "interpretation" of the Constitution.

The supremacy of Parliament · In England the supremacy of law merged with the supremacy of Parliament. As a result, English legal historians have been inclined to minimize unduly the importance of Coke's position. Certainly Cromwell and his followers were, as we have seen, deeply convinced of the need for some fundamental law limiting the power of Parliament. Sir Francis Bacon, Coke's opponent on the king's side, stressed the fact that English law "is grounded on the law of nature." The idea of such a relation between natural law and parliamentary legislation, stemming from Bracton, continued down to the end of the eighteenth century, and is clearly stated by Blackstone. But it became a rather empty formula after the evolution of cabinet responsibility in the eighteenth century. That the lawyers in England never placed any considerable obstacle in the way of this development had, as is justly argued by Professor Holdsworth, very important consequences for the English constitution and English law.[3] There was, nevertheless, a great accumulation of judge-made law in England, and it was against this power of the judges that Bentham uttered his vigorous polemics in favor of statutory legislation. The issue of law-making, by whom and for whom, was also involved in the American struggle for independence. Although Americans were explicitly challenging the supremacy of parliament in their cry against "taxation without representation," the anger with which people turned against the royal judges in the provinces was a clear sign that the issue of judge-made law was likewise involved. The whole issue evidently turned upon one of those principles of a fundamental nature which Coke and his contemporaries sought to except from parliamentary legislation. As Professor McIlwain has convincingly shown, justifiable doubt could be entertained by conscientious men as to the constitutionality of these acts of Parliament.

It was natural, therefore, that the framers of the American Constitution should have been divided on the issue of legislative versus judicial power. While the conservatives, that is, authoritarian members, were particularly sensitive to the chances of arbitrary usurpations of power by a legislature, the progressive, that is, democratic, ones were disturbed about the judicial usurpations. On the Conservative side, the magistral John Adams is full of thoughts on this subject, which were shared to a greater or less degree by his contemporaries. To these men, Hamilton's doctrine was most palatable, and Justice Marshall's famous decision of *Marbury v. Madison*, reasserting it, was equally so.[4] The issue flared up into open conflict in the famous struggle between Jefferson and Marshall when Jefferson sought the impeachment of Marshall. Were these issues appreciated in Europe by those who were inspired by American constitutionalism? On the whole, very little. On the Continent, people seem always to have been greatly concerned with securing bills of rights, but to have cared little about securing sufficient legal guarantees for their enforcement. The idealists who continued to cherish the French revolutionary ideals (the *droits de l'homme*) lacked the practical judgment to appreciate the importance of institutional safeguards. European lawyers and jurists, accustomed to looking upon government and politics in terms of "the state" and of "sovereignty," began to evolve the vacuous theory of "state sovereignty." Later formalists and positivists alike denounced the natural-law tradition as incompatible with this "state sovereignty." How indeed could institutional safeguards against the "sovereign state" be conceived? Bismarck's Imperial Constitution (1871), as well as the Constitution of the Third French Republic (1875), did not even contain a "bill of rights." On the other hand, the Weimar Constitution did, and so do the new constitutions of France, Italy, and Germany (see above, ch. IX, p. 156). In spite of this development, the Continental tradition of settling questions of principle by express statutory enactment is still strong. It calls for extensive codification of such principles as freedom of speech, of assembly, and of the press; it does not favor judicial development of practice from broad constitutional rights.

The impact of federalism · In the discussion of federalism it has been shown that a constitutional judiciary is an integral part of any federal structure. If there is to be a division of powers between the central and local authorities, conflicts over the respective spheres of authority are bound to arise, and a procedure for their settlement is obviously needed. Generally speaking, this need is analogous to the need for an arbiter between authorities dividing powers functionally under some kind of separation of powers. Therefore, it is not surprising that federalism should reinforce the idea of judicial review, along with the idea of a constitution which embodies "higher" law than ordinary legislation. Though judicial review of legislative acts has disappeared completely in the English constitutional tradition, it has reappeared as part of the pattern of the Commonwealth of Nations; it has also become an integral part of federalism in several of the Dominions, even though these Dominions are governed by cabinets responsible directly to a parliament. In Australia, judicial interpretation has developed important constitutional principles and resembles the American tradition most closely. Significantly, Australia is the most markedly federal of these Dominions.

It is, of course, possible to keep such a constitutional judiciary over federal-state controversies entirely separate and distinct, as was attempted by setting up the Court of State under the Weimar Republic. Explicitly, that was the position of the United States Supreme Court. But since the

Supreme Court, unlike the German Court of State, is also a court of final appeal in matters of federal legislation, it was natural for the several functions to merge. The Supreme Court is "the ultimate organ . . . for adjusting the relationship of the individual to the separate states, of the individual to the United States, of the forty-eight states to one another, of the states to the union and of the three departments of government to one another."[5] Short of constitutional amendments it is the ultimate federal constitutional authority. And since federalism could be maintained only with difficulty without such a constitutional judiciary, it is likely to remain so. Switzerland, by contrast, failed to establish so comprehensive a judicial control. But the inherent logic of the situation was so compelling that proposals for the outright recognition of judicial review over federal legislation have become more and more insistent. Professor William Rappard, in his *L'Individu et L'État*, shows pretty clearly that such efforts are rooted in part in a desire to curb the collectivism which Swiss democracy has increasingly adopted. It is doubtful whether a judicial body can serve as the moderating influence between rival groups and classes if it is thus recognized as a partisan instrument. Even so deep-rooted a federalism as that of Switzerland may be insufficient to insulate such a judicial body against the more apparent forms of partisanship.

In their provisional constitution or Basic Law, the Germans have not only revived the jurisdiction of the Court of State, but have merged this jurisdiction with that over other problems of constitutional interpretation in establishing a Federal Constitutional Court (art. 93).

Constitutional interpretation and due process · It would, of course, be vain to pretend that the American Courts, and more especially the Supreme Court, had not in fact been partisan. The whole setting predisposes them toward a conservative position (see ch. VI). To this setting must be added the distinct policy of conservatives, initiated by Adams and Marshall, to maintain control of the Court. In our own day, the great property interests have certainly been more alert to the Court's extraordinary importance in affecting the balance of interests and classes than have been the progressives. As William Howard Taft once wrote, in justifying his staying on the Court: ". . . I must stay on the Court in order to prevent the Bolsheviki from getting control . . ." At another time Taft said (in the presidential election of 1920): ". . . there is no greater domestic issue than the maintenance of the Supreme Court as a bulwark to enforce the guaranty that no man shall be deprived of his property without due process of law."[6] The Court, then, is likely to be on the conservative side. Recognition of this fact must be coupled, however, with the further recog-

225

nition that the public at large believes the Court to be relatively non-partisan. This belief is part of the belief in the Constitution which makes the Constitution a political force (see ch. IX).

There are three levels of political insight into the constitutional and political function of a high court: (1) the court interprets the constitution, the norms of the constitution being as clear as a mathematical equation (popular view); (2) the court is an instrument of party politics, it decides according to the political views of the judges, it is anti-democratic (political view); (3) the court is the high priesthood of the faith in constitutionalism, it rationalizes the new norm in terms of the old and thereby maintains continuity, if not consistency; in short, it arbitrates between the fundamental and ever-present rival forces under a constitutional system. It is this third level of insight which recognizes fully the function of a high court as an interpreter and guardian of the sacred word symbols that hold many men and many minds together in one organized community. As Mr. Justice Jackson put it, when he was still Attorney-General, "the Court keeps the most fundamental equilibriums of our society, such as that between centralization and localism, between liberty and authority, and between stability and progress."[7] At any rate, the Court *should* keep such an equilibrium. There is ever present the danger that its members become ensnared in their own logic, and in the effort to maintain the sacred words attempt to throttle life and life's progress. The Court, at such times, shifts from a conservative to a reactionary position. When it does, the future of constitutionalism is in jeopardy. In the *Dred Scott* decision, the Supreme Court held that there could be no compromise between the old and the new, between the maintenance of slavery and its abolition; the Civil War followed as a natural consequence, since an amendment to the Constitution to override the decision was impossible on account of the distribution of voting strength.

In the decades prior to 1937, the Court had been inclined to find ways to narrow some of the powers conferred by the Constitution upon the federal government, and more particularly Congress, such as the taxing power, while at the same time it broadened the meaning of limitations such as "due process." Due process provides in many ways the most interesting illustration of the working of constitutional interpretation. When the Constitution was adopted, its meaning was strictly procedural: in compelling public officials to act in accordance with established rules of procedure, it served a clear constitutional purpose; it prevented arbitrary imprisonments, seizure of possessions, and the like. It was not until after the Civil War that due process began to assume the substantive meaning which it has been given since. First through obiter dicta and dissenting opinions, finally in the decision of *Lochner v. the People of New York*, "a constitutional doctrine contrived to protect the natural rights of men against corporate monopoly was little by little commuted into a formula for safeguarding the domain of business against the regulatory power of the state."[8] In vain did Mr. Justice Holmes register his famous protest that a "constitution is not intended to embody a particular economic theory, whether of paternalism . . . or of laissez-faire . . ." But the wonder is not that business interests were given verbal protection under the constitutional roof, but that the protection was so vague and insecure. For the real forces molding the evolution of the doctrine of due process were generated by the development of large corporations, vast economic powers which found themselves challenged by a government whose decisions a democratic ideology seemed to make legitimate beyond dispute. The conservatism of the law held out against these forces of a new industrial revolution; forever it remained troubled by the old doctrines which gave government sweeping powers over public safety, public health, public morals, and public welfare. These powers are deeply rooted in the established objectives of modern government (see chs. III–VI). Far from frankly espousing the revolutionary forces which challenged these ancient governmental powers, the Court continually sought to hold back, to conserve and balance the old and the new. It was only in our own day, when the Court became dogmatic about the doctrine of due process which it had so hesitantly evolved, that it threatened seriously to upset the equilibrium. But when President Roosevelt poignantly reminded them of the fact that their position was no more than what the Constitution and the laws, that is, the people, made it, the judges beat a hasty retreat. Soon after the Reorganization Bill was introduced in 1937, the Court began to reverse its dogmatic stand by holding the National Labor Relations Act constitutional (almost too soon for dignity's sake). It confirmed the quip of Theodore Roosevelt: "I may not know much about law, but I do know one can put the fear of God into judges." In the period since then, the Supreme Court has considerably broadened Congressional power. Due process has not been employed to hold legislation unconstitutional which limits property rights. "Since 1937," one leading authority remarks, "due process has been more frequently the basis for holding interferences with civil liberties invalid than in any previous period of our history."[9]

In his famous treatise on the Common Law, Justice Holmes wrote many years ago: "The life of law has not been logic; it has been experience. The felt necessities of the time, the prevalent moral and political theories, intuitions of public policy, avowed or unconscious, even the prejudices which judges share with their fellowmen, have had a good deal more to do than the syllogism in determining the rules by which men should be governed. The law embodies the story of a nation's development through many centuries, and it cannot be dealt with as if it contained only the axioms and corollaries of a book of mathematics. In order to know what it is, we must know what it has been and what it tends to become." That is a beautiful statement of the deeper insight into the function of courts and judicial interpretation.

Constitutional interpretation is not limited to the courts; other departments of the government, though less highly placed in the priesthood of constitutionalism, share in this important function. To illustrate, the American pocket veto resulted from inaction on the part of the President; the Senate pressed for and the President conceded senatorial influence over appointments, known as the senatorial courtesy; the French Parliament, in 1924 and 1926, authorized the executive to modify by decree (*décret-lois*) existing laws, thus interpreting in a very controversial manner the provision of Article I, § 1 of the constitutional law of February 25, 1875, which provided that the legislative power shall be exercised by two assemblies: the Chamber of Deputies and the Senate. Analogous steps have been taken in many other countries during times of crisis demanding prompt action. (See Chapter XXVI for a discussion of such emergency government.) But the question we are here concerned with is primarily that of judicial review of legislative acts, viewed as a technique for preventing such "interpretations" from going beyond a reasonable point. By judicial review, in other words, the judicial sanction is denied to measures, even of the legislature composed of the representatives of the people, which according to the manifest meaning of the constitution are void. The crucial question, however, is that which inquires: "To whom is this meaning of the constitution manifest?"

Judicial review politically restated · The institution of judicial review substitutes the judgment of judges for the judgment of the elected representatives of the people whenever doubt exists regarding the full meaning of a constitutional provision. It is *not* a question of the *manifest tenor*, as Marshall maintained, but on the contrary a question of the doubtful meaning of various constitutional provisions, or the actual lack of any provision.[10] Courts have been in the habit of obscuring the bare truth of this statement by arguing about the "intention of the framers." But doubt usually has arisen where no intention was indicated in the debates. Indeed, how could the framers of the Constitution in the "horse-and-buggy" age possibly have had any intention concerning interstate commerce as it has developed in the age of railroad, steamship, automobile, and airplane? A striking case of this kind is the welfare clause in the American Constitution. That clause provides that "Congress shall have power—To lay and collect taxes, duties, imposts, and excises; to pay the debts and provide for the common defense and general welfare of the United States." In view of the semicolon, the courts have construed this clause narrowly, and on the whole have shied away from admitting that the taxing power might be used for the "general welfare." "It could not have been the intention of the framers . . ." ran the argument. Recent historical research, however, has brought to light the fact that the text of the Constitution which Washington signed had a comma and that the semicolon was entered by a clerk afterward. What, then, was the intention of the framers? Or take the case of the delegation of legislative powers to the executive departments. Under the National Industrial Recovery Act of 1933, the power to prescribe rules of conduct was delegated to the President and the representatives of various enterprises; this was later held to be a violation of Article I, 1 of the Constitution which forbade the delegation of legislative power. The court, in sustaining this argument, observed that there existed an old maxim of the Roman law that *potestas delegata non potest delegari*, that is, that a delegated power must not be delegated further. Since the legislative power, the argument runs on, is delegated by the constitution-making power to the legislature, the legislature cannot delegate it further. But were the framers of the constitution aware of this maxim of the Roman law? And has this maxim any application to a constitutionally delegated power, when it was originally evolved to maintain the hierarchy of Roman officials intact? These questions the courts do not ask, and do not answer, except by the cryptic statement that there is nothing to indicate that the framers did not intend it thus.

Judges and propertied interests · Those who, from Jefferson to La Follette, have attacked judicial review have argued that judges are conservative folk, and that the judicial attitude of mind is ill-adapted to the solution of problems which require striking out along new paths.[11] Judges sitting on the high courts are advanced in years. Though some brilliant work has been done by very old men, it is natural that a man should think in terms of a society with which he is familiar. If society is undergoing rapid change, it puts an elderly judge behind the times. It has often been pointed out by more radical reformers that judges are, through their training and upbringing, closely linked with the propertied interests. This may have thrown them on the side of the revolutionary middle classes in the days of Coke, when these classes were battling the king and his feudal landowning aristocracy. For many years, it put them with the big business interests opposed to the reforms desired by farmers and workers. Recently, however, a frank recognition of this problem has produced a marked change. No one familiar with the personnel of the United States Supreme Court in 1948 would charge them with excessive partiality to property.

Judges whose primary function it is to settle controversies between contending private parties when they disagree about the meaning of the law (see above, ch. VI) must in the nature of things be very careful to be consistent, lest the community feel themselves subjected to quite arbitrary rulings. All judicial systems are, therefore, careful in observing precedents at least within their jurisdiction. This practice in itself acts as a conservative force. It generates a habit of mind which turns to the past for guidance and counsel. This type of "reasoning" is not very helpful in dealing with distinctly *new* problems of a social or economic type. They require a scientific attitude of mind which is not authoritarian, but anti-authoritarian, which does not seek guidance from the past, but distrusts it. In support of precedent it is further urged that any new departure must be supported by a good show of supporting reason. This, however, is equally true of scientific work.[11] Still, a more or less public exposition of the reasons which led a court to decide as it did helps to settle the controversy by appealing to the reason of the losing litigant. It also serves the important legal and political function of holding the legal rules together so that they are something more than isolated bits, even if they do not, from a realistic point of view, constitute a coherent legal system.*

Disinterestedness and representative quality · As noted earlier, the judicial and scientific attitudes have one very important aspect in common, their "disinterestedness," or rather, their effort to be disinterested. It is admittedly easier to be detached when the issues are not of the human sphere. An economist studying the incidence of a certain tax and a judge deciding a case involving the conflict of interests between management and labor must both strive to detach themselves from their own personal bias.[12] This they can only do by realizing what that bias is presumably going to be. If they find themselves habitually on the side of management, they must be particularly suspicious of any conclusion which seems to favor management. To accomplish this is admittedly a great moral as well as intellectual achievement, and many, if not all, judges and social scientists fail at times to live up to this standard. The extent to which they do so, and are believed

*These two functions of legal reasoning are more or less impaired if judicial language becomes highly technical and incomprehensible to anybody but a trained lawyer. It will be found that the very great lawyer-judges, like Marshall, have usually been distinguished by a very lucid style. This lucidity may hide serious logical defects, but it serves the political functions just the same, as long as these defects are not discovered by any but very astute minds.

to do so, profoundly affects their political role. The willing acceptance of judicial review in the United States has been due to the fact that the community has had faith in the comparative disinterestedness of the judges composing it. This faith gave the Supreme Court a truly representative character, even though (or perhaps rather because) it was not elective and therefore not so obviously partisan. In countries where the courts do not possess that representative quality they cannot readily assume the arbitral function of interpreting the constitution.

From this standpoint, the tendency of the Europeans to make their new constitutional courts either elective *by* or outright committees *of* the legislature must be viewed very critically. In France, there is only a "Constitutional Committee" which determines "whether the laws passed by the National Assembly require a revision of the constitution" (art. 91). In Italy, a constitutional court is provided for, with the authority to declare laws unconstitutional (art. 137). The court, except in impeachment cases, is manned by lawyers, and under an implementing law, both parties to a controversy, as well as the lower courts, can bring action before this court. In the Basic Law of Germany, the Constitutional Court is to consist of judges and others elected by the two legislative bodies, each electing half of them. No member may belong to a governmental or legislative body. Thus, the German provisions go farthest in the direction of establishing a genuine court, certainly much farther than the earlier provisions of their several *Land* constitutions. But they are still frankly "political," at least in part.

Universality versus partisanship · When the case between a court and a legislature is put on the ground that one is elected by the people and the other not, as is still done in most French and English textbooks, the elected legislature appears to be "representative," the court "aristocratic." But once the legislature is viewed as divided into parties, its representative quality is seen to be of a more limited kind; for such majorities change, and the more universal and lasting aspects of community life may well require additional symbols (see ch. XIV). A court composed of the highest legal talent in the community, on the other hand, may often be representative of the community's beliefs as to what is just in a more real and universal sense.

But why should the ordinary courts be entrusted with this particular duty? Would it not be more in keeping with all angles of the problem if a separate body were set up to handle these thorny questions? The great French revolutionary politician, Abbé Siéyès, thought so, and accordingly expounded the idea of a constitutional jury in his famous speech before the

Convention on the 2nd of *Thermidor* of the year III.[13] The distinction between the amending power and the legislative power requires, he held, a guardian of the constitution. But this guardian cannot be the judicial power; it must be a special political representative body. "I demand," he said, "a jury of the constitution . . . or constitutional jury. This jury must be a real body of representatives which I demand should have the special mission (function) of judging all protests against any infringement of the constitution. . . . If you wish to give a safeguard to the constitution, a salutary curb which keeps each representative action within the limits of its special function, then establish a constitutional jury!" But no one heeded his advice. It was, of course, extreme in its rationalist disregard of political reality; the partisanship of the members of elected bodies. Curiously enough, this idea of a constitutional jury was supposed to be realized in the form of the *Senat Conservateur* of the year VIII. But of course its functions as the guardian of the constitution remained on paper under the autocratic rule of the first Napoleon. It is obvious that the new Constitutional Committee is derived from Siéyès' idea of a constitutional jury.

European constitutional tribunals · This idea of a special body charged with safeguarding the constitution had already gained much adherence in countries engaged in establishing new constitutions after the First World War. In Republican Austria, Germany, and Czechoslovakia, special courts were set up under the constitutions to examine the constitutionality of legislation. In Germany this court was primarily concerned with conflicts over jurisdiction between governmental authorities. The European concept of a "public corporation" offered, however, an entering wedge for extending the jurisdiction of these courts. Thus in Germany, parties were admitted as litigants before the Court of State in contesting an election procedure, and elections in certain states were actually held null and void because the election procedure did not correspond with the requirements of the national constitution. In Austria, under the constitution of 1929, a constitutional court was organized to deal with the constitutionality of laws, while the ordinary courts only had the authority to examine the formal aspects of proper publication, etc. Article 140 provided that the constitutional court might "suspend" laws which violated the constitution. In other words, the law was not declared null and void, as in the United States, but while contrary to law yet was legally binding until so suspended. This meant that only certain paragraphs might be so suspended, and that the suspension might be fixed for a later date than that of the court's decision. These provisions strikingly illustrate the different approach of Continental jurists to the entire problem of law and judicial review. More especially, the individual litigant is not recognized as entitled to contest the constitutionality of a law. This special issue proved to be the most difficult problem in connection with efforts of American Military Government to secure judicial sanctions for civil liberties, both under *Land* and federal constitutional reforms in Germany.[14] The functions of these bodies, then, while charged with guarding the constitution, are not to be confused with judicial review as practised in the United States. Nor are plans like that of Switzerland which provide for judicial settlement of conflicts between cantonal legislation and the federal and cantonal constitutions to be confused with the broad scope of American judicial review. Is the establishment of such bodies to be preferred to judicial review, that is, the power of *all* courts to inquire into the validity of national statutes under a constitution? Siéyès, in affirming this proposition, rested his case upon the idea that such a body would be political and representative. The American practice of judicial review, in denying the proposition, brings out that the courts, on the whole, are unpolitical and yet representative. On the whole, the judicial courts which a constitutional order inherits from the past are the residuary legatees of a great deal of power over the minds of the community, commanding much traditional respect and loyalty. French and German authorities opposing judicial review in their countries have rightly insisted that "in order to attribute to the courts so delicate and important a role, it is necessary above all else that the judiciary possess a very high authority: it is necessary that the people have a profound confidence in its wisdom and its professional and scientific standard." If this be accepted, there arises at once the objection that such function of interpreting the constitution, when attributed to the courts, will in time undermine their standing by making them partisan.

It is noteworthy that the Christian Democrats have been the protagonists of the broadening of judicial powers in France, Italy, and Germany. The efforts of the MRP during the constitutional convention in France were directed toward the establishment of something that might have been a genuine Supreme Constitutional Court. But, as one writer puts it, the Socialists were "obsessed by the memory of Roosevelt's struggle with the Supreme Court, [and hence] were determined to avoid any mechanism which might obstruct future social and economic reforms." It may seem strange that what happened under an eighteenth century individualist constitution should worry anyone concerning the future policies possible under a twentieth century constitution for a planned economy (*économie dirigée*), but it testifies to the continued absence of any real grasp of what has been called the "most characteristic, the most unique political institution" of the United States.

Representative quality of judiciary uncertain · Broadly speaking, it can be said that the question of how representative a judiciary a country possesses is a question of fact. The more deeply the community's respect for the courts is rooted, the less dangerous it is for such courts to assume the arbitral function of ultimate constitutional interpretation. This is particularly true if a workable amending process offers hope to the discontented that they may alter provisions in the constitution which irk them. The courts do not enjoy such an unqualified respect in those areas of Europe where the Marxist labor movement is strong. For according to Karl Marx's class-war doctrine, the courts are nothing but camouflaged exponents of the bourgeois class aiding in the exploitation of the toiling masses. In other words, they dispense class justice, instead of mass justice. It is evident that whenever such opinions have wide currency, general confidence in the "disinterestedness" of the judiciary will decline.[15] If courts under such conditions are called upon to decide cases which involve the "interpretation" of constitutional provisions, which may be partly socialist and partly not, the ensuing controversies will further undermine their position, no matter which way they decide. If, moreover, many of the judges are held over from a previous regime, and kept because of the principle of judicial tenure during good behavior, the loyalty of the courts to the new government may also become suspect. Such a situation developed in the United States when the Supreme Court declared a series of New Deal statutes unconstitutional. The issue was brought out into the open when Roosevelt proposed legislation to alter the composition of the Court. Violent partisan passions were aroused and conventional party lines collapsed as conservatives amongst Democrats as well as Republicans arose "to defend the Constitution." The President was accused of seeking "to pack the Court." A hallowed symbol of constitutional government appeared to be under attack, and many foes of the President's reforms saw clear proof of "dictatorship." So the plan was defeated; yet it had served the *political* purpose of calling attention to the Court's *political* position. Once the community had become conscious of the social and economic cleavage which divided it, the Court's representative quality was impaired by the mere fact of its identification with one side of partisan controversy. This reaction, however, was temporary. The country soon settled back into its traditional acceptance of the Supreme Court as the ultimate arbiter of its constitution, the more so since Roosevelt was able to alter profoundly the actual composition of the Court through entirely legitimate replacements. Since 1937 the Court has been rather partial to economic and social reform. Thus the crisis of the Roosevelt era has taken its place alongside many another political storm which the Supreme Court has weathered.[16]

We have mentioned the economic class conflicts first among the conditions depriving courts of their representative quality because they happen to be in the foreground of popular attention today, and they appear wherever modern industrialism prevails. But other basic cleavages can have the same disruptive result. Thus national minorities will rarely accept the decision of a court manned by the majority as rendering "disinterested" justice. They will always suspect partisanship on the part of a judge of the other nationality. Therefore a supreme court could not hope to be the effective guardian of a constitution which undertook to guarantee minority rights. None but an international tribunal or a mixed arbitral body containing members of their own nationality will be able to satisfy such a national minority. In other words, the actual disunity of the political community cannot be neutralized by even the most liberal-looking constitutional provisions or by stringent judicial safeguards.

Both these examples, but more particularly the economic class division, indicate that the political scientist is really confronted with a problem quite distinct from that outlined by Hamilton in the *Federalist*. There the entire emphasis is on which of the three powers will be least likely to extend its authority on its own initiative. Hamilton's conclusion has stood the test of a century, and there is not much actual fact which would oblige us to question it today. Hamilton, of course, in the fashion of his day, did not consider the function of parties under popular government. Yet, it is well known that the contest between the executive and the judicial power did not commence until the party issue was injected under Jefferson and Marshall. At that time, too, it was a matter of economic group interests. Marshall was an exponent of eastern business and manufacturing interests, while Jefferson fought for the southern and western farmer. However, the issues and the conflict were kept in bounds. These group interests did not crystallize into dogmatic and mutually exclusive positions. Nor have they done so in America at the present time. Still, the court is believed to be divided (as, of course, it actually is) into progressives and conservatives, and their respective balance is a matter of public controversy and great political pressure, as it used to be before the Civil War in connection with proslavery and antislavery members. Under such conditions the confidence of the community in the court is considerably shaken. A wise court with a sound tradition will seek to check that decline in public esteem by avoiding extreme positions on the most controversial issues. It may cease to perform the function of being guardian of the constitution when it accepts the "interpretation" of the legislature. Counterbalancing that, the legislature may try to avoid enacting measures which are too palpably beyond any conceivable "interpretation" of the existing constitution.

Conclusion · The political technique of judicial review can be employed only where considerable confidence in the integrity of the courts is generally entertained by the people at large. On the other hand, no "constitutional jury" other than such a judiciary will be sufficiently neutral and detached to exercise effectively the functions of a guardian of the constitution. We must conclude, therefore, that in the absence of a constitution deeply rooted in tradition, such as exists in England, Switzerland, or Sweden, a judiciary capable of exercising judicial review will be required if a constitution in the political sense of a set of techniques for restraining the actions of government is to be established. Only through the neutralizing and rationalizing influence of such judicial interpretation will the various interests, groups, and classes in the community be kept sufficiently balanced. Even such a judiciary may not be able to accomplish it. It is a wholesome sign of the strengthening of constitutionalism in Europe that the new constitutions in Western Europe all endeavor to establish some sort of judicial review of legislative acts. The extent of these efforts seems to stand in inverse relation to their experience with totalitarianism. In light of the history of the institution, it seems natural enough that those who have felt most intensely the results of the loss of constitutionalism should be most concerned with securing it against future undermining by anticonstitutionalist forces.

XIII

Local Self-Government and Grass-Roots Democracy

Introduction: Grass roots and the common man · Political philosophers on the best size of towns · John Dewey's approach · Growth of local governmental functions · The British tradition · Alternative patterns: (1) Great Britain, (2) France, (3) Switzerland, (4) Germany, (5) United States · Metropolitan problems · Middletown and Yankee City · Conclusion.

Introduction: Grass roots and the common man · The violent upheavals of our time have revived interest in the local community. Its importance for the functioning of constitutional government is common knowledge. But the local community has proved surprisingly resistant to the pressures of totalitarian government. When the Nazi armies conquered France and the central government of the Third Republic was swept away, the tradition of French life found refuge in the villages and small towns, where intimacy of personal contacts enabled people to know friend and foe. Again, when the conquering armies of the West had completely destroyed the government and party of Hitler, older and better German tradition re-emerged in the local communities. Local government turned out to be more disaster-proof than the broader, more far-flung structures of state and nation.

During the turmoil of the last great depression, a phrase became popular which was meant to express this foundational aspect of local government and the local community: grass-roots democracy. It was often used with conservative implications; as contrasted with the swiftly changing scene of national politics and the popular majorities which were presumably supporting these policies, "democracy at the grass roots" was supposed to represent the steady and persistent outlook of Americans in the local community, especially in the rural community with its settled ways.

Perhaps the most striking document of our time describing the rediscovery of the "small town" was written by a literary critic of distinction who had been deeply sympathetic with the outlook of Marx and Marxism. Granville Hicks, in *Small Town*, has recorded his experiences as a national and world-minded "intellectual" in trying to participate effectively in the self-government of a village in upstate New York. He concludes it with a highly significant reminder that such self-government constantly demands

237

that the reader make concrete what, for the "intellectual," is general and abstract: "As I write this, I think of the meeting of the board of fire commissioners that I must attend in a few hours. The outcome may be good or bad; all I can predict is that a considerable amount of time will be wasted in unnecessary talk. However it appears to be my job as much as it is any man's. . . . As a matter of fact, I expect to enjoy parts of the evening, as I have enjoyed parts—and rather large parts—of the whole experience with which this book has dealt." This outlook is part of the perspective, the slant, that this intellectual acquired when he learned that the resistances to proposed changes are not the product of stupidity. "People take what they can use without surrendering their way of life."[1]

Any thorough analysis of the way in which the "common man" participates in common concerns of the community will disclose that he hesitates to assent to what he does not understand. Hence his inclination to vote for persons, rather than policies, when it comes to national and international affairs. There are recurrent important exceptions, but as a general propensity it holds true in all Western countries. As a matter of fact, a certain amount of genuine local autonomy makes for a diversity; one community stresses public parks and other kinds of landscape beauty, another stresses schools, still another public safety. All these objectives have to be given some attention in every modern community, but there is considerable leeway as to emphasis, and the common man is able to make the decision. Whether to extend the town water line down in a certain direction and gain the added fire protection will be of vital concern to all citizens, for it will affect the future growth of the town. The decision they make may seem unwise from the standpoint of the expert town planner, the architect, the engineer—but if so, the citizens will discover it in time and they may learn a vital lesson in self-government. Popular government includes the right of the people, through their majority, to make mistakes.

Political philosophers on the best size of towns · Discussions about the optimal size of a community have been part of political philosophy since Plato and Aristotle. In keeping with their attachment to the city-state or polis of classical antiquity, these philosophers talked in terms of an independent community or state. Believing that a well-governed polis must rest upon a foundation of common beliefs, of shared convictions regarding what is right and wrong, and that such sharing presupposed leadership of the personal intimacy which the modern world has come to associate with churches, both Plato and Aristotle believed that the community, for good living, should be quite small. It should be small enough for everyone to know everyone else, Plato pointed out in his *Laws*, and he urged a regular system of festivals and rituals in order to acquaint the citizens with each other and to teach them a sense of mutual obligation. On the basis of such knowledge about each other, sound decisions could be arrived at concerning who should serve in public offices and similar matters. Both he and Aristotle suggested that 1000 citizens, i. e., about 6000 inhabitants, would be the best size; only in his *Laws*, in which generally, as an old man, he makes concessions to practicality, is Plato willing to go as high as about 5000 citizens, i. e., 30,000 inhabitants.[2] Growth of a city which goes beyond this, as had that of Athens in the fifth century B.C., when it reached perhaps 300,000, Plato condemned as disruptive of sound communal life and order.

The discussion of the best size for a city was resumed in the later Middle Ages, when the works of Aristotle were studied anew. Philosophers like St. Thomas seemed inclined to follow Aristotle's lead, in spite of the fact that the modern territorial state was in the making, containing many times the inhabitants Plato and Aristotle had thought right. In the Renaissance, the city-states of Italy, the Low Countries, and Germany played such a vital role that their size, not too different from that of the city-states of classical Greece (Florence, with perhaps 40,000 inhabitants in 1470, Cologne, with about 30,000 at the same time), seemed to support the contentions of the ancient philosophers. Toward the end of the sixteenth century, writers like G. Botero, J. Bodin, and J. Althusius became increasingly realistic about describing the growth of cities in relation to their location but continued to stress the importance of keeping size under control. But during the succeeding century, when the large territorial kingdoms definitely became the communities in terms of which the Western nation-state was conceived and governed, philosophers tried to find a basis in nature and reason for abstract law which was to regulate the relations between individuals as well as with the government. The close community corresponding to the old city was that of the monarchical court—but in contrast to these trends under absolutism England preserved the local autonomy of its towns and counties sufficiently to serve as a basis for her growing representative institutions. It was the French philosopher Montesquieu who clearly recognized and appropriately stressed the importance of this English tradition for the viability of her constitutional system. According to him, the intermediate powers, moribund in France under her despotic government, were the tap-root of freedom and constitutionalism. But it was Jean Jacques Rousseau, citizen of one of Switzerland's small cantons, Geneva, who dogmatically asserted once more, like Plato and Aristotle, that a "state" in order to be free and popular must be as small as a Swiss canton.[3]

John Dewey's approach · In 1927, John Dewey, after exploring the decline of democracy and the eclipse of the public, turned to the local community as the place where both might be reborn. For the troubled pessimism of Walter Lippmann's *Phantom Public* (as well as earlier studies), John Dewey sought to substitute a pragmatic ethic of neighbourly co-operation in *The Public and Its Problems*.[4] Dewey thought that the democratic public, still largely inchoate and unorganized, could not adequately resolve its most urgent problem: to find and identify itself. Perhaps it would be more in keeping with historical facts to say that this public is "increasingly" inchoate; it certainly was less so in earlier times than in mid-twentieth century America. If that is borne in mind, Dewey's entreaty that "democracy must begin at home, and its home is the neighbourly community," has a rather unpragmatic ring. For more than two thousand years, as we have just seen, philosophers have urged that the community should be small; yet for some centuries now, communities have been growing larger and more inclusive—having done the same in classical antiquity. At the very time of Aristotle's plea, the territorial dominion of Alexander the Great was superseding the small city-state, to be succeeded in turn by the Roman Empire.

But regardless of the homily, Dewey is undoubtedly right, if not very original, when he insists that only in the intimate contact of the neighborhood can the public, that is the mass of common men and women, become articulate. If this neighborly community is to be revived, it is important to understand the causes of its decline. The ideal which Dewey and other philosophers have portrayed is far from being a true description. In many American localities, hard-bitten machines are run by county sheriffs and town assessment boards. Fear and greed often play a greater role in the small community, with its weapons of social ostracism and personal discrimination, than in the more inclusive communities. Certainly Lord Bryce was rash in simply correlating the growth of machines to size. Genuine democratic constitutionalism calls for disagreement, open expression of conflicting views and responsiveness to divergent interests, as we have seen. The overemphasis on agreement which the philosophic partisans of the small community from Plato to Rousseau and Dewey have indulged in corresponds to boss rule rather than constitutional freedom. But whatever one's view concerning this aspect of the problem, the question as to the causes of the decline remains.

Unfortunately, several of these causes are so intimately linked with the development of modern industrialism that only very determined efforts to counteract them will have the desired result. If we agree with Dewey that "there is no substitute for the vitality and depth of close and direct intercourse and attachment," we have to ask how we may resolve such complex problems as the following: How can we induce the metropolitan cities to devolve into many smaller communities (see below, pp. 252 ff.); how can we provide adequate substitutes for the deep attachment which life-long membership in a local community gives, but which present-day mobility prevents; how can we counteract the constant expansion of central (federal and state) functions, impinging on every side upon the local autonomy (see above, pp. 216 ff.)? In view of such questions and in view of present trends, quite a few students of these problems incline toward abandoning any such attempts at reviving the dying local community, and instead tend to recognize the professional group, the trade union, and similar associations as providing that "direct and close intercourse"; they make these units the "living communities" of twentieth century man.[5]

In any case, the insistence upon the importance of direct intercourse is based upon the conviction that "the essential need is the improvement of the methods and conditions of debate, discussion and persuasion." Dewey's belief in this need rests upon his unqualified belief in the *rationality* of the citizen. He feels that it is easy to exaggerate the amount of intelligence and ability which may be required to judge the bearing upon common concerns of the knowledge, supplied by experts. He therefore pleads with the reader to help do away with secrecy, prejudice, bias, misrepresentation, and propaganda. The plea appeals to the idealism of the reader; but is it pragmatically based upon an understanding of how human relations actually work?[6] All Dewey thinks we need is greater publicity. This may be so; but how are we to get it? More concrete studies such as *Small Town*, *Middletown*, and *Yankee City* suggest that a more realistic understanding of the actual working of local communities calls for a reassessment of such rationalist appeals. Too much has been taken for granted in regard to the actual working of "democracy at the grass roots." New institutional safeguards are needed to reinforce the legal and constitutional position of these foundations of the constitutional order. But only a survey of what the comparative situation is in various constitutional systems will provide a firm ground from which to start efforts at reconstruction.

Growth of local governmental functions · The recognized growth of governmental functions at the national level has tended to obscure the parallel development of ever-wider local governmental functions. Actually, the technology of modern industrialism has produced many wants and needs which are of peculiar importance to local government. Thus, the rapid improvement in all kinds of motor-driven vehicles has challenged local communities by making available superior fire-fighting or snow-removal equipment. These matters often become simply problems of dollars and cents, comparatively. Thus, the increase in the tax rate resulting from the acquisition of such fire-fighting equipment may be balanced or outweighed by the reduction in fire-insurance rates which the householders have to pay, with a net saving for the citizen-owner. While the saving in automobile repairs which may be traced to more efficient snow-removal equipment may be more elusive, it may yet appeal to a community alert to technical progress.

Generally speaking, there has been a rapid increase in the number and quality of local functions, though in many countries, notably Britain, this increase has been associated with a decline in local independence and judgment. Recently, in Britain, it has been proposed to centralize by 1952 assessments of property for local taxes in a national revenue authority; such a move would remove the "power of the purse" entirely, limited as it is in Britain as compared with the United States. Nevertheless, it is true that the increase in technical services could mean that local self-government is of vital concern to the average citizen. Water supply, fire protection, sanitation, welfare, roads, gas and electricity, parks, libraries, building regulations and town planning, housing, and transportation are certainly matters which concern the daily well-being of the common man (and the uncommon one as well!) very greatly. If to these are added, as they must be in the United States, education and police functions, it is clear that active citizen participation in all these matters means tangible, concrete self-government.

The great problem is how to maintain local control over these varied services. Here the availability of adequate financial resources is of vital importance. The student of constitutional government has cause to regret the rigidity characteristic of most modern constitutional systems in this matter. In many American as well as European communities, the property tax on real estate is overworked and has caused the blight of central urban areas which provide many services for out-of-towners from the surrounding suburban areas and countryside. This in turn has given rise to various artificial devices, often highly undesirable from a social standpoint, such as sales taxes and other kinds of consumption taxes. These taxes fall with almost equal weight upon rich and poor alike. Yet so simple a device as a percentage addition to the state income tax is "constitutionally" prohibited.

Related to this problem of fiscal autonomy is the problem of optimal size. Functions are related to size. While a community of 10,000 inhabitants may be able to acquire a bulldozer for snow-removal purposes, a community of 2500 may not be able to do so. There has been a tendency in European countries, for example, in Britain, to decree alterations in size by legislative fiat. The *Local Government Boundary Commission*, an administrative body which in recent years exercised this discretionary legislative authority delegated to it by parliament, which retained vague supervisory control and could act on appeal (it was abolished in 1948), was reported to favor local government units of approximately 200,000. Communities of this size are clearly too large for effective sharing of experience. It is both characteristic and a bit alarming that the criteria which this body stresses are efficiency and economy; the problems of democracy and constitutionalism are placed in the background. Effective co-operation of several local communities through joint boards is more cumbersome, but it is probably sounder when effective citizen participation is considered.

The British tradition · Ever since Montesquieu wrote his praise of British constitutionalism and stressed the importance of the "intermediate powers" of local authorities, it has been customary to think of Britain as the home of local self-government. Yet in the strict modern sense there was very little self-government in the local sphere in Britain from the end of the Middle Ages to the nineteenth century. In towns and counties, in parishes and districts, the local gentry shared with the nobility and the patricians the privilege of government, largely upon appointment by the crown. To be sure, the crown chose these local authorities from among the local gentry, a natural thing, considering that the basis of parliamentary bodies was the corporate entity of county and town (the towns being greatly over-represented). Yet the fact remains that their authority, whether judicial, military, or ecclesiastical, was closely linked to the king and his ministers. It may be quite wrong to say, as has recently been done, that "the Justices of the Peace . . . exercised a benevolent dictatorship," for what these justices of the peace and other local officers could and did do was based strictly upon parliamentary authorization.[7] Yet the crucial characteristic of modern self-government, namely, the election of local officials by local popular vote, was restricted within narrow confines and was in any case only participated in by the property owners of substance.

Nevertheless, this British tradition of entrusting the local concerns to members of the local squirearchy was self-government in an aristocratic sense, especially after the crown, in the eighteenth century, became increasingly identified with the parliamentary majority through the development of the cabinet system of responsible government. There is a vital difference between such a system and the bureaucratic system of continental Europe, where officials unconnected with the local scene are sent out from an administrative center to handle local affairs. It is this system, in the France of Richelieu and Louis XIV, which Montesquieu believed to be the basis of despotism.

It was only in conjunction with the great reforms of the nineteenth century that true local self-government was adopted in Britain (see below, next paragraph). But the older "self-government" laid the basis for a striking feature of British local government tradition which is at variance not only with the United States (in those states where home rule prevails), but also with Continental practice. Rudolf Gneist, in his justly famous study of English self-government, noted that the concept had never been clearly defined by statute or judicial decision. Yet he found it a stable and firmly structured whole. This is the way he described it: "Legislation has regulated the exercise of governmental power since the days of *Magna Charta* in such a way that the responsible offices of internal administration are conferred upon locally resident persons and committees [of such persons] as *honorary offices* in accordance with statutory enactments [defining the authority] in county, town and parish. Likewise the funds required are raised by the *association of neighbors* [local community] according to legally established rates. Self-government appears thus as a mandate for [the carrying out of] the local governmental functions, through a relative distribution of the personal and tax obligations among the social classes in the neighborhood association which are suited [for these tasks]. Looked at from the local end, self government is an administrative system of the [local] community which is regulated by legislative norms in such a way as to represent the government's authority [*Staatsgewalt*] when it is locally active; and since this obligation is at the same time recognized as the right of the community, self-government constitutes the legal constitution of county, town and parish in England." What this means is that the British self-government tradition makes one and the same institutional structure at the same time a system of internal (national) administration and a system of local constitutionalism[8]. This emphasis upon local government *according to laws*, that is to say, in line with parliamentary and judicial authority on the national level, constitutes the significant contrast to continental Europe (except Switzerland). It has led to the British tradition of a local government of enumerated powers, that is, a local government empowered to do only what parliament has authorized it to do (in contrast with the United States, France, Germany, etc.

In view of the tendency to "idealize" British local self-government—a tendency which has produced some very odd efforts in the British Zone of Occupation in Western Germany—it may be well to conclude these observations on the British tradition by a statement made some years ago by Sir E. D. Simon, considered by many as perhaps the most eminent British authority on local government. Commenting upon local government in Stockholm, he found that "it was on about the same level as that in Manchester, that is to say, it is honest and fairly competent, without much energy or imagination; and there are few signs of any general or deeply felt sense of responsibility among the citizens for the government of their city."[9] The same would, I believe, turn out to be the conclusion of a candid observer in any of the countries we shall presently describe.

Alternative patterns · Patterns of local self-government are quite numerous. There is not only the obvious need to shape the pattern in such a way as to fit it into the broader constitutional pattern of each country, but even within a given country, numerous alternative patterns are found. If the constitution should be a federal one, as in the United States, the determination of local self-government law may be left to the several component units. If the constitution is a unitary one, traditional differences in different localities may be permitted to exist, as in Britain, or several possible alternative solutions may be offered the local communities for organizing themselves, as in Massachusetts. It is obvious that we cannot attempt here to give a complete survey, even in outline form; nor would any useful purpose be served by such a bare sketch.[10] The following subparagraphs are intended merely to provide an opportunity for high-lighting a few striking and instructive aspects of the several national traditions.

(1) *Great Britain.* The key aspect of the British local government pattern is a popularly elected council, supported by a professional civil service. It exercises both administrative and legislative functions but as previously noted cannot do anything which has not previously been authorized by either a general or a special act of parliament. The British like to think of this relationship as a partnership between the national and local authorities, but recent trends make it seem something of an euphemism. These elective boards with their reasonably well-defined territorial jurisdiction are a creation of the nineteenth century; they superseded a welter of overlapping boards and commissioners, dealing with welfare, highways, health, and so forth, and created *ad hoc* when the justices of the peace proved incapable of handling the multiple tasks resulting from the industrial revolution. First, in 1835, councils were established for the towns or boroughs, then, in 1888, for the counties and cities (called county boroughs), and last, in 1894, for the districts and parishes. A succession of local-government acts, down to the present, has dealt with assignment and reassignment of functions. Most important, from an American standpoint, is the fact that the control of education is not a local, but a national concern.[11]

The elective councils give a considerable uniformity to British local government. Concerned as they are with making ordinances, fixing the budget, determining such "policies" as are still left to them (not many) and working out their application, as well as selecting and appointing the permanent officials, the councillors are the mainstay of local democracy. Their qualifications, since 1945, are the same as for members of parliament and are no longer tied to property and real estate. In the smaller units all councillors are popularly elected, while in the larger units, one fourth of the councillors are co-opted and serve for six years, rather than the three years which are customary for elected councillors. Through staggering the elections, continuity is preserved in these councils in the larger local communities.

The mayors of British cities are elected by the councils from among their midst, serving usually for one year; in other units of local government a chairman is chosen. Ceremonial occasions, surrounded with the customary British pomp and circumstance, are deceptive in that they suggest a position of leadership which these chairmen and mayors rarely occupy. They resemble the president of Switzerland and the rector of a Continental university.

In recent years, the local sphere has increasingly become a battlefield of the national parties. The "welfare state" (see below, ch. XXIII) has proliferated programs calling for close co-operation of national and local government, and therefore the Labour Party has injected its party program into local elections. This has served to heighten interest in these contests which were formerly a matter of indifference to large sections of the electorate, participation falling at times as low as 5 per cent. (This is scarcely a pattern suggesting emulation in countries to be democratized (see below, (d)). Opinions differ widely as to the people's interest in local affairs; the pattern seems too impersonal to arouse popular interest and concern. The councils are large, thirty on the average, but running as high as one hundred, and their work is broken up into committees. These committees have a tendency to depend upon the permanent civil service engaged in the work they control. Considering the complexity of the technical work, it is only natural that these civil servants should carry great weight, but since they are appointed and paid by the council, the responsibility is clearly to the council. There are more than a million of these professional civil servants employed by local governments, and their general competence is high;[12] in fact they escape the elitism which is characteristic of the "administrative class" in the national government. The standards for many officials, notably teachers, are set by the national government.

The most important of the permanent officials in British local government is the town clerk, a general administrator co-ordinating the several special services. The British are inclined to consider this official a most valuable feature of their local government (and hence undertook to export him to British-occupied Germany). It is doubtful whether such a permanent official is really as desirable as the British think; he tends to legalize and thus to "bureaucratize" the local government, and thus stultify local democracy.

Even before the advent of the Labour Party to power, the growing need for town and country planning and their effective co-ordination led to the establishment in 1943 of a separate ministry to deal with these problems. Its tasks are defined as "securing consistency and continuity in the framing and execution of national policy with respect to the use and development of land throughout England and Wales."[13]

(2) *France.* The pattern of French local government is radically different, due to the fact that true local self-government has never been accepted in France. All the new constitution is willing to concede is that "the French Republic, one and indivisible, recognizes the existence of local administrative units." It states that there are two kinds, municipalities (communes) and departments. To these units, the constitution grants that they "shall be governed freely through councils elected by universal suffrage." This sounds as if there were to be established a system somewhat similar to the British, but such is not the case. In the next article, the constitution takes it all back by announcing once again the traditional centralist French doctrine that "the coordination of the activities of Government officials, the representation of the national interests and the administrative control of these units (communes and departments) shall be ensured within the departmental framework by delegates of the government appointed by the Council of Ministers."[14]

These "delegates" of the national government are the prefects, one appointed for each department, and they are directed by the Ministry of the Interior. The prefects are assisted by subprefects for each district (*arrondissement*) and, since 1948, supervised by eight general inspectors, one for each region (the original post-liberation effort to establish genuinely autonomous regions for purposes of decentralization, long demanded by the regionalist movement, was abandoned by the constitution-makers of 1946). Local government revolves around the prefect. Not only does he coordinate the agents of various ministries, but he appoints most of the local officials and may suspend mayors, council presidents, and councils. The prefect may even add to the local budget expenses he believes the laws make mandatory. Under the prefect, the elected councils, as well as their chairmen (called mayors in the communes and council presidents in the other units), play a decidedly subordinate role, except for the mayors of a few big cities who, like Édouard Herriot, may achieve such national prominence as to gain personal independence. This subordination is manifest in their lack of financial resources; the mayors and council presidents have no solid basis for taxation, they must provide for many activities in accordance with national legislation, and, when they fail to do so, are subject to administrative discipline by the prefect. But the councils cannot request the transfer of a prefect.

The prefects are administrative politicians, or political administrators. While no longer dismissed with changes in party control at the top, they have many tasks which might properly be described as those of a political agent, and their instructions from Paris are numerous and detailed. While the prefect is no longer the sole head of the department, the president of the council having acquired somewhat more the status of a local executive, the prefect still plays a predominant role. But all in all, the French pattern is one of central administrative control and direction to such an extent that the often-cited right of French local authorities to initiate anything they wish without having to wait for national authorization, as in Britain, is largely illusory, as a result of lack of funds. As a matter of fact, throughout the nineteenth century, France maintained extensive prohibitions against certain municipal and local activities in order to protect a "laissez faire" or free market economy. Under such regulations the communes could not enter any field where they would compete with private enterprise. These prohibitions are now gone. In fact, socialism is widespread in local government and in some communities the Communists take a large and growing part in local administration. (This is used as justification for continuance of prefectural control at the present time.)

(3) *Switzerland.* At the opposite pole from France is the local government pattern of Switzerland. Here much the most important protection of communal democracy is found in the constitution, which gives the cantons, as members of the Confederation, not only a clearly defined sphere of local autonomy but actually all residual power which the constitution does not specifically grant to the federal authorities. The cantons themselves are so small (see above, ch. XI) that the further local self-government granted by them under their cantonal constitutions to the municipalities, towns, and villages are merely a further reinforcement of the marked localism of Swiss government. This localism is rooted in ancient traditions and feeds the relatively strong interest in local politics which has often been stressed by students and observers.

Constitutional provisions and statutes vary from canton to canton, as does local government law in the American states, but the broad outlines of the pattern of government in the municipalities are similar throughout Switzerland. In the smaller of these "resident communes" (*Einwohnergemeinden*) the pattern is that of a town meeting, which decides upon broad questions of policy, passes ordinances, adopts the budget, fixes the tax rate, and elects the officials; in short, it operates very much like the New

England town meeting. Again, like the Board of Selectmen, a communal council (*Gemeinderat*), usually numbering from five to nine members, handles the administrative tasks. The council, presided over by a chairman (President), acts as a body in more important matters; this council is chosen by the town meeting. In larger communes (cities of considerable size), this council is chosen by popular vote and handles all but broad issues of policy which are submitted to popular referendum. There may be a smaller executive committee (*Stadtrat*) to supervise the administrative work, which the members sometimes divide among themselves as heads of departments. Finally, and again resembling New England, the town meeting elects some of the officials, while others are appointed by the council. Both councillors and officials serve for four years but they are often re-elected and reappointed.

It is evident that this system is truly democratic local self-government in a sense much more nearly in keeping with democratic constitutionalism than is either the British or the French. As a leading British student of local government has commented: "As regards village or city government, it seems to me that there can hardly be any doubt that this system is far superior to our British system . . ." and again ". . . not only is democracy in Switzerland based on the commune, but so also is culture . . . most villages have their art, their singing, their drama. . . ." The last remark coincides with the judgment of Professor Robert C. Brooks: ". . . the devotion of the Swiss goes out to his own canton, valley, or commune. . . ."[15] It is local self-government truly grass-rooted and supported by the citizen.

(4) *Germany*. It is perhaps the most striking feature of Germany's total collapse that self-government reasserted itself first on the local level. To be sure, Allied and more especially American policy was explicitly committed to building "democracy from the ground up" and thus making it secure. But there is little doubt that the same thing would have happened without Allied promptings. As a matter of fact, local government in rural as well as in urban areas tended to resume its pre-Nazi form upon the entry of Allied troops.

Unfortunately, some grave errors were committed as a result of an inadequate grasp of pre-Nazi German local government. Americans took the fact that German local government officials were charged with carrying out and enforcing state (*Land*) legislation to mean that they were lacking in independence, in spite of the fact that this situation is characteristic not only of Britain but of Switzerland as well.[16] British occupation officials and policy makers, on the other hand, felt that the managerial position of the Bürgermeister was undemocratic, and that the office should therefore be made elective, supported in professional administrative work by a town clerk of civil service status; this was felt in spite of the fact that the city manager movement in the United States had for years been promoted as the most promising pattern of administration under democratic conditions, provided this manager was responsible to and controlled by an elected council—which was precisely the German situation. As a result of these two assaults upon the traditional German pattern of local self-government, we find today a perplexing dichotomy.

The "traditional" pattern, prevalent under the Weimar constitution and derived from earlier patterns under the monarchies, varied to some extent in the different states, as it does now under the new state (*Land*) constitutions, since local self-government is a state prerogative. However, the Basic Law guarantees to the communes (*Gemeinden*) the right to decide on their own responsibility upon all matters of local concern within the framework of the laws, and it provides for popular representative bodies, based upon universal, free, equal and secret elections,[17] unless the commune wishes to assemble in its entirety, that is, hold a town meeting. In other words, the Basic Law returned to the "traditional" pattern of Weimar, under which local self-government was composed of three tiers of authority, all derived from the people: (1) the popularly elected assembly, (2) the assembly-elected council (*Kreisausschuss* in the counties, both rural and urban) or executive board (*Magistrat* in the cities), and (3) the chief executive (*Bürgermeister* or *Oberbürgermeister* in cities, *Landrat* (also other titles) in the rural counties) to be chosen by the council or executive board or sometimes by the assembly. However, in the name of democracy, the British and Americans have insisted that the chief executive be popularly elected, the British demanding that this be counterbalanced by the creation of a town clerk (*Stadtdirektor*). Furthermore, the Americans have tried to have all delegated administration eliminated, or at least reduced to a minimum. As a result, local self-government has been twisted out of shape. A deeper insight into German tradition would have shown what was admittedly needed to make local government less bureaucratic and more responsive to popular views, thus also permitting it to serve more effectively as the proving ground of grass-roots democracy. Generally speaking, needed German reforms pointed in the direction of Swiss practice: the use of referenda in larger communities, and the development of a true town meeting in the smaller ones. It seems more than likely that upon gaining strength, if it does, German democratic politics will develop its three-tiered pattern of local self-government, since German democrats know how misleading is the often-heard generalization that the Weimar constitution failed because local government remained "undemocratic." For it was in the local sphere that the Nazis succeeded last; they effectively destroyed local self-government only after they had conquered the central positions.

(5) *United States*. The characteristic feature of American local government is the "extreme freedom enjoyed by American municipalities, especially in the home rule states" (Robson). Considering the ever tighter central control in Britain, local freedom may well seem "extreme," but in terms of the analysis of constitutional democracy given here, this freedom is appropriate and sound. It resembles the situation in Switzerland.[18]

Under "home rule," the voters have a varying measure of freedom to adopt their own pattern of local government by referendum or even by initiative. While the several states have varying programs, the prevailing tendency is toward several basic patterns or "plans" among which local units may choose. There is more of this freedom for cities than for counties, but in New England, where the unit of effective local self-government is the town rather than the county, such freedom includes the towns. Without going into the details, it is worth remarking that American cities and towns are governed according to three primary patterns. The first and oldest is mayor-council plan under which both mayor and council are popularly elected (as are the judges and other officials); this plan is conceived in analogy to the broad pattern of American state constitutions, with their governor and state legislature operating in accordance with the traditional doctrine of separation of powers. The second pattern is the so-called commission plan under which a small elected body combined executive and legislative functions, each commissioner heading a department for administrative purposes. Finally, there is the manager plan, under which all administrative responsibility is centered in a manager who is a cross between the town clerk in Britain and the *Bürgermeister* in Germany. The manager is responsible to and controlled by a council presided over by a mayor or chairman (in rural counties).[19] There is sharp disagreement among Americans as to which of these patterns is the most desirable, but expert opinion leans toward the third alternative, provided popular referendum and initiative afford an opportunity for the citizen at large to participate in deciding the more important issues.

A special pattern is presented by the New England towns with their town meetings, to which the entire citizenry foregathers once a year (and more often, if necessary) to vote the budget and the taxes, elect town officers, and decide broad issues of town policy, usually in conjunction with an appropriation. In these towns, many small administrative offices are elective, including such ancient "honors" as "surveyor of fences." But the administrative nub of the town is the board of selectmen, usually three in number. The selectmen may meet once a week in the evening to handle current issues connected with the administration of the town's various departments. They may also head up one or more of the administrative

251

departments, although these are more often in the hands of another elected official (the selectmen, however, appoint some). Town meetings, like other forms of American local self-government, often suffer from a lack of interest on the part of a majority of the voters, participation falling as low as 10 per cent. This shows the limited importance of forms; in Switzerland, local self-government of the town meeting type in commune and canton is the mainstay of democracy and participation is lively and continuous. Yet Lord Bryce's judgment probably still holds: "Of the three or four types of systems of local government which I have described, that of the Town or township with its popular primary assembly has been the best. It is the cheapest and the most efficient; it is the most educative to the citizens who bear part in it. The town-meeting has been not only the course but the school of democracy."[20] The problem remains how a comparable "school of democracy" may be set up in the vast metropolitan areas or even in the large cities with which the United States is dotted today.

Metropolitan problems · In any event, the great metropolitan areas represent a most perplexing range of problems, technologically, economically, ecologically, culturally, and, last but not least, governmentally and politically. Efforts to solve these problems have been made in all major countries. They have taken three forms, governmentally speaking, all aiming at securing a workable pattern of over-all direction and control. These three approaches are (1) the creation of special boards or commissions to handle particular aspects, like the London Metropolitan Water Board, New York's Port Authority, or Boston's Metropolitan Transit Authority; (2) the consolidation of many smaller units into one larger unit; (3) the federation of the central urban core with the outlying suburban towns. Of these, the first appeals to the engineering-minded specialist, the second to the power-conscious politician and the efficiency-preoccupied administrator, but only the third offers an opportunity of combining the essential popular controls with the intimacy of close community contact which is necessary for effective local self-government.[21]

While these efforts and plans have been widely advocated and discussed, they have, except for the first, been mostly programs rather than realities in England and America. The strong democratic tradition and local autonomy and independence, and the extent to which these sentiments make themselves felt in legislative bodies called upon to authorize any proposed action, make it essential that public opinion be developed to provide a firm democratic foundation for both the establishment and the maintenance of metropolitan government. No program of simple annexation will meet the inherent requirements of this situation, as experience in Boston shows. In the second half of the nineteenth century, several immediately adjacent towns were annexed by Boston, but then the movement stopped; local resistance became too strong. Nor will a program of administrative bodies controlled by a national or state legislature meet the situation. Boston has had such a body, the Metropolitan District Commission, dealing since 1919 with metropolitan sewers, water, and parks. But while this commission has done very acceptable work, it has no broad popular base, and hence lacks the democratic support which would enable it to function aggressively as a metropolitan authority ready to expand into new fields.

Federalism, as we have seen, is the modern governmental technique for combining the effective management of common concerns of several communities with the continued separate existence of these communities, each attending to the management of their several local concerns. Constitutionally speaking, federalism ranges all the way from a loose federation of separate units agreeing by compact to establish a joint agency for the handling of common tasks, to the closely integrated federal union of such components into one joint government, with only residual powers remaining as the task of the united communities (see above, ch. XI). Whether, in a given metropolitan area, one or the other of these federalisms should be adopted or can be secured is a pragmatic question of political prudence and expediency—as it is likewise on the wider scene of Europe or the world.[22] Generally speaking, however, the history of federalism shows that it is wise to begin with a federation, and then allow the federation to grow into a federal community with its federal government if the centripetal forces are strong enough. It is at the same time more likely that the communities to be joined in such a federation will agree to do so if their local autonomy remains intact in all but the palpably common concerns calling for joint management.

In cities such as Boston and New York, it would seem best to organize a metropolitan authority to exercise those joint functions which are clearly metropolitan in nature. As a body politic it would provide the central organs of a federation of cities and towns in the area. Such a federal solution of the metropolitan problem could well be combined with the city manager type of governmental pattern. A representative council, based upon federally united local communities as electoral units (federal principle), would adopt the budget, make the basic policy decisions in the enumerated fields of the metropolitan authority, defend these policies before the electorate, and generally provide the political leadership in the metropolitan community. The manager, too, would have the usual functions, being selected and discharged by the council. While the cities and towns would retain their separate entity and autonomy, a measure of reduction in municipal activities and expenditures would take place, and the tax dollar would go farther than under the chaotic conditions of the present time. In any case, however, both the problems of the large community of the metropolis and those of the neighbourhood community would be attended to on a strongly democratic basis. Much of the corruption which afflicts metropolitan communities is due to the failure to organize the government in such a way that the people can control it.[23] In light of experience in Switzerland, as well as in the United States, it would seem desirable to explore fully the possibilities for utilizing referendum and initiative for certain very basic decisions affecting the metropolitan community at large. This would apply especially to decisions in the planning field involving preferences of the individual citizen. For example, one of the most elusive problems of metropolitan planning at present is how to spend the available funds in the metropolitan transport field: whether to expand rapid transit lines and other forms of public transportation, or whether to develop superhighways and great parking areas, linking the metropolitan core with the outlying communities. This problem cannot be answered except in terms of the preferences of the inhabitants of the area for use of public conveyances as contrasted with use of private automobiles. It is the kind of problem which, if conscientiously handled, might be most helpfully decided by the electorate itself.

Referenda have the additional and important advantage of arousing citizen interest in the area of their application. Since it will remain a very real problem how to secure that interest in the vast metropolitan areas of modern countries, the referendum may serve to keep citizen interest alive, and not restrict it to the infrequent use of the ballot. In addition, it may well be very desirable to organize advisory committees of citizens for each major field of metropolitan activity; such committees might be drawn from the civic associations and interest groups active in the particular sphere. To these might be assigned the role of shaping and recommending policies and program; they could work with the planning and programming unit in the metropolitan authority.[24]

Just before the Second World War, W. A. Robson presented a study of the government and misgovernment of London. In it he sketched the perennial struggle with London's vast urban problems. In spite of the fact that London is the capital, its problems have been inadequately attended to by parliament—in fact, Robson speaks of "neglect." Like Washington, London is too much controlled by men who are not responsible to the inhabitants of the city—a common source of metropolitan ills.[25] After critically assessing the irresponsible and undemocratic *ad hoc* boards and commissions and outlining a "regional authority" like the "metropolitan authority" discussed above, Robson points up his argument by the following general observations: "If we wish to preserve and strengthen democracy in this country, it is obvious that we must reject expedients of these kinds and acknowledge the necessity for a directly elected regional council for Greater London as the only type of institution which is satisfactory from a democratic view. . . . This aspect of the matter cannot be regarded as of secondary importance at a time when our democratic faith, and the institutions in which it is embodied, have acquired a new and enhanced significance in a world of competing creeds and hostile authoritarian doctrines. Democracy on the national scale can function in a healthy manner only if it is supported and nourished by democratic local government. It will be a disaster if the reform of the essential structure of London government is delayed and evaded by the introduction of piecemeal expedients without regard to their undemocratic or antidemocratic character. . . ."[26]

Middletown and *Yankee City* · The difficulties encountered in realizing such programs as have been developed by reform groups for the rebuilding of metropolitan communities are to a considerable extent due to lack of knowledge about these communities. It is, as a matter of fact, easy to realize that something on the order of the detailed information contained in studies like *Middletown*[27] would be vital for anyone desiring to bring about comprehensive reforms on a democratic basis. But that would be a gigantic undertaking for a metropolitan area of several million people. It is, as a matter of fact, rather interesting that the two most striking studies of urban life have dealt with rather small cities, but not with the close-knit intimate community. In the very small community, and especially in the rural community, the interviewer-investigator encounters extreme difficulties in establishing the necessary basis of confidence. The neighborly quality of small communities makes them very suspicious of outsiders asking "impertinent questions."[28] On the other hand, the metropolitan community staggers the potential inquirer by the range and complexity of its problems, as well as by the sheer mass of data to be gathered and analyzed.

Actually, there are some crucial methodological issues involved in both *Middletown* and *Yankee City*. The investigation in both cases was set up on the assumption that such an inquiry could be conducted without any value judgments being implied. In the usual terms, it was assumed that these inquiries could be "completely objective," "without any bias," "strictly scientific," and so on. They were, in other words, conceived as "demonstrating" what the authors as sociologists and anthropologists cherished as a desirable goal of scholarly studies of this kind. Anyone reading these books who happens not to share their particular ideas ("prejudices," these writers would call them) can readily identify the unexplained major premises in each case. In the case of *Middletown*, the antireligious, antibusiness, antibourgeois notions of the analysts stick out all over; in the case of *Yankee City*, the determination to find "classes" led the authors to discover them, when as a matter of fact the data merely supported a vague general recognition of "higher" and "lower," while no class consciousness or ability to act cohesively as a result of such consciousness could be demonstrated. These critical observations are not intended to belittle the significance of either *Middletown* or *Yankee City*. But they serve to contrast them with a study like *Small Town*, which is conceived in a different spirit.[29] In terms of our present concerns, it appears that the clearly apparent urgency of revitalizing constitutional democracy "at the grass roots" calls for intensive inquiries into the various factors involved in the blight of local self-government, both in the United States and abroad. There is little to be gained by anguished outcries or sermons imploring us to take greater interest in arrangements which do not interest us. In other words, unless we understand the "grass roots" better, we are not going to get the grass to grow more luxuriantly. For this task, *Middletown* and *Yankee City* provide striking challenges which the student of constitutional democracy may use as stepping-stones for the more clearly directed inquiry into the why and how of the functioning of local self-government, into the government and misgovernment of local communities.

Conclusion · Even so swift and general a survey as the preceding one provides many suggestions for needed thought and action in the field of local self-government as an essential part of the pattern and functioning of constitutional government. As the world is groping toward a federal organization for the world community, it is becoming increasingly evident that any such further broadening of government upward and outward will have to be accompanied by the extension of the federal principle downward and inward. There is need for federating adjacent communities for effective joint action where the constituent communities are too small for handling needed community services; there is need for federating many communities which have become part of a metropolitan region; there is need for giving local governments in general more nearly the autonomous status of component federal elements, comparable to the cantons of Switzerland, with firm constitutional guarantees for such local communities; there is finally a need for "regionalizing" over-centralized states (a problem discussed briefly under federalism). Everyone of these several federalisms can contribute to the "territorial division of power," and can thereby reinforce the stability of the constitutional order, while at the same time providing room for the democratic working of the local community as the "proving ground of democracy."

PART III

THE FUNCTIONING

PROCESSES OF

CONSTITUTIONAL

GOVERNMENT

XIV

General Problems of Representation

Introduction: representation as a method of securing responsible conduct ·
Representation in Rousseau · Representation in Hobbes · The dual nature
of representation · Representation and responsibility · Defining representation · Election and representation · Law and the legislative function ·
The views of Hooker, Locke, and Rousseau on the importance of laws ·
Fiscal matters · Representation and constitutional government · Reasons
for the late appearance of representative bodies · Conclusion.

**Introduction: representation as a method of securing responsible
conduct** · In discussing responsibility and its enforcement we pointed out
that one of its most important forms was electoral responsibility. From a
historical standpoint, efficacy in securing responsibility in government
must be considered the central objective in all the various schemes of
representation. In strongly religious epochs the notion that the king represents God on earth may be a most powerful impulse toward making him and
his officials responsible. But when such faith declined, the most arbitrary
tyranny might and often did grow out of such a scheme of representation.
The idea of toleration implies uncertainty concerning the absolute standards
upon which a religious sanction is built. As was said before, modern government can in some respects be interpreted as an effort to produce the responsible conduct of public affairs without religious sanctions and without
the standards supported by these sanctions. In the place of such standards,
mutually acceptable interests, public interests, so-called, become the basis
for evaluating the actions of officials and other public authorities (see
ch. XIX, p. 408). But who is the final judge as to whether governmental
action corresponds to the public interest? The orthodox answer is: the
public. In modern countries the public cannot, of course, foregather in the
market place, like the Athenian citizens of old. Hence the only possible
method of securing adequate controls is some scheme by which a small
selected group of citizens acts for the whole body. Such action is representative. Conflicting interests require compromise. Compromise results
from argument and discussion. Through such argument and discussion interests become articulate; they are rationalized. When the representatives
thus are exposed to full public view, it becomes increasingly desirable that
the methods by which they are chosen be likewise "rationalized," so that

favoritism and other personal motives would play only a minor role. The long struggle for parliamentary reform in England was fought over this issue; rotten boroughs, patrons, and all the paraphernalia of aristocratic nepotism became unacceptable. In spite of Burke's eloquent defense of irrational traditionalism, Bentham and his insistence upon rational standards prevailed. In the modern world, direct general election has been generally accepted as the most rational method for choosing representatives. There are, however, important exceptions. Courts, for example, are manned by a different method, which may be more rational, and probably is more effective. Their selection is based upon a relatively objective standard: technical competence. It could be argued that legislatures should be similarly selected. Their representative quality would not necessarily disappear; it might in fact be heightened. Burke, in his discussion of parliamentary representation (see below, pp. 264 f.), insisted that even the elected representative must conceive of himself as a guardian of national interests. Parliament, he said, was not a congress of ambassadors from different and hostile interests, but a deliberative assembly from *one* nation, with *one* interest, that of the whole; these representatives ought to be guided not by local purpose, but by the general good. Such an idealistic conception of the function of a parliament evokes the ridicule of moralists and cynics alike; they would maintain whatever a parliament ought to be, it is in actual fact a congress of ambassadors from different and hostile interests. Actually, Burke's view is not wholly mistaken, but is true only of the best Congressmen and M. P.'s—the cynical popular view is also partly wrong in that it applies only to the worst representatives.

Representation in Rousseau · In Anglo-Saxon minds the idea of representative government is firmly linked to that of democracy. It is, therefore, worth noting that Jean Jacques Rousseau, the most ardent and influential expounder of democratic ideas, rejects representation in the broad sense as contrary to the very essence of modern government. In his *Social Contract* he asserts that as soon as public affairs cease to be the primary occupation of the citizen, the state is bound to perish.[1] If it is a question of going to battle, the citizens prefer to pay mercenaries and stay at home themselves. If it is a matter of going into the assembly, they appoint deputies and stay at home. From indolence they allow paid soldiers to tyrannize the fatherland and "representatives" to sell it for profit. Therefore sovereignty cannot be represented, and for the same reason for which it cannot be surrendered: it rests upon the general will. The deputies of the people are, therefore, not its representatives, but merely its commissaries; they cannot give a definite decision. Every law which the people have not approved is null and void; it is no law at all. It is obvious from these remarks that Rousseau was misled by giving too much weight to the experience of the ancients. Where the active citizenry had been able to foregather in the market place, as in Athens or Rome, their failure to do so did indeed spell disaster to the commonwealth; what corresponds to it in modern communities is the tendency of the citizen to neglect his duty to vote and to participate in public affairs. If Rousseau were correct it would, in fact, make it impossible to organize responsible popular government in our modern countries with their millions of people. Rousseau, to be sure, does not bar the choice of professional magistrates to administer the law. But he does insist that legislation as an exercise of the "sovereign" power must be adopted by the people themselves. In truth, his arguments constitute the *reductio ad absurdum* of the idea of "sovereignty" in a democratic society. There is no good reason for singling out the making of general rules (laws) and saying: This only the people themselves can do. In legislation as in other concerns, where many people have the same right or interest, it is often absolutely necessary for them to agree upon one person to represent them lest their interest be neglected for want of unity in urging it. Nor is there any reason for drawing a hard and fast line between representatives and the agents, curators, and mandatories, as Burke did. They all are related types of human relationship recognized by every more highly developed legal system. Rousseau's violent hostility to any kind of representative scheme was no doubt stimulated by the fact that his great antagonist Hobbes gave it such a prominent place in his political system. Moreover, the small self-governing cantons of his native Switzerland provided a living model for active participation of the citizenry, which persists to this day.

Representation in Hobbes · It seems strange to us now that representation should at one time have been one of the most important ideas brought forth in the defense of absolutism. No writer offers a more striking illustration than Thomas Hobbes. Hobbes's entire conception of the state or even of a community rests upon the idea of representation. According to him: "A Multitude of men, are made *One* Person, when they are by one man, or one Person, Represented. . . . For it is the *Unity* of the Representer, not the *Unity* of the Represented, that maketh the Person *One*. . . . *Unity*, cannot otherwise be understood in Multitude."[2] Political writers in more recent times have often paid too little attention to the crucial significance of this notion when considering Hobbes's idea of the state. His notorious doctrine of the governmental compact, according to which every man covenants with every other man to make one man or assembly of men their representative, is rooted in this conviction that the unity of the state can in no other way be understood. And why can it not be understood? Because each individual composing the multitude is a being utterly apart, like a particle of matter, moving through time and space in search of "power after power unto death." Therefore, only the superimposition of one such individual over all others can bring unity and order out of multitude and chaos. It is quite evident that such a point of view was eminently fitted to the age of monarchical absolutism. The modern idea of representation is different, indeed. Avoiding the mysticism of Rousseau's general will, the modern conception is built upon the idea that the many specific interests in the community—local, professional, commercial, and social, to mention only the more important divisions—can by argument and discussion be co-ordinated and compromised, by public scrutiny and criticism be scaled down to become compatible if not identical with the public interest, that is, the interest of the community as a whole. It is the task of the popular representatives thus to co-ordinate and criticize. The necessary unity does not logically follow from the unity of the representer, as Hobbes would have it, but must be created and constantly recreated through a political process of dynamic activity. This process consists mainly of parliamentary action and elections. Since both involve multitudes of persons, those with relatively similar interests form parties, that is, groups of people with common interests and ideals. Therefore parties are of great importance in any discussion of representation. (See chs. XX–XXI.)

The dual nature of representation · Historically speaking, representative assemblies developed in most European countries in the course of the later Middle Ages as an important part of the medieval constitutional order. Very often the three "estates" were composed of nobility, clergy, and the merchants of the cities (the burgesses).[3] But the greatest variations existed in this respect. The most important of these assemblies is undoubtedly the English Parliament, where the higher nobility were joined with the higher clergy in the "Lords Spiritual and Temporal," while the knights together with the burgesses constituted the Commons. Thus the more important groups in the community—nowadays often referred to as "classes"—were represented and called together by the king through his "minister" for the purpose of securing their consent to extraordinary taxes or levies. This was necessary because the undeveloped state of central administrative systems and the absence of effective means of coercion (see above, Part I, and particularly ch. III) rendered the collection of such levies impossible without local co-operation. Quite naturally, these representatives when gathered together undertook to bargain for their consent to such grants of money;

they presented complaints and petitions, which the crown had to heed in order to secure what it wanted. These, then, were not national representatives but agents of local powers acting under special instructions or mandates. This was true, however, only as long as they acted separately. When the king and the two houses of Parliament acted together, after having settled their differences and reached a compromise, they were taken to *represent* the whole body politic. More particularly, they were supposed to represent the entire body politic of the realm of England when acting as a high court, which was taken to be their most solemn function down to the seventeenth century. Historically, then, one cannot draw a hard and fast line between agents with definite instructions or mandates and representatives empowered to attend to a general task. An elected body may and usually will be both a set of agents from different interests, and a representative group determining the common interest. Therefore, to return to our statement from Burke, a parliament is both: a deliberative assembly from *one* nation, with *one* interest, that of the whole, and a congress of ambassadors from different and hostile interests.

Older definitions of representation have tried to escape from this dualism, which lies deeply embedded in the political reality of representative schemes. But political thinkers, being philosophers or lawyers, sought some *logical* unity. Thus Hobbes, proceeding from his general theory of man as a machine propelled by irrational desires to make rational efforts toward their satisfaction, defined representative action as any action which actually served to realize the goals established by such human desires. To illustrate: the preservation of order by a monocrat, be he ever so tyrannical, is truly representative of the people simply because the desire for order is known to be a basic desire resulting from man's primordial fear of his fellows. It is evident that such a "definition" is much too broad. It neglects the conflict of interests and values, not only between groups, but within the individual himself. Hobbes's view has been revived in the contemporary Fascist and National Socialist doctrines of leadership; it also is implied in the Communist claim to represent the proletariat. Such self-appointed guardians of alleged proletarian or nationalist interests are in the last analysis basing their claim upon some kind of religious or inspirational sanction. Marx, Mussolini, Hitler, Stalin—all have been made to serve as inspired guides. The cult which grows up around such individuals places them into parallel with the demigods of old. In a sense, therefore, political representation has been transformed into religious representation once more.

Representation and responsibility · Whether the basis is religious or political, representation is closely linked to responsible conduct. If A represents B, he is presumed to be responsible *to* B, that is to say, he is answerable to B for what he says and does. In modern parlance, responsible government and representative government have therefore almost come to be synonymous. As our example shows, secularized political responsibility is conceived in terms of a relationship between human beings. There are two basic ways of securing such responsibility. One is the administrative and the other is the political or electoral form of responsibility. But in either case responsibility is measured in terms of service to interests determined by the preference of another. This means that responsibility always implies communication between human beings. Human beings will disagree as to what are their interests and, in the ensuing argument, the services are rationalized through which they are realized. But all rationalizations are bound to be more or less incomplete. Comprehensive notions, such as that of a "national interest," certainly lack definite content, and the conduct of officials in terms of them is therefore only vaguely rationalized, as Charles Beard has so learnedly shown with regard to the United States. Such notions possess rather the nature of a believed-in standard or value, and this is not at all surprising in view of the fact that nationalism has developed into a sort of substitute for religion. In fact, some writers have gone so far as to call nationalism a substitute form of religion. But even much more specific interests cannot be thoroughly rationalized by any means. How are we, then, to solve this problem of holding the several interests together and giving them a common direction, of integrating them into a more or less consistent whole? How, in other words, can the discordant private interests be converted into a common public interest? Authoritarians have always presumed to answer this question in an authoritative way. From Plato to Marx and Hitler they have been ready to say: I know! Leave it to me and all will be well. The classical doctrine of democracy answers: By the will of the people. But how is the will of this somewhat vague unity, the people, to be found? This question raises fundamental questions concerning electoral responsibility? With the development of modern means of communication and the vast scale of propaganda (see below, ch. XXIV), the "will of the people" concept has lost its magic. When smart public-relations men can substantiate the claim of changing the public's mind on basic questions, the belief in the common man, which was at one time such an obvious aspect of orthodox constitutionalism, must be restated to accord with the new reality. This is the second reason for seeking a new basis for responsible government. The problem, however, is not entirely new.

In a celebrated speech to his electors at Bristol, Burke enunciated the idealistic conception of political representation and responsibility thus: "My worthy colleague [his opponent for the seat] says, his will ought to be

264

subservient to yours. If that be all, the thing is innocent. If government were a matter of will upon any side, yours, without question, ought to be superior. But government and legislation are matters of reason and judgment, and not of inclination; and what sort of reason is that, in which the determination precedes the discussion; in which one set of men deliberate, and another decide . . . ? To deliver an opinion is the right of all men; that of constituents is a weighty and respectable opinion, which a representative ought always to rejoice to hear; and which he ought always most seriously to consider. But *authoritative* instructions; *mandates* issued, which the member is bound blindly and explicitly to obey, to vote and to argue for, though contrary to the clearest conviction of his judgment and conscience; these are things utterly unknown to the laws of this land, and which arise from a fundamental mistake of the whole order and tenor of our constitution. Parliament is not a *congress* of ambassadors from different and hostile interests; which interests each must maintain, as an agent and advocate, against other agents and advocates; but parliament is a *deliberative* assembly of *one* nation, with *one* interest, that of the whole; where not local purposes, not local prejudices ought to guide, but the general good. . . ." And pushing the matter one step further and into the realm of religion once more, Burke pointed out: "Certainly, gentlemen, it ought to be the happiness and glory of a representative, to live in the strictest union, the closest correspondence, and the most unreserved communication with his constituents. Their wishes ought to have great weight with him; their opinion high respect; their business unremitted attention. . . . But his unbiased opinion, his mature judgment, his enlightened conscience, he ought not to sacrifice to you, to any man, or to any set of men living. These he does not derive from your pleasure; no, nor from the law and the constitution. They are a trust from Providence, for the abuse of which he is deeply answerable."[4] This idealistic conception accords neither with the reality of politics, nor yet with the democratic conception of the "will of the people."

For the conflict of various interests and their possible relation to a more comprehensive public interest is the real issue. Ideally conceived, of course, a special mandate cannot be admitted, since it would make the members of representative assemblies into mandatories for special interests. But there is a vast difference between a special mandate and a broad indication as to the general line of policy to be pursued. The obvious question to be asked of Burke is: "Who decides whether you, Edmund Burke, have carried out this trust from Providence?" To which Burke could only answer: "The electors of Bristol!" "Very well," his cross-examiner would continue, "what about de Jouvenel's well-known squib about Parliament, that after having become a deputy, one need have but one essential preoccupation, to remain a deputy? Will it not be true that unless a representative does obey the mandates and instructions of his electorate, or of groups of them, he will fail of re-election?" Such thoughts are now common among people who consider electoral responsibility; for the actual behavior of most elected representatives belies the lofty sentiments of Edmund Burke. Even in Burke's own day, many a listener to his speech must have chuckled inwardly as he reflected upon the complete subservience of most members of Parliament to the great aristocratic landowners, who did not even have to issue instructions, so assiduously did "their" members study their every wish before each vote in Parliament (see below, ch. XXII, p. 462). As realistic students of political behavior we must conclude, therefore, that Burke's doctrine of reason and conscience as applied to representation and electoral responsibility was an untenable idealization even in his own day. Burke's argument is most persuasive; but it is built upon the false assumption that the major decisions in politics are purely reasonable when often they are not even partially so. Only to this partial aspect would his argument apply.

Defining representation · If then we avoid these extremes, which are at best rationalizations after the event, we find that the scope of political representation can well be indicated by adopting Robert von Mohl's unpretentious definition.[5] Representation is the process through which the influence which the entire citizenry or a part of them have upon governmental action is, with their expressed approval, exercised on their behalf by a smaller number among them, with binding effect upon those represented. Some aspects of this definition deserve further comment. We speak advisedly of *influence* rather than participation or control, since the large number of citizens is not very likely to participate in or effectively to control governmental action. We use the general expression "governmental action" rather than legislation, because all kinds of governmental activities might be subjected to popular influence. By suggesting, further, that influence of a part of the citizenry, as well as the whole, may be represented, we recognize the representative quality of the American Senate. Group representation is more ancient than the representation of the whole people, in any case. Finally, the most essential part of this descriptive definition is contained in the phrase: "with their expressed approval." This approval is expressed presumably in the constitutional provisions regarding representative institutions—the particular institutions of that constitutional order, as well as the general principle. In short, it is in this phrase that we recognize the constitutional setting of all such representation. The authority of the representatives is not only created by the constituent power, but it is subject to change by the amending power under the constitution.

Election and representation · The modern tendency has been to identify representation with election. What this means is that genuine *authority*, or legitimacy, as it is sometimes called, rests upon popular acceptance and support alone. The will of the people is the magic source of all legitimate power. And to discover this "will of the people," elections must take place at regular intervals to give the people a chance to express their approval or disapproval of the stewardship of key officials. The large masses of individual wills that are merged in this collective concept of the popular will have been personalized and symbolized, at least in America, in the normative idea of the "common man." So familiar have these notions become, and so generally are they accepted in the United States, that it is sometimes forgotten that a process of elections is not the only process for creating representativeness and representation. Representation is a matter of existential fact; up to a certain point it just "happens," and is generally so accepted. Why should this be? *Repraesentare* means to make present something that is *not* in fact present. A piece of cloth may in that sense represent a vast power complex, or the Stars and Stripes the United States of America. But when human beings represent other human beings existentially, it is usually due to their *belonging* to the same community of values, beliefs, customs, behaviors, and so forth. Elections, when seen in this context, appear to be a method of finding persons who possess this representative quality. But usually the persons so found also have to perform specific and often difficult tasks; for these they may not be the best qualified. Apart from the electoral method of selection, representatives may be chosen on the basis of technical achievements. The representative quality of the Supreme Court and other judicial bodies rests in part upon this foundation. There is also the older method of having the officials of constituent corporate bodies be *ex officio* members of a larger representative body. This method was seemingly employed in the Fascist Council of Corporations, but this Council was no genuine representative body because of the control which the government possessed over the corporate constituents. In other words, since these corporations were dependent upon the government, they influenced it only indirectly and sporadically. This method is genuinely used by the United Nations, where the foreign ministers of the various nations or their deputies are usually members of the assembly or the council or both. The German Federal Council, *Reich* Council, and *Länderrat* (States' Council) also belong in this category. Various economic councils, such as the French and Czechoslovak Councils, also were composed of this type of representatives. The German Economic Council of the Weimar Republic was similarly organized.[6] Another method of considerable historical significance is inheritance of the office. Older representative bodies, such as the House of Lords in England and some of the French upper chambers, rested upon this base. Inheritance as a basis of selection has become anachronistic for representative purposes. Election has superseded it almost completely.

If the election is envisaged as a method for securing people adequate for purposes of representation, it by no means follows that all those whose interests are to be represented should participate in the selection as such. The representatives may be dealing with the interests of children and imbeciles, yet most people nowadays readily admit that every voter should be able to read and write. Such a requirement is desirable, indeed, in a voter, who should certainly be capable not only of reading about what his representative is doing and saying in Congress, but also of writing to him concerning it (though some Congressmen might at times wish that there were fewer letter-writers in their constituencies). We may witness a considerable extension of such qualifications for the electorate. In the days when the American Constitution was made, property qualifications were often justified on the ground that they ensured a better education on the part of the voter. Democracy has found the answer to that argument by providing free public schools for all. The firm belief in the common man's judgment which democracy presupposes has thereby been given a firmer basis. Schemes of multiple representation have been advocated from time to time. It might conceivably provide a solution of the problems confronting democracies in foreign affairs. No such constitutional provisions would in and of themselves render a representative scheme less representative. But any proposal of this kind will have to make a hard stand against the ingrained equalitarian presumption that each citizen should have one vote.[7]

Law and the legislative function · How can we explain the fact that legislation came to be considered the peculiar province of representative, popularly elected bodies, when in fact medieval representatives had little or no concern with legislation? Because ever since the sixteenth century, legislation was believed to be the most striking manifestation of political and governmental power. Legislation entailed the making of rules binding upon the whole community. Bodin maintained that this power was the peculiar characteristic of a state.[8] As we have seen before, the medieval notion of law as eternal custom, as something already there and merely to be discovered by learned men, was giving way to a realization that laws are man-made, that they are essentially decisions as to what ought to be rather than as to what is. The shift, of course, was merely one in view and emphasis. The High Court of Parliament had changed the law in the process of finding it, and so had the other courts of the realm. But the great Coke, before his identification with Parliament, insisted at times upon the "higher law" as a standard and criterion by which to evaluate parliamentary enactments (see above, ch. VI, pp. 104 f.). He saw it as fixed and immutable, the peculiar and precious heritage of every Englishman, an embodiment of the principles upon which his life was built. This relation of general rules to religious, moral, and other principles was the other pillar upon which men's preoccupation with laws and legislation as a manifestation of governmental power rested. That human beings cannot be forced in matters of principle is the underlying idea. A specific act of government may be justified in terms of a specific emergency, but no general rule ever can be so justified. This leads to the important if elementary consideration that the making of a rule presupposes that there is a series of events which have certain aspects in common. In other words, there must be a "normal" situation. This means that time is available for deliberation to determine what had best be done regarding such a situation. Representative, deliberative bodies require time, obviously, and therefore legislation seems to be peculiarly fitted for such bodies. Some writers on the Continent have thereby been led into linking parliamentary deliberation to the romantic passion for everlasting conversation, a generalization which is as glittering as it is uninformed. For parliamentary deliberation is entirely focused upon and organized with a view toward action, the enactment of a general rule. The history and practice of parliamentary procedure proves this beyond doubt. But the enactment of such a general rule requires careful co-ordination of conflicting viewpoints. Really effective compromises must be reached. Such compromises are justified, because any considerable group of people in a given community possesses the capacity effectively to resist the enforcement of certain rules which they do not, or which they cannot, approve.

To put the foregoing analysis into a very abstract formula, one might say: the community requires recurrent integration. The failure to perceive this fact underlies the totalitarian contempt for elected representatives as valuable guides in the enactment of permanent legislation. The totalitarian emphasis upon the desirability of unity in a community does not solve the problems which arise from the diversity of actual interests. They assert that only a single leader, or a small elite, can achieve effective integration. They assert that when the conflict of norms in a given community becomes insoluble, when therefore the several groups have no common ground upon which to reach an effective compromise, the arbitrary superimposition of one possible solution is the only alternative to civil war or complete dissolution. Communists and Fascists both maintain that such was the case in recent times, and they both proceeded to impose their particular norms.

Once one grants their premise—and one has to when *their* factions grow to any considerable size—he cannot escape from their conclusion. But this is so not because there is a disagreement on fundamentals, for such we have had all the time. It is so because these particular groups have adopted organized violence as a method of party warfare. Constitutionalism and democracy, if they are true to themselves, will outlaw such methods of party strife as private uniforms, police, and the rest. This outlawing was done in the British *Public Order Act* of 1936 (see ch. IX, p. 161), and also in a number of American states. Federal legislation may be desirable. If this is done, there is no need for denying the rights of citizenship, such as our civil liberties, to people whose views are antidemocratic. The provisions exempting Germans with certain antidemocratic views from the protection of the basic human rights of the new German Basic Law (art. 18, see above, pp. 161 f.) appear much too broad from this standpoint; "abuse" of these rights "to attack the free, democratic basic order" seems much too vague a criterion for so dangerous a limitation on rights which the first article had declared to be "inviolable and inalienable." Compromise is, therefore, essential in making general rules; through argument and discussion the area of agreement is determined in the representative legislature.

The views of Hooker, Locke, and Rousseau on the importance of laws · To show the strong sentiment regarding the importance of laws and of legislation as the process of making such laws, it may be well to cite here three leading constitutional theorists, Hooker, Locke, and Rousseau. Rousseau describes the fundamental nature of a republic in terms of law: "I therefore give the name 'Republic' to every State that is governed by laws, no matter what the form of its administration may be: for only in such a case does the public interest govern, and the *res publica* rank as a *reality*."[9] Likewise, Locke's discussion of the forms of a commonwealth is based on the conception of law as the essence of a commonwealth: ". . . for the form of government depending upon the placing the supreme power, which is the legislative, it being impossible to conceive that an inferior power should prescribe to a superior, or any but the supreme make laws, according as the power of making laws is placed, such is the form of the commonwealth." And Hooker concludes his first book of *The Laws of Ecclesiastical Polity* thus: ". . . of Law there can be no less acknowledged, than that her seat is the bosom of God, her voice the harmony of the world: all things in heaven and earth do her homage, the very least as feeling her care, and the greatest as not exempted from her power: both Angels and men and creatures of what condition soever, though each in different sort and manner, . . . admiring her as the mother of their peace and joy."

270

Fiscal matters · This preoccupation with law and legislation must not blind us to the fact that representative bodies are not usually limited to that activity. At the very outset, representative institutions were brought into existence, as we have seen, by the ability of nobles, clergy, and townsfolk to resist the royal tax collectors, to assert their right of being asked for their consent to new or exceptional levies. The influence which one part of the citizenry, the nobles, and then another, the burgesses, actually possessed gave birth to representative institutions for the exercise of that influence. The purely negative power of resistance could thus be converted into the positive power of affecting the conduct of government through petitions, complaints, and so forth. This celebrated "power of the purse"[10] has remained one of the cherished activities of parliamentary bodies, although the English Parliament has delegated all detailed control to the cabinet. Closely related to this power is the power to determine the expenditures of the government. In the beginning the two were joined; Parliament granted specific levies for specific tasks. Today, the expenditures of the government are, under a representative scheme, fixed through an annual budget. Since many of these expenditures are the direct outgrowth of legislation, however, the lines of distinction cannot be clearly drawn. A final aspect of fiscal influence exercised through representative bodies in civilized countries is the accounting control usually carried out by some kind of independent officer or "court" directly responsible to the popularly elected body, such as the Comptroller-General in the United States, or the *Cour des Comptes* in France (see below, ch. XIX, p. 404). Their relation to the representative bodies is rather formal.

Representation and constitutional government · In our discussion of the separation of powers and federalism we showed that the problem of restraint is indissolubly connected with the problem of dividing governmental powers.[11] Such a division can take different forms, of which the most important are the functional separation of powers, in the traditional sense, and the territorial division through some sort of federalism. For both purposes, representation is of vital importance. Distinct divisions of the electorate, created and maintained under a constitution, require the selection of distinct sets of representatives between whom the several functions of government may be divided. The same is true under any kind of separation of powers. We have shown how in England the legislative power was divided between king, lords, and commons, and how the judicial power was separated from all of them. Likewise in the United States the separation of powers presupposes a variety of representatives for different constituencies. Looked at from this angle, these schemes for dividing "power" really amount to dividing the people in a number of different ways, and then giving these several subdivisions a voice through different representatives who are kept from abusing their power by holding each other in check. Such a plan could not have any effect unless the community were *actually* divided into a number of groups or classes, one of which might have a majority in one constituency, while another has it in another. We thus speak of farm states, Catholic states, and Negro districts, of a governor who is the farmers' man, but who battles the Senate dominated by a utility, etc. Without representation, such balances could not establish themselves.

This fact has given rise in recent years to demands for some kind of new corporative body to represent the various class and interest groups in the industrial society (see below, ch. XXII). Such occupational representation was offered after the First World War as the panacea for the admitted shortcomings of territorial representation. Occupational representation, based as it is upon the idea that man's true community in an industrial society is his professional or occupational group, such as his trade union, has great difficulty in determining clearly the actual size and conformation of a constituency of this sort on account of the overlapping and the difficulty of assigning appropriate weight to each organization selected. How do housewives compare with musicians? It also has been found difficult to cope with multiple representation of individuals belonging to several such groups. The tedious history of the efforts to carry out the mandate contained in article 165 of the Weimar constitution shows clearly how extraordinarily complicated these issues are. It is too early to assess the experience with the Senate under the Bavarian Constitution, based as it is upon an occupational plan, or, more important perhaps, the Economic Council established by the new French Constitution in article 25.

Reasons for the late appearance of representative bodies · It has often been said that representative schemes are of rather recent origin; they certainly were not found, as Montesquieu asserted, in the forests of ancient Germanic tribes. They arose as part of the medieval constitutional order when that order assumed proportions which forbade any direct action.[12] In the first place, the unitary organization of Western Christendom within the Catholic Church necessitated representative assemblies, the great councils, in which all the Christian people were believed to be present. It was natural to apply the same idea to the representation of monasteries and cathedral chapters within a secular feudal order. And when the cities and towns reached a place in the sun in the course of the thirteenth century, and had to be reckoned with as centers of wealth and power, a further extension of corporate representation of these municipalities was clearly indicated.

Was it a matter of peculiar genius or of pure accident that Simon de Mont-fort, in calling the Parliament of 1265, issued a summons to the knights of each shire, as well as to the burgesses? It has been suggested that the exigen-cies of the English crown, hard pressed by unruly and powerful barons, gave the minister of Edward I this idea as a matter of electoral strategy. At any rate, the shires were corporate entities, capable of representation by analogy to the towns. Apparently in all these cases the corporate spirit of solidarity was sufficiently developed to render the group willing to exer-cise its influence through agents or representative persons. Where personal attendance is practically impossible, and the result is considered more im-portant than personal participation, such corporate solidarity will appear. The whole preceding discussion has implied this result as a necessary corol-lary of representation. In classical antiquity the situation was quite differ-ent; personal attendance was quite possible in the small city-states, and the result was rarely considered more important than personal participa-tion of the citizenry. In fact, the prevalence of slavery placed the citizenry in the position of a small leisure class who immensely enjoyed the daily gos-sip in the market place. But this necessity for personal participation be-came fatal whenever such a city-state reached larger proportions. The at-tempts at solving this problem through a federal organization foundered upon the inability of the ancients to work out a representative scheme. Ingenious as were the arrangements of the Romans for their Latin Federa-tion, they could not get away from the idea of embodying the citizenry of each city in the Roman citizenry, with the result of swelling its numbers so unduly that eventually they had to abandon this practice altogether. As we have seen when discussing federalism, its embodiment in an effective political order has to await the completion of a representative scheme under which the whole people as well as the people of each component unit can be given a certain influence upon the federal affairs, and a firm and uniform federal authority can thus be established. Through participation in the representative bodies of the federal union the justifiable demand for in-fluence and control is being satisfied and the units are thus protected against total obliteration. From such a point of view logrolling is not a purely vicious practice, but one which secures a certain protection for local inter-ests. This being the case, the federal administration can be given more power and independence, and under certain conditions it may be directed by a few or even by a single person, as in the United States. Such an or-ganization is greatly superior to a congress of ambassadors, such as charac-terized the federations of old and was revived in the League of Nations and the United Nations. The many programs for reform of the Charter of the United Nations all seek to establish a federal system that will more adequately carry out the higher aspiration of a representative federal government of all nations. This may well eventually come to fruition. But what a real understanding of the problem of representation can contribute to this discussion is a better grasp of the basic rule that there can be no representation, federal or other, until there is a community to be represented.

Conclusion · It is difficult to draw conclusions beyond saying that representation and representative government are facing an uncertain future, since the communal bonds upon which their rationale rests are deeply disturbed, if not actually disrupted. It may even be considered doubtful whether governments which depend upon outlawing certain parties, the Fascists here, the Communists there, are truly representative, even though such outlawry is decreed by popular majorities. The argument that these parties are the agents of foreign powers undoubtedly carries some weight, but one must ask whether it would not be more in keeping with the spirit of constitutional government if specific acts of collusion with such foreign governments were outlawed rather than a party seeking representative support among the electorate.

In any case, neither in Europe nor elsewhere has the idea of representation been significantly advanced since the time when proportional representation was set against majority representation—unless one wishes to consider the declining support for proportional representation an advance. Occupational representation, which continues to claim some adherents, still founders upon the difficulty of finding the proper "constituency." It is generally agreed that the traditional method of basing representation upon territorial subdivisions is quite artificial since no genuine community corresponds to them any longer, especially in the great urban conglomerations. Yet no one has succeeded in discovering a really workable plan for a change that would take account of the transformation of communal bonds. While an old established democratic system might adapt itself through various devices, such as legalizing interest groups and the like, it is doubtful whether such devices do more than attenuate the decline in representativeness of the territorially based representatives. Yet the success or failure of efforts to re-establish and reform representative government will turn upon the finding of adequate techniques of representation through elections. Else the fragmentized mass feeling, lost and unrepresented in processes of would-be democratic government, will follow a "leader" of the inspired kind who sets forth a claim of representativeness on nonrational grounds of a transcendental community, whether of class or of nation.[13]

274

XV

Electoral Systems in Theory and Practice

Introduction: the problem · The English system · The proposals for proportional representation · Bagehot's view: the functional approach · John Stuart Mill's view: the individualist approach · The problem of "justice" · Gerrymandering (electoral geometry) · The different functions of proportional systems · Practical applications · Recent trends · Assessment of experience · Conclusion.

Introduction: the problem · Tom, Dick, and Harry trotting to the voting booth enact the most distinctive process of modern politics. There have been kings, revolutions, constitutions, and vast bureaucracies since time immemorial, but the mass voter is something quite recent. To Aristotle democracy (polity) meant that the vital decisions were made by the assembly of the whole citizenry in the market place. To us it means that the whole citizenry goes and elects representatives, after having read about their platforms in the newspapers, listened to them in a meeting or over the radio. As we saw in the last chapter, elections are not the only possible method for securing representatives. They are, however, considered the most democratic method. What does "democratic" mean in this connection? Should all those whose interests are to be represented participate in the selection of representatives?[1] A considerable number of people are quite obviously disqualified to select a modern legislator. To admit that obvious truth does by no means imply a plea for government by intellectuals. On the contrary, the real backbone of an elective system are the cautious, steadfast men and women of common sense who can see the forest rather than the trees. It is one of the recurrent errors of the Fascist and Communist critics of representative government to make light of the sound sense of the average citizen. They have been aided by the failure of the friends of popular government to evaluate critically the electoral methods which have been in use. This has made it easy for antidemocrats to denounce the whole "system" on account of the obvious flaws in it. A comparative estimate of electoral methods, therefore, is one of the most urgent concerns of the political scientist, as well as of the practical reformer.

The English system · Parliamentary government in England rested for a long time upon a strictly traditional system of elections. It had grown out of the corporational basis of early Parliaments. Until the Reform Act of 1832, it abounded with the most abnormal situations.[2] Districts which had once been populous centers, and therefore entitled to separate representation in Parliament, retained this representation after all just claims had gone. One such "rotten borough" actually had been swept away by the sea. On the other hand, in the industrial north of England thriving cities had grown up which had no member in Parliament at all. During the nineteenth century a series of parliamentary reforms undertook to cope with this problem. At first the expedient was used of giving several representatives to one district. This system lasted down to 1884–1885, when the single-member constituency came into general use. Since that time, elections in England have been held on the basis of what is known as the system of plurality, that is, relative majority. This means that the candidate who secures the largest number of votes (but not necessarily an absolute majority) wins the seat. At the same time, the elections are now secret. Formerly they were public and took place by a showing of hands. As a result, polling was an occasion for much brawling and merry-making. "Rivers of beer were set flowing; bribes were openly offered and accepted; organized bands of 'bludgeon-men' went about intimidating and coercing electors; non-voters thrust themselves joyously into the fray; political convictions were expressed in terms of rotten apples and dead cats; heads were broken and a generally riotous time was had by all" (Ogg).

Yet there is something to be said for an open election. As John Stuart Mill pointed out, the right to vote is a public trust, and should therefore be exercised in such a fashion as to give the public a chance to see how it is used. What is more, under proper conditions of free assembly, it develops in the citizenry that most desirable quality of civic courage which does not shrink from standing up for one's convictions. Unfortunately, economic pressures have introduced a new element into the situation which obliges us to forego these advantages in order not to deprive a large body of citizens of their "right of suffrage." Since 1885 then, England has adopted secret balloting under a system of single-member constituencies. The purpose of these constituencies is to elect a Parliament, which in turn will be ready to support a cabinet, which in turn is to govern the land. In other words, the English electoral system is clearly directed toward the goal of dividing each constituency and thus all England into two halves, the majority to govern, and the minority to criticize. This may mean permanent voicelessness for a man who belongs to a perpetual minority, like a Democrat in Vermont, or a Republican in Alabama. As Walter Bagehot told his readers many years ago: "I have myself had a vote for an agricultural county for twenty years, and I am a Liberal; but two Tories have always been returned, and all my life will be returned. As matters now stand, my vote is of no use. But if I could combine with 1,000 other Liberals in that and other Conservative counties, we might choose a Liberal member."

The proposals for proportional representation · The foregoing statement sounds like a criticism of the existing English electoral system; in fact it constituted part of a reasoned defense of that system against those who had just brought forward the plan known as proportional representation. To be sure, Thomas Hare's scheme, first expounded in 1857, cannot claim to be the first exposition of the idea of proportional representation.[3] The idea appeared in the French National Convention in 1793, without leading to action. It was further elaborated by the mathematician Gergonne (1820), and developed independently by an English schoolmaster, Thomas Wright Hill, whose son took it to Australia (1839). At about the same time, in 1842, the idea gained a foothold in Switzerland when Victor Considérant proposed a proportional-representation system to the Council of Geneva. Two years later Thomas Gilpin set forth yet another plan for proportional representation. Finally another twelve years later a Danish minister of finance, Carl Andrae, worked out a system resembling the Australian plan, but using ballots. The following year Hare published his tract. From this rapid survey it can be seen that proportional representation was "in the air."

The underlying idea of all the various systems is to secure a representative assembly reflecting with more or less mathematical exactness the various divisions in the electorate. Why should such divisions be reflected? They should be "represented"! The voice of minorities should be heard! Justice requires that no votes be lost, that the Bagehots be able to get together and send a representative to Parliament. A man of the eminence of John Stuart Mill extolled the virtues of the scheme in his *Considerations on Representative Government* and called it one of "the very greatest improvements yet made in the theory and practice of government." Yet proportional representation shifts the basic meaning of representation. An important part of representation, we saw (ch. XIV, p. 266), is to represent the citizenry as a whole, not just the divisions among them. Representation means the exercise of the people's influence through a smaller number acting in their behalf. Proportional representation, on the other hand, looks upon the divisions in the electorate as the only entities to be represented; in the last analysis it looks upon the individual as the representable element or unit.

Proportional representation has been a subject of heated debate for almost a hundred years now. It has been the inspiration of civic groups, such as the Proportional Representation Society in England, to which men of great ability and standing have devoted much time and effort. And yet, it is a curious fact that in the English-speaking countries (except Eire, a special case), proportional representation has not made any substantial headway in spite of the fact that these countries are the home of representative government. Is this due to the greater resistance of established ways to any innovation? Or to some inherent defect in the plan which reveals itself to the good sense of peoples with a sound political tradition? Or to conditions such as greater homogeneity in the electorate which would make proportional representation less urgently needed? These and related questions will be answered very differently by different observers, depending upon their general convictions concerning proportional representation. This fact suggests that broader political and moral issues are involved in this apparently technical problem of political machinery.

Bagehot's view: the functional approach · When two men of the ability, insight, and experience of John Stuart Mill and Walter Bagehot disagree sharply, in spite of their belonging to the same party, the issue is likely to be a deep one. They were both liberals and they were both economists, but while Bagehot was a liberal of the right, Mill was a liberal of the left. In spite of his socialist leanings, Mill was an ardent individualist. His adherence to proportional representation clearly reveals this. The real core of the disagreement between Mill and Bagehot can be found in the former's distinctive emphasis upon the rationalist aspects of the problem, as against the latter's insistence upon the functionalist aspects. Bagehot asked:[4] What will proportional representation do to the functioning of parliament as we know it? Bagehot's great achievement anyway was to spell out what everyone "knew in practice," namely that the function of parliament was two-fold: (1) for the majority to support the cabinet in its conduct of the government, and (2) for the minority to criticize the actions of the government. The combination of action and criticism enables parliament to represent the people as a whole both toward itself and toward the outside world. Of the two functions, Bagehot naturally considered the first more important than the second, and therefore he argued that no matter how great the gain on other accounts, proportional representation must be rejected if it seriously threatened the government's capacity for action.

Bagehot considers the basic difference between election by majority and proportional representation the fact that proportional representation makes the constituency voluntary; in other words, each voter individually is able to choose his own constituency in accordance with his personal preference. He votes as a voluntary member of a group which has no other common ties. A constituency being the group or segment of voters who are entitled to send a member to Parliament, this is indeed the basic point, although the language of proportionalists often obscures it. To put Bagehot's point another way, all proportional schemes say to the electorate: if so and so many among you can agree upon a candidate,* that candidate shall be elected; whereas the majority system says: so and so many among you shall constitute an electoral district or part of the whole people, and whomever the largest number among you elect shall be one of the members of Parliament. As Bagehot pointed out, the temptations of the idea of a voluntary constituency are very plain. "Under the compulsory form of constituency the votes of the minorities are thrown away. In the city of London now, there are many Tories, but all the members are Whigs; every London Tory, therefore, is by law and principle misrepresented: his city sends to Parliament not the member whom he wished to have, but the member he wished *not* to have. But upon the voluntary system the London Tories, who are far more than 1,000 in number, may combine; they make a constituency and return a member. In many existing constituencies the disfranchisement of the minorities is hopeless and chronic." "Again, this plan gets rid of all our difficulties as to the size of constituencies." "Again, the admirers of a great man could make a worthy constituency for him." Yet Bagehot saw defects in the scheme which overbalanced and outweighed these merits. Essentially, under the voluntary system, so-called central party organizations would acquire an overweening influence. "The crisis of politics would be not the election of the member, but the making of the constituency. . . . The result of this . . . would be the return of party men mainly. The member-makers would look, not for independence, but for subservience—and they could hardly be blamed for so doing. They are agents for the Liberal party; and, as such, they should be guided by what they take to be the wishes of their principal. The mass of the Liberal party wishes measure A, measure B, measure C. The managers of the registration —the skilled manipulators—are busy men. They would say: 'Sir, here is your card; if you want to get into Parliament on our side, you must go for that card; it was drawn up by Mr. Lloyd; he used to be engaged on railways, but since they passed this new voting plan, we get him to attend to us; it is a sound card; stick to that and you will be right.' Upon this (in

*The required number varies greatly. The following prewar list will give an idea:

Austria	39,500	Ireland	20,000
Belgium	40,000	Netherlands	70,800
Bulgaria	20,000	Norway	17,650
Czechoslovakia	45,400	Poland	61,200
Denmark	22,500	Sweden	26,100
Finland	17,125	Switzerland	20,000

theory) voluntary plan, you would get together a set of members bound hard and fast with party bands and fetters infinitely tighter than any members now. . . . The full force of this cannot be appreciated except by referring to the former proof that the mass of a parliament ought to be men of moderate sentiments, or they will elect an immoderate ministry, and enact violent laws. But upon the plan suggested, the House would be made up of party politicians selected by a party committee and pledged to party violence, and of characteristic, and therefore immoderate representatives, for every 'ism' in all England. Instead of a deliberate assembly of moderate and judicious men, we should have a various compound of all sorts of violence. The voluntary plan, therefore, when tried in this easy form, is inconsistent with the extrinsic independence as well as with the inherent moderation of a parliament—two of the conditions which, as we have seen, are essential to the bare possibility of parliamentary government." It seems desirable to quote this memorable passage at such length, because its conception has always remained dominant in England, in spite of persistent agitation for proportional representation over the last fifty years. What is more, it foretells in the most extraordinary manner the experiences which we have been able to observe where such systems have been put into force. On the other hand, these arguments do, of course, by no means exhaust the problem. They are applicable only to a parliamentary government. And what if the divisions or cleavages of the people have reached proportions where any electoral system would be abandoned which did not give these warring groups adequate representation in national affairs?

John Stuart Mill's view: the individualist approach · Had John Stuart Mill[5] thought of it in terms of this function of parliament, the function Bagehot later called the "elective" one? Obviously not. Mill was preoccupied with the issue of "representation." After briefly outlining Hare's scheme of proportional representation, Mill sets forth a number of reasons which in his opinion constitute "transcendent advantages." "In the first place, it secures a representation, in proportion to numbers, of every division of the electoral body: not two great parties alone . . . but every minority in the nation . . ." "Secondly, no elector would be nominally represented by someone whom he had not chosen. Every member of the House would be the representative of an unanimous constituency." He stresses the strong tie, the complete identification, the weakening of localism (N.B.!), the higher intellectual qualification of the representatives and avoidance of "collective mediocrity." Finally, Mill sees it as a check on "the ascendancy of the numerical majority" by offering "a social support for individual resistance, . . . a rallying point for opinions and interests which the ascendant public opinion views with disfavor." Characteristically, in his enthusiasm, Mill finally calls proportional representation *Personal Representation* offering a refuge to the "instructed élite." No objections of real weight could be discovered by Mill, though in his usual judicious manner he examines a few, but finds them wanting. He did not consider the function of parliament. He also failed to examine his major premise, namely, that there can be no representation of the whole without a representation of each of the whole's individual parts.

The extreme individualism of Mill's approach is further illustrated by an unexplained premise concerning *justice*. As the title of his chapter suggests, Mill was concerned whether parliament represented all or only a majority. Unless it did represent all it was not "truly" representative, it was false democracy. But since traditional constitutional law had always claimed that parliament represented all, Mill's challenge had to be based upon a new view of what constituted representativeness. "There is a part," he wrote, "whose fair and equal share of influence in the representation is withheld from them; contrary to all just government, but above all, contrary to the principle of democracy. . . ." Now we must remember that the word "democracy" did not at that time in England spell the almost universal approval which it today elicits in England, and even more in America. It was a symbol of the radicals. It deserves to be noted, moreover, that in Mill's thought the issue is a question of justice. "The injustice and violation of principle are not less flagrant because those who suffer by them are a minority, for there is not equal suffrage where *every single individual does not count for as much as any other single individual* in the community." This phrasing somewhat obscures the issue, since the minority in one constituency will be the majority in another, but this very obscurity is highly revealing. It shows that Mill is thinking of the particular *individual* who finds himself without a representative. The whole, seen as a compound of all these particular individuals, is therefore not "represented" if all the individuals as individuals are not represented. Is this true? The answer to this question turns upon a problem of "justice."

The problem of "justice" · No functional arguments will meet the moral and philosophical issue raised by Mill. It has been pointed out above that John Stuart Mill emphasized very strongly the basic issue of justice. Bagehot might well have been charged by his illustrious opponent with shifting the ground. "Nothing is more certain than that the virtual blotting out of the minority is no necessary or natural consequence of freedom; that far from having any connection with democracy, it is diametrically opposed to the first principle of democracy, *representation in proportion* to numbers."[6]

And again: "Real equality of representation is not obtained, unless any set of electors amounting to the *average number of a constituency wherever in the country they happen to reside* have the power of combining with one another to return a representative." What kind of concept of justice and democracy is this? Clearly it is one in which the individual is treated as unrelated to family or any other local attachments, so that "the people" are not seen as a whole, a distinctive entity, created out of smaller, more vital groups. Rather the people are merely the sum of the individuals composing it, atomistic units who require each their own representatives. But is representation possible on such assumptions? Is not this kind of reasoning subject to the *reductio ad absurdum* which Rousseau's denial of the possibility of representation foreshadowed? Furthermore, is this view of the situation realistic? It is significant that the intellectual Mill dwells at length upon the advantages to the intelligentsia of sending their own ilk to parliament. Were the numerous professors in the German Reichstag much help to the German republic?* The intellectual elite are, by their work and profession, the most individualized lot. Unlike workers, farmers, and other simple folk, they possess a high mobility and little attachment to any particular locality. They usually speak a high-brow, national language, untainted by much local color. All this is part of their function in contemporary society. The railing of the "blood and soil" fanatics is a senseless reaction. But if one belongs to this elite, one should beware of generalizing from one's own natural propensities, and of constructing institutional devices for society at large on that basis. Such uncritical disregard for reality and its functional needs is likely to spell disaster in the end. Can anything be just which does not work?

But let us assume for a moment that representation through a person elected by the majority of your fellow townsmen is "unjust" to some minority, and that this can be remedied by giving this minority a chance of combining with others constituting a similar minority elsewhere. If there were only one such minority, it would simply mean that there would be more men in parliament to criticize than before. This would mean less action, rather than different action. If there were many such minorities, so that no group any longer had a majority, it would mean complete inaction over long periods. In either case, is it not a question of competing claims? Why should the problem of what is just to a minority be given precedence over what is just to the majority? Admittedly the majority wants action.

*The British formerly made allowance for the professorial elite by providing a dozen special seats in parliament for the great universities. This survival of medieval corporate representation, although serving modern purpose, was abolished in the Representation of the People Act of 1948, which took effect in 1950.

Such action is, through Proportional Representation, or P. R., being delayed or altogether prevented. What is the justice of that? It would appear that Mill, in his concern over the minority, had neglected the majority. Problems of justice are problems of adjustment between conflicting claims. The election of representatives therefore always involves the paring down of *some* claims; justice can only be achieved if these claims are equitably adjusted. Presumably the majority's claims are weightier than those of any minority. Representation is a broad thing; representatives are elected so that many may participate indirectly in the essential tasks. The majority participates through acting, the minority through discussion and criticism. If the majority fails to be represented adequately, because its representatives are unable to act, the injustice is just as great, or greater, than if the minority fails to be represented adequately, because its representatives cannot talk as much as they would like to. It is not a question of justice, then, but of more adequate representation of minorities. This may or may not be a desirable thing. But it should be considered on its merits.

Gerrymandering (electoral geometry) · Besides providing for the representation of important minorities, proportional representation possesses the merit of getting rid of the difficulties as to the size and structure of constituencies. As long as the population shifts, periodic readjustments of the boundaries of electoral districts are necessary if gross injustices such as the rotten boroughs are to be avoided. In the United States that problem is a familiar one through the recurrent struggle over reapportionment.[7] In recent years a somewhat agitated controversy has been raging among statistical scholars regarding the "just" method of such reapportionment. It is this difficulty which affords many of the illustrations of those who argue for proportional representation. Unequal electoral districts are not of the essence of the system of plurality elections, but it must be conceded that this system does, *usually*, show considerable maladjustments in the size of electoral districts.

What is worse, under adverse conditions of unscrupulous party politics, it lends itself to the practice of gerrymandering, so-called after a former Governor of Massachusetts who perceived the potentialities of affecting the electoral result by manipulating the geography of the constituencies. Since all a party needs to gain a seat is a small majority (or in three-cornered fights a mere plurality) of votes, you can draw the boundaries of your electoral districts in such a way as to crowd large percentages of your party opponents into a few districts, and then divide the rest in such a way as to give yourself a majority. What you are thus doing is merely artificially creating conditions which resemble those which arise in course of time through the shifts in population. To give a concrete illustration: suppose you had an area which had to elect ten representatives for 100,000 voters. These voters are divided between party A and party B in such a way that party A is adhered to by most of the city-dwellers, whereas party B is counting most of the farmers as its partisans. There are three cities in the territory, one of 20,000 voters and two of 15,000 voters. If party A were in power and undertook to gerrymander this territory, they would want to get about 7,000 of their supporters into seven districts, thus giving them a clear majority in the representative body. They would do this by constructing mixed country and city districts, leaving the rest of the voters in solid agricultural areas. But the managers of party B also would want, if they were in power, to construct mixed districts, but in such a way as to leave some strictly urban districts. The two pictures would compare thus:

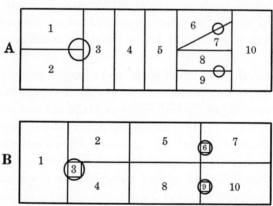

The districts under the gerrymander of A would be:

(1) A 7,000	B 3,000	(6) A 7,500	B 2,500
(2) A 6,500	B 3,500	(7) A 7,500	B 2,500
(3) A 6,500	B 3,500	(8) A 7,500	B 2,500
(4) A 0	B 10,000	(9) A 7,500	B 2,500
(5) A 0	B 10,000	(10) A 0	B 10,000

The district under the gerrymander of B would be instead:

(1) A 3,500	B 6,500	(6) A 10,000	B 0
(2) A 3,250	B 6,750	(7) A 2,500	B 7,500
(3) A 10,000	B 0	(8) A 2,500	B 7,500
(4) A 3,250	B 6,750	(9) A 10,000	B 0
(5) A 2,500	B 7,500	(10) A 2,500	B 7,500

These samples illustrate in a typical fashion how the same *total* electorate may give entirely the opposite result if divided along opposite lines. Many

American states show the most extraordinary shapes for electoral districts, shapes which are much more exotic than the "salamander" to which the "gerrymander" was supposed to be related. But even if party managers do not stoop to such tactics, it would be too much to hope for party managers to change electoral districts when the social forces have produced effects akin to our example but quite independent of any manipulation. Precisely this was the situation in England throughout a large part of the nineteenth century. The English reforms undertook to redistrict the country, and eventually in 1885 divided the whole realm into a fairly even number of single-member constituencies, probably because the more conservative Liberals, like Bagehot, could not see eye to eye with proportional representation. On the other hand, the German Social Democrats, who had advocated proportional representation under the Empire, stuck to their conviction after the revolution of 1918, and adopted a thoroughgoing system of proportional representation. This they did in spite of the fact that it would have been to their distinct advantage as a party to redistrict the country and hold elections in single-member constituencies.

The different functions of proportional systems · Unquestionably, Bagehot put his finger upon the central objection from a governmental standpoint.[8] But he did not formulate it in the most persuasive fashion. In terms of the accepted focal interests of political science, it is more important that a majority system of elections oblige the voter to *decide* between two or more alternatives than that the constituency be compulsory. The need of a decision is paramount when the representative body has over and above everything else the function of constituting either the executive or the government which is to hold office as long as the representative body is willing to support it. As everyone knows, such a system of parliamentary government makes the executive dependent upon and responsible to a majority in the representative assembly. For, if the assembly becomes divided into so many factions that there cannot be found a stable majority for the executive's support, all governmental activity becomes paralyzed. It is appalling to read with care the astounding documentation which Dr. Hermens has assembled to show how in country after country precisely this paralysis crept in. Eventually the people lost hope that effective action would ever be produced, and "parliamentarism" became a by-word for inefficiency and inaction. England resisted the lure of proportionalism. Sticking to their traditions, most Englishmen, including the Labour party, rejected P. R., recognizing it as the most important function of the English Parliament to support the government. For a long time this function was obscured by the doctrine of a separation of powers, particularly since such a separation prevailed in the United States. Parliament was looked upon as a legislative assembly. But while the legislative function is quite important, it is not *as* important as the maintenance and functioning of the government itself. The influence of the whole electorate upon this executive management must become focalized into a few clear alternatives. For, as Lowell has so clearly shown, large numbers of people cannot decide between any but two or three very simple alternatives.

But what if the elected representatives do not have this function of constituting the executive? It is, after all, by no means a foregone conclusion that the function of the representative assembly should be a decision as to who shall govern. Not only in the United States, but in Switzerland and in prewar Germany, the main function of the representative assembly was legislation. Such legislation, particularly modern economic and social legislation, touches the everyday interests of all citizens, and the divisions of interest between them are fairly persistent. It cannot, for example, reasonably be expected that the employer and capitalist would be persuaded to hand all profits over to his workers, nor can we hope that the workers will readily yield to those who expect them to be satisfied with the joy of work, and be content with long hours at starvation wages. Legislation touching these and many similar issues between the various groups in the community must be framed as an acceptable compromise in which all relevant views are voiced with a vigor approximately comparable to their actual strength in the community. A representative assembly, then, whose primary function is the framing of such legislation, would greatly benefit from a well-thought-out system which would bring into it the various groups in the community in rough proportion at least to their strength. But there must still be an effective majority ready to support a fairly coherent policy. The difficulties in the way of achieving that purpose are great under the American presidential system even without any multiplication of parties such as proportionalism envisages and engenders.

For no matter what the variations in detail, the fundamental principle of P. R. is always the same: to secure a representative assembly reflecting with more or less mathematical exactness the various divisions in the electorate. Now, there are two predominant ways of achieving that purpose, the single transferable vote advocated by Thomas Hare, and the list system of proportional representation widely used in Europe. The first scheme gives the voter leave to indicate first, second, and third choices (and more if there are more candidates in the district). Thus the voter continues to choose between individual candidates. The second scheme, on the other hand, asks the voter to choose between lists of candidates which contain as many names as there are representatives to be chosen. The particular forms they have been given in various countries are often combinations of the two basic types. A detailed study would offer an opportunity for an understanding of both. The most radical application of the list system of proportional representation was found in the Weimar Republic, whereas the single transferable vote is being tried in the Republic of Ireland. More or less mixed plans are being used in Belgium, Denmark, the Netherlands, Norway, Sweden, and Switzerland (among others).

Practical application · The oldest system of proportional representation for national elections is that of Belgium. Here the voter has to choose one of the several party lists, but at the same time he is entitled to indicate his preferences within the list.[9] It is noteworthy that under this system of proportional representation, a remarkable stability of party strength at first gave the strongest party, the Catholics, long periods of undisputed leadership. But more recently Belgium experienced marked ministerial instability, which undermined the long-felt satisfaction with proportional representation in that country.

Very similar in its conception to the Belgian system was the Dutch electoral plan, which was adopted in 1917 after very extensive deliberations and inquiries over many years. In the Netherlands, however, the entire country was constituted as one single electoral district. The Dutch system also led to a remarkable stability of party strength, and, on the whole, public opinion was satisfied. It is noteworthy that Holland as well as Belgium has a parliamentary system of government. It seems that the tendency toward a multiplication of parties was held in check by the very fact that parliamentary government renders small parties ineffectual. The experience of Belgium points even more definitely in that direction: we find only three great parties, the Catholics, the Socialists, and the Liberals, which stand for the three dominant creeds as well as the three dominant economic divisions of the country. To these must be added the Flemish Independence Party, which has agitated for the racially and linguistically distinct Flemish minority.

The three Scandinavian kingdoms, Sweden, Norway, and Denmark, also combine parliamentary government with proportional representation. Their systems are each different from the other, but both Sweden and Norway have list systems, whereas Denmark has tried to work out a complicated plan of combining single-member constituencies with proportional representation. In Sweden and Norway the voter has the sole voice in the rank order of the candidates on the lists. There are considerable variations in the extent to which the voters of the several parties exercise their own judgment in the matter of individual preferences. While the social-democratic electorate (labor) is very loyal, the conservative and liberal groups are more ready to bolt. In spite of these elements of flexibility, the Swedish electoral system has been considerably criticized in recent years, and occasional voices have been heard which demand the return to some kind of single-member constituency. The main point of attack has been the power of central party bosses and the lack of connection between the voter and the elected representatives. However, neither in Sweden nor in Norway does there seem to be any inclination to abandon proportional representation, and the same thing is true of Denmark. To be sure, Denmark has worked out a peculiar plan according to which the voter elects representatives in single-member constituencies, with certain complicated provisions for the transfer of his vote to adjacent constituencies combined into districts. The remainders are distributed nationally on the basis of the proportional vote for each party. The main objection to the Danish system is its complexity; but it does not seem to perturb the Danes, who are operating parliamentary government under its aegis with considerable success; whatever difficulties were encountered in connection with forming a workable ministry were not attributed to proportional representation.

Switzerland, without a parliamentary executive, has a federal system. Elections to the lower house of the federal legislature did not become proportionalized until 1919, and experience with this system is therefore limited. The Swiss system is another variant of the list system, made more flexible by giving the voter entire freedom in making up his list, as in Norway and Sweden, and adding the opportunity of voting twice for the same candidate. By the Swiss method an almost mathematical reproduction of the existing views in the community is achieved in the legislative body. The considerable division of parties under this system cannot, however, endanger the conduct of the executive government, since the Swiss Executive Council does not feel obliged to resign if the vote in the legislature is adverse to its recommendations. Instead, it sets to work on the preparation of a measure more in keeping with the wishes of the representatives. Though there are many complaints heard about the hardening of parties into class-interest pressure groups, to date the Swiss representatives seem to have performed effectively their one essential function, that of legislation.

Whereas Switzerland is on the whole a country famous for its moderation in politics, Ireland is noted for the violence of its political partisanship. Yet proportional representation seems to have taken root there without much friction. Indeed, it is claimed that the very intensity of political animosities necessitated a proportional scheme, because the lack of unity might have led the party defeated by an ordinary plural system to resort to violence. Be that as it may, the Republic of Ireland has adopted the single transferable vote system of proportional representation which the British Proportional Representation Society has so long been advocating. Each voter has only one vote, but if a candidate should receive more than his share of first choices, the second choices of his ballots are distributed among the other candidates to see which then gets the highest number. Although the parties may instruct their followers as to which candidate to put first, they usually content themselves with urging their voters to vote for the men on their list—or so it is asserted. At any rate, the voters can do as they please. The relative stability of party strength at the start prevented the extreme oscillations in the policy of the government which a new country with such passionate partisanship might otherwise have experienced. Since the necessary minimum quota of votes cannot readily be reached by groups which are too small to command solid support in at least one district, the number of parties is not exceptionally large. Yet, the breaking-up process seems to have commenced. In the general elections of 1948, no party received a majority, and Ireland had to choose between a minority and a coalition government. It chose the coalition which, combining all groups, has only 79 votes as against the largest party's 68. Once again, P. R. is proving its tendency to prevent the integration of political support for a responsible government.[10]

From the Republic of Ireland we must finally turn to the ill-fated German Republic of 1919, where proportional representation according to the list system was carried to its logical conclusion, and by some is held largely responsible for the collapse of the Republic. In contrast to the small or dependent states which we have so far considered, Germany was, even after the First World War, a large power with a complicated foreign policy of its own. Such responsibility for foreign affairs on a large scale broadens a government's political tasks, and enhances the importance of stability.

The German system was rather simple in its conception. The country was divided into thirty-five electoral districts. Each party prepared a list of candidates for these districts, the larger parties usually containing as many candidates as there were seats to be filled in the district. For each 60,000 votes this ticket received, one of its candidates was elected, and exactly in the order in which they appeared on the ticket. Remainders were transferred to regional and national tickets. The voter could make no changes; he really voted for a party, rather than a candidate. This was supposed to make it possible for national leaders to return to parliament without undergoing the exertion and sordidness of an election campaign. Actually these lists provided safe berths for the party managers and wirepullers behind the scene. It also kept them well-insulated from the people, thereby increasing the chances of a demagogue like Hitler. The very ir-

289

responsibility, or rather lack of responsibility, encouraged extremism in the electorate; for the electorate did not learn, through the competition of responsible parties, what the realities of Germany's political situation called for and what the available alternatives were. Consequently, and to make things worse, the radical wings hostile to the constitutional system gained at the expense of the more moderate and responsible parties and leaders.

Recent trends · If men were rational, P. R. would have been adopted only in countries prepared to work out a constitutional system which would not make the government dependent upon stable party support in the representative legislative bodies. People would generally have recognized that P. R., whatever its pros and cons—and that, as we have seen, is a complicated problem—leads to the fragmentation of parties and fails to give clear-cut decisions by the electorate. Actually, France, Italy, and Germany did just that: they adopted a parliamentary system of making the executive dependent upon parliament and provided for proportional representation besides. The French, in addition, resuscitated their system of double-voting, or run-off elections. However, in each case some modifications in both executive-legislative relationships and in the P. R. system itself were made which may help these countries to escape the worst results of this combination.

In France proportional representation lists were allowed on a district (department) basis only, but the voter, as in Belgium and Scandinavia, was enabled to change the order of candidates on the list, that is, express a personal preference. (Only 1.7 per cent of the voters made use of this privilege in the election of November 10, 1946.) This compromise which was first adopted by General de Gaulle for the constituent assembly's election in 1945 "contributed to the growth of a new political pattern, with four or five strong party machines replacing the undisciplined and flexible formations of prewar days." Men like Council-member (Senator) Michel Debré continue to attack the system as vicious along lines suggested in our own analysis.

In the opinion of Professor Einaudi, in Italy "the usual fateful consequences of proportional representation were avoided." Others are less optimistic. As in France, proportionality applies primarily to the districts; for the Senate, there is provided an opportunity to be elected on a single-member districts basis for those who can secure 65 per cent of the votes: the others are handled proportionally. In any case, Italy, like France, has stuck to the parliamentary system and is being governed accordingly. Due, however, to the exceptional threat of Soviet domination, the Christian Democrats, the Communists' main opponents, achieved an absolute majority in the important lower house.

The Germans, too, have modified P. R. somewhat. Abandoning the list system of Weimar days in the *Länder*, where a variety of electoral systems have been used, including a British-imposed straight majority system, the Germans have instituted two major innovations. One is the exclusion from all representation of a party which fails to receive a specified percentage of the total vote. In Bavaria this percentage is as high as ten per cent, and the Communists who polled just below ten per cent have not had a seat in parliament. Obviously, such a provision deals the death-blow to small splinter groups, but whether it is really democratic may be doubted. The other innovation is to provide, as was done in Württemberg-Baden, that no vote of nonconfidence could be taken without at the same time assuming responsibility for forming the new government; this plan has also been adopted in the Basic Law. Article 67 provides that the parliament "may express lack of confidence only by electing a successor," thus preventing two extremist groups, like the Nazis and the Communists, from stalling the system by irresponsible nonconfidence votes.[11] The new electoral law does not continue for the federation the device of excluding parties which receive less than a certain percentage. Instead, it seeks to combine majority and P. R. by providing that half of the representatives are to be elected by plurality in one-man constituencies, the other half on the basis of party lists, put forward for the parties in each *Land*. Each *Land* is given a certain number of seats to fill, from North Rhine–Westphalia with 109 to Bremen with 4, making a total of about 400. It is hard to foresee what such a compromise will produce, in the way of electoral contests. It is a hybrid which may fail to give either the clear decision of the majority system, or the "just reflection" of the P. R. system.

Assessment of experience · The P. R. system of the Weimar Republic was subjected to searching criticism by both theorists and practitioners. The most thoroughgoing student of this entire controversy arrived at very negative conclusions and goes so far as to assert that proportional representation "caused" the collapse of the Weimar Republic. Maintaining that democracy can reconcile liberty with authority only by subjecting the minority to the will of the majority, he finds that "certain fundamental tendencies are created by proportional representation which make this compromise impossible, replacing it by that kind of constitutional deadlock which is the ideal preparation for dictatorship." The expression, proportional representation, here refers of course primarily to the list system. But what were these "certain fundamental tendencies"? Perhaps most important was the fact that the list system not only stratified existing party organizations, but created new ones. It was much easier to found a new party under the German system than under a majority system. What is more, the parties under such a list system are controlled by the party bosses through the lists. Experience has essentially borne out the predictions of Bagehot as to the rigidity of party lines and the disregard for the marginal voter; it has shown further that the political consequence of that emphasis upon regularity, dogmatism, and creed was the rise of radical extremist parties. Hence the homogeneity which parliamentary government needs is not only not created, but is actually destroyed. Yet, curiously enough, this emphasis upon dogmatism has not banished the impact of special interest groups. On the contrary, each moderate party in Germany tended to become identified with some particular one of these interests, and some interests actually organized parties of their own. The result of such a combination of entrenched interests on the one hand and radical dogmatism on the other was a recurrent deadlock when it came to making up a cabinet. Under such a system, there is rarely any clear "decision" at the polls in terms of which a cabinet could be set up. The Italian elections of 1948 provide one of these rare exceptions, motivated in part at least by the basic issue of Soviet domination.

Internally, relations between members and leaders tend to become rather authoritarian. It is next to impossible for the party membership to dislodge entrenched leaders. The overweening position of the party bosses was further enhanced by the size of the electoral districts under the list system, which make personal contacts difficult, if not impossible. While a small constituency depends upon the co-operation of local volunteers for much of the work, such large constituencies allow the party to pay a permanent secretary and to become quite independent of genuine membership co-operation. Unlike the man who seeks election, such party functionaries remain unknown to the electorate, and dissatisfied groups in the party following are unable to make themselves heard.

This oligarchic and bureaucratic trend naturally also molded the relations between the rank and file of the representatives and the top men. Having no personal backing in the electorate, they had to look toward the party boss for support. Such boss rule is of course found everywhere, but P. R. greatly aggravates this evil. The result is a bureaucratic party leadership.

Where seats are personally contested under an electoral system, a man seeking election must be able to fight. This brings forward men of the "leader" type. Under the German list system, with its emphasis upon party regularity, a man seeking election had to conform; this brought forward the bureaucratic type. In the German parliament there were many excellent specialists on technical matters, but leaders were decidedly lacking.

What made matters worse was the premium such an arrangement places upon older men. Young men find it surprisingly difficult to break into the ranks of all but the most radical parties. Many more detailed demonstrations of the evil workings of the list system of proportional representation, especially under the list system, could be given, but it ought to be quite clear from this summary that it greatly increases certain defects in the democratic process.

Conclusion · Whatever the merits of other schemes of proportional representation, the proportional scheme which makes the whole country one constituency and bases its proportionality upon votes for unalterable party tickets (lists) has been found wanting and incompatible with parliamentary government. As to systems which allow the voter all necessary freedom to choose between individual candidates, the case is not so clear. In the first place, it must be admitted that in a system which clearly divides legislative from executive and administrative responsibility, such as that of Switzerland, a proportional system allowing the voter freedom of choice and requiring a considerable amount of local support is feasible. For here the main concern of the representative body is legislation. While a multiple-party system entails some difficulties, the adequate representation of all important groups in the community is in many respects desirable, particularly when social and racial differences are clear cut and well known. In the second place, under conditions of marked stratification of the social structure, that is, fixed political diversity in the community, proportional representation may be the only system acceptable to the larger minorities. The decisive question here would be how permanent these minorities are. Racial and religious minorities frequently have this rigidity which distinguishes them from traditional English and American conditions: they are quite permanent yet can never hope to grow into a majority. Where such minorities exist, and have reached a state of self-consciousness, they may feel the need for an electoral system which assumes stratified diversity. Yet even here it should be borne in mind that P. R. reinforces such stratification whereas the majority system tones it down. In any case, if P. R. is, adopted, probably the system of parliamentary government, if adopted, should be altered to make allowance for the conditions which the P. R. system is likely to bring about in the field of parties.

In answer to those who would point to the governments of Belgium, the Netherlands, Sweden, Norway, and Denmark, we would say that none of these countries are great powers. Their foreign policy was believed to depend on that of the greater powers. They all strove for neutrality, accepting internationalism as their natural course. When totalitarian aggressiveness, particularly Hitler's, rendered this policy impractical, they all began to flounder. While proportionalism can scarcely bear the sole responsibility, it certainly did not aid in producing an effective integration of the electorate and thus a clear decision.

But apart from this failure in foreign policy, there are special factors to be considered in these several lands. In Belgium, Holland, Sweden, Norway, and Denmark monarchy has survived in a form more nearly resembling older constitutional forms than is true in England. While these governments are parliamentary, in the sense that they must find support in parliament, the royal head of the government still exerts a certain influence in the selection of the candidates, and his moderating tendency is often apparent. It is obvious that the very smallness of these countries allows for an intimacy between court and parliament which would be hard to maintain in larger countries. What is perhaps even more important, it is notable that Holland and Sweden, which in many ways have the most distinctive foreign policy, have developed traditions in the administrative field which effectively neutralize a large part of the executive establishment and thus limit parliament largely to the legislative function, as in Switzerland under a separation of powers (see above, ch. X, pp. 182 f. for details).

All this goes to show that the prevalent English and American opinion against proportional representation is practically sound. There are special conditions which might mitigate this conclusion. But the proportional representation enthusiast, who would argue from the relative success of proportionalism in some small countries that we should try it in Great Britain and the United States, goes wrong. Although in the United States the constitutional order is based upon a separation-of-powers scheme, the President as chief executive must be elected by a simple plurality. While this might act as a deterrent to the development of minor parties, certain religious, class, and race cleavages might, in the course of time, emerge and plague us by their intransigeant attitude. The appeal of P. R. lies in the promise it holds out for breaking up corrupt machines. There can be no question that P. R. starts out by doing this quite effectively. But after the machine politicians have caught their breath, they are quite skillful in "taking over" proportional representation. Since proportional representation in the long run strengthens, rather than weakens party, that is, machine, control, the bosses return with another rampart added to their fortress. As Newton D. Baker put it in a communication to the *Cleveland Plain Dealer* on July 25, 1935: "We have groups of all sorts and kinds, formed around religious, racial, language, social and other contentious distinctions. Proportional representation invites these groups to seek to harden and intensify their differences by bringing them into political action where they are irrelevant, if not disturbing. A wise election system would invite them to forget these distracting prejudices."

Within the framework of most European countries, this conclusion against proportionality of representation seems, in retrospect, to have posed an insoluble dilemma. For apparently the divisive cleavages of the people often had reached such an intensity that any electoral system which did not give these warring groups adequate representation in the legislative process would have been unacceptable. It is so even after the Fascist catastrophe in Germany. The conclusion seems inescapable that the continent of Europe cannot be successfully organized in accordance with the parliamentary pattern of representative democracy. This conclusion has not been drawn, however, by the constitution-makers of Europe after 1945. There is much more vigorous opposition to P. R., to some extent influenced by the fact that the Communist parties throughout Europe have been firmly supporting it.

At any rate, electoral systems must be studied with reference to the whole constitutional order, as well as to the social and other conditions of the country concerned. No popular government can escape from the necessity of working out a system adapted to its peculiar needs.

XVI

Parliaments as Representative Assemblies

Introduction · Representation as integration · The importance of party structure for the work of parliaments · Social composition of membership · General problems of procedure · The House of Lords and second chambers · Bentham's views, their influence and results · Presiding officers: the English Speaker · The American Speaker · The chief whip · Procedure and parties · Majority and minority; the problem of consent and constraint · The representativeness of representative assemblies: quantitative approach · Conclusion.

Introduction · Parliaments until recently have been the institutional core of modern representative government. At present the executive, particularly when representing a majority party, is forging ahead and is tending to become the heart of representation, as shown in Chapter XVIII. Parliaments held the center of the stage until the First World War for many reasons. As election came to be looked upon as the primary basis of legitimate authority and hence of representative qualifications, the position of parliaments was enhanced. The emphasis upon legislation as a man-made body of rules (see above, ch. XIV, pp. 268 f.) helped to strengthen parliaments, because their public deliberations were peculiarly well adapted to the legislative process. Finally, the doctrine of the separation and balance of powers, particularly as applied to constitutional monarchies (see ch. X, p. 181 f.), strengthened the claim of parliaments, as the representatives of the people, to offer a counterpoise to the Crown. There is a difference between the procedure of such parliaments and legislatures in Switzerland or the United States, where constitutional provisions made executive and legislative authorities independent of each other. Yet it is difficult to appraise correctly the effect which this difference has had upon the inner working of parliamentary bodies; it seems that the effect is less marked than one might be led to expect. But an effect there is; the contrast in the position of the Speaker in the Commons and in the House of Representatives is perhaps the most striking illustration (see below, pp. 312 ff.). Whatever the difference, all these elected bodies have in common representative and deliberative functions which, though related, are quite distinct, and hence should be considered separately. The Fascist Grand Council also had representative functions; in letting itself be bellowed at by Mussolini it represented the Italian people as perfectly as the Nazi Reichstag represented the German people, but its deliberative functions were nil.

Representation as integration · Traditionally, legislation is considered the peculiar province of representative assemblies (see above, ch. XIV, p. 269). Representative assemblies are in fact referred to as *the* legislature, although it is always at once conceded that these assemblies do not have exclusive control over legislation nor are they concerned only with legislation. Nevertheless, legislation is traditionally looked upon as their primary function. Such a view is formal rather than political. Politically speaking, the function of making laws is nowadays at least as much carried on by the central bureaucracy, which drafts all important bills in England, France, and other European countries, and to an increasing extent in the United States.[1] The political function of representative assemblies today is not so much the initiation of legislation as the carrying on of popular education and propaganda and the integration and co-ordination of conflicting interests and viewpoints. The representative must be a master in the art of compromise. Parliaments and parliamentarians appear as integrating agencies through which the policy of the government and the claims of the various interest groups are expounded to the larger public with a view to discovering a suitable balance. There can be little doubt that this educational function is highly significant. The average citizen, that is, you and I, needs to have the pros and cons of pending proposals dramatized for him. The clash of argument in representative groups helps this greatly. The drama of the filibustering senator, though often arousing indignation, helps the citizen to appreciate the implications and significance of new legislation. The consequences of the lack of such contact between the government and the citizen are very apparent in totalitarian regimes. A great many measures of the government, which may be intrinsically necessary, meet with sullen indifference if not with hostility from the people merely because they are not understood. Occasional rhetorical outbursts on the part of a few leaders are not sufficient.

Integration is not, however, automatic, but highly dependent upon the structure of thought and outlook, feeling and interest, of the electorate. Hence the pious formula that representatives are not bound by mandate, that they are subject only to their conscience and are supposed to serve the common weal, which is repeated in so many European constitutions, while significant as a norm, may lead to differentiating as well as to integrating results. As in mathematics, so in politics, differential and integral functions are interrelated. One of the most dramatic instances of recent years in this field occurred in many countries, but more especially in the United States, just before the outbreak of hostilities of the Second World War. Popular sentiment became increasingly polarized as interventionists and isolationists in and out of Congress propagandized and educated the public to the dramatic issue of peace and war. Two large national organizations, the Committee to Defend America by Aiding the Allies (William Allen White Committee) and the America First Committee, spearheaded the contending forces. But while the sharp conflict—which was almost an even one, judging by the financial resources of each side—seemed to differentiate to the extent of almost dividing the American people into two halves, a broad integrating process was taking place on a deeper level. Both groups, and the many minor ones associated with them, were represented in the Congress; many Congressmen sought hard to maintain a middle ground and effect a compromise. The underlying integrating factor appears in the title of both organizations: "America." For what happened in the course of the struggle between the contending parties, both seeking to represent America, was to arouse the American people to the need to *defend* America. As was pointed out in the discussion of representation, it is the elected assembly as a whole which represents the people. Majority and minority acting jointly, therefore, have a powerful integrating effect. When, at the outbreak of war, all but a few act together in supporting the government, the unity of the people is strikingly represented, and integration reaches a high point. National emergencies, like the spring and summer of 1932, can have the same effect. No single executive, elected by a majority, can be as integrating as such a joining together of opponents.

We have seen in an earlier chapter (XIV) that representation and responsibility are closely linked. Representatives of the people are intended to be responsible to those whom they represent; in turn such responsible conduct enhances the representative quality. In fact, it is not too much to say that systems of representation developed out of the need of insuring constitutional responsibility. More especially elections, by permitting a recurrent review of the actions of representatives at regular intervals, are supposed to be the most rational method of establishing responsible government. This review brought about the development of parties (see below, ch. XX); they both differentiate and integrate. While trying to integrate as many voters as possible, they succeed in integrating perhaps half of them, the other half being integrated by a competing group of leaders. Such polarization of the electorate into two focal differentiations is characteristic of the majority system of representation, while the proportional system, as we have seen, produces multiple differentiation. Which of the two systems will more nearly facilitate over-all integration of the community for purposes of constitutional government depends upon circumstances; we have seen that the social composition and structure of an electorate, such as class, religious, and cultural groupings, are important in this connection. The problem is also intimately linked to the pattern of executive-legislative relationships, which are discussed below in chapter XVIII.

The importance of party structure for the work of parliaments · The organization and structure of parliaments is profoundly affected by party organization. A two-party system divides the house into two more or less equal parts. In line with this fact, the English House of Commons is divided into two halves facing each other. One half is supposed to be occupied by the party supporting the government, the other half by His Majesty's Opposition. In the American Congress, both Senate and House, the representatives are scattered according to seniority and personal preference. The Committees in the American Congress are composed of members of both parties, but the chairman is of the majority party, as is the Speaker of the House. This may tend to obscure political realities; in the United States, the genuine battle-line is that between conservatives and progressives, rather than between Republicans and Democrats. Hence the administration cannot "count" on the committee's staying in line. Another difficulty in the United States arises from the strength of sectional-interest and local-interest representation, especially in the Senate. Again, we see the impact of party organization here: senators and representatives are put forward by state party organizations.

Following the French tradition, a multiple-party system may range from conservatism to radicalism. Again, as in the German parliament of the Weimar Republic, it may possess a cluster of moderate groups at the center, surrounded by groups of radical extremists who might be either reactionary or revolutionary or both. The seating arrangements in parliaments often are expressive of the innate structure and relationship of the groups contained in it.[2] Thus, if the conservatives sit on the right side of the House and the radicals on the left, as was the case in the French Constituent Assembly and has been the case in France ever since, it is possible to speak of the "right" or "left" in a symbolic sense. It is a tribute to the force of French ideas that these expressions are now used in countries like England and the United States where no such seating arrangement is actually found.

It is obvious that the work methods of representative assemblies will be different, depending upon who sits in them. If each shade of public opinion is set off in a separate party, debates will tend to become a series of speeches, each speech representing one of those parties. Appointments to committees will be determined by party membership, since care must be taken that each party is represented, and so forth.

Social composition of membership · Even more important, perhaps, than the party system is the social composition of the representative assembly. There can be little doubt that the aristocratic backbone of the English Parliament which persisted throughout the nineteenth century was of great importance in giving to that body a certain homogeneity of outlook and a code of "gentlemanly" conduct which materially affected its mode of procedure.[3] What is more, the willingness of the English aristocracy to absorb new members who distinguished themselves in public affairs added a powerful social sanction to whatever conventional restraints were suggested by such a code. The reverse side of this gentlemanly tradition was described by George Bernard Shaw, albeit with typical satirical exaggeration, when he wrote: "It is the secret of our governing class who, though perfectly prepared to be generous, humane, cultured, philanthropic, public-spirited, and personally charming, in the second instance, are unalterably resolved in the first to have money enough for a handsome and delicate life, and will, in pursuit of that money, batter in the doors of their fellowmen, sell them up, sweat them in fetid dens, shoot, stab, hang, imprison, sink, burn and destroy them in the name of law and order." In France and Germany, where Parliaments arose in opposition not only to the monarchy but also to the exclusive hereditary aristocracy which supported it, professional men, particularly lawyers and to a lesser degree journalists, predominated in elective bodies at the outset. However, in more recent times, the peculiar feature of French Parliaments has been the relatively large number of farmers (and estate owners), with a fairly even distribution between other professional groups. The two outstanding features of the German and other parliaments of the 1920's were the numerous representatives of economic interest groups (the so-called *syndics*, lawyers for trade associations, and the trade-union officials) and the surprisingly large number of officials; there were between one hundred and one hundred and fifty outright governmental officials in the parliament of the Weimar Republic. Their entrance into Parliament had been facilitated by the constitutional provision which allowed them to attend Parliament irrespective of their administrative duties.

It has been reported that the same situation prevailed at Bonn where the assembly to draft the Basic Law of 1949 sat. This assembly contained 43 officials out of a total of 70, or roughly 60 per cent. In the states of the American Zone, the parliaments contain about 40 per cent of such officials. Military Government authorities have tried hard to alter this tradition. They have repeatedly urged the Germans to declare the holding of a government job incompatible with a seat in parliament. They even decreed so in the case of Bizonal officials. The German Social Democrats declare this to be undemocratic—as would the rest of continental Europeans. It is a difficult problem in view of the steady expansion of officialdom under socialization (cf. also ch. XIX).

European parliaments also contain a fair sprinkling of university professors, a group which is notably absent from American legislatures. Not only in the German parliament, but in all these parliaments, there has been a steady increase of members who formerly were workers. Almost all these so-called workers are, unlike the traditional farmer in American representative assemblies, not men who come directly from the factory, but men who have risen through the trade-union bureaucracy and are therefore actually trade-association officials when they go into parliament. The inclusion of labor representatives is an important democratic gain and one in keeping with the forward march of constitutionalism. The only real drawback is that it (along with other developments) has contributed toward a gradual increase in the heterogeneity of parliaments. This social heterogeneity has increased friction and complicated the course of parliamentary procedure.

General problems of procedure · Procedure, intrinsically a rather technical subject, is in its broad outlines essential for an understanding of the work methods of parliaments. Josef Redlich, in his celebrated treatise on the history of British parliamentary procedure, has done more than anyone else to show this vital relationship.[4] In the earlier period prior to the reign of Elizabeth, the fundamental procedural device of legislation by bill rather than by petition had been worked out. The later development can be roughly divided into four periods. During the time when Parliament was engaged in its struggle to curb the Crown, it was essentially a question of preventing the exertion of undue influence by the Crown's ministers over the deliberations of the House. Perhaps the most important achievement of this period was the establishment of each member's full right as an individual participant in the debates and decisions. It is to this period also that we owe the gradual separation of the Speaker's office from the Crown, as well as the development of separate readings. The provisions insuring the opposition a fair share of the time of the House, the famous protection of the minority, while begun earlier, were carried forward in the second period, when, after 1688, the House was divided by the two aristocratic factions which governed the country rather oligarchically, particularly after the accession of Walpole. In this period, the great conservative speaker Arthur Onslow and his colleagues thoroughly developed the institution of His Majesty's Opposition by the consistent refinement of various technicalities. Among the technicalities may be mentioned the employment of the committee of the whole for the debate on all bills, the use of the same form for all budgetary questions, and the many different techniques which make it possible to bring up any subject at any time. All these and many other provisions were meant to encourage the participation of members in the debate, which was often lagging. Since the whole Parliament was an instrument for the maintenance of aristocratic government, there was not much inclination on the part of the opposition to use its power for purposes of obstruction, nor did the majority care to do violence to the minority. Considering this, Redlich believes that the period from 1688 to 1832 could almost be called the golden age of the English Parliament.

Oligarchic rule evolved parliamentary responsibility. During the period after the Reform Act and down to the late seventies, when the Irish obstruction began, Parliament faced very different problems. The House of Commons was then the real core of the governmental system, as Bagehot showed in his famous treatise. Two fairly evenly matched groups were pitted against each other in the House under the able leadership of such men as Palmerston, Disraeli, and Gladstone. As industrial, social, and imperial problems multiplied, procedural reforms were concerned with expediting necessary business and preventing debate from being merely the occasion for the display of brilliant rhetoric. To this period, therefore, we owe the rules of debate and the elaborate system of interpellations and questioning. After the Irish obstruction arose, it became increasingly apparent, in the period from 1880 to the First World War, that the ministry was dependent not so much upon parliamentary as upon electoral support (see ch. XVIII). In other words, as party organization and the caucus supplanted parliamentary control, the dominant task of procedure became this: how to insure to the government as leaders of the majority party efficient control of the business of Parliament. To this period, therefore, we owe the development of closure and various other techniques for expediting parliamentary discussion.

It must be remembered that the obstructionist tactics which engendered closure and such tools are expressions of the fact that the community is rent by violent conflicts—conflicts which obstruct the maintenance of community and consequently of its representation. One way of escaping from the difficulties involved in such social cleavages is to reduce the representative importance of a parliament. Under the American Constitution, federalism and the separation of powers make Congress just one cog, though an important one, in the whole setup of representative organs, with the result that the burden of national representation does not fall only on Congress. The impact of the (absolutist) ideas of sovereignty and the consequent hankering after unitary representative decisions are correspondingly weakened. Stimulated by the confused developments during and after the

First World War, there has developed in Britain a demand for the curbing of this overweening governmental leadership. But as a matter of fact, the "national" government after 1931 seemed at times to proceed on the assumption that the opposition was no longer part of the parliamentary system; indeed, it was claimed by some that such opposition was merely factionalism. This "tendency to discount the validity of party conflict" (Laski) is akin to the Fascist intolerance of opposition and democracy. Yet we must beware of rash comparisons. Throughout history, the perversions of institutional development are exaggerations of persistent general trends, and a kinship thus links the useful change with the revolutionary and reactionary extremes. "The mother of parliaments," W. I. Jennings has written, "has discovered that the secret of perpetual youth lies in the ability to adapt the technique of its practice and procedure to meet the problems of new generations." To cope with the current trend toward the excessive power of the majority, some have urged the strengthening of parliamentary committees. Since 1907, standing committees have steadily gained in importance (see next chapter). But as yet their influence does not extend very far toward the control of the ministry. Indeed, the British Parliament's primary function today remains the representation of the people in the defending and criticizing of the government and of its policy.

The House of Lords and second chambers · In the preceding paragraph, the emphasis has almost imperceptibly shifted from Parliament as a whole, comprising Lords and Commons, to the House of Commons. In fact, since the Parliament Act of 1911, the question of whether or not there is a place for the continued existence of the House of Lords within the modern constitutional machinery has never ceased to command popular interest. The Conservatives favor its retention, even its extension, while many Liberals and the Labour party demand its radical change or abolition. This view is partly the result of partisan considerations: the House of Lords with its several hundred peers* has always contained an overwhelming Conservative majority. In spite of the very wide use made by the Liberal party after 1905 of the Crown's prerogative to create peers, there were in 1914 only one hundred and sixteen Liberal peers out of a total membership of more than six hundred. This development may be dated from 1886, when Gladstone split the Liberal party over the issue of Home Rule for Ireland; a great many members of rank and position went over to the Conservatives as "unionists." In the thirties, when the Labour party pro-

*In 1936 the House of Lords consisted of 681 hereditary peers of the United Kingdom, sixteen representative peers of Scotland and Ireland each, seven Lords of Appeal in ordinary, and twenty-six Lords Spiritual.

vided His Majesty's Opposition, the situation was even more marked. Of 746 Lords, 543 were Conservative or right wing, while 56 Liberal and 16 Labour peers formed the Opposition. There were also 126 peers who did not disclose their political views, such as the Lords Spiritual and the Law Lords.[5] The situation has not been substantially different since the Labour Party took over the government in 1945, although quite a number of Labour peers have been created.

The Labour government, while at one time committed to the abolition of the House of Lords, has to date only sought to reduce the period that the Lords may delay legislation. This is no doubt due in part to the large Conservative majority in the Lords showing a marked degree of self-restraint. In keeping with the traditional rule that the Lords should not negate any policy for which the government has a mandate from the people, the Conservatives have taken the view that "these proposals [socialization and other radical aspects of the Labour Party program] were put before the country at the recent General Election. . . . The Government may therefore fairly claim that they have a mandate." The Conservative Lords consequently took the position that it would be non-constitutional for them to oppose these measures, and they have not rejected any of them. In spite of this restraint, the Labour Party in 1947 proposed to make it possible for the Commons to overrule the Lords in the next session and within a year.

The whole problem of the House of Lords revolves around the question of representativeness. From the standpoint of electoral majorities, the House of Lords is merely an anachronism; "it represents," as one wit has remarked, "nobody but itself, and therefore enjoys the full confidence of its constituents." But representativeness is not necessarily insured by an election, by a simple counting of heads (see above, ch. XIV). It may be based upon objective achievement, and a variety of other believed-in qualifications, such as birth or the possession of property. Such qualifications may be wholly illusory. As Benjamin Franklin once remarked, to pick legislators on the basis of heredity is just as sensible as to pick professors of mathematics in that fashion. But elections by electoral majorities may also fail to produce representatives, as we have seen in our survey of electoral methods (see ch. XV). If it be true that the House of Lords is more concerned with the interests of big business, landed property, and the established church than those of other groups, it would not conclude the argument about their representative value, unless it were shown that these groups are no longer of great significance. The real issue was put by the Webbs speaking for the Socialists: "Its [the House of Lords] decisions are vitiated by its composition—it is the worst representative assembly ever created, in that it contains absolutely no members of the manual working class; none of the great classes of shopkeepers, clerks and teachers; none of the half of all the citizens who are of the female sex; and practically none of religious nonconformity, of art, science, or literature." Voices have arisen to suggest that the House of Lords be based upon proportional representation. At one time, the most imaginative proposal in view of the federalization of the Empire (see above, ch. XI, pp. 212 ff.) was that of "turning the Second Chamber to good account for the purpose of including in it persons who might be qualified both to express the views of the Self-Governing Dominions and other parts of the British Overseas possessions, and to join with full knowledge in discussing questions affecting them," as a parliamentary report put it.

All such proposals for change assume that a second chamber is intrinsically worthwhile and desirable. As was shown in the discussion of federalism above, such a body is important because it provides the basis for a balancing group of representatives, one house representing the majority of the whole people, the other the majority of the federated units. But there is also the question of a second chamber as a check upon the first. While such a check has appealed to some, it is this check upon the popularly elected majority which has brought forth the most virulent attacks as well. The *Labour Speakers' Handbook* declared in 1923: "Abolish the Second Chamber altogether; any second chamber would be a reactionary body. . . ." This is practical politics rather than sound theory; a second chamber composed in large part of the representatives of organized labor would evidently not be reactionary. But Labour's view is in the tradition of Benthamite radicalism, pure and unadulterated; a second chamber, Bentham regarded as "needless, useless, worse than useless." His objection was based strictly on logical grounds. Since the end of government is "the greatest happiness of the greatest number," a legislative assembly should be based on universal suffrage. There is no room for a second chamber. If it represents the general interest, it is useless; if it represents only a particular interest, it is bad. If the first chamber has not produced the proper kind of legislation, the right check is to turn it out (or to improve it), but not to establish a second chamber. This argument apparently holds only as long as one accepts Bentham's rational view of human beings. If all human beings acted rationally and farsightedly, there would be no sense in a second chamber except under federalism. But since they do not, such chambers may fulfill a variety of useful functions. The House of Lords does fulfill some such functions, through thorough debate of nonpartisan issues. While a large number of the members are of no use in either legislation or other matters, the limited group of genuinely interested lords (and these, incidentally, are much more nearly balanced between the parties) bring a degree of detachment, experience, and leisure to the discussion which is lacking in the House of Commons.

Bentham's line of reasoning also disregards the time factor. For it might happen, as it did happen in France in 1851, or in Germany in 1933, that "it is too late" for any turning out. Accordingly, the previously mentioned parliamentary committee agreed that it is desirable to interpose "so much delay (and no more) in the passing of a bill into law as may be needed to enable the opinion of the nation to be adequately expressed upon it. This would be especially needed as regards bills which affect the fundamentals of the Constitution or introduce new principles of legislation, or which raise issues whereon the opinion of the country may appear to be almost equally divided."[6] It is not really so much a matter of expression of opinion, as of crystallization. The Cabinet governs in accordance with the general mandate of the majority, but there are issues upon which more than a majority may be desirable (see ch. XVIII). As far as representation is concerned, it is all a question of who should be represented in the particular community. If persistent subdivisions entitled to separate representation are contained in it, or if certain interests are recognized as of paramount importance from a governmental viewpoint, two chambers may be desirable. It is undeniably true that such dualism raises grave complications, but these may be offset in part by the gain in providing for a reasonable and convincing division of powers, thus aiding the maintenance of a constitutional order.

Bentham's views, their influence and results · His unqualified rationalism not only led Bentham to demand the abolition of second chambers, but it also made him sponsor views on parliamentary procedure. These constitute, in the opinion of leading authorities, the only attempt at theoretical clarification of the immense mass of procedural detail which is found in the practice of representative assemblies throughout the world.[7] They are also worth considering on account of the influence they have exerted, on the Continent if not in England. The first impact of Bentham's ideas came through his brief sketch of the English procedure which he furnished Mirabeau as a model for the procedure of the French constituent assembly in 1789. But more important was the effect of his *An Essay on Political Tactics* (1816). This treatise undertook to fit the mass of detailed rules of procedure, particularly of the English Parliament, into a rational pattern; as a result, it greatly enhanced the general appeal of English procedure on the Continent. Through its Genevese editor, Dumont, it entered Switzerland. It also exerted some influence upon the French parliaments of the

Restoration, and through them down to the present day. It also helped to shape the procedure of the German National Assembly in 1848, and from there its influence spread over central Europe while the French procedure was molding Belgian and later Italian and other parliamentary practices.

The central purpose of the rules of procedure, according to Bentham, is to produce a majority and thus to discover the true will of the assembly. That the proceedings should be public is now generally conceded. Bentham offers a number of reasons: (1) to constrain the members of the assembly to perform their duty, (2) to secure the confidence of the people, and their assent to the measures of the assembly, (3) to enable the governors to know the wishes of the governed, (4) to enable the electors to act intelligently in elections, (5) to provide the assembly with the means of profiting by the information of the public, (6) to give amusement. The objections seemed to Bentham to resolve themselves into one, namely, that "the public is incompetent to judge of the proceedings of a political assembly." This objection he will not allow, because the public will judge, whether informed or not, because it desires to do so. If they were willing to forego judging because incompetent, they would be not common men, but philosophers. Omitting reference to those who do not judge at all, he argues further that those who judge anyway will judge ill upon incomplete information; they will, according to Bentham, judge better when fully informed. To deny them such information is to say: "You are incapable of judging, because you are ignorant; and you shall remain ignorant, that you may be incapable of judging." This argument would be conclusive if men were rational; overstating a good case, it has suffered from the hands of Fascist and Communist expounders of irrational human nature. In order to maintain Bentham's view, a restatement of his position, taking full account of man's irrational behavior, must be attempted. We shall return to this problem when considering the problems raised by the growth of committees in modern representative assemblies (see ch. XVII, pp. 330 ff.). For the time being, let us remember that Bentham's arguments prevailed and that publicity of parliamentary proceedings was instituted everywhere in the course of the nineteenth century, in England as well as on the Continent. At the time of Bentham this was nowhere the case, and his insistence upon publicity cannot therefore be called a rationalization of English practice. In fact, we find Bentham expressing himself very critically: "How singular soever it may be thus to see the deputies of the people withdrawing themselves with so much hauteur from the observation of their constituents . . ."; the public even in England did not particularly care. The Reform Act and the attendant popularization of the House of Commons changed all that in a generation. But at the time of Bentham's writing the

House of Commons was not really composed of the deputies of the people. Back of both Houses of Parliament stood an aristocratic *junta*.

Bentham saw parliamentary functions essentially as decisions about legislation (see above, ch. XIV, pp. 269 ff.). He consequently lists as inconveniences inaction, useless decision, indecision, delays, surprise and precipitation, fluctuation, quarrels, falsehoods, decisions which are defective in form, and others which are defective in substance. Ultimately, all these "inconveniences" come down to two: not reaching a good decision, when it might have been reached, or reaching a bad decision. Who is to judge what decisions are good? This question did not concern Bentham; he simply answers that good decisions are those which promote the greatest happiness of society. Such a reply recommends itself by its simplicity, rather than its adequacy. Yet Bentham's view of procedure aroused considerable enthusiasm when it was first expounded. English radicalism, with its faith in the rational nature of man, took it to be the final word. The more sophisticated, almost Machiavellian debating primer of W. G. ("Single Speech") Hamilton was condemned as "the wickedest book in the English language." Its failure to consider the general good earned it the most outspoken condemnation by Bentham himself. Yet intrinsically, Bentham's own *Tactics* does not lack a touch of Machiavellian preoccupation with pure *technics*.

The main shortcomings of Bentham's work result not so much from the general ethical purpose which he posits as from the neglect of certain factors in the real situation. In England, these omissions were perhaps not very serious, since the reader could supply them from his own experience. But wherever Bentham's theories were taken as realistic guides, as was the case among Liberals on the Continent, the effect was serious and has contributed its share to the breakdown of parliamentary politics. In considering it the main business of deliberative assemblies to make laws, Bentham had failed to recognize that it was as much a matter of fighting the opposition party. To be sure, he recognized the necessity of parties; but at the same time he viewed with indignation Hamilton's notion that "Parliament [is] a sort of gaming-house; members on the two sides of each house the players; the property of the people . . . the stakes played for; . . . what course will be most for the advantage of the universal interest, a question never looked at, never taken into account. . . ." He knew the fact, then, but he condemned it. Despising party strife, he would give as little consideration to it as possible in developing a theory of procedure. By doing so, Bentham fell into the error of neglecting the real value which attaches to securing effective party support. As a consequence, he failed to perceive the significance of the cabinet's responsibility to Parliament, which was just then emerging.

Debating laws *and* supporting the government, not debating laws *or* supporting the government, would seem to have provided the right approach to the problem. Since Bentham's time the need for governmental leadership in debate has caused sweeping changes in parliamentary procedure, such as closure.

In addition to minimizing the procedural significance of party struggle and governmental leadership, Bentham also misjudged the possibilities of organized obstruction. In many benign sentences, scattered through his *Tactics* and too long to quote here, he expressed his doubt as to such methods ever gaining a foothold. He considered them self-defeating. A permanent minority like the Irish Nationalists lay beyond the confines of his experience. In fact, parliamentary procedure everywhere has to some extent been affected by organized obstruction; the filibusters of small minorities in the American Senate are perhaps the best known, but the Irish Nationalists developed great skill in availing themselves of every conceivable procedural advantage. All such tactics have undoubtedly contributed much toward discrediting parliaments, the most striking illustration being found in the vivid description of the impressions Adolf Hitler gained when watching the proceedings of the Austrian Imperial Diet. But the writings and reminiscences of politicians of an antiparliamentary outlook in Italy, France, and other countries are equally filled with such observations. Bentham could not conceive of parliaments willfully discrediting themselves, because he never considered that popular forces might arise which would be utterly out of sympathy with representative assemblies. Through one of the paradoxes so frequent in institutional history, his radical views contributed toward the adoption of unrealistically rationalist procedure in countries where parliamentary government has since had great difficulties in taking root. Under his influence, continental parliamentarians failed to consider the problems of procedure in terms of the party system. Julius Hatschek has noted a considerable number of minor absurdities which crept into parliamentary practice in France, Germany, and elsewhere, because procedures well-adapted to the English two-party system as it existed in England in the time of Bentham were slavishly adopted in countries where very different conditions prevailed, such as a multiple-party system, permanent national minorities, and class-conscious groups.

Presiding officers: the English Speaker · If the effectiveness of a procedure is to be measured by results, perhaps the most important question is how to provide adequate leadership for a legislative program. In the United States such leadership is provided by the Speaker or the floor leader as presiding officers, with the aid of the Committee on Rules. Other representative assemblies, in following the theories of Bentham, adopted the idea of a neutral presiding officer, forgetting that in England such legislative leadership is provided for by the government. Curiously enough, at the time of Bentham's writing, the strictly neutral position of the Speaker in the House of Commons had not yet been realized. Bentham really anticipated developments. But his very success in forecasting the English evolution bolstered his authority elsewhere. Consequently, Josef Redlich could rightly conclude his discussion of the speakership with Bentham's dramatic statement: "Throughout the whole business, the grand problem is to obtain, in its most genuine purity, the real and enlightened will of the assembly. The solution of this problem is the end that ought everywhere to be had in view. To this end, everything that concerns the president, ought of course to be subservient.—The duty and art of the president of a political assembly is the duty and art of the accoucheur: *ars obstetrix animarum*, . . . —to assist nature and not to force her—to soothe upon occasion the pangs of parturition;—to produce in the shortest time the genuine offspring, but never to stifle it, much less to substitute a changeling in its room. It is only in so far as it may be conformable to the will of the assembly, that the will of this officer can as such have any claim to regard. . . . Any influence whatever that he possesses over the acts of the assembly, is just so much power taken from the assembly and thrown into the lap of this single individual."[8] This statement is not a descriptive generalization; it is a norm realized in the British House of Commons, but only because actual leadership comes from the cabinet, and not from the "real will of the assembly," as Bentham would have us believe. Where the peculiar conditions of British cabinet leadership do not prevail, the presiding officer cannot assume, and does not assume, such a neutral role; if he tries to, the result is chaos.

It is quite significant that the neutrality of the Speaker in England developed right along with such cabinet leadership. The first great example of a neutral Speaker, Arthur Onslow (1727–1761), falls into the period of Robert Walpole's and his successors' power and influence. Before his time, the Speaker had been oscillating between being an instrument of the Crown (More, Coke, Finch, Sir John Trevor) and the spokesman of the parliamentary party (Lenthal and others). Stubbs has shown how Sir Thomas More ran the House of Commons according to the directions of Wolsey. Of Sir Edward Coke's subservience as a Speaker (in great contrast to his later views) we have a graphic account, too. In the words of Redlich: "There can be no doubt that the absolutist domination of parliament by Henry VIII and his successors found its main support in the position of the Speaker as a servant of the crown and as a representative of the crown's interests." In other words, as long as the British constitution was built upon the medieval separation of powers between the king and the Houses of Parliament, effective leadership in the House of Commons had to come from the Speaker (just as in the House of Lords it had to come from the Lord Chancellor). In this period, the Speaker usually held a position under the Crown, as, for instance, Sir Edward Coke, who was Solicitor General. Such a situation would have been unendurable once the government (the cabinet) became a party government. Once the majority in the House of Commons supported the cabinet, there was an urgent need and a profound reason for developing the speakership as a judicial office mediating between the majority party and the opposing minority. Just as the judiciary itself in the course of the eighteenth century became independent of the party struggles and removed from the influence of both Crown and Parliament, so also this "moderator" and judge presiding over parliamentary proceedings became neutral and more and more effectively insulated against partisan influences. His decisions are "rulings," they "apply" the precedents of parliamentary law and custom according to legal logic, and whatever discretionary authority he possesses closely resembles the type of authority of a judge, and is derived from a skillful use of existing precedents. "Just as the immense, and many-meshed net of the common law binds the judge a thousand times in his decisions, but also offers him a thousand times the opportunity to develop the law through the employment of the stored-up precedents, and to create new law, in just the same way the Speaker faces the parliamentary law and customs. Here too vast fields extend beyond the limited line of positive norms, the vast field of parliamentary practice developed through hundreds of years as it is recorded in the proceedings." To develop new law is the highest function of the English Speaker. This state of affairs, however, must not blind one to the fact that ultimately Parliament itself is the sole judge of its procedure. By making a positive rule, it can sweep away whatever precedent may have grown up. Parliamentary supremacy is not subject to judicial fetters in this area any more than in other fields of legislation. No law behind the law can be appealed to.

Since the reform of Parliament, the independent judicial position of the Speaker has been generally recognized. Not only inside of Parliament, but outside of it as well, he must observe the strictest neutrality. According to prevailing practice he is not opposed in his own electoral district and makes no speeches nor even visits his former party club. He has an official residence, and is on all sides surrounded by the repressive pomp of royalty. His salary is £5000, and on his retirement he is made a peer and given a liberal pension. In every respect he resembles the highest judicial officer in the land. On account of this elevated position, reinforced by many cere-monial details inside of Parliament and out, the Speaker is enabled to main-tain that high order of efficiency and dignity which characterizes the pro-ceedings of Parliament. He can, with the aid of the Sergeant-at-Arms and the Metropolitan Police, arrest any person, whether a member of Parlia-ment or not, and deliver him into jail. There is no appeal against his de-cisions. This plenary power contrasts strongly with the helplessness of the president of the French chamber or those of other Continental countries, whose ultimate weapon, suspension of the sitting, is precisely the aim of obstructionist groups. Inside Parliament, all speeches are addressed to the Speaker, and his direction of the debate and other proceedings is beyond appeal. F. A. Ogg aptly cites Speaker Lowther's humorous remark: "The Chair, like the Pope, is infallible." If Parliament was once a court, today there is a judge that presides over Parliament, and that judge is as absolute, as final in his decisions as any in the realm. Only through such a device does the British constitution manage to combine great dispatch of all kinds of legislative and budgetary business, embodying the policy of the majority party, with an adequate protection of the minority's opportunities to speak and express their vigorous criticism. His Majesty's Loyal Opposition re-mains a recognized part of the government, even when it is as small a minority as it was between 1931 and 1935 when the combined opposition had only 59, as against the National coalition's 556 votes. As Jennings has put it: "Care for the rights of minorities is evidenced by the deliberate exaltation of the office of Speaker. . . . As often happens in British institu-tions, the Speaker's authority is greater than his power." The reason this can be so is that the Speaker is the representative of the unity of the House (and hence of the nation). His qualities must be representative qualities, that is, character will be more important than intellectual brilliance. It has been said: "The qualities required of a Speaker are not really very high, and so great is the prestige of the office, and so careful are all parties to maintain his independence and authority, that any reasonable man can make a success of the office." This is true only if by "qualities" are meant merely intellectual gifts. A Speaker, to be a success, must be an embodi-ment of those qualities of moderation, fairness, and gentlemanly conduct which are expressive of British tradition.

The American Speaker · Very different is the situation in the United States, and in the several states of the Union, as far as the position of the presiding officer in the deliberative assemblies is concerned. The tendency has been just the reverse of that forecast by Bentham.[9] Everyone knows that party leadership in the House of Representatives at least is provided from the chair, whether occupied by the Speaker or by the floor leader. Allusion has already been made to the underlying major factor explaining this complete difference. James Bryce, in *The American Commonwealth*, pointed out, "A deliberative assembly is, after all, only a crowd of men; and the more intelligent a crowd is, so much more numerous are its volitions; so much greater the difficulty of agreement. Like other crowds, a legislature must be led and ruled. Its merit lies not in the independence of its members, but in the reflex action of its opinion upon the leaders, in its willingness to defer to them in minor matters, reserving disobedience for the issues in which some great principle overrides both the obligation of deference to established authority and the respect due to special knowledge." Another writer elaborated this by saying that he wanted "a centralized, responsible authority, like the Cabinet of the British Government or of Canada, which will determine what laws are to be considered, and cast aside without mercy the mass of trivial and irrelevant bills that now discredit our legislative records. . . ." The presiding officers in American legislatures have often attempted to fulfill such a function. It was the explicit purpose of Speaker Carlisle, who considered it the duty of the Speaker to have a legislative policy and "to take every means in his power to secure its accomplishment." That view was continued and carried forward by his successors, Reed and Crisp. Each in his turn at the end of the last century made his particular contribution toward strengthening the power of the speakership, until at last in 1909–1910 revolt rose against their system as personified by Speaker Cannon. Robert Luce rightly observes that the epithet "Cannonism" was rather undeserved, as Cannon merely carried on what others had done before. It is curious that Carlisle himself, after having done so much to strengthen the power of the Speaker, should have attacked the system upon leaving the chair. He felt it to be an inevitable scourge. "Under any system of rules that can be devised, the presiding officer in a body so numerous as the House of Representatives will necessarily have more power than ought to be entrusted to any man in this country." Numbers alone hardly suffice as an explanation; for the British House of Commons is much larger. It is a question of the confusion resulting from lack of effective party leadership.

Reed, Cannon's successor, put the case for majority control this way: "The object of a parliamentary body is action, and not stoppage of action. Hence, if any member or set of members undertakes to oppose the orderly progress of business even by the use of the ordinarily recognized parliamentary motions, it is the right of the majority to refuse to have these motions entertained and to cause the public business to proceed. Primarily, the organ of the house is the man elected to the speakership; it is his duty in a clear case, recognizing the situation, to endeavor to carry out the wishes and desires of the majority of the body which he represents." Here it is frankly stated that "leadership" is the central task of the Speaker. Several devices, such as the absolute discretion as to whom to recognize, pre-arranged schedules for the debate and what should be taken up therein, extensive control over committee vacancies, all these contributed their share to the indignation which in 1910 led to the overthrow of the Speaker. A coalition of the Democrats, then in opposition, with insurgent (progressive) Republicans took away from the presiding officer much of his discretionary power; they enlarged the Rules Committee, provided that it should be elected (by the two caucuses in the ratio of six to four), and deprived the Speaker of a seat on it. A little later, it was further provided that all committees should be elected by the House. "Amid cheers for 'the fall of the Czar' and the end of 'despotism,' " C. A. Beard tells us, "a dissipation of leadership was effected." Yet, as Beard shrewdly remarks, this revolution did not destroy leadership. Concentration of power has remained. However, there is a certain distribution: leadership shifts about between the Speaker, the Rules Committee, the Chairman of Ways and Means, the floor leader, and the "steering committee" of the majority party. The resulting uncertainties have raised anew the demand for more effective leadership; in certain quarters the President is favored as the effective leader in Congress. Powers such as that of dissolution, the item veto in the budget, and so forth, are favored as desirable modifications to bring about such a change. If such presidential leadership were to become a reality, the Speaker of the American Congress could travel the road of the English Speaker, retire from active political leadership and make himself an impartial umpire or moderator for the House. Such was his position at the outset, but as long as measures vitally important to the majority party were delayed or even defeated by opposition tactics, the Speaker in conjunction with one or more of the other directing forces would be obliged to assume a measure of leadership. Such is his political function within the American setup, and what is true of the Federal Congress is largely true of the states as well, though the Speaker in Massachusetts, for instance, is much more nearly an impartial moderator than the Speaker in other legislatures (for local government, especially the "moderator," see ch. XIII).

The chief whip · To refer to James Bryce once more, he commented extensively upon the lack of any recognized leaders in either the Senate or the House.[10] How can such a statement be squared with the previous discussion? Was Bryce unaware of the existence of the Speaker, the Committee on Rules, and so on? Had he never heard of the floor leader at all?

Curiously enough, Bryce himself calls the Speaker "almost the leader" of the House; the importance of the floor leader he tended to overlook. The American Congress (and the same is true of American state legislatures) carries on most of its work in committees (see below, ch. XVII, pp. 332 ff.), and the votes in the whole House mostly ratify the committee reports. Nor does the position of the majority party in the House depend upon any particular vote. Only during the last few days of the session do conditions requiring something like the English parliamentary strategy prevail, and for these few days it is relatively easy for the caucus to keep members in hand. What Bryce was admittedly looking for was the "whip." It is desirable for a complete understanding of the contrast between the English Parliament and the American legislatures as representative assemblies to know what these whips are. Bryce considered them a "vital, yet even in England little appreciated, part of the machinery of constitutional government." The term, taken from the hunting field, denotes the men aiding the government in Parliament. The government party in the House of Commons appoints certain of its members as officials, nominally, whose real function it is to direct the party forces of the majority. The chief whip is the First (Patronage) Secretary of the Treasury, the others are mostly Junior Lords of the Treasury. Viscount Gladstone, chief whip himself from 1899 to 1905, claims that the office of the government whip originated about 1836 (note that this is after the Reform Act) and that the whip became ex-officio patronage Secretary of the Treasury in or about 1845. This meant that he kept his machine running by handing out jobs, titles and orders, and other favors. More recently, the favors have changed in accordance with the rise of the "social service" state (see below, ch. XXIII). Furthermore, the "peerage" has been protected by providing for review by the Privy Council. In a planned economy, effective contact with the planning center would be more valuable than most of the earlier "favors."

Under the direction of the cabinet, the chief whip, with the help of the assistant whips, lays out the plans for the parliamentary session, prepares a schedule, determines what opposition leaders are proposing to do, tries to arrange a fair distribution of work, and keeps the cabinet informed of important developments in the party. He may also smooth out difficulties between several leaders. Lloyd George, for example, claimed that the rift between him and Asquith would not have developed if the Liberal whip had not died and thus deprived the party of a skillful moderator. We are also told by Bryce that "a ministerial whip is further bound to 'keep a house,' that is, to secure that when government business is being considered there shall always be a quorum of members present, and of course also to keep a majority. . . . Without the constant presence and activity of the ministerial whip the wheels of government could not go on for a day, *because the ministry would be exposed to the risk of casual defeats.* . . . Similarly the Opposition . . . finds it necessary to have their whip or whips because it is only thus that they can act as a party. . . ." From these remarks it should be clear that the institution of the whip is clearly linked with the position of the English House of Commons as the supporter and critic of the cabinet. Gladstone has shown that in fact the role of the government whip and the opposition whip are quite far apart. The opposition chief whip, according to Gladstone, is more interested in work outside the House of Commons to prepare for victory in the next election. He collaborates with the party agent in giving financial assistance to candidates, in recommending and discovering suitable candidates, in keeping local organizations in running order, and so on. Robert Luce has pointed out that "most American legislators would strongly resent any such control" and, furthermore, that the power of American whips as they have functioned since 1900 is much more limited, and that "all we want and ask of them is that they shall incite members to be on hand at moments of party importance." And indeed, if any American were to be compared with the English government party's whip, he would be a representative of the President, such as the Postmaster General under many administrations, and more recently some of the "special assistants," such as Hopkins, who officially is concerned with patronage.

Procedure and parties · So far our discussion of the relation of procedure and parties has been mainly concerned with pointing out the effects of the party (and electoral) systems upon procedure. It is, however, a question of interaction, and one may ask what effect a certain procedure has upon party development.[11] We have already, in several connections, referred to the famous protection of the minority under English parliamentary procedure. Authorities are agreed that the several devices provided for this purpose greatly aided the Irish Nationalists in developing their party organization. The practice in France, only recently abandoned, of providing for the election of the all-important committees (see next chapter) by arbitrary divisions of the Chamber, the so-called *bureaux*, checked the development of real parties by emphasizing the individual member of parliament. In Germany, where the system of proportional representation adopted under the Weimar Republic (see above, ch. XV, pp. 289 ff.) produced many small "splinter parties," a rule was introduced according to which only parties represented by a certain number of deputies could claim seats on the committees. This was done in order to discourage the election of representatives of such small parties by making it impossible for such representatives to accomplish anything. In the United States Senate, the loose procedure providing for closure only in extreme emergencies, as Lindsay Rogers has shown, has greatly aided the maintenance of "independents" and other opposition groups.

In England many new and vexing questions arose after 1919 when the Labour party tried to carry on the government as a minority party with the "support" of the Liberals. It has been shown that the procedure in the House of Commons has in more recent times been developed in response to the system of a cabinet responsible to the majority of the House of Commons. This procedure proved very ill-adapted to the needs of a minority government, and it may well be questioned whether the Labour party was wise in accepting the commission without insisting upon sweeping changes in the rules of procedure. The difficulties became quite apparent during the very first debate on the Address to the Throne in 1929. The Labour government could not get preference for government bills, being opposed on this vital issue by Conservatives and Liberals alike. It is conceivable that it might have made this very issue a question of confidence; for here was the test as to Liberal "support."

While a Conservative attempt to force a commitment on the protective tariff was defeated with the aid of the Liberals, a Liberal effort to secure the repeal of the Home Rule for Scotland Bill (passed by the preceding Conservative government) was defeated with the support of the Conservatives. In other words, the Labour government was at the very outset shorn of real "leadership," such as Bryce had claimed existed in the House of Commons, because it did not command a majority. English procedure, developed for a two-party system, was unfit for the new situation (for which the procedure of the Swedish *Riksdag*, for example, is more preferable). As a consequence, procedural handicaps prevented the Labour government from doing any real work and measurably discredited it with the people. But that situation has now come to appear "marginal." The situation after 1931 returned to the "normal" two-party arrangement, except for the wartime coalition. Before 1939, the Labour Party, and, since 1945, the Conservative Party, have played the traditional role of His Majesty's Loyal Opposition. In 1950 the Labour Party met its first *real* test as a majority government facing a general election.

Majority and minority; the problem of consent and constraint · The impact of procedure upon parties is merely an institutionalized expression of the relation which exists between the problems of procedure and constitutional government. Rules of parliamentary procedure appear as restraints upon the exercise of power which the majority accepts as readily as the minority. Intrinsically, the majority could change the rules to give it complete ascendancy, as happened in the days of the Stuart Kings and Cromwell. Actually, such a change is out of the question as long as the other party is accepted as a partner in a contest requiring the participation of both—in the long run. In the United States, the constitutionally fixed recurrence of elections at stated intervals obliges the contestants to look beyond temporary advantage. In England, the periodic "appeal to the country" seems practically as inevitable, though a parliamentary majority could presumably change that as well as anything else in the constitution. But, of course, the protection of the minority does not extend to the point where it uses procedural means for the purpose of destroying the possibility of parliamentary work. Filibustering and various other devices resembling the boycott, when carried beyond a certain point, become attacks against the constitutional order as such. The power of the minority, as well as the power of the majority, can be abused and needs to be restrained. This limitation was exceeded by the policy of obstruction of the Irish Nationalists in the seventies of the last century in England, of the various subject nationalities in Austria before the First World War, and of the Communists and Fascists in Continental parliaments after the First World War. The Irish as well as their Continental brethren denied the constitutional order under which they lived, and therefore the right to exist of the Parliament to which they belonged. These developments have shown that the parliamentary system of modern constitutional government to some extent rests ultimately upon certain tacitly accepted conventions. Josef Redlich's treatise was devoted to unfolding this aspect in great detail.[12] From the vantage point of English (and Austrian) experience before the war he emphasized that the acceptance of such conventions depends upon a measure of general agreement amongst the people concerning their political order. But he went beyond that when he claimed: "Parties of such intransigeance that they reject the political order (*Staatsverband*) as such, which demand the subjection of this order to the Church, or which want to destroy the whole social order, parties, finally, which are rooted in a principle as deep as religious conscience, namely the principle of nationalism, such parties are in irreconcilable conflict with these conventions upon which parliamentarism rests. . . ." And Redlich continued: "Where political antagonisms of such force appear, that they destroy the political allegiance of the individual, because his political philosophy is rooted in still deeper and firmer political convictions, like his religious feelings, his national consciousness, or (in the future) his desire for social and economic equality, there the primary foundation of parliamentary government, the convention back of the majority principle, loses its moral force. With it the principle of the protection of the minority also loses its support." These prophetic words, written in

1905, foreshadowed the doom of the Hapsburg Empire; while not tenable in this pointed form (see above, p. 165), they yet indicate the point at which government by consent faces its most severe test.

The representativeness of representative assemblies: quantitative approach · We have so far considered parliaments as representative assemblies in terms of certain institutional devices and social conditions which these parliaments have developed in the past. It is, however, possible to study the representativeness of elected representatives and the behavior of such groups in terms of the statistical picture which their votes offer to the investigator. Stuart Rice has made a very interesting attempt along these lines. He analyzed the votes in selected American representative bodies in the hope of throwing light upon two moot points regarding such bodies. It is often assumed that a legislator is representative because voters tend to select men of their own "kind" to office, even though similarity in kind may be based on the voter's "identification" of himself with the social, economic, or intellectual attributes of the officeholder, Related to this is the second notion that such a legislator is representative because he responds to legislative issues on the whole in about the same manner as would his fellow group members in the constituency. In order to verify these assumptions or hypotheses, Rice undertook to correlate the "progressiveness" of Minnesota legislators with the "progressiveness" of their districts. The *indications* were that such a relation did exist, although the coefficient of correlation was no higher "than could be reasonably expected." This tested the first assumption; other experiments along similar lines would have to be carried on, however, before much weight could be attached to any conclusion. More particularly would it be necessary to construct tests referring to particular legislative issues rather than a complex such as progressiveness. In terms of our prior hypothesis (see above, p. 266), it may be found that the assumptions should rather be that a legislator is representative because he effectively correlates with existing notions legislative issues brought forward by special interest groups and is successful in selecting those for attention which, through education and propaganda, he can "put across" to his fellow group members in the constituency. In other words, he is a specialist in diagnosing group opinion in his constituency, and knows just how far to go in order to strike a balance between the pressure from various special groups and the resistance (passive pressure) from the group as a whole.

Now as to the first point, that voters tend to select men of their own "kind," Rice selected as the social factor the representative's *nationality*. He had already explicitly excluded as possible factors wealth, legal and political training, and possibly education generally. In order to determine the influence of nationality, that is, to find an answer to the question of whether voters tend to select as representatives persons of their own nationality, Rice studied the members of both houses of the legislature in Minnesota and Wisconsin for several years. These legislators were selected, he tells us, on the basis of availability, of personal familiarity with these states, and an arrangement of legislative districts generally conforming to county lines (which is the unit used by the census). More than a hundred of these legislators were born in foreign countries. A quotient which Rice called "the ratio of nationality excess" was calculated for each district in terms of its representative to determine whether there was a higher percentage of that nationality in the district than in the state at large. He found that there existed "a well marked disposition on the part of foreign-born voters to elect men of their own nationality to the legislature." While this is probably true, the data examined do not justify so explicit a conclusion, but rather the more modest one that there existed a well-marked disposition on the part of districts with an excess of voters of a certain nationality to elect a representative from that nationality; for as to who voted no data were examined at all. It must be remembered that where such an excess was found, a greater probability existed that men from that nationality would be available for election to a representative assembly. It would be highly desirable, if many more such explorations could be undertaken, to trace out the extent to which and the conditions under which the assumption from which Rice started is correct.

Comparative and historical material of a less quantitative though of a sufficiently definite sort suggests that under different social and political conditions the impact of nationality is even more pronounced than would appear from Rice's analysis. In Switzerland, for example, it is a matter of course that the French cantons elect French representatives, the Italian cantons Italian representatives, and the German cantons German. Of course, in most of these cantons there would appear a high "ratio of nationality excess." Again, in prewar Germany, the Poles elected Polish representatives. Czechoslovakia offered another interesting political arena of a similar sort, where the antipathy of nationalities toward each other was at times so profound as to make election of a representative of the other nationality utterly inconceivable. Germans, Slovaks, Hungarians, Ruthenians—all these struggled against the Czechs and against each other with such intensity that the nationality issue was of paramount significance, whereas in Minnesota and Wisconsin it is a minor factor. Again, Czechoslovakia and Switzerland have proportional representation, which favors the separate representation of distinctive groups; thus in Czechoslovakia you found German Socialists, as well as Slovak and Czech Socialists. Various factors, in other words, may carry different weight, depending upon the electoral system. Here would be a "political" condition, as contrasted with the previous "social" condition, affecting the weight of the nationality factor. What is true of the nationality factor is, of course, equally true of the factor of "class," for example. Restating the first assumption of Rice, and in keeping with our general analysis of representation, it might be better to say that a person is representative because voters tend to reject men who do not possess certain traits which correspond to dominant objectives and prejudices of the voters themselves. These traits could probably be arranged in an order of relative weight, such ratings presumably being subject to variations under differing social and political conditions. It is doubtful whether the distinction between rational and irrational objectives, interests, prejudices, and so forth, would serve any useful purpose in this connection. Rational interests, such as a trade union's interest in higher wages, may take precedence over any irrational prejudice against a representative of a foreign nationality, or vice versa. Whatever the further conclusions, Stuart Rice has opened up a rich field of enquiry bearing upon the representativeness of representative groups.[13] Perhaps further study will show that the preoccupations and prejudices of the voters today are themselves the force which is undermining the representative faculty of a numerous assembly, as contrasted with an individual or a small group girded for action without public deliberation.

Conclusion · After pointing out that parliamentary assemblies had become the core of modern representative government in the course of the nineteenth century, we showed that their prime function is not so much the initiation of legislation or the making of laws as the carrying on of popular education and propaganda and the integration and co-ordination of conflicting interests and viewpoints. Parliaments and parliamentarians, it was said, appear as integrating agencies through which the policy of the government and the claims of the various interest groups are expounded to the public, with a view to discovering a suitable balance. It was shown how important party structure is for the inner workings of such bodies, and the role which the social composition of members plays in their work. Procedure, though a highly technical subject, appeared in its broader phases to be closely linked up with what place representative bodies occupy in the constitutional order. The problem of second chambers was shown to be intimately related to the structure of the community, and to whether any permanent subdivisions required separate representation. Bentham's arguments against it were built upon the idea of a prevailingly homogeneous community. Such rationalist simplification of actual complexities pervades Bentham's unique endeavour at constructing a theory of parliamentary tactics. His thought is of significance today primarily because of his emphasis upon the importance of a working opposition. But it must not be dogmatically taken as complete or final. It is claimed that, where it was so taken, it materially contributed to the failure of various parliamentary regimes. England and the Dominions as well as the United States were not swayed by the logical brilliance of Bentham's deductions. While the development followed his demands, as far as the English speakership was concerned, it did so for different reasons and in a different way. The Speaker in the House of Commons did not combine leadership with impartiality, as Bentham had required, but abandoned leadership in favor of neutrality, while the leadership in legislation was assumed by the cabinet. In the United States, under the constitutionally safeguarded separation of powers, the Speaker of the House of Representatives abandoned neutrality in favor of leadership, and even though he today divides such leadership with several others, he still plays a decisive partisan role. Similar conditions exist in most of the American state legislatures. In the British Dominions which have adopted parliamentary cabinet systems of government, the Speakers have assumed the neutral position of their English colleague. The English cabinet's legislative leadership has been cemented by the development of the office of the whip, and even the opposition has found it expedient to co-ordinate its activities through such whips. While the party system, broadly speaking, has decisive effects upon parliamentary procedure, the latter often reacts back upon the parties. To the extent to which procedural rules become fixed, they can and do mold party development. They can thus become powerful tools in the hands of a majority. Ultimately, rules of parliamentary procedure appear, therefore, as self-restraints upon the exercise of power by a "sovereign" body of representatives. They are the heel of Achilles, the soft spot of the modern constitutional system. Redlich's recognition of the relation between these "conventions" and the future of constitutional government as a whole is now generally recognized. All such institutional studies of past practices require, it is submitted, implementation by statistical analysis of present practices as manifested in the voting behavior of representative groups under the most varied conditions, socially, economically, politically. Only a few pioneering efforts along such lines have been made, notably by Stuart Rice. They seem to suggest that the general assumptions underlying the present study, concerning representation and the function of elected bodies of representatives within the modern constitutional order, are in keeping with the facts. But much further inquiry is indicated.

Ultimately, the representative function of elected assemblies depends upon the general recognition that not the majority alone but majority and minority together represent the nation. As Jennings has put it, in concluding his work on *Parliament:* "The one permits the other to govern because the second permits the first to oppose, and together they lead their parties in the operation of the constitutional machine. The 'National' Government is truly national because it has a National Opposition and the people are free. The leaders of other Oppositions are rotting in concentration camps or have joined the noble army of political martyrs—and the peoples are slaves."[14] The ever-repeated claim of Hitler or Stalin to "represent" their peoples is hollow, because everyone knows, and no one better than they themselves, that the people would reject them if given a chance.

XVII

Parliaments as Deliberative Assemblies

Introduction: deliberation and representation contrasted · Speech and debate · Questions and interpellations · Closure · Parliamentary committees: England · Same subject: United States · Same subject: France · Fiscal and budgetary control in Britain · Congressional control over expenditures · The French finance committee · Administrative control · Control of foreign affairs · The problem of publicity · A glimpse at the caucus · Conclusion.

Introduction: deliberation and representation contrasted · Modern parliaments not only represent the "will" of the people, they also deliberate. Their political function is a double one: as representatives they integrate the community through periodic appeals, based upon a continuous process of education and propaganda; as a deliberative body they endeavor to solve concrete problems of communal activity: to do or not to do, that is the question. While the two functions are closely intertwined, they may, from the standpoint of political science, usefully be distinguished, as the present chapter will attempt to show. A parliament, it will be seen, deliberates upon many questions and decides many issues upon which it does not and could not consult the "will" of the people, nor does it attempt to develop such a will by education and propaganda. On all such occasions, publicity is unnecessary, often even undesirable. Procedural devices have been developed to guard the confidential nature of such deliberations.[1] In the age of Dr. Johnson no person with as much as a pencil was allowed within the halls of Parliament. An anecdote told of Johnson well illustrates this point. In a tavern, friends were discussing the quality of parliamentary oratory when one amongst their number recited verbatim a speech of the elder Pitt as an example of beautiful English diction. Upon turning to Johnson to hear his opinion, they were told that he himself composed that speech while working for a London paper, basing it upon a brief report by one of the attendants in Parliament! Only in the last quarter of the eighteenth century were reporters allowed, and regular publication of the debates followed. For a time the peculiar conditions of English electoral politics made possible a continuation of the deliberative function of Parliament in the full daylight of publicity, but under the impact of democratic forces Parliament in England gradually became less of a deliberative body; at the end of the century critics began to describe it as a "voting machine." It became, in the words of Finer, purely a "will-organization," and ceased to be a "thought-organization." This is probably an overstatement. The opposition still makes very vital contributions in the course of the deliberation of bills, not just in the whole house. How the English Parliament has undergone this transformation, and how it and other parliaments have tried to escape this transformation, will be the central topic of this chapter. Closure and committees are the two battle cries. For the rest, it will be shown that fiscal and administrative supervision by a parliament are entirely dependent upon the fact that it continues to be a deliberative body. Technical as these matters may seem, they are vitally related to the future of parliamentary institutions.

Speech and debate · Speech is the essence of parliamentary activity, it is the very lifeblood of parliament's corporate body politic.[2] But just as blood has to flow through well-encased channels in order to fulfill its salutary function, so speech has to be circumscribed and regulated in parliament. Not the bedlam of a multitude of voices, but the balanced and ordered procedure of speech and reply, of argument and of debate, is "speech" within Parliament. The privilege of "freedom of speech" is not an absolute privilege of the individual member, it is a relative freedom compatible with the freedom of others. In the words of the Marquess of Hartington, uttered when discussing closure in the House of Commons in 1882: ". . . the privilege of speech is a privilege which the House permits to be exercised for its own instruction, for its own information, in order to form its own opinion, and . . . [is] not a personal privilege to be used irrespective of the convenience and the efficiency of the House. . . ." He could, in the same vein, insist that the business before the House, and nothing but the business before the House, determined the rules and limitations of debate. When all relevant arguments have been advanced, debate ought to come to an end. But who is to say when this is the case? Modern English and American practice has given the decision to the majority party. This naturally raises the problem of constraint of the minority. But "filibustering," "talking against time," and similar practices in turn raise the problem of constraint of the majority. As in other political arenas, so in parliaments a certain measure of constraint is inherent in the situation. Effective political engineering needs to be directed toward achieving a minimum of such constraint, just as mechanical engineering aims at a minimum of friction in constructing a machine. The eighteenth century was occupied with the development of rules guarding against the restraining of private members; in the period of the Irish obstruction it became a matter of guarding against the restraint placed upon the majority by a recalcitrant minority. The latest problems, raised by the fact that there may be no majority party, have hardly been faced, except by academic discussions. But throughout these different phases certain ironclad rules have persisted which crystallized so early that their beginnings are obscure. Without wishing to go here into the many technicalities which the rules of debate in the House of Commons and other parliaments contain, it may be well to recall certain general practices which are of decisive importance. In order that there may be a debate, a definite proposal, called a motion, must ordinarily be before the House. Whatever anyone may say ought to be and ordinarily is germane to the subject matter of this motion. At any rate, no new motion can be introduced until the old one is disposed of. After those who wish to speak have each had their opportunity to do so, "the question is put" and a vote is taken. A proposal, a discussion of the proposal, a decision regarding the proposal—these are the ironclad stages of an orderly parliamentary transaction. It is evident that speech is the essence of it.

Questions and interpellations · One of the most important tools in the hands of members of Parliament today is the question. As private-member bills in the course of the nineteenth century were replaced by government bills, and as the government's administrative activities increased, private members—that is, members not connected with the government or the ministerial opposition bench—began to ask more and more questions. While at first intended to secure information, they have today become instruments for securing redress from administrative errors, as well as important occasions for embarrassing the government. Instances like the Savidge case[3] show that a question may become the starting point for extensive newspaper discussion, leading in turn to governmental and parliamentary action. Only the more important (starred) questions are nowadays answered by the minister, orally, and even these only when there is time. But the fact that the questioner (and others) have the right to ask supplementary questions, if the first answer does not satisfy, makes the question hour a chess game, and many oratorical questions are brought forward to dramatize a point which the opposition wishes to bring up. The right to ask such questions greatly strengthens the hand of the ordinary M.P. when asking a minister to look into a complaint of a constituent; for the minister who neglects to attend to such matters is likely to find himself embarrassed by a question in the House. At times, particularly during war, members will ascertain beforehand that a question will not embarrass the government in a manner contrary to the general interest; the minister may take an M.P. into his confidence and persuade him to withdraw the question.

The English system of questions cannot lead to a debate unless the questioner couples the question with a motion for an adjournment. Hence a question cannot ordinarily become the occasion for a vote of nonconfidence. In many Continental parliaments this was different. In these parliaments an institution known as interpellation was developed to do just that, and numerous French ministries went down to defeat after having thus been interpellated. Indeed, three fifths of all ministerial defeats were due to interpellations. The interpellation was the perfect expression of the multiple-party parliaments of pre-Fascist Europe. It has been revived in France, but not in Germany's federal system. It enabled the individual representative to challenge the government to an explanation of its policy in a particular branch of activity and to provoke a general debate in the course of which anti-ministerial sentiment could crystallize to the point where the assembly was ready to overthrow the government. In the French parliament the total number of interpellations between 1924 and 1928, which actually consisted of a discussion followed by a vote of confidence or no-confidence, was 152. The underlying conception is "control of the administration." But while the ever-present threat of such an interpellation certainly kept the ministries on the alert, in France and elsewhere, Finer rightly has observed that "it cannot be good for Ministers to be in hourly peril of fall." The interpellation, when not offset by the cabinet's power to dissolve the representative assembly, too readily produces impulsive reactions—gusts of popular passion, the fathers of the American Constitution would have called them—sudden decisions taken under the sway of effective oratory and without regard to the broader long-run results. The interpellation often produced brilliant debate; it precluded sound deliberation.

Closure · Even an ordered debate has to come to an end at some time. This fact has engendered certain rules from the very beginning. Short of the presiding officer "putting the question," the classical form for achieving this purpose of terminating the debate is motions for adjournment.[4] There were essentially three, adjournment to another day (fixed adjournment), adjournment without naming another day (indefinite adjournment), adjournment until after something else has been done, such as securing certain necessary information (relative adjournment). Each one of these motions became a tool in the hands of a determined obstruction. For as on each of them a vote (division) would have to be taken, and as these votes consumed a great deal of time, much delay could thus be effected. In other words, motions for adjournment could be employed much as the roll calls are being used in American legislatures. These motions for adjournment, as well as the inevitable extension of debate in a very numerous House of Commons, produced in course of time a demand for procedural devices which might be effective in expediting business. In France and in the United States such devices have had a longer history, but even in England the Speaker has for a long time had the right to bring the debate to an end by putting the question. This sort of closure, however, was not regularly used unless and until everybody appeared to have had a fair hearing. Only the crisis brought on by the obstruction of the Irish Nationalists in 1881 induced the then Speaker, Brand (later Viscount Hampden), to discard the ancient restraint and to bring a debate, which had lasted forty-one hours, to an end by putting the question. He explained his procedure in a short statement. After stressing the intolerable delays (five full days of debate) caused by the obstructionist tactics of a small minority, he declared that "The dignity, the credit, and the authority of this House was seriously threatened, and it is necessary that they should be vindicated. Under the operation of the accustomed rules and methods of procedure, the Legislative powers of the House are paralysed. A new and exceptional course is imperatively demanded; and I am satisfied that I shall best carry out the will of the House, and may rely upon its support, if I decline to call upon any more Members to speak, and at once proceed to put the question from the Chair. I feel assured that the House will be prepared to exercise all its powers in giving effect to these proceedings." The action of Speaker Brand had been taken with the understanding that the government (Gladstone) would at once proceed to alter the procedure in the House of Commons. This was done and, amended by minor innovations later, closure was introduced into the House of Commons, so that any member of the House may, with the support of one hundred members, move that the question be put. In the train of these reforms, even more coercive forms for limiting the debate were soon adopted, the so-called guillotine, and the closure by compartments. The former provides that after a set time, the question is brought to a vote, no matter what the state of the discussion; the latter, that a bill may be divided into sections (items), and a certain amount of time, agreed to beforehand, allotted to the discussion of each of these sections. Finally, in 1911 the so-called kangaroo type of closure was added, which permits the presiding officer to declare which of a number of amendments proposed shall be debated. When impartially employed, this type of closure can be highly beneficial. Yet it discourages active participation by members of the House. What is equally serious, it undermines confidence in the deliberations of the Parliament. If measures of the highest importance can be put through without even a word of debate, the deliberative function of such assemblies becomes a farce. This in turn weakens their representative position. To quote Finer again, it makes parliaments will-organizations, rather than thought-organizations. In terms of our own analysis, it curtails the deliberative function, thus depriving parliaments of their national representative position and placing them in the position of representatives of a party.

The markedly partisan exercise of the closure rules in the American Congress is more readily endured because this assembly is not at all taken as the sole national representative. Speaker Reed, who did as much as any man to strengthen the control of the majority over the debates in Congress, voiced sentiments much like those of the Marquess of Hartington, cited above, when he said that the purpose of a parliamentary body was action and not the stoppage of action. Hence he felt that if anybody undertook to obstruct the orderly progress of business even by regular and permitted means, it was right for the majority to refuse to have such motions entertained and to cause the public business to proceed. He and his successors were instrumental in bringing about the implied majority control by making it possible to discard motions, by forbidding speeches exceeding one hour except by unanimous consent, by allowing motions for putting the "previous question," and by placing the power of arranging legislative business at the discretion of the Committee on Rules, controlled by the majority. Since the American Senate admits closure only on the basis of a special vote by a qualified majority, measures fostered by the majority party will more readily meet an adverse vote in the Senate than they would in the House of Representatives. From this fact, Lindsay Rogers has rather persuasively argued that "with responsibility divided and confused, the check which is on occasion exerted by senatorial obstructionists is of great value. . . . Only the American Senate can act as a 'teaching apparatus' or bring about a 'catastrophe' of obstruction. . . . The Senate can help the country to form opinions and by its eternal vigilance . . . act as the 'real balance-wheel' of the Constitution." The absence of closure in the Senate, which many people so bitterly resent, does not prevent a reasonable amount of business from being attended to; but of course the Senate of the United States is a relatively small body. If a measure is opposed with real spirit by even a limited minority, it had better be abandoned, Rogers argues. Such a view is difficult to accept as regards the Senate's power in foreign affairs; it seems to lead to inaction. It is also questionable in matters where social reform is urgent, yet can be prevented by an interested minority. These issues were highlighted by the controversy over civil-rights legislation in 1949. It was striking how jealously the Senate guarded its right of debate. The anarchic potentialities of the *liberum veto* lurk in the background of such unlimited debate. (Rogers also argues the

329

value of having no closure for controlling the executive, a question which is dealt with below, pp. 344 ff.)

Closure, when applied with proper discretion, is to be viewed as a safeguard of the deliberative functions of parliaments. When deliberation is allowed to deteriorate into a circus by reading purely extraneous literary productions, like *Childe Harold* or the *Pilgrim's Progress*, into the record, it damages the deliberative as well as the representative function of parliaments.

Parliamentary committees: England · Since the pressure is undeniably great in the English Parliament as in others, critics of the system of closure have been looking for relief in other directions. As a consequence, they have advocated an expansion of the standing-committee system in the House of Commons.[5] This system is of rather recent origin, though it possesses historical roots. It grew out of the procedural reforms in the eighties. The arrangements have been fluctuating considerably as to both number and size of committees. The late appearance and the still rather limited scope of these committees is a peculiarity of the English House of Commons. Redlich has pointed out that the Commons could so long avoid a practice which had become very widely accepted elsewhere because of the procedural device of turning from the formal proceedings to what is known as the Committee of the Whole House. This committee is simply the House with relaxed rules of procedure; members may, for example, speak several times on the same matter. The Committee of the Whole has its greatest utility in the field of financial and budgetary functions (see below, pp. 341 f.). These functions, when referred to smaller permanent committees as in Congress, the Chamber of Deputies, or other parliaments, constitute the real strength of the committee structure. In England, where the whole House deliberates upon these matters in Committee of the Whole House, the demand for permanent committees arose in connection with the increase in all kinds of legislation in the second half of the nineteenth century and the increasing complexity and technicality of this legislation. However, these committees are not specialized, as in the United States; they consider every kind of legislation as it comes up. As Ranney and Carter have observed, in explaining the persistence of this system, "To the party in power it is obvious that the more able and expert the committee, the greater its power to make life difficult for the minister and the civil service. . . ." At present there are five such committees, designated by the letters A, B, C, and D, with a fifth committee devoted to Scottish affairs. The other committees are not specialized as to subject matter. Each committee has thirty to fifty members, with the possibility of adding from ten to thirty-five specially interested members. The members of these committees are nominated by a Committee of Selection. This Committee of Selection consists of eleven members nominated by the House. In nominating members, "regard to the composition of the House" is interpreted as meaning that the parties should be proportionally represented. The chairmen of these committees have been appointed by the Speaker since 1934. The chairmen are not necessarily members of the majority supporting the government, but the business of the committees is definitely and decisively directed by the government. It is a striking contrast to Congressional practice that M. P.'s are so little interested in committee membership that the fourth committee is often not set up at all. Also, M. P.'s get on and off committees with great ease, depending on their interest in particular bills. This, of course, is due to the relatively small power of the committees. While committees are formally allowed considerable scope in amending bills referred to them, they are in fact quite restricted. In the words of Finer: "Though the members in Committee are said by some to be freer from party alignment than members in the House, they are not much, if at all, freer, since the Minister in charge exacts the support of members of his party, of whom a majority are upon the Committee." Yet the same writer also reports that "it is universally admitted that they [the committees] do good work: considerable emphasis being placed upon the fact that they vote after hearing the arguments (this is unusual in the House) and that the Government is prepared to make concessions as the argument goes." Such concessions are of course in matters of technical detail; for the broad scope of the bill has been settled before it is referred to the committee. English parliamentary committees are supposed to aid and do aid Parliament in these matters of detail; very important bills are often reserved for consideration by the Committee of the Whole House. The committee's work is, of course, scrutinized by the whole House in what is known as the Report Stage; the tendency of the House to employ this discussion for doing over the work of the committee led to a rule that the discussion must stay within the ground staked out by the committee's recommendations.

The conception (and to a large extent the practice) of the English standing-committee system is perhaps most succinctly summarized by a quotation from Sir Courtenay Ilbert, at one time Clerk of the House. "It proceeds on the view that when the general principle of a bill has been affirmed, a reasonable chance ought to be afforded of having its provisions discussed, that this chance is improved by sending a bill to a Standing Committee, that, as a general rule, discussion in a Standing Committee is more business-like and effective than discussion in a Committee of the Whole

House, and that the time of the House is saved by dividing the House into compartments for discussing the details of legislative measures." Going well beyond these traditionalist arguments, various writers have advocated an extension of the committee system to improve the opportunities of members of the House to participate in the deliberative function of the House. A system of six standing committees, each concerned with the activities of one of the great "spending departments," Ramsay Muir has argued, would have most salutary effects. Such committees, he feels, could not only aid in considering bills, but they could also maintain a continuous review of the work of the departments with which they are concerned (equipped as they would be with full powers of investigation), and secondly, they could receive the estimates of these departments as soon as they were ready, go through them, and draw up a Report for the House when it came to consider these estimates. Another significant function, namely, the scrutinizing of all the orders and regulations issued by departments under statutory delegation, is now almost exclusively attended to by the House of Lords and forms a really significant function of that body. Whether the House of Commons could find the time for it seems doubtful. It would have to develop specialized committees. In opposing such a development, Englishmen have always insisted that they do not wish to see their Parliament go the way of the American and French assemblies. The different relation between Parliament and the executive seems to them to forbid it.

Same subject: United States · The extensive development of committees in American legislatures, though connected by a thin thread with early English beginnings, which "waned under the deadening influence of the cabinet system," commenced after 1800. There were committees in Virginia and elsewhere, and the experience of the former undoubtedly influenced the Constitutional Convention. Only in that colony had the committees started the modern American practice of framing and amending bills. Special (select) committees were, to be sure, common in England and in all the colonies for the work on particular bills, but in Virginia, as throughout the United States today, there were standing committees. In spite of considerable arguments to the contrary, it seems best to follow Robert Luce's judgment that "this process has been a matter of convenience, a natural development of orderly system, not begun with any deliberate purpose. . . ."[6] Congress, constitutionally separated from and therefore not subject to executive leadership, was soon confronted with the executive function of drafting new legislation (see ch. XVI, p. 313), of supervising the administration of such legislation (see below, p. 345), and of considering the expenditures involved in all such legislation. For these functions another method of procedure had to be adopted than the general debate, increasingly cumbrous in an ever more numerous assembly. Whenever a large group of men find themselves in such a situation, they are likely to resort to some form of committee for the preparation of decisions requiring attention to detail. As Luce remarks, this procedure is so obvious that it hardly would require comment if the committee system in American (and French) representative assemblies were not constantly subjected to a barrage of criticism. It is true that such committees are at variance with the representative function of parliaments. But, as was pointed out before, it greatly enhances the capacity of parliaments for deliberation.

Those who cry out against the secrecy of committee proceedings (see below, p. 349 ff.) forget what every experienced parliamentarian would tell them: "No man is the same in private and in public. The more numerous the observers and auditors, the less the frankness, sincerity, confidence. Universal experience tells us that in all manner of conference and deliberation, we reach results more speedily and satisfactorily if those persons directly involved are alone." It has been shown that the English Parliament, at the time when it was a deliberative body, closely guarded the privacy of its proceedings. Thus the baneful effect of "talking to the galleries" was eliminated. There is little room in a committee meeting for oratory. Businesslike procedure became essential in connection with the legislative and fiscal autonomy of Congress. While at first the committees "were looked upon as merely organs to investigate some fact, and to digest and arrange the detail of a complicated subject," in the course of time they have become the active, directing centers of congressional life. Bills originate with members occupying a powerful position on the committee to which the bill is bound to be referred, the advice of committeemen is sought by administrators, who thus anticipate the discussion of increased budgets, representatives of various interest groups are in constant contact with the members of the congressional committee charged with supervising the governmental activity which most closely touches their daily affairs— railroad representatives trail members of committees on Interstate Commerce, labor representatives pursue those concerned with labor, educators, patriots, farmers, women, all join in the fray (see ch. XXII).

In the United States Congress, where bills are at once referred to some committee without any previous discussion by the whole House or Senate (and the same is true of many state legislatures), many bills are killed in committee. This pigeonholing of measures has naturally and persistently aroused the ire of some part or other of the public (whoever happened to favor the bill); in contrasting the situation with that prevailing in England, these critics forget that such bills could not even get introduced into the House of Commons. It is reported that during the five Congresses preceding 1926, 29,332 bills and resolutions were introduced into the United States Senate, of which 3113 were passed, and during the same period 82,632 such bills and resolutions were introduced into the House, of which 2931 in all were passed. This is only a little more than 10 per cent in the Senate, and only about 3.5 per cent in the House. Since no distinction is made here between public and private bills, as is done in England, it is difficult to compare these figures with those concerning the House of Commons, but every writer on English parliamentary practices remarks upon the difficulty of getting any bill discussed which is not a "government bill." In the United States, the majority party will, if it is the party of the President, push "administration measures" whether advocated by a presidential "Message to Congress" or introduced by a Senator or Congressman favorable to the administration. But in either case, immediate reference to a committee merely insures it attention and possibly retention of its major "policy," but innumerable changes of real importance are bound to be made. There is hardly a piece of major legislation, even if introduced with the full support of the President, which will not thus be cast and recast in the process of Congressional work upon it. Take so important and permanent a statute as the Social Security Act: its legislative history is a tortuously winding road from the President through experts and the Department of Labor to the Congress and its Committees, checked and pushed by the interests, popular clamor, and the administration forces. The same kind of process may be observed again and again, for example, the globally important European recovery legislation, leading to the Economic Cooperation Act.*

In their effort to crystallize the policy which they are to recommend to Congress, congressional committees hold hearings. These hearings, being sometimes public and sometimes private, have also been subjected to a considerable amount of criticism. The length to which committees have gone in their efforts to compel witnesses to appear and testify has been denounced as autocracy, and the extent of the power of Congress in this respect is highly controversial, with the Supreme Court acting as a final authority. Since the investigation of past performance and the determination of possible lines of change and reform are closely interwoven, this usual distinction is more significant legally than politically. Private hearings before congressional committees have been defended on the ground

*As a staff member of the Special Committee (Herter Committee) set up to study the background of this legislation in Europe, the author was impressed with the range of uncertainty surrounding key provisions of the legislation to the end.

that witnesses can then more readily be induced to communicate confidential information. Certain it is that this is true at times. Yet Massachusetts, with her tradition of uniformly public hearings, has not been greatly handicapped. Whichever practice is better, hearings either public or private are an integral part of committee work. Considering the active leadership which emanates from the committees in American legislatures, naturally the question as to who selects them is of vital significance. Underlying the three formal alternatives of selection (1) by the Speaker, (2) by a committee appointed for this purpose (as in England), or (3) by the whole House, selection by the parties prevails today in practically all legislatures. Speaker Reed, in the heyday of power of that office, remarked that if he was a Czar, the power he had was held on sufferance of the majority of his party. Committee appointments entrusted to him reflected necessarily the preferences of his party colleagues. The questionable effects of the Speaker's power were mostly observable in his appointments of members of the minority party. It was here that tyrannical, unrestrained power could be exercised and not in the appointment of his own party colleagues. He might, and he often did, appoint strong minority members to committees overcharged with routine business in order to keep them away from an important policy-determining committee. Since the change of 1910 (see above, ch. XVI, p. 314), the party caucus, directly or indirectly, controls the membership of committees, as it long had in the Senate. From this it follows that what the change really did was to extend party control to the minority-party members of the several committees. Although the new arrangement has at times produced greater difficulties, and there are those who would suggest going back to the old plan, party control of both minority and majority members of the committees seems more in keeping with effective deliberation. In this respect, then, American and English practice are today much more nearly alike, for the Committee of Selection in the House of Commons, to which the naming of members for committees is entrusted, is subject to party control both as to majority and minority.

It remains to say a few words concerning the number of such committees. Apart from select committees, there were forty-four committees in the House at the beginning of the seventy-third Congress, and thirty-three committees in the Senate at the same time (1933). A number of these committees were abolished in 1946 when the reorganization was enacted. Committees ranged in membership from two to thirty-five in the House and from three to twenty-three in the Senate. The average important House committee has around twenty. Contrasting these figures with those in England, we find congressional committees to be more numerous, but smaller in size. The different nature of their work readily explains this difference. Accepting the complexity of modern legislation as inherent in the industrial society in which we live, we have only one remedy for the multiplication of committees in our legislatures, and that is to permit administrative bodies and officials to extend the range of delegated legislation as has been done in England, to allow them unrestrained and uncontrolled power in administering this trust within the limits imposed by intermittent appeals to the electorate, and to forego any effective scrutiny of expenditures by others than the leading members of the majority party. This (English) method of handling the problem has found so many well-informed detractors where it is practiced today that its desirability may be seriously doubted. The strength of the English Parliament lies in the broad integrating value of its debates upon issues of general policy, the strength of the American legislature in its deliberations upon specific legislative proposals and administrative activities. Whether a combination of the two could be effected, as some reformers on both sides of the water seem to hope, it is difficult to say. The two tasks of debating general policy and supervising the details of legislation and administration seem to take a large part of the time of any one set of men. Which will be given preference depends upon the political structure as a whole.

Same subject: France · The French parliament under the Third Republic came nearer combining English and American practices than many students of these problems appreciate. For that reason, an analysis is worthwhile, even though the weakness of French democracy and its swift collapse in 1940 have, for the time being, shaken confidence in the vitality of French constitutionalism and parliamentarism.[7] French parliamentary government under the Third Republic was almost government *by* parliament, not merely government under the more or less effective supervision of parliament. It took the French parliament just about the same twenty-odd years that it had taken the American Congress to evolve its system of committees. To be sure, permanent committees had been appointed in the revolutionary assemblies, notably the "convention." The experience with these committees, among which the Committee of Public Safety was the most notorious, brought on a violent reaction. The fusion of power which they effected and the resulting dictatorship led the Directory to forbid the formation of such committees by express constitutional prohibition. Reflecting the horror felt for the "Terror," such committees remained taboo until almost the end of the nineteenth century. Since that time they have emerged as perhaps the most distinctive feature of French parliamentarism.

The French committee system, like the American, was based upon the parties in the Chamber. Since 1909 the several parties were represented on the committees according to their numerical strength in the House. The parties, or groups, as they were called, made up their own panel, and through their leaders these panels were combined and presented to the Chamber for formal approval. Ordinarily, therefore, the coalition supporting the cabinet had a majority in the committees when it had a majority in the Chamber (for important exceptions see below, p. 342). In view of the decisive role the committees played in all matters requiring the action of the Chamber or touching the relation of the Chamber to the ministries, this arrangement was highly desirable, of course, and even indispensable for effective work. As in the United States, so in France, bills, whether coming from the government (called *projets de loi*), or from a particular deputy (called *propositions de loi*), as well as other matters coming before the house, were at once referred to the appropriate committees. The Chamber considered the bill as reported out of committee. The government often reintroduced provisions which had been changed in committee. But the committee, through its reporter, provided the leadership in seeing the bills or the budgets of the various ministries through the Chamber. Accordingly, these committees were placed in front of the house right next to the ministerial bench. This seating arrangement, characteristic of the French representative system, strikingly illustrated the difference between English and French parliamentarism. Parliamentary work was directed not so much by the government as by the committees. Nevertheless, the committees were, at least in matters concerning legislation, supposed to confine themselves to preparing the decision of the Chamber. Yet, many bills were simply buried by the committee. What is more, outside the field of legislation, for example in the realm of administrative supervision, the committees handled many matters without ever referring them to the Chamber. The powerful Foreign Affairs Committee attended to many issues which never came before the Chamber. In these fields, the committees were acting for the Chamber rather than preparing its work. The Chamber tended so much to be guided by the advice received from its committees that ministries often kowtowed to the views of committee members in drafting legislation. In the jargon of French politics, this art was called "to play the committees" (*jouer les commissions*), an expression supposedly invented by Briand.

The intimate collaboration between administrative officials and deputies was further facilitated by the French practice of having the committees appoint reporters so that the committees did not necessarily communicate with the Chamber through their chairmen. Rather, the committee members divided this reporting among themselves. It was customary to request one of the members to report on a matter before the committee, and then to appoint that member reporter (*rapporteur*) of the bill to the Chamber, if his report was, on the whole, acceptable to the committee majority. The reporter of a government bill was assumed to be collaborating with the government. The written reports, often very elaborate, were printed and distributed to members after having been introduced into the Chamber, and were published as *Parliamentary Documents*, of which they constituted the bulk. On the whole, the reporter was pretty free, as was the committee, to decide when to bring in his report, and efforts to impel deputies to come forth with their reports within a given time remained a dead letter. In fact, a deputy at times held out the report as bait to the government in order to exact a concession.

As the committee system more and more deeply entrenched itself in French parliamentary politics, the committees developed a formidable initiative in matters of general policy. When, in December 1932, M. Herriot wished to secure the Chamber's consent to a token debt payment to the United States, he found himself blocked by the two hostile committees on finance and foreign affairs; they listened to M. Herriot, adopted a joint resolution opposed to payments which the Chamber passed, 357 against 37, and thus forced the resignation of Herriot's cabinet. Such a role would have been unimaginable for the committees to play thirty years earlier. As a number of critics have pointed out, the fact that the chairmen of some of the key committees belonged to the opposition rendered the system incapable of action, since every major policy became a football of party politics, particularly as the interpellation discussed above provided the well-informed committee chairman with a powerful instrument for bringing his complaints before the house. The joint leadership of committee and cabinet in the French parliament was recognized in many rules of procedure; the chairman of the committee and the reporter of the particular bill were heard at any time, irrespective of the list of speakers; when the previous question was moved, the right to speak was limited to the mover, one member opposed, a speaker for the government, and a speaker for the committee in charge, and so forth. Only by moving the question of confidence could the government reassert its authority in a clash with such a committee. In a debate in the Chamber, discussion flew back and forth between the government bench and the committee bench a good part of the time. The committee as well as the government could demand additional meetings. Merely on the strength of the committee's work, many minor propositions were accepted by the Chamber without any discussion, or very little of it. As a result, there developed in France in recent years a procedural device known as "vote without debate." Matters which some committee or the government considered urgent were put upon the calendar with the provision that "there be no debate." If thirty deputies demanded a debate, it automatically went off the calendar. If one deputy wished to comment, he could do so in writing, and the committee then submitted a supplementary report in which it attempted to answer the particular member. He could repeat this process twice more; but after that only thirty members could prevent a vote without debate. This technique substituted written discourse for public debate. Such a procedure manifestly lent itself to abuse, since many deputies did not take the trouble to read the order of the day with care. The institution of the "vote without debate" illustrated perfectly what a learned observer pertly put thus: "To the Chamber, the votes, to the committee, all the discussion." The deliberative function of the French parliament had to a considerable extent been transferred to the permanent committees. But since the French committees were strictly confidential, even the proportional composition of these committees, representing as they did all groups in the Chamber, could not silence the fierce opposition which such frank recognition of the dwindling deliberative function of the whole house caused.

There can be little doubt that the French parliamentary committee system, combining the strength of American committees with the lack of any government and party control, was an important factor in the failure of French parliamentarism. Military defeat does not necessarily prove anything about the value of political institutions, but the lack of effective leadership, the absence of integrated national policy prior to the emergency measures of 1938–39, can be traced to this committee system, which was so intimately linked up with the French conception of parliamentary supremacy. For parliament's true functions of representation and deliberation there were thus substituted executive and administrative responsibilities which committees composed of a motley assortment of partisans were ill-adapted to discharge satisfactorily.

It is curious, in the light of this record, that the French should have returned to this system after the liberation. But since the French Constitution of 1946 revived the government *by* parliament, though not in as radical a form as the rejected draft of the previous spring had proposed, it is natural that the committee system appropriate to this type of government should also have reappeared. It is well to add that the change in the French party system (see below, p. 457) will probably also affect the committees, but it is too early to assess this prospect adequately. One significant change, meeting recurrent criticism concerning the secrecy of committee sessions under the Third Republic, is the provision that the meetings must be public if three members of the committee insist upon it.

Fiscal and budgetary control in Britain · There is one field of parliamentary activity in which the value of the committee system has been quite generally recognized, and that is the field of financial and more particularly of budgetary control. The committees dealing with these matters are generally looked upon as the most important ones in the system. In the United States the Chairmen of the Committees on Ways and Means and on Appropriations have traditionally been considered second only to the Speaker of the House. In Britain, on the other hand, expenditures (estimates) and revenues (ways and means) are traditionally handled by the whole House, sitting as Committee of the Whole. Since it is a fixed custom that the Commons must not increase items of expenditure, and since the cabinet would (and at times does) make any reduction in such expenditures a question of confidence, the discussions in the Commons have completely changed their nature. No detailed deliberation is devoted to the expenditures of the government; formal motions, for example, to reduce the salary of the Secretary of Foreign Affairs are made the occasion for a discussion of general policy. Thus this procedure produces deliberation upon issues of public policy, rather than fiscal control. "It is with no disrespect to this House that I say that it is not an efficient body for checking expenditure" was the verdict of one Chancellor of the Exchequer. W. I. Jennings has wisely commented that "expenditure depends primarily on policy, and the most efficient form of financial control can do no more than secure that due economy is observed in the execution of policy."[8] With great concern it was noted that twenty days in the parliamentary year were devoted to the Estimates of a score of Departments, some of which spent tens of millions of pounds and had enormous staffs performing very varied functions. In order to remedy this situation, a parliamentary committee in 1918 recommended the setting up of several Standing Committees on Estimates, and other authorities have followed it in urging such a change. The actual Select Committee on Estimates which was organized afterwards did not have the powers demanded, namely, to recommend the reduction or elimination of items which did not affect policy, to hear evidence of the administrative departments, and to secure the advice of accountancy experts. Nor was their work (backed by the power of the Commons when sitting as a Committee on Supply) extended to the point of disallowing minor budget items contrary to the wishes of the cabinet without such action becoming a question of confidence. It must be borne in mind that Treasury control, combined with the work of the Comptroller and Auditor-General (see below, ch. XIX, pp. 404 ff.), has succeeded in eliminating corruption almost entirely. A Select Committee on Public Accounts, together with these administrative officials, sees to it that no major expenditure unauthorized by

Parliament is incurred. But this type of control does not affect the authorizing of expenditure in the first instance. It is at this point that the English Parliament has abdicated its deliberative function, except for the broad lines of policy, as previously stated.

Congressional control over expenditures · The American Congress, in keeping with the general concept of congressional control over the executive, has always insisted upon debating the details of budgetary appropriations. However, American experience with committee control was rather deplorable as long as authority for making the appropriations was widely scattered among different committees and numerous appropriation bills. But these difficulties have now in a large measure been remedied by the Budget and Accounting Act (1921). Since that important enactment, the federal government has a comprehensive budget prepared by the Bureau of the Budget and presented to Congress by the President; this budget is then considered in conformity to its great divisions, corresponding to the organization of the government, and embodied in a series of related appropriation acts. Under the procedure which prevailed in the American Congress until the Second World War, all appropriations had to be reported by the Committee on Appropriations, which deliberated upon them after a preliminary survey by its subcommittees corresponding to the various administrative departments. Since the war, under the Legislative Reorganization Act, the Committees on Expenditures of the Executive Departments are "authorized and directed" to study "the operation of Government activities at all levels with a view to determining its economy and efficiency." This implies a further complication of existing machinery.

Whenever legislation is enacted which entails appropriations, such appropriations have to be passed upon by the Committee on Appropriations as well as by the committee concerned with that particular type of legislation. The reason is that such appropriations must be considered in relation to all other appropriations. Such a procedure naturally entails many delays, and by contrast English procedure is praised for its dispatch. There is nothing startling about this contrast; it is merely a special example of the technical efficiency of power when it is fully concentrated. W. F. Willoughby rightly pointed out that such concentration of power is at variance with the American governmental system. Moreover, he felt that the evils which were associated with legislative determination of appropriations in the past have been largely due, not so much to the possession by the legislature of such power over appropriations, as to the lack of any definite and comprehensive program such as the annual budget message of the President has since provided. It was, in other words, a question of redressing the distribution of power over appropriations so as to produce a clear division between the function of formulating a comprehensive program, which properly belongs to the administrative head of the government, and the function of deliberating upon this program and readjusting it in terms of an emerging compromise over major policies of the major party, a function which properly belongs to Congress. It is significant that even countries with executive establishments dependent upon parliamentary support, such as that of France, have developed committees specially charged with the supervision and control of governmental finances. In fact, these countries which adopted parliamentary government under the influence of the ancient slogan about the power of the purse have been inclined to look upon such committees as the very core of parliamentary prerogative.

The French finance committee · The French Committee on Finances (*Commission des Finances*) in both the Chamber and Senate occupied a very central position in the parliamentary system of that country. In recent years, a great deal of the criticism of the parliamentary system was focused on these all-powerful committees and on the role they played in connection with France's budgetary and financial difficulties.[9] These committees often were the center of parliamentary opposition to the government, in spite of the system of proportional representation. The leading position of the chairmen and reporters (as discussed above, p. 337) frequently gave opposition leaders their chance. It could, of course, be provided, that such presidencies and reports be given to members of the majority, as is in fact the case in the United States, but in France the chairmen (presidents) of committees often acquired a quasi-permanent position. What is more, the fluidity of French parliamentary groups often brought it about that a member delegated to a committee by such a group, but belonging to one of its wings, did not follow the majority of this group in relation to the government. Barthélemy went so far as to comment, "Under the French system the best of the majority are in the government, while the best of the opposition are in the Finance Committee." Yet it would be fallacious to assume, as was sometimes done, that the chairman and the reporter necessarily exceeded the finance minister in power; but they could be his powerful rivals. Under the Fourth Republic the status of the Finance Committee remains unchanged in all important respects.

Unfortunately, the discussion of the procedural issues involved in the Finance Committee's powers was carried on in a partisan spirit. Rarely were these questions detached from the writer's preferences in matters of policy. In keeping with the general practice of the French parliament, the budget used to come before the whole House in the form which the Finance

Committee had given it. Finally, the Finance Committee attempted to substitute its own budget for that proposed by the ministry, and to report a compromise between the two. Such a situation appears suicidal under financial conditions as difficult as those of France in recent years.

The French always retained a single budget law, the *loi des finances*, which was reported by the general reporter. In addition, there were a series of separate budgets for important services, each reported by a separate *rapporteur*, thirty-four such separate budgets being reported for 1933. The general report on the finance bill undertook to co-ordinate these separate budgets. While originally undertaken with the sound purpose of more effective scrutiny of the government's budget proposals, this division of labor gradually led to a deplorable lack of unity. The separate reports were not the result of any discussion and deliberation of the committee but were the work of the particular reporter. Since such reports came to be looked upon as rungs in the ladder toward a ministerial post, they gradually grew in bulk, until some of the later reports were huge quarto volumes. It is obvious that such reports have no practical relation to the work of the committee. The general budget received thorough discussion, but the special reports constituted rather a mine of detailed information on the conduct of French administration than a method of fiscal control. Cases were quite frequent when administrative abuses, after having been attacked in such reports, were later remedied. Such practices were naturally furthered by a member's reporting the same budget year after year; they led to a *camaraderie* of the specialists in the administration and in parliament, both maintaining a certain solidarity against the minister, the parliament at large, and the public.

Although, strictly speaking, the committee should not concern itself with anything but fiscal matters, it was inevitably drawn into a consideration of the relative merits of divergent policies. Consequently, the burden of work was enormous, with the result that discussion in the committee was cut short by tactical considerations, and considerable delays were occasioned. (In light of French experience, the above-noted innovation of further responsibilities along these lines in the Congress appears more than questionable.) These delays had a disastrous effect as the emergency deepened. Contrary to the rules which provided for distribution of the budget report well in advance, the committee often asked the Chamber to consider matters on which no report had become available. Toward the end, the finance committee had also commenced to unseat ministries by refusing consent to important measures (see above, p. 338). When taken together with the committee's substituting of its own budget for that of the government, France finally may be said to have had a dual government which produced anarchy, when effective action was required. Facing this situation, Barthélemy exclaimed: "The leftist group [in the committee] deliberates, the committee decides, the government follows." The lack of really effective leadership on the part of the government gave a great impetus to the Finance Committee's strength.

In the depression years, governments were very slow in submitting budgets, particularly the general *loi des finances*. Was this the result of too much divided responsibility? If the many discussions on this subject in France during the crisis are read, one definitely gains the impression that everybody was blaming everybody else for the troublous times. The problem of the Finance Committee cannot be separated, one may agree with Barthélemy, from the problem of parliamentary government, and, one might add, of constitutional government. It is a question of devising a procedure which will insure a competent decision after a sufficiently mature deliberation. Competence can be contributed primarily by the permanent administrative staff, deliberation and supervision by a limited group of people representing the major divisions in the community, decision by a large representative assembly. Unfortunately for France, her system moved farther and farther away from such a balance.

Administrative control · The discussion of the last two paragraphs has shown how intimately the problem of administrative control and supervision is bound up with the fiscal problem. It is nevertheless distinct. Both in the United States and in France (as well as in many other countries), the committee system, particularly when coupled with the interpellation, is an essential tool of parliament in controlling the administration.[10] It is natural, therefore, that voices should have arisen in England demanding a similar system of standing committees to restrain the "bureaucracy." In chapter XIX it will be shown that many techniques exist for making officials responsible for their conduct. Under modern conditions, parliamentary supervision has had a very strong appeal. Here were persons well acquainted with the particular matter in hand through their legislative activity; why should not they see to it that the laws were faithfully executed? It is hard to deny the good sense of such a plan, and particularly in the earlier phases of the movement for constitutional government such control seemed wholly beneficial. The deep-seated suspicion with which the average man in France and the United States viewed the "bureaucracy" served as a powerful drive toward the establishment of such control mechanisms.

As the century wore on, and as parties began to appear, it was discovered that such control by parliament and parliamentary committees was, in effect, control by parliamentarians. Such a system of control offered to these individuals and the party groups behind them opportunities of pressure which could be turned to quite different account than the protection of the public's interest against administrators. The evils of patronage, corruption in connection with governmental contracts, nepotism, and so forth, made their appearance. Parliamentary control soon began to look like parliamentary tyranny. Factionalism was introduced into the administrative services, with many an influential parliamentarian having a group of henchmen in various ministries who looked to him for promotion in return for assistance offered him in the promotion of various more or less legitimate interests. The difficulty lies in part in the intangible quality of such control. Unlike the preparation of a bill or a budget, we have conversations, questions, a certain atmosphere of either hostile criticism or collegial collaboration—all matters which are subject to a good deal of manipulation and diplomacy. This setting is further emphasized by the lack of publicity (in many cases) which raises further problems (see pp. 349 ff.). In spite of all these troublesome complications, detailed parliamentary control seems essential if the administrative services are to be held in check. Reliance cannot safely be placed upon control by the cabinet at the top alone. There are many minor abuses and irregularities which certainly do not justify the ousting of a cabinet. Such developments can readily be reported to the plenary session, and thus be given adequate publicity. What is more, the existence of such a watchdog keeps the officials on their toes. They will seek to anticipate the reaction of a parliamentary committee. It might be argued, of course, that an entirely separate body of quasi-judicial persons should be entrusted with this task, so as to forestall the development of the various forms of collusion of which mention has been made. But such a procedure would further complicate an already top-heavy structure, and it would deprive the members of legislatures of a most valuable school in which to learn about the difficulties of administering a certain body of laws. Nor is it apparent why such a group should not be likewise subject to the temptations which at present beguile legislators.

The great value of all parliamentary control is readily apparent to any student of contemporary dictatorships, which are honeycombed with corruption. This is often merely the result of inadequate supervision, as there is no one around to do the supervising. If one studies the cynical techniques the Prussian kings adopted in order to cope with this evil—techniques which did not outlast in effectiveness the reigns of their institutors, Frederick William I and Frederick the Great—he appreciates even more distinctly the difficulties which lie hidden here. Yet effective and reasonably efficient administration is of paramount value in modern life, and hence parliamentary work might be justified on that score alone. In order to exercise this function of administrative control, parliamentary committees have gradually evolved a large number of practices, such as hearings for taking evidence from officials as well as private persons, or direct inspection of the service (often involving the much-contested right to look into the files). In France one also finds the reporter system for the purpose of securing information. Through these procedures the many highly technical and complicated activities of modern governmental administration are brought up for discussion in a small circle of fairly well-informed men and women. Points of controversy can be thrashed out and a better understanding reached of the manifold activities of a modern administration. For that reason it is understandable that ministers have occasionally seen fit to resign after they encountered a hostile reception in a particular parliamentary committee. The Teapot Dome Scandal was uncovered by a congressional committee; indeed, the development of investigation as a primary task of Congressional committees has been an outstanding feature of the evolution of the American Congress. Since the cabinet does not require the confidence of Congress, as do European cabinets, investigating committees look into and in due course make public whatever abuses they may believe to exist. The impending threat of such an investigating committee fulfills somewhat the same role which the threat of a scandal involving the parliamentary support of the cabinet entails in England. Such an investigation brings to the attention of the public, frequently preceding an election, matters which will discredit the "ins." Such committees are naturally most likely to be appointed when the President has lost his majority in one of the Houses of Congress. The Legislative Reorganization Act of 1946 considerably broadened the scope of such congressional activity by authorizing substantially larger staffs for congressional committees which are intended to enable such committees to develop their own sources of information, because the Congress cannot depend upon the Executive Departments to supply all the information they need. In England, Royal Commissions of Inquiry are looked upon in a somewhat similar light, but since they are appointed by the Crown, that is, the government in power, they are more likely to explore and report upon areas where changes in basic policy are impending than into the administrative services themselves. The whole range of activities of committees involved in carrying out their supervision of administrative activities, however, remains geared to the legislative and deliberative function of parliaments; it is remote from the representative function.

Control of foreign affairs · A distinct set of problems is found in the realm of foreign affairs.[11] The English Parliament has been very slow to enter into this field, which was for a long time looked upon as a "preroga-tive" of the Crown. To be sure, the clash over the Bulgarian atrocities, between the humanitarian principles of Gladstonian liberalism and Dis-raeli's skillful diplomacy, afforded Gladstone the major plank for his famous Midlothian campaign, though the policy of collaboration with the Turk was blandly continued after he entered office. The shock of thus seeing prob-lems of imperial concern carried before the multitude in order to build popular appeal served as a considerable lesson to the British Foreign Office; henceforth it carefully guarded its secrets against Parliament. This system culminated in the complex situation preceding the First World War (see ch. XXI, p. 431), when fear of the parliamentary reaction induced Sir Edward Grey to pursue a more secret policy than had been followed for a century. France also carefully avoided parliamentary control of foreign affairs; the two parliamentary committees on the subject, which were beginning to build up a measure of surveillance, remained highly secretive themselves. Since the United States did not at that time carry on a very active foreign policy, but merely drifted along with the aid of a few "poli-cies," such as were supposedly contained in the "Monroe Doctrine" and the principle of the "Open Door in China," sporadic attempts by Presidents and Secretaries of State did not invite any measure of effective control. Hence not until after the First World War do we find anywhere a vigorous parliamentary participation in Foreign Affairs.

The general disaster of the First World War, the establishment of the League of Nations, the outburst of democratic and pacific enthusiasm, all aided in lending color to various efforts to realize the promise which had been held out by Wilson's "point" about the abolition of secret diplomacy and the substitution of "open covenants openly arrived at." As a technical device, the French and American system of a special committee made a strong appeal. In England it was ardently advocated by the Union of Democratic Foreign Policy; in Germany a special article of the constitu-tion was devoted to the establishment of a standing committee on foreign affairs; in Holland, in Sweden, in Norway, in Czechoslovakia, everywhere standing committees on foreign affairs were set up. The French committees in both the Senate and the Chamber became more vocal. But if the idea had at first been that parliamentary control would aid in making interna-tional relations smoother, the activities of the United States Senate Foreign Relations Committee in connection with the Peace Treaty and the League Covenant should have given a warning. It was soon discovered that every-where parliaments and their committees were inclined to outdo their minis-ters in insisting upon national "interest" and national "honor." The na-tionalist reaction first entrenched itself in Germany in the Foreign Affairs

Committee of the Reichstag, membership of which gave to the deputies the air of "being in the know." In the French parliament, nationalist elements likewise managed to dominate the scene in the plenary sessions as well as in the committees, and the more conciliatory policy of Briand met its first as well as its last serious defeat in these committees. Even in the small and pacific Netherlands the able Foreign Minister van Karnebeek was forced out by Parliament because he had made a conciliatory treaty with the Belgian government concerning the Scheldt which supposedly violated national "interests." Another almost insuperable difficulty appeared as a result of large Communist parties in many of these parliaments which, on the basis of the proportional principle, had a right to seats on these committees. They recurrently raised suspicions of collaborating with Moscow (the government of the Soviet Union, as well as with the Third International) and were therefore felt not to be entitled to any confidential information. Sometimes this difficulty was met by forming a more informal inner circle of members of the committee who received the really confidential information.

After Hitler's entry into power in Germany, parliamentary influence took yet another, and perhaps more disastrous, turn. In curious contrast to the preceding nationalist inclination, the parliaments of France, Britain, and the United States now became the decisive factor in fashioning a policy of appeasement. The United States State Department has issued a rather doleful document purporting to show that they did all that the Congress (and the people) would let them do. It is reported that at the crucial turning point of Hitler's re-occupation of the Rhineland, when the French government, or at least some members, wanted to act forcibly, the parliamentary committees forbade such action unless supported by the British and Americans. The British conservative majority preferred to conclude a naval agreement with Hitler, and to have its ambassadors pursue missions which were bound to fail. The indecisiveness, the confused and meandering course of foreign affairs, as conducted by the major democratic powers, while no doubt due in part to the novelty of the situation and the as yet "unknown" potentialities and dangers, nonetheless is traceable at least in part to the ineptitude of parliamentary committees of foreign affairs.

That situation seems to be somewhat changed since the Second World War. Whether as the result of experience, or of the more evident threat of Communist totalitarianism and imperialism, the parliaments of England, France, and the United States have shown a greater readiness to support a policy of containment of the aggressive tendencies, while at the same time the governments have displayed considerably greater vigor in shaping policies appropriate to this end.

The problem of publicity · The parliamentary control of foreign affairs squarely raises the issue of publicity. It is a question which has much bearing upon the whole system of parliamentary committees. Committee meetings are secret, either wholly or in part, and many of the most serious attacks are levelled at this feature of the system. No one has stated more forcefully the arguments in favor of making all deliberative transactions public than did Jeremy Bentham. He opens his classical *Essays on Political Tactics* with a discussion of publicity. "Before entering into the detail of the operations of the assembly, let us place at the head of its regulations the fittest law for securing the public confidence, and causing it constantly to advance towards the end of its institution. This law is that of publicity."[12] (For a summary of his arguments see the previous chapter, pp. 306 f.) Clearly, committees as ordinarily constituted violate this law thoroughly, more especially committees on foreign affairs. Regarding the latter, it should be noted that Bentham made an exception to his rule of publicity where "it would favor the projects of an enemy." It is, therefore, quite natural that the committee system should have been attacked on this score. Many prominent students of politics, including Woodrow Wilson, have bitterly condemned the secrecy of committee deliberations. Robert Luce, after citing Wilson's writings, asserts on the contrary that "the complete justification of privacy is that its absence would enure to the injury of the public business." He adduces the privacy of cabinet meetings in England and America, as well as the relations between doctor and patient, clergyman and parishioner, lawyer and client. It may be doubted whether such arguments meet the core of Wilson's objections to secrecy. "Legislation, as we nowadays conduct it, is not conducted in the open. It is not thrashed out in open debate upon the floors of our assemblies. It is, on the contrary, framed, digested, and concluded in committee rooms. It is in committee rooms that legislation not desired by the interests dies. . . . There is not enough debate of it in the open house, in most cases, to disclose the real meaning of the proposals made. . . . There is not any legitimate privacy about matters of government. Government must, if it is to be pure and correct in its processes, be absolutely public in everything that affects it." The last phrases are evidently an overstatement, but the objections to the secrecy of the deliberative process of legislation are not met by merely pointing out such exaggeration. Other things being equal, secrecy should be avoided as being undemocratic. As Bentham had noted, the objections to publicity reduce to one, "that the public is incompetent to judge of the proceedings of a political assembly." Would Bentham have taken the same view had he known our modern "yellow journalism" with its sensationalism, its irresponsibility, and the rest? As has been mentioned before (see above,

p. 308), at the time Bentham considered the subject the English Parliament was just emerging from its previous practice of carefully guarding the secrecy of parliamentary proceedings. Bentham himself, in surveying "the state of things in England," noted the contrast between the as yet unaltered rules designed to insure strict secrecy and the actual practice: "It is to these fortunate crimes that England is indebted for her escape from an aristocratic government resembling that of Venice." If the question be posited in terms of the double function of elected assemblies, it will become apparent that a measure of privacy is indicated by the nature of the deliberative function, while it is inimical to the representative function.

Robert Luce undoubtedly voices the experience of many conscientious representatives when he writes: "When a man thinks his words are to be repeated, he has an eye to the ultimate consumer. Instead of talking solely to those who are to make the immediate decision, he frequently talks with remote effects in mind. This would turn a public committee conference into a sparring spectacle for personal or party advantage." But elected assemblies *should* have an eye to the ultimate consumer, Bentham would reply. The conflict of ideas, therefore, cannot be resolved except in terms of an explicit recognition of the double function of elected assemblies and the consequent need for differentiating their techniques accordingly. A measure of privacy for deliberations should be provided, and the committee system provides that opportunity. But the ultimate value of publicity should likewise be recognized, and public debates, of either the whole house or some of its committees, be provided for. We noted above that the French parliament of the Fourth Republic provides for more publicity of its committee meetings. The same trend is observable in the post-war German constitutions (Basic Law, art. 42). But while publicity is acknowledged as desirable, the opportunity for excluding the public is generally believed to be essential. The American Congress, the English Parliament, the French Parliament, all provide for public debates as well as private (secret) deliberations. In England parliamentary procedure proper recognizes such privacy most sparingly, but all descriptive accounts of the English system point to one conclusion: the compactness of English party organization permits all essential deliberations to be carried on among party leaders outside of Parliament proper, the "ins" in the clubs and the cabinet, the "outs" in the clubs alone. Elsewhere, party organization being less authoritarian and the leadership less effective, much deliberation and the compromise which results from it are carried on in the committees.

A glimpse at the caucus · In the United States the problem of the "secret" party conclave is not unknown, of course. In fact, a great deal of controversy has surrounded the development of the caucus in the American Congress. It is significant, and in keeping with British experience, that the caucus should always have made its appearance in conjunction with strong presidential leadership, such as that of Jefferson and Wilson. But Luce asserts that the caucus is rather insignificant in American state legislatures, and more particularly in Massachusetts it has not been employed.[13] In the United States Senate it does not play a significant role either. Perhaps this weakness of the caucus in the Senate is directly related to the weakness of presidential leadership in the Senate. The caucus was somewhat strengthened in the House through the revolt against the Speaker in 1909–1910 (see above, ch. XVI, p. 314), but on the whole the privacy of committee proceedings in Congress has made the caucus a preliminary rather than a decisive stage. If genuine deliberation could no longer take place in these committees, the caucus might conceivably become increasingly the forum where actual deliberations would take place. Deliberation, with its need for privacy, will retreat to party conclaves if the regular legislatures do not provide suitable opportunities for the thrashing out of questions involving a frank facing of difficulties. The Senate has several times debated this subject, and in the course of these debates it has been stated that caucuses have rarely, if ever, undertaken to bind members to any particular action; their main power lies in the part they play in filling committee memberships and other such personnel questions, and in their ironing out dissensions over policy matters bearing upon party fortunes, particularly as they are related to presidential elections. These are matters of great political importance which do not come before committees, nor could they be considered in the presence of the opposition party. It is not readily apparent how national party organizations could be held together without some effort at concerted action of their national representatives. What is detrimental to the prestige of parliamentary institutions is the tendency of parliamentarians nonchalantly to allow the committees to take complete direction. The pressure of the mass of modern activity is, after all, the main explanation of that tendency. Each member of the assembly is so busy as the member of one or more of its committees that he would just as soon forget about the rest. All over the world committee work has been crowding out general debate in open session. And what time committee work would not take, the ever-increasing electorate with ever more efficient means of communication would absorb. The thousands of letters, telegrams, and telephone calls which many American Senators get at certain crucial moments are merely the peaks of this ever-rising curve of public business. Is it a fever curve? When the substance of our activities is mounting, we become indifferent to procedure; a very busy man is apt to be less polite than a man of leisure.

All this is widely admitted; reports on parliamentary procedure in the United States, in England, and elsewhere are full of such observations. Impatient men are ready to pronounce the breakdown of the system. In order to get efficiency, they would scrap all publicity and revert to the complete secrecy of bureaucratic direction.

As in the period after the First World War, so at present the tendency toward, and the willingness to condone, secrecy has been greatly increased by the fear that all Communists and "fellow-travelers" are in communication with the Soviet Union and its agents. Nor can this fear and suspicion be treated lightly by any reasonable man. All governments, but more especially totalitarian governments, are committed to secret service and espionage work. "Intelligence" functions have been growing by leaps and bounds in the United States. When a government is frankly committed to the espousal of world revolution, and the Soviet Union is so committed, all other governments, especially constitutional governments, are faced with the problem of how to avert their overthrow by these revolutionary forces. How far can one go in permitting advocacy of such views? How much of one's own policy can one permit the agents and accomplices of such a world-revolutionary organization to know about? These are two of the elementary and yet also the most persistent questions that face the student of constitutionalism, especially when concerned with constitutionalism's inherent requirement of maximizing publicity on all aspects of public policy and the discussion and deliberation upon such policy in the representative assemblies. No simple, dogmatic answers are feasible in this field. It all becomes a matter of judgment upon such elusive matters of "fact" as whether the danger is "clear" and is "present." Yet some such standard is the nearest criteria we have for coping with these complexities.[14]

Conclusion · In 1941 I wrote: "Dictatorial efficiency is at present impressing the multitude. But Napoleon, after winning all the battles, lost the war. Perhaps the sword of propaganda is made of lead, the party following disintegrates and becomes mute as dissenters are done away with, and parades turn out to be less interesting in the long run than parliamentary debates (since parades are always the same, whereas the argument varies). If experience should thus prove that the dictatorial alternatives to public debates in representative, deliberative assemblies are weak and temporary substitutes, and that the resulting actions and decisions are more frequently wrong than when they are the outcome of public deliberations, renewed efforts will probably be made in those countries which have abandoned them to organize them anew." Those sentences were, of course, written with the Fascist powers specifically in mind. However, they apply to all totalitarian regimes, even where a pretense is made of "public consultation." In any case, the documents we now have certainly prove amply how disastrous were the errors resulting from the concentration of power in the hands of the Fascist dictators. I believe that the policy of the Soviet Union since 1945 is similarly honeycombed with the most astounding errors and misjudgments, resulting from an almost complete lack of adequate deliberation upon vital public policies. On the other hand, Italy, Austria, and Germany have, as foreseen, organized representative and deliberative assemblies anew. At the same time, it would seem that some of the more mature parliamentary bodies are evolving toward a fairly equilibrated balance between their representative and their deliberative functions and the techniques required for the realization of both. The failure of French democracy naturally suggests that the emphasis upon debate characteristic of the French chambers was unwholesome. As far as greater publicity in America is concerned, adequate records might be kept for the committees dealing with financial matters. These could be open for study by the public after a suitable length of time, say six months. A larger amount of open debate might also be provided for, in case of disagreement within the committee. If, furthermore, certain specially qualified persons could be admitted into the committee upon special request after taking an oath not to publish what they had heard, a suitable corrective of present abuses might be provided. Whether reform should go further along lines suggested above will be a matter of disagreement for some years to come. The analysis of experience up to date has, it is hoped, shown that the representative and the deliberative functions of elected assemblies are both important, but that they are fairly distinct. Elected assemblies are responding to real needs when they differentiate their techniques to fulfill both functions. If men could deliberate without thinking of the reactions of those who are to elect or rather re-elect them, such differentiation would be unnecessary.

XVIII

Chief Executives and Cabinet Systems

Introduction · Leadership: mystique and reality · National emergencies and personal insecurity · Growth of social problems and planning · Policy-making and policy execution · Chief executives vs. cabinet · Model cabinet government: Great Britain · The cabinet subservient to parliament: France · An ill-fated experiment: Germany · The collegial council: Switzerland · One-man rule: the American President · Cabinet and presidential secretariat and the problem of informal advisers · Conclusion.

Introduction · Of the American President, Harold Laski has said that he is "both more and less than a king; both more and less than a prime minister." The issue of executive leadership is dramatically projected in such a comparison. The American President was conceived by the makers of the American Constitution as a republican equivalent to the hereditary monarch of British constitutionalism. Hamilton, in the *Federalist*, went to great length comparing the two offices, insisting that "there is no pretence for the parallel which has been attempted between him and the king of Great Britain."[1] He felt that anyone who thought that the President had anywhere near the power of the British king was absurd. Since that comparison was made, kings have vanished or become shadows of their former self, while the American President has assumed the central position in the American scheme. This, we saw in a preceding chapter, was at least in part the result of his becoming the leader of the majority party. In the meantime, in Britain the Prime Minister has emerged as the keystone of the arch of what is today a cabinet rather than a parliamentary government. The same is true of the British Dominions and Eire. Countries with less sound political traditions have struggled in vain to produce a similar integration, and when they failed have reverted to authoritarian schemes of executive leadership.

Along with the chief executives, their cabinets, or councils, have undergone considerable change. Their relationship both to the chief executive and to the elected representative assemblies has changed in accordance with the increasing emphasis upon executive leadership. Cabinets are older than parliaments. Princes surrounded themselves with councils or cabinets for the direction of their bureaucracies as soon as central administrative systems arose. In fact, these bodies, composed of leading administrative officials, are the very core of such centralized systems. It is therefore no wonder that the cabinet tends to occupy a somewhat independent position and is not ordinarily, as the phrase used to go, "an executive committee of Parliament." Cabinets today depend once again upon the chief executive, as they always have in the United States. What is more, the old formulas about policy-making and policy execution require extensive revision.

Leadership: mystique and reality · The crux of executive power is leadership. The doings of the Fascists have brought to the fore a conception which was dear to the hearts of romantic critics of constitutionalism and rationalism throughout the nineteenth century. Englishmen, Frenchmen, and Germans vied with each other in glorifying the hero, the Caesar, the superman. Carlyle, Maurras, Nietzsche, they all and many more vented their artistic spleen by contrasting the creative force of the leader with the equalitarian mediocrity of the majority and the mass. Nietzsche was inspired by Burckhardt, as Maurras was inspired by Taine, both great historians with a pessimistic bent of mind. Leopold von Ranke, greatest of German historians in the nineteenth century, while desirous of describing things "as they had actually been" (*wie es eigentlich gewesen ist*), nevertheless saw history essentially as the product of the great state-builders, the Cromwells, Richelieus, and the rest.[2] Looking at events primarily through the eyes of contemporary observers, like the Venetian ambassadors whose reports he so thoroughly explored, he too absorbed the Renaissance view of man and history.

Sociology and political science, psychology and economics, have more recently exploded a good part of these cherished historical premises. Indeed, economic determinism proceeded to interpret the leader as nothing but the product of favorable economic circumstance. "He thinks he pushes while he's being pushed"; this snarl of Mephistopheles would best describe the "leader" in a history preoccupied with price movements, inventions, discoveries, and trade. Meanwhile, Freudian hypotheses about sex as the ultimate propeller of human activity provided new hunches for an interpretation of history, not to mention the school of debunkers who delighted the reader by offering him the intimate view a butler takes of his hero, which proverbially destroys the illusion of greatness. Napoleon scolding Josephine for having mislaid his overcoat is a spectacle which suits the equalitarian impulse of democratic man. Increasing insight into the psychological processes associated with leadership, suggestions, egocentricity, and the whole range of propaganda, also contributed toward the eclipse of leadership as the decisive determinant of social development. But these mounting doubts of the intellectuals could not quell the psychic impulses which

355

are generated in men by a feeling of insecurity: the demand for the leader increased as international and class conflicts undermined the confidence of the masses in the future.

Many attempts have been made to discover the traits of *the* leader, to discover an abstract, general pattern of qualities or characteristics which constitute "leadership."[3] Indeed, many foundations, colleges, and other groups seeking to select the future "leader" cheerfully take it for granted that these qualities are known. Yet, actually, the greatest diversity of opinion prevails as to what constitutes even "executive ability," let alone leadership ability. A survey of the various inquiries, as well as our general knowledge, leads to the conclusion that these qualities depend very largely upon the conditions under which leadership operates. The nature of the group and of the task will make much difference. An American President needs different qualities from a British Prime Minister, and his qualities today need to be different from what they were a hundred years ago. Take only the single instance of radio appeal; we do not know for sure, but indications are that elections are being vitally affected by that intangible quality. No man can hope to be a success as Prime Minister in Britain who lacks the capacity of handling himself effectively in the give and take of parliamentary debate; the American President does not need that ability. This functional approach to the problem of leadership becomes even more essential when we go farther afield. A religious leader differs markedly from a business leader, and both contrast sharply with a military leader.

We are not at present in a position to "explain" leadership, and we may never be. When we consider a great religious or spiritual leader, like Luther or Jean Jacques Rousseau, we are apt to admit that we are facing the ultimate creative force in human society working through such a leader. The same would be true of the scientific or artistic leader. When we come to political and social leaders, to the shapers of organizations and governments, we are obliged to be more skeptical. Many students of history would see a clear analogy between a work of art and a "state"; indeed to Machiavelli the state appeared the greatest work of art of all. But recent history has shown or at least suggested that many, if not all, men can participate in the building and maintaining of a government; that a constitutional system is never the work of one great leader. Once law is placed in the center of attention, it is evident that many minds and many, many hands have gathered and are gathering the detailed insights, devising the particular solutions to particular problems, and that no one can know enough to devise a "state." As we have pointed out before, the "state" concept as such was an outgrowth of the opposite view,—a view constructed to justify and rationalize the despotic powers of monarchical rulers in the seventeenth century.*

It is possible, however, to spell out, so to speak, certain functional aspects of a leader. One such functional aspect is the leader's representativeness. We all know that an Irishman is more likely to get Irish votes than a Yankee. Likewise a man wanting to reform a church would have to be a member of that church. Again, no one who was not a member of a given profession or craft would be apt to succeed in "reforming" such a profession, no matter how sound his views might be. Representativeness is compounded of likeness of behavior, of outlook, and of general qualities of that sort (see above, ch. XIV). Another functional aspect of leadership is a capacity to find solutions to commonly recognized problems. Here the creative aspect is most apparent. The solution of problems presupposes intelligence; without intelligence there cannot be leadership—that much is certain. But intelligence unrelated to problems recognized by the group is unproductive of leadership. Intelligence is a matter of degree. Leadership, therefore, is likely to be a matter of degree also. A governmental system always presents many concrete problems; some are very small and specific, others vast and comprehensive. The man who suggests a convincing solution acquires leadership as others follow his lead.

A third functional aspect, related to the preceding, but distinct, is the capacity to foresee problems that are not yet generally recognized, to bring them into clear view and to dramatize their urgency. Again it is a matter of intelligence, but of analytical insight rather than inventiveness, plus the ability to generate and radiate emotion. All the progressive movements, particularly of recent times, abound with leaders of this type. They show, at the same time, how easily this capacity is stultified by unexpected developments. Thus, Marx's analysis, while a brilliant anticipation of the rising labor-class problem, overlooked the importance of the managerial class in an expanding industrialism by indiscriminately lumping it together with capital owners as the capitalist class.[4] His expectation of an inevitable labor majority has therefore remained unfulfilled, and the policies of socialist parties built upon that expectation have foundered. If the leader functions well as an anticipator and solver of group problems, he will naturally seem superior to his fellows.

---

*More detailed analysis reveals that the "great man" view is inappropriate in other fields, too. No one can go through the galleries in Holland without being struck with the many minor artists who preceded and surrounded Rembrandt; nor can anyone listen to the music of Bach's time and country without being struck with a similar "environment." It is clear that neither of these peaks of artistic achievement could have been achieved without the solid mass of less extraordinary, yet significant achievement. The "great man" view is one of decadent times in which none but the greatest are recalled.

Whether physical prowess distinguishes the leader, as it did Achilles, or whether a keen wit enables him to succeed where others fail, prestige will invariably be associated with his position. Prestige is not a separate result of leadership; it is part and parcel of it. Napoleon, the winner of battles, can afford to be a ruffian; a successful leader commands a margin of freedom from communal restraints. This fact is universally recognized. It is not limited to despotic regimes; everyone knows that there is such a margin in the most democratic constitutionalism, and when the British constitution to this day maintains that "the king can do no wrong," it gives symbolic recognition to that fact. Here we can see once again the root of constitutional restraints: they are designed to prevent the erstwhile leader from becoming a despot which he might otherwise do by utilizing this margin of freedom for the systematic destruction of his opponents.

National emergencies and personal insecurity · We have alluded, in the previous section, to the psychic impulse which a sense of insecurity generates in man, the impulse, namely, of either becoming or following a leader. There is nothing mysterious or novel about this; it is a most natural way to try to cope with pressing difficulties. Few are the people who, when seeing their house on fire, will calmly go their way, as if nothing had happened. Most men will either run in and get everybody to leave the house, form a bucket line, and send for help, in short *become* a leader; or they will call the fire department, that is, *seek* a leader. What an intelligent person will do depends a good deal upon whether the fire department is within easy, quick reach, whether the fire is far advanced, who is in the house—in short, upon all the conditions surrounding the concrete situation. This case, therefore, illustrates well the fact that the same person may elect to be a leader in one situation and a follower in another. The essential question always must be: what course of action offers the greatest probability of getting me out of the jam I am in. If I see no solution, I am likely to follow any man who asserts a reasonable claim to have a solution. Now it is an undeniable fact of our times that a great many people have a sense of personal insecurity, well-supported by incontrovertible evidence, such as the death of a close relative in war, bankruptcy, unemployment, etc.[5] All these anxieties have lately been reinforced by the mysteries of the atomic and biologic weapons.

In the good old days of quick recovery, the standpat solution of turning the rascals out worked. Maybe the rascals you turned in did not bring about recovery, but the sense of insecurity was once more lessened. What if you have turned in and out all kinds of rascals, and the sense of insecurity remains? Then the broader question arises: what is wrong with the system? None but those bold enough to allege that they know the answers can satisfy the psychic impulse which demands leadership. Here the horrible abyss yawns: that you accept as leader a man who has no solutions, a wild man who just wants to be captain of the boat, regardless of the storm. Some writers have denied the quality of leadership to such persons. Only he who convinces reasonable men of right solutions is a true leader. The other is a seducer. But a seduced girl has a baby as much as a loved one; the Don Juan remains a lover, even if a false one.

Can constitutionalism, can democracy, guard against the demagogue? Within limits, yes. Like the thoughtful parent, it can provide for cooling-off periods. Institutional restraints, such as have been surveyed in earlier chapters, can be provided. Even the constitutional emergency powers can be surrounded with safeguards (see ch. XXVI). But when the sense of insecurity becomes too extreme, when people in their search for some remedy become frantic, all these institutional devices will prove of no avail. That is the reason why the capacity of self-control, of facing emergencies calmly, of enduring an abiding sense of insecurity without losing one's head, is an essential condition of a lasting constitutional order. Those qualities, in short, which make a man a leader himself, which make him seek solutions to his problems, must be widely dispersed amongst a people to enable it to govern itself. Potentially a large part of a democratic nation is possessed of the capacity for leadership. That is the crux of the matter.

Growth of social problems and planning · The issues which give rise to the sense of personal insecurity just discussed are all more or less definitely rooted in the growing complexity of our industrial system. The restless forward march of technological change, the rapid succession of inventions which has brought the "power age," and the deepening awareness of class conflict have generated social tensions much more rapidly than the social inventiveness of man could cope with them. Some acute thinkers, like the late Lord Stamp, have gone so far as to suggest that there should be a general moratorium on all inventions.[6] Leaders in the most advanced nations, unable to cope with the total situation, have tackled now one aspect, now another, always finding their specific solutions defeated by unexpected secondary and tertiary effects in other spheres of social life. Take, for example, the field of agricultural policy in the United States. No one could deny that after the First World War the farmer's plight in America was serious. There was a rapid succession of remedial policies, trying to solve the problem first by stimulating exports, then by storing surpluses, then by restricting production; but in each instance the farmer was not materially helped, while other groups, foreign nations, taxpayers, consumers, raised a sharp protest against the consequences of the policy adopted. The same experience can be observed in the field of unemployment. Outright doles, insurance schemes, public works, they all have been tried in turn by all the industrialized nations and have been found impracticable in the end. The labor market became disturbed, insurance reserves could not be safely invested, the taxpayer objected to unnecessary public improvements, while his property deteriorated.

From a Communist viewpoint all this is inevitable; only an economy totally controlled by the government can cope comprehensively with this situation. But a thorough analysis of experience in the Soviet Union—not possible in this volume—reveals that over-all plans suffer from the same difficulty that a less comprehensively controlled economy encountered: unanticipated secondary and tertiary effects vitiate and upset the neatly balanced blueprint as much as such natural catastrophes as droughts. What is more, Stalin had at first a simple objective, that of industrializing Russia, which, when accomplished, will leave him confronting the same uncertainties with which planning is confronted in the United States.

Planning is, after all, no magic formula, no open sesame. Planning means anticipating problems and finding solutions for them, in short: leadership. And the unhappy fact is that no human individual is capable of comprehending all the social problems which our machine age presents. Or is it a happy fact? Is it not better in the long run that there be many leaders, and that planning (as actually conceived in America today) be pooling of resources, information, ideas? The roof of our house leaks, no doubt about that. Shall we tear the house down because someone claims that he will build a new one, even though he refuses to show us with what materials he proposes to do it? In communities accustomed to self-government, quite a few will prefer to look for a ladder, in the hope of repairing the roof, even though they get wet in the search. (For the administrative response to this situation, see the next chapter; see also the discussion in ch. XXIII.)

Policy-making and policy execution · In the last paragraph we spoke of an agricultural policy. Earlier in the volume reference was made to the modern shift in emphasis from legislation to policy-making. When, in Bentham's time, attention was focused upon legislation, men thought of it in terms of making rules. But Bentham dramatically insisted upon its embodying social "inventions." He saw it as what has become known as public policy. Public policy is a course of action, indicated by the need for overcoming a difficulty. Profoundly convinced of the possibility of "solving" problems in terms of increasing the sum total of human happiness, he was forever at work to find such solutions. His enormous direct and indirect influence upon English and American social reformers has helped to make his outlook an integral part of modern democracy. In fact, there can be little question that many of the American founders, notably Thomas Jefferson, shared his outlook.

It has long been customary to distinguish between policy-making and policy execution. Frank J. Goodnow, in his well-known work, *Politics and Administration*,[7] undertook to build an almost absolute distinction upon this functional difference. "There are, then, in all governmental systems two primary or ultimate functions of government, *viz.* the expression of the will of the state and the execution of that will. There are also in all states separate organs, each of which is mainly busied with the discharge of one of these functions. These functions are, respectively, Politics and Administration." But while the distinction has a great deal of value as a relative matter of emphasis, it cannot any longer be accepted in this absolute form. Admittedly, this misleading distinction has become a fetish, a stereotype in the minds of theorists and practitioners alike. The result has been a great deal of confusion and argument. The reason for making this distinction an absolute antithesis is probably to be found in building it upon the metaphysical, if not abstruse, idea of a will of the state. The problem of how a public policy is adopted and carried out is bogged down by a vast ideological superstructure which contributes little or nothing to its solution. Take a case like the AAA. In simple terms, AAA was a policy adopted with a view to helping the farmer to weather the storm of the depression. This admittedly was AAA's broad purpose. To accomplish this purpose, crop reduction, price-fixing, and a number of lesser devices were adopted. Crop reduction in turn led to processing taxes. Processing taxes required reports by the processors, inspection of their plants. Crop reduction itself necessitated reports by the farmers, so-called work sheets, and agreements between them and the government as to what was to be done, and so forth and so on. What here is politics and what administration? Will anyone understand better the complex processes involved in the articulation of this important public policy if we talk about the expression and the execution of the state will? The concrete patterns of public-policy formation and execution reveal that politics and administration are not two mutually exclusive boxes, or absolute distinctions, but that they are two closely linked aspects of the same process. Public policy, to put it flatly, is a continuous process, the formation of which is inseparable from its execution. Public policy is being formed as it is being executed, and it is likewise being executed as it is being formed. Politics and administration play a continuous role in both formation and execution, though there is probably more politics in the formation of policy, more administration in the execution of it. In so far as particular individuals or groups are gaining or losing power or control in a given area, there is politics; in so far as officials act or propose action in the name of public interest, there is administration.

The same problem may be considered from another angle. Policies in the common meaning of the term are decisions about what to do or not to do in given situations. It was pointed out that today most legislation is looked upon as deciding policy. Hence, policy-making in the broad sense is not supposed to be part of administration. While these propositions are true in a general way, they tend to obscure two important facts, namely, (1) that many policies are not ordained with a stroke of the legislative or dictatorial pen but evolve slowly over long periods of time, and (2) that administrative officials participate continuously and significantly in this process of evolving policy. To commence with the latter fact, it is evident that in the process of doing something the administrator may discover another and better way of accomplishing the same result, or he discovers that the thing cannot be done at all, or that something else has to be done first, before the desired step can be taken. In our recent agricultural policy, examples of all these "administrative" policy determinations can be cited, as likewise in our social-security policy. What is more, such administrative participation alone renders policy-making a continuous process. This process is so much in a state of flux that it is difficult, if not impossible, to state with precision what the policy in any given field is at any particular time. But, if this is true, it follows as a corollary that public policy will often be contradictory and conflicting in its effects upon society. Our myth-makers, of course, remain adamant in proclaiming that this should not be so, and let it go at that. It is hard to disagree with them, but we still have to face the question of responsibility, seeing that policies are in fact contradictory and conflicting. Who is responsible for what, and to whom? To what extent does such responsibility affect the actual conduct of affairs? (See next chapter.) No consideration of executives or cabinets can be undertaken without bearing the role of the administrator in mind.

In a very important discourse, Lord Stamp called attention to the creative role the civil servant is called upon to play in Great Britain. "I am quite clear that the official must be the mainspring of the new society, suggesting, promoting, advising at every stage." Lord Stamp insisted that this trend was inevitable, irresistible, and therefore called for a new type of administrator. An editorial writer of *The Times*, though critical of this development, agreed "that the practice, as opposed to the theory, of administration has long been moving in this direction." He added, "In practice, they [the officials] possess that influence which cannot be denied to exhaustive knowledge; and this influence, owing to the congestion of parliamentary business and other causes, manifests itself more and more effectively as an initiative in public affairs." Testimony of this sort could be indefinitely multiplied. It is no longer true that the mere dependence of a cabinet upon the "confidence" of an elected assembly ensures responsible conduct on the part of the officials in charge of the initiation and execution of public policy. It is objectionable to consider responsibility secure by this simple device, not merely because of interstitial violations but because there is a fundamental flaw in the view of politics and policy here assumed. The range of public policy is nowadays so far-flung that the "right" of the parliamentary majority to oust a cabinet from power is largely inoperative. The majority supporting the cabinet may violently disagree with this, that, and the other policy advocated and adopted by the cabinet, but considerations of party politics, in the broadest sense, will throttle their objections because the particular issue is "not worth a general election" and the chance of the M. P.'s losing his seat.[8] This is what gives the British Cabinet its key political function. This has often been described as that of "formulating policy." It is more correct to say that it is that of "making the major decisions." And yet, sometimes the most important decisions are made by the Prime Minister as leader of the party, and presented to the Cabinet as a *fait accompli.*

Thus, it is clear that the pattern of executive leadership is related to that of the representative assembly, when the executive depends upon parliamentary support. But cabinets may possess a very high degree of independence from such a representative assembly, like that of England before the time of Walpole, or of the United States at present, or of other governments molded upon the American pattern (for example, most of the American states). This interrelationship is, of course, important. On the whole, systems with a measure of independence seem to be more stable. As contrasted with the dependence of French cabinets, the English pattern seems to strike a happy medium. Here the Prime Minister's leadership of the dominant party gives the cabinet very comfortable independence without freeing it altogether from considerations of parliamentary support. Still different is the situation in Switzerland, where the cabinet, as in the United States, is constitutionally independent, but at the same time preoccupied with administrative problems, accepting in the realm of legislation the verdict of the representative body. From this quick survey it can be seen that the pattern of executive leadership shows numerous variations.

Chief executives vs. cabinet · The relative strength and power of the single executive as contrasted with some collegial body, like the cabinet, is today at least as important as the relation of either to a body of elected representatives. There is need for a broad comparative analysis of executive leadership in such terms.[9] Generally speaking, executive leadership may be vested largely in a single individual, as it is in the United States, where the Cabinet consists essentially of helpers of the chief executive. Or executive leadership may be exercised by a group of equals, as it is in Switzerland. Or it may fit somewhere in between—England, the Dominions, or France show intermediary patterns. Moreover, these national patterns have been changing gradually from the collegial toward monocratic control, owing to the development of large parties and the prime minister's increasing importance as party leader. The tendency toward the monocratic (presidential) pattern seems almost universal. Frequently it has been perverted into dictatorship; the slower evolution of the position of *Il Duce* merely foreshadowed the rapid rise of the *Führer*. The collegial pattern is more nearly compatible with parliamentary control (see above, ch. XVII), but it fails to produce the integration and symbolic representation of unity which the mass electorate seems to demand. In France, under the Third Republic, each of the several members of the cabinet figured as the leader of one of the groups which together constituted the parliamentary support of the cabinet. In Switzerland, the members of the cabinet (Federal Council) are not even necessarily leaders of groups or parties, but are merely representatives of such groups with high administrative qualifications. We find approximations to the collegial pattern in pre-Fascist Italy as well as in a number of the smaller countries of Europe. In many of these countries the pattern was subject to considerable variation, in response to different personalities—a fact which is of some importance even in more nearly monocratic systems. The instability of the pattern was particularly marked in Republican Germany. For a time, an effective leader such as Stresemann or Brüning would create a situation approximating the English arrangement. But the many parties would at other times, in the absence of such a leader, force a strictly collegial cabinet.

Model cabinet government: Great Britain · Combining strong executive leadership with parliamentary and popular influence, the British system of cabinet government is probably the most extraordinary masterpiece of constitutionalism. Both simple and subtle, it is the achievement of generations of people developing one of the soundest political traditions ever possessed by man. So remarkable has been its appeal that time and again admirers have sought to adopt and adapt it, never realizing its ever-evolving operational secrets sufficiently to understand its peculiar conditions of operation, its limitations as well as its strength. As has been well said, to pretend to a knowledge of its up-to-date functioning would predicate information where all is secrecy. The extent to which the idea of a governing class and of its exclusiveness continues to dominate the British executive is a heritage of the empire. In other words, empire prevails over commonwealth and the idea of a governing class over that of a self-governing people.

Historically speaking, the English cabinet developed as a committee of the Privy Council. It does not, as is sometimes assumed, comprise all the officials responsible to Parliament, but only the more important among them, including the heads of the principal departments. There are the First Lord of the Treasury, the Chancellor of the Exchequer, and the First Lord of the Admiralty, as well as the Lord President of the Council and the Lord Privy Seal. In recent decades the cabinet has usually had around twenty members, more or less. They are selected by the Prime Minister according to a variety of considerations. Among them, political expediency plays a predominant role. The man or woman who commands a substantial following in Parliament is likely to be the party choice. Various factions within the party must be taken account of; personal considerations and administrative necessities enter in. In view of this fact it is hardly appropriate today to call the Prime Minister *primus inter pares*, as is so often done. In fact he has been described as the central sun of a planetary system. While it would be inappropriate to call his cabinet colleagues his subordinates, it is clear that no individual could remain in the cabinet contrary to the Prime Minister's desire. Perhaps the most adequate statement would be that the Prime Minister is the superior of each individual member of the cabinet but not of the whole cabinet taken together. The actual relationships are necessarily fluid, since they rest upon the extent and effectiveness of the Prime Minister's party leadership, his personality, personal ability, and industry.[10] But in recent years, the Prime Minister's party leadership undoubtedly counts most heavily at least in peacetime. It is through this party leadership that his position has gradually been enhanced.

Leadership in the House of Commons is less important, for both the government and the majority party in the House are working under the same "mandate" of the people. Nevertheless, the party leader is chosen by a caucus composed of the members of Parliament in the respective parties supplemented by a few outstanding leaders from the outside. For this reason as well as for others it is not practicable to make too rigid a distinction between the cabinet's parliamentary majority and its following outside Parliament. As Lowell has put it, "the governmental machinery is one of wheels within wheels; the outside ring consisting of the party that has a majority in the House of Commons; the next ring being the ministry, which contains the men who are most active within that party; and the smallest of all being the cabinet, containing the real leaders or chiefs. By this means is secured that unity of party action which depends upon placing the directing power in the hands of a body small enough to agree, and influential enough to control." To these rings must nowadays be added the Prime Minister as an individual. Indeed, as was said at the beginning of this chapter, the British Prime Minister's position resembles more and more that of the American president in that the people go to the polls to vote for him and "his" government. Even in the days of Disraeli and Gladstone, this was beginning to be true, and in vain did Queen Victoria protest against the trend of the times when she requested that Mr. Gladstone abstain from speaking at railway stations. The Midlothian Campaign of 1880 marks the turning point; characteristically, Mr. Gladstone's great oratorical efforts in that campaign were referred to as "pilgrimages of passion."[11] The Prime Minister's pre-eminence among his colleagues is formally recognized in the fact that he attends to most of the dealings with the "sovereign"; it is upon his advice that the titular head of the government can request and has at times requested the resignation of individual ministers. The most striking recent illustration of the Prime Minister's powers in this respect was Mr. MacDonald's conduct in 1931. Having resigned with the King's consent as head of the Labour government which had been in power, he proceeded to form a National Union government with which he soon afterward "went to the country," as the British saying goes, in a general election.

The further extension of the Prime Minister's leadership is in part due to the development of radio broadcasting (see below, ch. XXIV). Like the American President, the Prime Minister can effectively appeal to the electorate at large; the cabinet as a group cannot. This trend became especially manifest under war conditions. In fact, the emergency powers discussed in chapter XXVI made the Prime Minister a constitutional dictator. But even before the war, the Prime Minister had incomparable opportunities for shaping the political views of the people. There is every indication that Mr. Chamberlain forced major decisions upon his cabinet. The circumstances surrounding the resignation of a number of cabinet members, like Mr. Eden, give clear evidence that the "appeasement" policy was Mr. Chamberlain's rather than the cabinet's. Until the spring of 1939 it was also that of the majority of the British people, as led by Mr. Chamberlain.

Formally speaking, of course, the cabinet is in charge; it is the cabinet which is responsible to Parliament. Apart from the legal responsibility of the entire ministry, this means that the members of the cabinet, both collectively and individually, are affected by certain actions of Parliament, which by convention oblige them either to resign or to dissolve Parliament and to call a general election. If none of these actions occur, new elections have to be called at the end of five years, except in wartime, thus preventing indefinite self-perpetuation. But by far the more usual occasion has been parliamentary action. These actions of Parliament are three. Parliament may pass a vote of "want of confidence." Such a vote would indicate disapproval of the general policy of the cabinet and is therefore unusual. This is also true of the vote of censure, by which the Parliament may criticize the cabinet or one of its members; still, the Labour government of 1924 was overthrown by such a vote of censure. More usual is the defeat of a measure which the cabinet has sponsored and refuses to abandon. Substantially identical with this is the case in which Parliament insists upon a measure along lines which the Cabinet opposes. Any one of these steps could be taken by Parliament only if a certain number of the supporters of the government had become sufficiently dissatisfied to vote with the opposition party. A development of this sort presupposes a considerable measure of confusion concerning a certain issue. This was the case with the Irish question, which frequently provided the occasion for cabinet changes in the later nineteenth century. In the period immediately before and since the First World War, cabinet changes have come about rather by the initiative of the cabinet itself, when it decided to appeal to the people in a general election, as it did in 1910, 1918, 1923, 1931, 1935, and again in 1945. At other times a reconstruction of the cabinet has been undertaken in order to anticipate an adverse electoral decision, as in 1905, 1915, 1931, and in 1940, when Mr. Churchill was called upon to form a national coalition to deal with the unprecedented emergency caused by the collapse of France and the danger of imminent invasion. What do these trends mean? They clearly indicate that the cabinet, and more particularly the Prime Minister, look toward popular party support for the maintenance of power. The compactness of party organizations, in other words, has brought about a gradual transition from a parliamentary to an electoral responsibility. To put it another way, the cabinet governs Great Britain today with the advice and consent of Parliament.

Serious difficulties have arisen through the rather considerable size of the cabinet. Twenty or more persons form a somewhat unwieldy body for the purposes of collective action. The recurrent demand before the war for a much smaller directing body led to the emergence of a small, informal group of five during the First World War. Under Lloyd George's active and energetic leadership this group took upon itself the making of the most important decisions, but the large amount of criticism which this arrangement engendered led to its abandonment after the war. Lloyd George's memoirs show, however, the great value which this instrumentality possessed in his eyes during the emergency. Formal recognition was recently given to that experience by the organization of the War Cabinet of nine members during the Second World War.

During the Second World War, Mr. Chamberlain likewise formed a War Cabinet and Mr. Churchill continued it. But these cabinets were the key of the arch mostly in name; both Chamberlain and Churchill themselves determined policy with the help of their own advisers. Churchill's War Cabinet grew beyond the original five members with which it started. The problem Churchill had to solve was to maintain an equitable balance in the cabinet between the Conservatives and Labour. He started with the leaders of the two parties, who were Lord President of the Council and Lord Privy Seal respectively, the Foreign Secretary, a Conservative, and a minister without portfolio, also representing Labour.

The functions of the cabinet are partly governmental, in the legal sense, and partly political. The governmental functions were characterized in the *Report of the Machinery of Government Committee* of 1918 as three-fold: (1) the final determination of the policy to be submitted to Parliament; (2) the supreme control of the national executive in accordance with the policy prescribed by Parliament; (3) the continuous co-ordination and delimitation of the authorities of the several Departments of the government. In commenting upon this description, W. I. Jennings remarks that the report "rightly makes no distinction between legislation and administration." In accordance with what will be said in the next chapter, Jennings states that "most legislation is directed toward the creation or modification of administrative powers," and furthermore that "the main function of government is the provision of services . . . for the welfare of the people." It might be added that the description is outmoded in its emphasis upon "policy"; Jennings himself gives many examples showing that it is the relative importance of the decisions which determines whether a matter belongs before the cabinet. To say that "the cabinet decides on the policy" obscures its function, which is to decide those issues that the individual ministers, including the Prime Minister, feel unable to decide by themselves. To this governmental function corresponds their political function of holding party support in Parliament and in the electorate together; for if the government makes too many unpopular decisions, the party will disintegrate and the government's popular support will be lost (see ch. XXI, above). However, pardons, personnel of the cabinet itself, and other appointments are usually not discussed in the cabinet, and the budget, while discussed, is taken up quite informally and orally, and not referred to a committee.

Regularly, in recent years, a matter is taken up in general form, is then referred to a committee, and is finally decided on the basis of a report circulated in writing. The cabinet, then, has worked more and more through these committees. The committees, of course, have no authority to make final decisions but only to report and recommend. The committee sittings ordinarily may be, and often are, attended by ministers who are not in the cabinet. The most extraordinary committee development before the Second World War was the Committee of Imperial Defense (it had started in 1904), which was not technically a committee of the cabinet at all, since it consisted of the Prime Minister as chairman, the political and technical heads of the defense services, the Chancellor of the Exchequer, and the Secretaries of State for Foreign Affairs, the Colonies, and India, as well as representatives of the Dominions, but was an important endeavor to develop an imperial executive besides the British cabinet—the cabinet being limited in its functions to the Empire outside of the so-called Commonwealth of Nations (see above, ch. XI, pp. 212 f.). It was not reestablished after the Second World War. Apart from these committees, the whole cabinet meets regularly once a week while Parliament is in session. In critical times, however, meetings may multiply. These meetings are quite informal and frequently of a rather conversational order.[12]

Such, to sum up, is the nature of the British cabinet, which has been described as the "pivot around which the whole political machinery revolves." Led by the Prime Minister, it directs the affairs of the country until its party support disintegrates. It does not merely execute and administer, as people who think in American terms are prone to assume. Except when the Prime Minister forces its hand, it makes all major decisions. It also decides upon, drafts, sponsors, and puts through Parliament new legislation, and takes full initiative in all fiscal and budgetary matters.

The British Dominions have, by and large, followed this pattern. Even where federalism was adopted, as in Canada and Australia, cabinet government under the leadership of a parliamentary prime minister has been evolved. Dominion experience shows, and *a fortiori* the case of Eire shows also, that this form of constitutionalism does not depend upon the existence of a hereditary aristocracy, nor upon the existence of an exploitable colonial empire, nor upon an advanced industrialism,—all arguments which have been set forth at one time or another. British cabinet government does, however, seem to depend upon (1) the capacity which is so deeply rooted in British traditions to accept as well as to provide leadership, (2) the existence of some kind of final arbiter such as the hereditary monarchy provides, and (3) a general acceptance of self-restraint and moderation as a virtue of all men when confronted with political responsibility. It is only with great peril that these moral conditions of political liberty are gainsaid.[13]

The cabinet subservient to parliament: France · Unlike Britain, France under the Third Republic failed to develop effective executive leadership. Twice France had succumbed to dictatorial perversion of its constitutionalism; no wonder that French republicans were unduly fearful of all extensions of executive power. What is worse, the French cabinet, or Council of Ministers, was not even cohesive as a collective group; it was a loose gathering of individual parliamentary leaders. The French cabinet, therefore, remained subservient to parliamentary groups and factions.[14] It could not possibly be described as the core of the government. Some thought that it too tended to become the center of gravity in the parliamentary system, but as such it certainly did not radiate energy and activity. It is quite significant that writers spoke of it as "the ministries," thus emphasizing the ministers' separate and individual roles. So realistic and perspicacious a commentator as Robert de Jouvenel in *La République des Camarades* discusses "ministres et ministères" without referring to a collective cabinet at all. He merely describes how an individual parliamentarian is put into a ministerial position and how this minister copes with the permanent administrative services, how he is surrounded by his personal and private secretarial staff (called in French *le cabinet*), and how he tries to get through his administrative functions without either previous knowledge or opportunity to acquire it while he is in office. "To administer," says this witty commentator, "is to appoint officials whom one does not know to positions of which one is ignorant, in other words to distribute promotions and decorations in the midst of solicitations, recriminations, and threats." But the all-engrossing task was that of keeping on good terms with parliament, and, more particularly, with one's own parliamentary group. The French cabinet was a group of individuals whose task it was to act as liaison between the dominant parliamentary groups and the permanent administrative staffs in the various ministries. Of course there were considerable differences due to personality in France as in England; for example, Delcassé managed to occupy a position of very great independence as Minister of Foreign Affairs between 1897 and 1905 and to conduct a policy which was largely unknown to the parliamentary groups supporting the ministries to which he belonged. Similarly, Ministers of War have been able to maintain a position of some independence. But on the whole, French cabinet ministers were the helpmeets of the parliamentary committees (see ch. XVII, p. 337) in supervising the permanent administration.

It has justly been said that the amount of changes to which French cabinets are subject is more apparent than real. The statistical picture in the fifty-four cabinets between August 31, 1871, and March 22, 1913, is twenty-eight Ministers of Foreign Affairs, thirty-two of the Navy, thirty-three of War, thirty-seven of Justice, and thirty-nine of the Interior. The same was true after the First World War. In the period from November 16, 1917 to July 23, 1926 we find that in fifteen cabinets there were seven Ministers of Foreign Affairs, eight of War, nine of the Navy, ten of the Interior, ten of Finance, and eleven of Justice. Correspondingly, we find some individuals holding parliamentary positions a great many times (one, in fact, twenty times). To put it another way, by taking all the cabinets from 1871 to 1930, we find that of a total of 1026 cabinet positions, 482, or almost half, were held by sixty individuals serving from five to twenty times. "The French democracy," M. Joseph-Barthélemy has written, "has been heavily blamed for its extreme fickleness and the reckless way in which its chambers have consumed one ministry after another. It has been described as a frenzied rush of cabinets across the political stage from one wing to the other. These criticisms, though perhaps justified to a certain extent by certain periods in the history of the Third Republic, are for the most part greatly exaggerated and the conclusions drawn from certain well-established facts are not always well-founded." He then gives a good many illustrations of the fact that ministers have often outlasted several ministries, continuing as ministers without interruption. This was quite natural in a situation where the cabinet was a loose collegial body and where the position of each minister was to some extent dependent upon his individual support in parliament. Certain groups could only be held in line by including the man whom they were willing to follow. These *ministrables*, parliamentarians with enough of a following to make them desirable members of a coalition, tended, of course, to return to office time and again.

In spite of the dependence of the ministry upon constant parliamentary support, French constitutional writers were much more inclined to emphasize the separation of powers than are Englishmen. They continued to take seriously to some extent the classical doctrine according to which the parliamentary system as established by the constitution of 1875 depended upon a balance of power with parliament on one side and the president on the other. This doctrine, according to which the cabinet was the link between the representative body and the chief executive, did not correspond to the French reality at all. For, elected by parliament and without the power of dissolution, the French President possessed no independent authority to match the power of parliament. Hence, neither he nor the chairman of the Council of Ministers, the *President du Conseil des Ministres* as the French Prime Minister was called, was in a position to establish effective leadership. To be sure, in the darkest hour of the First World War, after French armies had mutinied, Clemenceau was accorded genuine leadership. But the Tiger lost it as soon as the war was over. In the crisis of inflation, Poincaré also achieved a measure of genuine leadership; but both are really instances of constitutional dictatorship. Even in the terrible months before the outbreak of the Second World War, the French Republic struggled in vain to solve the problem. Though repeated grants of emergency powers enabled Daladier and Reynaud to undertake some of the most urgent tasks for the defense of the country, the authority remained divided; neither man achieved supremacy; both were at the mercy of certain parliamentary factions. Indeed, the very people who took over the government after the defeat of the Republic were, like Laval and Flandin, most responsible for the failure of effective armament. Whatever one may think of André Tardieu as a politician, the main argument of his critical appraisal of French constitutionalism, namely, that it failed to provide the opportunity for real executive leadership, can scarcely be denied.

All these difficulties were further aggravated by the fact that the French executive depended not only on the Chamber of Deputies, but on the Senate as well. Attempts to shake off the dual control of the Senate were only occasionally successful. Inasmuch as the composition of the Senate and the Chamber were often at variance, the forming of a cabinet was greatly complicated, at times producing well-nigh insuperable difficulties. The situation was endurable only because of the looseness and fluidity of the groups in both Houses. Once strongly organized parties or blocs came into existence, complete stalemates threatened. At the breaking point, the situation was often saved by the very disjointedness of the cabinet, since it facilitated the dropping of individual ministers who had lost the confidence of either house.

The whole French executive system was really incomprehensible, unless one remembered that the paramount concern of the men who developed this system was to control the permanent administrative staff. Just as the dislike of the French public for this staff found expression in the epithet "bureaucracy," so the long-established dominance of this centralized bureaucracy has been the main target of attack for popular movements throughout the nineteenth century. M. Barthélemy voiced this French viewpoint when he wrote that a change of ministers is very desirable because the minister is actually the controller of the bureaucracy. The minister must, therefore, not have the spirit of a bureaucrat, which he undoubtedly would have if he remained in office for extended periods. His vigilance must constantly be kept on the alert for parliamentary control and the threat of removal. He is not a technical expert, but rather the political superintendent of a stable and specialized bureaucracy. This view, which was typical for French liberalism, prevented the emergence of well-integrated executive leadership under the Third French Republic.

It is perhaps too early to assess the extent of the change produced by the Second World War and the constitution of 1946. Instead of a full power of dissolution, an "embryonic" one was provided: only after eighteen months of the elected assembly's life may the cabinet, after two successive crises engendering changes in the cabinet, dissolve the assembly and call for new elections. Apart from this important power, the cabinet's position continues to depend upon coalitions; in fact, the hardening of party lines under P. R. threatens the stability of such coalitions.

An ill-fated experiment: Germany · A study of executive leadership under the Weimar Republic would seem quite out-of-date were it not for the undeniable fact that we learn as much or more from failures as from successes. It may be unfortunate but it is not surprising that the makers of the Weimar constitution looked with a certain measure of sympathy upon the French cabinet system. Having just freed themselves from the clutches of a powerful bureaucratic tradition, they, too, felt that their ministry was to be primarily the political supervisor of a permanent bureaucracy.[15] The French system, with its polyarchic diversity in the cabinet, corresponded, they thought, more nearly to the needs of Germany with her many parties. Like France and unlike England, she faced the task of building up a parliamentary tradition in terms of the free professions, particularly those of law and journalism, since a republican order could not hope to command the allegiance of the aristocracy, which had at one time formed the backbone of the English parliamentary and cabinet personnel. On the other hand, the instability of French politics appeared in such an unfavorable light that arguments like the one set forth in the famous essay of Redslob, *Parliamentary Government, True and False*, made a deep impression. Consequently, the German Republican constitution provided for popular election of the president, thus giving the chief executive an independent basis. The resulting balance did not work, and in the end this popularly elected president became a mighty factor in the destruction of the whole parliamentary system. Owing to the double dependence of the cabinet upon the president on the one hand and upon the Reichstag on the other, both popularly elected representatives of the entire German people, it oscillated between the two masters. Unlike the unstable groups in the French Parliament, the several German parties were highly organized (see below, ch. XX). Unlike the English, none of these German parties ever commanded a majority. Since the constitution explicitly demanded (art. 54) that the Chancellor and his ministers needed the confidence of the Reichstag and that they must resign individually as well as collectively if the Reichstag withdrew its confidence, the president adopted the method of asking a certain parliamentary leader to form a cabinet and to appoint him Chancellor only after he had succeeded. This practice, which is also found in France, had the unfortunate consequence of calling to the attention of the public the bickering which is involved in forming a cabinet.

At first this method centered in negotiations between the parties for the formation of a coalition. Until 1923 cabinets were formed by the parties whenever they could get together, and when they could not, the initiative of the president sufficed to bring about a coalition with sufficient support to carry on. After 1923 cabinets were regularly supported by a minority in the center, in spite of constant efforts to broaden the base of support. After 1926 an increasing inclination developed to have the cabinet organized by presidential initiative and then have it seek the support of Parliament as it went along. Through this development the central idea of parliamentary government, namely, majority support, fell into discard. It was an endeavor to return to the German monarchic tradition of an independent government of administrators in terms of three slogans: "government of the middle way," "cabinet of personalities," and "government above parties." The most serious difficulty resulting from such an arrangement was the ever-present danger that the two radical wings of the House which were thus excluded from the cabinet would combine in a vote of nonconfidence without having any intention of combining to form a new government. The parliamentary maneuvering of Brüning sought to escape from this dilemma. Dr. Brüning always retained the idea that the cabinet must command the support of a parliamentary majority. How right he was is apparent from the hopeless impasse which resulted when the ministries of von Papen and von Schleicher, which followed his, attempted to conduct business without such a majority. It has often been felt that such a presidential cabinet system was bound to arise in Germany on account of the multiplicity of parties, but it has been cogently argued that this is not really true. Not the number of parties but their relationship to the electorate matters. Fundamentally, the German parties were so definitely linked with economic groups in the community that their leaders, when united in a cabinet, could not command a sufficiently representative position as long as they were believed to be the creatures of these parties. Only the president, as the representative of the entire people, could give them this broader appeal.

The complexities of the dependence of German cabinets were reflected in their internal patterns. While parties were themselves taking the initiative and bringing about ministerial coalitions, their delegates in the cabinet tended to occupy relatively independent positions in spite of the express recognition in the constitution that the Chancellor is the head of the cabinet. Later on, when the president became decisive in forming cabinets, particularly that of Brüning, executive leadership by the Chancellor closely resembling the situation in England seemed in prospect. In this connection it is important to remember that ever since Frederick the Great the Prussian kings had been convinced that the maintenance of royal power required their preventing the rise of a strong Prime Minister. Undoubtedly the innate centrifugal tendency of postwar coalition ministries was greatly aided by this traditional lack of co-operation. The fierce struggle between the permanent civil servants, proverbially a source of considerable difficulty, commenced to feed upon party conflicts. The permanent officials rapidly learned how to manipulate the party dissensions in the Reichstag.

As in so many other matters, so in its cabinet system also, the Weimar constitution combined too many discordant elements and was drafted with too little realistic consideration for the traditions of German politics and administration. If, instead of the popularly elected president, who, in spite of his national majority, was looked upon as a partisan, the system had been built around a hereditary monarch, it is possible that it would have worked as well as the constitutional parliamentary monarchies of Holland and the Scandinavian countries are working, for in all of them the party systems are very similar to that in Germany. There are many parties and they are fairly well organized and clearly connected with economic interest groups. On the whole, it is probably true that a cabinet system directly dependent upon parliamentary support is very hard to combine with a republican organization of government. France, though making a success of this combination for a while, encountered profound difficulties in later years, and her military defeat suggests caution in placing too much confidence in the precedent it established. Moreover, France has not had to battle with the complications arising from a federal setup. For a federal republican setup, the Swiss and American types would appear to be much more suitable. The attempt of German democracy to combine American, English, and French elements resulted in a complete failure.

Whether the provisions embodied in the Basic Law of 1949 will prove more satisfactory is doubtful. To be sure, the position of the president has been reduced; he has been deprived of his independent popular base, being elected by a special convention, consisting of the federal parliament (Reichstag) and of specially elected representatives of the state parliaments (art. 54). What is perhaps even more important, the parliament cannot overthrow the cabinet, including its head, the chancellor, except by electing a new chancellor; the ministers are the chancellor's appointees (art. 67). Finally, the German chancellor has been given a genuine, not an "embryonic," right of dissolution; this right comes into operation when and if the parliament fails to pass a vote of confidence. However, the parliament can prevent its dissolution by electing another chancellor (art. 68). This is decidedly a more stable system than that of the Weimar Republic. In the state of Württemberg-Baden, where a provision similar to that of article 67 has been in operation for two years, the cabinet, although a coalition affair, has been able to weather all parliamentary crises. But it is nevertheless surprising that the Germans should not have adopted either the American presidential or the Swiss Council system—both highly successful and stable forms of constitutional democracy. They rejected the American system because they feared that so powerful an executive might easily become dictatorial under German conditions. They rejected the Swiss system as not sufficiently responsive to changing situations to be suitable for a large country with weak democratic traditions.

The collegial council: Switzerland · The organization of executive leadership in Switzerland is different from that of any other independent government. Although there is a president, he is merely the chairman of the Council, usually elected for one year. He is a concession to the un-Swiss idea of a "head of government." Indeed, it is only by analogy that we can call the Swiss Federal (Executive) Council a cabinet; because there is no fictitious or real person whose cabinet it could be.[16] In other words, the Swiss setup is so strongly antimonarchical (much more so than that of the United States) that the nomenclature of Europe's monarchical past does not fit at all.

The Swiss collegial cabinet shares with the French system the tradition of polyarchic independence of the several ministers as department heads. But in spite of the fact that they are elected by the legislative assembly, they constitute a permanent and powerful executive, because the chief executives do not resign when defeated on any policy in the representative assembly. The ministers simply work out a new legislative proposal more in keeping with parliamentary views or they abandon the particular policy altogether. Professor Brooks has called this type of cabinet system "government by commission," and there is indeed some similarity between the relationship of, let us say, the Interstate Commerce Commission to Congress and the Swiss Federal Council to the Swiss legislature. The origin of this unique system must be sought in the Swiss cantons, which are organized on this pattern. But the adoption of this traditional cantonal organization by the federal government was greatly aided by the profound suspicion with which the constitution makers of 1848 looked upon anything resembling monarchy. It was a conscious decision by which they rejected the American plan of a popularly elected president.

Although this Federal Executive Council is elected by a joint session of both houses of the legislature after a new election, and although the terms of the councilors are three years, it has become the recognized custom, to which there are very few exceptions, to re-elect members as long as they are willing to serve. Consequently, members of the council usually serve many terms. Professor Brooks cites cases where members have served continuously for thirty-two, twenty-seven, and twenty-five years. When one considers that it is now usual to elect to the Federal Executive Council only men who have served for a considerable period in the representative assemblies, and that many councilors have previously served either in the cantonal representative bodies or in administrative or judicial posts, it is clear that the Swiss Executive Council is composed of men thoroughly seasoned in the art of politics and administration. The Federal (Executive) Council is presided over by the president who is, as was said, elected by the Federal Assembly each year. He has no powers over the Council. His bureau acts as a secretariat for the Council as a whole; in other words, unlike the English Prime Minister, he is a real *primus inter pares*. His office is an honor and his functions are "representative," that is, ceremonial. He is quite often in charge of the Department of Foreign Affairs, though he may be the head of any other. The several members of the Federal Council, while on an equal footing with each other and the president, act collectively on certain issues of general importance.

In the words of the Swiss constitution, the Federal Council is the "supreme directive and executive authority of the union." This general provision is implemented by another which gives a detailed list of particular functions. Related to the federal distribution of power, it indicates clearly that the Council has the same functions in the administrative field which the assembly has in the legislative field. Besides, the Council has to supervise whatever administration of federal legislation is entrusted to the cantonal authorities. The Council has to make detailed reports to the Federal Assembly. These reports are the subject of extended discussion, and as a result the assembly may address specific demands, known as postulates, to the federal councilors. A resolution to back such a postulate is unconditionally binding upon the Council.

It is clear that the Swiss Constitution wishes to make the executive a genuine administrative executor of the decisions of the representative assembly. It would, however, be very unrealistic to allow oneself to be blinded by these constitutional provisions. The members of the Federal Executive Council are leading politicians, often actually party leaders. When this party leadership is supplemented by the special knowledge which they possess as heads of the administrative departments, their word must necessarily carry a great deal of weight. Although the range within which patronage pressure can be brought to bear in Switzerland is very narrow, people have often claimed that it helps to consolidate the Council's leadership. Professor Fleiner has said that the continuous expansion of federal functions and of federal administrative authority has given the members of the Federal Council such a secure position that the Council has become more and more independent of the assembly and has extended its influence upon it. This is perhaps more significantly expressed in the fact that the Executive Council is not based upon a party majority in the representative bodies. Naturally, since councilors are continually re-elected, the party composition of the Council must vary considerably from that of the legislature. At the same time, members of the Council are elected from parties radically opposed to each other. Consequently, the Swiss Council is not like a coalition ministry in France or Germany. On the contrary, it traditionally includes representatives of all the important parties, even those which are in general opposition to the government's policies. From the point of view of those who are accustomed to think in terms either of single-party support or of an effective coalition, it may seem difficult to imagine such a plan. The deliberate emphasis on the administrative aspects of its work may save the Council from some of the pitfalls of such an arrangement. Nevertheless, very sharp differences of opinion are bound to develop from time to time, and occasionally a member of the Council will arise to oppose the proposal of a colleague before the legislature. Since ultimately the legislature can and will decide the issue, the necessary unity is imposed upon the Council from without.

Under these circumstances the Council will in a great many matters follow the decision of the member who has the particular matter in charge. Since Switzerland has developed an admirable civil service, many decisions are thus effectively neutralized and judicialized. This tendency has been enhanced since 1919, when it was decided to refer certain matters directly to the permanent administrative staff. (See next chapter.) Significantly, in all such matters appeal is allowed to an administrative court, thus further emphasizing the judicial controls. After much hesitation this administrative court was organized in 1928 as part of the Federal Court. It may be well, in conclusion, to quote an estimate of the Swiss executive which, written many years ago, would still seem to be correct: "Apart from all criticism and suggestions for reform, however, it is generally conceded that the Swiss executive has developed high efficiency within the limits of its powers and opportunities. In the opinion of two well-known English students 'the members of the Federal Council yield to no other government in Europe in devotion to their country, in incessant hard work for a poor salary, and in thorough honesty and incorruptibility. A diplomatist who knew them well and appreciated their good qualities aptly remarked that they reminded him of a characteristic industry of their own country, that of watchmaking. For, having to deal with very minute and intricate affairs, their attention is unremittingly engaged by the most delicate mechanism of government, by the wheels within wheels of federal and cantonal attributes, by the most careful balancing of relations between contending sects and churches and by endeavors to preserve the proper counterpoise between two (French and German), not to say three (the third being Italian) nationalities.' "

One-man rule: the American President · Swiss and American democracy have much in common. But their executive leadership is totally different, even though both countries separate legislative and executive establishments and therein contrast with the British system of "parliamentarism," that is, an executive dependent upon parliamentary support. Whereas in Switzerland, as we have just seen, the executive leadership is assimilated to the permanent administrative services, the American President has become the pivotal point of the American political system.[17] If his personality is powerful and his political support solid, he is today the ideal type of democratic leader. Though restrained by Congress, the states, and the courts, he provides the dynamic direction of national policy, but always with an eye toward public opinion. The fact that the elections come at stated intervals, so that their timing cannot be manoeuvred to suit the party in power, helps to keep this great power under popular control. Not only the President's own desire either to be reelected or to determine his successor after four years of service, but also the congressional elections every two years have this effect; for the President must seek to keep his congressional support unimpaired. Insofar as this desire to anticipate popular reaction works as an influence upon the President's policy, the *Federalist's* contention that the President's position could not be compared with that of the British king still has merit. But as the successful leader of the majority, the President has more power at his disposal than any constitutional monarch could ever dream of.

The makers of the Constitution were much concerned to secure for the President a position removed from politics and the "gusts of popular passion." The *Federalist*, inspired by the monarchical leanings of Hamilton, is almost lyrical in its enthusiasm for the electoral college as a device for insuring that independence. When the Constitution was drafted, the party had not yet emerged as the mainstay of popular government which it is today. All that remains of the electoral college is a system of electing the President by majorities in the states, rather than by a majority of the nation as a whole. A number of proposals have been made to alter or abolish this system. It usually creates the impression that the President has received a much larger majority than he actually had in percentage of all voters. Thus Roosevelt in the 1944 election had only 53 per cent of the voters, but carried all but ten states—many with very slight majorities. In view of the fact that only one President has ever been elected by a minority (President Hayes in 1876), a change does not seem very urgent, particularly as the present system has the value of maintaining federalism by giving strength to state party organizations. This latter fact, it must be admitted, has the counterbalancing disadvantage of obliging a Presidential candidate to seek and make compromises with state leaders prior to the election, and hence has been urged as a primary argument for change. But since the President-to-be would still have to get the votes, it may be doubted whether pre-election deals would be eliminated.

Much has been made of the fact that over the years the election has usually been won by the candidate who had the largest campaign fund. It has been an arrow in the quiver of those who maintain that America has become a plutocracy. This interpretation of the facts is too strained. Since those who contribute money to campaign funds are a widely scattered cross-section of the electorate, it is only natural that their verdict before the election should roughly resemble the verdict of the election itself. Claims by the Socialist and similar parties that they are being defeated by the money power fail to take into account the fact that in a democracy appeals to the masses for small contributions are as productive of funds as the large donations of a few rich individuals. Socialist parties in Europe have always been maintained by such contributions, and on the whole their financial position, more particularly that of the British Labour Party, has been quite strong as a result. It would be strange, indeed, if those who strongly favored a president and his policy were unwilling to contribute their small share to the expense of running the campaign; in fact such willingness is in itself a gauge of popular interest and support.

Is it proper, then, to say that Franklin D. Roosevelt was more powerful than Thomas Jefferson, or Andrew Jackson, or Abraham Lincoln? Only in the sense that the power of the United States has greatly increased. As one of the world powers, America has made her President a personage of extraordinary prestige and influence in international affairs. But in terms of the internal balance of forces, it would seem that the earlier Presidents had relatively as much power. The vastly increased service functions of modern government have enhanced the position of all governmental authority, but, along with the President, Congress, the courts, and the state and municipal authorities all share in this expansion of power. Indeed, two modern developments have brought with them something of a curb to presidential power as contrasted with Jackson's days: one is the professional expert and administrator (see next chapter), and the other is the technique of mass communication and of polls (see ch. XXIV) which has brought the citizen's view into the limelight.

It is obvious, then, that the position of the cabinet in the United States is very different from that in Switzerland. The American cabinet consists of the heads of departments. Since Washington's administration they have been his "secretaries." The President appoints the cabinet without any interference; the cabinet is his. And yet the exigencies of party support give certain secretaries a position of their own. Often the choice falls upon men to whom the President owes his election—indeed, pre-election deals are not infrequent in order to build up the necessary support for the nomination or to secure the funds with which to carry on the campaign. If the party following of the President is rent by factions, it will often be necessary for him to include leaders of the several contending groups so that their support may be gained and maintained. Lincoln's appointment of Seward and Chase in 1860 would be a historical example, to which Wilson's appointment of Bryan, or the second Roosevelt's choice of Farley, might furnish parallels, not to mention the deals of Harding or Coolidge. Men appointed under such conditions are difficult to dislodge. It is unrealistic to look upon them as merely the administrative subordinates of the President. Today, at any rate, they are of vital importance to him in his national representative function. It is only through them that he can associate with himself a number of representatives of the different social forces which make up the support of his political party. One may "represent" the business man, another the farmer, a third labor, and so forth. Similarly, allowance will be made for regional interests and claims. All in all, the President must take into account personalities which have become associated with broad groupings in the electorate, if he is to be a representative of the nation. This system illustrates in a particularly striking way the interrelation and interaction of the two aspects of representation. Not only an elected body, but even a single elected individual will be, through his associates, both a representative in terms of the common interest and an agent for different interests (see ch. XIV, p. 262). While the difference between a collegial cabinet, such as the Swiss, and our own is very great, the distinction should not be made absolute. Through both systems the decisive social forces will secure a share of the government's power. The share may vary, as the balance of social forces shifts, but no considerable group can be excluded for any length of time without the government's losing its representative position, and thereby its power through consent.

It is inescapable that under such conditions, where the President and his cabinet are viewed as the representatives of the common national interest and the representatives of various social groups, respectively, a good many important policies will be determined by discussions not of the cabinet collectively, but of the President with individual cabinet members. Sometimes, of course, an important piece of legislation, particularly when it touches several departments, will be discussed in the cabinet. But votes are seldom taken on such matters, and they are considered mere expressions of opinion. There is a well-known story told about President Lincoln who concluded a discussion in the cabinet during which everyone had taken sides against him by remarking: "Seven nays, one aye, the ayes have it." And yet, it is true only in a limited sense that "the cabinet is merely the kind of organization which the President wishes to make of it and is his own council in a very peculiar sense," as Charles A. Beard claims. Lord Bryce once observed that "There is in the government of the United States no such thing as a cabinet in the English sense of the term." While this may be less true today, due to the changes in the English pattern itself, the difference still vitiates suggestions for changes in American practice based upon English practice. In a stimulating study of the American president, Harold Laski has argued that "a good cabinet ought to be a place where the large outlines of policy can be hammered out in common, where the essential strategy is decided upon, where the president knows that he will hear, both in affirmation and in doubt, even in negation, most of what can be said about the direction he proposes to follow." He adds that "few American Cabinets have been of this quality." If Mr. Laski had inquired into the reasons why American cabinets have not functioned the way he thinks they ought to, he would have readily seen (he himself brings forth much evidence to that effect) that the cabinet is now formalized in function, that it consists therefore not of confidants but of "representatives," as we have seen. Likewise, the argument that cabinet members should be drawn from the elective bodies is not in line with American reality. Laski is very right when he urges that a President who is likely to be successful must have about him men who are capable of taking a line of their own. But the extent to which this will be true is likely to be a measure of the President's intrinsic ability, not the result of institutional devices.[18] In short, the American President and his cabinet are a working group of political leaders and administrators, dependent upon popular support through a party which may, and often will, also control the Congress. There have been recurrent "kitchen cabinets," small, ephemeral, informal groups of advisers whom various Presidents have employed; more recently, the President has been provided with a regular secretariat (see next paragraph), and three co-ordinating agencies, to wit:

the Bureau of the Budget, the Office of Government Reports, and the National Resources Planning Board have been put directly under the President. But informal advisers are so essential that no institutional arrangement will take their place. Having once been invested with his monocratic powers, no President is likely to distribute this power to others, and if a particular President should, out of indolence or altruism, move in that direction, his successor is likely to redress the balance on assuming office. The concentrated powers of the American President are a part of the pattern of constitutional relationships established by the separation of powers; they are endurable only because that pattern provides other restraints through limiting the concentrated powers themselves (see ch. X, pp. 177 f.). It is another method of coping with the problem which in the opinion of Lord Bryce (and many another liberal thinker) is the greatest which confronts free peoples: how to enable the citizens at large to conduct or control the executive business of the government.

Executive leadership in the United States is not limited to the federal government, of course. As several times noted in the preceding discussion, the states play a vital part, as do some of the great cities, notably New York. There has been a natural tendency for the chief executives of the states, the governors, to be looked upon as roughly parallel to the president. In the course of the nineteenth century, the governors became more independent of the legislatures as direct popular election was adopted for them. But unlike the cabinet of the President, the chief officers of the state governments were made elective in turn and this made them largely independent of the governor altogether. Thus a plural executive resulted which had the effect of dissipating executive leadership in the states. The only way a measure of integration could be recaptured was through effective party control, and hence the bosses became supreme.[19] However, the expansion of governmental activities has created, since the turn of the century, an increasing demand for reforms and they have been making slow headway in recent years. Especially the budget has been seized upon as a promising mechanism for enlarging the governor's power of control and integration. But in a serious emergency, the existing confusion may lead to serious strains and the adoption of rather radical measures for overcoming them. The recurrent labor strife in a number of states, leading to the calling out of the state militia, is an ill omen.

Cabinet and presidential secretariat and the problem of informal advisers · The increasing scope of governmental activity has seriously impeded efficient direction in all major industrialized countries. We therefore find a general trend toward strengthening the administrative effectiveness of the chief executive as a co-ordinator. Both in Britain and in the United States there have recently been created special secretariats whose function it is to deal with these over-all questions. The Cabinet secretariat owes its origin to the First World War. Until that time, British cabinets had been conducted in the most informal way, with matters coming up and being decided without any clear record. Since there were no minutes of the meeting, it was difficult, later on, to ascertain what the decision had been. This war secretariat developed as the secretariat of the Committee of Imperial Defense. Although it was proposed to abolish this secretariat after the war, the *Machinery of Government* Report recommended its retention. It operates essentially as a co-ordinating office by circulating memoranda and other documents, preparing the agenda for the Cabinet and its committees, as well as the minutes and reports, and, finally, keeping the records unless instructed otherwise.

The American President's secretariat is similarly designed. It is, however, concerned with strengthening and making more effective the president's relations with the public, Congress, and the numerous governmental agencies which should somehow be co-ordinated and made to contribute toward the President's national policy. We consequently find one secretary dealing with each of these tasks, as well as one dealing with Latin-American problems and one with economic issues. The *Report on Administrative Management* (1937), which first suggested explicitly the organization of such a secretariat, spoke of ". . . men with a passion for anonymity." This phrase elicited a good deal of laughter at the time, and yet there can be little doubt that these men, if they are to be effective as spokesmen for the president, must possess the capacity of keeping themselves personally in the background. On the whole they have been remarkably successful in doing so.[20]

The Hoover Commission in 1948 made further significant recommendations with regard to the President's immediate office. Among these was the recommendation (no. 10) that "the President should be given funds to provide a staff secretary, in addition to his present principal secretaries, to assist him by clearing information on the major problems on which staff work is being done within the President's Office, or by Cabinet or interdepartmental committees." The Commission also came out in favor of an Office of Personnel, similar to the Office of the Budget (to replace the present Bureau of the Budget), this Office to be headed by the Chairman of the Civil Service Commission. The director should provide the President with continuous staff advice and assistance relative to matters affecting the career civilian service of the Federal Government (no. 11). The Commission also specifically urged that the President be freed from restrictions and rigidities in running his own office and immediate staff agencies (no. 4).

Do these secretariats provide that opportunity for critical advice which Laski demanded? Hardly. Strong executives who perceive the need for such independent judgments will always seek it more informally, and preferably from persons who do not officially depend upon them. Such men have undoubtedly wielded a great influence upon public policy precisely because they brought to the problems of the chief executive detachment and a nondepartmental, nonbureaucratic viewpoint. It is an everpresent need of men in positions of leadership to find some such persons of discretion, judgment, and insight. In a constitutional democratic system this is always possible, and famous instances can be readily cited, such as that of Colonel House's work for Wilson. It is one of the incurable weaknesses of a despot that he encounters insuperable obstacles in the way of securing such advice, because he lacks all effective means for checking upon the dubious or sycophantic advisers. Napoleon and Frederick the Great, the Tsars of Russia and Oliver Cromwell, all struggled with the same difficulty in vain. There is no more telling symbol of the isolation of the absolute ruler than Harun-al-Raschid prowling about the city in disguise to learn what the people think of this rule.

Conclusion · Executive leadership has at all times been essential to the success of government. Constitutionalism and more especially constitutional democracy have been confronted with a most delicate task: how to discover institutional patterns which would provide vigorous and effective action, without allowing those who were called upon to take such action to turn into irresponsible despots. Two countries have evolved outstandingly successful executive leadership: Great Britain and the United States. Very different in conception and practice, each subtly fitted into a distinctive tradition, they each possess peculiar elements of strength and weakness. But so organically have both the British cabinet system and the American presidency evolved in relation to the governmental pattern as a whole that the numerous proposals which have been advanced for overcoming the weakness of one by altering it to be more nearly like the other have rarely met with more than literary and academic approval. There are operative behind and underneath them both, however, responsible administrative services which are becoming continually more alike and which infuse into them both the continuity and competence without which no lasting work can be done in our technological age.

XIX

Responsible Government Service

Introduction · Growth of the professional administrative service · Problems of recruitment and training · Recent American developments and problems · Responsibility and dismissal · Five ways of enforcing administrative responsibility · Disciplinary measures · Promotional measures · Fiscal measures · Judicial measures · Governmental versus personal liability · Measures based upon an objective standard · Conclusion.

Introduction · "For forms of government let fools contest; Whate'er is best administer'd is best"—wrote Alexander Pope in 1733. This sentiment has been gaining ground again in recent decades. It is not sound constitutional doctrine, but it rightly focuses attention upon the importance of effective administration as a test of government, whether constitutional or not. For a government that is badly administered can never be expected to last long. Allusions in the preceding chapter were necessarily made to administrators and administrative systems. Indeed, patterns of administration have a way of persisting through diverse regimes and many of the basic approaches and techniques are hundreds of years old. In France, the land of restless constitutional change throughout the nineteenth century, the officials, *les fonctionnaires*, remained essentially the same. An official of the French Foreign Office in 1930 would have been at his ease in conversing with an official of the same office a hundred years earlier.

The core of government in modern times has been a rationalized administrative service, a bureaucracy. We have sketched its rise and general nature earlier in this book. We have pointed out that the failure to perceive its central position has led many writers to place bureaucracy in juxtaposition to democracy—as if a democracy could get along without an effective administrative service. There are those who would try to construct a contrast between England and the continent on this score. Actually, England developed a rationalized central administration at an even earlier time than continental countries simply because such a development went hand in hand with national unification; this unification the English kings succeeded in achieving at an earlier date than most other rulers for a variety of reasons. Tout, in exhaustive studies, has unraveled the growth of this central administration. He has shown the impact of ecclesiastics at a time when few others could read or write. It was only *after* the establishment of that central core of administrative government that the constitutionalizing could make real headway. We have shown how this constitutionalizing process was aimed at placing restraints upon the administrators, at making them responsive to popular preferences, by subjecting them to elected representatives. The constituent group in nation after nation arose to demand that the administrators be subjected to a constitution giving the ultimate power of direction to the people ever more comprehensively defined. It is, therefore, not a question of *either* democracy *or* bureaucracy, of *either* constitutionalism *or* efficient administration; the task of our industrial age has been and remains the achievement of a combination of the two, of a working balance between them, in short, of a responsible bureaucracy.

Growth of the professional administrative service · In his comprehensive discussion of modern administration, Herman Finer writes: "It is clear . . . that some of the cardinal and least-questioned principles of modern civilization brought about the establishment and growth of a professional Civil Service. . . ."[1] Among these principles he lists (1) the idea that talent should be the primary basis of selection, and (2) the division of labor. Both are part of that economic rationalism which shaped the industrial revolution. There can be little question that the abler monarchs, in search of administrative talent, went beyond the nobility who traditionally composed the ruling class. Indeed, as we have shown in Chapters I and V, the monarchical governments succeeded in direct proportion to their readiness to be coldly rational about their personnel. England, France, Prussia, and Hapsburg were all equally ready to grab talent wherever they could find it. England was in many ways the most practical; the titles of nobility remained continuously at the disposal of the crown and were liberally handed out in recognition of new talent. In the course of the nineteenth century all the more highly industrialized countries developed administrative services based upon tested qualifications. This rationalization went forward in inverse ratio to the strength of constitutionalism, however, owing to the simple fact that fully developed constitutional governments, like those of Britain, the United States, and Switzerland, had to overcome the vested interest of entrenched political-party organizations. The pressure of need was everywhere great enough to bring about a fully developed bureaucracy sooner or later.

What was this need? The two principles of the recognition of talent and of the division of labor do not seem quite enough. It was not merely a question of catching up with business. The growth of the government's administrative services parallels that of business; the best governmental services have right along been the equals of the very best business concerns in the mastery of the art of large-scale organization. The answer to the question lies in the very nature of government and its function in society. One of its outstanding objectives is to regulate the relations between individuals and groups in a society, to keep them at peace and enforce their mutual obligations, to maintain the general as against particular interests, and to restrain the abuse of power by individuals or groups. These tasks, which have always been recognized, are bound to multiply as a society increases in size and complexity. Take as an example modern traffic. There was no need for many traffic policemen at a time, only a bare hundred years ago, when the streets were primarily occupied by a leisurely assortment of pedestrians and horsedrawn vehicles. But as cities became more and more populous and mechanical means of locomotion greatly increased the speed of vehicles, traffic police became ever more numerous. The regulatory or police function of government necessarily increased the number of government servants. Nor was it a matter only of the police. As motor vehicles became more numerous, the government found itself obliged to develop a licensing system which required quite a few officials for its administration; hospital services had to be increased to handle the numerous accidents; courts had to be stepped up to render judgment in controversial cases. The same picture can be seen over and over again. There is little value in emotional outbursts over this development. If we have a "wonderland of bureaucracy," it is the natural accompaniment of our wonderland of industrial progress.

Various attempts have been made to gauge the increase in the number of government officials and employees. Finer, in an interesting compilation, presented approximate figures for comparing England, France, and Germany. These figures reveal that there has been a markedly greater increase in officials than in population. In France the population increased about twenty per cent between 1841 and 1928, while the government services numbered about ten times greater at the end than at the beginning of the same period. In England the population grew to about two-and-a-half times its size in the same period, the service to about sixty times its size, while in Prussia the population grew about as rapidly as in England, but there was only a twenty-fold increase in officials.[2] Clearly, then, in the ratio of growth of population to growth of officialdom, we are facing a geometrical proportion which is roughly analogous in all these countries. The comparison of France, England, and Prussia suggests that the *complexity* of our industrial society, its machines and other modern features, is more likely to be responsible for the growth in administrative services than the increase in the size of the population. But is it not rather a result of socialistic theories, many ask? While such theorizing has played its part, a realistic view of society demands the counter-question: why did such theories arise? Are they not themselves expressions of the need of an industrial society? In Chapter XXIII, where we discuss at some length the relation between government and the economy, these problems are more fully explored.

Problems of recruitment and training · It has been said before, but must be said again, that all effective administrative work depends upon successful training and recruitment of personnel. European kings developed educational systems in large part for the purpose of providing themselves with trained personnel. In doing so, they followed the example of the churches, which had always been intensely interested in education for precisely that reason. Many of the great European universities owe their beginnings to this desire of church and government for trained personnel. In modern times the increasing specialization of the services has raised the issues of scientific training in a more pointed form. A thorough discussion of recruitment and training problems falls outside the scope of the present volume. There are, however, certain general aspects, vitally affecting the securing of responsible conduct, which we should consider here. In an earlier chapter (II) it was shown how the educational system and the recruitment of government officials depend on each other in a general way. The nations, however, have developed marked differences in the training for the public service; these differences are bound up with the entire pattern of folkways and national traditions. On the Continent a government-supported system of schools and universities forms part of the bureaucracy itself; democratic Switzerland does not differ in this respect from authoritarian Prussia. In England and the United States nonpublic schools and colleges and universities are found alongside the public institutions of learning which more nearly correspond to the concept of democracy. But even today the endowed schools play a vital role; their relative independence from communal restraints often allows them to take the lead and thereby to enrich and to hasten educational progress. In times of stress the private institutions of higher learning also seem to be better capable and more inclined to offer resistance to inroads made by public agitation and leading to interference with academic freedom.

A comparison of England, France, and Germany reveals an interesting contrast in educational objectives for the higher grades of governmental service. These contrasts are gradually being blurred as the impact of common economic and industrial conditions makes itself felt. But they are still important as persistent influences and deserve a brief sketch. In England social and cultural values have been given the central place. The idea that a higher servant of the Crown should be a cultured gentleman seemed a matter of course in the Victorian age. It was embodied in the rules and regulations of the famous reform of the Indian service, and was later applied to the home services as well.[3] This "imperial" origin has affected the British Civil Service to this day, though less and less strongly. Originally it was a question of securing representatives of a "governing class"; through school and college the selective process was at work, even while a strenuous effort was being made to find those young men who showed marked intellectual ability. The ancient traditions of literary and classical scholarship at Oxford and Cambridge, when combined with the pride and *esprit de corps* of their highly selective student body, were, it was felt, likely to secure the kind of man who would with "equanimity" shoulder the "white man's burden" in India. As Robert Moses summarized the situation: "Like the English Cabinet and the English aristocracy, the Indian civil service was to be opened to gentlemen who had inherited breeding and culture, and to those of the middle class who had made themselves gentlemen by acquiring the same breeding and culture."[3] In the decades since that was written, India has become divided and has achieved Dominion status, and the situation at home has changed much. The Labour party has acquired many strong adherents among both faculty and students at Oxford and Cambridge; the great municipal universities of Birmingham, Edinburgh, and the rest have forged ahead and provided an increasing number of highly qualified civil servants; and the rigid distinction between the upper grade, the administrative class, and the lower grades is weakening as exceptionally able men are given an opportunity to rise from the bottom in the bureaucracy. But this forward march of democracy must not blind us to the persistence of the traditional outlook; an American is likely to be amazed by the fact that even ardent Labour party folks do not send their children to the public school, and when queried reply that "they would not learn to speak properly." In short, both recruitment and training for the public service remain strongly affected by the country's aristocratic past.

The British civil service has been increasingly under attack for these "elitist" or aristocratic aspects. H. R. G. Greaves has stressed, as we have done, "the preoccupation with the social background and antecedents of those who were to be recruited for the reformed service" which characterized the original conception of the civil service. He has likewise emphasized the failure of these reforms to demand certain essential qualities of the recruit: initiative and enterprise, originality and constructiveness of mind, human understanding and contact, scientific and social studies and training. These points and other related ones were even more sharply attacked by an American analysis. Recognizing that there has occurred an "enormous increase" in the power of the permanent officials, Donald Kingsley approvingly quotes Laski's striking phrase that "administrative discretion is the essence of the modern state." Kingsley, too, stresses the lack of initiative. "Their ideal became the safe man, the passionless man, the man who would not upset the apple cart." This author, like Mr. Greaves, is a partisan of the planning state, and he is certain that this means "a huge expansion of the bureaucracy." The problem, therefore, is how to make this bureaucracy "representative," that is, responsible. He notes that the civil service, during the first three years of the war, increased 72 per cent, and, without the Post Office, 137 per cent. As a result, the composition of the civil service has changed; there was the usual influx of outsiders, and technicalities went by the board when recruiting went from the civil service to the Ministry of Labor and National Service. In view of a parliamentary select committee's judgment that the Treasury had failed to bring expert judgment to these administrative and management problems between 1919 and 1939, this is hardly surprising. The "complete revamping of the entire system" which Kingsley envisaged as part of the arrival of the "planning state" has not been undertaken by the Labour Government; in fact, its failure to do so has been alleged by some to be the cause of its not becoming a socialist state. The changes are occurring gradually, as is the habitual British way. It may well be right that the new situation requires more men of action, rather than political philosophers who are Latin scholars; it is certainly true that more technical expertise will be required. But the prediction that a Labour government would "reform the civil service from top to bottom" has so far proved premature.[4]

In France, which combines a strong bureaucratic tradition with great emphasis upon the humanistic, linguistic element in education, logical and literary brilliance used to be given great weight in the training and selection of future officials. The famous *Ecole Normale Supérieure* and the equally famous *Ecole Polytechnique* were veritable hothouses for budding literary genius, and a large percentage of the future holders of France's most prized honor—membership in the *Académie Française*—found themselves in the same classroom at one of these *Ecoles*, which were open only on the basis of competitive scholarship. In the preparation of future civil servants, Romanist legal training, in spirit so closely related to humanistic studies, also played a vital part. That training covered both private and public law, but it was primarily a study and inculcation of principles, rather than an analysis of cases. This literary-legal conception of French training for public service dates back to the French revolution, with its battle cries of *raison* and *nation*. The cult of the French language, seen as the most logical product of this heritage of revolutionary ideals, was the natural one. To be a great Frenchman, a man had to be a near-genius in the use of the French language, and it is extraordinary how many notable French politicians, known to the outside world for their political achievements, men like Poincaré and Herriot, were writers of note and real artists in the use of the mother tongue. What is even more startling to the outsider is that men who hated and detested each other politically, like the Royalist Charles Maurras and the Republican Raymond Poincaré and the Socialist Léon Blum, found themselves united in this cult of the French language. It is only natural, therefore, that logical and literary achievements should have been given a decisive place in the training and recruitment of French officials. The French revolutionary tradition of strong central control has aided the imposition of rigid standards through a government-controlled school and university system. The same methods of teaching and the same subjects taught throughout France created a common intellectual atmosphere among all strata of educated people in France, which of course permeated the governmental services. But again developments in recent decades tended toward a change in the direction of recognizing technical efficiency and ability in engineering and other scientific specialties. These technicians, however, did not gain ascendancy over the brilliant lawyers and orators whom the literary tradition favored.[5]

An extensive reform of the French civil service was one of most generally agreed upon policies advocated by the resistance movement. It was in measure achieved. The central aspect of this reform is the establishment of institutes of public administration at the universities, and at the *Ecole Nationale d'Administration* in Paris. Here the higher civil servants, the *hauts fonctionnaires*, are to be trained in the social sciences and certain tool courses, such as statistics and management. Since this is clearly very much of a long-range program, it is difficult at the present time to assess its eventual success.[6]

Germany, much influenced by French traditions, nevertheless developed an emphasis of her own. Without a national cultural capital, her cultural life remained divided between Vienna and Berlin, Munich and Dresden, Frankfurt, Hamburg, Cologne, and the many other regional centers of distinctive speech, architecture, and folkways. The training of potential civil servants focused upon legal and social studies. While these legal studies were carried on dogmatically and logically, as in France, nevertheless there was considerable stress placed upon the historical and practical aspects of the law, and periods of apprenticeship were interwoven with theoretical studies. What is more, the cameralist tradition of economic training led to the inclusion of economics and of political and administrative science,[7] with a good many variations in emphasis in different states and universities. With schools and universities under state control, legal training always retained an element of localism; even though the great national legal codes, enacted after the establishment of the Empire, provided an impulse toward unification, it was not until the coming of the Weimar Republic that effective moves were initiated for the unification of training requirements. Among the genuine achievements of the several monarchies was the development of standards of severe probity for their officials—standards which freer governments often envied, but eventually succeeded in emulating (especially England and several of the small countries, like Sweden, Norway, Denmark, Holland, and Switzerland). The emphasis upon legal training had its share in developing high standards of probity; rightly conducted, education in the law has that effect. But although Germany clung to the idea that a man whose logical faculties had been highly developed would be able to turn his hand to any concrete task, the increasing complexity of our technological civilization brought about a gradual increase in technical personnel. Undertakings like the governmental railroad administration called, of course, for large staffs of engineers and other experts.

The Hitler dictatorship, after purging the civil service of all "politically unreliable elements" (in other words, all strongly democratic officials), proceeded to adopt a far-reaching national law for the civil service. It brought complete unification, and if read without reference to the Nazi party and its strong corrupting influence, sounds in many of its provisions like a realization of democratic trends. It is nevertheless true that under it the professional civil service in Germany was perverted into an instrument of the ruling party clique. Fritz Morstein-Marx, in his assessment of the law, asserted that "the general civil services statute of January, 1937, consolidates the new tradition of an ideologically homogeneous people." In spite of this alleged "homogeneity," Morstein-Marx felt that the German bureaucratic tradition worked as a "powerful counterpoise" to the Nazi movement. It can hardly be said that the documentary sources which have become available in connection with the Nuremberg War Crimes Trials bear out this estimate. Karl Loewenstein's view seems more nearly right when he wrote that "the membership badge as technical qualification for office is . . . responsible for decay of administrative efficiency in almost all walks of public life." Civil service, for which Germany was famed for centuries, may be one of the fields in which the havoc wrought by the Third Reich is irreparable. There can be little question that so far all efforts have been unsuccessful to reform the German public service and rescue it from the morass into which the Nazi dictatorship plunged it.

Both American and British military government have been deeply and earnestly concerned with reform of the German civil service. They, and more especially the Civil Administration Division of the Office of Military Government (United States), have tried to persuade the parliaments of the several states, and eventually the Economic Council in the Bizone, to pass civil-service reform legislation. Among the points of greatest emphasis was the need for separating the civil service from politics, especially by eliminating the civil servant from parliamentary bodies, and secondly the need for democratizing the service by converting it into a career service open to talent, rather than maintaining it as a preserve of the privileged classes. As part of this latter objective, a great effort was made to introduce the system of competitive examinations for entry and promotion. These efforts have encountered the most stubborn resistance on the part of politicians and officialdom in spite of a considerable amount of support for it among the general electorate. When, in the winter of 1948, after protracted delays, military government decreed a "reformed" law for the officials of the bizonal administrative services, it received much popular acclaim. It is doubtful, however, whether a reform thus imposed by occupying foreigners will remain in force.[8]

Many of the smaller countries developed along lines similar to those of Weimar Germany. Among the smaller countries, Switzerland is of particular interest to America because of the similarity of her governmental pattern. Besides, Switzerland was a full-fledged democracy when she began to enlarge and rationalize her governmental service. Except to the extent to which she was helped by the example of France and Germany, she is full proof of the contention that a democracy is able to do a better job, in fact, than other systems. For there can be little question that upon close scrutiny by an unbiased investigator the Swiss appear to have a more effective, democratically responsive officialdom than any other country except Sweden —and Sweden also is very democratically governed. The probity, industry, and general ability of the Swiss official are striking to all but the Swiss, who are possessed of a hypercritical, almost carping, attitude toward their government. The Swiss railways, for example, demonstrate the efficiency of Swiss officialdom; the railways, which face an extremely difficult operational task because of the mountainous terrain of most of Switzerland, are about as well run as any railroads in the world; the service is punctual and surprisingly reasonable. Another task of especial difficulty which the Swiss government has been handling with exceptional ability is the administration of the forests. Owing to the many avalanches, all forest land in Switzerland is operated under close governmental supervision if not actual control, and the results are outstanding. The Swiss have given continuous recognition to technical expertise. Their nonparliamentary system has permitted the several members of the Council-Cabinet to become successful administrators as the heads of departments and thus to help integrate the service as a whole.

Recent American developments and problems · The rapid survey of four European countries has shown that in spite of marked differences in tradition they resemble each other in the conviction that very thorough training is necessary for a permanent government service which is to cope successfully with rapidly expanding governmental functions in an industrial age. America has been slow in recognizing this task. Until very recently, the specter of bureaucracy has stood in the way of clear thinking on the subject, in spite of almost unanimous protestations from students of government and administration. Certain powerful economic interests were inclined to the view that a weak governmental service was less apt to bother them. Such a view is correct only as long as these interests themselves do not need the governmental service. The catastrophe of the great depression opened the eyes of the more intelligent leaders of industry and commerce to the advantages to be derived from an effective administration of statutory regulations, which the popular majorities insisted upon putting on the statute book in any case. As a consequence, the great universities have all undertaken the job of "training for the government service." However, down to the present all this training is carried on without detailed integration with the requirements of the services themselves. A somewhat antiquated Civil Service Commission interposes itself between the universities and the great administrative services and imposes "examinations" which more often than not disregard what is relevant. Even a casual study of the examinations given to establish a panel or "register," as it is called, reveals a lack of constructive co-operation between the universities and the public service.[9] Indeed, the instructors in charge of training future government officials are ordinarily denied access to the examinations, which are treated as closely guarded official secrets, nor would they derive any suggestions concerning the course of study of these future officials if they did peruse the examinations. Fortunately, the unsatisfactory state of affairs has led to gradual improvements. Men like L. D. White, Arthur Fleming, and a determined group of experts in personnel administration are making some progress, and the example of the independent personnel administration of the TVA demonstrated how much can be accomplished once outworn conceptions of training and recruitment are scrapped and the issue of technical competence is squarely faced. The Hoover Commission Report insisted upon this recently.

There lurks in this general approach, however, a very serious danger.

Federal as well as state agencies in the United States have hitherto seen improvement largely in terms of acquiring people on the basis of their technical achievement, engineers, chemists, geologists, and so on. Even the lawyer is found in these agencies as a technician: as solicitor, land-law or oil-law expert, and so on. No general conception, such as the cultural, literary, or legal education of European countries, has given a common framework to the entire bureaucracy. On the whole this has left the coordinating strictly administrative jobs unprovided for. Whenever an expert or technician had an aptitude or knack for it, he would take on the job, or he would drift into it as it were. There is much that is healthy in such a haphazard development, and yet there is today such a vast body of special expertise in the art of administration as such that the administrator has come to be recognized as a specialist himself. The Bureau of the Budget, especially through its management experts, has stimulated much constructive thought and some action. So did the Hoover Commission. The special problems which arise in connection with operating larger and larger organizations has brought into existence a special field of training and study, just as the growing complexities of business organization have led to the establishment of graduate schools of business administration. The recognition of such specialists has the added advantage of fitting right in with the American constitutional pattern. An attempt to formulate and implement a general government-guided system of training and education would probably run afoul of established traditions of constitutionalism in America. Such a scientifically trained specialist may in time satisfy the requirements without which a functional responsibility, such as will be sketched presently, would be difficult to achieve.[9]

Responsibility and dismissal · We have seen that the constitution is essentially an instrument through which the arbitrary power of government is restrained. The generations which fought for a constitution to restrain the concentrated power of monarchical governments tended, therefore, to identify such restraints with responsibility. It thus became customary to consider government according to a constitution "responsible government." People remained perfectly aware in practice of the decisive importance of impelling action as well as of restraining it. But formulas such as "that government is best which governs least" show an inclination to minimize the errors of omission. The Victorian age was likely to be more exercised over mistakes a government had made by acting than over the failures resulting from a government's not acting. In a rapidly expanding economy there was enough of a margin to take care of such failures. It is, however, significant that in countries where that margin was less sizable, public opinion remained more favorable to governmental efforts. No issue is more typical as an indicator than social insurance: Germany, though the least democratic, had done the most by 1900, while the United States had done the least. The situation is, of course, greatly altered today. Governmental activity has been on the increase everywhere; governmental services have been multiplying in response to recognized welfare needs; that government is responsible which responds to the demands for *action*. Even in England and the United States, the classic homeland of "let-well-enough-alone liberalism," the growing complexity of modern government and administration has brought about the organization of a permanent civil service whose responsibility cannot be enforced through changes in cabinets except on lines of broad general policy.[10]

As we have said, the key problem of constitutionalism in an industrial society is how to render the activities of these governmental services responsible. Generally speaking, this problem has been obscured by "liberal" demands that we return to nineteenth-century methods of parliamentary and electoral debates. But since the electorate can do no more than either re-elect or defeat a Congressman or an M. P., this means that the discussion has been arbitrarily limited to the question of "hiring and firing" Congressmen who cannot possibly undertake the creative direction of the public services of what Marshall Dimock has engagingly called the "Creative State."

It is in keeping with this general preoccupation with dismissal as a technique for enforcing responsible conduct that the Supreme Court of the United States, in its celebrated decision of the *Myers Case*, proceeded essentially on the assumption, embodied in an *obiter dictum*, that the power of removal was a necessary part of making officials responsible to the President.[11] For that reason, the court held, the President must have unlimited power of removal in order to retain responsibility for the administration of his office. This view is questionable, to say the least. The learned judges might have taken a different view if they had examined administrative experience elsewhere; in several constitutional democratic countries of Europe, with not only efficient but responsible administrative services, practically all the officials are appointed on life tenure. The power of dismissal is, in other words, only one of many techniques for making official conduct responsible. In fact, dismissal is not even a particularly effective method for producing responsible conduct, but has many disadvantages and shortcomings, which ought to be considered for purposes of comparing the removal power with other means or techniques for producing responsibility. Again, the problem of how to produce responsible conduct cannot be considered without reference to the nature of the activities which are being carried on. Evidently the Supreme Court would be prepared to grant that its own conduct is "responsible" without anyone having an unchecked power of removal. Recently the Supreme Court itself seems to have partially recognized its mistake in the *Myers Case* when it ruled in the *Humphreys Case* that Congress could lay down for officers possessing quasi-legislative or judicial functions such qualifications as it saw fit. In case of controversy, such qualifications would be interpreted by the courts, which further extends the judicial power into the administrative field. This, however, raises other difficulties in connection with administrative justice.

Five ways of enforcing administrative responsibility · Whenever the need for action is paramount, the technique of dismissal is decidedly crude as a method for securing conduct responsible and responsive to the wishes of the principal. Hence modern governments have had to rely to an increasing extent upon other methods to induce their officials to act in accordance with the wishes of the people. Dismissal remains, of course, as the ultimate sanction, but immeasurable damage can have been done. Where the official acts in collusion with private interests, he may even do so in anticipation of being hired by these interests, so that dismissal holds very little punishment for him. On account of the preoccupation with electoral forms of representation and responsibility (chs. XIV–XV), there has been a tendency in Anglo-Saxon countries to overemphasize the power of hiring and firing, appointment and removal. We criticized former President Taft's view that the President would have to have the power to fire any and all administrative officials of the federal government, if he were to be held responsible for the administration. What is the experience in other countries and what does it suggest? It seems that one can distinguish five types of measures which contribute to the actual realization of such administrative responsibility as one would want to secure in a functioning administrative setup. First, there are the disciplinary measures which are based on the psychology of discouragement. Second, there are the promotional measures. These are based on the psychology of encouragement. Third, there are financial measures of control and audit of expenditure, based on the rule of anticipated reactions. Fourth, there are the judicial measures based upon civil and criminal law. Such judicial measures are necessary concomitants of a legalized order or a constitutionalized government; they, among all administrative methods, have been most emphasized in English-speaking countries. Fifth, there is the spirit of craftsmanship, of a thing well done. This spirit embodies critical standards in terms of objective achievement. This fifth method of enforcing responsible conduct is becoming increasingly important at present. It has for a long time played a very important role in all the professions and therefore it has profoundly influenced the judicial branch of the government (except where judges are elective). It is in some respects akin to religious responsibility; for the standards of science are taken as relatively settled absolutes.

Disciplinary measures · Partly as a result of this religious element disciplinary measures based on the psychology of fear have always loomed large in the efforts to enforce responsibility in administrative setups. In fact, many persons would try to persuade us that only the harshest disciplinary measure, dismissal, affords an effective technique for enforcing responsible conduct of officials. That this view is erroneous we have already shown. That disciplinary measures are, nevertheless, an important weapon in the armory of the enforcer of responsibility must be admitted.[12] But before the extreme penalty of dismissal or removal is applied, five other measures are available, each of them a valuable tool and effective within limits. They are reprimand, fine, temporary suspension, reduction of salary, and transfer to another, presumably less attractive, post. To neglect all these and to focus exclusive attention upon removal is like trying to set up a criminal law with capital punishment as the sole penalty. According to administrative experience elsewhere, removal should only be used when all the other disciplinary measures have failed; it should, in other words, be recognized as the extreme penalty for the worst offenses, and it should never be used except on the basis of an established judicial procedure. Here, in fact, lies the core of the administrative law which we have discussed above (see ch. VI, pp. 113 f.). Preferably, all these disciplinary measures should be imposed only after a hearing.

It seems desirable to consider one further problem of especial significance in this area, and that is the role and the importance of contacts with the public. Private employers are becoming increasingly aware of the decisive role which all their employees must play in the public relations of business concerns. Competition through service is becoming an ever more important factor, and the contact of the general public with particular businesses is through their employees. It is evident that the government through its expanding services is placed in a similar position.[13] The Postal Service has long recognized this and has evolved careful regulations concerning the dealings of its employees with the public. As a result, the letter carrier has become a symbol of cheerful service. By contrast, the arbitrary official of authoritarian regimes abroad has always been acknowledged as the antithesis of democracy. Although such conduct was often condoned as part of administrative efficiency, we know today that this view is mistaken. Just as morale within the service is of decisive importance in bringing about responsible administration, so likewise morale should extend beyond the confines of the service itself.

The most serious disciplinary issue revolves around the problem of the employees' right to organize, to bargain collectively, and to strike if their demands are rejected. It is difficult to see how popular government can recognize a right to strike, though it seems equally questionable to deny it. Whatever the abstract arguments, the right of public officials to strike is not recognized by many democratic governments. In the United States, most public employees recognize that such strikes really are not in their true interest. But it is obvious that in lieu of the possibility of bringing their complaints and grievances forcibly to the attention of their employer (the government), public officials must be provided with carefully devised institutional safeguards for mediation and arbitration. Such mechanisms have a fairly long tradition in some countries; they are rapidly developing in the United States. The American Federation of Government Employees has always staunchly defended this right of government employees to organize and present their views collectively. Recently, a CIO union, the United Federal Workers of America, has taken an even more militant attitude, including a demand for the recognition of the right to strike. Here, again, it is evident that a democracy has to face the issues which are being raised by the ever-expanding size of its administrative activities. It cannot possibly hope to develop and maintain responsible conduct unless it accords its employees a status at least equal in dignity and self-respect to the status its labor laws impose upon and demand from private employers. The problem is one of considerable scope and concern for the Labour Government in Great Britain. Here the rapid expansion of the public services, due to nationalization of basic industries, has brought into governmental employment many workers formerly in private business and accustomed to the right to strike. Unlike the Communists, who simply ruled that any worker striking against the workers' republic was a saboteur, the Labour Government has had to deal with recurrent and at times crippling strikes. Its trade-union element is naturally very adverse to any curtailment of its right to strike. The situation represents one of the toughest issues of democratic socialism. In sum, even though the government does not feel justified in conceding the right to strike, it should not discriminate against employees who join an organization which advances this claim. For merely to demand this right is not a crime, since reasonable men may differ as to the right answer. Employees who are denied the rights of ordinary citizens cannot possibly be expected to remain loyal and responsible public servants.

The right policy is to be sure that all necessary disciplinary rules are loyally accepted by the entire staff, irrespective of the organization to which they belong. This formula works well as long as those responsible for the rules respect the rights of the persons working under them. It must be kept in mind, however, that there are quite a few difficult borderline cases, where the infraction of a given rule has been due to faulty behavior or hostile attitudes on the part of the higher-ups. Possible frictions of this type are endless; it is evident that adequate representative organization of the employees is the only possible way of coping with the situations as they arise.

Promotional measures · Promotional measures are based upon the psychology of encouragement. They consist essentially of promotions themselves, salary increases, titles, orders, and decorations. A considerable amount of responsibility can be secured from officials by a judicious employment of all of these; but most of these possibilities have been badly neglected in the United States. In the thirties the Commission of Inquiry on Public Service Personnel Problems, in a notable report, insisted upon the decisive importance of promotion when it wrote:

There can be no career service in government, or anywhere else, without promotion. The creation of promotion opportunities, however, is not easy to bring about, especially in large organizations, because the top officials with the power to appoint and promote may not know the younger subordinates or have any contact with their work. . . . A regularly organized system of promotion, maintained by the chief executives through a properly established personnel office, thus performs three indispensable services: first, it makes the service attractive to promising young men who will not enter an employment which is known not to give the opportunity of advancement based on proved merit; second, it results in an energetic staff by displacing the stagnant atmosphere of a stationary service; and, third, it brings to the top positions men who combine energy with knowledge of public administration, rather than partisans, amateurs, or men, with or without energy, who do not know the public service. From the standpoint, therefore, of the establishment and maintenance of a career service, the promotion system is indispensable."[14]

The educated young man of ambition who enters the civil service of England, France, or other European countries is driven by competition with his equals to exert himself to the utmost in discharging his duties. To strengthen further the impetus toward self-exertion, the British have developed a system of annually certifying that service has been satisfactory as a condition for promotion as well as for salary increases. In the United States the situation is not nearly so satisfactory. Until recently it was difficult to get young people of ambition and ability to enter the government service, except as a stopgap, because there was no clear road to promotion. While there has been considerable improvement in recent years, there are still many uncertainties and the person who exerts himself to conduct his office responsibly often finds himself unrewarded by promotion. It is a curious thing that in a country in which the lure of promotion is generally recognized by business leaders as of decisive importance in managing a large-scale organization efficiently, the need of a career in government has been overlooked. To be sure, one should avoid making a fetish out of the career element in enforcing responsibility. The overstimulation of ambition may lead to very undesirable practices. Students of the problem of promotion have sometimes tended to neglect its dangers and to make it a panacea for all ills. What must particularly be guarded against are schemes which seek to provide for a certainty of promotion. If a career in government service is taken to mean that, a good part of the value of promotional opportunities in stimulating responsibility is lost. The possibility of promotion, not the certainty of it, is necessary in order to be assured of responsible work. As A. Lawrence Lowell used to say, those who are unwilling to gamble with themselves are not safe as a gamble for anyone else.

Closely related to promotion are titles. If the greater responsibility of a higher office is to be publicly recognized and honored, an appropriate title has to be provided for such an office. Since much valuable ambition is generated by the desire for honor, it is almost absurd to fail to make use of the opportunities which human nature offers in this respect. Generally speaking, America's tradition is opposed to the use of titles. However, courts, universities, and the defense forces, three very important branches of national life, employ them extensively. Titles such as "colonel" are even used as a form of address in strictly private business relationships. The steady increase in the use of titles in American life testifies to a growing consciousness of rank and status. It could be correlated to rapid stratification in some sectors. It is, however, not easy to prove this contention. It is quite possible to argue that these titles, associated as they are with churches, universities, the military service, and certain honorific positions in the government, and devoid as they are of any hereditary element, constitute survivals resulting from the autonomous traditions of these non-modern segments of the society.

Certain offices are generally conceived as honorific in their very names. A powerful impetus for responsible government service may thereby be secured. Yet much that is most valuable in this sphere is beyond human control. Titles seem to follow something which corresponds to Gresham's law in economics—their value seems to decrease with the increase of the numbers acquiring them. The history of titles shows that you can never recoup a deteriorated title. The only possible method is to impose a still higher rank. The history of both the M.A. and the Ph.D. in the United States is a significant illustration. When the Ph.D. first appeared, it was usually the degree of a foreign university and was supposed to confer the distinction of foreign study. Gradually, as American universities developed their graduate research work, they offered the Ph.D. degree, with very stiff requirements, patterned upon the tradition of the European universities, notably Oxford and Cambridge. But in the decades past, it became more and more common to demand a Ph.D. in academic life and in the public services. Hence the institutions conferring it multiplied, until finally a foundation for advanced study was set up to enable students of exceptional ability to pursue their study in the Society of Fellows at Harvard—provided that they did not seek a Ph.D. degree. Any effort to create titles must be guided by what people desire as an honor.

Orders and decorations, on the other hand, can be and have been created. Therefore, if the growth of titles does not proceed fast enough honors can be established through orders and decorations. However, there are here other considerable limitations. For the honor which is attached to such orders and decorations is great only if there is a general belief in the traditional significance of the person who establishes the order. If a king sets it up in a monarchical country, the decoration has that quality, but if the President of the United States does it, it does not necessarily have the same effect. For the President is a party man. This point is well illustrated by the history of congressional decorations. Honorary degrees by universities also have a very limited appeal, particularly because of the abuse made of them by various institutions in search of funds. This is quite natural, for orders and decorations are likewise subject to the law that the value of a thing is enhanced by its rarity.

There has always been a tendency to associate orders and decorations with aristocratic and therefore exclusive tendencies and they are instinctively felt to be undemocratic. Consciously democratic constitutions are inclined to forbid the accepting or the wearing of foreign orders and decorations. In the United States, only the military have developed an elaborate system of orders and decorations, but the trend is toward decorations in the civilian sector of public life. For one thing, decorations, like titles, provide a very inexpensive reward for public service. Nevertheless the Swiss, in 1931, extended to all citizens the prohibition of foreign decorations, titles, presents, and pensions, formerly limited to government officials. While electoral participation was limited, the debate was highlighted by the conflict in principle between such decorations and democracy.

Fiscal measures · Time-honored and yet often not sufficiently appreciated are the fiscal techniques for securing responsible conduct of administrative business. They are essentially three: forecasting the expenditures through an appropriate budget, controlling the payments when they are being made in order to insure their consonance with the budget, and auditing the accounts afterward.[15] In relation to the administrative organization itself, these controls are partly internal and partly external. Budgeting is both internal and external. The drawing up of the budget (with which the President with the assistance of the Bureau of the Budget is charged in the United States, while in England it is the Treasury, and in other countries the Ministry of Finance) is internally done by administrative officials. The approving of this budget, on the other hand, is external and entrusted to parliaments (see above, ch. XVII, pp. 340 f.). The controlling of the payments as made is internal in Europe, where the Treasury or Ministries of Finance have ultimate control, though in England the Comptroller and Auditor-General has some share in the control. In the United States, on the other hand, the Comptroller-General as an independent "legislative" officer has complete control (short of court review), an arrangement which has led to very serious friction. Auditing, finally, is external everywhere. Highly judicialized techniques are preferred on the Continent (*Cour des Comptes* in France, *Reichsrechnungshof* in Germany), executive work in England, (Comptroller and Auditor-General) and in the United States (Comptroller-General). But everywhere parliamentary supervision, by some sort of committee on accounts, implements this machinery wherever there is parliamentary government. Probably the preference of Continental countries for a judicial setup in the audit field is due to traditions derived from their monarchical past. Some sort of independent body, like the *Oberrechnungskammer*, established by Frederick William of Prussia as early as 1711, or the *Cour des Comptes*, established by Napoleon, is essential for the maintenance of financial integrity. These bodies continued to develop into courts, because under the separation of powers as practiced by monarchical constitutional governments (see above, ch. X, p. 179) judicial safeguards of administrative integrity were compatible with monarchical traditions; these monarchies looked upon them as acceptable alternatives to parliamentary supervision. When, later on, parliaments were able to extend their jurisdiction, they found these independent bodies quite acceptable as aides in discharging their supervisory function. From this circumstance, as well as from the general theory of the separation of powers, it might be argued that the United States would be well advised to follow the pattern of a judicialized procedure for auditing, and such a change has indeed been advocated. The present fusion of controlling and auditing functions in one "independent officer" certainly has not produced results which argue for the continuance of such an arrangement. Hence if a Court of Accounts were set up, the controlling function could then be put back under the administrative direction of the Treasury Department, where it belongs. The Hoover Commission, taking a line similar to the one here stated, proposed to divest the Comptroller-General of his accounting responsibilities (even now not well worked out and integrated) and to set up an Accountant-General in the Treasury Department. He would have authority to prescribe general accounting methods and enforce accounting procedures. He would be charged with "combining agency accounts into the summary accounts of the government, and produce financial reports for the information of the Chief Executive, the Congress and the public." (Section II.) The report pointed out that "there are serious weaknesses in the internal operations . . . in the fiscal field. These weaknesses penetrate into the heart of every governmental transaction. . . . Some of the fiscal concepts of the Federal Government come down from Alexander Hamilton. They were archaic when the total expenditures of the Government were $4,000,000,000 per annum. Now . . . they are totally inadequate."[16]

Whatever the general framework of government, these several techniques have been found invaluable aids in securing financial responsibility. Politically speaking, they operate largely in accordance with the rule of anticipated reactions. It is, as in all such cases, futile to offer elaborate statistics as to what items have been disallowed, or what misdemeanors have been detected. They are, taken individually, important enough. But a much larger result is due to the fact that administrative officials who know that their expenditures must first be approved, and later audited, are much more careful in their financial conduct.

Judicial measures · The preceding discussion of disciplinary, promotional, and fiscal measures has sketched a wide variety of techniques for making the conduct of governmental officials more responsible. But most of these measures presuppose a willingness at the top to employ them when necessary. They are largely administrative in nature. Suspicion, first of the king, and later of party bosses, has inclined the majority of people in Anglo-Saxon lands to look for outside controls. The judiciary provides the most obvious and ancient technique for this purpose. Judicial methods for rendering official conduct more responsible are, therefore, of great importance. Modern conceptions of the rule of law demand that all officials be subject to civil and criminal law. Whatever exceptions may be necessary regarding certain actions taken in the course of official duties, it goes without saying that no civilized community will suffer its government personnel to steal, cheat, or rape with impunity. But such checks upon personal misconduct of officials can only take care of a minor part of the task of enforcing responsibility.

Even if it be admitted that such judicial methods make an official responsible for doing something which should not have been done, they certainly do not provide any safeguards against the failure to do what should be done. The common law has developed certain special writs like *quo warranto* and *mandamus* to prevent or enforce official action. By these writs the courts may, in the name of the "sovereign," compel an inferior official to comply with the law. Yet, since administrative action is largely positive and an administrative agency must primarily be interested in "getting something done," judicial measures are narrowly limited in their effectiveness in securing governmental responsibility. What is more, many things which officials should not do are beyond the reach of the judiciary. Take, for example, offensive and overbearing conduct toward the public. This is certainly a bureaucratic vice of widest occurrence. Yet courts cannot deal with it at all; rarely will the offense reach the point of extremity where the offended citizen could sue for tort. Again consider the case of slothful red tape or even deliberate lying. The damage to individuals may be very great, but nothing can be accomplished through the courts. Take the following case: a subaltern clerk in an American Consulate rejected an invitation from an American citizen to a foreign relative (which is required as evidence of a *bona fide* visit), claiming it was not properly executed, and requested a duly sworn invitation instead. The clerk added that the visa could not be issued unless the duly executed form were in the hands of the consul four weeks before the intended departure. But there were only five weeks left, and consequently it was impossible for the alien to secure such an invitation within the time limit stipulated by the official. However, inquiry at the State Department revealed that no such rule existed; was there any judicial remedy for the improper and irresponsible conduct of the clerk concerned?

Governmental versus personal liability · Not only are courts largely unable to bring about official action, and partly unable to prevent irresponsible conduct, but they are furthermore hampered, in the United States, by the ancient rule that "the king can do no wrong." This rule means that the government cannot be held liable for acts committed by an official in the discharge of his duty. Damage suits against officials must, therefore, always establish that the official acted *ultra vires*. If the court finds that he acted *ultra vires*, the claim of the individual has to be enforced against the individual officer. It is evident that in many cases the individual officer is totally unable to pay the claim. If, on the other hand, the court finds that the official did not act *ultra vires*, then the damaged party is dependent upon the grace of a "sovereign legislature" for adequate compensation. The disadvantages of this situation are, however, by no means limited to the "public" which may sustain damages. Inasmuch as it exposes the official to constant danger of a ruinous suit for personal damages, it makes him overly cautious and thus irresponsible from the point of view of a vigorous pursuit of his duties. The recognition of this exceedingly unsatisfactory state of affairs has led legislative bodies to provide specifically for the responsibility of certain large-scale government enterprises in the case of torts committed by any of its officials. Certain municipalities have recognized their obligation for damage done by their fire departments, and the federal government has provided similarly in the case of the TVA. It is indeed as evident as anything can be that the government should take the same responsibility for any large-scale service enterprise which it manages as would be provided for if that enterprise were privately owned and operated. If it is to the community's benefit to undertake such tasks, the community and not the damaged individual should bear the losses involved in its operation. Actual experience in local government bodies where a certain amount of that type of corporate liability is allowed tends to show that objectively responsible conduct in terms of the particular service can be secured by internal measures such as we have sketched earlier in this chapter.

To put the matter positively, it appears that relieving the officer of the government from this type of personal liability has the great advantage of placing the responsibility where it belongs. If, let us say, a man lying asleep on his porch is accidentally shot by a policeman, the important point is not whether the policeman acted according to his legally defined duties. Even if he did not, it might be a gross injustice to burden him with the liability as long as he believed that shooting was the only effective means of handling the situation. If an American citizen is seriously damaged without due process of law by an officer of the government trying to maintain law and order, he is entitled to just compensation. This compensation should come from the party responsible for the damage, namely, the American government and the American people as a whole. It is then up to the government to determine whether its officials acted responsibly or not, and to collect, in the latter case, what they can from the official, or to punish him according to established disciplinary procedure. All the facts point toward the conclusion that responsibility is more effectively enforced by such a provision. In fact, only such a plan will insure that a government service wielding vast powers of control, supervision, and regulation in every phase of the public's activities will not deteriorate into an irresponsible bureaucracy, now irremediably damaging private individuals in executing "laws" however bad, now timorously shirking from responsible action because of the absence of unequivocal "legal" authority. The problem of how to "judicialize" such a responsibility, how to organize courts which would specialize in adjudicating controversies arising out of administrative action, is a grave one. We have treated it in broad outline when dealing with the judiciary as a governmental technique (see above, ch. VI).

Measures based upon an objective standard · It remains to inquire into what we called methods based upon an objective standard of performance as a possible technique for insuring responsible conduct. It is a question of craftsmanship, of sound professionalism, extremely important as a basis for "sound" action. Perhaps the most ancient instance of the application of such an objective standard is found in the judiciary itself. As we pointed out when discussing the judiciary in relation to the bar (see ch. VI, pp. 106), judicial decisions are relatively responsible, because judges have to account for their action in terms of a rationalized and previously established set of rules. Any deviation from these rules on the part of a judge will be subjected to extensive scrutiny by his colleagues and by what is known as the legal profession. The judges' sensitivity to criticism of their brethren off the bench, their feeling of responsibility toward that wide fraternal community, is a typical illustration of the kind of objective standard of performance with which we are here concerned.

Administrative officials seeking to apply scientific standards similarly have to account for their action in terms of a rationalized and previously established set of *hypotheses* or *rules*. Any deviation from these hypotheses will be subjected to thorough scrutiny by their colleagues in what is known as "the fellowship of science." If an official in the Bureau of Standards, let us say, should make regulations which would show lack of acquaintance with the essential knowledge in his field, he would be criticized so strenuously by fellow engineers that his authority would presently vanish. There are, of course, here as well as in the judicial field, wide areas where doubt and controversy prevail. With regard to those activities, indecision or arbitrary selection among possible alternative solutions remains unavoidable. But it should be evident that even in these cases the necessity for justifying the choice will impose enough responsibility upon the official to make him wary of changing his conduct in a similar matter without weighty evidence. Thus a certain amount of regularity and predictability is secured.[17]

Conclusion · The ways, then, by which a measure of genuine responsibility can be secured under modern conditions appear to be manifold, and they must all be utilized for achieving the best effect. No mere reliance upon some traditional device, like cabinet dependence upon majority support in parliament, or popular election of the chief executive, important as they are, can be counted upon to render the vast public services of a modern government responsible. Traditionalists have continued to take it for granted that in England, at least, such cabinet responsibility effectively ensures responsible conduct of public affairs by officials high and low. Some of these men have gone so far as to suggest that the United States will never have a healthy political system until the British scheme is adopted. Actually, the task of making the administrative services responsible leads much farther afield. At best, responsibility in a democracy will remain fragmentary because of the indistinct voice of the principal whose agents the officials are supposed to be: the heterogeneous masses composing the electorate. But it can be approximated. Appropriate training, reasonable care in selection at recruitment time, a well-ordered system of disciplinary procedure, a sound system of promotion, tight fiscal controls, and a strong sense of professional pride and craftsmanship are all necessary parts of a democratic administration that is truly responsible. If all these devices are kept operative while the leaders, the executive and legislative representatives, respond to the majority's preference in matters of general policy, democratic government, by pooling many different interests and points of view, continues to provide the nearest approximation to a policy-making process which will give the "right" results. For right policies are policies which seem right to the community at large and at the same time do not violate "objective" scientific standards.

Responsibility to the people does not require partisans of a particular general outlook, whether Republican or Democrat, conservative, progressive, or socialist, but it does require specialists who know their job and will, therefore, effectively execute the general rules decided upon by executive or legislative leadership in accordance with popular preferences. Fortunately, people aware of such "objective" standards and sensitive therefore to objective responsibility within a given function are often glad to be relieved of the obligation of making decisions where no objective standards are available. The very passion for objectivity and impartiality which renders them judicially or scientifically minded makes them shrink from any rash and arbitrary decision. They are delighted to leave that task to the "people" or to their elected representatives. For such specialists often do not realize that *some* decision has to be made. To the representatives of the people, both executive and legislative, falls the difficult task of working toward such decisions by bringing together the judgment of the expert and the "will of the people."

XX

Political Parties: General Problems

Introduction · Party origins and the cabinet system · A two-party system grows out of one party. The policy of the government as a factor in the development of parties · Ideal and material objectives · Material interests and majority rule · Hatschek's law regarding English party development. Parties secure power for their leaders · A definition of party · Parties and factions · Lowell's theory of political dispositions · Parties in relation to class structure · Conclusion.

Introduction · Parties are, it is now generally agreed, indispensable features of democracy. Yet, one hundred and fifty years ago, their place and function were generally unknown.[1] At the founding of the United States, the "people" were looked upon as capable of acting as a unit. Washington, as everyone knows, warned in his farewell address against "factions." Later historians have mockingly remarked that Washington was inclined to look upon efforts to disturb Federalist rule as "factionalism." This is true, except that Washington did not think of the "Federalists" as a party; what came to be the platform of the Federalists was to him still the one sound, patriotic, American policy to which there did not exist any well-defined alternative. To be sure, in England in the course of the eighteenth century the idea of parties as a part of the governmental scheme had been dawning on the minds of the most acute observers; but Bolingbroke's persuasive arguments against such a system, his readiness to identify it with "corruption" and to extol the ideal of a patriot king, still dominated many minds. Curiously enough, the American colonists were revolting at the same time against this corruption in Parliament and against the tyranny of the king who tried to cope with it. To understand this paradox, one should recall that George III had been emulating the technique of Walpole and the Whigs by building up a royalist faction of henchmen in Parliament. He was, in other words, tarred with the same brush of "factionalism." But his underlying ambition was to become such a patriot king as Bolingbroke had depicted. He was going to rule as an independent chief executive according to the original scheme of the constitution of 1688. But by organizing a party, he acknowledged the place and function of parties in the constitutional order; it is no wonder that the party outlived him and his personal ambitions.

410

Party origins and the cabinet system · Historically speaking, the English cabinet's parliamentary responsibility arose out of the party struggle; it is generally agreed that the evolution of the party and of parliamentarism is inseparably intertwined. It is therefore rather difficult to discuss the development of one without the other.[2] But since the Whigs and Tories of the last years of Charles II's reign are admittedly the prototype of the modern English two-party system, it must be conceded that the parties antedate the cabinet system. We may say, as we did in the previous chapter, that the single-member constituency with plurality elections is peculiarly adapted to the two-party system under responsible parliamentary government, because it forces the electorate to make up its mind between two clear-cut alternatives. But we must remember that the plurality vote and the resulting sharpness of party division preceded the cabinet system. The reason why the responsibility of the cabinet to Parliament (the cabinet system) was engendered by the party strife is that each party in its effort to buttress its position, but more particularly the Whig party under Walpole and Pelham (1715–1760), sought to secure for itself a solid majority in Parliament. Such a majority greatly facilitated the realization of all policies for which the co-operation of Parliament was necessary. Walpole proceeded to secure such a parliamentary majority for himself and his cabinet by a carefully worked out system which to his contemporaries and to moderns alike can appear only as a system of corruption. Wraxall tells us in his memoirs that the government under Pelham handed each of their partisans in Parliament from five hundred to eight hundred pounds at the end of a session, the amount varying according to the services rendered. These payments were official enough to be entered on a record kept in the Treasury. More recent investigations have shown that the Whigs at that time had worked out a very elaborate system of governmental favors, ranging from direct payments to voters and members of Parliament, to patronage and the various favors available in foreign trade and the privileged trading companies. All this is well enough known, since it was so intimately bound up with the struggle for independence waged by the American colonies a few years later. What is less readily seen is that the English two-party system was rooted in a traditional struggle for spoils between two distinctly aristocratic factions or divisions of the (aristocratically controlled) electorate. In fact, Walpole once remarked that he and Lord Townshend constituted the "firm" to which the king had entrusted the country's government.

A two-party system grows out of one party · It would, however, not be generally conceded today that the long Whig rule under Walpole was the true origin of the English parties. Historians have for a long time argued about this problem and while some, with Sir Erskine May, have dated party growth back to the Puritans under Elizabeth, others, like Lord Macaulay, have refused to admit anything worthy of the name prior to the Roundheads and the Cavaliers of the Long Parliament.[3] The truth lies in between. Some of these differences in opinion are traceable to different conceptions as to what constitutes a party. Obviously, the more one stresses organizational features, the later one will have to put "party origin." When party is taken to mean something akin to faction, the partisans of the Red and the White Roses in the fourteenth and fifteenth centuries were members of a "party." But since these factions of nobles were baldly striving to seat their head on the throne, no question of principle entered in. On the other hand, the Puritans under Queen Elizabeth lacked all effective organization, and they hardly attempted to control Parliament (without parliamentary responsibility, such control was not particularly important). They had deep-seated convictions, to be sure; but many of these beliefs transcended the strictly political sphere. Under James I, however, the Puritans took on something of the quality of a party which developed into the Roundheads of the Long Parliament. While the Puritans did not explicitly claim it, they really sought the control of the government. Or, to put it another way, they sought to escape from the control which the king had hitherto exercised over the government. The Tudor kings had developed a system of patronage and corruption for the purpose of keeping Parliament in line. What matters to us is that the Puritan party developed as an opposition to the government as such, and more particularly to so-called royal prerogative. This remained so down to the Long Parliament period, when the Puritans themselves gained ascendancy. Then they in turn claimed an exclusive control, which eventually called forth the Cromwellian dictatorship. This Puritan party was not recognized as a legitimate undertaking; the government belabored them by calling them rebels, and they returned the compliment by denouncing the crown as tyrannical. It was only after these violent revolutionary experiments with one-party rule had proven abortive that the English people settled down to a mutual acceptance of each other's political viewpoint. Thus we find that a two-party system develops out of a one-party predominance. Only after the resulting civil war had shown a people the danger of party violence did the two-party system with its dependence upon a certain amount of tolerance become acceptable to the group at large.

The policy of the government as a factor in the development of parties · Why should the two-party system have taken hold in England and nowhere else? What conditions favoring its development in England

were absent in all these other countries? The development of a cabinet
system was an important contributing factor. Another very important
condition is the *early* development of the parties.[4] England escaped the
religious division (and the consequent development of a Catholic party)
on account of the overwhelmingly Protestant nature of the country, but-
tressing this religious uniformity by depriving Catholics and other religious
dissenters (nonconformists) of political privileges until well into the nineteenth century. As a result, England could evolve the fundamental and
simple division of conservatives and liberals (with some reactionaries and
radicals thrown in on each side) during the course of two centuries of more
or less undisturbed domestic peace. She could therefore enter into the era
of the industrial revolution with that pattern firmly established. What is
more, the radical tendencies engendered by this industrial revolution for a
long time found an acceptable voice in the traditional Liberal party. A
distinct Labour party arose only in the twentieth century. This party, after
four decades of growth, seems now definitely to have superseded the Liberal
party as the party of progress.

On the Continent conditions were vastly different. After the restoration in France, a major cleavage existed between Republicans, in favor of
the principles of 1789, and those opposed to these principles on various
grounds. But the French restoration ministers, unlike those of the Stuarts,
never attempted to organize a party of the crown, for they knew that such
a party was liable to call forth an opposition which would eventually establish parliamentary supremacy. So the tactics of Louis XVIII and Louis
Philippe followed the maxim of divide and rule so as to avoid the consolidation of parties. Thus a multiple-party system established itself in France,
but the situation remained unstable, as the revolutions of 1830 and 1848,
the Second Empire, and its overthrow in 1870 clearly show. By the time
the Third Republic had firmly established itself, the Socialists had got under
way as a factor to be reckoned with. Since socialism assumes a fundamental
cleavage in the electorate, class antagonism between capitalists and workers,
the party divisions of the electorate assumed the proportions of a permanent disruption of the people into mutually exclusive and lastingly hostile
interests. In Germany the development took a different course, but the
result was the same. Here the Socialists could consolidate their position
even more definitely before a cabinet system supported by parliamentary
majorities was set up by the constitution of 1919. The Prussian development before 1871 was indicative of the future. Bismarck, instead of seeking
majority support for the government's policies, openly flouted the parliamentary opposition. After his internal and external victories, he made no
attempt to collaborate with the party most ready to support him—the

National Liberals—but sought to secure his majorities as he needed them. When the Socialists, as a result, were forging ahead rapidly as the party of progress, he attempted to suppress them by force; toward the end of Bismarck's career the failure of these efforts brought the Socialists back into parliament as a firmly entrenched party proclaiming the Marxist doctrine of inexorable class warfare. Disunity thereafter became the earmark of German representative bodies.

Party development appears, therefore, greatly affected by the policy of the government in the period of the beginnings of parliamentary, representative government. Does this mean that we are confronted by situations totally at variance with one another in the several countries? Evidently not. In spite of a number of variations, there remains much similarity in the party formations of all the European nations. And while the two-party system, so-called, has its distinct advantages from the standpoint of parliamentary responsibility, we should not deceive ourselves into overestimating either its importance or its permanence. After all, the two large English parties have frequently been divided into warring groups; such groups have often caused the downfall of the government. Besides, even in England since the Reform of 1832, two parties have been the exception rather than the rule. The Peelites, the Radicals, the Liberal Unionists, the Irish Nationalists, and the Labour Party have followed each other as third parties, and it would, in the light of all the facts, be more appropriate to describe the English as a two-and-one-half-party system.

Ideal and material objectives · The English evolution suggests another hypothesis to the student of politics: parties in order to live and function must be compounded of ideal and material purposes or objectives.[5] A party, to achieve any degree of permanency, must and will have both an interest in certain ideas concerning law and government and an interest in securing the power of government and all that goes with it in the form of patronage and the rest. In other words, the distinction between patronage parties and parties of principle, which is so popular among writers on politics in Europe, is untenable. There is no such thing as a party which lacks either of these elements. Moreover, this is a distinction of which one should be particularly wary from a practical viewpoint; it is one of the most common errors made in dealing with politics to contrast the ideal aspirations of one's own group with the actual performance of one's opponents. Politicians continually build appeals on this presumption. A measure of sophistication apropos of such claims is an indication of political education in an electorate. In countries with limited experience in democracy, many people are readily beguiled by such claims.

414

But a realistic recognition of the material advantages which parties seek must not become the ground for undiscriminating denunciations of parties as such. "Parties are inevitable," Lord Bryce justly said, "no free large country has been without them." Conceding this claim, quite a few insist that for that reason popular government must go. There is, we are told, always much corruption and patronage connected with party government. This cannot be denied by anyone who studies the historical records attentively. But what can be denied is that this tendency toward corruption and patronage is in any way peculiar to party government. Authoritarian regimes do not differ in that respect; they, too, are never free from corruption and nepotism, and in periods of decay are notoriously honeycombed with both. The recently revealed records of the Nazi regime show that it was no exception. The real difference is that the dirty laundry of popular regimes is washed in public, whereas under authoritarian rule it is washed behind the scenes or not at all. For that reason, it is justifiable to describe any type of authoritarian regime as essentially a one-party government. This means that the control which comes from alternation with another party is lacking. It is difficult to see why the absence of all criticism should make for greater purity in the conduct of the government. The authoritarian regime which strives for the good of the country all of its own free will is to be found only in the blue skies of the philosophers.

A realistic political science can state with some confidence that all parties strive for a combination of ideal and material objectives. What is more, observation of the actual working of government points toward the conclusion that the ideal objectives are forced upon parties by their struggle for gaining control of the government. It is a platitude of practical politics that the outs are invariably more emphatic in their advocacy of principles than the ins. Therefore authoritarian (one-party) regimes are apt to be more corrupt and venal than two or more party set-ups. So-called "historical" instances pointing supposedly in the opposite direction, like the Prussian monarchy under Frederick William I and Frederick the Great, turn out upon closer investigation to have been subject to very special conditions which account for the relatively small amount of corruption *in spite* of the authoritarian nature of the regime. Frederick William I was fired with a passionate ambition to clean up the vast corruption which had prevailed under his spendthrift father and at the same time to overcome the large remnants of feudal dispersion and corruption which disunited and weakened his scattered domains. Frederick the Great was engaged in very extensive foreign warfare, which necessitated as high an efficiency as was attainable in his administrative staff, and the later phases of his reign were filled with an unceasing effort to rebuild and consolidate his exhausted kingdom. But as soon as he was dead, a process of large-scale corruption set in and brought this authoritarian government to the brink of complete disaster during the Napoleonic wars. All this suggests the conclusion that corruption is even more common in authoritarian than in popular government.

Material interests and majority rule · Although it is true that all organized parties strive for material as well as for ideal objectives, considerable differences exist between parties regarding the balance between the two. Continental European observers have often commented upon the relatively large role which material objectives seem to play in the history of English and American parties. This is undoubtedly in part due to the fact that the parties in these countries have had a real prize for which to fight, namely, the actual control of the government, whereas in many of the continental countries, but particularly in Germany, the limited power of the representative body has tended to keep a considerable section of the public and the parties speaking for them on the outside of actual government, and consequently emphatic in their advocacy of ideal purposes. Both Liberal and Socialist parties were deeply affected by this; they developed, on the Continent, a programmatic dogmatism which goes ill with practical politics (see next chapter). Furthermore, all evidence seems to point toward the conclusion that the larger the party, the more pronounced are its material interests. Professor Holcombe has shown this quite convincingly for American parties, which throughout their history have been sensitive to the broad economic interests of various sections of the country.[6] It is evident that a party in order to hold together a rather heterogeneous following (and any party aspiring to an actual majority must do that) will shun a decided stand on questions of principle, while at the same time making concessions to a variety of theoretically perhaps incompatible interests. By such a policy a party manager may gain the adherence of sufficiently large groups to lead his banner to victory. The attitude of many an American politician toward some of the demands of labor and socialism illustrates this point. Theoretically, socialism is based upon the idea that the interests of employers and employees are incompatible, and that capitalism must eventually be destroyed and supplanted by state or government control. Practically, the interests of workingmen are in higher wages, lower hours, better working conditions generally, in unemployment and old-age insurance, and so forth. These material interests are precisely those which an American politician will quite readily support, if working men's support is essential for his being re-elected, whereas he probably would contemplate with horror the possibility of becoming a "Socialist." Of course, in the United States both Republicans and Democrats expound a long series of "principles" in their official platforms, but most of these principles are so vague as to turn out to be almost identical for both parties on closer inspection. As a result, the material interests, including patronage, remain as the real cement of parties wherever the system of election by plurality prevails—and as we have seen in the previous chapter this is made one of the points of attack upon this system by the proportionalists. There is, to be sure, a considerable difference between the several kinds of material interests. Patronage is one thing, concessions another. An act prohibiting child labor, while a material interest to some, is very much fraught with ideal issues for others.

Hatschek's law regarding English party development · The preponderance of material objectives in large-party organization has led Julius Hatschek to suggest a rule regarding English party development which may have more general significance. He finds that this development follows a definite course.[7] First, a party with a distinct and coherent program comes into power. This program gradually loses its appeal in the course of the party's efforts to realize it. Some parts turn out to be impossible of achievement. Others arouse the antagonism of some of the party's own following when the practical implications become apparent. The party then breaks up into divisions. This disintegration offers to another party, irrespective of whether it has evolved a distinct and realizable program or not, the chance of concentrating and unifying its forces; then that party gains ascendancy. After a while, this party is subject to the same process of disintegration. This means that once party organizations have come into existence, the existence of a realizable program is no longer necessary. A party can not only continue to live, but may be able to displace the other party in the government, merely because its organization under a powerful leader is more effective than is that of the other party. The party lives by the strength of its organization, and therefore the organization is the main thing, the program a side issue. This fact was already noted in the eighteenth century by David Hume, who in his *Essay on Parties* remarked: "Nothing is more usual than to see parties which have begun upon a real difference continue even after that difference is lost." Putting it simply, and in analogy to the hypothesis discussed in the previous paragraph, one may propose the law that *the older the party, the more pronounced its concern with material interests.* Hatschek believed this to be a peculiarity of English party life, but if he had considered American parties, he would unquestionably have concluded that the situation was much the same here. A similar trend occurs in other countries and under very different conditions of party life.

417

Parties secure power for their leaders · We have now found that parties live independently of their programs, although programs are vital at their inception. We also have seen that parties pursue material as well as ideal objectives. A third general rule or law is that parties strive to secure power for their leader or leaders, rather than for themselves. For only through such leaders can the body of the party membership hope to secure the material and ideal gains which they seek. The leaders may, of course, cheat them. Thus MacDonald in 1931—for whatever motives—unquestionably betrayed the trust which his Labour followers had put in him. This inevitable preponderance of the leader is the result of the same forces which produce monocratic leadership in government; for the party is almost constantly in the position of a nation at war. The unceasing struggle either to maintain or to gain ascendancy in the government provides that pressure from which we saw monocratic, or at least strictly hierarchical, leadership to result. It has been argued that this dominance of the leaders is something peculiarly English. But this is not true; wherever a party is seeking actual control of the government, such hierarchical structure is bound to develop and to maintain itself. Starting from a large body of careful observations, Robert Michels showed that (in keeping with the law just stated) parties advocating democracy and equality are just as prone to be authoritarian and boss-controlled as authoritarian parties.[8] Michels's particular interests centered around the German Socialist party, which showed this hierarchical, bureaucratic trend in a very marked degree. It was with acute insight that the leader of German Social Democracy was often jokingly referred to in international socialist congresses as "Kaiser Bebel." In fact, the authority of his position corresponded much more nearly to the popular conception of a *Kaiser* than did that of the German Emperor. But there is nothing particularly shameful about the existence of such leadership, as the innocent reader of Michels's study might be led to infer. Nor yet can this trend be entirely explained by the bureaucratic tradition of Germany. The Socialists were violently opposed to this tradition. It was the difficulty of their position and the resulting intensity of party warfare which necessitated such strictly hierarchical organization. The essential identity of the situation in England may be indicated by a citation from the memoirs of an English parliamentarian under the younger Pitt: "I was never present at any debate I could avoid, or absent from any division [that is, vote] I could get at. I have heard many arguments which convinced my judgment, but never one which changed my vote. I never voted but once according to my opinion, and that was the worst vote I ever gave. I found that the only way to be quiet in Parliament was always to vote with the ministers." That many of the contemporary lamentations about the decline of Par-

liament lose much of their force when considered in the light of such statements (and they could be many times multiplied) was shown more specifically above (see ch. XVII). What matters here is that monocratic, or
at least oligarchic, leadership is inherent in party organization, because
parties are fighting groups.

A definition of party · We are now, I believe, ready to pull together
our several hypotheses or rules into a "definition" of a party. We may say
that a political party is a group of human beings, stably organized with
the objective of securing or maintaining for its leaders the control of a government, and with the further objective of giving to members of the party,
through such control, ideal and material benefits and advantages. A
political party, that is, a group operating to secure control of a government,
state, or country, could be contrasted, for example, with a church party.
A definition broad enough to cover all these other cases would have to speak
of the control of an organization rather than just "the government." This
definition, while developed from earlier ones, differs from them in two
important respects. In the first place, we speak of *control* of an organization,
rather than power within it, because the latter way of putting the definition
would make a group of men founding a newspaper a party, since they surely
seek to secure power within a country.

Parties, because they seek the control of the government, are structured
in accordance with the governmental structure. This is the fatal flaw in
Professor Schattschneider's proposal that what is needed in America is the
reconstitution and reconstruction of party government along British lines.
He criticizes those who would seek to reform the governmental structure as
attempting the impossible. That may be true enough; but his own remedy
is equally unattainable. All that Americans need to do, according to
Schattschneider, is to make of the party that integrated and effective representative of the majority's will which modern policy requires. This argument overlooks the central point, namely, that a party system, precisely
because it is directed toward the control of the government, will closely
resemble the government's pattern. If the government is divided federally
and functionally, the effort to control it will be similarly dispersed. There
is much trenchant criticism in Professor Schattschneider's argument, particularly in what he has to say concerning the squeamishness of Americans
about facing the realities of party government. His argument proceeds on
the sound basis of the first part of our definition, but it goes astray because
he does not ask: what is *the* government in the United States? It also goes
astray because he neglects the second part of the definition; while I am prepared to agree with him that the parties are hardly "associations" in the

usual sense, nevertheless the "partisans," as he calls the members, still demand both ideal and material benefits and advantages. These advantages, in the United States, are as scattered as the governmental authorities which dispense them.[9]

Max Weber used to emphasize the fact that parties rested upon "formally free recruiting," that is, that they allowed anyone to join up. Weber introduced this criterion to differentiate parties from aristocratic factions and the like. But since it is never practical for political science to deviate markedly from common usage, and since we are nowadays accustomed to speak of the Communist party in Russia, and so forth, it is no longer possible to insist upon that criterion of free admission. The distinction, however, is quite important. We may therefore say that parties either will allow free recruiting, and then may be called constitutional parties, or they will not, and then are autocratic. Constitutional parties are part of the functioning process of the constitution as a system of effective restraints. In England, the two-party system has been particularly important in this way. But what if there should be only one party, as in many American States? The expression "one party" is very deceptive. Actually, there are in effect two parties in such states. In Wisconsin, for example, there are progressive and conservative "Republicans." The same is true in many other states. As long as there is a constitution, and hence free recruiting of membership, this could not be otherwise.

Autocratic parties, on the other hand, constitute the organized following of an authoritarian group which has gained complete control of a government but which feels the need for large-scale popular support. If differences of opinion and clashes of loyalty occur in such a following, they cannot under such a government lead to the formation of new parties, and they therefore result in factional strife. Such factionalism is, of course, violently denounced by the preponderant group, and may be forcefully suppressed, as was done by Hitler in the course of the so-called *Purge* of June 1934. But these denunciations bring us back to our starting point, when, in the days of Cromwell, if not of Washington, parties generally were decried as factions.

Parties and factions · It is very common among political writers, after defining a political party, to remark that their definition historically fits many contending groups, such as the patricians and plebeians of Ancient Rome, the Guelfs and Ghibellines of the Middle Ages, and so forth, but to add that such groups had perhaps better be called factions.[10] Such vagueness is quite undesirable. If a definition does not distinguish a party from a faction, we must either hold the two to be identical in fact, or alter the definition so as to distinguish them.

Our definition of a party contains elements which suggest a clear-cut distinction between party and faction. In the first place, the requirement of stable organization is a distinguishing feature of a party. In the second place, the ideal benefits of which our definition speaks are, as we know from previous discussion, related to principles or ideals believed in and pursued as desirable objectives for the corporate body as a whole. It may often be difficult in actuality to determine whether a stably organized group pursues such objectives if there is no recognition of free speech by the group in power. But eventually, after a certain lapse of time, it will almost always be possible to answer this question one way or the other. Thus, both of the historical examples cited above must be admitted to have pursued such objectives. What gives them the character of factions is rather the absence of stable organization; for a group with scattered leadership, such as the Ghibellines, cannot be said to possess a stable organization.

Lowell's theory of political dispositions · In the concluding chapter of his *Public Opinion in War and Peace*,[11] A. Lawrence Lowell presents an essay on the changes in the disposition of men which will help us in painting the comparative panorama of European party politics. It will reveal the large measure of similarity between the party systems of various countries. Discarding an old classification of people into those desiring liberty and progress on one side and the defense of the established order on the other, Lowell suggests that people be divided into the contented and the discontented, and into those who are sanguine or not about possible changes. By combining any two of these traits, one finds four groups of people: those who are discontented with present conditions and sanguine about improvement, the radicals; those who are contented and sanguine, the liberals; those who are contented, but not hopeful of improvement, the conservatives; and finally those who are not content with existing conditions and at the same time see no prospect of better things to come, the reactionaries. A graphic representation of these divisions can be given thus:

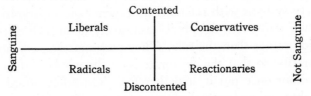

Then in considering the change from one of these dispositions to another, Lowell, following Röhmer, speaks of the tendency of men to run the cycle from radical to reactionary as they grow old. In the same connection he points out the rarity of persons changing from one disposition to another diagonally opposed, the reason being that two basic changes would be involved, that from content to discontent and from sanguinity to despondency, a combination which is not very likely to occur at the same time. Now, the combination and relative prevalence of these four dispositions is a matter of great importance concerning the politics (and the party structure) of various countries. For they determine both the stability of the order and the probability of change. If the people at large are represented as enclosed in a circle, four diagrams can be used to illustrate the results: Lowell believes that the first diagram represents the situation in England

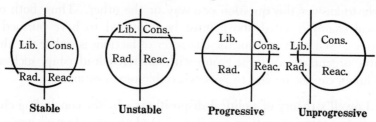

| Stable | Unstable | Progressive | Unprogressive |

from the reform of the House of Commons in 1832 to the First World War, while the second is characteristic of France from the fall of Napoleon until the stabilization of the Third Republic in 1889 (defeat of Boulanger). The second diagram was also strikingly true of the German situation between 1918 and 1933, and the French situation since the liberation. Since the surrender, the German situation resembles the first diagram, at least on the surface. Again, the United States illustrates the third diagram, but may shift to the fourth. While these observations regarding popular dispositions will aid us greatly in untangling the party developments in Europe, it would be quite wrong to identify political parties with such dispositions. As we shall see, some very important parties are built upon racial and religious cleavages.

Parties in relation to class structure · Racial and religious as well as social-class groupings of one sort or another suggest that it is not possible to analyze party systems with reference to psychological dispositions and attitudes alone. Party cleavages built exclusively upon such dispositions are the exception rather than the rule. They presuppose a very homogeneous social substratum so that the electorate is on the whole "fundamentally at one," as Balfour once put it, and therefore "can safely afford to bicker." It follows that an understanding of party systems really presupposes a thorough knowledge of the various layers of the social substratum, the class structure of society, if you please. The student of politics must go to school here with the sociologist and the social anthropologist and perhaps the geographer. We are just beginning to work out this background. Recently,

Stuart Rice offered some novel statistical approaches to the problem. In his justly celebrated *Political Panorama of the West of France* André Siegfried, originally a geographer, studied the problem in a limited region, district by district, seeking to discover interrelations between social and political party change.[12] But a clear correlation does not exist. The area which Professor Siegfried investigated is relatively static and conservative, yet Siegfried could not discover any definite correlation between changes in social structure and party development. Under conditions of highly dynamic flux, such as those of postwar Germany, the lack of correlation is even more marked. The rise of a party like the National Socialists is hard to account for in terms of any equivalent change in the class structure. Arguments based on the destruction of the German middle class are not entirely convincing. In Germany prior to the First World War, the shift in population was reflected in the rise of the Socialist party. In 1870 more than 50 per cent of Germany was rural; in 1914 less than 30 per cent lived in the country. After the First World War, the leaders of German socialism thought their party's postwar continuance and growth assured by this as well as by other factors. But National Socialism proceeded to crush these hopes by splitting the following of the Socialists wide open, detaching almost completely the artisans from the workers. By similarly breaking up the bourgeois alliance which had coalesced in opposition to the Socialists' ascendancy, and by detaching from the parties composing this alliance the small farmers and the lower commercial groups, shopkeepers, white-collar employees, officials, and so forth, the Nazis secured a following which believed in a pink socialism and a red-hot nationalism, a mixture better suited to the predispositions of these groups of people than either the antinationalism of the Socialists, or the antisocialism of the bourgeois parties of various shades. But while this party *change* cannot be entirely explained in terms of a *change* in the social substratum, an understanding of this substratum is essential for the understanding of party growth. Parties will, we have seen, appeal to men in terms of their ideal and material interests. Naturally, therefore, they will respond to the groupings among them. Churches, classes, and cultural (racial) and occupational groups are indubitably the most important such divisions amongst the electorate. Fortunately for the analyst, the nations with which we are here concerned show many similarities, enough, in fact, to enable us to treat them as if they had the same social structure. They all are industrialized. Hence they all have the division between capitalist, management, and labor. They have a technical intelligentsia, a middle class of engineers, lawyers, doctors, teachers, scientists, and officials. They have a farmer class which (outside the United States) is divided into big farmer-landowners, and peasants and farm workers. Their

423

traditional religion is Christianity, as divided into Catholics, Protestants, and various shades of agnostics. Besides these, they possess a certain number of Jews. The only grouping with regard to which they differ markedly from each other is national-cultural (racial) divisions, and these are static and hence more or less continuous in their impact.

Stress has been laid by certain writers upon the factor of *stratification*. We indicated in the last chapter how such stratification may explain the need for P. R. This stratification of the class "structure" is supposed to explain difficulties in the establishment of "democracy." In such simple terms, the proposition is untenable. Historical and comparative analysis shows that such stratification may actually be helpful to constitutional government. But political parties certainly bear a demonstrable relation to this stratification.

Conclusion · The general problems of the political parties, then, are threefold: the party's relation to the pattern of the government whose control the party seeks to secure; the relation between leader and followers; and the relation of the party to the social structure of the society in which it seeks to appeal for support. Through their leadership the parties establish and maintain the contact between the government and the people. In a democracy this contact is likely to be continuous and full of dramatic incident. The citizen seeks participation in communal affairs, and he achieves it through membership in a party. To recoil from entering the fray simply condemns the supercilious and the timid to sterile passivity. A man may well refuse to commit himself to either Republican or Democratic regularity if he feels that these are outworn labels and that the real division is between, say, conservatives and progressives. He should not avoid making up his mind and throwing in his weight, however small.

XXI

Political Parties: A Panorama of Their Comparative Development in Europe

Introduction · Liberal parties: their relation to conservatism · Liberal parties: the dissolvent of social reform · Liberal parties: the blind alley of nationalism · The Liberal party in Germany and Italy · Socialist parties before 1914 · The British Labour party · Socialism during the First World War and the beginnings of Communism · Communist parties · Socialist parties in power · The British Labour party as a minority government · The *Front Populaire* in France · Catholic parties, particularly in France · Catholic parties in Germany and other countries · Bonapartism, Fascism, National Socialism · The "restoration" of parties · Conclusion.

Introduction · The panorama of party development all over Europe, the comparative analysis of Liberal, Socialist, Catholic, and, finally, of Communist and Fascist parties, amply documents the generalizations of the preceding chapter. A full-length portrait would only be possible within the scope of an exhaustive history of Europe during the last hundred years. Recent historical researches have provided much material and some brilliant analyses. No general treatment could possibly rival the insight afforded by a careful study of E. L. Woodward, *The Age of Reform, 1850–1870,* or of R. C. K. Ensor, *England, 1870–1914.*[1] But there still seems to be a place for a rapid, thumbnail sketch of the high points as silhouetted against a systematic analysis. No separate treatment is given conservative parties in spite of the important role which they have played throughout. They will be referred to wherever opportunity arises. Conservatism shows very diverse forms in different countries and at different times, for it is by definition concerned with maintaining the existing order. It is primarily compounded of the groups and interests who happen to be "in possession," the "haves," the *beati possidentes.* Conservatives are content with things as they are, and inclined to believe that change will come gradually and the less done about it the better. A conservative in the United States is a constitutionalist, a conservative in prewar Britain was an Imperialist and a believer in parliamentary government under the Crown, a conservative in pre-1914 Germany was a monarchist. Sometimes, then, there will be no conservative party; only a very few people want to keep things as they are.

But in most countries and at most times there are enough such people to constitute a sizable group in the community. Hence the programmatic viewpoint, the ideal objectives of conservatives are variable in the extreme. By reversing the positions taken by the leading advocates of change, whether they be called Liberals, New Dealers, or Socialists, it is always possible to derive the position and the interests back of the respective conservative parties or groups.

The first comprehensive challenge to things as they were, by an orderly constitutional party, comes in the form of the Liberal party in England. This challenge presents phases which constitute the evolution of Liberal parties. In its first phase, the Liberal party forms an aggressive opposition to the traditional monarchical government; in England this occurred from 1680 down into the nineteenth century, and on the Continent since the French Revolution, or more explicitly, since the Napoleonic Wars. In its second phase, the Liberal party attempts to cope with the social problems raised by industrialization, but inasmuch as the more radical Socialist elements are becoming the effective opposition, the Liberal party begins to adopt a defensive attitude, and in so far as it does, it becomes conservative. In its third phase, the Liberal party gets embroiled in the conflicts engendered by the rising nationalism everywhere without being able to offer a clear-cut answer in terms of its own tenets, and therefore it breaks up into nationalist and internationalist factions. The acute crisis of the second phase is reached when socialism triumphs or at least supersedes liberalism as the main opposition, while the acute crisis of the third phase culminates in the Fascist dictatorship exterminating the Liberal along with all other parties.

Liberal parties: their relation to conservatism · There was *one* party in the English Parliament between 1600 and 1641, the party of opposition to the royal prerogative. A similar party developed toward the end of Charles II's reign, when Shaftesbury organized the "Green Ribbon Club," the nucleus of the Whig party organization. This "Country" party, as it was called in contrast to the "Court" party, was animated by hostility to the crown's subservience to France and its tendency to favor the Catholics. Foreign policy and religion, both rooted in strong national sentiments, provided its main arguments; the economic interests of the rising mercantile classes also were a powerful cement. That the rights of Parliament should have become another central tenet is only natural under the circumstances; the king being supposedly beyond reach, any effective opposition had to seek a strengthening of Parliament. If we remember that opposition to Catholicism was already to some extent opposition to orthodoxy, that the banner of toleration had been raised, and that deism and atheism had made their appearance, we are justified in saying that all tenets of orthodox liberalism except the doctrine of free competition were already implied in Whig doctrine, and the transition to the nineteenth century Liberal party was by no means such a break with the past as has occasionally been assumed in our time. The tenets of the Tory party were implied in the viewpoint of the Whigs; the Tories constituted essentially a reaffirmation of the traditional mode of life and thought. Thus, as against toleration, parliamentary rights, and mercantile interests, the Tories stood up for the Church of England, the royal prerogative, and landed interests. The Tory party was the party of squires and parsons. Essentially concerned with maintaining the existing order, English Toryism in the eighteenth century yet became a party of "Reform." The Whigs having put over the Hanoverian succession, and thereafter ruling England for decades under Walpole and Pelham, drifted so markedly into the position of the government, that the Tories lifted the banner of "reform." They did so, as we have seen, in the rather ineffectual manner of demanding that the "corruption" of the Whigs be remedied. Thus, even though the Tories insisted upon the rights of Parliament, they never adopted a position frankly demanding the change of existing institutions. As a result, the growing forces of public sentiment in favor of parliamentary reform tended to associate themselves with the Whig party, and by carrying their viewpoint to triumph in the great enactments of 1832, more fully treated in the next paragraph, they transformed the Whig into the Liberal party. All the way through, the mercantile interests had continued their association with the Whigs. For the great centers of industry and commerce were discriminated against by the then existing electoral districts (see above, ch. XV). A redistribution of parliamentary seats, so it seemed, would greatly increase the representation of these mercantile interests. The Tories could hardly be expected to foster such a scheme. But as a matter of fact, another problem was steadily coming to the fore, and by the time the Parliamentary Reform Act had become law, the Liberal party was beginning to face a dilemma touching the very foundations upon which its ideology was built. That was the social problem. Before entering upon this second phase of the evolution of Liberal parties, it may be mentioned in passing that nowhere except in Sweden had a party in the eighteenth century made its appearance which as closely resembled the later Liberals as the English Whigs. In France, Prussia, and the Hapsburg Dominions absolutist monarchy reigned supreme, and whatever enlightenment found expression in governmental policy did so through the benevolent despots ruling these lands. Frederick the Great, Joseph II, and Louis XVI were all profoundly influenced by certain basic tenets of liberal philosophy, such as toleration and the furtherance of trade and industry, but no parties corresponded to or supported these monarchical policies.

Liberal parties: the dissolvent of social reform · After the French Revolution and the Napoleonic wars, liberal parties appeared in almost all countries of Europe.[2] Often in collaboration with Free-masonry and other "enlightened" currents of the times, they advocated policies in the representative assemblies which bear a close resemblance to the major policies of the Whigs. In France, men like Benjamin Constant undertook to combat clericalism, royalism, and the landed interests, and when their opposition proved of no avail, staged another coup which, in 1830, placed a bourgeois king on the throne. The notorious words of this king, Louis Philippe, "Enrich yourselves," embody the doctrine of progressive industrialism which these dominant commercial classes preached to the "people." A similar situation prevailed elsewhere. In England the mercantile interests back of the Whigs had gradually, during the eighteenth century, become articulate. Their faith in individual initiative was closely linked with the desire to see the fetters removed which hindered the expansion of industrialism. These fetters at that period undoubtedly inhibited the teeming energies of industrialism. They were often denounced as feudal by writers at the time, but in fact they were of much later growth, in part the result of the stagnation of the artisan craft guilds, in part a natural outgrowth of the monarchical efforts to develop various manufacturing and other economic activities (see above, ch. V). But now the time was at hand when it seemed best to do away with all such restrictions, and the Liberals were voicing this demand. At the same time, new problems began to make their appearance which were closely related to this expansion of industrialism, the problems of the worker in industry. These problems called for effective restrictions of commercial and industrial activity rather than for *laissez faire*. As a consequence, the English Liberals, faced by an insistent wing of Radicals, found themselves obliged to enact legislation aiming at the reform of factory and laboring conditions. So apparent were the needs for change in this respect during the thirties of the last century that even a certain group of imaginative Conservatives, like the young Disraeli, sought to capture this field of reform and thus to push the Liberals out of the position of fostering the interests of the working man. But they were unable to detach the trade-union leader from the radical wing of the Liberal party. Bismarck made a similar effort in his struggle with the Socialists. His policies illustrate the dilemma into which continental Liberals had already drifted before the middle of the nineteenth century.

Unlike English Liberals, they found themselves confronted with the necessity of neglecting social reforms in their efforts to push forward the fight for constitutional representative government. Consequently, those who believed social reform more important, or at any rate more urgent, than parliamentary government, began to organize new parties, Workers', Labor, or Socialist parties, whose early aspirations culminated in the *Communist Manifesto*. Continental Liberals could not absorb the new forces as readily as could their English partisans. We have here a striking illustration of the importance of an already existing organization, like the English Whigs, seeking to win the support of as many concrete material interests as it possibly could. In the end, the English Liberals have proved to be as unable as their continental brethren to assimilate the interests of labor. The almost heroic intellectual efforts of thinkers from Bentham through John Stuart Mill to Hobhouse to interpret the various restrictions which a program of social reform entailed as part of real "liberty" have not been able to alter the fact that the dominant groups, to whose advantage a minimum of such restrictions undoubtedly redounds, have drifted away from the Liberal and into the Conservative party, while those seeking a realization of a maximum of such restrictions have found a program unencumbered by "bourgeois" subtleties more inspiring and have therefore flocked to the Labour party. Perhaps it could be argued that the Liberal party might have become the Social Reform party if its leaders had shown sufficient suppleness to abandon early enough the liberal political philosophy of "as little government as possible." Perhaps this is too much to ask; for while the transition from whiggism to liberalism was a gradual one, and implied no clear-cut rejection of one of the major tenets previously held, a complete turnabout would have been necessary to pass from liberalism to socialism. From this viewpoint, then, the rise of parties of social reform, replacing the liberal parties, or pushing them into the position of conservative parties, appears inevitable. Nor is it difficult to understand why it should have happened much earlier on the Continent than in England. Since Continental liberalism had not inherited any effective party organizations, nor any secure claim to recurrent participation in the government, it found itself readily rivaled by groups proclaiming radical social-reform programs. Not so the English Liberals. They, as we have seen, received the Whig legacy. It is quite possible that this long delay, in the course of which the Liberal party may be said to have acted as an incubator for the insurgent forces of socialism, has had the important effect of "liberalizing" the new elements sufficiently for these groups to preserve what remains of value in the older liberal creed. Evidently, the story of F. D. Roosevelt and the New Deal closely parallels the English pattern. It remains to be seen whether the Democrats can achieve what the English Liberals found impossible: to amalgamate Liberalism and Socialism. There are special conditions in the United States, suggested by the expression Progressivism, which may make this possible.

Liberal parties: the blind alley of nationalism · The English Whigs were animated by national sentiments from the very outset. Likewise, the French Liberals of the revolutionary period, like Mirabeau, objected to the monarchy partly on the ground that it endangered the national existence. Siéyès went further and actually identified the Third Estate with the nation.[3] Again, under the Restoration monarchy French Liberals were aggravated by the king's dependence upon foreign support, and it was indeed difficult to deny that Louis XVIII ruled by the grace of Metternich and Castlereagh. Humiliations in the field of foreign policy contributed their share to the overthrows of the restored French monarchy in 1830 and 1848; in 1870 actual defeat on the battlefield destroyed Napoleon III. The Liberal elements under Gambetta, who took over after Napoleon's collapse, were naturally animated by passionate patriotism. As a result, the Liberals of the Third French Republic remained rather outspoken nationalists to the end.

But to return to the French Revolution and its liberals, the Jacobins. Their nationalism was so ardent and all-engulfing that they identified their revolutionary doctrine with a French civilizing mission. This *mission civilizatrice* served as the basis for Napoleonic imperialism. But if the French Revolution proclaimed nationalism, the reaction abroad was not very slow in meeting the challenge. In England Whigs and Tories alike thundered against the atrocities of the hereditary enemy; the wholesale executions of noble families touched the very foundations of sentiment in aristocratic England. To be sure, radical clubs in England took up the revolutionary doctrines, but the public at large did not follow them, and general patriotic agitation did not subside until the Napoleonic Empire had been downed. This injection of fervent nationalism the English Liberals have never entirely outlived. The issue of Irish Home Rule squarely raised the problem of imperial control. When Gladstone decided to make Home Rule for Ireland a plank in the Liberal platform, some of the more nationalist elements in the Liberal party under the leadership of Chamberlain broke away, calling themselves Liberal Unionists. They were eventually absorbed by the Conservatives. When, in 1905, the Liberal party came back into power with a very large majority, the nationalists and imperialists had, however, once more gained the upper hand in the party, as the appointments of Sir Edward Grey and Lord Haldane to the Foreign Office and the

War Office showed. Haldane himself has told the impressive story of this Liberal clique's ascendancy, and of their determination to seek another showdown if the party should be unwilling to put them into power. In spite of very strong international sentiments in large groups of the Liberal following, an effective union of liberalism and nationalist imperialism remained part of the actual policy of the party. There was something anomalous in this position. Doctrinaire writers on liberalism usually try to minimize the significance of this factor. And yet, certain manifestations of expansive nationalism and imperialism are liberal rather than conservative. The Whig foreign policy from Pitt to Palmerston shows this clearly. The tendency of Conservatives to assume the imperialist position, particularly since Disraeli, is to be understood only if we see it as part of the Conservative party's trend toward the former Liberal position. This nationalist and imperialist implication of liberalism is quite understandable once we consider the material interests of the mercantile classes, which constituted such a large part of the Liberal following. It is these classes which profited most by the colossal colonial empire which afforded markets as well as raw-material resources. It is these classes, again, which were most embarrassed by the rise of any potential rival of truly competitive powers, such as the Napoleonic or the Bismarckian Empires. On the other hand, the laboring classes, which throughout the nineteenth century were inclined to support the radical wing of the Liberal party, and the leaders of this wing, animated by radically rationalistic and humanitarian views, had a strong predilection for peace and international solidarity. By wishing to make the Liberal the "Little England" party, they voiced the sentiments of large groups of this progressive electorate. After the Midlothian campaign in 1880, during which Gladstone violently attacked the methods of British imperialism in the Near East, and after the adoption of the Home Rule platform in 1886, the situation changed. The remaining nationalist and imperialist elements in the Liberal party leadership decided to keep the *arcana imperii*, the secrets of empire, that is, of foreign and colonial policy, out of popular discussion. Under Grey the whole gamut of imperialist foreign policy became veiled in mystery; the outer appearance of Liberal strength was being maintained by the leaders at the cost of deceiving their own following. The Liberal party, in the long run, was bound to be destroyed by such practices. If leading liberal historians admit today that a full and frank statement of Grey's policy would have led to the downfall of the ministry— an argument which has been advanced to excuse his failure to make such disclosures—they imply by such an admission that the conflict between nationalist and internationalist elements in the Liberal party had become irreconcilable. Tactics of equivocation will never solve the dilemmas of a party's ideal objectives. An attempt to do so has disastrous consequences, not only for the party itself, but for all the institutions which its power affects by such a fraud. The First World War and the speedy eclipse of the Liberal party afterward are only the most portentous results of this devious double-dealing. It was not only understandable but inevitable that many men of character should quit the Liberal and join the Labour party.

The Liberal party in Germany and Italy · If the English Liberal party was rent asunder by the explosives of modern nationalism and imperialism, it can hardly surprise us that the same development occurred in Germany and Italy. At the beginning of the nineteenth century national unification, the central goal of a nationally minded people, had not been achieved. Therefore, when liberalism got under way after the French Revolution, it adopted the founding of a free national government as a major plank. In Germany, this meant first of all the throwing off of Napoleon's foreign yoke, and after that was accomplished, opposition to the petty monarchical governments dividing Germany; in Italy, where a good part of the nation lived under Austrian dominion or within the Papal State and the remainder in small tyrannies controlled by the Hapsburgs, Liberals made opposition to the imperial rule of the Hapsburgs and to the international ambitions of the Papal State.[4] Since the Hapsburg Empire actively supported the petty German princes, German and Italian Liberals had one common enemy, Metternich, who ruled supreme in Austria until 1848. Since Metternich upheld the ideas of monarchical absolutism, Liberals used quite a conservative platform. In thus adapting themselves to the exigencies of the situation, the Liberal parties in these countries were finding themselves in a hopeless dilemma. Nothing illustrates this dilemma more strikingly than the ill-fated German National Parliament of 1848–1849. This assembly of brilliant and well-intentioned leaders foundered because it was confronted with the task of at once uniting and liberalizing the governments of Germany. Since unification remained the uppermost concern of the majority of Germans, the Parliament's failure to achieve it produced a setback from which German liberalism never recovered. When afterwards the methods of military force employed by Bismarck succeeded where the parliamentary methods of German Liberal parties had failed, it imbued large numbers of Germans with a lasting antiliberal bias. The National Liberals under the Empire consequently occupied the unenviable position of the dog which, while wagging its tail at the master, is being kicked about without mercy. Until the end, Bismarck treated them with studied contempt; yet they were the only group to raise their voices in protest against the veteran statesman's abrupt dismissal. Having learned nothing from past experience, these National Liberals, as they called themselves, later felt obliged to support the nationalist and imperialist policy of William II's chancellors, while another group, calling themselves Progressives, challenged this tradition and sought under the able leadership of Friedrich Naumann to discover new paths for a more international outlook. The division of Liberal party strength, which was none too considerable anyway, contributed its share to the puny role which this party was forced to play. After the First World War and the collapse of the Empire, the fatal division continued. The Democrats, successors to the Progressives, collaborated with the Socialists in building a republican government, while the so-called People's party, which had taken over the legacy of the National Liberals, joined forces with the reactionaries, the German Nationalists. Gustav Stresemann, the able leader of the People's Party, and Briand, the architect of the Locarno treaties, sought leftist connections after 1924 in order to support international policies. But these efforts proved merely an Indian-summer interlude before the eclipse of German liberalism. The superhuman efforts of Stresemann to hold together the coalition backing his policy were in a sense necessitated by the earlier failure of German liberalism to find a solution for the dilemma which nationalism had posited. Perhaps there was no solution; at any rate, the decomposition of German Liberal parties was almost complete before they ever had a chance to show what they might have done for the country.

In Italy the development was similar, yet different. Here nationalist liberalism triumphed completely under the brilliant leadership of Mazzini and Cavour and solved constructively the twofold problems of national unity and free constitutional government. Nowhere has the Liberal party had a more successful or a more brilliant record. What then can account for the complete eclipse of Italian liberalism in the twenties? The Fascists who destroyed the Italian Liberal parties came to the fore as an opposition to the Socialists and Communists. The rise of these latter was inevitable, once the problems of social reform became clearly visible. The industrialization of Italy brought them to a head in that country as elsewhere. Mazzini's early dream of combining liberalism and socialism did not come true any more than that of his English friends in the radical wing of the Liberal party. The Italian Labor Movement soon was carried away, first by the anarchism of Bakunin, and later by Marx's doctrine of the class war.

Socialist parties before 1914 · If the story of Liberal parties begins with England and ends with Germany, the situation is reversed when we come to socialism. The reasons for this situation are implicit in the history of Liberal parties.[5] It seems at first sight as if the strength of the Liberal party in each country between 1848 and 1914 stood in inverse proportion to the growth of an organized Socialist party. Where the Liberal party did not fulfill the function of an effective opposition, the Socialists pushed forward to take their place. But of course the Liberals also were not an effective opposition where they more or less dominated the government, as in Italy. This destroys the validity of the impression first gained; if the, Liberal party is very strong, the Socialists also grow rapidly. This seems to suggest that the growth of the Socialist parties is dependent upon whether they represent the most clear-cut alternative to the party in power. Whether this party is Conservative or Liberal does not seem to matter. This fact is explainable in terms of our second hypothesis, according to which a party requires for its growth valid ideals as well as material objectives. What were these ideals of the Socialist parties? They addressed themselves to the solution of the social problems raised by industrialism, proclaiming them more important than any other matter within the purview of politics. Religion, foreign policy, constitutional government, all these can wait until the pressing needs of industrial society have been successfully met. The great dogmatic thinkers of this new creed, like Karl Marx, theoretically justified this subordination of all other issues to the social problem by insisting that the problems of religion, foreign policy, or government were all rooted in the social problem, were in reality an outgrowth of the conflict of social classes. The state was proclaimed to be an instrument for the exploitation of one class by another. Such a position would naturally find its most ardent supporters among the groups who suffered most under the industrial system, the factory workers.

Both in France and in Germany (as well as in other continental countries), the first beginnings of parties with programs taking some or all of these positions got under way in the thirties of the last century. In Germany the organizations of journeymen under Weitling and others became the incubators of socialist thought, whereas in France original thought along socialist lines had been growing in intellectual circles. This earlier theoretical interest in socialism initiated the "splintering" of French socialism. The situation was further complicated by the fact that several Socialist thinkers, notably Fourier and Proudhon, were anarchists. The German movement, on the other hand, was primarily practical and concerned with the needs of the workers. But neither in France nor in Germany do we, as yet, find durable organizations. To be sure, the Revolution of 1848 brought a certain number of socialist leaders to the fore. In France three such men participated in the provisional government following the February Revolution. Their insistence upon the social problem helped to frighten the bourgeoisie into later accepting the dictatorship of Napoleon III. In

Germany, where they had some voice in the liberal Frankfurt Parliament and in the Prussian revolutionary assembly, the Socialists were not as yet strong enough to do more than weaken, as in France, the liberal cause in the eyes of the propertied classes. It was only after the reaction to these revolutionary upheavals had spent itself that genuine parties of socialist outlook got under way, in the early sixties in Germany, in the late seventies in France. Ferdinand Lassalle in 1863 founded the General German Workingmen's Association, the first organized German Labor party. It was out of this party that the German Social Democratic party developed. Until Geman unification was accomplished, the German Socialists were much divided by the question as to whether to include or exclude the Hapsburg Empire in a united Germany. This question mattered greatly to German workers, since their party from the beginning expected the solution of the social question from the state. The political philosophy of Hegel, that quaint mixture of ideas derived from Rousseau, the Greek city-state, and Prussian bureaucracy, animated Lassalle even more than Karl Marx. Although materialist ideas gradually permeated the German Socialist party, idealist and nationalist ideas always retained a certain influence among German Socialists.

In France orthodox Marxists remained a minority, yet state action similarly occupied the foreground of attention among Socialists. During the German siege of Paris in 1871, the most radical elements of the movement, together with a group of bourgeois Radicals, seized power and tried to organize popular resistance to the enemy by instituting a communist regime. The inevitable collapse of this ill-considered move cast a shadow over French socialism, and prevented party organization until 1876, when Jean-Joseph Barberet got together a National Labor Congress which endorsed his mild reformist program for trade unions, stressing technical education, the creation of employment bureaus, the establishment of cooperative bureaus and mutual aid. But as early as 1879 leadership had passed to the revolutionary elements led by Jules Guesde. At the Congress of Marseilles in that year Guesde declared that the collectivization of all the instruments of production should be pursued by all available means. This radical collectivist position was associated with a deep distrust of any kind of collaboration with existing bourgeois parties, and with an insistence that the only possible way to realize the goal was a social revolution. Guesde was admittedly and dogmatically Marxist and remained so to the end of his life. The struggle between his followers and those who, like Paul Brousse, believed in the possibility of co-operation with liberal and progressive bourgeois elements (therefore called *possibilistes*) continued throughout the party's prewar life. When Millerand entered the cabinet of Waldeck-

Rousseau (1899), the party split wide open over the issue of whether or not ministerial participation of a Socialist could be condoned, but reunion was effected in 1905. These internecine struggles were part of another peculiarity of the French Socialist party, its continuous controversies with the trade unions. Unlike trade unions in other countries, the trade unions in France were the more radical elements of the socialist movement. Jules Guesde's influence was most securely anchored here. With France a parliamentary republic, it was natural that members of a political party should be tempted by participation in the government, particularly those sitting in parliament. But the trade-union elements, made suspicious by the repeated "treason of intellectuals" who had used the workers' support as a stepping stone for a political career, followed those who, like Guesde, preached revolution of the proletariat as the only means of seizing power permanently preliminary to inaugurating an all-round collectivism. Thus it may be said that the Socialist party did not really seek power within the existing government, but rather the overthrow of it. In terms of our definition, the French Socialist party leaned toward totalitarian views; it was not thoroughly "constitutional" at that time. There was, however, another group of people organized as a powerful party seeking to realize certain measures of social reform, the Radical Socialists. This party, in spite of its name, was not socialist in any strict sense of the word. It was radically progressive and democratic, and was widely supported by the small shopkeepers, artisans, and farmers. Since industry played a minor role in France, this party continued to hold its own against the Socialist party, really the party of the industrial workers. However, so strong was the impact of the forces behind the Radical Socialist party that the French Socialist party, in contrast to its German counterpart, sought and in some measure found a bridge to small farmers and artisans. This was essentially the work of Jean Jaurès, a brilliant leader who was assassinated at the outbreak of the First World War. Jaurès deduced his socialism from democratic ideas. The socialization of capitalist property he held to follow logically from democratic equality. As a result, the property worked by one's own hands, such as the workshop of the artisan and the farms of the smaller peasantry, are beyond collectivization and will be preserved in the social democracy which is dawning. This kind of stand is radically at variance with orthodox Marxist views. Consequently it had a following in Germany only among the left-wing Catholics, the Christian trade unions, and some of the bourgeois progressives.

The German Social Democratic party was dogmatically Marxist, although after the Congress of Gotha (1875) the democratic reformist "interpretation" of Marx became dominant in guiding the political conduct of the party. The rapid growth of the party (1871: 102,000 votes; 1874: 352,000; 1877: 493,000) created consternation among the conservative elements, just the same, and when in 1878 two attempts were made upon the life of the aged Emperor, William I, Bismarck secured the passage of the so-called "Laws against Socialists." Under these laws, the government could prohibit associations which through social-democratic, socialist, or communist tendencies seemed to aim at the overthrow of the existing political and social order; it could also prohibit papers and books advocating these views. Moreover, the government could, after declaring an emergency, deport socialist "agitators." The penalties under this law were very severe, the possibilities of arbitrary action considerable. These laws were in existence until 1890 and they influenced the development of the German Social Democratic party deeply. Liberal writers have felt that it thwarted the party's natural development toward a constructive attitude; it strengthened the revolutionary drift in the party councils. Socialist radicals, on the other hand, have repeatedly pointed out that these laws prevented effective criticism from the rank and file, thus strengthening boss rule and bureaucracy in the party. As the leaders grew old, this stratification of the party opened the doors wide to bourgeois reformist tendencies. The writers representing these reformist trends emphasize that the re-interpretation of Karl Marx in an evolutionary sense occurred in this period. Significantly, Karl Marx's scathing criticism of the program of Gotha was withheld by the party leaders until 1891. Whatever the merit of these observations, the progress of the German Socialist party was delayed only temporarily by Bismarck's measures. After their inglorious abandonment, the growth of the party resumed its rapid progress. In the election of 1890 they secured 1,427,300 votes, in 1903, 3,010,800, and in 1912 they reached 4,250,400, thus being the largest party in the German parliament, a position which they retained until the advent of Hitler in 1933. As remarked before, the Social Democrats were *the* party of effective opposition and social reform. They, too, like their French brethren, demanded basic changes in the form of government, being avowed republicans and antifederalists; before the outbreak of the First World War, they could justly entertain the hope of capturing an actual majority and of then forcing the adoption of parliamentary government. No one can tell whether these hopes would have been shattered, as were those of the Prussian Liberals in the sixties, by the government's adopting a dictatorship such as that which Bismarck had assumed in the earlier conflict. If such a conflict was looming, its outbreak was forestalled by the First World War. Some writers have held that the German government's readiness to enter the war was the result of their seeing it as a way out of the impending social conflict. It cannot be doubted that there were people in influential quarters who justified to themselves the going to war by the rising power of the masses and their threatening conquest of the government; how far such views can be taken to explain the position of the government is a difficult question. It is beyond controversy that the policies of parties and governments in pre-1914 Germany were profoundly affected by the rise of the Social Democratic party.

The British Labour party · The rise of the British Labour party raises very special problems. It has been pointed out before that the English Liberal party throughout the nineteenth century was successful in absorbing the elements interested in radical social reform. Particularly after Karl Marx's abortive efforts to organize a *Workingmen's International* (1866 and after) and the ill-fated experiment of the Paris Commune which Marx had had endorsed by the *International* (1871), English trade-union leaders remained attached to the Liberal party. They strengthened the Liberals' "radical" wing, though from a Socialist viewpoint their attitude was obviously very "conservative." But English liberalism could only with subtle dialectics manage to foster such more advanced social reform programs. Such dialectics did not appeal to the laboring masses. It also seemed pale when subjected to the searchlight of radical analysis, such as the theorists of the Independent Labour party (organized 1893) and of the Fabian Society (organized 1884) were inclined to focus upon the liberal doctrines. The Fabians, emulating the tactics of *Fabius Cunctator* after the battle of *Cannae*, admittedly wished to go slowly; they resembled the French *possibilistes* in their belief in democratic, parliamentary government. But they held the central aims of social reform to be incompatible with the policies of a party directly descending from Manchesterian free-competition liberalism. Constant contact with Continental Socialists, many of them the leaders of powerful parliamentary parties, who were working through a revived *International* for the pacific parliamentary conquest of power in other highly industrialized countries strengthened the theoretical conviction of these radicals that England must have a Labour party too. The most prominent persons in this group were Ramsay MacDonald, Sidney and Beatrice Webb, Bernard Shaw, and H. G. Wells. Their outlook was not dogmatically Marxist, but rather akin to that of Jean Jaurès. In the pre-First World War period, although they did not found the Independent Labour party, they succeeded in permeating this party with their views. The party began to play an increasingly important role, particularly in local government. In Parliament it was not strong enough to pursue a very independent course. In the election of 1905 Labour won twenty-nine seats, in the two elections of 1910, forty and forty-two respectively. The Labour Party generally supported the Liberal party, though in debates on foreign policy Labour tended to assume a strongly critical attitude toward the imperialist group in the Liberal party. During the war, Arthur Henderson and the more patriotic trade-union members supported the government, and "Uncle Arthur" actually entered the cabinet. But the radical group, notably Ramsay MacDonald, steadfastly refused to collaborate. They thus provided the ferment which later led to the break between Henderson and the government. These episodes indicate, in all their complexity, the ideal and practical conflict between national and international labor interests which became the touchstone of socialism in the period after the First World War.

Socialism during the First World War and the beginnings of Communism · Like the English, the French government during the First World War attempted to secure Socialist support. The gloomy specter of the murdered Jaurès plus the imminence of national catastrophe, as symbolized by the invasion of France, combined to persuade even very radical French Socialists to support the Tricolor. Not many of them did it, however, in such poor taste as one Gustave Hervé who, having harassed French Socialists before 1914 with his pacifist extremism (he advocated a general strike at the outbreak of a war), rebaptized his newspaper, *La Guerre Sociale*, called it *La Victoire*, and joined the front rank of extreme chauvinists. Most of the Socialists sadly persuaded themselves that the bourgeois Republic's fight had to be supported, because it was, after all, France that was being invaded, and their friends, the German Socialists, seemed ready to support what appeared to French Socialists rank imperialist aggression. There were, however, some stout souls in France as in England, men and women who took their lead not from what others did, but from what they themselves believed in. The same was true in Germany. The majority of Social Democrats, confronted with the imperial oratory of: "I know no more parties, I know only Germans" (August 4, 1914) considered that they were Germans first, and Socialists and pacifists afterwards, and voted war credits. For in Germany it was "of course" no question of entering the cabinet. But the matter of war credits was crucial and so was service in the army. But there were others, a small minority, with Liebknecht at their head, who saw things in another light. Avowed Marxists, they did not care about the destruction of the bourgeois government. The German people would remain. The specter of Russian Czardom did not frighten them. Lenin and Trotsky would finish that in course of time. On all fronts, the battle of an uncompromising struggle must be waged against the established authorities, their prestige undermined at home and abroad, their power destroyed. To the men fighting this battle, it did not matter much who lost the war. Whoever it was would see the triumph of Marxist socialism, the dictatorship of the proletariat, and the establishment of the classless society. These fervent views could not be squelched by throwing Liebknecht and his friends into jail; there were others to carry on the struggle. It was this group of small minority leaders in France, in Germany, in Russia, in Italy, who during the war came together in secret conclave in Switzerland to agree upon a common strategy for the overthrow of the capitalism which had brought on this terrible slaughter.

The break between majority and minority Socialists in France, in Germany, and in other continental countries during the First World War marks the birth—or if one accepts their own ideology, the rebirth—of militantly internationalist communism such as Karl Marx had dreamed of in the days of the First International. Bourderon, Cachin, and their friends in France, Liebknecht, Rosa Luxemburg, and those who after their death carried on in Germany, and above all Lenin and Trotsky, constituted the group around which the Third International eventually emerged.[6]

The process of disintegration of the united front of industrial labor which had been built up before the war was a slow one. The turning point came with the Russian Revolution and the Stockholm Conference in 1917. Originally this conference was to unite Socialists of all shades of opinion in an effort to stop the war. Radical ideas were spreading rapidly through the war-weary ranks of labor throughout Europe. But the allied governments professed to see in the conference a plot of "Prussian" socialism, a super-Machiavellian move of Imperial Germany. Samuel Gompers, a lifelong foe of socialism, obligingly provided the entering wedge by refusing to have American labor represented at the conference. England, France, and Italy refused passports. The urgent request of the more moderate Russian Socialists to allow the conference to take place proved of no avail. "Uncle Arthur" Henderson, sent to Russia to investigate, came back a supporter of the Russian viewpoint; his advice was disregarded; he quit the cabinet; the war went on; the radical Bolsheviks in Russia gained the upper hand with their cry of "Bread and Peace." It is not too much to say that these fatal blunders of the allied governments materially contributed to the victory of militant communism.

Communist parties · The First World War acted as the incubator of communism as we speak of it today; not a theory, but a stern reality of a new managerial bureaucracy where the managers of great industrial and agricultural production units direct masses of serfs in accordance with what the bureaucrats at the top consider best. The new "International" became permanently located in Moscow, the capital of one of the world's great empires. The Third International carried on a militant policy of stirring up revolutionary unrest wherever it suited Stalin's diplomacy. In this work it was backed by the vast physical power of the Soviet Union, although the Soviet government recurrently washed its hands of the business and finally dissolved the International when, as one of the "democracies" fighting for the Four Freedoms and the Atlantic Charter (signed by the Soviet Union in 1944), it no longer fitted the Soviet Union's role. Since the revival of the world-revolutionary policy of the Soviet Union, the International has reappeared in a new guise, the *Cominform*, or Communist Information Bureau. This situation contrasts profoundly with the internationalism of Socialist parties before the First World War, which consisted largely of periodic conventions meeting in different cities of Europe (Brussels, Amsterdam, Copenhagen, Stuttgart) and discussing resolutions which might express the sentiment of Socialists throughout the world. After 1919, most of their practical work was taken over by the International Labor Office in Geneva.

The Communist parties which sprang up all over the world after 1918 were from the beginning to some degree dependent upon the center of Communist power in Moscow. But for some time, while Lenin and Stalin consolidated their control over the Soviet Union, these parties retained a measure of autonomy. In some countries, where they actually triumphed, as in Hungary and Bavaria, their ascendancy was short-lived. Several attempts to radicalize the German masses in 1918–1919 and in 1923 also miscarried. Thereafter, for twenty years, the Communist parties worked to undermine the existing governmental systems and spearheaded the anti-Fascist underground. Since they were the only parties which received a substantial measure of outside support, they were enabled to play a leading role in such situations. Alongside with such anti-Fascist activities, however, in Italy, Hungary, Spain and Germany, went a readiness to make common cause with the Fascists, or at any rate not to resist them whenever the strategy of world Communism deemed it appropriate. Thus the Communists helped to undermine the Weimar Republic's tenuous fabric and contributed to its downfall, and again the Communists failed to support the French Republic when assaulted by the Nazi armies, presumably because of the Soviet's deal with Hitler. This deal itself, made at the expense of Poland in August 1939, brought forth startling turnabouts in the Communist parties of many countries which had previously been lambasting the Hitler regime.

The question may well be raised whether organizations which are to such an extent dependent upon a foreign power are parties in the democratic sense. At times, as in Switzerland and in some American states, the Communists have therefore been outlawed. They certainly fail to show one typical feature of democratic parties discussed above: formally free recruiting. Candidates for party membership are not only very carefully screened, but purges are at times carried out. However, the British Labour party and the German Social Democrats, as well as other parties, have at times engaged in such practices. A proposal to outlaw certain practices believed to be typical of Communist parties, such as foreign financial support, while presumably sound, would probably not change the situation materially.

Electoral support for Communist parties varies considerably from country to country. While very weak in the United States, Britain, and the Dominions, they commanded almost a third of the votes in France and Italy after the Second World War and continue to receive about a quarter of the votes. In Germany and Austria Communist strength has waned, after reaching almost 20 per cent before 1933, and after 1945. In the elections of August 1949, the Communists only received about 8 per cent of the votes in Western Germany and prevailing estimates suggest that their true strength in Eastern Germany is not much greater. In Austria, in October 1949, the Communists polled 41 per cent of the votes. Generally speaking, it may be said that the Communists have become increasingly suspect as to their national loyalty under the impact of the "cold war," since they have been uniformly found to be supporting the policies advocated by the Soviet Union, regardless of the implications for the country whose electorate they are appealing to.

Suspicions of the Communist parties have also deepened as a result of the methods employed by them in securing power in the Central and Eastern European belt of satellites, more especially Poland, Czechoslovakia, Hungary, Yugoslavia, and Rumania. These countries have all experienced "seizures of power" by the Communist parties, constituting limited minorities but employing violence in order to achieve their revolutionary aims. These spectacles have strengthened the general impression that Communist parties are dangerously subversive as they practice what they preach: class war and revolution as the *Communist Manifesto* of 1847 demanded. These events are in sharp contrast to the efforts of the Socialist parties which have made every effort to retain and indeed to strengthen constitutional democracy in the various countries. These efforts deserve separate treatment, since they have vitally affected the development of Socialist parties. Confronted with a ruthless and totalitarian opposition from the Communists, the Socialist parties have found themselves in a much more difficult position than had been assumed by them.

Socialist parties in power · The collapse of the central empires carried the moderate Socialist parties into power along a considerable front. Before the fall of 1918 the Socialists had already taken over the government in Sweden. The German revolution of November 1918, initiated as it was by the radical and communist elements, miscarried; the moderate Social Democrats were able to maintain themselves in power with the effective support of what was left of the German army.[7] The frightened bourgeois element came to their support also. The Social Democrats, while holding the communist uprisings at bay, thus could combine with left-wing reformist groups and the Catholic Center party to form the "Weimar Coalition." For the constitutional convention had been convened at Weimar in a half-hearted attempt to rally to its support the spirit of Goethe and Schiller, at the same time removing the convention from the pressure of the street fighting which was going on in Berlin. Similar activities were being carried on all over Europe, in Austria, in the several succession states, in Poland. Everywhere moderate socialism proceeded to establish lengthy constitutions embodying mild provisions which looked toward the realization of a socialized community, but establishing them only with much caution and after constant consultation with the existing administrative staffs, their experts and specialists. These measures seemed rather pale in comparison with the red-hot dictatorship of the proletariat which was being forged in Russia. Throughout this period the Social Democrats were harassed by their communist opponents for being traitors to the workers' cause, and ridiculed for their pusillanimity and readiness to compromise with the "bourgeoisie." Unfortunately, a certain measure of patronage and corruption crept into governmental activities along with this extension of party control. In ever-repeated harangues the workers were reminded by antidemocratic elements, Fascists and communists alike, of the various "failures" of the Socialists, their failure to nationalize even the key industries (railroads had been governmentally owned and operated in Europe before 1914), their failure to tax big business, their failure to bring about real peace in the international sphere, and so forth. The tendency of parties to espouse lofty rectitude in matters of principle while out of office (see above, pp. 414 ff.) worked in this instance with particular vehemence, because the Marxist movement is cast in strongly dogmatic terms anyway. It was not very long before the Socialists lost control of the government. Having instituted proportional representation, they lost in the elections to the communists as well as to the Leftist bourgeois forces. Their recurrent participation in the government on a coalition basis (in Prussia during the entire period from 1919 to 1932) obliged them increasingly to seek protection of their interests with the aid of the accepted methods of parliamentary politics:

compromise in principle, compensation in the shape of offices for the party bureaucracy. In Germany as well as in other countries this state of affairs produced a stratification of the party itself. The old leaders, monopolizing the party caucus and the conventions, forced the party to move according to the tactical considerations of coalition needs, backed by the older workers who had grown cautious and disillusioned in the service of the party. Recurrent movements among the younger elements to stage an overthrow of this hierarchy met with defeat; the brilliant group of "Young Socialists" could not secure enough influence to inject new vigor into the general outlook of the party. In the foreign-relations field the party pursued a policy of national reconstruction, but kept on talking as if they were of the same mind as Moscow; no effort to reconstruct party ideology in terms of the actual new policy succeeded. This conflict between word and deed served as a constant basis of attack, the communists denouncing the Social-Democrats as betraying the German worker to Western "Big Capitalism," the Nazis railing at the old Marxist ideology of internationalism as an irrefutable proof of the unpatriotic attitude of Social Democracy. The party possessed many good men who did their best to remodel Germany along lines which would have given her a decent popular, if not a socialist, government and who proved competent administrators when confronted with specific tasks. But the party lacked really brilliant leadership. Not a single genuinely great man appeared amongst them. Friedrich Ebert, the Republic's first president, comes nearest genuine stature as a statesman, and both Loebe and Severing were men of high moral caliber, but Social Democracy did not provide the names which shine in the annals of the Weimar Republic. The absence of really prominent leaders is a rather difficult thing to explain; it seems highly improbable that the human material was not there in view of the large size of the party. One encountered men with the making of really remarkable leaders, but they were thwarted by the bureaucratic machinery of this highly organized party. The power of the organization, developed in prewar days in response to the difficult position in which the party found itself under the imperial government, proved its undoing.

A rather unusual situation developed in Austria. Here supporters of the various strands of socialism remained a compact party, pledged to the revolutionary principles of orthodox Marxism. At the same time, the able leaders of Austrian Marxism refused to associate themselves with the communist Third International. They decided to play their own little fiddle, and their ventures into international action were dubbed the two-and-one-half International. Within the small rump of German-speaking Austria which was left over after the disintegration of the Hapsburg Empire, the Socialists at first had a clear majority and could establish a thoroughly social-democratic constitution to suit themselves. Hans Kelsen played a prominent part in this work. But no constitution could have halted the economic collapse resulting from the dismemberment of Vienna's economic *Hinterland*, and the Socialists had to bear the brunt of the blame and rapidly lost their hold upon the government, except in Vienna. In this large and beautiful city and its many industrial suburbs the Socialist power was solidly anchored in the industrial masses. There consequently developed a rather clear-cut antagonism between the progressive, socialist metropolis and the conservative, Catholic countryside.

The British Labour party as a minority government · In France and England, whose governments emerged victorious from the First World War, the course of development has been rather different from that in Central Europe. After their severe defeat in the Khaki elections of 1919 the British Labour party staged a brilliant comeback on December 6, 1923, when they were returned as the second largest party in Parliament, though without a majority. They then decided to take over the government with the support of the Liberals in Parliament. The wisdom of this decision, which was in keeping with English parliamentary traditions, has been questioned in the light of later developments. As Asquith observed: "You cannot achieve legislation on an heroic scale . . . when you are in a permanent minority in this House . . . and when, in consequence of that, you are denuded of . . . the power of taking the time of the House, moving the Closure, and of regulating its proceedings in accordance with your wishes."[8] The weakness of such a minority government was strikingly illustrated by the troubles of the Labour party in 1924. "The present Government again and again have said that they stand in a peculiar position because they do not command a majority in this House." It was particularly unfortunate for the Labour party to take over the government under such conditions, because they were pledged to extensive social reforms which were violently opposed by Liberals and Conservatives alike. The very essence of their party outlook was bound up in these reforms, like the nationalization of the coal industry, for example. But the Labour party fell because of their Russian policy. It was a matter of course that the Labour party should seek the recognition of the Soviet Union and the establishment of effective trade relations with this socialist republic. In the matter of recognition they were supported by the Liberals, but difficulties soon developed. What was worse, the cautious course indicated by their difficult position in Parliament (192 Labourites with the (uncertain) support of 159 Liberals, against 258 Conservatives) created internal conflicts. In a different context, and in different form, we have here the same conflict as in Central Europe and more particularly in Germany after the war. To be sure, the radical wing did not split off into a Communist party. But the insurgent left-wing Labourites were able to force the dropping of one governmental measure, the prosecution of Campbell, a Communist writer, and the adoption of another measure, the signing of the Russian Trade Treaty. The very rigidity of party principles characteristic of Socialist parties enhances the probability of sharp doctrinal conflicts and consequent breakups. When the regular party has only a minority behind it, it cannot effectively deal with disaffected individuals or groups within its own ranks.

The difficulties which the British Labour party had encountered when trying to govern with a minority did not dissuade its leaders from trying again when, after the elections of 1929, they were returned with a following slightly larger than the Conservatives (Labour 288, Conservatives 260, Liberals 59, Independents 8); they again decided to take over the government, this time with the compelling argument that the losses of the Conservatives had largely been their gain, and that parliamentary precedent compelled their "assuming responsibility." This in spite of the fact that Liberals and Conservatives were moving closer together. The government's difficulties began at once with the debate on the Address to the Throne. Stanley Baldwin, as leader of the opposition, pointed out: "The Government is a minority Government and, therefore, the House of Commons as a whole has its rights. . . . Nevertheless," he added, "it is . . . essential for the Empire, that we face the world as a united Parliament." At once the government found itself thwarted in its desire to secure the procedural aids which precedence for the government's business affords (see ch. XVII, pp. 327 ff.). Only after a very lengthy debate could it get the Address to the Throne through, and in the divisions it had to rely now on support from the Liberals, now on that from the Conservatives. Without going into the tortuous history of the Labour party's ministerial fortunes, it may summarily be stated that things went the same way they had in 1924. Cautious governmental maneuvering aroused a spirit of defiant opposition in the more radical circles of the party. This insurgent attitude was intensified by the economic difficulties centering around the maintenance of the pound and the unemployment insurance which was sapping the financial strength of the country with ever-mounting payments to be made. The great debate on the Unemployment Insurance Bill No. 3, in July 1931, foreshadowed the conflicts which brought about the disintegration of the cabinet, its resignation, and the great defeat of the party in the ensuing elections (after the government of national coalition had been formed by MacDonald). It took the British Labour Party thirteen years of vigorous effort to recover from the shock of this internal conflict and subsequent electoral defeat, though it should be noted that its loss in votes was much less considerable than the number of parliamentary seats would indicate. This was due to the vagaries of simple majority elections.

The *Front Populaire* in France. In France, the Socialists for a long time stood aloof. Under the leadership of Léon Blum they refused to enter into coalition with bourgeois governments, although they lent considerable support to the Herriot ministry in 1924, particularly to its policy of reconciliation with Germany. French Socialists long debated the question of coalition. As already noted, Millerand's entry into the cabinet of Waldeck-Rousseau in the early 1900's actually provoked a break in the party which was only healed in 1905. A resolution forbidding a Socialist to become a minister was adopted. Small groups calling themselves Socialists, such as Aristide Briand and his following, pursued a different course. However, only with the election of 1936 did the orthodox Socialists abandon this policy, take over the government, and start what became known as *l'expériment Blum*, a belated, ill-considered attempt at social reforms in the face of the threatening international situation. They found themselves confronted, of course, with some of the same troubles against which their German and English comrades had battled before them. But these troubles were greatly enhanced and in some respects basically altered on account of the threat of the Axis. This threat seemed to suggest a coalition with the Soviet Union; the Socialists seemed well-qualified to cement such coalition. But events proved that the masters at the Kremlin were as ready to discredit the French Socialists as they had been to discredit the English and German ones. Hence the Blum government, hindered by coalition and compromise with bourgeois liberals, harassed by radical agitation and communist opposition, was hard put to it to maintain governmental prestige. Paul Reynaud, one of the few conservatives willing to form a national-union cabinet with Blum after the seizure of Austria by Hitler, remarked pointedly: "We cannot fight Hitler with the two-Sunday week."[9] The Socialists were caught between the Scylla of external pressure from Hitler and the Charybdis of internal pressure from the communists. Like the German socialists, they were being crushed between the upper millstone of nationalist militarism and the lower millstone of industrial strife, loosed by a policy of half-hearted reforms. Even superb leadership could not have succeeded under such conditions. After the Blum cabinet was overthrown, the reaction under Daladier and Reynaud dismantled step by step, first haltingly, finally with brutal swiftness, the "reforms" which the Socialists had initiated. In November 1938, after the surrender at Munich, when the government by emergency decree abolished the 40-hour week, the once-powerful General Federation of Labor declared a general strike which quickly collapsed. Although they knew that they could not succeed, once again and for the last time the Socialist leaders yielded to radical pressure, only to be denounced by the communists for their failure afterwards. *La Front Populaire* had become a term of derision.

Catholic parties, particularly in France · The alliance between Catholic-Conservative and Fascist-Royalist elements in France raises the general issue of the role of political Catholicism.[10] In many countries, particularly those with proportional representation, Catholic parties have played an important role. It is, therefore, necessary briefly to examine their background and compare their position in various lands. Like the socialism back of various parties of workers, Catholicism is an elaborate creed, a philosophy of life, and transcends all national boundaries. Indeed, as everyone knows, Catholicism has an international organization of wide ramifications, older and more tradition-bound than any of the governments of present-day Europe. It is a heritage from an age when no national governments were in existence. Those who are strongly attached to this creed are almost bound to carry their convictions into politics. But whereas in the United States the impact of Catholicism upon politics has until lately been local and indirect, the peculiar conditions of European politics have led to the formation of Catholic parties, particularly where the Catholics have constituted a numerous minority, or a bare majority.

The formation of parties upon the foundation of the Catholic faith is conceivable in two ways, ideally speaking. Since the Catholic faith espouses an active ethic, it maintains a very definite belief about the end of all government as an aid toward man's ultimate end: the salvation of his soul. But there is also the more practical proposition of fighting for greater freedom and independence of the church whenever the government attempts to interfere. In either case, the Catholic parties appear as the mainstay of a comprehensive program of opposition to Marxist materialism, at least to their own followers. From this point of view it is no longer a question of independence of the church from the government, but of protection for the government by the church. To these ideological objectives are joined, as in all parties, the concrete advantages to be derived from securing adequate or favored treatment for faithful members of the church. But the historical origins of Catholic parties in Europe are sometimes more clearly related to one or another of these objectives.

In France, the aggressive hostility of the revolutionary government and its interference in church affairs (by secularizing church property and by attempting to separate the clergy from Rome) called forth political activity of the Catholics which accrued to the support of the first Napoleon and the restored Bourbons as well. The new Catholic view found brilliant expression in de Maistre's *Du Pape*. He argued that Catholics must rally to the leadership of the Pope now that the governments were becoming anti-clerical. Gradually these battlelines, as drawn during the revolutionary period, became transformed in the course of the nineteenth century into a bitter hostility between liberalism and radicalism on one side and Catholicism on the other. Four great encyclical letters by Leo XIII present the issue comprehensively: *Diuturnum* (1881), which deals with the nature of political power; *Immortale Dei* (1885), which deals with the nature of the state; *Rerum Novarum* (1891), which deals with the social problems; and *Sapientiae Christianae* (1890), which deals with the duties of citizens. The mixed trends of French politics during the greater part of the nineteenth century prevented the crystallization of a compact Catholic party, though Catholicism is a constant issue between various party groups. When *l'affaire Dreyfus* had thoroughly aroused the French public and rekindled a spirit of republican enthusiasm, a group of Catholic politicians sought to compromise with certain tenets of liberalism and founded the *Action Liberale Populaire*, a rather conservative group with a mildly reformist program, the three R. P.'s: *Représentation Proportionnelle, Représentation Professionnelle*, and *Répartition Proportionnelle des Crédits Scolaires*. The issues of *l'affaire Dreyfus* also created, or rather revived, a militant form of reactionary conservatism, the royalist and Catholic *Action Française*, which flourished intellectually, if not politically, for about thirty years under the brilliant leadership of Charles Maurras and Léon Daudet, until it came to an ignominious end through its association with Vichy. But since this group was condemned by the church in 1926, it can hardly be considered a Catholic party. Minor groups on the left further illustrate the lack of unity in French Catholicism under the Third Republic.

Catholic parties in Germany and other countries · Very different has been the role of political Catholicism in Germany. Here the original impetus was provided by a struggle against the monarchs.[11] In Catholic countries, like Bavaria, the government after 1804 had seized all church property, and in return had guaranteed the church an income. In Protestant monarchies, like Prussia, the government had undertaken to foster such measures as mixed marriages, which the church opposed. In either case, the inevitable conflicts with the government could be influenced in favor of the church if her interests were represented in the elected assemblies. The transformation of clerical representatives in diets of the estates, where they had constituted one estate, into a parliamentary party was a gradual one in these German principalities. Even at best the church could not hope to achieve a position rivaling that of former days. But even a minority group could achieve results by compromising on other issues. This primary interest in certain issues touching the position of the church explains the shifting position of the Catholic parties. Under the constitutional monarchies they were prepared to support the throne. In Weimar Germany they were equally ready to collaborate with democracy.

Throughout the nineteenth century the central objective of these Catholic parties remained the same: to free the church and certain areas of social life which she considered vital as much as possible from interference by the government. In the earlier period its constant argument was that the Catholic Church is the best bulwark against revolution; but she can fulfill this function only if she is left in charge of education, family life, and so on. Napoleon the First set the pattern for the sort of relationship between church and state characteristic of the nineteenth century by concluding his Concordat with the Holy See in 1801. Bavaria and other South German governments followed later. By thus concluding "international" agreements with various governments, the church reasserted its independent position and the fact that the church is not a governmental institution and never should be one. The priests, therefore, are never civil servants, even though they receive their salary from the government. This they do only because the property of the church was secularized by force, that is, confiscated, and the governments had accepted the obligation of supplying the wants of the church. Besides these questions of mixed finance, by far the most important practical aspect of clerical politics is the conservation of clerical influence in the schools of all grades, whether through separate parochial schools or through direct influence upon public schools. Whereas the Catholic parties in various South German principalities had been ready to collaborate with the monarchs, another group of Catholics succeeded in organizing a Catholic Club within the revolutionary Constitutional Convention at Frankfurt in 1848 with the express purpose of defending the political rights of the Catholic Church. Under the able leadership of Radowitz and Reichensperger this Club secured the support of the Catholic masses as almost all trends of political attitude were represented with the moderate elements predominant; all were united in the effort to secure an independent position for the church through a federal organization of the dreamed-of popular *Reich*. When these dreams faded, the local clubs became important starting points for further political activity.

Though Catholic party activity flared up in 1852 in Prussia in opposition to constitutional violations of the constitution by the government, still it might have died away for lack of any real issues, as it did in France, had not Bismarck ventured forth into his ill-fated *Kulturkampf*. Around the issues of this struggle Catholic politicians were able to organize a lasting party organization in the eighteen seventies. The party of the Center, so-called because their seats were in the center of the assembly, had been reorganized in 1870. Catholics had, through the exclusion of Austria, become a minority. Their hope of a Germany federally united under Austrian leadership had been destroyed. At the same time, the recently declared infallibility of the Pope had complicated the relationship between the Catholic Church and the governments, since it raised anew the issue of allegiance. The unification of Italy and the consequent destruction of the Papal State, making the Pope a voluntary "prisoner in the Vatican," had added further complications, particularly for Prussia, since Bismarck had supported the Italian unification. Unhappily, some of the non-German subjects within the Empire happened to be Catholics, like the Poles in the East and the French in the West. The Catholic clergy shared the feelings of these national minorities. It favored the use of their mother tongue in schools and churches. Some French bishops, whose dioceses included territory which had passed from France to Germany, fanned the flames by ecclesiastical decrees. The newly formed Catholic party naturally became the mouthpiece of these various sentiments. Consequent upon the *Kulturkampf*, the Catholic Center Party became the second largest party, with fifty-seven seats in the newly elected *Reichstag*; it proceeded to demand intervention of the Reich in favor of the Pope's right to stay in Rome and to retain the city as his worldly dominion. To help the minorities, it demanded the inclusion of the Prussian bill of rights in the imperial constitution. The Bavarian particularist elements, hostile to the Prussian leadership, allied themselves with the party. Under skillful tactical leadership, the Catholic party became the most effective opposition to Bismarck's government. This changed only in the nineties when, because of the rapid increase of the Social Democrats, a *rapprochement* between the various bourgeois groups seemed indicated. The appointment of a Catholic and an experienced parliamentarian as chancellor, cemented this reconciliation of the Center party with the Empire. But the Catholics retained their rather independent position, often making opposition on particular issues, like the treatment of Alsace-Lorraine. They freed themselves more and more from strictly clerical influences, and through the powerful Christian Trade Unions maintained a strong connection with the labor movement and other left-wing tendencies. During the First World War these elements in the Catholic party gained the upper hand. The appointment of the Catholic Count Hertling to the chancellorship was an indication of the growing influence of the party. The radical group under Erzberger took a prominent part in forcing the adoption of the peace resolution in the spring of 1917, at the same time persuading the Pope to make his several overtures for a negotiated peace.

It was quite natural for left-wing Catholics to play a prominent role in the reshaping of Germany after the First World War. Through Erzberger, the party became deeply involved in the Versailles settlement. The Nazi agitation against the "stab in the back" always was in part directed against the Center party. Erzberger, by disposition an optimistic tactician rather than a statesman, had firmly expected Wilson's Fourteen Points to prevail. When they did not, he nevertheless was among the most ardent advocates of accepting the peace of Versailles. In the meantime, the party had helped to draft the Republican constitution. At that time many non-Catholics looked upon the Center party as their salvation from outright state socialism, such as was expected from the Social Democrats. It is undoubtedly due to the conflict between the Catholic and Socialist views that the German constitution embodied so many contradictory provisions on various phases of national life, such as religion, the schools, property, and so on. As the reaction against this progressive national charter set in, the Center party gradually drifted to the right. At first in Bavaria, whose Catholic group split off from the Center party as the Bavarian People's party, and later elsewhere, the drift of the Catholic majority was toward a reassertion of authoritarian ideas. Successive Catholic chancellors under the Weimar Republic mark the phases of this shift. At the same time, the Center party proved its suppleness by continuing a member of the Weimar coalition of leftist groups in Prussia throughout the entire period, with the unique result that when von Papen undertook to expel the Prussian government in the summer of 1932, he was proceeding against his own former party colleagues. The fruit of this policy was a position of unique influence for certain Catholic parliamentarians, who assumed the role of bringing together the rival administrators of the Reich and Prussia. When the National Socialists came into power, the Catholic party was obliged "voluntarily" to disband along with the rest.

Similar problems have arisen elsewhere. Other European countries with solidly organized Catholic parties are Switzerland, Belgium, the Netherlands, and Austria. As noted before, the presence of a Catholic minority has served to emphasize the need for proportional representation in the former three countries (see above, ch. XV). In Switzerland, Catholicism and conservatism have always gone hand in hand, and the Catholics have never quite recovered from the loss of prestige which the ill-starred War of Separate Union (*Sonderbundskrieg*) brought upon them. In Belgium, too, the Catholic party has always been associated with conservatism. As elsewhere, the orthodox peasantry was solidly behind the Catholic leadership. The attachment of many peasants was strengthened by the cultural conflict between the Flemish and Walloon elements, the latter French-speaking and inclined toward Liberalism, predominantly urban and industrial, the former speaking a language akin to the Dutch, predominantly rural and agricultural and inclined toward Conservatism. The split between Liberal and Socialist elements, together with the large number of Catholics in that country, gave the Belgian Catholic party for a long time an almost uninterrupted control of the government. The broadening of the electorate after the First World War brought this Catholic regime to an end. But the Catholic party's influence has remained strong.

In Austria, in the twenties, the Christian Social party was able to secure a predominance similar to that in Belgium. The Alpine peasant, orthodox and patriotic, was the backbone of this Christian Social party. Under the skillful leadership of a Catholic clergyman, Dr. Seipel, this party succeeded in monopolizing the opposition to the Socialists, and the issues were so clear-cut that a two-party system developed in spite of proportional representation. The international position of Catholicism was shrewdly used by the leaders of the Christian Social party who increasingly assumed a stand hostile to unification with the German Republic. The best argument against advocating the *Anschluss* in the eyes of Seipel and his brethren was a good one: that the *Anschluss* was not practical politics. Furthermore, such unification seemed to close the door to the Hapsburgs' return. The Christian Social party was conceived in terms of social conservatism, if not reaction. Eventually, when the indignation of the masses over the economic troubles of the depression threatened the Christian Social party with electoral defeat under Chancellor Dollfuss, popularly dubbed Milli-Metternich, the latter proceeded to suppress the Socialists (July–August 1933), egged on by his Fascist and legitimist associate Prince von Starhemberg. But the Austrian Socialists were determined not to let themselves be pushed aside like their ill-fated German comrades in Prussia. They prepared for another coup to dislodge their Catholic adversaries, by force if necessary. Dollfuss thereupon proceeded to break their resistance and in unexpectedly brutal proceedings had the army attack and partially destroy the modern workers' quarters, and jail and shoot the leaders, including Vienna's able Socialist burgomaster, Karl Seitz; he then promulgated another "constitution" which forever barred such popular elections as might have displaced him. But as history was to show in 1938, the Austrian clericals, by going Fascist, had destroyed the only basis for effective resistance to Hitler, if indeed there was such a basis.

The tactical alliance, if not spiritual kinship, between clericalism and Fascism also has been operative in Italy. To be sure, the Catholic party of the Popolari was dedicated to reconciling Catholicism and social reform; its leader, Don Sturzo, was exerting an increasing influence in the days preceding the Fascist March on Rome. But when Mussolini had firmly entrenched himself, the Catholic Church preferred to conclude a concordat with him, and to request Don Sturzo to go into exile. Mussolini's concordat bore a close resemblance to Napoleon's. The anticlerical elements in the Fascist party were violently opposed to it. But it gave to Mussolini the support of the church, and to the church the support of Mussolini. At last the Italian government had recognized the international position of the church and the territorial existence of the Vatican, concessions which perhaps no Catholic party could have wangled out of more liberal and popular governments.

Bonapartism, Fascism, National Socialism · Throughout Europe, the Catholic, or Christian, opposition to socialism could not be effective wherever the underlying religious faith had been shattered, even though the opposition itself was firmly rooted in property and other interests. If the tradition of self-reliance, of self-government, of self-restraint is weak in these masses, and if they therefore demand or rather yearn for authoritative leadership, the "nation" or the *Volk* offers itself as another goddess. Around this golden calf the Fascist masses of Europe danced for twenty years.[12] There was good precedent for that. The French Revolution, though enthroning the goddess "Reason," had already shown a decided penchant for the rival goddess "Nation." Many thinkers see the birthplace of modern nationalism here. Reason having become discredited by the Terror, Napoleon led the French armies to victory after victory for the greater glory of *La Nation*. Carlton J. H. Hayes has emphasized the profound conflict between the religions of nationalism and Christianity. Bonapartism, Fascism, National Socialism were three forms of the same nationalist religion, each born of the terror of the middle classes at seeing their security threatened by the masses. In the ancient world the challenge of Christianity was directed against the tribal multiplicity of gods, each protecting his or her particular city. In contemporary civilization, the challenge of Fascism is directed against the catholicity of a Christian faith transcending all national loyalties. Communism, cherishing the ideal of a mankind composed of workers and united by an international bureaucracy of supermen, attempts to substitute a millennial hope of all-round material prosperity for the transcendental faith in eternal salvation of the soul which the Christian churches espouse. The terrified small property owners, farmers, peasants, shopkeepers, craftsmen, white-collar employees, professional men, and their like, unwilling to become mere "workers" under an international bureaucracy, yet unable to maintain a faith in Christian views, return to the tribal fetishes which once dominated the minds of men. The parties dedicated to these views proved themselves as intransigent as the Communists.

Events in 1939 and after 1945 have made amply clear that all the totalitarian dictatorships have a good deal in common. Unnoticed by many, Stalinism has emerged as the dictatorial reaction to revolutionary communism. Stalin, like Napoleon, uses the revolutionary slogans, but kills those who take them seriously. Fascism and Nazism were similarly the reaction to the revolutionary socialism of Central Europe. They both derived a great many of their slogans from Socialism, the Nazis even their name. Fascism and National Socialism were post-revolutionary developments, and in spite of certain differences which were often emphasized for political reasons, they were fundamentally alike. They were for maintaining property, but professed to hate big business. Actually, Fascist regimes collaborated closely with monopoly capitalism. For faith in democracy, however, they substituted faith in the leadership of one man. In this they resemble the Communists, although originally the latter emphasized the party rather than the leader. In practice Stalin has come to occupy a position much like that of Hitler and Mussolini. The Fascist leaders made their "program" themselves and to order, whereas the Communist masters continue to acknowledge the writings of Marx as their inspirational source. This Communist willingness to follow a "Bible" introduces a measure of argument into the party councils. Orthodoxy remains a controversial matter. A man like Trotsky could go about in other countries denouncing the doctrines and actions of Stalin as being not thoroughly Marxist.

The Nazi party was slowly built up under the Republic from 1921 onward, and the organization was honeycombed with factionalism. Labor battled with business interests, farmers fought both, the doctrinaires of race purity were scorned by the groups interested in economic welfare, and so forth. This was a natural result of the party's willingness to appeal to everybody on his own terms: farmers were promised higher prices for their produce, workers were offered a lower cost of living at better wages, yet the employing group were cheered by expectations of seeing the trade unions destroyed. While debtors heard the "slavery of interest" denounced, creditors discovered a silver lining in the proposed return to good old-fashioned German honesty. All this sort of straddling of real issues is familiar enough in the United States, where party managers have always been obliged to placate many factions and interests in order to hold a majority together. In Germany it was startling, since the more limited appeal of parties had allowed a sharper focusing of issues. The Nazis were rewarded by eventually becoming the largest German party before coming into power. It is noteworthy that they rallied to their many-colored banner more followers than any other German party ever did in the history of German party development. And while they were in the opposition, the self-contradictions in their appeals could not readily be revealed except to the thoughtful. After all, any one group or interest had at least a betting chance of coming out on top after the party took over power. At the same time, it can readily be seen that Hitler could not possibly be expected to take over power unless he could hold it secure from criticism for a long time; for these contradictory promises would otherwise have led to his very speedy downfall, the more so since he did not even possess a simple majority in the *Reichstag*. Hitler would have been, as so many politicians before him, the captive of his own rhetoric. By indoctrinating the mass of his followers with the belief that parliamentary machinery is useless or worse, he protected himself while turning radical democratic ideology inside out. For if the majority of the people were willing to sanction such a procedure, who could question it from a democratic standpoint? Actually, the German Nazis never secured a majority of the electorate.

Omitting discussion here of antiparliamentary, totalitarian parties in some of the smaller countries of Europe, such as Hungary, Poland, Serbia, and Rumania, we shall add just a few observations concerning the Italian Fascists. The Fascist party was rather small and insignificant until Mussolini assumed the headship of the government (*il capo del governo*). Mussolini had a Socialist past which gave him a comprehension of the social conflicts of our day. He was deeply dyed in the color of nationalism, however; Mussolini had fought out a bitter controversy with the strongly internationalist and pacifist Italian Socialists during the war. Like Hitler, Mussolini was able to appeal to unsatisfied nationalist emotions, and on a strongly personal basis to build up a following resembling in social and economic structure the Nazi following. Mussolini publicly declared that the Italian peasants were always the most loyal supporters of his regime. If socialism is the ideological weapon of the labor movement, Fascism in its various forms served the same purpose for the farmers' movement until 1945. In many European countries the peasants constitute as large a minority as the workers, if not a larger one. It is a group which never before was really awake to its political power. In Germany as well as in Italy the peasants uncomprehendingly supported the interests of the large estate owners, or were divided between the several bourgeois parties, none of which gave them a feeling of solidarity.

The violent anti-Semitism of the Nazis had its deepest roots in this rural population. It continues to be a factor of considerable force with the rural masses in Continental Europe. Of course, anti-Semitism also has a great appeal to the frustrated lower middle classes in the cities. We cannot hope to deal here with the complex issues of anti-Semitism in contemporary society. General feelings and attitudes should be distinguished from the open and approved violence characteristic of the Nazi regime. The bewildered frustration of postwar politics, accompanied as it was by constant international humiliations, cried for some group to blame for it all. The Nazis seized this demagogic opportunity—or rather their own predilections made them stumble upon it. But this is only a partial explanation, especially since in Italy the same thing did not happen. The reason is not, as apologists of Fascism would have us believe, any innate superiority in the strictly Fascist creed; the fact that the Jews in Italy offer no such golden opportunity for baiting was undoubtedly one aspect of the situation. The Ethiopian campaign proved beyond doubt that the inherent need for such opportunities was the same. The essential fact is that the tribal religion of Fascism invariably carries with it a ruthless readiness for war against any outsiders, whether they are physically located within the boundaries of the country or beyond them.

The "restoration" of parties · Since 1945, and the defeat of Fascism, the political parties of pre-Fascist days have experienced a rebirth. While Britain voted the Labour Party into full power for the first time in history, Continental European party development has seen several new factors; the situation is highly unstable, but must not be interpreted in terms of analogies to the twenties when the meaning of Fascist dictatorship and its deleterious effects were not known and appreciated by the middle classes. These elements of the population, never too enthusiastic about democracy, even in France, are now definitely antidictatorial. There is, as a matter of fact, a general negativism about European political attitudes which resembles the outlook of other restoration periods (see above, pp. 151 f., for the discussion of this "negative revolution"). Among the new aspects of the party line-up, the more important are the definite crystallization of the Christian Democrats as the major party of the middle class in France, Italy, and Germany, with the corresponding disappearance of nineteenth-century liberalism, and the effective collaboration of these Christian Democrats with the moderate Social Democrats and Socialists. A majority of both Christian Democrats and Social Democrats favor planning and socialization; they are definitely middle of the road, and commonly referred to as the "third force." They are the third force actually only in France, where they occupy the middle ground between the radicals of the right under General de Gaulle and the radicals of the left under Communist leadership. As contrasted with this tenuous situation in France, the Christian and the

Social Democrats between them have a solid majority in both Italy and Germany, or at least Western Germany. What the situation in the Soviet Zone of Germany might be, if free elections were held, is a matter of guesswork. The best-qualified observers believe, however, that the party structure in Eastern Germany would be very similar to that in the West, once Communist terror methods were removed. It is one of the most striking developments of the post-1945 period that after an initial burst of pro-Communist sentiment, the Communist parties have been losing in all three countries. This decline in Communist support is especially striking in Germany, where it has fallen to below 10 per cent of the total vote, but it is also quite marked in Italy and in France, where the voting strength of the Communist party is down to around 25 per cent of the total vote. The development has been accelerated and reinforced by economic assistance and military and political support from the United States, but that is not the only factor; the sense of apprehension of (and in Germany the experience with) Soviet totalitarianism is of at least equal importance.

Specifically, the Socialists are pretty much the straight-line descendants of the prewar parties. Both in leadership and in program they follow the old line of a moderate "Marxism," and their voting support is largely that of organized labor, with some intellectuals in the leadership from the middle class. But while some prewar figures, like Blum in France and Loebe in Germany, are still enjoying a measure of leadership and support, the dominant figures, like Kurt Schumacher in Germany and André Philip in France, are younger men who played no role in earlier days.

Conclusion · Throughout the preceding discussion the intermingling of ideal and material objectives in the development of parties has been quite evident. The mercantile class battling the landed interests, the workers the businessmen, the farmers the city-dwellers—we observe a constant procession of thesis and antithesis, the latter always posing as a new synthesis, which it actually fails to be. Party development, more than any other sphere of political life, displays a dynamic evolution. There is here no final rest, as in the Hegelian metaphysics with its ultimate synthesis, nor any harmonious swing of the pendulum so often alleged as a "law of politics," but constant change in one direction or another, with never a return to the starting point. The great panorama of the history of modern parties is a reflection of the secular evolution of modern society in the mirror provided by the elected assemblies of modern constitutional governments. A thorough treatment would therefore be a history of our times. The psychic dispositions so lucidly portrayed by Mr. Lowell are ever present, but they attach themselves to different ideologies expressive of different configurations of interest. One hundred and fifty years ago, the theory of absolute democracy reached its abstract perfection in the glittering generalizations of Jean Jacques Rousseau. The great French Revolution, as well as the dictatorship of the first Napoleon, is anticipated in its brilliant passages about the unlimited power of the sovereign majority, whether expressed directly or through a divinely inspired lawgiver. Not a word about parties occurs in this penetrating tract. No wonder that Communism, Fascism, National Socialism, as well as Bonapartism, should have felt satisfied when assured approximate majority support. They are all children of nineteenth-century democracy. They are all drunk with the will of the people. Nations whose familiarity with the working of constitutional government was largely academic and theoretical, whose thinking was confused on the difference between constitutional government and absolute democracy, have surrendered themselves to the leadership of one man or of a few who claimed such divine inspiration. The longing for unity has issued into a make-believe unity of one party identifying itself with the whole people. "All good Germans are National Socialists," cried Adolf Hitler; "All good men are Communists," echoes back Stalin. The plurality of parties, though generally admitted by political observers to be an essential feature of working constitutional government, has not found its apologist. Yet if parties are organized for securing power within a group, is not that very fact objective proof of the need for several parties? To deny this proposition, we should have to assert that men when holding all the power concentrated in their hands are never likely to abuse it. Political experience points in the opposite direction. In order to prove the superiority of one party, people have argued against innumerable parties. But are not two parties better than one or three? Neither monism, nor pluralism, but dualism corresponds to the harmonious equilibrium. To permit this equilibrium enough flexibility to move with the changes in the evolution of society is the touchstone of an effective constitutional order.

XXII

Interest Groups and Economic Councils

Introduction: the deterioration of political representation in terms of the general interest · General interest and special interests · American lobbies · Chambers of Commerce and similar semiofficial bodies in France, Germany, and other countries · Central banks · Trade unions · The Russian Revolution and the trade unions, particularly in Germany · The German National Economic Council · The Fascist "corporative state" · National Socialist "estates" · Communist councils · Pressure groups in the United States today · Conclusion.

Introduction: the deterioration of political representation in terms of the general interest · Interest and pressure groups are the living "public" behind the parties. Such groups were viewed with moral indignation and alarm by the last generation. They were held up to scorn both by muckrakers and by sane students of politics. They were the sinister force gnawing at the foundations of modern democracy, of representative government, and the word "lobby" supposedly comprehended a whole congeries of abuses, corruption, fraud, and the like. There was and is more than a kernel of truth in these assertions. The activity of these "interests" has manifestly weakened the belief in *popular* government by undermining the faith in a united *people*. Wilson's attack upon congressional government, and its committee system (see above, ch. XVII, pp. 352 f.) was built around allegations concerning the power which interest groups had arrogated unto themselves. "It is in committee rooms that legislation not desired by the interests dies. It is in committee rooms that legislation desired by the interests is framed and brought forth."[1] Even earlier, a searching appendix to Bryce's *American Commonwealth* was devoted to the "lobbies." While in the United States and in the British Dominions, as well as in England, the "interests" worked and pressed upon each party, in countries with a multiple-party system the interests often associated themselves to a greater or lesser degree with particular parties as we have seen in the preceding chapter. The rise of Socialism and of Socialist parties identified with the industrial workers' interest provided an ideological framework for special parties of workers. As the workers united, other special interests, too, sought effective political organization. As parties thus became identified with special interests, or members of representative assemblies yielded to special interests

460

and thus appeared as their tools, the representative quality of these assemblies changed. When, in the depths of the crisis of German democracy, a German minister asked, "Shall we forever remain a collection of special interest groups, rather than become a united people?" he was voicing a doubt regarding representative government which has grown strong in the minds of intellectuals the world over. The ill this German was crying out against was troubling not only Germany, as so many Germans believed. Marxists of various shades had been indoctrinating the masses throughout Europe with the theory of "the economic determination" of human activity. Royalists and reactionaries had preached with wit and passion that the Third Republic was honeycombed with the corruption of big business. The United States, as we saw before, was reverberating from time to time with the revelations of the dark machinations of interest groups, and the high protective tariffs stood as a lasting memorial to the logrolling proclivities of Congress, a reminder to anyone who had eyes to see or ears to hear. It is natural that plans should have made their appearance for legalizing these pressures and influences, for co-ordinating them with and fitting them into the regular framework of government. In France, economic advisory councils representing the "interests" had come down from the days of the "estates" and the mercantilist efforts of Henry IV. In Germany, Bismarck had tried to bring together the representatives of management and labor through an Economic Council, but had failed, since parliamentarians feared that he wished to balance the popular forces as represented in the *Reichstag*. After the First World War, such councils appeared everywhere as part of the new constitutions. Fascism and National Socialism seized upon these trends and developed comprehensive corporative setups. These corporative structures were supposed to replace the traditional representative scheme; whereas the economic councils are intended to function as a complement rather than a substitute. The trend has re-appeared now: the new French constitution in its article 25 provides for the establishment of a national economic council; in Italy, corresponding efforts of the Christian Democrats to have interests represented in the Senate were defeated. Apart from the Bavarian Senate, which is partially based upon such interest representation, the idea seems buried in Germany. Whether this is due to inhibition imposed by the military governments is hard to tell. American military government's insistence that such occupational representation is not "democratic," because it is reminiscent of the Fascist corporative state, and hence cannot be permitted, may be considered extreme in view of the French constitution if not of the Weimar one, but it may yet be well to keep the Germans away from this sort of difficult experimentation. The problems such occupational representation raises are certainly difficult. Are these movements expressing a rapid stratification of our modern industrial society? Are these organs capable of effective operation, of fulfilling the deliberative function which once fell to elected assemblies?

General interest and special interests · We must now go back to some of the general points made in the course of our analysis of representation (above, ch. XIV). In discussing representation, it was shown how Burke formulated the classical norm of a representative's task: to consider issues and to decide them in terms of the general interest. A reminder of how far from a description of reality such a view was at the time of Burke may be had in an autobiographical remark of his contemporary, "One-Speech" Hamilton. Before retiring from parliamentary life he wrote his patron, who had requested his continuance, that he might consider the request were he permitted to vote according to his own convictions. The permission was not granted![2] Apart from the reality, the difficulty with Burke's view is that most people are quite positive that they are "considering the general interest" even when they are concerned with very special interests; for it is usually possible to rationalize the special interest as an essential part of the general interest. Thus the welfare of, let us say, the shipping industry is of paramount importance to the English people, and therefore its continued existence "a matter of general interest." The same can and will be said of the workers, the farmers, the doctors, either in whole or in part, and always with some show of truth. It seems, therefore, that the "general interest" is similar to Rousseau's "general will": a metaphysical entity, a yardstick of indefinite length with no inches or feet marked on it. Considered in such broad terms, the general interest is obscure, remains undefinable. And yet there is a difference. It is a question of more or less. The interest of farmer Jones is different from the interest of the farmers of Windham County or the American dairy farmers. Again, the interest of these groups of farmers is different from the interest of all American farmers. In other words, some interests are more general than others. A true and ideal "American" representation would therefore consider the interests to be most important which all Americans have in common and which are therefore most "general." It is obvious that no man is likely to be able to "represent" the American people in such abstract, ideal terms. The nearest approximation is oftentimes the man who owes his seat in parliament or his place in Congress to a particular, powerful patron. One of the shrewdest observers of Congress once told the writer that a certain senator, now dead, although well-known for his subserviency to one big corporation, was nevertheless one of the most useful members of Congress, because once the interests of that corporation were taken care of, he was free to consider the general public interest. This is a strange approximation to an ideal, and yet Mr. Burke made much the same point when he defended the "rotten boroughs" in England: "You have an equal representation, because you have men equally interested in the prosperity of the whole, who are involved in the general interest and the general sympathy; and perhaps these places furnishing a superfluity of public agents and administrators, . . . will stand clearer of local interests, passions, prejudices, and cabals than the others, and therefore preserve the balance of the parts, and with a more general view and a more steady hand than the rest. . . ." This is a far cry from the norm of an "ideal" representative, and yet it shows the extent to which representativeness is a matter of more or less. This is equally true of the representativeness of particular parts of the government. The American President would seem to be "more representative" than any individual member of the House or the Senate, but the Senate and the House, when acting with large bi-partisan majorities, would be "more representative" than the President (who is necessarily of one party). In relation to certain functions, the Supreme Court, as we have seen, is "more representative" than either Congress or the President because it is "nonpartisan." The narrower the special interest is, the lower is the representative quality of those whose actions are directed toward its realization. And an interest is narrow or broad depending upon the number of human beings whose interest is identified with it. The most general interest is the interest of widest application, conceivably comprising all humanity. The great appeal of the Marxist view lies partly in its claim to universality, at least as far as all workers of the world are concerned. The same is true of peace and pacific endeavors. At the same time, interests of very general application are frequently lacking in intensity of appeal to the interested party.* They are for that reason of rather remote interest to the man seeking re-election to Congress. He must, necessarily, be more concerned with the fortunes of the local soap factory, the needs of the farmers in his district, or whatever may be indicated by the particular social pattern of the community in which he is being elected. Such a state of affairs is less perturbing from the viewpoint of modern political science than from that of the standpat democratic doctrinaire. The more general interest is recognized as a compound of many less general interests, and by bringing spokesmen for these various interests together, such a compound may emerge if the working conditions are right. Faulty electoral methods, outworn procedures for deliberation

---

*The fervor of the advocate of such interests cannot be argued to invalidate this conclusion; for such fervor is engendered by other impulses than the "interest" of the advocate himself— except in so far as he may sense the immense potential power to be derived from the effective realization of a universal interest.

463

and action, and unrestrained license of the press may, however, bring about conditions under which the less general interests become so hardened and so violently pitched against each other that no working compromise can result. Then the complex mechanism will stall and eventually break down. Such breakdown is not, however, the result of special interests dividing the community, or of the advocacy of such views by elected representatives (as the Fascists and Communists allege); it is rather the result of the particular maladjustments which prevented compromise between these interests.

American lobbies · Whatever the reasons, it is a fact that the pressure of special-interest groups manifested itself in an organized form quite early in the United States. The large size of the country, the legislative initiative assumed by Congress, the comprehensive vagueness of party programs, all contributed to a development which brought interested citizens together in support of or in opposition to legislation which was of special interest to them. The farmers' organizations, seeking governmental control or at least supervision of the railroads, are one striking illustration. The number of such organizations and the interests they represent have more recently become so impressive that they are nationally recognized. Broad surveys of the whole range of activities, as well as searching and detailed studies of particular activities, have appeared in the course of the last decade, analyzing the rise of this "assistant government," as it has aptly been called. Since the administrative departments have been taking a greater part in legislation, and since they have been vested with ever more discretion in administering them, they also have become the target of the pressure of these interest groups. The following are of outstanding importance: the Chamber of Commerce of the United States, the National Association of Manufacturers, the American Farm Bureau Federation, the National Grange, the National Education Association, the American Federation of Labor, the railway brotherhoods, the Congress of Industrial Organization, the American Legion, the American Railway Association, the Committee of Utility Executives, the Federal Council of Churches, the American Medical Association, and a dozen strong trade associations, such as those of the woolgrowers, and coal, oil, lumber, meat packing, and sugar interests. It is a far cry from the activities of these large, publicly conducted organizations to the scheming and usually corrupt methods of the early lobbyist, looking for land grants and similar concessions. Every one of the modern organizations more or less persuasively identifies itself with the public or the national interest. "The American Federation of Labor talks of working for 'labor and the people.' 'Its accomplishments have benefited all the people, for the trade union movement is as deep and wide as human life.'

The Chamber of Commerce of the United States takes the position that 'what is good for business is good for the country.' The Farm Bureau Federation states that 'in reviving and invigorating American farm life, we are regenerating and preserving the nation.' Similar statements may be encountered in the literature of others of these associations."[3] These statements are not untrue, but they hardly describe adequately the purpose for which these organizations were created. The nature of interest is such, however, that in the long run the subjective purpose pales into insignificance beside the objective reality in which various less general interests merge into the more general interests of the more comprehensive community. There are today hundreds of such organizations voicing the "will of the people" in one field or another. To the older institutions, more particularly Congress, falls the difficult task of weighing these pressures and effecting the necessary compromise.

Chambers of Commerce and similar semiofficial bodies in France, Germany, and other countries · In Europe the development of pressure groups has been influenced more extensively by the government. In England certain reform movements played an altogether decisive part in the parliamentary history of the nineteenth century. Such great names as Bentham, Cobden, and John Stuart Mill are definitely associated with these activities. All these movements played their game *in* Parliament, rather than *upon* it, and associated themselves with parties or founded them, rather than standing aloof, distributing praise and blame as the modern American organizations do. On the Continent, organizations constituting the counterpart of the American private associations have flourished with bureaucratic sanction. Some of these organizations have for a long time been officially recognized. In France and other countries, the Chambers of Commerce constitute semipublic authorities. The personnel of these Chambers acquired semiofficial status and the government delegated important functions to them. The nearest American analogy is the American Farm Bureau Federation which, through the county agent, shares with the government the task of local agricultural extension work. In Europe, analogous activity was developed through the Chambers of Agriculture, organized in direct parallel to the Chambers of Commerce. While these two sets of organizations concerned themselves with the promotion of agriculture and commerce, Chambers of Handicraft were organized to protect traditional craftsmanship against the inroads of either.

After the First World War, the Social Democrats promoted the corresponding Chambers of Labor to look out for the interests of the industrial worker.[4] In a sense, the multiplication of these organizations amounted to a *reductio ad absurdum* of the original idea of promoting trade and commerce, and yet in a democratic society, such competition was bound to result. But owing to the link with the government which was in keeping with European bureaucratic traditions, they tended to become popular extensions of the particular national ministry. There are other organizations which have played a conspicuous role in politics, notably the trade unions and central banks. Still others, particularly in the field of reform, have lacked the financial backing for effective organizational activity. There was, however, a tendency for the government to assist financially organizations which made it their business to promote ideas which the government officials approved, and to resist those which they frowned upon. Thus, organizations fostering patriotism and similar purposes were promoted by the government in France. The same tendency was even more markedly observable in Germany. Under the Weimar Republic, by contrast, the government sought to counteract the nationalist tendencies by supporting the League of Nations Association, as well as international student exchanges. The French Government likewise helped the International Student Center in Paris. Oftentimes, conflicts in outlook between the ministries and their officials led to their supporting competing organizations here, as in the economic field. The same spectacle could have been seen in Germany under the Republic. This intermingling of governmental and civic activities was inimical to the long-run interests of both. It decreased genuine civic participation in these organizations, as expressed through the pocketbook. It also involved the government in conflicts which it should have been in a position to mediate.

Since 1945, American Military Government has taken the lead in seeking to have German Chambers of Commerce and the like dissociated from the government and deprived of the monopolistic position which they occupied in the past. Perhaps Military Government authorities were motivated largely by the avowed hostility of the Allies toward the corporative system associated with Fascism and Nazism. But a realization of the corrupting and distorting influence of such private organizations having the sanction of the public authorities has also played a role. The resistance from the Germans has been very strong; they have rarely seemed to appreciate that the existence of such organizations conflicts with the spirit of constitutional democracy. They apparently had a hard time grasping the fact that once "public authority" has become the "people's authority," you cannot invest an organization representing a partial interest with such public authority. (As a matter of fact, that grasp is weakening in the United States.) It remains to be seen whether the efforts of American Military Government will bear fruit, considering the contrary views of the French and Russians.

Central banks · Differing from each other in structure and function, central banks have nevertheless been of decisive importance in influencing the policy of popular governments. Although a good part of their influence has been clandestine, it has nevertheless been powerful. There is general agreement that in times of financial stringency the paramount need of the government to have adequate credit resources may bring about a questionable degree of political dependency upon those who hold the strings to the credit resources of the country. Since it is the primary function of central banks to maintain the liquid banking reserve of the country, the central bank in turn finds itself obliged to insist upon conservative methods of governmental conduct which may ill accord with the popular majority. Andrew Jackson's famous fight with the Second Bank of the United States provides a striking illustration of the political issues involved. But owing to its abundant tax and credit resources, the American government has not been seriously troubled with the issue since. As in so many cases, the issue was seen most candidly, and fought over most bitterly, in France, where the *Banque de France* had become the stronghold of conservatism. Through Empire, Restoration, Monarchy, another Empire, and Republic, the Bank remained in the hands of the "two hundred families."[5] Under the Napoleonic Law of 1806, which remained essentially unaltered down to 1936, "the powers of the shareholders were vested in the general assembly composed of the 200 French citizens who held the largest number of shares for six months before an election." Since the minimum thus established was eighty-five shares and the shares were quoted in 1935 at 10,000 francs, it took 850,000 francs to qualify. "Small wonder that membership came to be regarded as a sign of financial importance and that a list of members read something like a social register with counts, dukes, and representatives of the *haute finance*." The French party system and the ascendancy of parliament over the cabinet underlaid the political powers of the bank.

The great parliamentary debate preceding the basic changes in the position of the Bank in 1936 reviewed once more all the arguments brought forth from time to time by the long-drawn tug-of-war between the Bank and successive governments throughout more than a century. The Socialists and their friends proceeded under the slogan "Let's make the Bank of France France's Bank" (*Faire de la Banque de France la Banque de la France*). These were sharpened, however, by the economic problems of the depression and the role which government spending should play in dealing with these problems. There had been bitter clashes between the Bank and the government during the inflation ten years earlier, but the Bank's position had on the whole been the popular one, since it tried to resist inflation. Now it was a question of credit expansion which the Bank opposed, and the voters, restless and impatient to see something done, turned toward those who proposed to break the stranglehold of the Bank's anti-inflationary position. Here we face the crux of the whole issue: governments today are so intimately connected with the whole economy that the control of spending by the government is almost the key to controlling governmental policy in the economic realm. The government's credit, in other words, can no longer be equated with that of a small commercial enterprise and its right to borrow established on the basis of a simple balance sheet. What is this balance sheet, anyway? What, specifically, is investment and what is current expense? Is the government justified in considering as investment all expenditures made for the purpose of conserving natural resources? If not, how much of it? The answer to these questions strikes at the very core of public policy; it is evident that the answer cannot safely remain lodged in a bank whose directors are chosen by a small group selected on the basis of their wealth, such as the general assembly of the Bank of France constituted. For even granting that these groups of people possessed special qualifications which enabled them to form a more "expert" judgment, the fact remains that their activity did not maintain the credit of France. Denying the *government* credit may indeed, by causing a complete stall, bring about the collapse of the credit structure. Like a steam boiler without a safety valve, a democracy without an outlet for popular policies is liable to explode when tension rises. The French system fortunately had such a safety valve. The Bank's position rested upon a statute which could be changed, once the situation got serious enough.

Politically, the basic charge was that the Bank consistently favored governments of the right and repeatedly made it clear that the credit of the government would be better if the government would be a more conservative one. Since credit means confidence, there can be no doubt that the conservative big-business representatives would have more confidence in a government controlled by their own group. But such dependence evidently was intolerable to many. The defenders of the Bank's "independence" contended that great instability would result from the Bank's transformation into a political weapon of the dominant party; by such claims they obscured the undeniable fact that great instability also resulted from the Bank's remaining a political weapon of one class, regardless of the will of the majority. Attempts were made to cope with the problem by distinguishing between control of the Bank by the "state" and control of the Bank by the "party." But of course no one could suggest how under democracy the party and the state could be separated,—a striking instance of the tyranny of the word "state," which is meaningless under democratic conditions, as we have seen.

468

The Act as finally passed, while democratizing the Bank and placing it under government control to some extent, did not achieve nationalization. Representation on the Board of Directors (*Conseil de Regence*) was divided between the government, the banking interest, and the users of credit. Twelve of the twenty-three directors were to be appointed by the government, thus giving the government clear control. The same was true of the Executive Committee, and to insure that no inside group could entrench itself, elections were staggered and self-succession barred. Broader control was vested in the stockholders, who each received one vote, regardless of holdings, as in the elections to the Boards of Federal Reserve Banks. Thus the Bank was allowed to operate for private profit, but its policies were under government control. This meant that the Bank was no longer able to dictate the government's spending policy, but it also meant that all bars to uncontrolled government spending were removed. This cannot be helped. If democracies cannot learn to control spending, they cannot hope to exist for long. The experience in Sweden, Switzerland and other highly democratic, yet industrialized, countries with relatively sound practices in this field holds out hope that there may yet be majorities for sound fiscal policies. In 1946, as we shall see, the Bank of France was nationalized and is now part of the planned and directed economy (see next chapter).

In England the same issue of central banking control came to a dramatic head in the summer of 1931. Conservative investors both in Britain and abroad were seriously aroused over the fiscal policy of the second Labour government. They wanted to see drastic cuts made in the various social benefits, particularly in the unemployment benefits. The Cabinet of Ramsay MacDonald was deeply split; MacDonald himself and his Chancellor of the Exchequer, Snowden, desired to make the cuts and rehabilitate the government's credits; but the larger part of the Cabinet, including Henderson and other conservative trade-union leaders, were not prepared to make such concessions. The powerful Trades Union Congress was adamantly opposed. MacDonald, caught between these two irreconcilable powers, resigned and formed a new Cabinet consisting of a coalition of Conservatives, Liberals, and National Labourites (as he called them). In the ensuing election, the issue of the currency was made a central point, and the small investor was terrified by the assertion that the Labour Party was committed to a policy of currency inflation. Interestingly enough, after winning an overwhelming victory to "save the pound," the Cabinet of National Union proceeded to devalue the pound. Hence, in England, the conservative forces allied with the Bank triumphed over the progressive elements. Indeed, the Bank of England and its governor, Sir Montagu Norman, played an important part in driving Labour from power. It is not surprising, therefore, that one of the central planks of the Labour party should have been the nationalization of the Bank of England, which has since been achieved.

In the United States, where the entire Federal Reserve Board is appointed by the President with the advice and consent of the Senate, and where three out of nine directors of the several Reserve Banks are appointed by the Board in turn, the problem is not likely to arise in the form in which it has plagued European politics; control is already securely lodged in the government as supported by the majority of the voters. Characteristically, the chairman of the Federal Reserve Board under the New Deal was one of the outstanding defenders of the government's spending policy.

Trade unions · If central banks have provided the most effectively organized rampart of business and general capital interests, trade unions have been the defenders of workers and general labor interests. And just as central banks have at times tried to thwart the decisions of the majority by refusing to grant credit to the government, so trade unions have made analogous attempts through general strikes. The analogy between the two operations was brought out by the slogan about the "strike of capital"; a general strike of either capital or labor is indicative of a clash between the majority and a minority which is powerful enough to risk a challenge, through a test of strength, to the constitutional authority. As was pointed out earlier (see pp. 135 ff.), such conflicts cannot and need not be outlawed; they *need not* be outlawed, because they are not sanctioned by the law to start with, and they *cannot* be outlawed, since they are essentially appeals to force "to right a wrong" caused by the breakdown of law and the constitution.

The trade-union movement is more than a hundred years old.[6] In its origins it goes back to the craft guilds of the Middle Ages. The craftsmen, dislodged by the factory system in the industrial revolution, found themselves at the mercy of employers and hence proceeded to organize for collective bargaining. Numerous obstacles were placed in their way. Through use of all the resources of the law, as well as through extralegal and even illegal methods, employers sought to weaken the trade unions in virtually all industrial countries. But the organization of the workers went relentlessly forward, born of inherent necessity. While imaginative thinkers and writers spun out elaborate systems of socialism and constructed utopias of communist havens—men like Saint Simon, Fourier and Proudhon, Marx, Engels and Bakunin, Owen, Emerson, and many others—the hard-headed secretaries of trade unions hammered into shape first one union and then another, then federations of unions covering entire industries, countries, continents, reducing working hours, improving working conditions, raising wages, until in retrospect the achievements of the communist Utopia which Marx and Engels projected in their Manifesto look like the mild liberalism of a friendly college professor. Today, the International Labor Office stands at the apex of this vast network of workingmen's organizations. It could be pointing the way toward the democratic world order which peoples and governments have not yet managed to achieve were it not for the dissensions which the Communists have injected into the movement by trying to convert it into an instrument for furthering the political aims of the Soviet Union.

The forward march of the trade-union movement has been beset with internal as well as external difficulties, of course. As we noted in the discussion of party development, unions have been deeply divided in their general outlook. While the majority of trade-union officials have been conservatively progressive, slow to accept Marxism on the Continent, slow to accept the Labour party in England, slow to go into party politics in the United States, there have always been more radical elements like the followers of Jules Guesde in France who preached the general strike as the signal for the inevitable revolution, or the Communist unions in Germany which demanded that the bourgeois republic be destroyed. There have also been powerful Christian trade unions wherever Catholics had organized a party of their own. These unions, while rejecting Marxist and other forms of a secularist and atheist outlook, strove just as determinedly to accomplish the practical objectives of the trade unionist everywhere.

It is only with the coming of totalitarianism that trade-union power and progress have been halted. To be sure, there are organizations formally called trade unions in Russia as there were in Germany and in Italy in the thirties. But these organizations, far from being trade unions in the old sense of being free associations of workingmen, freely organized and open, are closed regiments whose leadership is controlled by the government. From being instruments for pressing the workingmen's interests against the employer and the government, they have become organizations for regimenting the workers and pressing the interests of the government and the party against the workers.

A peculiar break has occurred in the United States. Here the trade-union movement has until very recently been relatively weak as compared to Europe. Among the many causes two stand out: the individual worker's opportunity for personal betterment and the generally high standard of living for skilled workers. But its very weakness obliged the trade-union movement to remain united; the American Federation of Labor followed persistently for many years the policy of the most skillful pressure groups

471

in giving and withdrawing support from politicians in the light of their "labor record." Under a plurality system of elections, organized labor could thus be the balancer and decide the election in many a closely contested district.

But the system of craft unions upon which the American Federation of Labor was reared tended to be dominated by the most highly skilled workers, the steamfitters, the precision mechanics, and dozens of other highly paid technicians; it tended to neglect the interests of the vast army of the semiskilled and unskilled. These workers had come to play an increasing role in the mass-production industries. For some years there had been murmurings of revolt against this system, and a demand for organization by industries had been heard to an increasing extent. After all, such organization had been the basis of trade unionism in Europe for many years; no reason existed why it should be barred in the United States. When the open break came, in 1935, it led to the establishment of the Congress of Industrial Organization, the CIO, under the aggressive leadership of John L. Lewis. The movement has scored striking successes in the mass-production field, such as automobiles, electrical-equipment manufacture, and transport. Of course, the United Mine workers were, in a sense, an industrial union right along. (They have since left the CIO.) This split in labor's ranks, while probably difficult to avoid, has had very unfortunate immediate effects upon labor's dealings with the government. Regulatory mechanisms, set up for the benefit of labor, such as the National Labor Relations Board, have been torn between the rival claims of the two great organizations. But there can be little doubt that under severe strain a merger of the two great trade-union federations will be effected. Even if it were not, relationships will gradually become stabilized, just as they were between Christian and Free trade unions in Germany. The need for effective co-operation is so great that differences in point of view can only temporarily interfere with its operation. Charges have frequently been made that Communists were dominating the CIO. While Communists, or rather Stalinists, undoubtedly saw a golden opportunity in the split between CIO and AFL, because they had never previously been able to make any substantial inroads upon American trade unions, their hopes have largely been disappointed. In some CIO unions they have played a dominant part, but the Congress as a whole is anti-Communist since the start of the "cold war" and a veritable purge of party members has been effectuated in many unions.

The Russian Revolution and the trade unions, particularly in Germany · It is undeniable that Communism, since the establishment of the Soviet Union, has had a disruptive effect upon the trade-union movement. In Imperial Russia the trade unions were outlawed. They afforded no outlet for the activity of even the mildest social reformers.[7] Sporadic and clandestine attempts were made to organize the workers, but usually the initiators ended up in Siberia, if they were not shot. The daily contact of factory workers nevertheless afforded an opportunity for skeleton organization. Councils or soviets composed of these more progressive elements in the factories (and in the army) offered themselves, therefore, as the most readily available means of organized support after the revolution. The Communist party, politically speaking, was an organization bringing these elements together in a Pan-Russian and comprehensive group. Therefore, if later all the councils were found in the hands of the Communists, there is nothing startling about that. The soviets are the natural arena of Communist party activity (see below, p. 481).

As is so often the case, what was an inherent necessity in one political arena is carried by doctrinaires into another where it has no such place. Thus we find that the revolutionaries in Germany and other parts of central Europe who were partisans of the Russian revolution set up councils of workers and soldiers. But here they ran afoul of the well-established and highly disciplined Socialist trade unions and the bureaucracy of the Social Democratic party securely backed by its following. The Workers' and Soldiers' Councils consequently did not have any specific function. The great congress of such councils, which convened at Berlin in December 1918, was readily dominated by men connected with the old trade-union hierarchy, and refused to foster the erection of a Soviet or conciliar Republic. When, thereupon, the radical followers of Liebknecht, calling themselves Spartacists and Communists, went into the streets and began to barricade themselves, civil war broke loose. The radicals were bloodily suppressed, since the Soldiers' Councils were unable to prevent the support of the moderates by the remnants of the imperial army. Since social democracy had been effectively organized for years, there was no real value in the councils. Very soon after their first appearance, Hugo Preuss had formulated the fundamental objections to this sort of hidden dictatorship in a famous article. "In the old bureaucratic state," he wrote, "the citizen had little to say; in the present state he has no say at all; at this moment more than ever before the people as a whole are nothing but the object of a government which is set above them by inscrutable council. The only difference is that it rests its authority not upon God's grace, but upon the equally obscure people's grace. . . . Not classes and groups, not parties and estates in isolated opposition, but only the entire German people represented by a democratically elected National Constitutional Convention can create a truly popular government." Such thoughts made a great appeal to the more moderate elements (which did not cherish the thought of a fate similar to that of the Mensheviks in Russia), backed as they were at this time by a large number of the bourgeoisie who were prepared to give support to whoever seemed ready to prevent real revolutionary violence. For the highly educated German middle classes did not only think of Russian developments; they also had before their minds the course of the French Revolution, which they had learned to detest from their childhood. This revolution, as well as the Commune of 1871, had shown what absolute power concentrated in the hands of self-appointed councils meant. Theoretically, of course, these councils had been subject to recall at any time, as was in keeping with Rousseau's ideas of direct democracy. But how could such recall be effected when anyone advocating it was immediately carted off to the guillotine as an enemy of the people? The masses of German workers as well as the middle class (in so far as they actively participated in political life at this time) would have none of such concentrated power in anybody's hands. In fact, the general attitude toward Workers' Councils became so hostile that the efforts of radical elements to work such a structure into the proposed constitution met with defeat. A compromise provision was appended to the document as its last article to bring to an end a new armed uprising which had been raging in Berlin in March, 1919.

The German National Economic Council · The National Economic Council[8] with its never completed substructure of regional, district, and factory councils was a confused compromise substitute for the National Workers' Council which the radicals had demanded. It placed all groups in the economic life of the country on an equal footing, or attempted to do so, thus realizing a highly conservative set of ideas for functional or occupational representation. Catholic parties had long advocated such a return to medieval, static forms of representation. As mentioned before, even Bismarck had evolved such a plan after the adoption of his tariff system in 1879. As a first step, he organized a Prussian Economic Council in 1880 which, however, met only three times. A bill for a similar council for the nation failed of acceptance because the *Reichstag* remained suspicious of the project. But the idea never died. These undemocratic ideas of conservatives and reactionaries were merged with the equally undemocratic ideas of the social revolutionaries. It was perhaps the first time that the totalitarian alliance of right and left against the democratic middle found active expression. As far as Germany is concerned, it fitted well, of course, into the pattern we have just described of interrelated interest groups and government departments. This realistic basis assured the National Economic Council of a measure of success, even though the first exaggerated expectations were sadly disappointed.

The German National Economic Council as organized under Article 165 of the constitution was not wholly unique. Similar organizations with similar powers were found in France, Japan, Czechoslovakia, Poland, Spain, Mexico, and Yugoslavia. It is characteristic that most of these countries had leanings toward dictatorship and strong remnants of feudalism in their social structure. France, under Vichy, experimented with such a corporative system with little success. But the Economic Council under the Third Republic was rather a technical advisory body than part of the constitutional order. This is different under the new constitution which provides for such a Council in article 25 as we have noted. In the period between the two world wars, the German Council best illustrated the possibilities and the limitations of such councils as parts of a constitutional order. As an experiment, a provisional council was organized in 1920. This provisional council was never replaced by a permanent one, although a bill for its establishment was under consideration when the Hitler forces came into power. But even this provisional council was an independent part of the German constitutional order, and its relative success is indicated by the fact that the bill pending in 1933 for the establishment of the permanent council measurably increased the powers of this body; it proposed to give it the right to initiate legislation.

What were the functions of the provisional council, how was it composed, and how did it work? The functions of the council were concentrated in the fields of business regulation, social welfare, and finance. It played a part in both the legislative and the administrative work in these fields. The government was obliged to submit to the council all legislation dealing with such matters, and it submitted the reports of the council to the other two legislative bodies together with its own memoranda. In the administrative field, the council was called upon in many laws to nominate representatives on various technical boards in the field of economic regulation, labor, and so forth. On the whole it is believed that the council made substantial contributions in these activities. It goes without saying that it slowed up the process of such legislation, and consequently voices were heard in Parliament and among permanent administrators which denounced the council as an unnecessary encumbrance. It was claimed that the various interest groups organized in the council proceeded to press their claims again when the bill came up in the Parliament for decision, after having tried to exert their influence when the bill was being drafted by the administrators. But on the whole, the body could be made to work within the parliamentary system.

More serious problems arise when one turns to the question of its composition. It was generally agreed that the provisional council was too large, and this was due to the fact that every pressure group tried to secure as many seats as possible. What indeed is the relative importance of various activities within the whole economic life of the nation? It is clear that a certain measure of arbitrariness is unavoidable. The provisional council was composed as follows: there were six groups, so-called, Agriculture and Forestry with sixty-eight representatives, Gardening and Fisheries with six, Industry with sixty-eight, Commerce, Banking, and Insurance with forty-four, Transportation, Communication, and Public Enterprises with thirty-four, and Handicrafts with thirty-six. To these were added thirty representatives of the Consumers (for example, German Association of Housewives, with four representatives), sixteen representatives of the officials and the free professions, and twenty-four members appointed by the government. This makes a total of three hundred and forty-six members. In the first six groups employers and employees were jointly represented, each nominating half of the members. In practice, this hitching together of management and labor did not work. The labor members of the various groups all collaborated, being directed by the united German trade-union organization, and thus established what became known as a division (*Abteilung*) to which the division of the employers corresponded, supplemented by the others as a third division. We thus find eventually three divisions, management, labor, and groups not identified with either. The pending bill had recognized this development and proposed to assign membership in the council on the basis of these divisions. Thus in Division I, the various great organizations of industry, commerce, agriculture, and so on, were each to name their representatives, while all the members of Division II were to be nominated by the General German Union of Trade Unions (*Allgemeiner Deutscher Gewerkschaftsbund*). Actually this had been the situation even in the provisional council. The original pretense of effectively integrating employers and employees had not materialized. The government in order to break the deadlock which resulted at times from the opposition of these two groups, particularly in social questions, fell back upon the third division, composed of consumers, officials, free professions, and appointees of the federal government and the state governments.

The gradual ascendancy of the divisions over the groups brings us to the inner working of the council. After a first outburst of enthusiasm when the great captains of industry participated in the deliberations of the council, the plenary sessions atrophied. After 1924 no more plenary sessions were held at all. All the work of the council shifted to the committees. Three of these committees were of leading importance, corresponding to the three main fields of council activity, one dealing with business regulation (*wirt-schaftspolitisch*), another with social reform (*sozialpolitisch*), and the third with financial matters (*finanzpolitisch*). The government voluntarily granted them an advisory supervision of ordinances and decrees as well as participation in legislation. The members of these committees were designated by three divisions of the council, each naming an equal number. Under the provisional council, the chairmanship of these committees was entrusted to members of the permanent civil service designated by the respective ministries (Economic Affairs, Labor, Finance), but the draft changed this and had the committees elect their own chairmen. As the business of the council had developed, the major committees were really to all intents and purposes the council. Working through numerous sub-committees and temporary committees, they received the drafts of the bills directly from the government, with the steering committee, composed equally of members from the three divisions, acting merely as an intermediary.

It is obvious from what has been said that the German Provisional National Economic Council, as it functioned under the Republic, served essentially to co-ordinate the manifold organizations which modern economic life has brought into existence and to legalize or constitutionalize their participation in legislation and administration. In Czechoslovakia, where a similar council was at work, the experience with it was very much like that in Germany. Such councils can undoubtedly fulfill a useful function under modern conditions, but it seems arguable whether the amount of additional work involved is worth the result. In truly democratic countries, where the interest groups are largely independent of the government, considerable objection arises to such "co-ordination." Perhaps if they are kept advisory, councils have a permanent role to play. It is as yet difficult to say whether such more restricted bodies, attached to the cabinet itself, are preferable. In the United States, where, in spite of expanding executive leadership, legislation is still to a large extent the work of Congress, and where the greatest pressure of organized groups is brought there, novel problems would undoubtedly arise. It seems highly improbable that a body composed of the representatives of interest groups could resolve the conflicts which the Congressman struggles continually to compromise in his efforts to retain the support of his constituency.

The Fascist "corporative state" · As noted before, the idea of representation by interest groups has roots in antidemocratic traditions, sentiments, and viewpoints. It is therefore hardly surprising that bodies built upon this principle should have been features of totalitarian systems. Indeed, these bodies are at times represented as alternatives to popular representation by districts or territorial subdivisions of the electorate. They are an extension of the government's long arm into the economy; the co-ordination of all organizations, the abolition of all freedom and independence of association, make the managers of economic interest groups part of the governmental and party hierarchy and bureaucracy. Following the pattern of the Provisional German Economic Council, there was, in the Fascist Grand Council of Corporations, a threefold division of economic activities, as well as several groups such as agriculture and industry. The threefold division was that of employers, employees, and others (consumers, professional people, and the like). These divisions and groupings were composed of various organizations. Each activity was recognized by the government through *one* organization only. Though the officers of some of these organizations were "elected," they practically all owed their offices to the government which either directly appointed them, or maneuvered their election through effective pressure. A measure of autonomy was, perhaps, preserved by some of the organizations of large business interests, banks, and so forth. But essentially the government and the party behind the government used the "corporate" or rather associational structure of modern economic life for the purpose of co-ordination and control. Associations which before the advent of the Fascists maintained a vigorous life of their own, particularly in the labor field, were all fascistized. In the conflicts between Fascist trade unions and Fascist employers' associations the government rendered the final decisions. It inclined now to the one side and now to the other, as the exigencies of general policy seemed to suggest, but on the whole the workers, being the weaker party of the two, came out at the short end. Fascist mythmakers looked upon this setup of bureaucratized associations as a first step in the direction of complete pacification in the industrial realm, when workers, employers, and consumers would be united in real "corporations"; but there were no signs, except in official speeches and writings, to indicate that any such trend was materializing. As H. Finer, in his able analysis of the Fascist system, remarked: "the term 'corporative' has been used, if not invented, to rouse a sense of wonder in the people, to keep them guessing, to provoke inquiry, and to contrive, out of the sheer mystification of an unusual word, at once to hide the compulsion on which the Dictatorship finally depends and to suggest that a miraculous work of universal benevolence is in the course of performance. . . . The 'corporative state' is a tool of propaganda." To this G. Salvemini, an Italian scholar of high repute and an avowed enemy of Fascism, rightly added: "From 1926 to 1935 the sole reality in Italian political life was the dictatorship of a man and his party. But side by side with this reality a new myth had grown to gigantic proportions—the myth of the 'corporative state.'"[9] Hence, apart from Mussolini's propaganda, the discussion of this governmentalization of all associational life leads back to the ordinary problems of bureaucracy previously discussed.

National Socialist "estates" · In Germany, where the tradition of looking upon the government as the cure-all was very strong, the development of occupational representation under Hitler took place along lines very similar to those in Italy, though accompanied by a different verbiage. Here the mythmakers talked about professional estates (*Berufsstände*) or guilds. Actually, the organizations functioning in conjunction with the National Socialist government and administration had little in common with the late medieval estates except the name. For whereas the estates proper were autonomous bodies and the mainstay of the medieval constitutional order, the Nazi "estates" were, as we just said, prolongations of the governmental bureaucracy like the syndicates, federations, and "corporations" of Fascism.[10] There was the National Economic Chamber, with regional chambers below it, composed of chambers of industry, of commerce, and of handicraft. There was the National Estate of Agriculture (*Reichsnährstand*, sometimes translated German Food Estate), composed of all the organizations of agriculture and allied businesses. There was the German Labor Front (*Deutsche Arbeitsfront*), composed presumably of all working Germans (the claimed membership was 23,000,000). There was finally the National Culture Chamber (*Reichskulturkammer*), composed of all the "free" professions: doctors, writers, artists, and so forth. Each one of these "estates" was hitched to one of the ministries, Economics, Agriculture, Labor, and Propaganda respectively. Thus, final co-ordination could come only through the *Führer*, Adolf Hitler, as boss of the several ministers in his cabinet. But in the meantime, each one of these estates was free to reach out and to gather as many Germans into its fold as would "join." Thus individuals and firms might belong to both the Chamber of Agriculture and the National Economic Chamber. Again, they might combine allegiance to the National Economic Chamber and the German Labor Front. This depended entirely upon the nature of their business or activity. The German Labor Front was very keen about gathering into its fold employers as well as employees—as a symbol of industrial pacification and community. There existed, however, at the base of the industrial system in every factory, so-called shop communities (*Werkgemeinschaften*) in which the employer was, according to law, the "leader" and the workers the "followers."

What this all adds up to is this: after the destruction of the German

Socialist and Christian trade unions, the National Socialists had to cast the relations of management and labor into new forms. The recreational and fraternal activities of the trade unions, as well as the representation of the "labor interest" in the formulation of national policies, were taken over by the German Labor Front; the determination of wages, working hours, and other practical questions were turned over to the individual employer as "leader" in his factory or place of business, but under the constant supervision of the government. Watchdogs, the Trustees of Labor, were created under the Ministry of Labor to settle any disputes. Such disputes were brought before them by "confidential councils" established in each factory. The members of these councils were annually proposed by the employer-leader and either accepted or rejected by the worker-following. When rejected by the worker-following, the Trustee of Labor for the district stepped in and appointed a council. It is obvious that such a system of compulsory arbitration favored the employer as the stronger party in any dispute, and on the whole tended to keep wages, hours of work, and all the other conditions more or less stable. With constantly rising prices, such as prevailed in Germany, the "real" wage of labor steadily declined.

In order fully to appreciate the measure of constraint, or indeed terror, which this comprehensive co-ordination (*Gleichschaltung*) of all associational life implied, it is necessary to look at it from below rather than from above. With the "leadership principle" prevailing throughout this hierarchy, any person who incurred the displeasure of his superiors at any point in this vast network of interrelated organizations practically speaking faced starvation. A worker fired from a factory, for example, found it exceedingly hard to secure a place elsewhere; his "Labor Passport" immediately told any prospective employer of his past. If he was talented enough to earn his living by writing, he was blocked because enrollment under the National Culture Chamber was denied him. If he had been willing to begin anew in some handicraft, he would have found himself blocked because of the compulsory guild membership under the National Chamber of Handicrafts, a part of the National Economic Chamber. But unemployment relief was also denied him because of his status. The prospect of such a pariah status might well have deterred even a stout soul from offering effective opposition. And what was true of a worker was equally true of a professional man, or in fact of anybody who did not enjoy unearned income from capital. Unfortunately the person provided with such an income was the most vulnerable of all potential oppositionists; for the confiscation of all his property for "treason" was easily possible through judgment of a regular court and was in fact effectuated on a large scale in the last years of the regime. The terrifying perspectives of such controls condemn the centralized governmental direction of associational life as quite contrary to the spirit of constitutional democracy. Any moves in that direction deserve to be scrutinized with the greatest care.

Communist councils · It was shown above how the Russian Revolution and its conciliar (soviet) structure influenced the thought of German radicals and thus indirectly prepared the ground for the National Economic Council which sought to integrate autonomous associations, whether of manufacturers, farmers, or workers, with the government in its various activities of legislation and administration. How did the Russian institutions themselves develop? Do they offer the solution which Fascist and National Socialist experiments evidently failed to provide? The conciliar structure of the Soviet Union is the core of the whole system. From factory and village soviets or councils, through county, district, and regional councils, to the All Russian Congress (itself a vast council of more than two thousand members, convened once a year) the structure rises by which the Communist party controls the community in all its phases of economic life. Just as in the German shop communities, the members of the incoming soviet are proposed by the executive officer of the council next higher up in the ladder. But these councils of workers are the only organizations recognized by the Soviet Union. It must be remembered that Russia under the imperial government did not possess any such rich associational life as other countries. Trade unions were outlawed. On the other hand, what organizations of employers and agriculturists there were could not have any place in a classless society as envisaged by the Communist doctrine. Only workers' organizations could be recognized, and they remained weak from the outset, being limited to recreational and fraternal activities. As pointed out before, the officialdom of the Soviet Union constitutes a managerial bureaucracy. The problem of the relation between "capital" and labor in industry is "solved" by confiscating all capital; but the problems of management and labor not only remain, but are aggravated. With the governmental bureaucracy in charge of the central administration of the entire economy, the workers are by no means permitted direct participation in this administration; they are merely allowed to protest against their own wages and working conditions, and may console themselves by the fact that it is all done on their behalf and for their ultimate benefit, and that some measure of social equality between the official bureaucracy and the other and dependent workers is being maintained. The setup is even more paternalistic and autocratic than the Fascist and National Socialist schemes and the individual, especially the non-Communist, is practically at the mercy of the officials. Therefore, even opposition on a limited scale indicates a very large measure of profound dissatisfaction with the government. In fact, such opposition is occurring all the time. Publications like *Vlast Sovietov*, meant for circulation amongst the officials, are full of incidents illustrating this desperate and stubborn resistance. In meetings for the election of factory and village councils (soviets) the majority will defy the local party boss even by a public showing of hands. The sham endeavors on the part of the Soviet government to introduce a greater measure of "freedom" into the system of "elections" did not alter this situation; they are claimed by many to have been instituted merely for purposes of foreign propaganda, and recent developments certainly would strengthen that inference. Ideology and myths aside, it may therefore be doubted whether the Communist procedure of a self-appointed bureaucracy of "Marxists" administering the country's capital in the name of the "working class," but at their expense, is a solution of the problem of the relation of social classes and economic groups under modern industrial conditions. Granting the rather imposing achievements of the Soviet government in industrializing Russia, one is nevertheless compelled to conclude that the manifold groupings of modern industrial life have been held in check only by setting up a rigid grouping of the people into a governing "elite" of Communist bureaucrats and politicians, and a mass of passive followers, exploited to a very high degree for the purpose of enhancing the future industrial power of Russia, that is, the self-same Communist elite. To what account this "elite" will ultimately turn this gigantic power it is hard to say. But as foreign conquest and personal aggrandizement have been the common uses to which power has been put when uncontrolled and undivided, it is quite probable that both of them will play a role in the future evolution of the Soviet Union.[11]

Pressure groups in the United States today · Ever since Pendleton Herring's *Group Representation before Congress* was published in 1929, there has been developing a more constructive attitude toward these organized interest groups. This attitude is helpful, if it is not carried to the point of cynical disregard for the key aspects of constitutional democracy. Such an outlook is becoming more general; it tends to look upon the voter with an independent mind of his own as a weird or undesirable citizen. These pressure groups fit in better with the idea that it is all a matter of trends and forces. "The" farmer and "the" worker displace in this view the citizen who as a common man participates in the common concern of the community. No doubt this concept of a common man, that is to say of a man as free citizen, has a distinctly normative flavor. Even so, the discarding of this norm spells great dangers for constitutional democracy. Happily, it is still a rather far cry from the operation of the Soviets to the position of professional groups and associations in the United States today. All these associations are democratically organized.[12] Control over them is, at least according to the by-laws, exercised by the rank and file in the various organizations. This democratic pattern is recognized by the Chamber of Commerce just as much as by the American Federation of Labor. But none of the labor unions, and only a few of the professional associations, like the American Medical Association and American Bar Association, are actually in control of their trades. Others, like the American Association of University Professors, occupy an intermediary position with their members exercising a varying, but rarely decisive, influence in the colleges and universities of the country. Still others, like the associations of school teachers, have as a rule even less control. All these occupational and professional groups have as one of their primary functions the representing of the interest of the particular group for which they speak. As pressure groups before legislatures and administrative bureaus, they watch over whatever governmental policies would affect their members. The extent of such activity is, of course, affected by the measure to which the government has adopted any policies, and it therefore varies greatly; on the whole, it has been increasing in the last few decades.

Perhaps the most startling extension of pressure group activity occurred, when the National Recovery Administration undertook to co-ordinate the American economy on a vast scale with the help of these organizations. This experiment, even though it failed, signalized the rise of organized interest groups and their potential claim to participate in the government in an active and legal way. During the Second World War, trade associations again exercised governmental functions in various ways. Even in peace time, numerous advisory bodies in various fields of governmental endeavor are staffed by the representatives of organized interest groups. Indeed, successful participation in such groups is one effective road toward participation in government today.[13] Another striking instance of the close collaboration between occupational interest groups and governmental agencies is presented by the county agents. These are officials who are connected in an administrative-executive way with all three levels of the American government, federal, state, and local, as well as with the Farm Bureau Federation, one of the three great farmers' organizations. The United States Department of Agriculture, the extension services of the schools of agriculture in the state universities, the counties, and the farmers individually through affiliation with the local Farm Bureau, all contribute toward the maintenance of the administrative work which this official and his staff carry on.[14] In the labor field, similar developments are in the making through the National Labor Relations Board of the federal government and cognate agencies in the states. In Massachusetts, for example, definite co-ordination has been worked out through administrative measures. All this goes to show that occupational groups are beginning to play a role in the American governmental process, just as they have been doing in other highly industrialized countries. Perhaps this approach is more promising than the one comprised under the formula of "legalizing the lobby." It is not so much a question of giving a legal status to these pressure groups as it is a matter of transforming them from mere pressure groups in their relation to the government and the general public into groups taking an active part and a measure of responsibility in the conduct of modern administration.

Conclusion · In conclusion, it may be said that the genuine representative significance of all organizations arising in connection with men's activities within the total context of modern industrial life has become sufficiently apparent to make it necessary to reckon with them as pretenders to the throne of government. Where the interests are sharply divided, certain of these groups have proceeded to take over the government and to revolutionize it in such a way as to suit their particular needs and conceptions. Such efforts have been accompanied by dictatorial methods—relapses into crude techniques of government which violate the fundamental premises of constitutional limitations. In order to overcome the one-sidedness of their representative basis, they have sought to extirpate the groups which they did not represent. Constitutional governments of the established kind have seen a widespread movement for the participation of all kinds of occupational and professional groups in the administration of that part of national life in which they happen to be particularly concerned. Such participation saddles the administration internally with all those conflicts which it is supposed to mediate. Functional representative devices must be considered with great care; they tend to have a divisive, rather than an integrating, effect. The task remains of distilling the general, public interest out of the often-conflicting special interests which constitute part of the whole. But it looks as if functional representative devices are here to stay as elements in any pattern of constitutionalism under modern industrial conditions.

PART IV

TENSIONS

BREAKDOWNS

ADJUSTMENTS

XXIII

Socialization and Planning

Introduction · The nature of planning · The nature of socialization · Bureaucratization · Socialization and planning in Great Britain · Socialization and planning in continental western Europe: (1) France. (2) Italy. (3) Germany · International planning: the Marshall Plan · Conclusion.

Introduction · Since the emergence of modern constitutionalism in the seventeenth and eighteenth centuries, some unforeseen tensions have developed throughout Western society. Of these, some are of a spiritual and moral nature and are associated with the decline of Christianity as a living and vital force; as such they lie beyond the scope of this study.[1] Others are of a more earthy and pragmatic sort and have themselves been nurtured to some extent at least by constitutionalism and democracy. Among them planning, propaganda, and plebiscitary mass action (direct democracy) are of major importance; they in turn have occasioned the ever more frequent employment of emergency powers. Such "constitutional dictatorship" was superseded in a number of countries by totalitarian dictatorship, both of the right and of the left. The aggressive propensities of the latter, whether under the banner of world revolution or world conquest, have precipitated wars, both hot and cold, which have further extended the employment of emergency powers, and have called for planning, propaganda, and plebiscitary mass action on an unprecedented scale. No study of constitutional democracy in the mid-twentieth century could overlook these tensions, breakdowns, and resulting readjustments. If there has been a reaffirmation of constitutionalist principles and practices in Europe, in France, Italy, Austria, and Germany, it is counterbalanced by the disappearance of constitutional democracy from Czechoslovakia, Yugoslavia, Poland, and China, to mention only the most important countries.

Each one of the tension areas raises a problem of readjustment. Can the particular practice be combined with constitutional democracy? Can it, in other words, be constitutionalized is the anxious question. Nowhere is this questioning more persistent than in the field of "planning" and socialization. There are many who would maintain that planning of a central kind means the end of constitutional democracy.[2] Others have on the contrary insisted that planning is simply an extension of constitutionalism into broader fields, that a constitution is itself a plan.[3] The same range of arguments has been urged with regard to socialization and socialism. A sizable group of writers link constitutional democracy with a free-market economy, including free enterprise.[4] The traditional view of moderate socialists, from Lassalle to the Labour Party and Social Democratic parties throughout Europe insists on the contrary that socialism is the fulfillment of democracy, that "political" democracy without "economic" or "industrial" democracy is incomplete or worse.[5] We have had occasion to sketch some of these ideological aspects in Chapter XXI, above. It seems desirable, however, to explore this vital issue in greater detail and in concrete rather than in ideological terms. It is worth noting, moreover, that the negative view which insists upon the ideological and practical incompatibility of planning and socialization with constitutional democracy is shared by conservatives and by the totalitarian enemies of constitutionalism. Here lies the key to the strange and often disastrous combinations in electoral and parliamentary politics that seem so illogical from a rational standpoint.

One other introductory remark is in order. It is customary to speak of planning and of socialism in virtually the same breath. This is in part due to the fact that socialist ideology has always stressed its interest in a rationalized, planned economy. The assumption of a necessary link between the two is reinforced by the fact that the Soviet Union, believed and represented to be a "socialist state," has engaged in large-scale planning and is by many economists credited with having achieved "the highest state of development" in planning.[6] But the fact that socialism and planning have been thus linked in theory and practice does not mean that planning is necessarily so linked. Nor indeed does it mean that socialization, as distinguished from socialism (for instance, a country may "socialize" its railroads without embracing socialism as a system for all or most economic activity), need necessarily imply planning. To illustrate the latter argument, one may point to the socialized utilities in many European countries completely devoid of economic planning twenty-five years ago; to illustrate the former, one only has to think of the considerable planning for war mobilization of the economy in the United States and other countries[7] involving no socialization at all. It is clear, or should be, that while planning and socialization are closely related tendencies or approaches to the economy, they should be clearly distinguished and treated accordingly as far as their relation to constitutional democracy is concerned. They are two distinct attempts to "rationalize" economic life by eliminating those aspects of economic activity in a free-market economy believed to be contrary to rationality: in the case of planning, competition and its attendant evils of advertising and related distribution costs are to be eliminated; while in the case of socialization, it is profit and the related divergencies in the distribution of wealth which is to be done away with.

The nature of planning · Like any descriptive concept, planning can be given a very wide or a very narrow connotation, often qualified by such adjectives as "national," "regional," "international," or "economic." Planning may at one point almost merge with any predetermined policy for the execution of which a "plan" is made. Thus Alexander Hamilton's *Report on Manufactures* (1795) is often considered as planning of an early sort. Narrowly speaking, planning is restricted to the activities involved in setting up an over-all plan covering an entire economy in most of its ramifications and, according to some writers, in being worked out in quantitative statistical terms. Thus conceived "planning can be defined as guidance of economic activities by a communal organ through a scheme which describes, in quantitative as well as qualitative terms, the productivè processes that ought to be undertaken during a designated future period" (Landauer).[8] The trouble with this definition (and with similar ones given by other economists) is that it fails to take account of a basic distinction arising for the student of democracy from the fact that the ends or purposes of such a planning process may be determined in radically different ways. For if the end or purpose of the planning is authoritatively determined by a body such as the Politburo, the planner's task is reinforced by that body's compulsive force, whereas planning under democratic conditions has to treat its end as variable in terms of popular approval or disapproval, and the resulting difficulties of enforcement raise in many people's minds the question as to whether planning can be carried on under such conditions at all. To illustrate from recent experience with the European Recovery Program (Marshall Plan), the planners have had to deal with strong pressures exerted by American business and agricultural interests which insisted that the funds under the Plan must be used to buy their products, regardless of the effect of such purchases upon the Plan. In view of agricultural surpluses, pressure in this field has been especially strong, and the pervasive power of the agricultural lobby has aided this cause to the point where the Congress was prepared to impose "reservations" upon the planners. To many thoughtful persons this appears as incontrovertible proof that planning cannot be combined with democracy. From this conclusion they then proceed to argue either that planning must go or that democracy is out of date. The seriousness of this issue cannot be denied.

It is, nevertheless, our contention that a certain kind of planning is not only compatible with constitutional democracy, but is its natural extension in a mature industrial society. But this planning is not the same as the "blueprint planning" of a totalitarian system. In fact, it is its diametric opposite[9] in the very same sense in which legislation, government information, parties, unions, and a host of other public activities are opposites of a totalitarian system. In fact, properly considered, a constitution is itself an ambitious "plan." It is well known that the primary task of the men who projected our constitutional plan at Philadelphia was an economic one: interstate commerce, tariffs, currency, and debts were among the primary problems for which the Constitutional Convention sought a solution. As Mr. Walton Hamilton has shown in his brilliant study on the commerce clause, the makers of the Constitution had a definite ideal society in mind, economically as well as politically—and it was not simply a free-market economy either, but to some extent at least a mercantilist directed economy.[10] What was true at Philadelphia was equally true of the Weimar Republic. Here a socializing commonwealth was envisaged, and an unsuccessful attempt made to order and plan a "social democracy." The new constitutions of Europe, more especially the constitutions of France, Italy, and Germany, are likewise "plans" and much of the discussion in the constitutional conventions was concerned with such crucial issues of the modern economy as what was to be the extent of socialization. These plans were evolved in public debates, and were accepted or rejected by the electorate in mass referenda. The provisions for constitutional amendment provide machinery for the periodic revising and recasting of these plans. It is inadmissible to insist that because these constitutions are not stated in quantitative terms they are not plans. As a matter of fact, ends or purposes which are universally admitted to be key aspects of any plan can rarely be stated in quantitative terms. A constitution outlawing forced labor (Constitution of the United States, Art. XIII) is providing a very important ingredient to a particular society, as is the corresponding guarantee of freedom of choice in one's occupation (German Constitution of May 8, 1949, art. 12).[11] It is part of a definite plan—an open society—which that constitution seeks to organize.

It is, from this standpoint, unfortunate that economists (who necessarily emphasize the economic aspect in planning and whose technical services are of decisive importance) should have pre-empted the discussion in the field of planning to the extent to which they have in fact done so. For economic values, while of great, even paramount, importance in the general outlook of the mass of humanity, are not by any means the only ones. Freedom of speech, to give only one example, may not seem important to those who have it, and security in one's person even less so—but the statement often heard that people cease to care about freedom when they have no bread may well be true in countries which have enjoyed freedom over a long period or which have never known it. People who have enjoyed the blessings of a system of planned economy in which unemployment was eliminated by regimentation and forced labor show little enthusiasm for that "solution." In short, a planning process which involves coercion in any considerable scale will be unenforceable in a democratic society.

We cannot escape from the difficulties which this situation presents by interpreting planning to mean any rational effort to utilize social intelligence in the determination of public policies (Merriam). We have distinguished the authoritarian approach which insists that "an economy is planned when one central authority adopts and carries out a program designed to realize a single and unquestioned end to the whole of the community over which it has jurisdiction," because an "unquestioned end" is incompatible with constitutional democracy. It is the very essence of the democratic process to permit the questioning of any end at any time.[12] But to assume that this questioning will necessarily proceed according to rational methods is basically unrealistic and not in keeping with our knowledge of man either histori- cally, psychologically, or economically. Planners proceeding on such as- sumptions will fail to meet popular needs and demands, and theorists of planning in such terms will be easy prey to the criticism of both Marxists and Fascists. In short, since interests and values are not wholly rational, any deliberate rational coordination of values and assignment of priorities in accordance with such coordination is inhibited.

Democratic planning, dedicated as it must be to achieving the greatest satisfaction for as many as possible, cannot neglect the reactions of all those whom a given policy affects. Based upon the primary decision of the elec- torate which the constitution embodies, the broad pattern of such a plan will be submitted to and periodically reviewed by the representative legis- lative bodies. Where the referendum is an established institution, it may be employed for clarifying some basic aspects. But generally speaking the procedures applicable to sound budgeting (itself a plan for government operations) are *ceteris paribus* the procedures applicable to democratic planning. It is, however, characteristic of the as yet primitive state of affairs in this field that none of the new constitutions, let alone the old ones, deal with planning as they do with budgeting, even though the category of "extraordinary expenditures" which wrought such havoc in European fiscal affairs points toward planning, as does any proposed budgeting over several years.

It is in the nature of things no easy matter to state the objectives of planning in a given democratic society, except in such platitudinous gen- eralities as "general welfare" or "the greatest happiness of the greatest number." A totalitarian society can fix such a goal: industrialization in the case of the Soviet Union, preparation for war in the case of Hitler's *Reich*. But the democratic process, as we have seen, consists in compromises on concrete and specific policies, with different groups and individuals going along, although with different purposes in mind. (There is also the problem of multiple motivation in the individual himself to consider.)

In short, co-operative, democratic planning under a constitution may be defined as guidance and co-ordination of the community's activities through an over-all program, especially in the use of economic resources, in accordance with the community's preferences, as expressed through the constitution and through representative bodies. This over-all program describes, in quantitative terms where possible, the various measures required in guiding production and distribution over a projected planning period of, say, four years.

The nature of socialization · The term "socialization" is often used interchangeably with "nationalization." This is unfortunate, as there are several ways of socializing property which does not transfer title to the "nation," but to other entities. It is more precise to speak of nationalization as a subordinate concept of the more general socialization concept. Thus, a city may socialize its street railways, or a state under a federal system may provide for socializing banks within its jurisdiction.

As everyone knows, socialization has for many generations been associated with the political, social, and economic philosophy known as socialism. It was an old story when the Communist Manifesto, in 1847, demanded the "centralization of control in the hands of the state" of such key enterprises as banking and transport.[13] But in spite of this fact, it is necessary today to dissociate the two concepts, for socialization is a recurrent event in contemporary society, often accepted and even promoted by nonsocialists, while socialism is an ideology, a system of ideas concerning desirable social changes. The many publicly controlled and publicly operated utilities may be a source of greater joy to socialists, but they are accepted by nonsocialists for purely pragmatic reasons unrelated to any ideological preconceptions.

The preceding remarks imply a conception or definition of socialization as the process of transforming private into public property, ordinarily followed by governmental operation and management of such enterprises. However, besides such governmental operation, other forms have been recognized, such as semi-autonomous government corporations and even union-managed enterprises (see discussion of Italy, below). Socialization is recognized in the new constitutions of France, Italy, and Germany.[14] In all these constitutions it is associated with the statement of basic rights as a limitation upon the right of private property. In the French constitution, the provision is, like all basic rights, found in the preamble; socialization is made dependent upon either of two criteria: (*a*) that an enterprise have the character of a national public service, or (*b*) that an enterprise be a monopoly in fact. The German constitution (Basic Law) is more detailed and specific; its provisions are also broader in that not only monopoly but any kind of "abuse of economic power" serves as criteria. The Italian constitution follows the same line, but speaks of "public interest" and "social utility" as criteria as well as of monopoly, and seeks to restrict private initiative where it damages "security, liberty, or human dignity." A similar provision was contained in the rejected (socialist) constitution of France (May 5, 1946), and it is amusing to see that even here property is described as an "inviolable right." But this right was defined as "the right to use, enjoy and dispose of the goods guaranteed to each person by law." Needless to say, it excluded property required for public service and monopoly in fact. We shall discuss presently what has happened under these constitutional provisions of the several countries.

Even where the constitution does not now provide for socialization "in the public interest" (whatever the phrase may be is unimportant, since only the people and their representatives decide), socialization seems to be going forward. Marx and Engels would indeed be surprised if they could see how much of their original program is now realized in "capitalist" states. Socialist governments, though constitutionalist, have gone further. In Britain, under a Labour government, socialization has been adopted for the central bank, inland transport, and the basic sources of industrial production (coal, electricity, and gas), while steel is to follow next.[15] Without a written constitution, Britain was able to accept the basic decision of her electorate in lieu of the more elaborate process which would be required in the United States. How these decisions might be modified, if the electorate changed its mind and returned the Conservatives to power, no one can know at the present time. But the Conservative party has given indications that it will continue most of the socialization measures which have been effected.

In view of the role of government in all socialization, it has become customary in France to describe as "*étatisme*" this general tendency toward socialization, that is to say, toward increasing the role of the "state." Lately certain circles have introduced into English the term *statism*, mostly in order to decry it. In view of the lack of resonance for the term "state" in America, if not in Britain, this word lacks punch, and should be replaced by "governmentalism." This "governmentalist" trend is also more in keeping with the general meaning of socialization, since a municipal, as well as a state or national, government can readily be envisaged as engaged in "governmentalizing."

Some measure of socialization is clearly compatible with constitutional democracy. The opinion often heard in the United States that socialization subverts constitutionalism is palpably contrary not only to the experience of many European countries, where socialization of, say, railroads, has for a long time been accomplished without any destruction of the constitution. But even in the United States, socialization has gone forward, especially on the local level. As a matter of fact, close government control of a given industry such as the railroads, under the Interstate Commerce Act (1920), is sometimes referred to as "cold socialization." If property is seen as a bundle of legal relationships or, as Walton Hamilton once put it, "an accepted medley of duties, privileges and mutualities,"[16] that is, of rights and obligations, then any legislative (authoritative) act by which some of these rights or privileges are transferred from private persons to the community should, broadly speaking, be included under socialization. Even though the transfer of such a right or privilege may only prevent an owner of cattle from selling milk if the animals have not been tested for T. B.—a step obviously desirable from the standpoint of health—it would still be part of the broad socializing tendencies of our time. It is a denial of the harshly individualistic doctrine of "buyer beware" and substitutes governmental for private action. But it is also possible to continue to speak of such cattle as "private property" simply by defining property as consisting of a different bundle of relationships or "miscellany of equities." When seen in this perspective, it becomes clear that private and socialized property are not simple, absolute antitheses, but are a whole series of gradations. What property "means" depends in any case upon definition by law and sanction by public authority. It is in this sense that the new constitutions are justified in stating that "private property" is protected. It is a bitter lesson, but an inescapable one, for the property owner to learn that the meaning of property is itself subject to constitutional determination.

Bureaucratization · The early advocates of socialism were curiously naïve regarding the remedial potentialities of the "state." Having seen with their own or their fathers' eyes the realities of the police state, of the despotic governments of "enlightened absolutism," it would seem that they might well have been as cautious concerning the wielders of power and authority as were the political leaders who founded the United States and wrote the Declaration of Independence. But they evidently believed that a state, once it was controlled by the right kind of people, that is to say, socialists, would be a "creative" and wholly beneficial agent. Later, as the nineteenth century wore on and the blessings of liberty turned out to be somewhat less unmitigated than had at first been hoped, many socialists pinned their hope on some kind of disappearance of the state, in short, on anarchism. Of course, they themselves (and more specially Marx) would have strenuously objected to any such suggestion in spite of their explicitly stated expectation that "the state will wither away," and that there will ensue a spontaneous co-operation without any coercive organization. The anarchist implications of such socialist doctrines as those of Fourier and Proudhon are more generally admitted, especially since Marx castigated them as "Utopians" for this very reason, among others. It is important to recall this excessive hopefulness of the older socialist doctrines because it focuses attention upon a striking blindspot in their social analysis. This blindspot is the inability to visualize clearly that a socialized society would be a bureaucratized society and, what is even more important, that a *socializing* society is a society considerably advanced on the road toward bureaucratization.[17] For as Marx himself pointed out, the increasing concentration of economic power in a relatively small number of large-scale enterprises with the consequent rise of monopolies is the stepping-off stone for socialization. Marx' analysis was probably too crude and too simple; but it nevertheless contained a very important insight into the degree of ripeness of a given economy.

But a factor to which Marx and many of his followers paid slight attention was the extent to which such large-scale enterprises themselves become bureaucratized until a point is reached where the transfer of top control to public authorities calls for hardly any changes in organizational pattern or in relations to the general public. Whether it is therefore desirable to centralize control administratively in the government, rather than to provide the government with the supervisory and inspectoral authority for which monopoly power calls, is another matter. Bureaucratization is a general trend in contemporary society; it is as noticeable in American universities with their tens of thousands of students as it is in industry and government. The key problem from a democratic and constitutionalist viewpoint is how to render and keep these bureaucracies responsible. About this problem we have written earlier (see ch. XIX). If the problem of responsibility can within reason be taken care of, then a "commonwealth of mutual servants" may in course of time be inclined to treat the question of socializing a given economic activity purely in terms of administrative rationality; the criteria would presumably be linked to such issues as the nature of effective incentives and the like. (It may be either profit or power, or it may be a combination of these and other incentives.)[18]

But probably the most difficult issue confronting such a commonwealth of mutual servants is the ability of the workers in any one of its sectors to stall the entire economy, or a large part of it, through the strike weapon. Traditionally, democratic constitutionalism has been very hostile to strikes in the government service. In the United States, where even unionism in the government service has always been sharply criticized, such strikes are completely taboo; they used to be in Britain. But as important and highly unionized segments of the economy become part of the public service, that is, bureaucratized, the strong pre-existing union organizations, accustomed to collective bargaining, are loath to and in fact refuse to surrender the strike weapon. Since the rationale of unionization is the overcoming of the weakness of the individual worker as he faces the larger and larger corporate organizations in industry, the government, being the largest and most anonymous employer of them all, certainly confronts organized labor as perhaps the most difficult and powerful employer of them all. It is often said that the government under constitutional democracy is after all subject to the influence of popular control. While this corrective may be of some value, especially in the long run, it will hardly satisfy a unionized labor force which finds itself confronted with declining real wages, as is often the case under socialization. This is a development which earlier socialist theory tended to neglect almost entirely. In the socialist fatherland, the Soviet Union, strikes are completely outlawed since it is part of the totalitarian position to "co-ordinate" all independent organizations. Therefore, the labor unions become subordinate to governmental control there, as they do in Fascist states. This policy is rationalized in terms of the over-all ideological pattern which claims that the Soviet Union is the people's government, the "true democracy," and therefore entitled to the loyal support of all. No challenge to public authority can be permitted. But a constitutional democracy, especially one whose constitution guarantees the right to strike as part of the freedom of association, cannot adopt such a method. Whether there are any other workable methods must at present be considered an open question. Neither the denial of the right to strike, nor the crippling of all plans and programs decided upon by the government representing the majority and occupying a strategic monopoly position, can be accepted as a true solution. The road toward such a solution would seem to lie in the direction of developing adequate criteria for and against the calling of particular strikes in the public services, but the experiences to date are not encouraging.

Socialization and planning in Great Britain · Since Britain has a Labour government, committed to a planned socialist economy as a long-range policy objective, planning and socialization have been closely linked.[19] However, it is desirable even so to keep the two processes apart, since the policy of planning may be a relatively greater success than socialization, or vice versa. This might mean that under democratic conditions, the more successful policy may gain greater majority support than the other. On the other hand, either policy may prove the more insistently necessary, even though no more successful; or again, socialization may prove more difficult to abandon as a policy, because "an omelet once made cannot be unscrambled." It is a fact that few industries that have been socialized anywhere have been afterwards unsocialized again, American railroads after the First World War being the one major exception.

The objectives of the Labour government's planning have been described very differently by different authors, as our general analysis would lead us to expect. Among the major objectives more or less generally recognized must certainly be included the following: reconstruction and more especially increased industrialization to replace foreign assets consumed during the war, relocation of industry to provide a more rational distribution of the population and greater security, stabilization of prices and wages and the maintenance of a high level of employment such as resulted temporarily from war and postwar exigencies, and finally the maintenance and possible extension of a free democratic society.

Apart from controls which owe their continued existence not to any plan, but rather to continued scarcities and other difficulties resulting from the last war, British planning must be considered on two levels: national economic planning and town and country planning. NEP, as we may call the former, proceeds along two main lines.[20] Before stating what these are, it should be emphasized again that these activities are embedded in the procedures of a constitutional democracy and are hence quite different from planning under a totalitarian government. There is much effort at joint consultation with both management and labor, and a great part of the economy is therefore "surveyed" rather than "planned." The result is a "program" which is being urged by "discussion and persuasion," reinforced by the "indirect influence" exercised by price controls, import and export licensing, raw-material allocations, and the like in shaping the decisions of business management.

There is first of all, then, a central planning set up which in its various branches is trying to estimate the national income and the division of expenditure between capital and consumption, as well as manpower and raw-material resources in their relation to the foregoing, and, finally, export and defense needs. There is secondly a long-range development planning which divides into three main sectors: (a) the sector of socialized (nationalized) basic industries, (*b*) the sector of agriculture, and (*c*) the sector of relatively free private industry and trade (about 80 per cent of the economy). The first socialized sector is by many believed to be the real nub of the NEP setup; for seemingly the government can more readily direct through and in accordance with its plans those industries which are owned and controlled by the government. Due, however, to international competition and new inventions, this idea may prove to be a false one. Certainly some of the greatest difficulties in the planning of the Labour government have been encountered in this very field (for instance, in coal).

Before we describe the scope of these socialized industries, however, it may be well to point out that the early period of labor peace has more recently given way to protracted strikes in nationalized industries, with promise of more to come. This problem of strikes against the government, as we have already pointed out, is perhaps the most touchy issue of a partially socialized economy. The British Labour government, as long as it upholds the tradition of constitutional democracy, cannot travel the road of a totalitarian dictatorship which, like the Soviet Union, outlaws the strike. Hence, consultations with autonomous unions controlled by their membership rather than by the government must be held regarding wage policy, relating this policy to other aspects of the planning program. Unfortunately, like other rights, the right to strike is a weapon in the hands of enemies of the constitutional democratic system. Thus, in the recent dockworkers' strike, the Labour government found itself compelled to recognize Communist agents as major factors in the situation. The same difficulties present themselves when an approach to a solution of this problem is sought through work councils, which are intended to enable the workers to participate in management. The British tradition of councils of officials in service should be of some help, but the problem remains a serious one. It imposes limits upon the scope of socialization in a democratic society which parallel the limits imposed by excessive bureaucratization.

The scope of nationalization in Britain largely coincides with the Labour Party's program. Through the Bank of England Act and the Borrowing Control and Guarantees Act, banking is largely nationalized and the flow of credit controlled. We have already mentioned that the basic power sources of industrial production, coal, electricity, and gas, are nationalized. Steel is to follow, while inland transport has already been taken over. It should be remembered that telephone and telegraph services, as well as radio broadcasting, have been governmental services almost from their beginning, in accordance with the European tradition of governmental control of communications (see ch. XXIV). Accordingly, cable and wireless services were nationalized, as well as civil aviation. But whereas in the railroad field public ownership is usually justified on the ground that it is a "mature" industry, aviation was believed to need public ownership because it could not be developed without government subsidies. In point of fact, the governmentally controlled airlines in Europe are very costly compared to the United States lines, and governmental control is exercising a deleterious effect upon transoceanic air traffic development.

While the aforementioned industrial sector is a decisive part of the economy, it is a minority of the whole economy. According to the Labour Party's program and concept, it will remain so. As one writer, speaking for the government, put it recently: "What is aimed at is a partnership involving public ownership of basic common service industries on the one hand and private ownership in a numerically much larger group embracing the vast majority of manufacturing industries, commercial enterprises, and distributive trades on the other."[21]

In order to effectuate such a partnership, a considerable framework of organization and instruments of control is required. Wherever the task can be accomplished by general rules (laws) it should, in keeping with the requirements of constitutionalism, be done. Thus administrative controls and discretion can be kept within limits. Nevertheless, there are possible areas of incompatibility between administrative rationality and constitutional processes which may be serious since administrative initiative and direction remain of decisive importance. They are concentrated in three boards or councils subject to over-all cabinet control. The final authority of the cabinet in the British setup is paramount from the standpoint of constitutional democracy. For the cabinet, and more especially the Prime Minister, holds the mandate from the people, and the people can repudiate them at least every five years. At the same time, the clear-cut support upon which the British cabinet system is built, and which its electoral system favors (see above, chs. XV, XVIII, and XX), gives the cabinet enough stability to carry out a broad plan once it is approved by the electorate in a general election. The high integration of the British system encourages the testing of a plan, especially since the opposition is able to criticize and query at every turn. As Herman Finer has put it: "The Cabinet is the formal, authoritative embodiment of the will to plan of the majority party; it decides the main objectives, and from it the main orders descend; the figures, facts, and the advanced stages of all plans are prepared by its subordinate agencies." My only quarrel with this summary is the contention that the cabinet "decides the main objectives"; it seems to me that these are decided by the electorate, and more specifically by the agents of its majority, the cabinet.[22]

From the cabinet stem a number of committees, boards, and offices which reflect the complexity of a modern government in all its ramifications. Among these, the most important is the Lord President's Committee consisting of the Prime Minister as chairman, and the Lord President, the Foreign Secretary, the Minister for Economic Affairs, the Chancellor of the Exchequer, and several other ministers. Besides this, there is a Committee of the Minister of Economic Affairs, a Defence Committee, and several more specialized committees. In addition to this proliferation of cabinet committees, there is a planning staff, a statistical office, and an economic section, all of the Cabinet secretariat, as well as three different advisory bodies, including the Joint Planning Board, the National Joint Advisory Council, and the National Production Advisory Council. These boards are used to sound out representatives of labor, management, and the general public on proposals of the staffs and offices, as well as to consider general information. Anyone familiar with the ways of bureaucracy cannot but regret this multiplication of committees, boards, offices, and staff units; for no matter how sound may be the theory of responsibility associated with any and all of them, a very considerable twilight zone is bound to be created in which irresponsibility, arbitrariness, and downright inefficiency flourish. If anything should be clear in this vital field, it is the fact that the larger the sweep of an organization, the more firm and clear-cut must be the controls.

One tool or device deserves special attention, the Industrial Working Party. Composed of representatives of employers, labor, and the government, these Parties are set up for a particular industry to study and report on its possible improvement, its efficiency, capital requirements, labor conditions, and so forth. These Working Parties are to draw up a plan for a whole industry on which the government may act.

Finally, for town and country planning—the second level, as we called it—there now operates the Ministry of Town and Country Planning, established in 1943 following the Barlow Report. Under the Town and Country Planning Act, this department is charged with securing a more rational distribution of the population and a corresponding rationalization in the location of industry. It works with the Board of Trade and the various NEP planning outfits and has published a number of very useful studies. Central in its attention is the problem of planning Greater London.[23]

Socialization and planning in continental western Europe · As already mentioned, the new constitutions of France, Italy, and Germany all contain provisions for the socialization of monopolies, basic public services, and industries. Besides, socialization has always been more common in continental Europe, with municipalities producing their own gas and electric power, and the like, and with the national government operating telephones and telegraph, as well as railroads. This is as true of democratic Switzerland and Sweden as it was of authoritarian Germany. The constitution of the Weimar Republic, adopted in the wake of the Communist revolution, contained very broad and explicit provisions (arts. 7, 13) for the socialization of natural resources, as well as any businesses, whether engaged in production or distribution. A Socialization Commission busied itself for some time after 1919 with plans for the carrying out of these enabling provisions of the constitution, but the political reaction as well as the divisions in their own rank cut down the strength of the Socialist parties, and no comprehensive plan materialized. In Switzerland, while the free market and free trade are still recognized, the exigencies of war and the pressure of socialism, especially since 1945, have produced constitutional provisions in support of social security, regulation of monopolies and cartels, and of banking and the like; however, no broad provisions of this kind which have been accepted in France, Italy, and Germany are as yet supported by the majority; even the right to work was rejected as a constitutional principle by an overwhelming majority (525 against 125 thousand, roughly). In Sweden, planning as well as socialization have been pushed vigorously. Sweden (under a Socialist government) has adopted the "double budget" which is in effect a plan to level out the business cycle by making annual budgets show either deficits (in depression years) or surpluses (in boom years).[24]

In contrast to Sweden, the three major European countries here under review have been long on socialization but short on planning. Until the advent of the Marshall Plan in 1947, comprehensive planning was a matter of blueprints and general debate in France, Italy, and Germany; even the famed Monnet Plan was a nice blueprint rather than a workable program. As for the so-called "level-of-industry plan" for Germany, it was no plan in the sense of the democratic planning we are discussing here but an ill-considered attempt to implement an unsound policy by a good deal of highly speculative statistics.

(1) *France.* At the time of the liberation, French public opinion inclined to look upon socialization as a panacea for all the ills and weaknesses of the country's economic and industrial life. The shock of France's collapse had convinced most Frenchmen that there was something radically wrong with their society and their economy. The collaboration of a number of top-ranking industrialists with the Fascists, from whom they expected the same crushing of progressive and labor forces that had occurred in the Fascist regimes, had discredited big business and made them appear ripe for liquida-

tion and nationalization. Few realized the kernel of truth in Herriot's mot: "Nationalization is like a drum: it makes a lot of noise, but there is nothing inside." To nationalize without a detailed plan for the economy of which these nationalized industries would form a part made little sense. Yet even the details of the execution of these nationalizations were not at all clearly worked out. As a matter of fact, when the Socialist-Communist predominance in the constituent assembly became dubious in the spring of 1946, there developed a rush to put nationalizations through at all costs. An observer could not help but feel that the Communists, at least, were 'to some extent motivated by an indifference to the chaos these measures might create, if, as has frequently been alleged, they did not actually wish to promote such chaos.

In the course of 1945–1946 a string of industrial and mining enterprises were nationalized, including: coal, gas, and electricity; the Renault automobile works; some airplane manufacture; central banking and a large share of deposit and credit banking; as well as insurance in considerable part. All these enterprises were put under boards of a mixed composition, with the government, labor, and management represented, but the undertaking is perhaps best characterized by one observer of coal nationalization who wrote that it was "jammed through on the eve of adjournment after a ludicrous debate of an hour and a half on the floor."[25] It is hardly surprising that the gravest difficulties should have developed in industries and businesses socialized in so casual a fashion. In fact, each sector of the economy remained largely independent, without co-ordination by the national government. And since the French "right to strike," guaranteed in the constitution, was not abrogated or even more closely defined for these socialized enterprises, a series of disastrous strikes have rocked the French economy and made it a prey to Communist disturbances of the gravest sort. In other words, the reality is far different from the ideals enunciated at the time of the liberation: the setting up of a true economic and social democracy entailing the eviction of the great economic and financial feudalities and the return to the nation of the monopolies, the sources of mineral wealth, of power, and so forth.[26] Yet, in the spring of 1946, members of parliament could not get any information on the operation of these governmentalized activities, nor have they been able to since. The same is true of planning.

Early in 1946 General de Gaulle had appointed a Planning Council or Commission and the Commissioner of the Plan was presumably at work, but no plan was divulged in spite of repeated protests by members of parliament until the Monnet Plan, so-called after its author Jean Monnet, made its appearance in January 1947.[27] But in the elaboration of this plan, in spite of its vast implications for French economic development, the

French parliament took no part, nor was the Plan a subject of intensive parliamentary scrutiny during either 1947 or 1948 (until August). The Planning Council is assisted by an administrative office, the *Commissariat General du Plan*, working under Jean Monnet. Such an arrangement is sharply at variance with the principles of democratic planning stated above and endangers the future of constitutionalism in France.

The Plan was and is directed toward four main goals (as originally laid down by de Gaulle): (1) to increase French production and foreign trade, (2) to raise the productivity of French labor, (3) to ensure full employment, and (4) to raise the standard of living and housing. Some progress has been made in France on all these fronts, but it is doubtful whether this progress is due to the Plan. In any case, none of these objectives were submitted to parliamentary, let alone popular, discussion—nor was there any attempt to secure a decision as to how they rank when in conflict with each other. It is therefore hardly surprising that neither labor nor anyone else in France feels identified with the Plan, or considers it his own and co-operates accordingly. The parliamentary debate in August 1948 brought out that an increasing number of deputies were critical of the lack of opportunity to examine and evaluate the Plan in its broad outlines and basic objectives. The government seemed inclined to feel that the wide participation of representatives of labor, business, and the general public through the eighteen "modernization commissions" for the leading industries was giving it a broad popular base. But this view was objected to on sound grounds of parliamentary government. The Deputy Commissioner of the Plan had described the members of these commissions as chosen not for their titles but because of their active participation in their industries, because of their personalities and leadership, and because of their determination to modernize France's economy.[28] Such a procedure for consultation is indeed valuable for any comprehensive planning, but it cannot take the place of the democratic process of seeking broad popular support through parliament and through appropriate legislative action. Whether the sector is the nationalized one, where the public is vitally concerned with the rates charged by nationalized enterprises, or the private sector, regulated in varying degrees, where business and labor may find themselves affected in hundreds of ways, the government, in keeping with democratic methods, should keep the public fully abreast of developments and should secure at least majority support. Yet no adequate report was rendered for months following this debate in spite of parliament's adoption of a specific instruction to this effect. What changes were being made in the original plan as a result of the Marshall Plan and the development of European reconstruction remained vague. To be sure, the Deputy Commissioner, M. Robert Marjolin, became Secretary-General of the Office of European Economic Co-operation (OEEC), which indicates the strong link between the two plans. Presumably the philosophy of a "concerted economy" rather than a "directed economy" permeates the thinking of both. Yet no amount of consultation with experts can be considered an adequate substitute for democratic planning. It is apt to remain a pious hope that "such a plan . . . is essentially a method of making action converge (*convergence dans l'action*) and a means by which each can place his effort in relation to that of all."[29]

The proof of the pudding is in the eating. Although France has made considerable strides toward reconstruction and modernization of her industry, the goals of the Plan are far from being met, in spite of the hundreds of millions of dollars of American aid made available under the Marshall Plan. Indeed, it seems doubtful whether any significant progress would have been achieved without this aid. The doubts which the ECA mission has expressed are reflected in the cold figures. The production levels projected in the plans have not been attained, and without most determined support by the entire people probably cannot be attained. Of course, there have been many factors disturbing the situation, but some of the worst, like the great coal strike, are themselves related to the democratically unsound pattern we have described. Over-all planning in mid-twentieth century Europe and America is as vital in its political ramifications as the celebrated purse-strings once were. Indeed, it may be doubted whether under article 13 of the French constitution, which vests legislative (policy-making) power in the National Assembly and forbids its delegation, the failure of the government to secure legislative support can be considered "constitutional."

(2) *Italy.* Italy's planning has been carried out more nearly in keeping with democratic and constitutional procedure. This is at least in part due to Italy's experience with Fascism. Indeed, this experience has caused Italy to approach socialization and planning with a more cautious, not to say suspicious, attitude. For since both nationalization and planning were initiated by the Fascist government, most Italians are anxious to avoid anything that might mean the reappearance of Fascist practices. Yet there can be no question that measures adopted by the Fascists continue in force in these fields. The Institution for Industrial Reconstruction (*IRI* or *Istituzione per la Ricostruzione Industriale*), which was established by Mussolini in 1933 to ward off a collapse of the banks by taking over their industrial holdings, continues to exercise the functions assigned to it at that time and later. Likewise, the right to strike in publicly owned enterprises, abrogated by Mussolini in 1923, was also denied in 1948 by de Gasperi, the Italian premier, at which time the government reaffirmed the Fascist decree.

Socialization in Italy has taken three major forms, all envisaged by the constitution. First, there is outright government ownership and operation, as in posts, telegraphs, and telephones. Second, there is partnership between government and management, as in many of the enterprises under the Institution for Reconstruction which holds varying amounts of stock. Finally, there is socialization of the kind which vests operational control in corporate entities below the national government, like municipalities or even trade unions. The latter program is an outgrowth of the syndicalist tradition in Italy. The constitutional provisions are contained in article 43 which reads as follows: "To the end that general utility may be attained, the law may from the outset reserve or may transfer, by means of expropriation and with indemnity, to the state, to public bodies, or to groups of workers or of users, specified enterprises or categories of enterprises which relate to essential public services or to sources of energy or to situations of monopoly when the foregoing are characterized by outstanding public interest."[30] These constitutional provisions rest upon the general conception of property outlined in the previous article. This latter divides property into public and private property, recognizes and guarantees private property, but only within the framework of statutory law which determines how it may be acquired, enjoyed, and limited. The purpose of such statutory determination must be to assure "social needs" and to render property accessible to all. It is obvious that such a social conception of property would lead straight to the proposition that it may be expropriated by law in the general interest against compensation. The one important safeguard is that such expropriations must be *by law*; as long as law-making remains democratically controlled, the essential condition of constitutionalism or *Rechtsstaat* appears to be preserved (provided minority rights are adequately protected by the constitution).

In spite of the broad sweep of a socialized conception of property, Italian practice in this field has socialized risks and profits rather than property itself in the broad sector covered by the *IRI*. Contrary to impressions one might derive from the text of the constitution, the situation is largely what it was under the Fascists. Their very simple solution had been to transfer blocks of shares from the banks to the government's *IRI*. No effort was made to direct existing management until the exigencies of war preparations necessitated it.[31] In other words, the *IRI* is still the old holding company of Fascist days which operates as a sort of government insurance against risk; it eliminates the sanction of failure through bankruptcy, upon which capitalism depends, without substituting the governmental sanctions upon which socialism or governmentalism must be able to count. Thus Italy's intrinsic advantage in possessing a concentrated control mechanism for effectuating a unified policy is not being employed for the one purpose which might have justified such socialization.

Italy is the one country in which planning is in a sense institutionalized by the constitution. After stating that private initiative, though free, must not conflict with social utility, security, liberty, or human dignity, article 41 of the constitution announces that "the law determines the suitable programs and controls so that public and private economic activity may be directed and coordinated toward social ends." In spite of this broad grant of power, the Italian government has done less real planning than is required under the European Recovery Program. American aversion to planning in principle has not prevented ECA officials (after the United States yielded to the need for planning European recovery in practice) from sharply criticizing Italian practice. They called the Italian government's long-term program "a very tentative expression of views rather than a firm program of goals and of the means to achieve them,"[32] and recommended "vigorous public action" in the form of more effective planning and public investment. Such planning, in the American view, would not stifle private initiative but would promote it; there is too little of that, also, and it results, as we have seen, from the unsatisfactory socialization program. Independent American observers have come to the conclusion that the political and social climate of Italy actually rules out the possibility of effective planning.[33]

(3) *Germany.* It is too early to assess socialization and planning under the new German constitution (Basic Law) adopted in May, 1949. Socialization has been provided for in a number of state constitutions, notably Hesse and Bremen.[34] However, little had been done to implement these provisions by the time the Basic Law came into effect because both British and American military government took the view that socialization measures should wait until the federal constitution was adopted and a determination made by it as to what should be done by the states and what by the federation in this controversial field.

Actually, the Basic Law, as far as property and socialization are concerned, follows a philosophy very similar to that of Italy. This is not surprising since the same parties with the same Social- and Christian-Democratic ideologies arrived at this compromise. In articles 14 and 15 of the Basic Law a social conception of property is outlined, stressing the obligations which property entails as much as the rights, and permitting expropriation with compensation when the public welfare requires it. Land, natural resources, and means of production may be socialized, and under article 74 such actions may be taken by either the *Bund* (federation) or the *Länder* (states), that is, they are subjects of concurrent legislation.[35]

The same article states the antimonopoly position more broadly as "prevention of abuse of economic power." There is, however, no explicit recognition of planning or programming for the economy as a whole, although the broad grant of concurrent legislation to make laws for the economy could presumably be used as a valid basis for claiming such jurisdiction. Since the German Republic is part of the OEEC, a substantial amount of planning will have to be shouldered by its government.

In fact, such planning as has been undertaken for Germany has until now been the joint responsibility of the Western occupying powers and the German officials acting in an advisory capacity. The *Long Term Program* put forward by the ECA and based upon this co-operation lacks, therefore, the democratic basis to an even greater extent than other European plans. The assumptions made by the planners with regard to investments and consequent restrictions on consumption, in view of the present tax burden and low income level, are highly speculative, to say the least. It seems more than doubtful that a responsible democratic government, such as has now been set up, will be able to secure popular support for this program.

In view of the federal structure of the German Republic it is especially unfortunate that no attempt was made to project into the field of planning the compromise arrived at in the fiscal field (taxation and budgeting). With legislative and administrative responsibilities, that is, policy-making functions, in a number of vital fields such as agriculture assigned to the *Länder*, effective planning will be well-nigh impossible without elaborating integrated procedures which would tie in the Federal Council (*Bundesrat*) as well as the Parliament (*Bundestag*)—not inherently impossible under the constitution. The gravest difficulties are to be expected otherwise, since the party composition of the federal authorities is bound to differ from that of some of the states, and smooth co-operation is going to be hard to achieve when the one favors a free-market economy while the others want a socialized and directed economy.[36]

International planning: the Marshall Plan · We can only briefly and from a governmental standpoint comment upon the ambitious project in international planning which the United States inaugurated with the proposal that the European nations get together for the purpose of planning their reconstruction so as to qualify for large-scale American aid. It was an unheard of challenge to the European nations, accustomed as they were to think of planning entirely in terms of national advantage and international competition. It is therefore not to be wondered at that the conferences held during the summer of 1947 in Paris did not produce a well-integrated plan for reconstruction and development, but rather a "shopping

507

list," as critics called it.[37] As a result, requirements were overestimated and had to be paired down rather mechanically after American protests. The greatest difficulty, however, resulted from the fact that the several European nations were not, as we have seen, really ready for planning such as this United States proposal implied. There resulted, as a consequence, the rather paradoxical situation in which the United States, while unofficially and sometimes (in Congress) officially voicing protest against Europe's liking for socialism and a directed economy, was at the same time urging the European governments to engage in over-all planning on an unprecedented scale. As we have noted, the officials of the Economic Cooperation Administration (ECA) have had occasion to criticize sharply the failure of Europe's presumably Socialist or socializing governments for their failure to plan effectively as well as for their failure to implement such plans and programs as they had adopted. In these criticisms one finds much more frequently the voice of the exasperated technician and planning expert than that of the representative of constitutional democracy. There is a notable lack of stress to be found in American official observations on the need of securing widespread popular support for these plans, nor is there adequate analysis of the extent to which European governments have informed the public and its representatives of the basic policies involved in these plans.[38]

This indifference to the democratic basis for Europe's planning efforts is curious in light of the fact that these plans have been, as far as ECA is concerned, subjected to detailed scrutiny by the Congress of the United States. In fact, a Joint Congressional Committee, the so-called "watchdog committee," has had highly qualified experts in the field to check on performance and to advise the Congress on the basic issues involved in the plans. There can be little doubt, in light of the record, that the ECA Administrator, Mr. Paul Hoffmann, has been obliged to render a more detailed account of the past and future operation of the plans than any of the European officials occupying corresponding positions in their countries under OEEC. It would seem that this paradoxical situation illustrates well the fact that such democratic controls are a vital aspect of democratic planning.

Conclusion · In the field of socialization and planning any conclusions at the present time are highly tentative. Perhaps it would be wiser not to attempt to state any conclusions at all. But at the risk of landing between two chairs, I am prepared to argue that the adherents of constitutional government are confronted with two equally uninviting alternatives. Discussion of the problems of socialization and planning is largely carried on in terms of negatives. The friends of planning demonstrate with cold facts and inexorable logic that an unplanned economy produces very undesirable results, economically and otherwise. The adversaries of planning proceed to describe the "road to serfdom" which a planned economy has involved and will involve. The trouble with the two contending parties is that they are both close to being right. Both the free-market economy (or approaches to it) and the planned economy give us much to complain about; there is either lack of security or lack of freedom. To those who are willing to face the facts there can be little question that the starry-eyed expectations of earlier generations concerning socialism are doomed to disappointment. But this recognition of the shortcomings of socialism does not oblige us to resume an attitude of smug acceptance of the existing state of things. Planning may not of necessity be the road to serfdom. But if it is not, the supporters of planning will have to give a great deal more constructive thought to how planning may be fitted into the processes of constitutional government.[39]

At this stage in the development there is great lack of clear thinking on this subject by both friend and foe of planning. As our all-too-brief sketch of developments has shown, European governments have pushed socialization without any clear plans as to how such socializations integrate with, or form an essential part of, an over-all plan. Such planning as has taken place has been overtaken time and again by so-called unpredictable factors the recurrence of which is perfectly well-known: bad crops, strikes, inefficiency, and so forth.

Very fine achievements have been recorded in more limited fields; some of them, like the TVA,[40] we have not been able to review here, because of their specialized character. But while the TVA has been supposed to be a planning agency for the region in which it operates, former Chairman Lilienthal's suggestion that the life principle of democratic planning is "an awakening in the whole people of a sense of common moral purpose" is too broad and vague, and his related suggestion that "the TVA idea of planning sees action and planning not as things separate and apart, but as one single and continuous process," while sound as far as it goes, forgets that the TVA had its basic plan handed to it in the form of enabling legislation. Its fundamental objectives were settled for it, and therefore TVA did not have to grapple with the most difficult task confronting democratic planning, that is, the task of correlating conflicting purposes involved in any over-all plan. The TVA was like a war, and all democracies have proven their ability to handle the planning task under such conditions of *simplified* purpose. This is not said to belittle the splendid efforts of the TVA in keeping democratic processes at work; far from it. But the issue posited by planning and socialization is deeper and more perplexing.

Some time ago I wrote that "the road to serfdom lies through the timid disbelief in the capacity of the people to rule themselves." And in the last analysis, this is the nub of the problem, as it is in the other tension areas we shall have to consider. There is a democratic way. Whether it lies through assimilation of the planning process to well-tried budgetary and fiscal techniques, as I am inclined to believe, or whether it can be accomplished through syndicalist methods, as guild socialists argue, or whether planning can be made part of responsible administration, it is in any case clear that we cannot surrender to chaos and despair, because we may have to restrict one freedom in order to make another freedom secure. Freedom, like property, is a bundle of rights and privileges, changeable in its composition, yet basically interrelated. If too much of the bundle is lost by the failure to make a plan, free men may find some way of planning the way out. There is enough concrete experience at hand to show that it may be done.

XXIV

Propaganda and the Control of Communications

Introduction · Propaganda · The beginnings of the press as an instrument of opposition, particularly in England down to the end of the eighteenth century · Toward an "independent" press: England · France: the press as an agent of revolution · The problems of the American law of libel: no restraint · The political effects of a commercialized press · The forces behind the mass press · A comparative survey of the nature of the modern press in certain leading countries · The English press · The American press · The news agencies · Radio: new medium of political influence · The American system of broadcasting · Federal regulation · Press and propaganda under contemporary dictatorships · Press and propaganda in wartime · Governmental control and censorship · Conclusion.

Introduction · When we speak of "the people," we may think of a vague mass of unassorted individuals. But from the point of view of the member of the legislature this public is largely represented by three identifiable and institutionalized elements, namely, the modern means of mass communication, especially the press and radio on one hand and the interest groups on the other. Of these, the press, in all its shades, represents opinion to such an extent that as a forum for the discussion of public questions it still holds the foremost place. Hence freedom of the press is considered a cornerstone of constitutional democracy (see above, ch. IX). At the same time, press, radio, and to some extent interest groups are of great importance as channels of communication from such representative bodies (as well as the government's executives) to the public at large. In view of this fact it is significant that parliamentary debates do not find their way into the press as they used to. The London *Times* still gives very extensive extracts from parliamentary debates, but this is unusual. In the United States speeches of individual Senators and Representatives, and in France and other countries the discourses of ministers, are fully reported. But the debates as such do not mold public opinion. When President Hoover insisted that Congress give him the right to raise or lower tariff rates, his appeal appeared on the first page of the newspapers, but arguments made in the Senate against his demand, speeches of the highest quality and under-

511

standing based upon careful study of the circumstances, received relatively little consideration. In fact, the most searching of all these counterblasts received almost no attention at all.[1] In recent years, such instances have multiplied. Due partly to the increasingly representative position of the President, it is also in part traceable to the much greater "news value" which the President has as compared to Congress. There is only one President, whereas there are many Senators and Representatives. Consequently, from the news reporter's point of view any slight move on the part of the President is worthy of attention.

In spite of the profound impact of the newspapers and of the press in general upon government and politics, political science has tended to neglect the press. Some years ago Walter Lippmann called attention to the fact that political science, as expounded to future businessmen, lawyers, public officials, and citizens at large, paid little or no attention to the sources of popular information. The will of the people was treated as if unrelated to the information available; news-gathering was not considered a part of the political process. Actually the emergence of constitutional government, and in particular the crystallization of the systems of popular representation as we know them, are inextricably interwoven with the growth of the modern press. Without it constitutional government is unimaginable. Thomas Jefferson dramatized this view by saying that if he were confronted with the choice of having a government and no newspapers or newspapers and no government, he would have no hesitation in preferring the newspapers; as an ardent believer in minimizing the role of the government, he realized that the government could not be restrained without independent newspapers ready to criticize.

The press in all countries remains, of course, subject to governmental regulations. Such regulations may help to fit the papers into the institutional pattern as well as into the economic organization and physical environment of the community. The most striking instance has been provided in occupied countries after the Second World War, where licensing and strict control of the press was imposed by the Western democracies in the avowed interest of "freedom of the press," because it was, and is, felt that only thus could the enemies of freedom (Nazis, Fascists, militarists, and eventually Communists) be "kicked out and kept out" of positions of influence. The success of these techniques has been discouragingly limited (see ch. XXVI, below). But there are other problems, even in free countries. The size of the United States, for example, produces a press markedly different from that of England. The literary preoccupations of the continental press are an outgrowth of the governmental censorship to which that press has been subjected for long periods of time. In spite of these contrasts, there is a considerable measure of uniformity. This has been enhanced in recent decades by the leveling impact of technical processes, such as the telegraph, and the general impact of modern economic forces implied in large-scale production. All in all, the press is an important concomitant of political processes in modern times. But in considering the press as a political instrument, we must not forget that we are dealing only with one aspect. Some time ago an inquiry at Harvard showed that a majority of undergraduates were taking the Boston *American*, a Hearst organ. Someone, disturbed by the political implications of this discovery, inquired into the reasons for their doing so. It was found that in the opinion of the students the Boston *American* had the best comic strips; as for the rest, they did not care.

Propaganda · The mass-communication media have produced one of the most dangerous tensions in contemporary constitutional democracies. The role of the reactionary chain of newspapers and magazines, owned by one Hugenberg, leader of the nationalist party, in undermining the Weimar Republic was possibly decisive, and in any case its disturbing influence was profound. Walter Millis has described the frightening effect of the jingo press in the United States in bringing on the Spanish-American War. Similar situations have appeared elsewhere.[2] Any student of constitutional democracy today must face the issue raised by propaganda. But what is propaganda? It seems to many to have arisen as an "inescapable trend" from the very workings of a free industrial society, with its market mechanisms developing monopoly situations. To others it appears an evil machination of willful and wicked men which may be eliminated by an appeal to man's rational faculties or by some kind of regulation. Still others would trust the spontaneous working of competitive drives; so they exclaim that "the cure for propaganda is more propaganda." The difficulty with much of this discussion is the failure to describe with sufficient precision what is meant by propaganda. From the popular notion that propaganda is simply lies or, perhaps, the other fellow's opinions to the often highly sophisticated views of social psychologists there is a plethora of "definitions." These definitions are often useful within their context, but they do not necessarily bring out the aspect which is of primary importance to the student of constitutional democracy. From the governmental standpoint, the crucial aspect is that of power, control, and organization. Hence the description of propaganda should be approached in terms of those originating it, in short, we should look at it from the vantage point of the propagandist.

Even a casual inspection of the propagandist and his purposes yields a definite distinction between several communication processes. If all propa-

513

ganda presupposes a propagandist, such a person (or group) may be descriptively defined as one who hands out information in order to gain ideal or material advantages for himself or the group for which he is acting. The tie-in between propaganda and parties as defined earlier (see ch. XX) is very close. Indeed, modern parties are large propaganda organizations. Like every propagandist, they seek to get people to take or not to take particular actions, and yet these activities are accepted as part of the democratic process. (The widespread unpopularity of parties is, however, related to their propagandistic efforts to present the issues.) Party life illustrates an important generalization about propaganda activities, namely, that propaganda is frequently directed toward one of two objectives: to persuade people to join an organization, or to persuade them financially to support an organization. This, from a political standpoint, is the hard core of the work of a propagandist, while around it cluster the more general activities which are concerned with attitudes, propensities, and states of mind which dispose people toward joining or supporting an organization (these psychic dispositions constituting the focal interest of the psychologist).

With this general description in mind, it is possible to relate propaganda to constitutional democracy. For such propaganda may obviously be available on a broadly competitive basis to all comers, including, of course, the government, or it may be the monopoly of the government or nearly so. The latter situation is, broadly speaking, characteristic of authoritarian, and more especially of totalitarian, governments. In such closed societies, one group, often referred to as the "elite" or "ruling class," will control all major channels of communication. The classic doctrine of such a society was developed by Plato in his *Republic*, *Laws*, and *Statesman*, but it has had numerous adherents throughout history, and more especially recommends itself to all fundamentalists with a firm and unshakable faith in the righteousness and truth of their own doctrine. It has therefore always been a favorite of dogmatic religious organizations and organized churches. Constitutional democracy, on the other hand, will try to ensure a "free market of ideas"; it will try, through appropriate legal safeguards, to ensure to every citizen and group of citizens the opportunity to counter a particular propagandist and his campaign by counterpropaganda to the limit of his resources. These resources may well be of a nonmaterial sort: enthusiasm, devotion, superior knowledge, may count for more than money. This has often been overlooked by critics of democratic society; observing the undeniable effect of financial support given by vested interests to propaganda campaigns and organizations favorable to their interests, they have argued that the "free" society is not free at all. But the cases are numerous in which even a single individual has in course of time defeated such entrenched interests, provided the legal system is protecting the citizen's right to carry on a campaign (for example, consider the case of Senator Norris and others in favor of public ownership of electric power). Thus, whatever the particular campaign may be concerned with, under the competitive conditions of constitutionalism there are usually opposing groups on hand to point out the fact that propaganda is being made. War, antiwar, isolationist, interventionist, socialist, capitalist—these are typical of competing campaigns. In the process, a good deal of propaganda is neutralized. Thus the partisanship of a good part of the American press in some of the recent presidential campaigns failed to sway the electorate sufficiently to bring about the defeat of the candidate the press was opposing. Other propagandists were at work to counteract what the press was saying.[3]

The beginnings of the press as an instrument of opposition, particularly in England down to the end of the eighteenth century · The medieval constitutional order passed away before the powers divided under it could avail themselves of the new opportunities which the press offered. The tremendous outburst of pamphlet literature in the sixteenth century, of which the writings of Martin Luther stand as the most lasting monument, heralded the coming of the press. Even more important were the regular "newsletters" which had made their appearance still earlier. In the course of the sixteenth century these became more and more elaborate.[4] Wealthy merchants particularly, like the Fuggers of Augsburg, organized a regular service. Printed periodical publications containing news reports and opinions did not get under way until the seventeenth century. In 1609 two printed weeklies made their appearance, one in Augsburg and another in Strasbourg, probably the oldest regular periodicals. Soon after, another one appeared in Leipzig. While these were independent commercial enterprises, in England and later in France the governments, which at that time maintained a strict control over all printed matter, usually had a hand in it. The *Weekly News* started in England, and in 1622 was devoted to what purported to be foreign news. "The transition from the spasmodic series of reports from abroad published before 1622 . . . to the not altogether regular issues of the newspaper is easy and natural. At the start it had nothing in common with what we understand by a newspaper today except the fact that it was a continuous enterprise." Thus Shaaber summarizes the beginnings of the newspaper. Nine years later, in 1631, the first French newspaper, called the *Gazette*, was started at the instigation of Richelieu, who granted it a monopoly in the distribution of news. Since Richelieu was able to control this paper, he was subjecting to governmental supervision the entire process of distributing news. In a sense, this system has continued, not only in France, but in other large European countries, down to the present day. The great news agencies, the Agence Havas in France, Wolff's Telegraphenbüreau in Germany, and Stefani in Italy, unlike the Associated Press in the United States and the Reuter Agency in England, were always subject to governmental supervision, rather than under the influence of the commercial groups controlling the enterprise (see below, p. 527).

The first genuine challenge to the system of governmental direction occurred in the course of the English Civil War. It is natural that during that period when Parliament and the Crown were fighting for supremacy, the parliamentary party should demand freedom of the press along with other instruments of popular opposition. Yet when the Puritans came into power, they in turn commenced to oppress the opposition, and Parliament repeatedly enacted measures for the suppression of what seemed to it objectionable publications. Still, John Milton's ardent appeal for liberty and the unsatisfactory experience which the official licenser reported at the end of one year (1649) led to a certain leniency. Cromwell, to be sure, could not suffer an independent press, but his natural tendency was in that direction. After the Restoration, suppression once more became the order of the day. Charles II adopted the policy of Richelieu, and licensed the publishing of an official newspaper by L'Estrange, the *London Gazette*. This same gentleman also acted as censor and prosecutor of unlicensed publications. Nevertheless the Whigs continued to publish, particularly after 1679 when the licensing law was repealed. James II, on his accession, attempted a revival of rigid censorship, but the developments overtook him. After the Glorious Revolution the publishing of newspapers became more general. A series of Intelligencers made their appearance. Partisanship availed itself to an ever-increasing degree of the opportunity the press offered, particularly as the public acquired the taste for constant news. The literary talents of Addison, Swift, Bolingbroke, and Steele were all placed at the disposal of this rising tide of journalistic effort. The opposition party in particular derived considerable benefit from the constant agitation in the daily press. Yet all these Intelligencers, Journals, and the like lacked the institutionalized security which the modern press commands. The lack of power of the press during the entire eighteenth century is indicated by their not being allowed to report parliamentary debates. Privacy of debate was still considered the privilege of the aristocracy which was directing public affairs.

Toward an "independent" press: England · The press in England during the eighteenth and the first half of the nineteenth century was essentially partisan. There can be little doubt that it helped materially in holding a parliamentary opposition together. It was in this period that the reporting of news was merged in one paper with interpretation and opinion, and to these were added literary and other items.[5] It was natural that this should have been so, for it helped to secure readers who might be indifferent to the political controversies. During this entire period, however, and down to 1855, the so-called stamp tax handicapped those who might want to start new papers. It made it easier for the governing classes to regulate the contents of the press. Since the party controversies in England flowed in more or less established channels, this handicap was not seriously objected to until the time of the French Revolution. But after English radicalism got under way, a movement, it will be remembered, which was directed against the aristocratic nature of English politics in general, the restrictions imposed by the stamp tax as well as by the libel law and the import duties on paper (abolished in 1861) were bitterly attacked. In spite of these restrictions, radicalism was able to carry forward its struggle for the reform of Parliament, that is, the electoral system, considerably aided by the press. After all, the financial restrictions could be overcome by sufficient zeal. The libel law, which during the Napoleonic era had been interpreted to mean that to criticize the ills of the electoral system was "to utter seditious words against the matchless constitution," could not well be used against the revelations of outright scandal and corruption, nor could the libel law cope with the fervent pen of a writer like Charles Dickens (after 1836), who was a trained journalist. It is therefore not surprising to find that Cobden's famous struggle against the tariff on grain (1838–1846) was already largely fought out in the press. Nor is it any cause for wonder that in the decades which followed, the restrictions on the press were removed one after the other. After 1860 the press entered upon its new career and commenced to rival Parliament as a platform of political discussion.

France: the press as an agent of revolution · In France, where governmental restrictions persisted up to the Revolution and were revived by Napoleon, the opposition nevertheless availed itself of the press, which was largely clandestine, as is the opposition press in totalitarian countries today. The periodic upheavals in France during the nineteenth century were accompanied by extensive changes in the position of the press. The press itself, of course, was instrumental in bringing these changes about. The revolution of 1830, for example, is generally believed to have been maneuvered by a group of newspaper editors. At the critical moment in July 1830, the journalists met first.[6] This is not surprising, since the first of the oppressive ordinances that the government had decided upon outlawed any publication without governmental authorization. The opposition journalists asked Thiers to draw up a protest. In it he announced: "The legal regime has ended, that of force has begun. Obedience ceases to be a duty. We shall try to publish our journals without asking for the authorization which is imposed upon us. It is for France to judge how far resistance should go." The statement was signed by forty-three journalists and appeared in *Le Temps* and in Thiers' *National* on July 26th. This is perhaps the most dramatic occasion upon which journalism opposed a government. Here the press took over the function which was exercised by Parliament in England during the Commonwealth. It was the first time that the "fourth estate" emerged as politically decisive. In the course of the latter half of the nineteenth century the vital role of the press became so generally accepted a fact that it seems unimaginable for a political opposition to survive without developing an effective press of its own.

The problems of the American law of libel: no restraint · The development of the press, of course, could not have taken place without considerable changes in the legal framework which prevailed earlier. Freedom of the press has been looked upon as perhaps one of the most essential features of political bills of right and there is no democratic constitution which does not expressly provide for it. American politics have been carried on without any material restrictions upon the conduct of the press, except the common law of libel. There is, then, no statutory inhibition[7]. As a result, when the British Foreign Office made its survey of press laws throughout the world, it reported that it could find none in the United States. Actually there are some state laws dealing with particular matters affecting moral standards, and the federal government enforces some standards through its control of the postal service. But by and large the legal restraints under which the press of the United States operates are covered by the common law of libel. This holds the press responsible civilly and criminally for defamation of character. How very limited that restraint is may be gauged from a report that one of the most sensational of the tabloid newspapers paid $5,000 in all for libel suits totalling $7,000,000 in claims. Nevertheless the liability for libel does make the press wary in dealing with private citizens and corporations. This is not the case when they report governmental or other public affairs. For protection of the press from prosecution for libel in reporting and commenting on governmental performance is connected with the peculiar nature of the common law of libel which demands that the party bringing suit show that damage has been done to it. Moreover, a suit for libel, on the precedent of Zenger's case, requires of the plaintiff that proof be brought to show that the alleged statements are untrue, proof which it is often impractical for governmental agencies to furnish. In Zenger's case the issue was clear, for he was put in jail for printing reports about the government the truth of which nobody denied, but on its precedent papers nowadays frequently print news the falsehood of which nobody doubts. It is a question, in part at least, of where the burden of proof shall fall. In the eighteenth century all that the government had to do was to allege that the statements were libelous, and all that it had to prove was that they had been printed by the person being prosecuted. The interest of the government was the sole consideration. It was unhesitatingly identified with the public interest. Such an arrangement is manifestly unacceptable from a democratic point of view, but whether the exactly opposite arrangement of leaving the determination of what is in the public interest to privately controlled business enterprises is the solution to the problem may be seriously doubted. Perhaps D. M. Keezer is right in saying that those who led the struggle for freedom of the press would probably have lost much of their enthusiasm if they could have foreseen this outcome. More recently, constitution makers in Europe have concerned themselves with the problems resulting from the abuse of freedom of the press (as well as other freedoms by antidemocratic elements and movements). Since the rise of these movements to power was often associated with an unprecedented campaign of antigovernmental propaganda, the tendency is now (see above, ch. IX) to deny the protection of these rights to such anticonstitutional propagandists. The dangers inherent in such attempts are great, since they undermine the basic principle of "free competition" in the market of ideas. Much detailed inquiry is needed for developing more precise and specific criteria than "subverting the constitution" and the like.

The political effects of a commercialized press · The question of irresponsible comment on and slanting of the news has raised a general problem of economic versus partisan and political control. It is a problem which is confronting democracy in all the more highly industrialized nations. The tendency for advertising to go to the papers with the largest circulation combined with the mechanical developments of the last fifty years have converted a large part of the great metropolitan press into a few huge corporations linking already powerful and highly organized papers in extensive chains.[8] Such is the case in the United States with the Hearst, Scripps-Howard, Time Inc., and other organizations. Such is likewise the story of the Northcliffe, Rothermere, Inveresk, and other trusts in England. The Hugenberg concern offered a German parallel. Only France, of the large countries, has retained a more divided press, though François

519

Coty also commenced to build a chain of rabidly nationalist papers. It is perhaps no accident that these great corporate enterprises tend to deteriorate the quality of the news and to throw their weight to the support of jingoistic nationalism. At any rate, even if one concedes that the masters of these undertakings are not the scheming and undemocratic plotters that they are sometimes depicted to be, the problem remains as to how to cope with organizations that look upon the process of opinion formation, so essential to the conduct of democratic government, as secondary to that of making money. The accepted American doctrine of the difference between facts presented in the news and opinions expressed on the editorial page is too superficial to serve as an adequate basis. It is obviously a situation arising from very powerful underlying trends which may be quite indirect and unrelated.

The forces behind the mass press · What are some of these phenomena to be considered here which seem definitely related to the rise of the mass press suggested by the names of Hearst, Pulitzer, and Northcliffe? Certain technical developments since the American Civil War, such as the conversion of wood pulp into newsprint, the invention of the linotype machine, and many others, cheapened the cost of production. At the same time the spread of popular education constantly expanded the available reading public, and the rapid increase in population did the rest. We find that between 1850 and 1900 the number of daily-newspaper publishing establishments, as classified by the United States Census Bureau, increased in America from 254 to more than 2000. At the same time the circulation of their publications increased from 750,000 to 15,000,000 per day. Between 1900 and 1910 both figures continued to rise, but the increase in establishments was much less than that in circulation, namely from 2226 to 2600 and from 15,000,000 to 24,000,000 per day. After this the number of papers actually began to decline, and by 1920 had fallen to 2441. This decline continued, and in 1930 there were 2293 such papers in the United States. In the same period circulation rose to 42,000,000. These figures suggest something of the enormous transition that was taking place. Pulitzer, Hearst, and Harmsworth, afterward Lord Northcliffe, are simply individuals who rode the crest of the wave. They were essentially skillful businessmen who perceived the possibilities of cheapening the wares which journalism had to offer, from both a material and cultural point of view, and in making a profit from the broad market. Sensationalism gained an ever more extended hold upon the press in this period. Scandal and corruption in the government were as acceptable as any other untoward developments. The implications of the profound cynicism thus engendered in the masses did not worry these master showmen of the press. They did, however, markedly alter the configuration of modern politics. Of course these popularizers of journalistic goods did not completely displace the older and more established papers. Their inventions and discoveries were bound to spread as they were being imitated by competitors. Eventually, after the First World War, so-called tabloids actually outdid Hearst and his brethren. In order fully to appreciate this mass press one must compare it to the older and more traditional patterns of the press of the leading countries.[9]

A comparative survey of the nature of the modern press in certain leading countries · In any comparison of the press in relation to the government in the various leading industrial nations one must keep in mind the differences between these countries as far as the place occupied by the government in the whole political process is concerned. But it would be misleading to cast the analysis into a rigid pattern of "national" types. The comparison of governmental systems should not obscure other similarities and differences. Thus the labor press in all these countries bears a marked resemblance in its tendency to focus interest upon trade-union activities. As was said before, there are also marked differences which have only an indirect relation to the governmental structure, such as the geography of the country.

A brief survey of the press in terms of governmental structure reveals some interesting correlations. In America, where the government is federally divided and where a major political interest is focused on the contest between two large political parties of somewhat similar outlook, the press tends to be restrained on strict party politics (though there are many exceptions, for instance, *The Chicago Tribune*). In any case, much of its interest is centered upon local matters. England's centralized government is contested for by parties which are sharply divided by their ideology. Hence the press is vigorously partisan. Besides, Britain's world empire causes the British press to be much concerned with affairs in distant lands. (This tendency has been sharply on the increase in the United States.) Moreover, the possibility of distributing a paper overnight throughout the country makes it possible to serve certain groups, such as finance or labor, by a paper distributed from a single center, like *The Times* or the *Daily Herald*. This phenomenon has lately made its appearance in the United States, due to air-mail service, but is restricted to a few papers, especially to *The New York Times*. In France, where parliament is supreme and divided into many contending groups, the editorship of a moderately successful paper is one of the safest careers leading into politics, and many prominent politicians, like Clemenceau or the brothers Sarraut, have been editors. It is not likely that such men will give up their independent control. Consequently the French press is divided into many individual enterprises. At the same time, the dominant position of Paris in the country's politics offers the same opportunity for distribution of a paper from a single center and gives the Parisian press national scope. Germany, as long as it had constitutional government, was federally divided; its party politics were rent by sharp ideological conflicts between a number of highly organized parties. Here the press again tended to be strictly partisan, but with many different organs, to serve the different parties, available to the reader seeking a cross section of the opinion of various groups. There were also significant papers in different parts of the country. A number of other European countries have a similar party structure possessing an analogous press. We see, then, that there is a definite correlation of pattern between government and press which testifies to the vital role the press plays in political life under constitutionalism.

The English press · English politics today revolve around two primary poles, the leader of the majority party, who is Prime Minister and who directs the government, and public opinion, which criticizes and in a measure controls this government (see above, ch. XVIII, pp. 364 ff.). Such public opinion develops influence and maintains it through many different channels, but the strongest position here is occupied by the press. In spite of the vast extension of the sphere of personal contact through the radio, the printed word remains the most widely scattered influence.[10] Particularly since the eighties of the last century, when the curtailment of parliamentary debates began, the press has become the most effective critic of the government. In spite of all the emphasis upon mere reporting of the news, the selection of items is of such importance that it is, from a political viewpoint, decisive. So-called slanting of the news, which may take the form of continued emphasis or merely passing notice, as well as many other forms, makes the newspaper a "views"-paper. Perhaps the most important technique of slanting the news is the tactics of appropriate headlines. What is particularly interesting in England is the dovetailing of this general newspaper technique with the work of Parliament. The method of questions (see above, ch. XVII, pp. 326 f.) would be utterly ineffective today if it were not for the potential interest that the press might take. Parliament itself can hold a debate, of course, but a newspaper can work up a question by giving it appropriate attention through editorials, related news items, letters to the editor, and so on. In spite of the vigorously partisan nature of most of the English press, a tradition of fairness toward the party adversary has been maintained. Speeches of opposition leaders are faithfully reported. Deliberate lying is frowned upon. In return the government is inclined to treat the papers with respect, even to take them into its confidence. Since the First World War, however, the rise of the Northcliffe and Beaverbrook press has undermined this tradition. Situations like that which arose between the Northcliffe press and Lloyd George in 1921, the attitude of the *Daily Mail* and others in connection with the Zinoviev letter incident in 1924, and the atmosphere which developed at the time of the forming of the National coalition in the late summer and fall of 1931 showed a degree of bitterness and unfairness such as had not been witnessed in England since the agitation over the Reform Bill. These events focused attention upon the fact that the newspapers are, after all, privately owned and capitalized enterprises. When confronted with the policies of the Labour Party it is difficult for them to maintain the degree of neutrality which they could maintain toward parties which never questioned the foundation of their own existence.

As long as the country's electorate was divided between Conservatives and Liberals there was some positive advantage, from the point of view of party management, in not having the papers too closely tied with the parties. Thus, while *The Times* might be Conservative, the *Daily News* Liberal, and the *Manchester Guardian* radical, their editorial staffs developed personalities of their own which gave to each paper a more distinctive flavor than the broadly conceived party platforms under a two-party system would indicate. This situation was helped, of course, by the fact that in England, as elsewhere in the nineteenth century, these and many other leading newspapers were owned by families injecting a personal element and tradition into the policy of the paper. Through the papers, these families were permanent factors in the politics of the land. The family of John Walter, who had founded *The Times* in 1785, the Taylor Scotts, who have owned the *Manchester Guardian* since 1821, the Rowntrees and Cadburys with their *Daily News*, all possessed a directing influence in their respective party councils. Under such conditions it is quite natural that England should not possess a governmentally controlled press. It does not need and could not have such a press, since whichever party was in power would have the necessary publicity channels. The British are masters at informal techniques of securing co-operation. The aristocratic tradition of England, with its orders, decorations, and titles, is one of these techniques which is in many ways more effective than any official press organ of the government could be. This informal co-operation has been particularly remarkable in the conduct of foreign affairs. *The Times* especially has been a leader in this field. Since the days of its great editor, John Delane, *The Times* has been a factor of independent importance. While usually collaborating with the Foreign Office, it has often profoundly influenced its policy. In every important capital of the world *The Times* has correspondents of its own, very well paid, sometimes rivaling the position of the Ambassador as a representative of British policy. As in foreign policy, so in many other matters, *The Times* would have the leading specialists as contributors. One very striking instance of great political importance was the position occupied by *The Times'* military correspondent, Colonel Repington, who acted as a highly confidential go-between for the Foreign Office, the army, and the French Embassy in the difficult negotiations concerning the military collaboration between England and France in 1906 and later. After the First World War the *Manchester Guardian* made considerable strides toward fulfilling a role somewhat similar to that of *The Times* for the more radical elements in the country. Though not in any sense an official Labour organ, the *Manchester Guardian* became sufficiently favorable to the Labour Party to occupy such a position. More recently, the rise of the *Herald*, out-and-out Labour in its outlook, has come to occupy that role. Yet as far as foreign affairs are concerned, the lack of effective support in the press has had a good deal to do with the difficulty the Labour Party has experienced when in office, particularly since the Northcliffe and other papers of the mass press have not hesitated to carry on rather violent campaigns. While no other papers can be compared with *The Times* as far as power and influence are concerned, it may be well to mention some of the more important ones. On the Conservative side there are *The Daily Telegraph* and the *Morning Post*. The former caters to the higher middle class, the latter to the aristocracy and to Society. On the Liberal side there is the *Daily Chronicle*, which is democratic and popular, and on the Imperial side of the Liberal tradition, the *News-Chronicle*. While all these papers rest upon the foundation of private capital and are in the last analysis business enterprises, the Labour Party recurrently endeavored to develop an organ of its own, the *Daily Herald*. This paper, as long as it was a party organ, had a very hard time competing with the powerful journalistic appeals of the mass press. Today the *Daily Herald* is one of the most widely read papers in England. Yet the gradual conquest of newspapers by profit-seeking, large-scale business enterprises has led to an increasing emphasis upon magazines and reviews as the true focal point of opinion, at least among the educated classes. The Liberal *Edinburgh Review*, started in 1802, and the Conservative *Quarterly Review*, founded in 1809, set a tradition of high achievement and represent the most effective efforts at long-range influence in politics. Although most of these magazines are again identified with some political party or group, they are not in any sense dependent upon them. On the Conservative side we have the *Spectator*, the *Saturday Review*, the *Outlook*, and J. L. Garvin's *Observer*. On the Liberal side the *Nation* used to be of great significance. It is now merged with the Fabian publication, the *New Statesman*. The *Labour Leader* was a more radical Labour organ. It has now become *The New Leader*. Somewhat more remote from party politics and therefore perhaps even more influential are the Conservative *Fortnightly Review* and *Nineteenth Century*, the Liberal *Edinburgh* and *Contemporary Review* and the *Review of Reviews*. Besides these the strictly economic journals, the *Economist* and the *Statist*, must also be mentioned.

The American press · In America—to summarize well-known material for purposes of contrast—the press used to be far removed from the government. The ideological conflicts engendered by the New Deal policies have somewhat changed that. Though some journalists have been prominent in party councils, the American press does not have the same intimate personal relations with the parties which we find in England. Until quite recently the American press has been largely guided by the business considerations of securing large circulation. Since many readers were not very vitally interested in party politics and only quadrennially, in connection with presidential elections, cared to hear much about it, the adoption of a partisan viewpoint would deprive the paper of a good deal of its circulation. This was not always so: in the early days of the Republic, the conflict between Federalists and Republicans was highlighted in conflicting newspapers. The same thing may be said of the Civil War period. But the coming of the mass press changed all that. It is natural, therefore, that the American press should be independent of party politics. Papers like *The New York Times* will even come out for a Republican candidate, though traditionally Democratic. It is widely believed, however, that the American press has exchanged dependence upon parties for the dependence upon business influences which might be exerted either through ownership or through advertising. It is difficult to get adequate factual information upon which to base a judgment concerning this question. Since advertising depends upon circulation and circulation depends upon reader interest, it is obviously not possible for a newspaper to heed the wishes of advertisers beyond the point where reader interest would be lost or reader antagonism aroused. On the other hand, reader interest is a somewhat intangible matter, leaving a fairly wide margin of discretion to the editorial office. Adolph S. Ochs, the long-time owner of *The New York Times*, once remarked that the more readers a paper has, the more independent it is of any advertiser. But this consideration does not apply to problems where all advertisers feel more or less the same way about an issue. The Commission of Inquiry of the Interchurch Movement, investigating the steel strike of 1919, felt that

525

"it is inconceivable that the public which relied upon the Pittsburgh newspapers could, by any human method of reading newspapers and allowing both for exaggeration due to bias and inaccuracy due to haste, have understood either the causes of the steel strike or the significance of its incidents." It is widely believed that similar situations are frequent where the conflict between management and labor is involved. There has been some improvement in this field in recent years. In any case, newspapers often give very complete accounts of developments which the owners of the papers do not like at all, and it is for that reason difficult to draw any definite conclusions. Newspapers as business enterprises are torn between the desire to utilize fully the sensational quality of this struggle and the owners' and advertisers' desire to have it settled in favor of the business interests. The outcome of this conflict of motives is naturally uncertain. A recent avenue of escape has been the use of "columnists" of not only divergent but of antithetical views, giving both the titillation of disagreement and the satisfaction of being reassured. It is part of the striving for political neutrality. In relation to deeper political issues, the role of the American press has not been one of leadership and guidance such as we find in Britain. Rather it has been that of voicing the reactions of particular groups of interest or of the readers at large. Newspaper editors in the United States share with other people the desire to climb on the band wagon.

What has been said of the newspapers is equally true of magazines, except that small group of weekly and monthly journals which are devoted to voicing the opinions of those who are opposed to the present order of things. Unlike the English magazines, a great many American journals used to be quite indifferent to government and politics. The challenges of the New Deal and the Fair Deal, however, have caused the large-circulation magazines to show a strictly partisan outlook. This is an important development in view of the wide distribution of these journals. While most of their contents are in the form of stories and similarly neutral material, it is possible to inject a certain measure of partisanship. This has become a more noticeable trend under the impact of the "cold war" because of the constant attacks upon the capitalist order by the Soviet propaganda machine and its avowed as well as its unsuspecting partisans. There can be little question that if the American party structure corresponded to the division between Conservatives and Progressives, as it does at present only to a limited extent, American magazine journalism and perhaps even newspaper journalism would take on a much more vital relationship to politics, and, to the extent to which the division between Progressives and Conservatives is the true political division of the country, that is already the case. Whatever the outcome of the present developments, there can be no doubt that such magazines as the *New Republic*, the *Nation*, and *Commonweal* represent a vital body of political opinion in the United States whose influence and significance seems to be in inverse proportion to the number of its readers. To these magazines of longer standing may be added a whole flock of journals of more recent origin representing various shades of radicalism, such as the *Partisan Review*, which is leftist, but anti-Soviet, or *The New Leader*, which speaks for anti-Communist trade-union intellectuals.

Extending corporate control has been a factor of importance in the American magazine field no less than in newspapers. Among these trusts, the most remarkable is Time Inc. Although developed originally as the publishing company of the magazine *Time*, it controls today, under the shrewd leadership of Henry Luce and Roy Larsen, a whole group of communication media. *Time* itself, presenting the week's news from its own viewpoint, has a circulation of 1,588,000. The pictorial magazine *Life* actually reaches more than five million readers today, while *Fortune* makes its appeal to the rich and the would-be rich through an ingenious technique of combining costly research and skillful writing. Time Inc.'s motion-picture serial, *The March of Time*, has revolutionized the newsreel field. The power which, through the control of this trust, has been concentrated in the hands of the managers of Time Inc. is assuming questionable proportions.

Perhaps even more remarkable is the rise of the *Reader's Digest* and its many imitators. Without any advertising at all, it has achieved the largest circulation of any magazine at any time in history: nine million, to be exact. It has also a foreign circulation of over four million. Based upon articles in other magazines which it condenses, *Reader's Digest* has at times been sharply criticized for its editorial policy and for the influence it exerts by "suggesting" articles and the like, but its growth continues unabated.[12]

The news agencies · In European countries, the governments have sought to influence the press through controlling the news channels. Governmental ownership and operation of the telephone and telegraph facilities made it possible to develop the news agency as a monopoly under government control. Thus the French l'Agence Havas controls not only the ordinary channels of news communication but also possesses a virtual monopoly in many sectors of the advertising-agency field. The government subsidizes this agency, so it has a double control over its operations. It is not too much to say that news unwelcome to the French government never has had much of a break over French wires. The situation in Germany has been virtually the same. American military government made a determined effort to break down this tradition, and the DENA agency, while centralized, is supposedly free from government control (though not from military government control); how long it will remain so, only the future can tell. Reuter's, the British agency, while occupying a somewhat more independent position, nevertheless has always co-operated closely with the Foreign Office in handling its news so as not to interfere seriously with the interests of Britain's imperial domains.

America, in keeping with the general commercial and unpolitical spirit of its press, has developed a markedly different system. Since the government does not own or control, but merely regulates, the telephone and telegraph wires (as well as radio), it does not have the same hold over the facilities needed by news agencies. The weakness of imperial and class interests in determining governmental policy (as compared with other countries) combined with the democratic traditions of a free press to foster the development of news services as competitive private enterprises. The Associated Press, the United Press, and the other smaller agencies are so definitely private that governmental subsidies would seem quite unthinkable. Systematic news-gathering developed naturally as a part of the competition of newspapers for sale. The drama and romance of the early competitive struggles have even been popularized on the screen. While fanciful in detail, those pictures brought out correctly the way in which, in ever more rapid succession, one novelty in speeding the news led to another. From the rowboat and the Boston Exchange Coffee House to the almost instantaneous transmission of news today, American methods have been commercial, competitive, nongovernmental.

The oldest and largest of these agencies, the Associated Press, came into existence in 1848 as a co-operative enterprise of six New York publishers.[13] It has remained on that basis through the years, with all members paying toward the cost in accordance with their circulation. But it is not open to anyone who wishes to join: hence, membership in the AP is a valued asset of any paper. There has been a good deal of criticism of this exclusive feature, and some changes have been made, in any case, to counteract any monopolistic tendencies. The United Press and the International News Service (Hearst) were organized as purveyors of news on a simple profit basis. Between them, they serve just about as many papers as the Associated Press. Besides these general agencies, supplementary news bureaus have sprung up in considerable number to gather particular kinds of news. Radical groups in the United States have tried to cope with the inadequacy of the general agencies, but for obvious financial reasons they have never been very successful.

Though it is undeniable that certain conflicts, such as strikes, raise problems in the news services similar to those we noted in connection with newspapers, the problem of political limitations upon news became really serious only with the rise of totalitarian dictatorship. These dictatorships forced the big news-gatherers to toe the line by the threat of excluding them from their territory altogether. Only complete co-operation and a united front quite at variance with the intense competitive spirit in this field could have been successful in combating such intimidation by ministries of propaganda in the totalitarian states.

In recent years, there has been more and more sharp competition between the news agencies of the press and the radio industry. A pattern of co-operation has been worked out whereby AP and other press news is presented over the radio, the listener being referred to the papers for further details. But the radio industry has scored remarkable successes in direct word-of-mouth reporting from Europe. In times of crisis, such as the war scare before Munich and the actual outbreak of hostilities, these reports direct from the news centers supplanted the traditional news agencies: for reasons not yet fully known, the average American as interviewed by the Institute of Public Opinion showed more confidence in these radio news reports than in the press news, even though they often originated from identical sources.

Radio: new medium of political influence · The possibility of broadcasting the spoken word to the four corners of the globe has profoundly altered the realities of modern politics. Whether political leadership is contested, as in the democracies, or imposed, as in the despotisms, the opportunity of reaching millions in the direct, personal way which only the spoken word offers has turned the modern community into a market place. The conditions under which Athenian democracy flourished in the days of Pericles have once again been provided by this newest means of mass communication, which at present is being implemented and rounded out by television. Inevitably, therefore, the issue of who shall control this channel of communication presents political problems of decisive importance, at least in a constitutional democracy. Authoritarian governments see only one obvious answer and that is that the government must control. This very fact will cause doubts as to the appropriateness of government control under democratic conditions. And yet Great Britain, as well as France, has adopted such a system, as contrasted with the American system of governmentally regulated commercial enterprise. This divergence is quite in keeping with the differences between Europe and America in the field of news dissemination, which has just been described.

The British, after a period of experimentation in the early twenties, organized the British Broadcasting Corporation (BBC) by Act of Parliament[14] in 1926. It was set up as a government corporation under a charter which gave it considerable independence from partisan influence, provided the governors, originally five in number, desired to exercise such independence. Actually, their predominantly conservative outlook inclined them toward an unprogressive program policy. During the early years this took the form of frowning upon political and controversial broadcasts altogether —always a safe policy for conservatives, as any crusading reformer will testify. The charter ran for ten years, when, after an extensive discussion in parliament, it was renewed in 1936. It was debated at great length in 1946 when the Conservatives put forward a proposal for increasing the independence of the BBC, but these proposals were defeated.

Under the charter, the Director-General is responsible to the Postmaster-General, thus emphasizing the parallel with other channels, such as telephones. While the British Postmaster-General is not the patronage chief of the government, as in the United States, his is a party outlook like that of any cabinet officer. In spite of this, the BBC has, on the whole, been free from the grosser forms of party politics. But there have been instances when the BBC has been the vehicle for effective political moves. For the rest, the corporation's executives have conceived of their task in terms expressive of the aristocratic conception of political leadership which gives Britain's democracy its peculiar flavor. In the words of the BBC's autocratic, yet able, first Director-General, it must "carry into the greatest possible number of homes everything that is best in every department of human endeavour and achievement." An American scholar has rightly commented: "A constant attempt has been made to intermix culture and entertainment, in order progressively to raise the public taste and enable general enjoyment to be afforded by that higher quality of artistic accomplishment appreciation of which was formerly limited to a select few." Though this conception is very different from that prevailing in America, very effective arguments can be advanced in its favor.

But this is not the place to enter upon a general consideration of the cultural significance of such an educational conception of radio. As far as the immediate issues of politics and government are concerned, we find that the BBC has evolved policies which make the airwaves available to the major political groupings in a spirit of remarkable fairness. This spirit is essentially an application of the traditions of parliamentary debate discussed in an earlier chapter. Although talks are unimportant as compared with music and other entertainment so far as amount of time is concerned, they are the crux of the problem of control. It has been pointed out repeatedly by non-British observers that definite preconceptions have largely been taken for granted: the monarchy, the constitution, the Empire, and

Christianity. But the belief in these institutions is not peculiar to the BBC; a large percentage of the listeners feel the same way about them. American radio, though subject to "private" control, has developed very similar taboos. The situation is somewhat different when a commentator of great popularity was eased out because he expressed "questionable opinions," that is, opinions not in keeping with the Chamberlain government's "policy for the promotion of peace."

The issue involved in the expression of controversial opinion by a news commentator is one which has raised considerable difficulty in America as well as in Britain. But since any selection of facts is actually an expression of opinion, it is obviously impossible for any commentator to remain neutral, and hence, under a government monopoly, news broadcasts by a single commentator present an insoluble problem. During the early years, the BBC banned controversial matter completely. It was only after 1928, and after extensive agitation, that the BBC, upon Cabinet action, could announce: "Controversy, political and economic, will be admitted on clearly defined occasions with adequate safeguards for impartiality and equality of treatment. . . . Debates and discussions will be the normal procedure." Such standards are more easily enunciated than executed. If a broad view of political controversy is taken, practically any topic of a sociopolitical nature is controversial, if controversial is defined (as it has been by the BBC) as "any speech regarded as controversial by any reasonable section of the public." Consequently, successive difficulties have been encountered, and the material offered has been often insipid and lacking in "punch."

When one turns to party politics proper, one finds that the BBC has taken the view that broadcasting "can exercise a greater influence over public opinion in matters of politics than can the press. . . ." But in spite of this programmatic declaration, the BBC has not provided nearly the amount or intensity of party controversy over the air which American broadcasters have conceded. This is, in part at least, due to much more limited facilities, but on the other hand, the taxpayer and listener are paying for the BBC facilities, whereas the advertiser pays for them in the United States. With minor exceptions, this field of party politics is limited to the parties represented in parliament. Through an advisory committee the BBC has kept in touch with the parties, a fact which in turn raises the question of the danger of limiting such broadcasts to party regulars. The division of time between them has been made in proportion to their parliamentary representation, but without rigidity. The party in power gets the lion's share, however, through the rule that it is entitled to explain major policies.

The great advantages of a governmentally controlled and operated system of broadcasting became apparent during the Second World War. The BBC could and did become the mainstay of British overseas propaganda. Postwar investigations have shown that the BBC was far more effective than American facilities in reaching the Continental listener, whether it be a resister in France or a disaffected enemy national. Similar advantages are now accruing to the British in the "cold war." Far from having to fight from appropriation to appropriation for its program, as is the fate of the "Voice of America," the BBC is in a position to execute government policy without any uninformed interference from Parliament or the public. Parliament, of course, could challenge the government in a major issue as always, but until it does, the BBC remains an effective tool of British policy in the cold war.[15]

The American system of broadcasting · The American system reflects the peculiarities in the general political pattern of the community, just as does the press. Indeed, the study of the control pattern of radio derives part of its fascination from the fact that it so strikingly mirrors the distribution of power in the community. The government was not, in America, in a position to assume outright control or operation of radio broadcasting; such governmentalism was quite unacceptable to the majority of the people in the twenties. As a consequence, since the wave lengths and hence the available facilities were strictly limited, creating a natural monopoly, the government assumed the role of umpire in granting licenses for the use of these facilities, and in imposing certain conditions of financial responsibility and technical competence upon prospective licensees, but amplified these by the vague general standard that the facilities should be used "in the public convenience, interest, or necessity." Before the issues raised by this formula of regulation are explored more fully, the general pattern of control needs to be broadly outlined.

Radio broadcasting has remained essentially a business enterprise in the United States. Although the statute dealing with the licensing system enunciates the people's general claim to the "air,"[16] it vindicates that claim only in times of national emergency, when the president is given power to "suspend or amend, for such times as he may see fit, the rules and regulations . . . and cause the closing of any station for radio communication, . . . or he may authorize the use or control of any such station . . . by any department of the Government." The radio broadcasters, the advertisers, the public, and the regulatory agency all share in the "control" of radio. Their control is divided in a complex way. The control is ultimately control of programs, that is, of the content of the broadcasts. An error frequently made by people is to assume that the control of facilities necessarily gives control over program content. Documentary evidence is quite scarce, but the following general formula will give some indication of the distribution of control over programs. A large part of the programs are commercial; that is, they are sold to advertisers and hence are not political, since the big broadcasters do not sell time for "controversial" subjects. The latter are broadcast on "sustaining time"; that is, time not paid for, but contributed by the broadcasting company. It is on the latter programs that the interest of the student of politics must center. It is here that the broadcasters exercise their most definite control. Since the broadcasters' primary interest is the profitable use of their facilities, they exercise their control primarily where program content either increases or decreases listening. They are indifferent to programs which have little listener appeal, unless the programs arouse listener antagonism; the broadcasters prevent the appearance of such programs if they can. Justice Holmes's "inarticulate major premise" plays quite a role in guessing at listener appeal. Advertisers, though not primarily concerned with sustaining programs, take a vivid interest in excluding from the air any programs that might be said to question the so-called "capitalist" system. Hence organized labor has had a very small percentage of sustaining time. Advertisers also interest themselves in moral issues, such as birth control. But the general impression that you can buy air time for popularizing particular minority views is erroneous, especially as far as the big networks are concerned. It is much more nearly possible on small stations. A striking illustration was provided by pro-Nazi and pro-Fascist broadcasts which came over quite a few local stations before the Second World War—broadcasts which could never have been offered over the big networks. Italian olive oil thus could become the vehicle for extolling the "grandeur that was Rome." The public participates in the control in two ways: as it is the general listening public, and as it participates in pressure groups that secure time for the airing of particular views. A good measure of the hostility of the public toward radio is owing to the fact that none of these pressure groups is satisfied with the amount of time nor with the latitude for the programs which they are able to secure. And yet the total amount of programming provided for by such groups in America is quite considerable. The general public's control, which broadcasters like to stress, is largely powerful in a negative way, in direct contrast to the pressure groups. The latter succeed in getting on the air what would otherwise not be there; the general public keeps things off the air which might otherwise be present. It is the same kind of control that all customers exercise over the wares they buy. Their control cannot be much more than the rejection of what they do not like, since they are not sufficiently informed about the medium or its potentialities to become aggressively and positively interested. Hence their judgment never can be taken to settle the positive merits of program content.

Federal regulation · Federal regulation of the broadcasting industry is built on the concept that "the air belongs to the people." The right to use a certain frequency is acquired under a license, and can be revoked for due cause. AM stations must submit to review and receive renewal of their license every three years, FM stations approximately every two. As a matter of fact, such revocations have been exceedingly rare for all but very small stations, but the government's power to revoke nevertheless continuously influences the broadcasters. Anticipating the reactions of the regulatory agency, station owners and managers stay within what they believe to be the government's concept of "public convenience, interest, and necessity." The regulatory power was exercised by the Federal Radio Commission between 1927 and 1934, and it has been in the hands of the Federal Communications Commission since that time. The Federal Communications Act charges the Commission with a contradictory objective in imposing upon it the duty to see that broadcasters operate "in the public interest," etc., but at the same time in outlawing "censorship." The act nowhere indicates how the Commission is to determine whether a station has been operated in the public interest without considering the nature of the programs offered by the station. The explicit rule against censorship may have had a good effect, however, in that it has kept the Commission from laying down positive rules for broadcasters. Any such good effect must be weighed against the disadvantage of encouraging, nay almost forcing, the broadcasters to do some tall guessing about the Commission's views, and hence leaving everything to guesswork.

The Act places enormous powers in the hands of the Commissioners when it enables them to destroy the profitable and flourishing business of a good station management. The sparse use of the power has not prevented the regulatory agency from being the target of recurring charges of corrupt practices. Congressional debates are full of such charges, alleging that Commissioners can be bought to license stations—in fact, that each Commissioner has "his price." Since no investigation has ever taken place, though demands for it have been perennial in Congress, it is difficult to secure any adequate evidence either to prove or to disprove the charges.

What role, then, does the Federal Communications Commission play in determining program content? Since almost all its influence comes through what the broadcasters themselves anticipate to be its reactions, the role of the Commission varies greatly. At times, as in the case of the wartime agitation over foreign-language broadcasting, the Commission's anticipated views were practically decisive. At other times, broadcasters will feel so completely within the range of established broadcasting practices that they will not give the Commission's views a single thought.

In 1946 the FCC created a considerable stir by the publication of a special report dealing with the public-service responsibility of broadcasters. While recognizing the primary responsibility of the broadcaster, the Commission pointed out that it was "by statute required to review periodically the station's operation, in order to determine whether the station has in fact operated in the public interest." This was certainly an unassailable position; but when the Commission went on to claim that "the establishment of sound station policy with respect to news, information, and the discussion of public issues is a major factor in operation in the public interest," it stepped into the hornet's nest of "censorship." Loud outcries were raised by the trade journals, even though the report showed clearly that the Commission was primarily concerned with such matters as time distribution. "The carrying of any particular public discussion, of course, is a problem for the individual broadcaster. But the public interest clearly requires that an adequate amount of time be made available for the discussion of public issues." Yet the Commission's investigations had shown that "few stations are staffed adequately to meet their responsibilities in serving the community . . . particularly at the local station level." In its summary and conclusions, the report appealed to the industry for more effective self-regulation, but also emphasized the responsibility of individual licensees. The Commission in addition called for the development of radio critics, the establishment of radio-listener councils, and the participation by colleges and universities through workshops and research. But above all the Commission reasserted its own responsibility in determining whether licenses should be renewed, and indicated four factors which would be of especial concern to it in this task: (1) the carrying of sustaining programs so as to balance program structure, (2) the carrying of local live programs, (3) discussion of public issues, and (4) advertising excesses.[17]

In 1940, the FCC embarked upon an ambitious program of counteracting what it described as monopolistic practices in the broadcasting field. In June of that year it released a preliminary Committee Report, which it followed by a formal "Report on Chain Broadcasting" in May 1941.[18] In these reports the Commission ordered discontinued certain practices which were mainstays of the great national networks, such as the exclusive contractual relationships between a network and its affiliates. It threatened that it would refuse to grant licenses to stations which did not obey its orders. The objective of the Commission in making this attack appeared

535

to be to insure "competition." It is an understandable, and yet a curious, objective. Certainly the radio industry combines monopolistic practices with the fiercest competition. In fact, this competition, whatever its results, has been the outstanding feature of the American system of broadcasting, and most of this competition is network competition. The situation is not unlike that in the newspaper field, with its multiplication of "columnists" and other "features." The reason one local paper after another finds itself obliged to go in for these syndicated materials is "reader demand." The local stuff rarely can compete.

The development of radio commentators is generally speaking of great importance. Owing to the responsiveness of press and radio to "public appeal," these commentators are "popularly elected" almost as definitely as are the political leaders of the country. They represent a most interesting extension of democracy into the field of thought. Being in continuous contact with the masses, they act as popular tribunes in our contemporary society, and thus restrain those who in government and politics are clothed with the more traditional symbols of authority.

For years, after its "Mayflower" decision in 1941, the FCC held to the view that radio broadcasters must, especially in news broadcasts, avoid the expression of political views. That case had arisen over the highly colored broadcasts of a crusading-editor type, attacking local politicians in Boston, over the local Yankee Network. The politicians organized a company to seek the radio license of the network's Boston station on the ground that its broadcasts were not "in the public interest, convenience and necessity." The FCC, while turning down the "Mayflower" group, enunciated the principle that broadcasters must abstain from this sort of pronounced partisanship. In 1947, the FCC reversed itself on this issue and "permitted" a certain amount of such partisanship. While hailed by the industry as a contribution to "freedom of the air," it has not radically changed the actual content of American broadcasting.

Press and propaganda under contemporary dictatorships · France, Germany, and Italy all had very brilliant journalistic traditions before the Fascist reaction set in. Their papers had achieved a key position of leadership in politics, and their editors had become what commentators and columnists are in America today: the intellectual mentors of the nation. The collaborationist prostitution of leading French journalists was as disheartening as was the surrender of Italian and German writers to Fascism.[19] Since the overthrow of the Fascists, the press in Italy and Germany has sought to recapture its place in national life, but the lack of trained journalists combined with financial difficulties have hampered these efforts.

All mass communications in totalitarian systems are seen as vehicles of official propaganda. It is not merely a question of censorship, but, following the example set during the First World War, a constant stream of governmental news material is poured into the press of these countries with a view to holding public opinion in line. Primitively simple, the system maintains a certain amount of consent without permitting any public discussion. In this area, at least, all totalitarian systems are very much alike. The enforcement of discipline amongst journalists is accomplished by requiring every writer on a newspaper to be enrolled in an association which is controlled by the government; without such enrollment no person can be a member of a paper's staff. In other words, each newspaperman is held in line by the threat of losing his job.

As if to convince free peoples that there is no difference between the Soviet Union and the vanquished Fascist regimes, the Politburo and other party agencies have, during 1947–1949, instituted purge after purge of journalists, writers, and even of musicians and natural scientists because they were "out of line" when the party masters came to change policy. No doubt some of these purges reflect internal party struggles—there has been much speculation about the relation of Zhdanov's death to some of them—but they are evidence, anyhow, of the complete dependence upon the official machine of all means of communication; they have all become propaganda agents.

The major difference between Fascism-Nazism and Sovietism in the field of mass communications results from the survival of some "private" capitalism under the former. To be sure, in the vampire economy no enterprise is really "private," but there is a difference, just the same, between the Fascist-Nazi "control" of all means of mass communications, and the methods of the Soviet Union where all channels are part of the same party-government setup.

The Fascist-Nazi control was (and in Spain still is) operated through compulsory associations of the writers, performers, and so on. In Nazi Germany the "Chamber of Culture" to which the journalists belonged was not technically a subdivision of the Ministry of Propaganda, but the actual control was complete. No avenue of escape was left. Special standards were established for editorial behavior. No one unacceptable to the Propaganda Ministry could be an editor. To remain acceptable, an editor had to "withhold from publication everything which (1) confused selfish with common interests in a manner misleading to the public; (2) could weaken the strength of the German people nationally or internationally, the German nation's will toward unity, German defensive capacity, German culture or German business, or might have hurt the religious feelings of others; (3) was offensive to the honor and dignity of a German; (4) illegally injured the honor or the well-being of another person, hurt his reputation, or made him ridiculous or contemptible; (5) was for other reasons indecent." This list of "standards" was a veritable hodgepodge of ideals shared by newspaper people throughout the world, of equivocal generalities, and of invitations to a callous disregard of truth. Very similar regulations prevailed in Italy under the Statute of the National Fascist Union of Journalists. The attitude of the rulers of this kind of press had been well stated by Dr. Joseph Goebbels: "Since we National Socialists are convinced that we are right, we cannot tolerate anybody who contends that he is right. For if he, too, is right, he must be a National Socialist, or if he is not a National Socialist, then he simply is not right." The paradox of this pedantic tirade provoked the bitterly sarcastic commentary: "The real will of the people claims precedence over the will of the people."

But it is not merely a matter of silencing possible critics, but of making them extol the virtues of their new masters, or, to use a familiar American expression, of making them eat their own words. The Soviet Union has carried this technique farthest. The spectacle has by now become familiar to the point where few are surprised when a Communist denounces what he has just been extolling, whether it be men or ideas. Soviet control, as already stated, is more complete than was the Fascist-Nazi manipulation of the press and all culture. In the Soviet Union the disappearance of private ownership has swept away all but Communist press organs. The Communist press consists, pure and simple, of governmental newssheets. Apologists have alleged that this gives the Communist party a "positive and constructive power in the shaping of the press" as distinguished from the restrictive power of Fascist governments. Obviously, this is a Communist party view; a totalitarian press is constructive from the partisan point of view in that it spreads the party's creed.

The Communist press has been gaining enormously, owing in part to the rapid disappearance of illiteracy. In 1932 there were in the Soviet Union 2230 newspapers printed either every day, every three days, or every five days, with a total circulation of 33,000,000, whereas in 1913 there were 859 newspapers with a circulation of about 2,500,000. This great increase is related to the reduction of illiteracy in the Soviet Union, often praised as a "positive" aspect of the Soviets' policies. But the ability to read and write is valuable only when it is part of the freedom to think, speak, and write. In a country where an encyclopedia takes 23 years to appear, where all its editors are liquidated in the process, and where this self-same encyclopedia has to be suppressed and its export forbidden before it is finished, literacy serves to enslave rather than to free the mind. In fact, the great Russian

538

Communist organs, *Pravda* (for the Communist party) and *Izvestia* (for the Soviet government), each with a circulation of 2,000,000 copies daily, have a semantic, priestly role to fulfill. It is their task to interpret the developments of the day in terms of the elaborate Communist theory which underlies the whole institutional framework of Communist Russia. Their vigorous competition is cast in this pattern of dogmatic orthodoxy.

Evidence about the breakdown of the Nazi system suggests strongly that these rigid systems of control of the press defeat themselves, that a saturation point is reached beyond which news offered through such propagandistic channels is no longer accepted by the reader. Such a reaction has even been observed in free societies, especially after a war with its attendant propaganda.[20]

Press and propaganda in wartime · The division between constitutional and nonconstitutional systems of government in the field of propaganda and communication, while of great importance in differentiating these two types of government, tends to become blurred in wartime. Both in the First and the Second World War, democratic governments found themselves compelled to institute official propaganda on a large scale, to operate official censorship, and to exercise a substantial amount of control over all means of communication. The old Latin dictum, *inter arma leges silent*, applies with peculiar force to the constitutional law of freedom of expression. Mr. Justice Holmes's famous criterion of "imminent danger" is broadly applicable to wartime situations (see above, ch. IX). While the general problems raised by such emergencies will be dealt with below (ch. XXVI), some special aspects relating to the press and other means of mass communication may well be remarked upon here.

Basically, all problems revolve around the central wartime objective of how to defeat the enemy. Opposition to this objective will not be tolerated by a democratic community, even as a minority right, to any considerable extent. The more desperate the struggle becomes, the more disinclined will be the majority to allow any serious dissent. Hence, competition will be replaced by monopolistic control wherever these vital wartime issues are involved. This raises the central issue of informational strategy: how can information be made a part of the grand strategy of a total war?

During the Second World War, the information services in the United States, especially the Office of War Information, took the line that the problem could be resolved in terms of the "strategy of the truth" or "the propaganda of truth." It was claimed that this was democracy's answer to the incessant barrage of totalitarian phrases, slogans, and word-symbols. Truth, it was said, will fight our battles for us in the great struggle for the mind of mankind. In so far as the propaganda of truth is merely a rejection of the propaganda of lies, it has much to recommend it. Every propagandist worth his mettle will use the truth in preference to lies whenever he can—even a Dr. Goebbels. And a determination to avoid saying anything when you would have to lie is admittedly the better part of wisdom in a democracy, where public discussion even in wartime is relatively free and hence apt to uncover lies rather quickly. "Lies have short legs," a German proverb says.

But the decision to avoid telling lies does not give us a positive standard as to what to say. What information to give out relative to the myriad happenings in any war calls for more selective principles than the proposition that we shall tell the truth. Also, in many important situations there remains the old query of Pilate's. Demagogues may orate: "Give us the facts, all the facts, and nothing but the facts," but the student of the contemporary social scene knows that it is impossible to live up to any such directive. If he is semantically sophisticated, he will hardly be able to suppress a wry smile at the confused thinking of such oratory.

In short, the slogan about the strategy of the truth does not offer us an answer to our prayer for a strategy that would make the best use of all available information for the winning of the war. Indeed, no such simple formula will do the trick. Informational strategy, like all strategy, while not very complicated, calls for a clear analysis of the functional relation between such information and the task in hand. Like all weapons, information has a task to perform in a comprehensive undertaking such as "victory."

Victory, in the democratic perspective, means (1) the defeat of the enemy, and (2) the making of a better peace, that is to say, the establishment of a social order sounder and more workable than the one which issued in war. Informational strategy which neglects the second part in pursuing the first part of this total objective is false and will lead to disaster, as did the propaganda carried on by the Committee on Public Information in the First World War.

Unfortunately, no such counsels were followed by those responsible for government propaganda during the Second World War. Who is willing to assert today that the American people were told "the truth" about the Soviet Union when they were being told that the USSR was a democracy, that her fighting on our side made her a peace-loving nation, and so forth? Or that it was wise, or necessary, to broadcast such misrepresentations in the face of the most conclusive evidence to the contrary? If one asks oneself what are the ingredients of an informational strategy that might have avoided these grave errors, the following criteria suggest themselves: war requires the considerable backing of a majority of a nation, and any public policy calling for action on the part of a number of people should be considered a battle which can be won only if advance preparations are made to prepare the people involved for the actions to be taken by them. This calls for (1) research to determine whether prejudices, ignorance, or other grounds obstruct the likelihood of such action being taken when requested; (2) the channeling out of information in such amounts as will overcome these obstructions; (3) further research to determine whether the information is being absorbed and is having the desired effect; (4) announcing the policy in such a manner as to anticipate the major obstructions by highlighting the information previously broadcast.

Any program of channeling out information to prepare for a proposed policy of the government is bound to encounter a variety of difficulties resulting from counterpropaganda unloosed by hostile special-interest groups. It is one of the most important tasks of effective informational strategy to determine what these groups are and to anticipate their campaigns by appropriate information which would be designed to "blanket" their slanted statements, rumors, and the like. Rigid rules for such strategy cannot be formulated, because the strategy needs to be shaped in the light of the total situation.

It is generally agreed that political warfare seeks to accomplish two things: (1) to undermine the enemy's will to fight, and (2) to undermine the will of allies of the enemy to support him. A special case of the latter is the task of diverting neutrals from the enemy and turning them into more or less active supporters of one's own cause. It is evident that these tasks call for a concrete and realistic understanding of *who is the enemy* and *who are his allies*. A great deal depends upon doing this with the necessary precision and accuracy. No effective informational strategy can be devised unless the addressees of such information are known.

On the whole, it is fair to say that the United States and her allies were more successful with the second than with the first objective. The United States Bombing Survey's Morale Division has been able to show how limited were the achievements in undermining the enemy's will to fight. In part the difficulty resulted from the failure to define the enemy clearly. Fascists and anti-Fascists were often treated alike. Informational strategy could conceivably become the way of going about propaganda objectives in a democracy. It could be made compatible with the basic limitations of governmental propaganda in a free country, even when at war. But this result is not likely to be achieved if the direction of such efforts is in the hands of men who do not understand the issues involved. The deleterious effect of both World Wars upon the functioning of constitutional democracy is in no small degree traceable to the unrestrained, and at times totalitarian, handling of the necessary propaganda machinery, both in facing one's own people and when addressing the enemy.[21]

All governments have had recourse to censorship in wartime. Where the immediate danger was small and popular fervor considerable, as in the United States during the First World War, such censorship did not have to be carried very far. In England and France, where opposition to the War developed almost immediately after the outbreak of hostilities and gradually became more and more insistent, censorship was applied with considerable rigidity, and more so in France than in England. Long white columns in many French papers attested to the effectiveness of the working of this machine. Clemenceau, who chafed under these restrictions, published his paper *L'Homme Libre* under the significant new title *L'Homme Enchaîné* after the censor had deleted one of his editorials. But while censorship may be used for a brief period, it is highly unsatisfactory as a control mechanism.

Governmental control and censorship · In a sense the war merely highlighted issues of longer standing. The capitalist basis of the press in free societies has been a source of contention which recent American elections have merely emphasized. There can be little doubt that a press largely hostile to the present popular trend in favor of governmental restraints, and consequently oblivious to what is believed by many to be the public interest, raises very serious difficulties in a democratic age.[22] The present state of affairs cannot be looked upon with indifference. The public at large is increasingly dissatisfied with the newspapers. In towns where a single individual controls the one or more papers, intolerable conditions can easily develop. But a constructive solution is difficult. Few would advocate a licensing system, such as was instituted in conquered Austria, Germany, and Japan. Recent emergencies have intensified the issue.

The new constitutions in Europe vary in their approach to the problem. The French constitution is silent in the matter. The Italian constitution, in article 21, after outlawing censorship, admits nevertheless that publications as well as shows and demonstrations that are "contrary to good morals" are forbidden. Even more pioneering are the provisions of the German Basic Law. While outlawing censorship in article 5 and guaranteeing freedom of the press, of radio and motion picture reporting, article 18 declares that anyone abusing freedom of expression in order to attack the free democratic basis and order shall forfeit these basic rights (the same applies to other rights—see above, ch. IX) by judgment of the constitutional court. It is difficult to see how the court is to carry out this difficult and dangerous duty without inquiring into the content of publications and other communications with a view to determining whether they do attack the free democratic order; in other words, they are to institute *ex post facto* censorship. This attempt at judicial determination of what is inadmissible in the field of press and communication constitutes an interesting attempt to avoid administrative control. For outright administrative control, particularly in matters of public policy, defeats itself because it undermines the confidence of the public. In course of time it would be inevitable that the same results would follow such administrative interference on the part of a constitutional government as have followed in dictatorial regimes. These problems of the control of channels of communication, and particularly those of the news, are, for technical reasons, inescapable in the sphere of radio broadcasting, but they present themselves for all mass-communication media. Everywhere the public is awakening to the fact that we are not settling the political problems which are involved in these situations merely by insisting that the government not interfere. In fact, those groups which oppose the present order of things are emphatic in their demand for precisely such governmental interference. From the standpoint of the scientific analyst, both arguments are misleading, one because it treats private capital as a neutral control, the other because it treats the government as a neutral control. Whether we think of the newsreel, the radio, or the press, in every instance we are facing the same set of problems in contemporary constitutional systems.[23] How can we prevent the exclusive control of these channels of communication, and therefore of public opinion, by any one of the contending groups?

Conclusion · Grave difficulties threaten constitutional democracy from a commercialized press that lacks responsibility, and from other mass communication channels, especially radio and the movies.[24] Equally great dangers must be faced from an extension of governmental controls in these fields. The democratizing efforts of the United States and Britain have further emphasized the issues and difficulties. But an attentive perusal of the growing literature does not produce the impression that a simple solution to these growing difficulties is very likely. The Commission on the Freedom of the Press, actually concerned as it was with freedom of all mass-communication channels, struck a surprisingly hopeful note when it announced that the problems have been pretty well worked out as far as the restrictive activities of the government are concerned. The crux of the problem of the control of mass communications in contemporary society is their deleterious effect upon the beliefs which are vital to the life of free societies. To trace the vicious circle by which every new technique begets a new servitude is the primary task; the Commission miserably failed in this vital task. In reading these reports, one has the impression of being in some fairyland. It seems as if the crisis of constitutional democracy were not confronting us at all.

Constitutional government rests upon the provision of effective restraints on the exercise of institutionalized power. The press of today is thoroughly institutionalized in its corporate structure, and yet we talk about it simply in terms of individual liberty. We realize its representative position, particularly in such cases as *The Times* (London) or *Le Temps*, yet we have not evolved any effective technique for coping with the problems involved. To be sure, an attempt has been made in England to nationalize *The Times* by making it a trust akin to the great universities. But this solution does not face the most pressing problem of all: class control versus governmental control. It is not the task of the present volume to suggest concrete practical measures in this any more than in any other field of political activity. It may be permissible, however, to indicate certain contemporary trends and to comment upon them in conclusion. Various methods which have been suggested for constitutionally restraining the press all amount to administrative censorship. Constitutionality apart, censorship raises the problem of standards, which is insoluble in a constitutional democracy. There is no group which is recognized as knowing what is good for the rest. The Second World War brought a temporary censorship, but the experiences during that war as well as during the First World War and under dictatorial regimes since that time do not encourage further experimentation. Censorship in particular fields, as it is practiced in many American states, is almost as unqualified a failure. How, then, shall we ensure that the press is really free: that it is not the instrument for propagandizing the views of one class as against that of others? This question has been asked time and again by thoughtful students of modern journalism. It is not easy to suggest answers. One suggested remedy would be the breaking up of trusts and monopolies. You could perhaps try to withdraw the legal foundation of the large-scale newspaper chain by appropriate changes in corporation law.

The exigencies of modern newsgathering and the cost of a modern plant would still render the press subject to some of its owner's "inarticulate major premises." The radio, of course, has provided important competition and has thus in recent years contributed to the progress of the press. But, as has been shown, the broadcasting industry, in turn, is influenced by the same major premises. Indeed, advertisers have an even more complete hold, and the "editorial judgment" of the broadcaster is exercised under conditions varying widely from those prevailing in the press.[25]

In spite of these differences, there is a broad similarity. This similarity results from two common, unproved major premises, (1) that news is purely factual and hence not influenced by the general political outlook of the owners of communication media, and (2) that such communication media depend for their success primarily upon their users, readers, listeners. These make-believes, though certainly possessing a kernel of reality, are even in their more fanciful forms important factors in rendering the owners and operators of such media responsive to public criticism, preferences, and tastes. This general view is, as Dexter Keezer has pointed out, peculiarly an American conception. It is a symbol of democratic virtue. No study of the realities of communication control can afford to neglect it, even when it makes allowances for the element of pure myth which it contains.

XXV

Direct Popular Action

Introduction · Propaganda and the effects of the mass-communication media are, as we have seen, of great importance as factors causing stresses and strains within the fabric of modern constitutionalism. Apart from readjustments peculiar to their field of operation, such as constitutional limitations upon the rights of anticonstitutional forces, a more direct participation of the electorate in the major decisions of policy has suggested itself as a remedy. Indeed, the ever-recurring problem of "legitimacy," that is, the question of how authority can be made to appear legitimate to those over whom it is wielded, seemed to many ardent democrats at the beginning of the twentieth century to call for an ever greater extension of personal participation of as many citizens as possible in as many decisions as possible. Basic constitutional questions and crucial issues of foreign policy, especially going to war, are particularly suitable for direct submission to the people. The activating of the citizen seemed further to suggest that any substantial group of them should be in a position to put a law before the electorate at large.

The totalitarian dictators of this century, following the example of Napoleon, have in turn relied upon such referenda or plebiscites for legitimizing their unconstitutional and anticonstitutional regimes. Such direct popular approval provides an impressive propagandistic screen for the dictatorial *coup d'état* and can be used against democratic opposition at home and abroad on the pretense that "the will of the people" has been consulted. That true freedom for this will of the people presupposes available alternatives is an aspect usually obscured in the shuffle of claims and counterclaims, though it should be obvious to all.

The tendency toward securing popular acclaim by plebiscitary appeal is also apparent in stabilized constitutional systems. The general elections in Britain and the presidential elections in the United States have exhibited an increasing plebiscitary character. In continental Europe, the reconstruction of constitutionalism has brought new incentives for such direct popular action. Where the basis of traditional legitimacy has disappeared, an appeal to the people sounds like a solution. Thus the sharp disagreements among members of the French Resistance, and between them and de Gaulle as well as the older leadership of the Third Republic, was resolved by a referendum on October 21, 1945. In this case, the electorate was asked to decide between three alternatives: revival of the old constitution, establishment of an all-powerful constituent assembly, or formation of a more restricted assembly with limited powers of provisional government. The last alternative won and naturally so, since the first and second possibilities were blocked by powerful emotional predispositions: shame over the fall of the Third Republic and fear of Communist and Soviet domination.

These recent developments are a far cry from the early hopes and aspirations associated with referendum and initiative which first manifested itself when provisions for a popular referendum (incorporated in the Swiss constitution of 1874) spread rapidly through the United States after the turn of the century. In Switzerland, direct popular action had remained the traditional form of political activity in some of the small rural cantons, and the modern referendum was essentially an adaptation of these methods to more numerous electoral bodies.

Rousseau's objections to elected representatives · The great apostle of democracy, Jean Jacques Rousseau, had strenuously objected to the employment of representative assemblies for the purpose of enacting legislation[1]; the argument that Rousseau accepts magistrates does not go to the heart of the issue. For laws, he felt, were so important that they must be a genuine expression of the general will, of sovereignty, and he felt that all such assemblies tend to pervert the "general will" (see above, ch. XV, pp. 260 f.). Though the complexities of Rousseau's doctrine of the general will cannot be considered here, we may say that we are inclined to understand the general will as referring to an objective thing, like the general interest, rather than to the subjective element of will. There are many passages in Rousseau which carry the implication that the general will is the voice of reason, others which suggest that there is a concrete, living superentity, an organism which is acting and deciding for itself. The vote of a majority of the individuals composing it is merely an indication of what this will might be, and the good citizen, when participating in such a vote, should not ask himself what *he* wants, but what is good for the com-

547

munity. That voters do not actually do this is apparent enough. Hence Rousseau on one hand would restrict democracy to small units, such as the Swiss cantons; he would also leave room for the constitutional dictator, the great legislator of Greek antiquity. On one hand, then, the general will is not merely the dictates of right reason in the traditional sense of rationalism and natural law; on the other it is not the will of the majority. It is curious that Rousseau should have believed that a majority of the citizens were the most promising source for discovering this general will. On Burke's theory of a good representative (see above, pp. 264 f.) the majority of elected representatives would seem a better bet.

Rousseau's animosity to representative assemblies may perhaps be explained by his observations in Switzerland, where the aristocratic government of Geneva contrasted strongly with the simple democracy of the rural cantons. Indeed, his attempt to resuscitate the older democratic forms in his essay on the government of Geneva (for which he was exiled) stands as a vivid reminder of his intense interest in these contrasts. The general idea of radical and direct democracy and the gradual spread of the referendum as an instrument of practical democracy in the second half of the nineteenth century are parallel developments mutually intensifying each other.

The Napoleonic plebiscites · Rousseau's views were applied in the course of the French Revolution (or so it seemed to the actors on the revolutionary stage). The Committee on Public Safety claimed to act on behalf of the general public because the members were supposed to be subject to recall by the public at large. Unhappily, it remained quite obscure how this public was supposed to swing into action, since every opponent of the Committee promptly landed on the guillotine. Such a condition could not long be endured; but the efforts toward returning to a constitutional order ended in the ascendancy of Napoleon Bonaparte, who in turn claimed to be the executor of the general will, on behalf of the people, thus fulfilling the role of the (divine) legislator whom Rousseau had envisaged as a necessary corrective of human frailty in large political bodies. Napoleon, however, who in his youth had been deeply attached to the doctrines of Rousseau, and had rendered a measure of lip service to them all his life, went further than the Committee on Public Safety had done.[2] At certain crucial moments in his career, such as his election to remain First Consul for life and his assumption of the position of Emperor, he called for popular plebiscites which would indicate what the public thought about these changes. Such was the theory. In practice, open registers produced a large measure of coercion, and the percentage of favorable votes was correspondingly high.

In the first of these plebiscites it was found, on August 2, 1802, that 3,568,-885 Frenchmen had voted "yes," and only 8374 "no" on the proposal of making Napoleon consul for life. In spite of local frauds, these figures are generally believed to be accurate. Undoubtedly the prefects and military officials exerted extensive pressure, but on the whole the vote was due to Napoleon's victories and the re-establishment of the church. The second plebiscite produced similar results. Assent to the establishment of an hereditary empire was given by 3,372,329 voters, while only 2569 objected. In this case we know Napoleon himself corrected the result, and the number of abstaining objectors may have been appreciably larger. There was also a great deal of local fraud. Voters who could not write were summarily reported by the authorities, and no real vote ever took place. A good many cases of actual intimidation are known. To proclaim such a popular vote an expression of the general will was a sordid sham, or a bad joke.

When the third Napoleon executed his *coup d'état* in 1851, he at once revived the practice of his illustrious uncle and ordered a plebiscite to be held on the question of whether the French people approved of his action. They did. On the 31st of December, 1851, an electoral commission could report to the new dictator that 7,439,216 people had voted in the affirmative, and 640,737 in the negative. This dissent of about 7 per cent of the voting citizens considerably exceeds the opposition under the first Napoleon. The technique of open registers was discarded when loud protests were raised against it, but almost the same results were achieved by supplying only an insufficient number of ballots with "no" printed on them so that those who wished to object were obliged to write out their votes, which made them readily recognizable. It is now generally believed that the vote as reported is fairly accurate; nor is the difference between it and the vote given to Napoleon at the time of his election to the presidency (1848) so large as to imply the extensive use of force. A later plebiscite instituted to legitimize the elevation of Napoleon to Emperor yielded similar results, though the actual percentage of negative votes was smaller. There were 7,824,189 votes for and 253,145 against the empire, or only about 3 per cent negative. But the abstentions are reported as amounting to 2,062,-789. In certain parts of France, like the Vendée and the Rhône Valley, they ran to 40 per cent and over. Just the same, Napoleon seems to have gained further adherents and could claim solid popular support. When, in the course of the evolution of the empire toward a measure of liberalism, a limited parliamentary regime was to be instituted in 1870, the proposed constitutional change was again submitted to a plebiscite. This time the outcome was more equivocal, which is important since the electorate had come to look upon the vote in terms rather of endorsing the government of

Napoleon than in terms of the proposed liberalization. Particularly in the cities this plebiscite revealed massive opposition. To a considerable extent, this opposition came also, of course, from those followers of Napoleon who believed in the thoroughly authoritarian and dictatorial conduct of the government. Indeed, on the night of the plebiscite, when the first returns were coming in, things looked very black; for in Paris and the Seine department there were 138,000 "yes" votes, 184,000 "no" votes, 83,000 abstentions, and about 10,000 invalid votes. But the rural population solidly supported the Napoleonic dictatorship. For the whole of France there were 7,358,786 affirmative votes, and 1,571,939 negative ones, with about 2,000,000 abstentions and invalid votes. It will be seen that the latter remained about the same, but that about 20 per cent of the voters at this juncture turned out against the empire. The government did not attach too much importance to this trend. Yet within a year the empire had collapsed and its inner hollowness had been revealed.

The referendum and initiative: Switzerland · In Switzerland, direct popular action was put to a very different use.[3] The radically democratic elements fostered it as a curb on the ruling Liberals. After a rapid spread of the movement in the cantons during the sixties, the referendum (and the initiative) were embodied in the constitution in 1874. They were organized according to ancient traditions as a restraint upon the governmental agencies established under the constitution. To consult the majority of the people at large as well as the majority of the people as divided into cantons was made obligatory in all matters affecting the constitution itself. Moreover, with sufficient backing any matter could be embodied in the constitution through a popular initiative followed by a referendum. Both methods have been extensively used since that time and a considerate judgment is possible today.

There can be no question that these methods of direct popular action as used in Switzerland are working fairly satisfactorily. It has been rightly remarked that in Switzerland the popular votes have tended to be on the conservative side, but in certain matters of social reform they have tended to favor progressive measures, such as the referendum on compulsory insurance for workingmen (1891), or the law for the purchase of railroads by the government (1900). When such measures tended unduly to enhance the power of the central government, they were, before the First World War, rejected, as happened to the constitutional amendment to extend the power of the federal government to uniform legislation on trades (1894), or the constitutional amendment for direct federal taxation (1918).

Since that time, the trend has been toward increasing governmentalism.

This is especially true of the referendum of 1947 on "economic questions." By this comprehensive referendum, the growing governmentalism (*étatisme*) of Switzerland was sanctioned. According to Professor Rappard, this constitutional revision eliminated a great many inherent contradictions between the constitution and legislation of an "interventionist" sort. Many of the fields of activity associated with the progressive and New Deal legislation in the United States as well as with those of national (military) security were sanctioned by the Swiss people (556,803 for, 494,414 against) and the road cleared for a closely regulated market economy.

The workings of the obligatory referendum on constitutional amendments proposed by the federal legislature are simple. On the whole, the referenda have been positive. From 1874–1948, forty-five amendments were passed by the legislature, and only seven of these were rejected by the people. There were fewer rejected between 1896 and 1948 (three in thirty-five) than between 1874 and 1895 (four in ten). None have been rejected since 1926.

The obligatory referendum procedure is implemented, as noted above, by a constitutional initiative according to which 50,000 voters can demand a constitutional amendment. It has been said that this method acts as a spur in the flanks of the legislative steed, while the obligatory referendum is a bit in the mouth. The constitutional initiative finds favor with the voters less often than does the obligatory referendum, even though the percentage of voting is somewhat higher. The fact of the matter is that the initiative proceedings are employed for highly controversial subjects such as the right to work and the duty of the government to provide work (1894), or the estate tax (1922). With the present method, dating from 1891, there have been thirty-seven such initiative proposals, and of these thirty have been rejected, down to 1948. Economic and social measures have been the most frequent subject of initiative and obligatory referenda. After an initial period of extreme proposals, the measures put forward under the initiative procedure have on the whole been moderately progressive. They have helped in the process of democratic popular education; they have given the Swiss people a feeling that the constitution is theirs for the making and unmaking. This means that not infrequently an initiative which was rejected has given rise to a counterproposal by the legislature which may then be submitted to the people, like the question of private manufacture of armaments in 1938. A proposal for the total revision of the constitution was made by initiative in 1935, but decisively rejected by the electorate. Nevertheless, in the opinion of Swiss students of their constitution, there are increasing signs of "old age"; the constitution of 1848 is proving more and more inadequate for the age of governmental participation in the economy, for it was conceived in the heyday of liberalism. The broad revision obtained through the amendment of 1947 would seem to prove the viability of the constitutional system, however. Similar methods prevail throughout the majority of the cantons. The federal constitution requires cantonal constitutions to be submitted to popular referendum. Initiative also is found in many of them. Thus the problem of constitutional amendments, always a thorny question in connection with constitutions (see above, ch. VIII, pp. 135 f.), has found a significant solution.

Direct popular action, however, is not limited to constitutional amendments. The constitution also provides for a referendum on important legislative measures if eight cantons or 30,000 voters demand it. It is reported that of three hundred and thirty laws and resolutions which might have been subjected to such a referendum, thirty-five were actually so tested down to 1922, and of them nineteen failed of acceptance. Between 1922 and 1940, thirteen statutes were subjected to referendum, and ten of these were rejected by the voters. These were not necessarily the most important measures, but rather the ones which had aroused popular interest. While the federal constitution does not recognize a corresponding right to initiate legislation, this is provided for in many of the cantonal constitutions and is extensively used. The percentage of the voters whose signatures are required varies between 3.09 per cent in the canton of Basel Stadt to 12.77 per cent in the canton of Schwyz. In the federal realm, where the actual numbers are fixed at 30,000 and 50,000, the percentage has varied from about 12.5 per cent in 1848 to 6.1 per cent in 1910 (for initiative petitions). During the same period, the participation in these forms of direct popular action has been changing, downward in the case of compulsory referenda, upward in the case of initiative and optional referenda. Optional referenda and initiative proceedings are extensively propagandized beforehand in connection with the collection of the necessary signatures for the petition, while the obligatory referenda come from the legislature with the official approval which tends to insure them success at the hands of the electorate. Swiss experience has been well summarized in the following phrases: "Direct legislation in Switzerland has not realized all the extravagant anticipations of its friends. But on the other hand it has completely falsified the dismal prophecies of chaos and revolution uttered by the conservatives of an earlier period. It has become a vital and freely functioning part of the Swiss political organism." The recurrent refusal of the general electorate to sanction constitutional and legislative measures designed to benefit particular groups suggests the referendum as an integrating mechanism, where the representative bodies may be inclined to yield to the pressure of particular interest groups. This, however, does not always work. When the law for the reduction of the salaries of civil servants was submitted to a popular vote, at the request of the unions of civil servants, it was defeated (1933), though by a narrow majority.

We cannot close this discussion without brief mention of a further extension of the referendum system in Switzerland—that is, the addition, in 1921, of a constitutional provision to the effect that treaties with foreign powers must, when requested, be submitted to a referendum if they are concluded for more than fifteen years. There can be little question that this provision is a logical consequence of the idea that the popular referendum is the truest expression of the popular will and should therefore be applied to all really important matters. Even before the enactment of this provision the referendum had been used in connection with the entry of Switzerland into the League of Nations (1920). Indeed, this entry was accepted by a very narrow majority of 56.3 per cent of those voting, with 77.5 per cent of those entitled to vote participating in this momentous decision. A later treaty, which was to settle the long-drawn-out controversy between France and Switzerland concerning their boundary, was rejected by the electorate. Whether this decision was a wise one and augurs well for the application of direct popular action in the field of international affairs is very questionable. The percentages against the proposed treaty were very high in many cantons, but they were significantly lowest in the cantons most immediately affected, Freiburg and Waadt actually having a majority in favor, and Geneva almost so (48.9 per cent).

The referendum in the United States · The constitutional referendum migrated from the United States, where it was first employed in Massachusetts (1788) and again in connection with the ratification of the federal constitution, through France to Switzerland. But while it disappeared in the United States for almost a hundred years, it was developed and extended in Switzerland, as we have seen. To it was added the initiative in both constitutional and ordinary legislation, and toward the end of the century these various methods for direct popular action were reintroduced into the United States, there to sweep through the several states, beginning with Oregon in 1904.[4] On the whole, the experience has been the same as in Switzerland; neither the ardent hopes of its first expounders nor the dire apprehensions of its opponents have materialized. Both referendum and initiative have become recognized parts of the American political machinery. But whereas in Switzerland referendum and initiative have been developed extensively in national affairs, in the United States they have so far been used only in the states. To be sure, at least one of the methods for constitutional amendment is a form of indirect popular referendum, for special conventions, as provided for in Article V, would presumably act in accordance with the "will of the people."

We find, in the several states, and in many different forms and combinations, referendum, both compulsory and optional, and initiative, the latter two applicable to legislation as well as to constitutional amendment. Compulsory referenda are the most frequently used of these methods. It is said that during the ten years from 1899 to 1908, 472 constitutional questions were submitted to the electorates of forty-three states, and from 1919 to 1925 more than 600 such measures were thus voted upon. The optional referendum (also called popular referendum) has been put to the test between 1906 and 1925 173 times in sixteen states. Finally, the initiative has been brought into play 440 times during the same period, but of these, 120 times in Oregon. A few states with a highly developed interest in direct popular action, such as Oregon and California, contribute a considerable part of the total sum. As in Switzerland, we find that the optional referendum and the initiative elicit a higher percentage of voter interest than the compulsory referendum. Regarding the latter, the figures are very discouraging, rising only in a few localities above 50 per cent of the vote for Governor, for example. Voter interest in Switzerland is higher than that. This is undoubtedly in large measure attributable to the peculiar nature of American state constitutions. The mass of legislative detail included in many of them, when combined with the compulsory referendum, necessitates the submission of a large number of trivial and uninteresting matters to the electorate. Optional referenda and initiated votes usually reach as respectable a percentage as 75 per cent of the vote cast for governor; even this percentage is materially below the Swiss figures. While these procedures seem to arouse a larger amount of public interest, it cannot be said that the measures brought before the electorate are, on the whole, either foolish or extreme, nor does the action of the electorate itself seem irrational. As in Switzerland, there is a higher mortality amongst optional referenda and initiated proposals, more than half being rejected, but it is rare that measures are either proposed or passed which have not also been proposed or passed by some state legislature. One difficulty with ordinary legislative referenda is that they might be employed by special-interest groups for the purpose of delaying the enactment of necessary, and sometimes even of urgent, legislation. States have tried to cope with this situation by excepting emergency legislation from the operation of the optional referendum. The difficulty is that no agreement exists as to what constitutes an emergency (see below, ch. XXVI). Under the optional referendum and the initiative, the desire of the voters is ordinarily registered in the form of a certain percentage of voters subscribing to a list under a petition. Upon investigation it is found that these signatures rarely indicate any real urge on the part of the signer. Yet it is hard to see how the popular demand should otherwise be indicated. The trouble is that it favors petitions supported by financially potent groups. It may be pointed out, however, that other groups, like trade unions, command a sufficiently numerous following to secure signatures without any appreciable outlay of money. Social-reform initiatives in this country as well as in Switzerland have been brought forward by these groups. Inasmuch as one of the greatest advantages of direct popular action flows from the educational stimulus which results from the attendant agitation, official literature on the subject of referenda has in certain states been provided by the government, giving, in the case of California, the arguments pro and con. It seems that such arrangements materially increase the voters' interest. These instrumentalities for direct popular action are not perfect mechanisms. Only an inveterate Rousseauist could survey the experience to date and still maintain that they provide a panacea for the difficulties of popular government. The electorate is quite liable to abuse its power. Inasmuch as all the forms of direct action have been developed in the states, they are subject to the constitutional limitations of the federal constitution. Occasional tendencies to invade the sphere of private rights or to neglect the rights of minorities (racial and others) have thus been checked. One must agree with A. N. Holcombe that "there can be no doubt that the referendum is now permanently established among the political institutions of the states. There is little question of abandoning it," he continues. "The only questions concerning which there are still serious differences of opinion relate to the form in which, and the conditions under which, it shall be used." What is even more important, it is undoubtedly true that "the best effects of the popular initiative should be found, in the long run, not in the legislation placed by its use directly upon the statute books, but rather in the improvement of the legislation placed there by the legislatures."

Direct popular action and the general problem of representation · The political problems created by the spread of the several methods of direct popular action, their tendency to corrupt the people and to weaken the representative assemblies, have been urged time and again.[5] The low percentage of voters participating in many of these decisions has raised the problem of the trustworthiness of the result. In the case of the compulsory referenda in the United States with their very low percentages, this trustworthiness has been widely questioned. Cases can readily be cited where the electorate reversed itself in short order. The possible delays involved in referendum procedure serve as another point of attack. Besides these specific difficulties there is the broader issue of just how direct popular action fits into the general pattern of democratic representation. It has generally been assumed that there is a conflict between representation and direct popular action, and those who stress the representative features of constitutional government tend to question direct popular action. But does not direct popular action itself possess representative quality? In the first place, it is exercised by the electorate on behalf of the people. Furthermore, the electorate itself is represented by those who are participating in the vote. We have seen above that the voting in these referenda is rather limited. Our definition of representation held that representation would be the process through which the influence which the entire citizenry or a part of them have upon governmental action is exercised on their behalf by a smaller number among them, with binding effect on those represented as well as on those participating in the decision. It is evident that the voters participating in a referendum stand in precisely such a relationship to the total electorate and to the people at large. The real difference between direct popular action and the action of legislatures and other "representatives" lies in the field of deliberation. The voters cannot assemble and discuss matters. But under modern conditions it may be said that this difference is not more apparent than real. A constant meeting of minds is made possible through newspapers and other communication media. All questions of general public interest stir up discussion and argument. The big shot makes speeches which are reported in full columns; average Mr. Citizen writes a "Letter to the Editor." But both participate in the deliberation. What is more, many vital issues are thrashed out within the organized interest groups. The referendum within the United States Chamber of Commerce is a striking illustration. The representatives of these interest groups in turn participate in the public discussions through speeches, articles, and other communications. The day-to-day history of any referendum reveals the wide extent of actual discussion which goes into such a decision. And after all, the discussion in deliberative assemblies is not as unrelated to these forces as earlier views tended to imply. We have seen how party, press, and interest groups are influencing what is being said in the halls of legislatures, if they do not actually dictate it. In other words, our modern means of communication have set up a context within which representative action by a much larger part of the electorate than formerly has become practicable. It remains to remark in this connection that the contrast between England, the classical country of representative government, and countries like the United States and Switzerland must not be overstressed. After all, whenever an English election turns upon a hotly debated issue, as it did in 1923, 1924, 1931, and 1945, it amounts almost to a popular referendum. This has often been pointed out, and acute students have related this emergence of the general electorate alongside the cabinet as a primary aspect of the decline of Parliament (see above, p. 366). Whether it is actually caused by these developments may well be doubted, however; the two go hand-in-hand as parallel changes in connection with the changes in the underlying social and industrial pattern of life. If constitutionalism is to continue, direct popular action will continue to find effective constitutional channels. It will, in a sense, be self-restrained. In the United States, the most important check results from the fact that direct popular action is limited to the States. In Switzerland, the constitutional initiative opens up a practically unfettered realm for the exercise of unlimited power, but so far the Swiss voters have shown great restraint in extending their own influence. It may be different, however, in countries with a less firmly rooted tradition of political democracy, particularly if rent more violently by the controversies of contemporary social conflict. Even in Switzerland, the introduction of direct action into the field of foreign affairs is a matter of some concern; in a larger country with a real foreign policy such a step might be disastrous.

It proved itself so in the Weimar Republic. Although an attempt was made to guard against the demagogic abuse of the referendum, the relevant constitutional provisions proved wholly ineffectual. Since the referendum was difficult to put into motion, practical politicians of the more moderate parties did not employ it for such purposes as are giving life and meaning to the referenda in Switzerland and the United States. No such scruples handicapped the Communists and National Socialists. Thus, the referendum became a vehicle for the expression of irresponsible mass nationalism and contributed its share to the disintegration of the constitutional order.[6]

War referendum proposal · Mass emotionalism is the most dangerous force generated by democracy in foreign affairs. Macaulay once wrote to an American congressman that on account of it, democracy would deliver every country with a foreign policy into the hands of a dictator within ten years after it had been established. That, of course, was an exaggeration born of the fear of the mob which the liberal aristocrat instinctively felt. Still, nobody would question today the terrific strains which mass nationalism has created throughout the world. How, then, is it possible that a proposal has been made and ardently supported for submitting the declaration of war to a popular referendum in the United States?

There can be no doubt that those who advocated this arrangement were animated by a deep desire to "keep America out of war." But the means which they chose were likely to make it more certain that the United States would be plunged into war. Here is the amendment to the Constitution originally proposed: "Except in the event of an invasion of the United States or its territorial possessions and attack upon its citizens residing therein, the authority of Congress to declare war shall not become effective until confirmed by a majority of all the votes cast thereon in a nation-wide referendum. Congress when it deems a national crisis to exist may by concurrent resolution refer the question of war and peace to the citizens of the United States, the question to be voted on being 'Shall the United States declare war on ——?' . . ." Regardless of the minor changes which were later made in various bills along this line, there remained two decisive political objections which cannot be eliminated, because they are inherent in the referendum. As long as the United States is not completely neutralized, that is, as long as war remains a possibility, the first political objection is that a nation on the brink of war ought to be, needs to be, united as far as possible. If a referendum is held, a partisan spirit is bound to associate itself with the issue and produce a dangerous split. If the war party loses (as the proponents of the referendum, of course, *hope* it will) nothing would prevent the government, nothing could prevent the government, after some further incidents, from holding a second referendum. In the meantime public agitation could be further increased. The entry of America into the First World War, often cited by friends of the referendum plan, shows this very clearly. For Wilson's re-election was in effect a referendum on this issue. "He kept us out of war!" was Wilson's slogan in the campaign. Yet, when a year later he sought congressional support for a declaration of war, he was given an overwhelming majority. He probably would have got a majority of the electorate.

After the outbreak of the Second World War, a violent disagreement developed between those who would support the Allies fighting the Fascists and those who would not. Down to the attack on Pearl Harbor, this controversy divided the American people into almost equal halves. Urgent measures of preparedness, such as the Selective Service legislation, passed with as perilous majorities as did legislation aiding the Allies, such as Lend-Lease. The extraordinary way in which the people were united by the attack on Pearl Harbor led some of the more ardent opponents of intervention to accuse the government of having "provoked" the attack.

The foregoing reflections lead to the other objection, which is really more fundamental and conclusive. The student of foreign affairs and propaganda cannot help feeling that a referendum provision simply means that every time an administration is approaching a war-threatening situation, it will build up a martial spirit in anticipation of the referendum. The public will be exposed to most of the pressures of war propaganda, even before there is a war. This will greatly heighten the danger of its coming about. In fact, from this standpoint such a referendum is about the most dangerous thing imaginable; it would turn every chance of war into a probability.

In light of the attack on Pearl Harbor, as well as the attack on Finland and Hitler's various unprovoked acts of aggression, it is hard to see how constitutional democracies can afford to cripple themselves in the face of totalitarian dictatorships by providing for a popular referendum on the question of war. On the other hand, in a completely constitutionalized world, the situation may be different.[7]

In any case, how conclusive is the argument for direct popular participation in foreign-policy decisions? Is it not rather *un*democratic to demand that the "will of the people" should be consulted on a matter which the people cannot properly judge because they lack most of the relevant information? Such a decision would not be democracy, it would be demagogy. Even a radical democrat like Rousseau would reject this proposal; for a declaration of war is not a law but an executive decision. Its tremendous importance does not alter the fact that it is beyond the knowledge of the electorate. All the people can do is to elect the man who commands their confidence in the expectation that he will decide as they would if they had all the facts.

In terms of sound constitutionalism, the effective participation in such organizations as the United Nations, properly approved by the people or their representatives, appears a more democratic solution than a popular referendum on war. For through such participation, co-operative decisions are made possible between nations. Thus the danger inherent in democracy that the "sovereign will" of one people becomes pitched against the equally "sovereign will" of another is attenuated if not altogether eliminated (see above, ch. XI). This argument would be altogether conclusive if the international organization were composed only of constitutional democracies, or at least of constitutional governments. Difficulties arise as a result of the participation of totalitarian dictatorships which exclude the informal contact between individual citizens of the several countries and upon which the pattern of co-operation and effective compromise rests. As a result, constitutional democracies are forced back into a measure of authoritarianism in their foreign relations.

The "will of the people" in the international field: plebiscites before the First World War · Ever since the French Revolution, direct popular action has also played a role in international affairs. Referenda concerning the territorial status of controversial areas have been held from time to time.[8] The doctrine of popular sovereignty, as expounded by the French revolutionaries logically following Rousseau, led to the idea of national self-determination. At the same time, it proved a potent instrument in furthering the expansive aims of the Revolution in its later phases. In Avignon, in Savoy, in Nice, as well as in Belgium and the Palatinate, Mulhouse, and in Geneva, plebiscites were held to determine whether the voters favored the attachment of their territory to France. The methods were fairly constitutional at first, but they gradually became more arbitrary. Military occupations preceded and accompanied the popular votes, and pressure was exerted everywhere. As may be surmised, the monarchical reaction had very little use for this method of consulting the people, and consequently no plebiscites were held until after 1848. Cavour extensively relied upon them in his efforts to unify Italy, declaring that "the dukes, the archdukes, and the grand dukes will be found buried under the pile of ballots deposited in the electoral urns." And so they were. In all the Italian principalities the popular referenda went strongly in favor of unification. With the emergence of Bismarck's empire the plebiscite suffered another eclipse. The consolidation of national states throughout Europe did not offer promising opportunities, except in areas where the existing powers would not even contemplate such a method. Obviously, the plebiscite might well have exploded the Hapsburg Empire by the end of the nineteenth century if it had been offered to the subject nationalities. Its potentialities in the colonial sphere were even more portentous. The nascent "nationalism" in India and elsewhere might well have adopted the plebiscite as a promising weapon of combat had it been allowed to do so. After all, had not the American colonies broken away by precisely this method? What was the Declaration of Independence but the harbinger of just such a plebiscite? It is not to be wondered at that the age of imperialism would have none of so dangerous a technique. Nevertheless, isolated instances occurred. After the forcible separation of Norway from Sweden, in 1905, the latter insisted upon holding a plebiscite, despite the overwhelming sentiment expressed in favor of such a separation. All these instances suggest that the technique of direct popular voting seems relatively well adapted to the settlement of territorial controversies. Two major difficulties arise in connection with plebiscites. First, the policing of the voting is burdensome, but necessary, in order to prevent intimidation of the voters. Also, appropriate methods for interpreting the results of the plebiscite are hard to agree on beforehand, and yet without such agreement the controversy is likely to be more troublesome after the plebiscite than before.

Plebiscites after 1918 · The principle of the self-determination of nations which Wilson had made a part of his peace program led to the most extensive application of the method of plebiscites, although Wilson himself did not entirely favor this particular technique for settling boundary problems. While he enunciated the general idea that "national aspirations must be respected," and furthermore that "peoples and provinces are not to be bartered about from sovereignty to sovereignty as if they were mere chattels and pawns in a game . . ." (February 11, 1918), he apparently became convinced, by the time the peace was to be made, that plebiscites were unsatisfactory. Did they sanction secession? After all, what would have happened if such a doctrine had been preached and accepted before the outbreak of the Civil War? The anarchistic potentialities of radical democracy made Wilson and his advisers recoil. But there were so many points in the territorial settlement of Europe which seemed beyond the scope of any rational compromise that the exigencies of practical politics resulted in the provision for a number of such plebiscites. At the very outset, the Danes came forward with the demand for a plebiscite in Northern Schleswig, such as was supposed to have been held in 1867, but which had been discarded by Bismarck.[9] This plebiscite led to a division of the territory between Denmark and Germany. Held under the supervision of allied troops, it was attacked by Germans as unfair; yet it was probably the most acceptable plebiscite held under the peace treaty. Other important plebiscites were written into the treaty as a compromise between the Allies themselves. Thus the plebiscites in East Prussia and in Upper Silesia resulted from the insistence of the English that the cultural composition of these territories should be ascertained. Again, the plebiscite in the Saar valley was the compromise secured by France when she was forced to relinquish her claims upon the left bank of the Rhine, which were being resolutely opposed by the English and Americans. In all these plebiscites the voting was supposed to be supervised by police forces controlled by governments other than those involved in the decision of the plebiscite. The troops and the higher officials of both contesting parties were removed. It is, perhaps, unfortunate that such policing could not have been undertaken by neutrals as the Germans repeatedly demanded. Particularly in the case of the Upper Silesian plebiscite, this failure of really neutral police supervision had the result of discrediting the outcome of the plebiscite. But as we shall see later, it was not only the voting which caused trouble in that case but also the interpretation of the vote. Adequate arrangements for the interpretation of the vote would seem as important as the neutralization of the contested territory. Undoubtedly the most acceptable plan is one whereby it is definitely agreed beforehand just how the outcome of the vote is going to

561

be applied. For obviously a great difference may result from treating the territory as a whole, or from dividing it into several parts. The latter method lends itself to extensive "gerrymandering." It was undoubtedly one of the best features of the Schleswig plebiscite that here the division of the territory was made beforehand. The map illustrates well what can

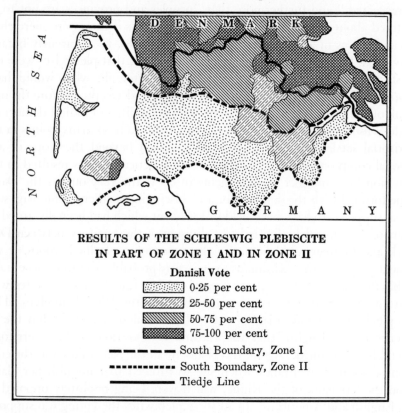

**RESULTS OF THE SCHLESWIG PLEBISCITE
IN PART OF ZONE I AND IN ZONE II**

Danish Vote

0-25 per cent
25-50 per cent
50-75 per cent
75-100 per cent
South Boundary, Zone I
South Boundary, Zone II
Tiedje Line

thus be accomplished. By dividing the Schleswig area, a Danish majority appeared in the upper zone (I), whereas if the territory had been taken as a whole, the majority of the votes being for Germany, it would all have gone to Germany. Fortunately, this method of division had previously been agreed to by Germany, so that no controversy could afterwards result from it.

Different was the case of Upper Silesia. Here, too, the whole territory went for Germany by about 65 per cent, but it was quite feasible to divide it and cut off a part which would have a Polish majority. This was actually done, but unfortunately no adequate agreement had been reached beforehand concerning any such zoning. Consequently Germany smarted under what appeared to her as cheating. It is undoubtedly true that little con-

UPPER SILESIA, RESULTS OF THE PLEBISCITE

GERMANY

POLAND

CZECHOSLOVAKIA

96%
68.1%
74.9%
53%
50.6%
61.6%
59.3%
50.1%
51.1%
80.5%
51.9%
99.6%
70%
62.5%
74%

German majority
Polish majority
District boundaries
League line

troversy can be justified concerning the major lines of demarcation, and yet the plebiscite as a whole cannot be considered a success, because the methods of interpreting the result were not agreed to in detail beforehand. What aggravated this particular situation was that according to the vote, practically the entire industrial part of Upper Silesia, which was by far the most important, should have gone to Germany, except for the gerrymander constructed by the Interallied Commission. It may well be doubted whether true neutrals such as Sweden or Holland, or even America, would have consented to the boundary as actually drawn.

For a while the plebiscite as a technique for settling boundary disputes seemed to hold distinct possibilities in a democratic age. The leading American authority on the subject rightly observed that the plebiscite is not to be considered a perfect tool, but that since there is no perfect method of establishing national boundaries, "the problem is one of alternatives, a choice between methods varying in imperfection." In the context of the present discussion we can push this view a bit farther and say that only such popular votes seem to possess the representative quality which is necessary for any permanent settlement. Only this method seems to correspond to the ideas prevalent today as to what constitutes a legitimate, basic decision concerning cultural autonomy and the inescapable consequences of national attachment. While it is intrinsically possible to let representatives elected in the controversial district speak for their community, as was done repeatedly in the nineteenth century, the possibilities of misrepresentation in an act as final as inclusion within the territory of a certain country makes such a method inconclusive, since the people would have no way of reversing the decision by recalling their representatives if they disagreed.

The plebiscite under dictatorship · As in the days of Napoleon, plebiscites have proved a favorite method of dictators seeking a legitimization of their power. This was especially true of Hitler.[10] According to an official authority, "the meaning of such a 'consultation' of the people by the Leader was to be seen in the fact that the relation of confidence between the Leader and the people as followers receives tangible political expression on the occasion of important political decisions." The National Socialists used the plebiscite primarily to demonstrate a united front in support of the aggressive foreign policy of the government. When Hitler, in the fall of 1933, decided to quit the League of Nations and the Disarmament Conference, he appealed to the German people to sanction this act. The move was designed to "prove" to the whole world, presumably hostile to Hitler's action, that this demand for "equality of treatment" was a demand backed by the entire people. Such a plebiscite mobilizes the democratic myth of the "will of the people" for the attainment of international concessions. The violent propaganda campaign put on by the Nazis in the fall of 1933 consolidated the attitudes which had already become dominant amongst Germans of all classes. The referendum, which was held on November 12, 1933, produced the desired results: of 45,176,713 qualified voters 43,491,575 or 96.3 per cent participated in this ballot, and of these, 40,-622,628 or 95.1 per cent were reported as voting "yes," 2,101,191 or 4.9 per cent as voting "no"; the remainder were invalid. It is impossible to determine whether this result was achieved without dishonest counting, open threats, or bribery of voters. It had its internal as well as external advantages. It undoubtedly enhanced the majority the government was able to roll up in the "election" it proceeded to hold on the same day. The relation of the two votings to each other is suggested by the fact that in the "election" the government only secured 92.2 per cent of the votes as against the 95.1 per cent in the referendum. To be sure, this election was nothing else than a repetition of the Napoleonic plebiscites; it was an opportunity for the voting masses to acclaim the regime of the Nazis; for only the regime and its friends were presented to the voters. The opposition had to make the fruitless gesture of turning in an invalid ballot.

The technique worked out by the Nazis for this first "democratic" ballot was applied again and again. After President Hindenburg's death on the last day of July, 1934, Hitler had all presidential powers transferred to himself as Chancellor and Führer, thus avoiding the choice between two undesirable alternatives: either to have a president over himself in form, or to have a chancellor beside himself in reality. This bold measure was secured against criticism by another appeal to the people. "Steeped in the conviction that all authority of the State must proceed from the people and by them be ratified in a free, secret election [sic!], I request you immediately to lay the decision of the cabinet before the German people for a free plebiscite." The results were somewhat less imposing than those of the previous plebiscite; of 45,474,157 eligible voters 43,530,232 or 95.7 per cent participated, and of these 38,368,195 or 89.9 per cent voted for, and 4,294,727 or 10.1 per cent voted against Hitler's proposal to take all power to himself. Since the invalid votes were mostly spoiled ballots, we get an opposition of almost 12 per cent. In certain urban centers, like Cologne, Hamburg, and Berlin, the opposition vote admittedly reached 20 per cent and more.

When Hitler reoccupied the Rhineland in the spring of 1936, he immediately proceeded to appeal to the German masses, as he had done in the previous year when announcing German rearmament in defiance of the

Treaty of Versailles. A similar appeal was made after the seizure of Austria in 1938. Here the evidence about falsification of the vote was quite specific as far as Austria was concerned, due to the direct reports received in adjoining Switzerland. In some parts of the conservative Catholic Tyrol the percentage in favor of *Anschluss* did not reach 50 per cent, in spite of all the pressure. Yet results were reported with almost nauseating uniformity as approaching 100 per cent. Hitler's international antagonists, particularly the French, were stunned, and they recoiled from forceful measures in the face of such solid popular support.*

The popular referendum or plebiscite did not form as essential a part of the Italian Fascist pattern of government as it did of the National Socialist. Unlike the Nazis, who placed the people above the state, the Fascists, proud of their Roman tradition, and with no appreciable numbers of their people outside the national boundaries (except in America), extolled the state. Italy did not face the same number of international grievances as Germany. Mussolini's Fascist organization was a relatively small body of determined men who supported him in imposing his conception of politics upon the rest of the Italians. There was no vast popular movement behind Fascism which had to be held together, a movement rent by violent conflicts of interest and principle. The pattern of Italian Fascism, moreover, was profoundly affected by the fact that the king, following Mussolini's conception of the monarchy, had conferred upon Fascism the legitimacy which the National Socialists had to seek in popular plebiscites. "The monarchy," Mussolini once said, "is the sacred symbol, glorious, traditional, millenary, of the Nation; we have strengthened the Monarchy and made it more august." With his prestige thus heightened, the king helped to legalize the Fascist power. But the plebiscitary element is not wholly lacking. The "march" as a symbol of Fascism embodies the desperate search for a magic "unity" through patent uniformity. Indeed, totalitarians are veritably obsessed with unanimity. In order to secure this measure of popular approval, the parliamentary "elections" provided a suitable occasion for the unloosing of official propaganda to drum up the desired "acclaim." All the machinations of modern propaganda were brought into play, but the voter, though he voted, remained indifferent. The Italian "Parliament," which seemed such a grotesque and impotent parody of its English namesake, primarily served the purpose, perhaps, of affording the Fascists the occa-

*In 1937, the author stated, in *Constitutional Government and Politics:* "At critical moments in the life of the Nazi dictatorship one may, therefore, always look for some bold action in the international sphere, with a plebiscite following it to reintegrate the crumbling mass support. The limited supply of any safe outlets for that tendency augurs ill for the Nazis as well as for Europe." It is put here as a matter of record. Hitler did not hold a plebiscite after the invasion of Poland.

sion for that periodic appeal for general popular acclaim, the need for which seems to be felt in this democratic age just as much by dictators as by the leaders of constitutional governments.[11]

The contrast of the Soviet Union · A somewhat different situation has prevailed in the Soviet Union. Here the lack of any preceding experience with democratic procedures among the people has enabled the Soviet government and the Communist party to work uninhibited by older patterns and to create its own framework of "democratic" life. In fact, however, elections in the Soviet Union have, in more recent years, taken on the clear connotation of a plebiscite. This is especially true of the election of 1946 in which Stalin submitted himself and his new Five-Year Plan to popular acclaim. The elaborate tier of councils, governing soviets, trade unions, consumers' co-operatives, and so forth, are all dominated by the Communist party, without any alternative. The Bolsheviks themselves designate this elaborate method of indirect election as democratic centralism.[12] There is some measure of democracy in the local bodies if by democracy is meant discussion and argument. But such discussion and argument cannot, of course, extend beyond the scope of the actual autonomous sphere of the particular body. It may, at any time, be invaded by the higher-ups. The Soviet Union attempts, therefore, a somewhat different solution to the problem of how to combine the urge for popular participation with the need of autocratic direction. One authority recently remarked: "The soviet system left no room for a referendum, or even for a parliamentary general election. It was the reverse of government by the mob." This is, in a measure, true; though a little later the same authority cites the general discussion invoked about the change in family law as an instance of general popular consultation. Certainly in a "consultation" held on a similar issue, there was much discussion, but the authorities calmly flouted the sentiments brought forth, and went ahead with their original proposals. There is a great deal of discussion, and as far as technical matters of strictly local concern are involved, these discussions are decisive. But as to any matter of policy, it is authoritatively decided by Stalin and his group.

Characteristically, the acclaim of the people for the constitution in 1936 was sought at the very time of the great purges. Thus what was alleged to be the most "democratic" constitution was adopted in the midst of terror and violence. The constitution having been drafted by a commission under Stalin's chairmanship, it was a foregone conclusion that the special congress would ratify it without much delay—ten days in all.

The whole setup in the Soviet Union is permeated by the fact that a

567

carefully worked-out intellectual pattern, the Marxist-Leninist-Stalinist conception of social life, provides the base line upon which all action is molded. It is not the will of the people, but the ideas of Marx and Lenin, which ultimately legitimize action. Consequently those who most effectively interpret this creed are secure in the conviction of righteousness; they crave no popular acclaim. There is a profound strain of intellectualist aristocracy in the Marxist doctrine of the Communist believers as the *avant-garde* of the "proletariat." It is on behalf of the proletariat that these guardians in the true platonic sense wield their benevolent and yet autocratic power.

These techniques have been studiously followed by the Communist governments in the "satellite" states. Plebiscitary elections and constitutional referenda have been used to provide the appearance of "greater" democracy. The Soviet Zone of Germany has been democratized in the same way. Its constitutions were passed with no more time to discuss and ratify them than the Soviet Constitution of 1936.

Postwar constitutional referenda in Europe · Contrary to prevailing European tradition, constitutions have been the subject of referendum procedure in many cases. But unlike the totalitarian plebiscites, these referenda presented genuine alternatives between which the majority could choose without fear of reprisals, and did. The preconstitutional referendum in France (October 21, 1945) by which the method of arriving at a constitution was determined has already been mentioned. The constitution resulting from the deliberations of this elected constituent assembly was submitted to the French people on May 6, 1946, and was rejected. A leading student of the events leading up to this direct popular action has expressed it as his opinion that the referendum "turned into a plebiscite for or against the Communist party . . . in the minds of many citizens." In his view the vote was the result of a battle of slogans rather than a mature decision on the constitutional draft. But when the actual content of the constitution, with its radical majoritarian bias in favor of parliamentary supremacy is considered, it would seem that the voter did, in point of fact, reject this Communist pattern. The fact that the Socialists had gone along with the Communists does not really alter the situation; the Socialist party did not fight hard for adoption. For a short moment it had seemed as if Communists and Popular Republicans (MRP) might compose their differences; but such near compromises often occur in political situations fraught with conflict. The next constitution, written by the same assembly and submitted to the people on October 21, 1946, was adopted by the French electorate, but it was adopted under conditions which leave its legitimacy in considerable doubt. About nine million voters voted for it, eight million against it, and another nine million abstained. "All Gaul is still divided into three parts," it was said with Gallic sarcasm, "those who say reluctantly yes, those who say unconditionally no, and those who simply don't give a damn." In a very dangerous sense, General de Gaulle's sharp opposition had gained its objectives; for the General, realizing that he could not defeat the constitution, had set about to discredit it by securing a two-thirds majority of voters who did not vote for the constitution. Another aspect of this situation is the expressed expectation of the Popular Republicans that the constitution will be amended in important respects. In keeping with this expectation, the French adopted provisions for amending the constitution by popular referendum, though parliament can eliminate the need by higher, qualified majorities.[13]

In Italy the referendum was employed first of all for the basic decision regarding the monarchy. On June 10, 1946, the Italian people adopted the republican form of government by a substantial majority. Having settled this problem, the Italian constitution was drafted in a fairly long-drawn-out process and submitted to the people a few days after the last occupation troops were withdrawn, in December 1947. Again, the referendum is retained for the purpose of constitutional amendment, but only if demanded by one fifth of the membership of either house, or by 500,000 voters, or by five regional councils, and then only if the amendment was adopted by less than two thirds of the two houses of parliament. But fortunately the constitution itself was adopted by a substantial majority.

In Western Germany, where the referendum had had a rather stormy career under the Weimar constitution, and where the Nazi plebiscites had raised substantial doubts in many minds as to the soundness of this device of "radical" democracy, constitutional referenda were nevertheless held on the state constitutions in the American and French zones. These referenda produced very large majorities, upward of 70 per cent, largely because they were the product of genuine compromises between the two major parties, the Christian Democrats and the Social Democrats. Consequently, the two parties, commanding over 70 per cent of electoral support, could go to the people together.

A very difficult situation arose in connection with the Basic Law. It had originally been agreed on between the three Western allies in London to submit the draft constitution to popular referendum, largely on American insistence. German political leadership rejected this plan on two grounds, one a matter of politics, the other a matter of principle. As to the latter, they argued that no true constitution could be made, except by a "sovereign" people, and that the German voter should not be duped into thinking that such was the situation. The Basic Law, a provisional charter, concludes with an article decreeing its disappearance as soon as the German people can freely decide upon their constitution. The political objection was that a referendum would oblige the two great parties to go before the electorate together, a task which would make compromises in the constituent assembly more difficult. Reluctantly, the allies yielded to these views. What it means is that constitutional democracy lacks a strong framework and is legitimized by allied occupation policies rather than by popular will. On the other hand, the extent to which strong party organizations control the electorate would have made any such referendum a foregone conclusion once the Christian Democrats and the Social Democrats had decided to support it.[14]

Conclusion · In theory and in practice modern democracy has been haunted by the specter of direct popular action as an alternative to all kinds of representative schemes. The manipulation of mass psychology with a view to destroying any and all constitutional restraints in the name of His Majesty the People has taken concrete form in recurrent dictatorial regimes. Some of these regimes have sought to legitimize themselves by securing popular majority support. Napoleon I, Napoleon III, Mussolini, and Hitler, all were found to be alike in their search for popular acclaim. The suddenness with which these dictatorial regimes, apparently reared upon so broad a foundation of majority support, have caved in under the impact of victorious foreign armies suggests the unrepresentative quality of this primitive substitute for effective representation. Such forms of direct popular action, when introduced into the pattern of constitutional government, have worked with a reasonable degree of smoothness; in both Switzerland and the United States they serve a useful purpose in offering yet another technique for the division of power among distinct constituencies. But the difficulty of placing effective restraints upon its exercise makes it a questionable device in communities not thoroughly seasoned in popular politics and thoroughly attached to their constitutional morale.

All political power is subject to abuse no matter what the legal form of its exercise. But concentrated power is very much more easily abused than divided power. Direct popular action, while it is not concentrated power under a constitutional setup, is its nearest kin. At any rate, it may well be doubted whether Jean Jacques Rousseau after watching the operation of modern plebiscites nationally or internationally, would be inclined to consider them very useful tools for discovering the "general will." But then, it is only fair to add that he concluded his famous discussion of democracy by the apodictic remark: "If there were somewhere a people of gods, it would govern itself democratically. So perfect a government does not suit human beings." Considering that Rousseau meant direct democracy, this observation is borne out by political experience. Contemporary American democracy is not an argument against Rousseau's conclusion. For as commonly used among us, the word democracy means constitutional government. It means divided powers. It means civil liberties. It means that there is a moderator as well as a Town Meeting. It means concern for minorities, as well as decision by the majority. It means that the people are living in time as well as in space; that their good life will not be jeopardized by inexorable decisions of a temporary majority. It is up to the majority—for in the last analysis free government depends upon the decisive group of common citizens which we have called the constituent group. It depends upon their determination to remain free, they themselves and their fellow men. As John Stuart Mill put it: "A people may prefer a free government, but if, from indolence, or carelessness, or cowardice, or want of public spirit, they are unequal to the exertions necessary for preserving it; if they will not fight for it when it is directly attacked; if they can be deluded by the artifices used to cheat them out of it; if by momentary discouragement, or temporary panic, or a fit of enthusiasm for an individual, they can be induced to lay their liberties at the feet even of a great man, or trust him with powers which enable him to subvert their institutions; in all these cases they are more or less unfit for liberty: and though it may be for their good to have had it even for a short time, they are unlikely long to enjoy it."[15]

Direct popular action in its several forms serves to strengthen the democratic element. But if the dose is too strong, it will destroy the balance. In spite of these handicaps and shortcomings, the methods of direct popular action, if guarded and circumscribed by constitutional provisions guaranteeing a free choice to the electorate, provide a modern constitution with an integrating device by which the dissensions of parties, pressure groups, and propagandas can from time to time be overcome. The "will of the people" has lost some of its luster as a basis of legitimacy and as a ground for securing universal acceptance. But there is still no better one in sight in this age of secular outlook and pragmatic doubt. Direct popular action thus provides a genuine adjustment for modern constitutionalism.

XXVI

Constitutional Dictatorship and Military Government

Introduction · The commissioner · The (Roman) constitutional dictatorship contrasted with the commissioner · Martial rule · State of siege · Legislative emergency powers · Modern constitutional limitations inadequate: (1) The appointment of a dictator · (2) The determination of an emergency · (3) The precise time limit · The legitimate objective: the defense of the constitution itself · Explanation of inadequacy · The pattern of transition from constitutional to unconstitutional dictatorship · Military government · Experience prior to the Second World War · Military government and democratization · Military government and the rule of law · Military government as constitutional dictatorship · The future of military government · Conclusion.

Introduction · In three preceding chapters, three major areas of tension, breakdown, and adjustment of modern constitutionalism have been discussed. But the most dangerous and serious of these areas is caused by war, both foreign and internal. Modern technological warfare is all-engulfing and calls for the participation of everyone. It causes casualties on a huge scale among the noncombatant population whose productive and morale potential is being made the target of enemy action. This type of warfare has rightly been called "total." It is truly a marvel of the vigor and resilience of constitutionalism in Britain and in the United States that the constitutional framework continued to function, and that in the United States even a presidential election (not to speak of minor elections) could be carried through without endangering the conduct of the war. Few would have been willing to predict beforehand that this could prove possible.

In the late Middle Ages, the concentration of powers was brought on by the exigencies of religious upheavals, of increasing and technically more formidable warfare, and of the economic revolution accompanying them.[1] The violence and the constant recurrence of these emergencies during the latter half of the sixteenth and throughout the seventeenth century made it possible for certain gifted individuals to break down the medieval division of powers to a very large extent and to concentrate these powers in their own hands. Owing to the military and administrative requirements of the

emergencies, the princes who had been charged with military and administrative powers in medieval society were rather advantageously placed for a
successful usurpation of this kind. Today, we are told, the necessity for
such concentration arises once again from the emergencies with which we
are confronted: the conflict between classes in our industrial society and
the exigencies of modern mass warfare. Is our constitutional government
likely to be able to cope with these situations of unprecedented magnitude
and gravity? Many answer no, and turn toward dictatorship as their solution. Every modern constitution has recognized the problem of temporary
emergencies and has sought to provide for a temporary concentration of
powers to be used in overcoming such emergencies. In Britain and in the
United States, emergency power and martial law are the legal institutions
which have been developed; in civil-law countries these problems are dealt
with on the basis of the "state of siege" and the "exceptional state" (*Aus-
nahmezustand*). Constitutional dictatorship is the term we shall use to
designate all such methods for the temporary concentration of powers.

The commissioner · Similar methods were recognized by the medieval constitutional order, but the princes ultimately succeeded in transforming them into instruments for the destruction of medieval constitutionalism itself. How was this result accomplished? Essentially through the
institution of extraordinary commissioners or *commissarii* whom the princes,
following the papal precedent, appointed out of the fullness of their authority (*plenitudo potestatis*).[2] For it was held to be part of the royal prerogative to determine when an exceptional situation required exceptional
measures. Thus in place of the regular officials with legally, if not constitutionally, defined spheres of jurisdiction, there appear specially appointed
delegates of the king who, on the basis of a special instruction, are called
upon to handle particular situations. We find commissioners authorized to
inspect markets, to requisition food and other support for the army, to carry
on negotiations, and so forth. Perhaps the most celebrated historical form
of such commissioners are the intendants whom Henry IV of France employed to such a remarkable degree. These commissioners aided him materially in securing the revenue which enabled him to dispense with the
Estates. But even before Henry IV the institution of commissioners had
been developed by the French crown. A striking chapter in Bodin's
treatise on the state is devoted to a discussion of the legal and practical
aspects of such commissioners (he himself occasionally acted in this capacity).
Bodin clearly distinguished the commissioner from the regular official.
Since the latter's activities were created by express and public law, his
office was more or less permanent, and the official had a sort of right to his

office. On the other hand, the commissioner, relying on a royal ordinance for his right to act, exercised only a temporary function, and therefore had no right to his office but was completely dependent upon his master. Therefore the commissioner's activities were determined by his instructions, while the regular official could practice a certain amount of discretion. If the tenor of the instructions was narrow, the commissioner's powers were correspondingly limited. But if the prince saw fit to make the instructions very comprehensive—for example, by requesting a commissioner to employ all necessary means for quelling a rebellion—then such a commissioner, unlimited as to the means he might use, was very likely to suspend existing laws and rights on a considerable scale. It is at this point that the analogy between these commissioners and the office of the dictator becomes apparent.

The (Roman) constitutional dictatorship contrasted with the commissioner · The Roman dictator was appointed for a given task like that of concluding a war or suppressing a rebellion, and as soon as his commission was carried out his office similarly came to an end. Therefore, a Roman dictator could only be compared to a commissioner with very extensive powers; for he became the chief executive of the Roman Republic for the period of his appointment, whereas the commissioners in the sixteenth century and later were usually agents of a king who remained the chief executive and who employed them for more or less limited tasks.[3] In the Roman Republic for several centuries, dictatorship remained a bulwark for the Republican government and did not lead to a usurpation of powers. It afterwards became obsolete, until revived by Sulla during the civil wars. The constitutional bases of the earlier dictatorship essentially seem to have been four. In the first place, the appointment of the dictator took place according to precise constitutional forms. Secondly, the dictator himself could not at his discretion declare the state of emergency. A third condition of great importance was a strict time limit imposed upon the dictator for the fulfillment of his task, never to exceed six months. Finally, the dictatorship always was instituted in defense of the existing constitutional order, never with a view to destroying it. Obviously, all these conditions are themselves dependent upon the constitutional order, and can therefore properly be called constitutional limitations. When Sulla revived the dictatorship for the novel purpose of making a constitution, he violated these constitutional limitations in essential respects. He caused himself to be appointed by an *interrex* especially named by the Senate for that purpose, and he continued in the dictatorial position for three years, finally withdrawing from it on his own volition. The same restraint was not shown by Caesar. He mocked at Sulla for having resigned, and eventually, in 44 B.C., assumed a permanent dictatorship. This step was nothing else than a disguised assumption of monarchical power.

The commissioners of the royal governments were, on the contrary, personal servants of the king in whose hands power was being concentrated. Their object, therefore, was not so much the maintenance of a constitutional order, but of order as such. Their purpose was conceived in technical terms, and evaluated in terms of pure expediency, the so-called reason of state. It is thus quite apparent that from a political as compared to the legal standpoint, constitutional dictatorship is the very antithesis of such commissionerships (or commissioned dictatorships, as they have been called). Nothing shows this more clearly than the fact that when these commissioners became permanent, they formed the core of the monarchical bureaucracy. When the constitutional dictatorship becomes permanent, it becomes unconstitutional and leads to the perversion and eventual overthrow of the constitutional order. A concentration has replaced the division of powers.

Modern constitutional provisions for martial law and the state of siege cannot, therefore, be placed in a parallel with the commissioners of old, as has sometimes been done. As so often in the history of political institutions, a legal continuity hides a fundamental transition in political function. For it is undeniable that both martial rule in common-law lands and the state of siege on the continent of Europe are derived in part from institutions similar to the commissionership. Yet, like the Roman Republican dictatorship, martial rule, emergency powers, and the state of siege are all conceived in terms of maintaining a constitutional system rather than destroying it (until they are perverted into a usurpation of concentrated powers). To be sure, the apologist of absolutism would insist that the kinship of the two institutions lay precisely in the fact that both were extraordinary means for maintaining "the state." But the word "state" is itself a propaganda tool of the absolutist. It hides the fact that order for its own sake is being substituted for constitutional, legal order as the primary objective of the exceptional concentration of powers. Political science must keep the two methods quite distinct. This distinction, therefore, is not one of formalities, such as might be suggested by the terms commissioned and noncommissioned (sovereign) dictatorship, but one of objectives, properly designated by the terms constitutional and unconstitutional (unrestrained) dictatorship. The modern forms of constitutional dictatorship are martial rule, the state of siege, and constitutional emergency powers. The first is found, for example, in England, in the Dominions, and in the United States, the second in France, in Germany before 1918, and in many other Continental countries, and the third is characteristic of the American federal government, among others.

Martial rule · As we have already mentioned, the differentiation between martial rule and the state of siege is essentially related to the difference between a common-law and a civil-law system. The concept of martial rule is understandable only in terms of the rule of law which it replaces. Where this rule of law is taken to be the core of the legal system, because it alone guarantees a calculable stability of legal relationships, an emergency is essentially a condition of things which threatens the continued maintenance of this rule of law. The most decisive evidence of such a disturbance would be the fact that the courts are closed and can no longer perform their function. This the American Supreme Court held to be the condition for the application of martial law.[4] Similarly, Judge Mackintosh once said that when it is impossible for courts of law to sit or for the executive to enforce the execution of their judgments, then it becomes necessary to find some rude substitute for them and to employ for that purpose the military, which is the only remaining force in the community. But on the whole, the English courts have not been quite so strict. The important point is that ultimately the judiciary are the arbiters who determine whether or not the actions taken by excessive organs are in fact necessary. On the other hand, there is no limit beyond which the authorities exercising such constitutional dictatorship may not go if they can afterward convince the court of the necessity of their action. It is hard to say much more about it, for the law of martial rule is very vague and is obscured by a maze of conflicting precedents. Nor is there any clearly defined measure by which the initiation of such a system of martial rule is definitely indicated. Although it is customary for the executive "to declare martial law" before initiating extraordinary measures, this declaration does not entail any very definite consequences. It may be a mere threat. It may presage the most extreme measures, violating all the customary constitutional limitations upon governmental powers. Sir James Fitzjames Stephen described it thus: "The common law right of the crown and its representative to repel force with force in the case of invasion and insurrection, and to act against rebels as it might against invaders." Whatever measures are taken, they must be defensible in terms of the nature of the emergency, which arose from the onslaught of hostile forces against the customary rule of law.

State of siege · Rather different is the state of siege. Here a specific declaration by the legislature or by the head of the government or by both is required by law, or even by the constitution. Thus, the French constitution of 1815 (*Acte additionnel*) required that the declaration of the state of siege take the form of a law.[5] What is perhaps more important, the state of siege is defined in terms of a suspension of certain enumerated individual rights, more particularly the right to be tried in an ordinary court, the right to free speech, and the right to free assembly. It is at this point that the contrast with common-law practice can be most clearly seen, and it is indeed of decisive importance in civil-war situations. Whereas the executive and/or the legislature have the final word as to whether an emergency situation has arisen, the courts have this function under the common law. Politically speaking, this means that a political body, an admittedly partisan organ, has the ultimate authority in Continental jurisdictions, whereas a nonpolitical authority, which presumably tries to be nonpartisan, has the last word in Anglo-American jurisdictions. Continental countries seem to see the emergency in an effective threat against public safety and order, whereas in common-law countries emphasis is placed upon the suspension of the rule of law. In practice the two states of fact may largely coincide; but the concept of public safety and order focuses attention upon the political system, or "the state." On the other hand, the rule of law seems preoccupied with the safety of the private individual. This difference is undoubtedly responsible for the inclination of common lawyers to look upon the state of siege as an objectionable institution, traceable to the heritage of the Continent's monarchical past. Under the new French constitution, the emergency powers, like the civil liberties which they might suspend, remain undefined. Whether this strange silence of the constitution means that emergency powers will be broadly or narrowly defined is yet to be seen. Presumably traditional approaches, as described above, remain largely in force. But the failure to define and clearly circumscribe these dangerous powers, from a constitutionalist viewpoint, must be considered a definite weakness of the Fourth Republic.

The Basic Law of the German Federal Republic likewise is very circumspect about emergency powers. The experience with article 48 of the Weimar constitution has created a deep-seated suspicion of such powers, and the Western allies reinforced this tendency by explicit warnings. Hence neither the president nor the chancellor and his cabinet nor the parliament have well-defined emergency and war powers. The occupying powers have reserved to themselves an ill-defined emergency power to deal with all threats to their own security, for the exercise of which under the occupation statute not even a formal declaration is required. However, the established practice of American military government makes a formal proclamation highly probable.

Legislative emergency powers · Basically and ordinarily, constitutional dictatorship applies to executive action. But under modern conditions, where a complex industrial society is conducted in accordance with correspondingly complex statutes, emergencies are likely to require adequate powers for legislative change as well as for administrative action. Most modern constitutions are silent on the subject. But since the need is paramount, emergency powers have come into existence, sometimes by usurpation, at other times by express delegation. When Lincoln, after the start of hostilities, found himself without an adequate army, but also without a Congress to authorize one, he proceeded by measures not authorized by either the Constitution or Congress to achieve his apparently necessary purpose. Congress *afterwards* authorized what he had done and passed an act of indemnity. As long as such action as Lincoln's is taken for the manifest purpose of maintaining constitutionalism, as interpreted by the majority, this method "works"; it is subject, however, to the objection that all breaches of the law are destructive of the general belief in law upon which constitutionalism rests (see ch. IX).

Actually, the Constitution of the United States is distinguished by its broad grant of war powers to the President of the country as "commander-in-chief" of the army, the navy, and the militia, when called into actual national service. The broad legislative powers of the Congress notwithstanding, these war powers, when taken in conjunction with the President's duty to see to it that the laws are faithfully executed, give him extensive emergency powers, especially since the Congress has been inclined to back the president in dealing with insurrection and civil war. The courts (for instance, *Luther v. Borden* (7 How. 42)) have been inclined to interpret the President's authority broadly. Subsequent history has thus borne out Alexander Hamilton's brief but emphatic statement in *The Federalist* that "the direction of war most peculiarly demands those qualities which distinguish the exercise of power by a single hand," and that "the direction of war implies the direction of the common strength; and the power of directing and employing the common strength, forms a usual and essential part in the definition of the executive authority." On this basis, the President is likely to be led to assume all the powers which the emergency requires, as Bryce noted, and the Congress can make him "almost a dictator," as it did in the Civil War* and the two World Wars. It is the marvel of American constitutionalism that this temporary grant of dictatorial powers has not brought the constitutional system to an end, but that after each such trial it has re-emerged virtually unchanged in its basic pattern.

Emergency powers of legislation were extensively granted during the First World War, none of which powers given to the President going farther

---

*I prefer the neutral term "Civil War" to the too-partisan terms often used (especially in public places) by the North and the South respectively: War of the Southern Rebellion, and War between the States.

than the British Defense of the Realm Act, which authorized the King in Council for the duration of the war "to issue regulations . . . for securing the public welfare and defense of the realm."[6] The power hereby conferred was used for matters rather far removed from the defense of the realm, but as long as the war lasted, no one minded. A similar statute (the Emergency Powers (Defense) Act) was passed in England at the beginning of the Second World War and considerably broadened after the invasion of the Low Countries. Under it, the King in Council was empowered "to make such regulations as appear to him to be necessary or expedient for securing the public safety, the defense of the Realm, the maintenance of public order, and the efficient prosecution of any war in which His Majesty may be engaged. . . ." He could also require "persons to place themselves, their services and their property at the disposal of His Majesty. . . ." In the United States, similar powers were granted the President by a series of Acts such as the Lever Act, Selective Service Act, Espionage Act, Priority Shipment Act, Trading with the Enemy Act, Overman Act, and others. But whereas the delegation of such legislative authority was part of the accepted pattern of British constitutionalism, the issue had never been fully faced in the United States. The delegation during the First World War was, to be sure, never effectively challenged in court. But a similar delegation in a number of statutes during the Great Depression (NRA, AAA, etc.) was held unconstitutional by the courts (see ch. XII), notwithstanding the fact that the courts had allowed the concept of quasi-legislative power to develop under the Interstate Commerce and other regulatory acts for some time. Such a judicial denial of Congressional readiness to delegate is, of course, unthinkable in England, where the courts accept acts of Parliament as definitive, since Parliament can change the constitution as well as the ordinary statutes. In so far as the common-law tradition and its martial rule provide for judicial rather than legislative checks upon the exercise of emergency powers, the American practice is more nearly in keeping with it. Does that suffice to justify it? The argument is, of course, that only the amending power is available for changing the distribution of power, but we have seen how unrealistic that contention is in fact. Had Congress retained the right to revoke executive orders that seemed manifestly unreasonable, it might have been argued that the powers conferred were only quasi-legislative and hence constitutional. But was such a provision really necessary? Did it not go without saying that Congress, by changing the statute, could revoke the executive regulations that had been issued under it? The real issue would appear to lie hidden behind the fact that the solid New Deal majority in Congress had full confidence in the executive's general policy and hence was disinclined to be jealous of its authority. For the Supreme Court to substitute its judgment for that of Congress on the ground of the Roman-law dictum that delegated power cannot be redelegated* was to drag a dubious formalistic red herring across the path of a democratically arrived-at policy. It was a usurpation of emergency powers by the Court.

But the distinction between legislative and executive or administrative powers in an emergency is as such questionable. For these emergency powers are being exercised to accomplish a definite result; they involve decisions large and small which together constitute the policy to be pursued in the accomplishment of this end: to overcome the emergency and to maintain constitutional government intact. There must be a broad grant of powers, subject to equally strong limitations as to who shall exercise such powers, when, for how long, and to what end.

Modern constitutional limitations inadequate: (1) the appointment of a dictator · If we now ask ourselves to what extent the four criteria of a constitutional dictatorship outlined above are realized in the various provisions for martial rule, for the state of siege, and for constitutional emergency powers, we have a test by which to evaluate these arrangements. This test may afford us some clue as to the relative value of these several arrangements. At the same time, such testing will reveal a considerable amount of similarity between the three forms of constitutional dictatorship. As to the first criterion, it must be admitted that only constitutional emergency powers regularly fulfill the condition laid down by it, to wit, that the appointment of the dictator take place according to precise constitutional forms. In England, where the application of martial rule occurs at the discretion of a cabinet supported by a legally and constitutionally unlimited majority in the House of Commons, the appointment of the dictator may be said to be thus defined, but it is a pretty vague definition at that. In France, where the state of siege was defined by the laws of August 9, 1848, and of April 3, 1878, it was provided that it shall be declared by legislative enactment, and when the legislature is not in session, by executive decree, later to be confirmed by the legislature. Presumably these arrangements continue in force. Here again an aggressive majority in the legislature, by changing the existing laws, could alter the provisions for the appointment of a dictator *ad hoc*. Although it is traditional under parliamentary government that the cabinet assume dictatorial functions, as happened in the case of Poincaré's dictatorship of 1926 for the stabiliza-

---

*Nowhere in the Constitution is there any mention of *potestas delegata non delegari potest*, nor even any statement to the effect that the legislative power is a "delegated" power. The power is said to be *granted* to Congress, presumably by the Constitution.

tion of the French currency, grave consequences may follow from a parliamentary majority's using this traditional power for the purpose of forestalling the emergence of incipient opposition forces.[7] Yet, with the intensification of social strife, this possibility cannot be brushed aside. The fact that the constitution is at the mercy of the parliamentary majority weakens, if it does not actually destroy, the dependability of the state of siege or mere martial rule as a technique of constitutional dictatorship. Only a constitutional order like that of the United States measures up to the first criterion with precise constitutional provisions concerning the appointment of a dictator when it provides, in Article I, Section 8: "Congress shall have power . . . (15) to provide for calling forth the militia, to execute the Laws of the Union, suppress Insurrections, and repel Invasions." But the constitutional provisions omit the naming of a distinct dictator. This brings us to the second point.

(2) The determination of an emergency · Martial rule in England, the state of siege in France, and the constitutional emergency powers in the United States all seem to square with the second criterion, according to which the dictator himself must not be vested with discretionary powers for declaring or calling off the state of emergency. This implies that someone must determine it. Who should that be? The American Congress, the English or the French parliament, do indeed appoint someone else, and therefore these constitutions seem to be in accord with the second criterion of sound constitutional arrangement for the exercise of these extraordinary powers. But this seeming accord is too formalistic. For these legislatures (the English and French always, the American a large part of the time) are led by the executive leaders whom their majority supports. Their position of party leadership makes these constitutional dictators too unrestrained. Too much depends not only upon their own good will, but also upon that of their compound following. Hitler gained his first opportunity by distorting the election results in March, 1933, through the unsubstantiated claim that the Reichstag fire proved that a state of emergency had arisen. His own supporters in the Reichstag did not, of course, question his allegation. But even where the political purpose is not clearly anticonstitutional, as it was here, but merely a partisan view of what is needed for the maintenance of constitutionalism, that difficulty must be faced. The danger from recurrent "emergencies" to the constitutional system is intensified by the presence of sizable Communist parties, as in France and Italy, because of the contact these parties maintain with a foreign power.

Where no constitutionally fixed time limit is provided, the issue is even more serious at the end than at the beginning of an emergency. In contemporary social conflicts it is easy to prolong and deepen the "emergency." This difficulty arose in both France and Germany. Needless to say, Hitler never bothered with the account which he at one time promised after four years of his rule; nor was anyone in a position to question his use of the emergency powers he had illegally acquired. The succession of emergencies in France before the outbreak of the Second World War, as well as in Germany before the advent of Hitlerism, shows that parliamentary majorities, bound up in their fate with the constitutional dictator, become more and more emergency-conscious as the day of reckoning approaches. This is no empty hallucination. As one authority puts it: "In view of the fact that all stand to gain by a common party victory there is no reason to suppose that the rank and file will be any less complacent than their leaders toward abuses . . . Where common party interests are at stake, therefore, it is clearly unrealistic to rely on a government-controlled majority in the legislature. . . ."[8] We must conclude, therefore, that the present systems of constitutional dictatorship in the leading countries do not accord with our second criterion. Whether their constitutional orders will therefore be perverted into governments with concentrated powers, as happened in Germany, France, and Italy, would seem to depend upon the extent to which recurrent crises will entail the employment of presumably temporary emergency powers brought into play for lengthening periods of "emergency." The "cold war" provides a comparable frame of reference, and in the loose employment of the term "cold war" there lurk very real dangers for the future of constitutionalism. It is not without significance that the "cold war" was "declared" without the Congress in spite of the fact that the Constitution requires declarations of war to be by the Congress. The retort that the "cold war" is simply a state of fact is not effective, since the same can be said of all war. Its formal "declaration" is vested in the Congress precisely because from this state of fact are supposed to flow legal results which require legislative authorization.

(3) **The precise time limit** · The third criterion, namely, the imposition of a strict time limit during which concentrated powers can be exercised, is not rigidly fulfilled by any modern constitutional order. To be sure, there is supposed to be an implication of such a time limit in the provision of a legislative check upon the exercise of these powers. The constitutional limit of four years for a presidential term may also be said to constitute at least some time limit. Various constitutions and laws provide for the immediate reporting of any measures taken by the dictatorial executive and for their revocation if the legislature should demand it. But by such provisions this criterion merges with the second one, which would

withdraw from the dictator the discretion of determining the end as well as the beginning of the emergency. It was shown with regard to these provisions that in view of parliamentary dependence upon executive leadership under the cabinet system no real check is provided against the arbitrary abuse of this discretionary power. At any rate, such a procedural rule cannot be said to take the place of a fixed limitation of time such as that which was imposed by the Roman Republican constitution. It may be true that the six months which the Roman constitution provided is not a suitable period in which to deal with the emergencies which are likely to arise in an industrial society. But whatever the particular period of time, a constitutionally fixed time limit is a vastly different thing from any check which with proper manipulation is capable of indefinite extension. It is a curious thing that modern constitutional systems have never faced this problem squarely, though with the vagueness surrounding so-called social crises and emergencies it would be most important. Even a constitution so deeply permeated by a distrust of power as the American Constitution fails to insist upon some such limit.

The legitimate objective: the defense of the constitution itself · The final condition for the exercise of constitutional emergency powers is that the objective be legitimate, that is to say, that the concentration of powers be employed for defending the constitutional order, and not for destroying it. Changes may be required, but they must not touch constitutionalism itself. It is very disquieting that no explicit provisions safeguard the employment of martial rule and the state of siege in this regard. The purely military background of both institutions, and the consequent preoccupation with the technical problem of producing a certain effect, are inimical to adequate consideration of this problem. On the battlefield victory is an ascertainable technical goal, and the emergency evidently has passed once victory has been achieved. But in social and economic crises the matter is not so obvious and the tendency of partisans to identify their particular solution with the only solution is strong. Hence measures of extreme violence, like, let us say, the forcible destruction of all labor unions, may appear to be a necessary condition of social pacification to one group, while the forcible expropriation of all private industries may seem equally unavoidable to the other. Some would say that at such a point a constitutional order becomes impossible. It is undeniable that neither martial rule nor the state of siege under a parliamentary regime offers any safeguards against abuse by violent partisans in a civil-war situation. Hence these modern attempts at constitutional dictatorship are liable to be the first step in the destruction of an existing constitutional order. Constitutional emergency powers need not be exposed to this objection. The arbitral position of the courts in determining the *constitutional* exercise of all governmental powers can to some extent be brought into play in order to insure that the dictatorial powers be confined to defending the existing constitution. The United States Supreme Court gave striking illustrations of that fact in interfering with the atrocities of the reconstruction period. But unless the judiciary or some other magistrate can thus be brought into play, the situation is likely to get out of hand. Moreover, the judicial power is also subject to abuse, and courts are likely to prove helpless in the face of a real emergency. As Robert H. Jackson reminded us, in vain did Chief Justice Taney cry out against Lincoln in *Ex parte Merryman*. Convinced that he was protesting at great peril to himself, "the weary and weatherbeaten old Chief Justice thundered forth the fundamental principles of civilian freedom," but had to admit in the end: "I have exercised all the power which the Constitution and laws confer upon me, but that power has been resisted by a force too strong for me to overcome."[9] While the judiciary, therefore, may act as a sort of keeper of the President's and the people's conscience, there are no ultimate institutional safeguards available for insuring that emergency powers be used for the purpose of preserving the Constitution. Only the people's own determination to see them so used can make sure of that, provided the constitution has placed the limitations upon the exercise of dictatorial emergency powers which have been discussed. Unhappily, all modern constitutions are defective in this respect. Yet, how are the people to exercise their restraint, when the constitution does not contain effective working limitations? Therefore, emergency powers which are supposed to support a constitutional dictatorship may change into concentrated powers directed toward the destruction of the constitution.

Explanation of inadequacy · All in all the quasi-dictatorial provisions of modern constitutional systems, be they martial rule, state of siege, or constitutional emergency powers, fail to conform to any exacting standard of effective limitations upon a temporary concentration of powers. Consequently, all these systems are liable to be transformed into totalitarian schemes if conditions become at all favorable to it. The failure to deal with this issue altogether, which we noted in the most recent constitutions of France and Germany, is an ostrich policy which leaves the government without the constitutional resources which an emergency is likely sooner or later to present. One hesitates to contemplate what might have happened in the United States at the start of the Civil War, if the President had not been able to act decisively. But as we saw, even the provisions of the American Constitution, though much the best, are too loose. Unless changes are made to tighten constitutional provisions for the exercise of emergency powers along the lines here indicated, the kind of civil war emergency which the rise of the Soviet's world revolutionary policy and power presages may well destroy constitutional systems from within and/or from without. To repeat: even such provisions are merely technical improvements, and no constitutional order can maintain itself which is not supported by the loyal enthusiasm of its citizens.

Why then do modern constitutions so uniformly neglect this problem of constitutional limitations? It may well be that the emphasis upon legislation as the real core of governmental action is responsible for this.[10] From Rousseau to the present time, martial rule, the state of siege, and constitutional emergency powers have been taken to be largely limited to executive action. Indeed, they have been looked upon as extensions of this "power." At the same time, the doctrine of the central importance of rule-making was retained, and all such emergency powers as were wielded by executives could only be used to suspend the laws but not to alter them. When extensive delegation of legislative powers occurred in France, Germany, and elsewhere, it was thought such delegation could be permitted because the elected assembly, the "legislature," remained as the guardian of legislation; it could revoke any rules it did not like. Thus the legislative body appeared as the guardian of the constitution. The more strictly executive or administrative phases of the process did not seem to matter in comparison. The notorious power of the Roman dictator over life and death might not be equalled on account of *habeas corpus*, but a boundless extension of administrative competence would be accepted, although it might endanger the lives of thousands or even millions. Such a doctrinaire approach to the problem overlooks the potential cumulation of such practices into a fixed pattern. Orthodox tradition looked upon the whole process as merely temporarily enlarging executive power. But in terms of the actual distribution of power, the process appears as a rapid concentration of power in the hands of a ruling oligarchy, represented by an individual capable of effectively dramatizing its position. The traditional and legalistic attitude is too legalistic. It appears to be that an emergency such as war or insurrection is an undesirable state of fact. For this undesirable state of affairs it seemed evidently sufficient to find a specific technical solution. The phrase "state of siege" is indicative of this attitude. The siege must be lifted; that is all. An executive officer is seen in analogy to a military commander; he must take command and accomplish the desirable end. This done, nothing really fundamental has happened; things have returned to their normal state. The rule of law having been re-established, everything is precisely where it was before. Such a view now appears shortsighted. The temporarily concentrated powers cannot be separated and distributed again unless residuary power is left somewhere for that purpose. Recurrent measures crystallize into rules, and under crisis conditions a continuous state of emergency arises. It is curious that the later nineteenth century should have failed to revise its notions on this score in spite of the spectacle of the actions of Napoleon III and of Bismarck right before their eyes. The general optimism prevented a searching consideration of deeper springs of action in such situations. Rigid constitutional limitations such as the one suggested by the present analysis will not save a constitutional regime which prevents the realization of what is considered right by the community. But they will add a most powerful brake which in the day of crisis may be decisive in bringing the skidding constitutional order back into its groove, while the necessary adjustments are made in the distribution of power according to the believed-in standard of justice.

The pattern of transition from constitutional to unconstitutional dictatorship · The details of the transition from a constitutional government to an unconstitutional one are not yet known. But the broad outlines of the process are distinctly discernible.[11] The following sketch may give an idea of the kind of situation that is typical. The constitutional government is weak. It lacks the support of tradition. The division of power under the constitution is faulty, resulting in too much friction or in too much power for small groups in the community. The constitution provides channels for the manifestation of mass emotions, however. Typical tools of radical democracy, such as general elections or referendum machinery (plebiscitary apparatus), are available under it. The dissatisfied groups throw their strength in this direction. They thrust forward one or more leaders who are able under the constitution to secure positions of power, and thus legitimate authority. They buttress intransigeant demands for broader channels of mass emotionalism by appeals to the tenets of radical democracy. In the meantime their mass supporters carry on guerilla warfare against all opponents, thus creating a civil-war situation. The attendant disorder and the eventual anarchy stir the indifferent elements in the community into action. The tension rises. More disorder, clashes between groups of citizens, murders, burnings, follow. Dictatorial methods for the maintenance of the constitutional order, indeed any order, appear inevitable. The resulting constitutional dictatorship lacks drive, because of the weakness of constitutional morale. It consequently tends to succumb to anticonstitutional elements, working either from within or from without. At the decisive point, these elements will seize the initiative, with the mass of the citizens unable to counteract such an initiative or to seize it in their turn.

This, roughly speaking, has been the pattern of "transition," regardless of whether the particular totalitarians were coming from the right or from the left. Italy, Spain, Germany, France, or Czechoslovakia, Hungary, Eastern Germany, it is a similar story again and again.

If one asks what measures might be suitable means for preventing this development, the answer seems at first to be: more radical measures for dealing with the emergency. But such measures usually will violate the constitutional tradition, and hence must be justified. This problem of "justification" is politically of crucial importance, because as the latent civil war develops, the decisive question is which side the army will take. In Russia the army was revolutionized through the war; the decision of the Kerenski government to continue the war was its fatal error. In Italy the army remained neutral, which was enough to give Mussolini the upper hand. In Germany the army refused to march against Hitler, as it looked upon the nationalism of the masses as the most effective support for the rearmament and remilitarization it desired. In Poland the army always supported Pilsudski, their own general. Likewise in Yugoslavia, the army supported *their* supreme commander, the king. It appears, in other words, that the concentration of powers cannot be forestalled if the armed forces remain indifferent. They must be positively attached to the constitutional order. It is here that the problem of constitutional morale meets its crucial test; the failure to perceive this problem spells eventual disaster. The Communists have learned this lesson and have seen to it that their partisans either infiltrated the army (Czechoslovakia) or developed a revolutionary army of their own (China). Neither Locke nor Rousseau saw this problem clearly, and much constitutional doctrine was equivocal about this matter. But the Swiss people have always been keenly aware of it, and their views have had a measure of resonance in the United States. Curiously enough, the keenest exposition of the problem in theory is offered by none other than Machiavelli. In his *Discourses on Livy*, as well as in his other works, he always returns to the *militia* as the central theme. In doing so, he rationalizes the historical conceptions of Livy. By this token, the democratization policy of the Western allies has been crucially handicapped because it was prevented by its demilitarization objective from permitting the German democrats to organize a "militia" with which to maintain themselves. Continued occupation is, under these conditions, the only possible thing to do; but it means that constitutional government exists by grace of the allies. The full measure of the gap implied here may be seen when one recalls that the American revolutionaries proudly claimed the "right to bear arms" as one of the basic rights of all free men, while the German Basic Law contains the provision among its declaration of rights that "no one may be forced against his conscience into military service." Whether the Basic Law's attempt to forestall an assault upon the constitution by outlawing the "threat of force" against the constitutional order succeeds remains to be seen. At least it should handicap those who would seek to effect a transition from constitutionalism by the methods employed in the recent past. But in any case, what is the constitutional significance of military government?

Military government · All writers on comparative government neglected the questions of military government until the course of the Second World War forced its problems upon their attention. This in spite of the fact that military government was a recurrent phenomenon throughout the nineteenth century and played a significant role during and after the American Civil War. Its normative aspects formed a part of international law, but they received scant treatment since its major aspects did not appeal to a liberal age.

Military government needs to be distinguished clearly from martial rule, military law, and civil affairs. For military government is the government by the military of the civil population of occupied enemy territory, whereas the term civil affairs, properly speaking, is used to designate functions of liaison and supervisory direction in occupied territory belonging to friendly powers, while military law is the law applying to persons in the military forces, and martial rule consists in rule by the military of domestic territory and citizens.

Military government may be of two kinds when considered in relation to constitutionalism. It may be wielded on behalf of a constitutional government or on behalf of an authoritarian (totalitarian) regime. In the latter case, it is an extension of the authoritarian methods to an enemy population which in the case of contemporary totalitarian dictatorships means the application of the terroristic secret-police-state techniques with their characteristic total disregard for the basic human rights of all who are subject to their control. There is obviously no reason why an occupied enemy territory should receive more lenient treatment than the government's own subjects. On the other hand, the military government of a constitutional system is an "exceptional state" resulting from an "emergency" and hence it has the characteristic features of a "constitutional dictatorship." Such military government is not bound by the constitutional limitations, of course, but it will partake of the "constitutional morality" of the home government. Indeed, the American Army's Field Manual on Military Government which was in use at the beginning of the Second World War laid it down as an objective of military government to "protect the welfare of the governed." In other words, within the scope and limits of military necessity, military government was and is inspired by humanitarian considerations for the subject population. This intrinsic tendency of military government when carried out on behalf of a constitutional democracy is enhanced if it is the objective of the occupation to seek the establishment of a constitutional democracy in the occupied area. For in the latter case, military government becomes a "constitutional dictatorship" in the more specific sense in which such a dictatorship is directed toward the maintenance of constitutional government. In other words, a "democratizing" military government is in a particularly close sense committed to the constitutional traditions of the people for whom it acts and speaks. The failure to grasp this fundamental fact has caused some of the most embarrassing situations arising out of the Second World War.[12]

Experience prior to the Second World War · Experience with military government in modern times has been quite varied. Ranging from the merciless burning and pillage of the religious wars, as exemplified by the deeds of a Wallenstein, a Richelieu, or a Cromwell, to the highly civilized occupation of the Rhineland by American armies, military government has tended to reflect the spirit of the times and of the government responsible for its execution. Francis Lieber in 1863 formulated the latter conception when he wrote: "As civilization has advanced, during the last centuries, so has likewise steadily advanced, especially in war on land, the distinction between the private individual belonging to a hostile country and the hostile country itself, with its men in arms. The principle has been more and more acknowledged that the unarmed citizen is to be spared in person, property and honor as much as the exigencies of war will permit." This philosophy was codified in the Hague Convention of 1907 which provided in its article 32 that ". . . the occupant . . . shall take all measures in his power to restore, and ensure, as far as possible, public order and safety, while respecting, unless absolutely prevented, the laws in force in the country." In view of what happened during and after the Second World War, this article sounds like an echo from another world. Perhaps even more idyllic is the sound of article 46: "Family honour and rights, the lives of persons, and private property, as well as religious convictions and practices, must be respected. Private property cannot be confiscated."[13] These ideas dominated the *Basic Field Manual on Military Government* of the United States War Department, published in June 1940. It is fair to say that they dominated American military government practice in most cases. They were part of that "civilized warfare" which had originated with Hugo Grotius' *Law of War and Peace* (1625), inspired as it had been by the revulsion humane men had come to feel over the barbarities of the religious wars. But there were exceptions even in American practice, for example, during the Civil War, and most European countries have seldom lived up to these lofty conceptions, especially in their colonial warfare.

Experience with military government after the end of the religious wars rarely involved the notion that it was the task, let alone the moral duty, of the occupying power to reform or make over the occupied country or its people. This idea did play a role in the conduct of military government by the first Napoleon and during and after the American Civil War, the latter being a special case precisely because it was a civil war. Napoleon I, considering himself the "son of the revolution," had encouraged revolutionary changes in many of the countries he conquered, such as the establishment of the Helvetic Republic and the dissolution of the Holy Roman Empire and the creation of the Federation of the Rhine. It is worth noting, however, that the idea of encouraging self-government has been an aspect of American military government for a long time. This idea, in such cases as the Philippines, has served as a moral justification for ruling a foreign people. It gradually spread to other colonizing peoples and was dramatized in the slogan of "the white man's burden." Yet, while connoting a greater moral concern on the part of the occupant with the assumed welfare of the occupied people, it heightened the intrinsic offensiveness of foreign rule for the latter by its implied superiority of the conqueror. In the case of the Rhineland occupation, the situation was further complicated by the conflict between the liberal-conservative outlook of the American and British governments as contrasted with the liberal-socialist revolution which had occurred in Germany at the time of the surrender. Experience in most of these cases might have served to caution one against this kind of reformist military government, but the lesson of history was, as usual, largely lost.[14]

Military government and democratization · After some preliminary hesitations, democratization was made the major positive objective of military government after the combat phase. This constituted a marked deviation from earlier ideas which had clustered around the twofold objective of (1) military needs, and (2) restoring law and order. The latter objective is not unrelated to the first, but it was intended to serve and implement it. After the end of fighting, it would assume primary significance, however, and may be said to have been expanded into the task of establishing constitutional democracy. For such a democracy is readily conceived by its adepts as the only sound basis of "law and order." Such a view was encouraged by the obvious absence of law and order in the Fascist and militarist regimes which the victorious allies proposed to displace.

That a comparable lack of law and order characterized at least one of the major allies was glossed over in such elusive phrases as "peace-loving nations."

Unfortunately for all concerned, the term "democratization" had completely divergent connotations for the Western allies and the Soviet Union. Agreements, such as the Potsdam Agreement, embodying this phrase were therefore in reality no more than compromises in terms of a formula. As events were to prove, these divergent conceptions of democracy were in a number of vital respects antithetical. The historian finds it difficult to accept the now often heard excuse that Western allied policy-makers had to learn by experience that this was so. Actually, the contrasting and mutually exclusive conceptions of democracy were a matter of full and well-established record and even the most casual inquiry would have revealed the clash of views. In what follows we shall use the term "democratization" exclusively in the Western sense; the policies and practices of the totalitarian people's democracies are not properly a part of a study of constitutional democracy.

Democratization, however, is not a controversy only between the West and the Soviet Union. It is also a bone of contention between the Western powers and among their citizens. In spite of the comparative evaluations of such writers as Lord Bryce, each democratic nation inclines to identify the concept of democracy with its particular institutions, and each party is similarly inclined to identify its outlook with "truly" democratic views. Therefore, such issues as the importance of a free-market economy, the compatibility of socialism with a free society, and the like are bound to inject themselves into a policy which merely speaks of democratization without spelling out what is to be understood by the term democracy.[15] The experience with military government after the Second World War is replete with difficult situations and breakdowns resulting from disagreements over what democratization calls for. Whether we consider denazification, decartelization, re-education, or any one of a great array of vital areas of military-government activity, the same basic issue appears to be involved.

In an effort to clarify the resulting situation and to guide the Germans who were approaching the task of formulating constitutions in three states of the American Zone, American military government issued a statement of policy which defined "democratization" in terms of eight criteria which may be summed up thus: basic political power stems from the people, and those who exercise power must submit their program and policies to frequent popular elections; such elections must be competitive between at least two parties; such parties must be democratic, voluntary associations of citizens; basic rights of these citizens must be firmly guaranteed; public-opinion channels must be kept free of governmental domination; the "rule of law" must be recognized; and the exercise of governmental authority must be decentralized.[16] By this statement, the line was clearly drawn which separates constitutional democracy from the "people's democracy" of the Soviet Union and its satellites, including the Soviet Zone of Germany. Had such a basic definition been developed prior to Potsdam, and submitted to the Soviet representatives, the presumably hidden conflicts over democratization could have been brought to light. This might have eliminated democratization as such from the agenda, but it would at the same time have greatly reduced the area of potential friction, and left the democratic elements free to accomplish their task.

Military government and the rule of law · It was the contention of the writer, since borne out by events, that it would be wiser to restrict military government objectives to the establishment of government according to law in the conquered countries. Historically speaking, such government according to law has been the basic condition for the growth of constitutional democracy. This government according to law, comparable to the German concept of *Rechtsstaat*, is characterized by the general respect for and observance of law on the part of the governing authorities. It is frequently rather inaccurately referred to as the "rule of law."[17] Such an approach would have provided a common core for the different views on democracy, and it would have obliged the Germans to shoulder the responsibility for democratization. It would also have enabled the allies to avoid making "democracy" appear responsible for the painful tasks involved in liquidating Fascism.

The almost complete destruction of government according to law under the Fascists called for two interrelated steps: (1) to purge the law of those accretions which embody Fascist and National Socialist policy and prejudice; (2) to do everything possible to strengthen the authority of the regular courts after eliminating judicial personnel with markedly Fascist records. Of these two steps, the first proved easier of execution than the second, largely because the judiciary had become Fascist and Nazi to a much greater degree than had originally been thought probable. Indeed, one of the most difficult aspects of denazification resulted from the fact that so many judges were suspect that it seemed impossible to assign the task to the courts. The suspension of all specifically Fascist and Nazi laws was decreed at the outset, and more detailed "purging" was carried out by the joint effort of military government and the Italian, Austrian, and German authorities.[18] It was, in fact, Law Number 1 of the Allied Control Council which repealed the Nazi laws on September 20, 1945. It listed specifically twenty-five laws, but implemented the list by outlawing any injustice or inequality which might be caused by discriminating against any person by reason of his race, nationality, religious beliefs, or opposition to the National Socialist German Workers' Party or its doctrines. Considering the actualities of government in the Soviet Union and the United States, this provision was indeed a counsel of perfection well calculated to suffer in concrete application. In spite of it, Control Council Law Number 1 constituted the basic step in the re-establishment of government according to law which the adoption of the Basic Law of the German Federal Republic on May 8, 1949, completed. For in this Basic Law the principles of the *Rechtsstaat* were unqualifiedly reaffirmed and reinforced by the Allied Occupation Statute which subjects the occupying authorities to comparable restraints. In Italy the same result was achieved by the Constitution of 1947; in Austria by the revival of the Constitution of 1929.

Military government as constitutional dictatorship · The complex and in many ways unfortunate record of allied military government must be seen in the perspective of the establishment of constitutionalism in Italy, Austria, Germany, and Japan. Ever since the policy of democratization was first formulated, American criticism has been directed at it in some such general terms as "You cannot impose democracy by force." Much of the best liberal and democratic tradition in the United States has been cited in support of the contention that democracy cannot develop as a healthy and lasting form of government unless the people want democracy and have fought for it. From the viewpoint of those who, without deeper knowledge or insight, proceed on the assumption that democracy is something wholly new in the several countries subjected to Fascist and militarist rule in Europe in recent years, and that therefore it is to be bestowed upon them by outsiders, the objection is fatal indeed. But fortunately the situation is not as desperate as all that. Allied policy has been directed in each case not toward "imposing democracy," but toward imposing restraints upon those elements of the population—demonstrably minorities —which would prevent democracy from becoming established or, if established, would undermine and eventually destroy it. Force can be used, and has been used, for suppressing the Fascists, the Nazis, and the militarists. Force can be used, and has been used, for reducing the power of the big landowners and of the industrialists who supported the Fascist movements. Anyone who is even casually acquainted with the history of the first German Republic and of its institutions as depicted in preceding pages of this study will realize that a substantial reduction in the power of these anti-constitutional elements will substantially assist those Germans who desire to rebuild a constitutional democracy. The situation in Japan is similar.[19]

When seen in this perspective, the policy of democratization as carried forward by the Western allies is a policy of employing emergency powers of a dictatorial kind to re-establish constitutionalism. It therefore differs only in degree from the broad policy implied in the "hot war" against the Axis powers and in the "cold war" against the Soviet Union. In Asia and in Europe, the policy of democratization is the spearhead of a general policy of supporting constitutional and democratic forces. Force is being employed for "containing" the antidemocratic forces throughout the world. These antidemocratic forces, whether Communist or Fascist, have created in the past and continue to create a state of universal emergency throughout the world community by their appeal to force. As the *Communist Manifesto* made clear, and as the masters of Stalinist Russia have repeatedly reaffirmed, their appeal is to revolutionary forces. We have seen at the outset of this chapter that war and insurrection are the states of emergency which call for the establishment of constitutional dictatorship. Thus, an evaluation of military government operations on the part of the constitutional powers of the West cannot penetrate to the full significance of many detailed items without comprehending the world revolutionary situation of our time.

It is noteworthy, however, that military government corresponds more nearly to the four criteria for organizing a constitutional dictatorship that were outlined at the beginning of this chapter. The constitutional dictator who is military governor is in fact appointed by a constitutional government he does not control, the exercise of his powers is expressly defined, and since he is subject to recall, his term may be said to be subject to a clear time limit. Full, and at times sharp and even unjust, criticism by the representative bodies and the public both in Britain and in the United States has tended to ensure the employment of these dictatorial powers for "constitutional" purposes.

The future of military government · Military government has ended in Italy and Germany, and is slated to come to an end in Austria and Japan in the foreseeable future. In 1947 a thoughtful student of the development of military government policy sized up the situation thus: "The paradox which American military government confronted at the termination of hostilities both in Germany and Japan, was that it sought to build the peace with policy weapons forged in the heat of war. Clarity there was on what was to be destroyed or eliminated. But much more difficult was the realization that political reconstruction carries with it other imperatives—encouragement to groups that have repudiated Nazism or militarism, and the creation of conditions that make it possible for such groups to provide constructive leadership in new directions."[20] It is the hope of all well-intentioned citizens of the constitutional democracies, as well as the vast majority of subjects of the totalitarian dictatorships, presumably, that no war of the shooting kind will break out between the power groups contending for world unity under their leadership. But such hopes should not prevent students of constitutionalism, as it did in the past, from formulating basic policy for military government as an important phase of any possible future war between a world "half free and half slave." Such a formulation, if the analysis here offered is sound, calls for a clear recognition of the constitutionalizing task of military government. It would undoubtedly be a more gigantic task than the one faced after the Second World War. The peoples involved would be more numerous and their experience with constitutionalism practically nonexistent. Still, only an approach in terms of a firm belief that these peoples can achieve constitutional freedom and democracy will provide sound policies of occupation and military government.

What does this mean? It means that military government in the post-combat phase would be directed toward the establishment of government according to law and that the formation of groups of persons in the occupied areas ready and willing to initiate and that promote democratic movements and constitutional efforts "at the grass roots" would be encouraged immediately. Such groups would presumably be led by democratically sound men and women who had escaped from the totalitarian terror. Finally, military government policies would be formulated and executed by men thoroughly familiar with the culture and the past traditions of the countries to be occupied. What is perhaps even more important, however, is that such policies and their execution should be in the hands of persons who would understand the nature of the world revolutionary situation and would appreciate the limits of force in dealing with a conflict of this type. This implies that they would understand the genesis and functioning of constitutional democracy and appreciate the conditions for its maintenance and growth. This prescription may sound like a twentieth-century call for the philosophers made kings. It is a fact that the constitutional dictator occupies a position which would be akin to the Platonic guardians, were it not for the fact that he remains responsible to a democratic people at home.

Conclusion · Constitutional dictatorship, on the surface a contradiction in terms, is the final test of constitutionalism. For a government which cannot meet emergencies is bound to fall sooner or later. There is no object in arguing against such emergency powers on the ground that they endanger the constitutional morale, and hence the maintenance of the constitutional order. Of course they do. Any suspension of legal norms, no matter how temporary, raises doubts concerning their validity. But after all, what does an emergency mean if not that the constitutional order is threatened? Imminent invasion and civil war are only the most blatant final stages of such a danger. No one in his right mind can argue that their emergence should not be forestalled. Unfortunately, no man can foretell the future. Hence, it will always be a matter of judgment, a matter of weighing risks as to which is more dangerous: the threatening emergency or the powers for combating it. Humanly enough, the more uncertain the choice, the more emphatic become the partisans. Nothing shows that more clearly than America's dilemma in the face of the world revolutionary situation that has been briefly sketched. It is similar to the dilemma we confronted in the rise of Hitler. Few would question in retrospect that even rather far-reaching measures designed to forestall that rise would have been in America's interest; yet at the time, in 1936, 1937, 1938, few were prepared to adopt such measures because they miscalculated the danger ahead.

Although modern industrialism forbids the employment of the Roman pattern of constitutional dictatorship, its underlying conceptions are still valid. Emergency powers should be very broad in scope, but the conditions for their exercise should be rigidly defined. The constitutional dictator should be appointed by a body which he does not in fact control, he should not be in a position to declare the emergency himself, and a fixed time limit should be attached to the grant of powers. But behind all these procedural devices there must stand an alert people, a real constituent power, determined to see to it that these limitations are effectively utilized to insure the legitimate employment of these emergency powers: to strengthen the constitution, if necessary, by timely changes. What can never be timely is a change in the basic pattern of constitutionalism itself. The problem of constitutional dictatorship, therefore, presents a more acute case of the general problem of constitutionalism. How are we to get effective, vigorous governmental action, and yet limit the power of governmental bodies so as to forestall the rise of despotic concentration of power? Logically it is a paradox, but practically it has been done. The task requires all the wisdom man can muster. The prize is his greatest achievement: freedom.

Bibliography

I · *A Historical Sketch of Modern Constitutionalism in Theory and Practice*

REFERENCES

1. Since this chapter attempts to place the systematic analysis of the whole volume in historical perspective, many of the statements made are more fully elaborated in other places. It did not seem necessary to give specific references in each instance, as the analytical table of contents, as well as the index, readily enables the reader to check any point of special interest.

2. For the Aristotelian political philosophy, Ernest Barker's book, *The Political Thought of Plato and Aristotle* (1906), is probably still the best, although its point of view is diametrically opposed to that adopted here; it is inspired by the traditional acceptance of the Greek view of politics. Against this see the author's "The Deification of the State" in *The Review of Politics*, Vol. I, No. 1, pp. 18–30 (Jan. '39). Werner Jaeger's study of *Aristotle* (1934) is important in showing the development of the Aristotelian position.

3. The illustration of monarchy is elaborated in an article by the author and F. M. Watkins, "Monarchy," in the *ESS*. See also "Oligarchy" and "Tyranny." The "Spenglerian" touch of this paragraph must not be taken as an indication of the author's acceptance or approval of that writer's general philosophy of history, which he, in fact, rejects. The aspect brought into the analysis here was derived by Spengler from Burckhardt and Dilthey.

4. The most challenging work treating the relation between capitalism and liberal constitutionalism is Harold Laski's *The Rise of Liberalism* (1936). It makes free use of the concept of the bourgeois class, but, while the writers on constitutionalism are shown to have been members of the professional middle classes, little attempt is made to show in what way that class membership affected their writing. More light is shed upon this aspect of the matter by Bernard Groethuysen, *Origines de l'Esprit Bourgeois en France* (1927). The relationship between imperialism and constitutionalism is stressed by certain writers under Marxist influence who desired to explain the persistence of free institutions under capitalism, more especially Rosa Luxemburg, *Die Akkumulation des Kapitals; ein Beitrag zur ökonomischen Erklärung des Imperialismus* (1922).

5. The objections to defining scientific base-line concepts are stated well in A. N. Whitehead, *Process and Reality*, pp. 6 ff. The axiom stated here is often seemingly denied by men striving after a "scientific" outlook, but what is denied under the heading of purpose, value, or objective reappears in another form. Charles Merriam (*Political Power* [1934], p. 7) has said that "political power lies in a definite common pattern of impulse." A. F. Bentley took a somewhat similar view (*Process of Government* [1908], pp. 171–172). It has often been assumed that an introduction of objectives unavoidably plunges politics into the controversies of ethics and metaphysics. The fact that Plato (*Republic*, Book VI, for example) stressed the common pur-

pose of all men seems to substantiate such a view, but it does not. For a correct modern statement, see M. R. Cohen, *Reason and Nature*, pp. 342 ff.

6. National unification has been emphasized in the writings of the German historical school, and more particularly Gustav Schmoller, "Das Merkantilsystem in seiner historischen Bedeutung" in his *Jahrbuch* (1884). For England, compare William Stubbs, *English Constitutional History* (1874–1878). In a very stimulating article "Power versus Plenty as Objectives of Foreign Policy in the Seventeenth and Eighteenth Centuries," in *World Politics*, Vol. I, pp. 1 ff., Jacob Viner has argued that wealth as well as power was a prime objective of government in this period. He is right, but the view to the contrary that he imputes to Schmoller, Cunningham, and Heckscher is not, in my reading, held by these writers.

7. See William Cunningham, *The Progress of Capitalism in England* (1916); Adam Smith, *Wealth of Nations*, Book IV, Ch. I, and Book V; Werner Sombart, *Der Moderne Kapitalismus* (1916), Vol. I, 1, Chs. XXI–XXVIII; and R. H. Tawney and E. Power, *Tudor Economic Documents* (1924). See also below, notes to Ch. V.

8. The problem of how much weight to attach to the "nationalist" sentiment and appeal in Machiavelli is a difficult one. Ever since Fichte (whose views were brilliantly restated by Macaulay in one of his *Essays*), who, in his nationalist period, undertook to rehabilitate Machiavelli in his *Über Machiavelli als Schriftsteller* (1807) it has been taken for granted by many that Machiavelli was a "nationalist." I rather incline to feel that national sentiment is too emotional a basis for Machiavelli's thought and that he was more truly interested in the state as a work of art. The doctrine of the reason of state derived from him is the outgrowth of Machiavelli's preoccupation with power as the essential resource of the state builder. See P. Villari, *N. Machiavelli* (English translation by Linda Villari); O. Ferrara, *Machiavelli* (French translation by F. de Miomandre, Paris, 1928); F. Meinecke, *Die Idee der Staatsräson* (1925), Chs. I and III; and G. Ritter, *Die Dämonie der Macht* (1940, 1947).

9. See Hans Delbrück, *Geschichte der Kriegskunst* (1900); M. Oppenheim, *A History of the Administration of the Royal Navy* (1896), Vol. I; Sombart, op. cit., Vol. I, 2, Ch. XLIX; and H. T. Buckle, *History of Civilization in England* (1857). See also below, notes to Ch. III.

10. A very interesting treatment has been published by Derwent Whittlesey, *The Earth and the State* (1939). He builds on the earlier work of R. Kjellen, *Grundriss zu einem System der Politik* (1920), and *Die Grossmächte der Gegenwart* (1916). See also Friedrich Ratzel, *Politische Geographie* (1897).

11. For a systematic treatment see Reinhold Niebuhr, *Christianity and Power Politics* (1940). Further, see R. H. Tawney, *Religion and the Rise of Capitalism* (1926); C. J. Friedrich, *Introduction to Johannes Althusius' Politica* (1932), particularly Chs. II and IV; J. G. Droysen, *Geschichte der Preussischen Politik* (1868), Vol. II, pp. 2, 383 ff.; Otto Hintze, "Kalvinismus und Staatsräson in Brandenburg zur Anfang des 17. Jahrhunderts," in *Historische Zeitschrift*, Vol. CXLIII (1931); E. Troeltsch, *The Social Teachings of the Christian Churches* (1923; tr. O. Wyon, 1931); Max Weber, *Protestant Ethic and the Spirit of Capitalism* (tr. T. Parsons, 1930); and Hans Kohn's magistral *The Idea of Nationalism* (1944).

H. Sidgwick, *The Development of European Polity* (1903); James Bryce, *The Holy Roman Empire* (1904), and *Modern Democracies* (1921).

C. J. H. Hayes, *Essays on Nationalism* (1926). For further suggestions, consult K. S. Pinson, *A Bibliographical Introduction to Nationalism* (1935). For a more recent survey, see E. H. Carr and Associates, *Nationalism* (1940).

12. Georg von Below, *Die Ursachen der Rezeption des Römischen Rechts* (1905); Otto von Gierke, *Das Deutsche Genossenschaftsrecht* (1868), particularly Vol. II; H. Sidgwick, op. cit. Lectures XXII and XXIII; Fritz Schulz, *Principles of Roman Law* (1936); for a summary see Max Radin, *Handbook of Roman Law* (1927 and later).

13. The famous definition is found in Jean Bodin's *De Republica, Libri Sex* (Paris, 1576; Latin translation by the author, 1586), Bk. I, Ch. VIII, and reads: *Majestas est summa in cives ac subditos legibusque soluta potestas.* Later on he adds the important stipulation that *summa* means that *majestas* recognizes no earthly superior, which shows that the definition was politically

directed against the authority of Pope and Emperor. Bodin also insists that *majestas* is *potestas perpetua*, thereby excluding all temporary grants of power from the definition. For Bodin see Roger Chauviré, *Jean Bodin* (1914). It is my hope that a new English edition will soon be published by the Harvard Classics.

14. For the idea of the state as "sovereign association" see F. M. Watkins, *The State as a Concept of Political Science* (1934). For a trenchant criticism of much jurisprudential claptrap see the recent article by Kenneth C. Cole, "The Theory of the State as a Sovereign Juristic Person," *APSR*, XLII, pp. 16 ff. For an elaboration of the ideas stated briefly in the text, more especially as they relate to democratic theory, see the author's *The New Belief in the Common Man* (1942), especially Ch. II, and the literature cited there. The idea, curiously, is also stated by Thomas Paine, in *The Rights of Man*.

15. A brilliant sketch, from a sociological viewpoint, of the idea of the state is offered by Alfred Weber in his *Die Krise des Modernen Staatsgedankens in Europa* (1925). See also the author's paper in *Synopsis—Festgabe für Alfred Weber* (1949), pp. 135 ff., entitled "Constitutionalism versus Absolutism—Main Currents of Political Thought, 1610–1660." Great stress was laid by Max Weber in his various writings upon "monopoly of force," for which see now the translations made available by Talcott Parsons (with A. M. Henderson), *The Theory of Social and Economic Organization* (1947) and by H. H. Gerth and C. W. Mills, *Essays in Sociology* (1946).

16. C. H. McIlwain, *The Growth of Political Thought in the West* (1932); John W. Allen, *A History of Political Thought in the Sixteenth Century* (1928). See also the recent study by Francis D. Wormuth, *The Origins of Modern Constitutionalism* (1949), especially Chs. IV and V. See below, "Remarks" in Chapter XI.

17. The entire medieval literature on the prince is permeated by the idea of ecclesiastical sanctions for "just" conduct. See the essay by John Dickinson, "The Medieval Idea of Kingship and Some of its Limitations, as Developed in the *Polykraticus* of John of Salisbury," in *Speculum*, Vol. I (1926), pp. 308 ff.; R. W. and A. J. Carlyle, *History of Medieval Political Theory in the West* (1903–1916), passim; and (for an authoritative source) Thomas Aquinas, *De regimine principum*. For Henry II, see Rosenstock-Wittig, *Das Alter der Kirche* (1928), pp. 561 ff. Concerning Protestantism, see Hintze's article cited above, note 11, as well as Max Weber's pointed essay, *The Protestant Ethic and the Spirit of Capitalism* (tr. T. Parsons, 1930), pp. 79 ff.

Concerning the *Anti-Machiavel*, see Friedrich Meinecke, *Die Idee der Staatsräson in der neueren Geschichte* (2d ed., 1925), pp. 340 ff.

18. Reason of "state" has been given wholly inadequate attention in England and America. Concerning Botero, see Friedrich Meinecke, op. cit., pp. 81 ff., and his own work, *De Ratione Status* (ed. Conring, 1666). Meinecke's work is of general importance here; but compare the author's review in *APSR*, Vol. XXIV, pp. 1064 ff. Concerning the divine right of kings, see John N. Figgis's classical treatment of the subject *The Divine Right of Kings* (2d ed., 1914). See also his *Churches in the Modern State* (1913). On the deification of the state, see the author's article by that title in *Review of Politics*, Vol. I, No. 1 (1939).

19. For the wide ramifications of the issue of toleration, see the comprehensive monograph by W. K. Jordan, cited above, Ch. VII, note 5. Charles A. Beard's volume, *The Idea of National Interest* (1934), was followed by another, *The Open Door at Home; A Trial Philosophy of National Interest* (1934). C. J. H. Hayes's views are set forth in *Essays in Nationalism* (1926), especially Ch. IV, "Nationalism as a Religion."

20. A very interesting modern analysis of the importance of objectives for organization is found in Chester I. Barnard's *The Functions of the Executive* (1938).

21. The definition by Hobbes is found in *Leviathan*, Book I, Ch. X. Locke's thoughts on power in the *Essay on Human Understanding*, Book II, are as follows: "Power, thus considered (namely, in reference to the change in perceivable ideas), is twofold, viz. able to make or able to receive any change: the one may be called active and the other passive power" (Ch. XXI, §2). Locke then goes on to point out that we derive a clear idea of active power from the mind, not from external observation (perception). "This power which the mind has thus to order the

consideration of any idea, or the forbearing to consider it; or to prefer the motion of any part of the body to its rest, and vice versa, in any particular instance; is that which we call the will." This statement is preceded by the important sentence: "This at least I think evident, that we find in ourselves a power to begin or to forbear, continue or end several actions of our minds, and motions of our bodies, barely by a thought or preference of the mind ordering, or, as it were, commanding the doing or not doing such a particular action" (ibid. §5). And again: "All the actions that we have any idea of, reducing themselves, as has been said, to these two, viz. thinking and motion; so far as man has power to think or not to think, to move or not to move, according to the preference or direction of his own mind, so far is a man free" (ibid. §8). And further: "Liberty is not an idea belonging to volition, or preferring; but to the person having the power of doing, or forbearing to do, according as the mind shall choose or direct." And later, after his well-known argument on the so-called freedom of the will: "For *powers are relations*, not agents: and that (agent) which has the power, or not the power to operate, is that alone which is or is not free, and not the power itself. For freedom, or not freedom, can belong to nothing, but what has or has not the power to act" (ibid. §17). Note that this view, rather dogmatically expressed, is found in Bentley, op. cit. The contrast between consent and constraint is implied in Tönnies' fundamental distinction between *Gemeinschaft* and *Gesellschaft*.

22. The importance of the time factor for political analysis has not as yet been adequately developed,—certainly nowhere nearly so adequately as in economics. Yet it is undoubtedly true that certain generalizations are vitally affected by the segment of time to which they are supposed to apply. See, for some sample suggestions, Stuart Rice, *Quantitative Methods in Politics* (1928), and P. Sargant Florence, *The Statistical Method in Economics and Political Science* (1929).

23. See Eli F. Heckscher, *Mercantilism* (1935; 2 vols.). For a somewhat studied, but stimulating criticism, see the article by Viner, cited in note 6, above.

24. Cameralism received careful treatment at the hands of Albion Small, *The Cameralist* (1909). See also the author's "The Continental Tradition of Training Administrators in Law and Jurisprudence" in *The Journal of Modern History*, Vol. XI, No. 2 (June, 1939).

25. Insofar as constitutionalism is related to liberalism, Guido de Ruggiero's *The History of European Liberalism* (1927) is excellent. Catholic political philosophy, of course, has always stressed the idea of governmental restraints in connection with the Church's efforts to prevent secular absolutism. From St. Thomas to contemporary writers such as Jacques Maritain the idea has found ever new expressions. See John A. Ryan and F. J. Boland, *Catholic Principles of Politics* (1940), and Heinrich A. Rommen's magistral *The State in Catholic Thought* (1945). The stress, however, is upon natural law, and the role of institutional sanctions is minimized. The word "constitution" characteristically does not even figure in the index.

26. For the Marxist crisis see Eduard Heimann, *Communism, Fascism, or Democracy?* (1938).

27. See the author's "European Union in Theory and Practice" in *Memorial Volume for Charles Payne* (ed. by Stuart Brown [1949]); for the earlier movement, initiated by A. Briand, see William E. Rappard, *Uniting Europe* (1930).

28. See Charles A. Beard's two articles on the origin of representative institutions in the *APSR*, [Vol. XXVI], 1932, pp. 28 ff., as well as William Stubbs, *English Constitutional History*, and F. W. Maitland, *Constitutional History of England*; in addition, G. P. Gooch, *English Democratic Ideas in the Seventeenth Century* (2d ed. with notes by Harold Laski; 1927), is important.

29. The view here adopted of emphasizing the constitutional issues in the American War of Independence is that found in C. H. McIlwain, *The American Revolution* (1924). See below, Ch. XII, note 3. There is no good comparative constitutional history tracing the spread of English constitutional ideas on the continent. Some interesting special points are developed in *The Constitution Reconsidered* (1938): Robert Binkley, "The Holy Roman Empire versus the United States: Patterns for Constitution-Making in Central Europe"; Hajo Holborn, "The Influence of the American Constitution on the Weimar Constitution"; W. Menzies Whitelaw, "American Influence on British Federal Systems"; Geoffrey Bruun, "The Constitutional Cult in the Early Nineteenth Century."

30. An able analysis of these writers is given by Benjamin Lippincott, *Victorian Critics of Democracy* (1938). Macaulay's famous letter to a congressman, as printed in *Harper's Magazine*, Vol. LIV, pp. 460 ff. (Feb., 1877), should be consulted. The vast literature on democracy, of course, cannot be summarized here. Much is propagandistic rather than scientific in its tenor, but Vernon L. Parrington's volumes, *Main Currents in American Thought* (1927–1930), and R. H. Gabriel, *The Course of American Democratic Thought* (1940), offer a wealth of insight into the process of democratization in America. A comparable treatment for England is not available, but the two volumes by E. L. Woodward, *The Age of Reform, 1815–1870* (1938), and R. C. K. Ensor, *England, 1870–1914* (1936), provide an excellent general panorama.

31. Arthur Rosenberg, *Democracy and Socialism* (1939). See also Harold Laski, *Parliamentary Government in England* (1938), and H. R. G. Greaves, *The British Constitution* (1938).

32. See especially Leslie Lipson, *The Politics of Equality; New Zealand's Adventures in Democracy* (1948), skillfully weighing the impact of socialism upon the citizen's freedom.

33. W. E. Rappard, *L'Individu et l'État* (1938), the main thesis of which is that expanding governmental activities, by threatening individualism, also threaten constitutionalism. In the United States the view was presented in somewhat popular form by James Beck in *Our Wonderland of Bureaucracy* (1932). The point has since been made so frequently by columnists as to have become almost a commonplace. See Mark Sullivan and David Lawrence. The argument, in turn, has been picked up by American fascists such as Lawrence Dennis, who in his *The Coming American Fascism* (1936) makes much of this contention. It is likewise a weapon in the armory of Marxist critics such as Max Lerner, who in "Constitution and Court as Symbols," *Yale Law Journal*, Vol. XLVI, No. 8 (June, 1937), has taken a view analogous to that of Laski.

34. See Harold Laski, *Parliamentary Government in England* (1938), especially Ch. I. The argument that the Labour Party has not realized socialism (an argument expounded by Paul Sweezey in his *Socialism* (1949), pp. 40 ff.), even if true, does not mean that Laski's prediction may yet come true, since the gradual adaptation noted in the text is the crucial point. See also Francis Williams, *Socialist Britain* (1948), for a broad statement of the situation.

35. Rosenberg, op. cit. p. 216.

II · The Core of Modern Government: Bureaucracy

REMARKS

The literature on "bureaucracy" is very extensive, if that term be taken to comprehend "administration and administrative personnel." Current developments and theory have been given an admirable platform in *Public Administration Review* since 1940. It reflects the rapid growth of the science of public administration, as suggested in works like John M. Gaus' *Reflections on Public Administration* (1947). I wish to draw attention also to two articles which sharply focus some of the issues: Robert A. Dahl, "The Science of Public Administration: Three Problems," and Herbert A. Simon, "A Comment on the Science of Public Administration," *PAR*, Vol. VII, pp. 1 ff. and 200 ff. (1947). J. M. Juran's *Bureaucracy: A Challenge to Better Management* (1944), while focused on American problems, deserves mention, as does the excellent case study by Taylor Cole, *Canadian Bureaucracy* (1949). Outstanding contributions to the historical origins are: Thomas F. Tout, *Chapters in the Administrative History of Medieval England* (6 vols., 1920–1933); Jean Brissaud, *History of French Public Law* (tr. J. W. Garner, 1915); Gustav Schmoller, "Der Deutsche Beamtenstaat vom 16.–18. Jahrhundert," in *Jahrbuch für Gesetzgebung, Verwaltung und Volkswirtschaft*, Vol. XVIII (1894), and "Über Behördenorganisation, Amtswesen und Beamtentum," introduction to *Acta Borussica*, Vol. I (1894), particularly Chs. II and VII; Otto Hintze, "Die Entstehung der modernen Staatsministerien," in *Historische Zeitschrift*, Vol. C (1907), pp. 53–111. Also C. J. Friedrich and Taylor Cole, *Responsible Bureaucracy* (1932), particularly Chs. I and II (Vol. I of *Studies in Systematic Political Science*, etc.); Max Weber, *Wirtschaft und Gesellschaft* (*Grundriss der Sozialökonomik*, Vol. III) (1925), Ch. III, §§3, 4, 5, of the first part, and Ch. VI of the third part; Alfred Weber, *Der Beamte* (in *Ideen zur Staats- und Kultursoziologie*) (1927). These three attempts at systematic treatment are closely related to one another in their terminology and in the effort to avoid ideological distortions. Such distortions intrude themselves to some extent in: Herman Finer, "The Civil Service," in *The Theory and Practice of Modern Government* (1932), Vol. II, Part VII; Leonard D. White, *Introduction to the Study of Public Administration* (2d ed., 1939). To this must now be added the same author's fine historical study, *The Federalists—A Study in Administrative History* (1948), which describes the establishment of the core of America's federal bureaucracy. An interesting challenge to these approaches is offered by Dwight Waldo, *The Administrative State* (1948), stressing the importance of values. Excellent special studies on personnel devoted to American practice are: Lewis Meriam, *Public Personnel Problems* (1938), and W. E. Mosher, *Public Personnel Administration* (1941). Other general references are found in Sarah Greer, *A Bibliography of Civil Service and Personnel Administration* (1935).

REFERENCES

1. See Tout, op. cit.; J. F. Baldwin, *The King's Council in England during the Middle Ages* (1914).

2. Tout, op. cit. Vol. I, p. 181.

3. W. Altmann, *Ausgewählte Urkunden zur Brandenburg-Preussischen Verfassungs- und Verwaltungsgeschichte*, Vol. I, pp. 55 ff.; Gustav Schmoller, "Über Behördenorganisation, Amtswesen und Beamtentum . . . ," which is the introduction to Vol. I of *Acta Borussica* (1894).

4. See E. B. Greene, *The Provincial Governor in the English Colonies of North America* (1898), for discussion of early American development.

5. Leonard D. White, *The Federalists—A Study in Administrative History* (1948). See also Carl Russel Fish, *The Civil Service and the Patronage* (1904).

6. The importance of "rationalized" conduct was first stressed in broad cultural terms by Jacob Burckhardt in his justly celebrated *Die Kultur der Renaissance in Italien* (1860), especially Ch. VII. The idea gained ground and was given very general sociological significance by Pareto and Max Weber. Antecedents of a rather speculative type are to be found in Condorcet, Auguste Comte, and Spencer. The most significant philosophical statement in historical terms may be found in W. Dilthey *Einleitung in die Geisteswissenschaften* (1883). It is central to H. Simon's analysis. (See below, note 8).

7. These categories are developed in their application to modern administration by Leonard D. White, *Introduction to the Study of Public Administration*, Ch. III. See also C. J. Friedrich, op. cit. pp. 29 ff.; Herman Finer, op. cit. Vol. II, p. 1362.

8. See Chester I. Barnard, *The Functions of the Executive* (1940) as well as Ch. XVIII of this volume. Herbert A. Simon, *Administrative Behavior* (1947); Otto Hintze, "Behördenorganisation und allgemeine Verwaltung in Preussen," the introduction to Vol. VI of *Acta Borussica* (1901); Walter L. Dorn, "The Prussian Bureaucracy in the Eighteenth Century," *Political Science Quarterly*, Vols. XLVI and XLVII (1931, 1932); C. J. Friedrich, "The Continental Tradition of Training Administrators in Law and Jurisprudence," *Journal of Modern History*, Vol. XI, No. 2 (1939); René Hugot-Derville, *Le principe hiérarchique dans l'administration française* (1913). This trend serves as the basis for Burnham's much discussed *Managerial Revolution* (1941); see also S. de Madariaga, *Anarchy or Hierarchy* (1937). The problem of the conditions under which monocratic leadership occurs has not as yet received the attention it deserves. Certain phases are considered below in Chs. XXII and XXVI. See further R. C. K. Ensor, *Courts and Judges in France, Germany, and England* (1933).

9. See the works cited in Greer, op. cit. pp. 79 ff.

10. Morale has been the subject of extended discussion among philosophers, psychologists, political scientists, and administrators. We may note H. D. Lasswell, *Propaganda Technique in the World War* (1927); F. C. Bartlett, *Psychology and the Soldier* (1927); William Ernest Hocking, *Morale and Its Enemies* (1918); and the recent striking study by Samuel Stouffer and associates, *The American Soldier* (1949), especially Vol. I, Chs. I–VIII.

11. See Herman Finer, *The British Civil Service* (1937); also Walter R. Sharp, *The French*

Civil Service—Bureaucracy in Transition (1931), Chs. IV, V, VI, and VII; for recent developments, see Fritz M. Marx, "Civil Service in Germany," in *Civil Service Abroad* (1935), Chs. VI, VII, VIII; also Franz Neumann's penetrating analysis in *Behemoth* (1942); C. J. Friedrich, "Responsible Government Service under the American Constitution," in *Problems of the American Public Service* (1935), Ch. VII; Harvey Walker, *Training Public Employees in Great Britain* (1935). On the British civil service, two sharply critical evaluations have appeared recently: H. R. G. Greaves, *The Civil Service in the Changing State* (1947), especially Chs. III, IV, and VIII; and Donald Kingsley, *Representative Bureaucracy* (1944). Both books express Labour Party views now current in Britain. No scholarly assessment has yet appeared of the struggle over civil service reform in occupied Germany, but the Monthly Report of the Military Governor in both the American and the British Zones contains much relevant material.

12. The Presidential press conference is analyzed in several of the volumes dealing with the presidency, as cited below, Ch. XVIII.

13. The struggle for greater publicity of what goes on in the government has been highlighted by the efforts of the occupation officials to have appropriate provisions inserted into the legislation dealing with civil service reform. See above, note 8.

14. The problem of the expert is further developed below, Ch. XIX. Here we may note *The New Belief in the Common Man* (1942), Ch. VI, "Responsibility and the Sense of Workmanship."

15. The clash between the idea of constitutionalism and secrecy was stated with greatest emphasis by Immanuel Kant in a number of works.

16. See J. Donald Kingsley, op. cit. and L. D. White, *The Federalists*, cited above.

III · *Territorial Expansion, Security, and the Military Establishment*

REMARKS

The literature on territorial expansion and more especially on modern imperialism is very large, while that on the interrelation between military and governmental development is thin, considering the tremendous importance of the power to kill in the establishment of lasting control patterns. Neither the expansion of Rome nor that of modern Europe is conceivable without discovery of superior military techniques. But the Second World War has produced some interesting studies. Pendleton Herring's *The Impact of War* (1941) explores the problems of the military in a free society from a fresh viewpoint. It contains a good annotated bibliography and provides a skillful antidote to such sharply antimilitary studies as R. Leigh's *Conscript Europe* (1938). Leigh thought that "if Germany wins," it might lead to a revival of the League of Nations. A significant collaborative work, edited by Edward Mead Earle, is entitled *Makers of Modern Strategy* (1943). Several of its studies are quoted specifically below. The contributors were mostly historians, and their comments on the political and constitutional aspects of the military thought they examine are incidental. Yet, much of the most interesting material is found in the work of historians; see particularly William L. Langer, *The Diplomacy of Imperialism* (1935), Ch. XIII. A certain amount of work has recently been done in anthropology and comparative cultural sociology along these lines. But for the period here in question, the outstanding recent contribution is Alfred Vagts, *The History of Militarism* (1937). Also, the editors of the Journal of the American Military Institute, *Military Affairs*, have at last provided a forum for a discussion. But the great classic is Alfred T. Mahan, *The Influence of Sea Power upon History* (1890). Besides this, one should consult Hans Delbrück, *Geschichte der Kriegskunst im Rahmen der Politischen Geschichte* (1900–1926), which unfortunately remains untranslated, even in part. This remarkable work leaves something to be desired from the standpoint of the student of political institutions, because, in spite of its avowed intention of showing the connection between the constitution and tactics and strategy, it is not permeated by any carefully developed ideas on government and constitutionalism. See Gordon A. Craig's "Delbrück: The Military Historian" in *Makers of Modern Strategy* with whose general estimate of the importance of the work I agree.

Before the Second World War, many a priori assertions were heard concerning the devastating effect which war was supposed to have on "democracy." Factual support was usually lacking. The many volumes of the Carnegie Endowment's *Economic and Social History of the World War* (1924 and later) should have offered a welcome antidote, since they showed that democracy in fact *advanced* in the course of the First World War. A striking analysis of the decisive economic aspects was offered by Max Werner, *The Military Strength of the Powers* (1939).

REFERENCES

1. Henry Sidgwick, *Principles of Political Economy*, Ch. XVIII, §§4 and 5.

2. Arnold von Luschin und Ebengreuth, *Österreichische Reichs- und Rechtsgeschichte*, pp. 397, 411, 466–467 ff., 479.

3. Arnold J. Toynbee, in his *Study of History*, Vols. I and II (1934), has gathered much significant material on this point.

4. M. Oppenheim, *A History of the Administration of the Royal Navy, 1509–1660* (1896). See also Mahan, op. cit. For the American parallel, see Harold and Margaret Sprout, *The Rise of American Naval Power* (1939). See also W. C. Abbott, *The Writings and Speeches of Oliver Cromwell*, 4 vols. (1937–1947) under "Navy"; G. M. Trevelyan, *English Social History* (1942) especially pp. 194–195; and J. L. de Lolme, *The Constitution of England* (1775) 1807 ed., pp. 453 ff.

5. See G. M. Trevelyan, *English Social History* (1942), p. 194. For de Lolme see *The Constitution of England* (1775) (new ed. 1807), p. 453, for the quote. De Lolme, in the preceding pages, from 439 ff., takes Adam Smith to task for saying, in *The Wealth of Nations*, Book V, Ch. I, that "the English government derived the singular stability it manifests from the standing force it has at its disposal."

6. Delbrück, op. cit. pp. 255 ff. Also Sombart, *Kapitalismus*, Vol. I, 1, pp. 342 ff. The description of Prince Eugene is found in Ernest F. Henderson, *A Short History of Germany* (2d ed., 1917), Vol. II, p. 51.

7. The generalization advanced in this paragraph is sometimes advanced by historians in their special treatments of a specific history. Thus J. Beloch, in his *Griechische Geschichte* (1893–1904), explains the dispersion of political authority characteristic of the city-state in these terms. See especially Alfred Vagts, *The History of Militarism* (1937).

8. See the Report of the Atomic Energy Commission, Dept. of State, No. 2498 (1946).

9. See Henry Guerlac, "Vauban: the Impact of Science on War," in *Makers of Modern Strategy* (1943), pp. 26–48, and the literature cited there. See also the same author's unprinted dissertation, *Science and the War in the Old Regime. The Development of Science in an Armed Society* (1941). See also Max Scheler, *Versuch zu einer Soziologie des Wissens* (1924), pp. 99 ff.

10. Interesting material is found in Pitirim Sorokin, *Social and Cultural Dynamics* (1937), Vol. III, Part II, Ch. XI.

11. H. Nicolson, *Public Faces* (1932). See also *Geschichte der K. und K. Wehrmacht von 1618 bis Ende des XIX. Jahrhunderts* (her. v.d. Direktion des K. und K. Kriegsarchivs). See also P. Herring, *The Impact of War* (1941), passim. Not exactly the point of the text, but related problems of the link between technology and science are touched upon in the following: Ch. XI of C. Bouglé's *Leçons de Sociologie sur l'Évolution des Valeurs* (tr. H. S. Sellars as *The Evolution of Values*, 1926); E. Mach in *Erkenntnis und Irrtum* (1905; 1926); the same author's *Die Mechanik in ihrer Entwicklung* (1883–1933) (tr. by T. J. McCormack, with later additions by P. E. B. Jourdain, 1915); and Max Scheler, *Soziologie des Wissens*, pp. 129 ff., as well as the other authors cited there.

12. Oppenheim, op. cit.; Sombart, *Krieg und Kapitalismus* (1912), pp. 66 ff.; J. W. Fortescue, *A History of the British Army* (1899); and similar works for France, Germany, etc., cited by Sombart. See also Albert T. Lauterbach's *Economics in Uniform: Military Economy and Social Structure* (1943), for recent trends.

13. As in other parts of this chapter, considerable literature is provided by economic history,

for example, regarding the debasing of the coins. Eli Heckscher's *Mercantilism* (1935) provides far and away the best general comparative treatment. Regarding trading companies, G. Cawston and A. H. Keane, *Early Chartered Companies* (1896), and S. van Brakel, *De Hollandsche Handelscompagnieen der Sewentiende Eeuw* (1908), are worth consulting, along with the standard economic histories. Regarding the estimates on benefits derived from confiscation of ecclesiastical property, Thomas Tanner's *Notitia Monastica* (1744) has been consulted; see also F. A. Gasquet, *Henry VIII and the English Monasteries* (1888–1889). The figure regarding the price of the Ark Royal is found in E. Keble Chatterton, *Sailing Ships* (1909).

14. Present-day issues are the theme of J. M. Keynes' *How to Pay for the War* (1940). A different approach is set forth by Robert Warren and others in *Financing the War* (1942). On the historical side, a thorough comparative study based on the extensive new material for developments throughout Europe unfortunately does not exist; the article in *ESS* is confined to France. For Germany, see particularly Georg von Below, "System und Bedeutung der landständischen Verfassung," in *Territorium und Stadt* (1900), pp. 163 ff., and the same author's *Landstandische Verfassung von Jülich und Berg* (1885). For France, see Georges Picot, *Histoire des États Généraux* (2d ed., 1888). The essays on the several parliaments in the *ESS* afford some guidance. For the battle on the White Hill see Julius Krebs, *Die Schlacht am Weissen Berge* (1879), and the summary in Delbrück, op. cit. Vol. IV, pp. 223 ff.

15. For the doctrine of the prerogative see Francis D. Wormuth, *The Royal Prerogative, 1603–1649* (1939). The French *intendants* are treated with discrimination by G. Hanotaux, *Origines de l'Institution des Intendants des Provinces* (1884), of whose views an adequate summary is found in Herman Finer, *Modern Government*, Vol. II, pp. 1223 ff. These problems are discussed further below, Ch. XXVI.

16. The problem of war in Marxist theory is discussed with insight by S. Neumann in "Engels and Marx: Military Concepts of the Social Revolutionaries," and by Edward M. Earle, in "Lenin, Trotsky, Stalin: Soviet Concepts of War," in *Makers of Modern Strategy*, Chs. VII and XIV. Earle makes the point that it was the Fascists rather than the Marxist Soviets who turned this war into a revolutionary one. The problem stressed in the text is now troubling European reconstruction; see esp. Ch. IV. For an earlier theoretical analysis see Gerhart Lütkens, "Das Kriegsproblem und die marxistische Theorie," in *ASW und SP*, Vol. XLIX (1922), pp. 467 ff. See also the author's *Foreign Policy in the Making* (1938). Acute specific comments are found in W. P. Maddox, *Foreign Relations in British Labour Politics* (1934), pp. 53 f., and elsewhere; and in Merle Fainsod, *International Socialism and the World War* (1935). Much good material is also found in Louis Fischer, *The Soviets in World Affairs* (1930), passim, and in the collective volume *War in Our Time* (1939), edited by Hans Speier and Alfred Kähler.

17. For the German events touched upon here, see Herbert Rosinsky, *The German Army* (1940); Alfred Vagts, "Land and Sea Power in the Second German Reich" in *Journal of the American Military Institute*, Vol. II, pp. 210 ff. (1939); and the detailed treatment, some of it biased, in Bénoist-Méchin, *Histoire de l'Armée Allemande 1919–1930* (two vols., 1938). See also Karl Loewenstein, *Hitler's Germany,—the Nazi Background to War* (1939). An essay deserving special consideration is C. Malaparte's *Coup d'État* (1932).

18. See for this problem (as far as the Soviet Union is concerned), Leon Trotsky, *My Life* (1930); John Wheeler-Bennett, *Brest-Litovsk, The Forgotten Peace* (1938); T. A. Taracouzio, *War and Peace in Soviet Diplomacy* (1940); Erich Wollenberg, *The Red Army: A Study of the Growth of Soviet Imperialism* (1940); D. F. White, *The Growth of the Red Army* (1943); and the chapter by Earle cited in note 16 above. For the Hitler army and what preceded it, see note 17. The common aspect of the army in the totalitarian scheme of things is brilliantly analyzed in Sigmund Neumann's *Permanent Revolution* (1942), Chs. VIII and IX. He shows how war is related to the "boundless dynamics" of a totalitarian dictatorship.

19. Besides the general studies on the National Socialist dictatorship, see especially John Wheeler-Bennett, *Wooden Titan* (1936), Part III; Arnold Brecht, *Prelude to Silence* (1944); and Hans Ernest Fried, *The Guilt of the German Army* (1942), which, although somewhat in-

fluenced by the passions of war, presented the crucial issues which have since been confirmed by the documentation developed in connection with the War Crimes trials. This vast material will yield much additional material awaiting systematic analysis.

20. In this connection, one might quote a sentence from Herring's book: "We can recognize the need of central controls and discipline without making these needs the central article of our faith. The point really is that a democracy to succeed must take for granted the social integration . . ." (p. 281). The rather extreme theme of Silas Bent McKinley, *Democracy and Military Power* (1934), that the military are necessarily the dominant class is diametrically opposed to this view and cannot be accepted for a constitutional democracy.

21. The enormous literature on disarmament cannot be cited here. For a convenient reference selection, see the article on disarmament in the *ESS*. The demilitarization aspect of the post-surrender policies of the Allies in Germany and Japan has been one of the least controversial so far. However, any withdrawal of the occupation troops will raise very difficult problems of re-armament unless international security forces have by that time grown sufficiently strong. The problem of these international military forces remains, at least for the time being, insoluble within the context of the United Nations. But the close collaboration developing in this field between Western European nations, reinforced by the Atlantic Pact, foreshadows some partial internationalization of the military establishments of these nations.

IV · *Peace and Diplomacy*

REMARKS

There has been a striking output of general treatments of foreign policy in the last few years. Apart from the discussions in the leading texts on international relations and world politics, four books may be mentioned as representing dominant trends: Nicholas J. Spykman, *American Strategy in World Politics* (1942); Walter Lippmann, *U.S. Foreign Policy: Shield of the Republic* (1943); Sumner Welles, *The Time for Decision* (1944); and Charles A. Beard, *American Foreign Policy in the Making* (1946). In addition there are some very forceful statements of the case for world government, such as Emory Reeves, *The Anatomy of Peace* (1945), and Cord Meyer, Jr., *Peace or Anarchy* (1947). See also the books on federation and related subjects cited below, Chapter XI. To these might be added the Harris Foundation round table, entitled *The World Community* (1948), edited by Quincy Wright.

Among the many treatments of diplomacy in all modern languages, the political scientist will find three most suggestive. These are: Ernest Satow, *Guide to Diplomatic Practice* (1917); Jules Cambon, *Le Diplomate* (1922); and Albrecht Mendelssohn-Bartholdi, *Diplomatie* (1927). Harold Nicolson's biography of his father, *Sir Arthur Nicolson* (1930, published in the United States under the title *Portrait of a Diplomatist*), is also most instructive, as is the same author's *Peacemaking, 1919* (1933). Regarding the general problem of democracy and diplomacy, there are also a considerable number of works; among the more important ones in English may be noted: Arthur Ponsonby, *Democracy and Diplomacy* (1915); George Young, *Diplomacy Old and New* (1921); P. S. Reinsch, *Secret Diplomacy* (1922); Aubrey L. Kennedy, *Old Diplomacy and New* (1922); DeWitt C. Poole, *The Conduct of Foreign Relations under Modern Democratic Conditions* (1924). These and other points of view are considered in another volume by the author, *Foreign Policy in the Making* (1938). Since that time, three very suggestive volumes have appeared, all especially concerned with this problem in the United States: Kenneth Colegrove, *The American Senate and World Peace* (1944), Joseph M. Jones, *A Modern Foreign Policy or the United States* (1944); and Robert Bendiner, *The Riddle of the State Department* (1942). See also *How Foreign Policy Is Made* (1949) by Kurt L. London.

REFERENCES

1. The importance of the distinction between policy determination and negotiation is emphasized by Harold Nicolson, *Curzon: The Last Phase, 1919–1925* (1934), in a terminal essay containing "some remarks on the practice of diplomacy." It is an old distinction, but in

constant need of re-emphasizing. D. J. Hill, *A History of Diplomacy in the International Development of Europe* (1905), Vol. III, gives significant critical comments on the failure of Louis XIV (pp. 282 ff.) and Frederick the Great (pp. 537 ff.), but the judgments expressed in the text are *communis opinio doctorum*. For Louis XIV, see G. Pagès, *La Monarchie d'Ancien Régime en France* (1928), pp. 134 ff. For Frederick the Great, see G. Küntzel, "Die Drei Grossen Hohenzollern," in *Meister der Politik*, ed. E. Marcks and K. von Müller (1923), Vol. II, pp. 391 ff. Re Napoleon, see J. H. Rose, *The Life of Napoleon I* (1901–1924), Vol. II, pp. 213 ff.

2. See the general treatments cited above, and also Hans J. Morgenthau, *Politics among Nations: The Struggle for Power and Peace* (1948). They all assume, more or less explicitly, that a coherent foreign policy is possible. Lippmann goes so far as to suggest that the foreign policy be adopted first (by whom?) and that the people be then somehow brought into line.

3. A brilliant example of the "art of negotiating" is offered in Crane Brinton's treatment of Talleyrand's diplomacy, *The Lives of Talleyrand* (1936), pp. 166 ff. The general problem of this paragraph has been taken up at greater length in C. J. Friedrich, *Foreign Policy in the Making* (1938).

4. For the Franco-Russian alliance see W. L. Langer's study, *The Franco-Russian Alliance, 1890–1894* (1929), p. 399. For the problem of Anglo-German relations see F. Meinecke, *Geschichte des deutsch-englischen Bundesproblems, 1890–1901* (1930).

5. For the problem of official language, see Satow, op. cit. Vol. I, pp. 58 ff. See *New York Times*, January 28, 1934, for the Soviet remark; for Curzon's breach, see Nicolson, op. cit. p. 358.

6. The relevant sections of Ch. XIX, "Responsible Government Service," should be consulted here. See Otto Krauske, "Die Entwicklung der ständigen Diplomatie," *Staats- und sozialwissenschaftliche Forschungen*, Vol. XXIII (1885). For a general summary, see F. L. Schuman, *International Politics* (1933 and later editions). See also D. J. Hill, *History of Diplomacy in the International Development of Europe* (1905–1914), particularly Vol. I, pp. 359–360.

7. Besides the works by Nicolson, see Cecil Spring-Rice, *The Letters and Friendships of Sir Cecil Spring-Rice* (1929); *The Life and Letters of Walter Hines Page* (ed. B. J. Hendrick, 1923); the memoirs of Stimson and Byrnes, as well as of Robert Sherwood; *Roosevelt and Hopkins* (1948) reproduces the atmosphere of the newer international politics from on high. The worm's view, if one can put it that way, of the lowly consular official is realistically and humorously presented by Donald Dunham, *Envoy Unextraordinary* (1944). Another work of unusual interest, showing the frustrations of the professional diplomat under democratic traditions, is Ambassador Joseph C. Grew's *Ten Years in Japan: A Contemporary Record* (1944); A. Whitney Griswold's *The Far Eastern Policy of the United States* (1938) provides the setting.

8. For this problem see Cmd. 6420 (1943), "Proposals for the Reform of the Foreign Service," and the critical article by Ivor Thomas, M.P., "The Reform of the Foreign Service," *The Political Quarterly*, Vol. XIV (1943).

9. This issue was at the core of the protracted controversy regarding the relation between the State Department and the organization to be set up for European Reconstruction. See Seymour Harris, *The European Recovery Program* (1948).

10. See H. K. Norton, *Foreign Office Organization* (1929); and more recently J. Rives Childs, *The American Foreign Service* (1948), which contains the text of the Foreign Service Act of 1946; and three papers in *The Public Service and University Education* (ed. J. E. McLean, 1943), Part III. The work by Bendiner, cited above in "Remarks," contains a highly critical appraisal. Dunham's study, above, note 7, should be compared for a more sympathetic view of the facts. A more extensive, comparative study of why the foreign service in all democratic countries is so unpopular is urgently needed.

11. See Martin Hill, *Immunities and Privileges of International Officials* (1947); the earlier study by Egon Ranshofen-Wertheimer, *The International Secretariat* (1946); and Chester Purvis, *The Internal Administration of the International Secretariat* (1946). I profited from helpful advice by Dr. Daniel S. Cheever, Chairman of the International Affairs program at Harvard University.

12. A fuller treatment of this point will be found in the author's *Foreign Policy in the Making* (1938), particularly pp. 116–133. Edward H. Carr, *The Twenty-Years' Crisis* (1939), was generally hailed at the time, although it presented a counsel of despair in face of the totalitarian challenge of the Fascists; the same author more recently has counseled appeasement of the Soviet Union. For the problem of the balance of power, see also Spykman's general treatment, cited above, especially pp. 20 ff., and the broad historical treatment in Charles Dupuis, *Le principe d'équilibre et le concert européen de la paix de Westphalie à l'acte d'Algeciras* (1909); Dupuis stresses the use made of the concept of a balance of power as a tool of negotiation. An interesting historical study by Alfred Vagts deserves notice: "The United States and the Balance of Power," *Journal of Politics*, Nov. 1941.

13. The passages quoted from Lippmann, op. cit., are found on pp. 50 f., 149 ff., 164 ff., 169 f.

14. Hans J. Morgenthau, op. cit., takes the view that the struggle for power and peace go hand in hand; like Spinoza, he seems to feel that "the big fish devour the little fish by natural right," a view which certainly can be supported by a great deal of historical experience.

V · *Prosperity, the Police, and Legislation*

REMARKS

Obviously, a general bibliography for this chapter would have to cover the entire field of modern economic history, manifestly an impossible task. Reference may be had to any one of the more recent and competent texts in the field. I like G. M. Trevelyan's *English Social History* (1942) for its attention to governmental and administrative aspects. In addition to this, attention may specially be called to Eli Heckscher's masterly all-European treatment of *Mercantilism* (1935). It is a veritable monument to the cosmopolitan scholarship of the smaller countries of Europe. To it may be added four somewhat controversial and yet very significant works: W. Cunningham, *The Progress of Capitalism in England* (1916), and his *The Growth of English Industry and Commerce* (5th ed., 1910–1912); W. J. Ashley, *Introduction to English Economic History* (1888–1925); and Werner Sombart, *Der Moderne Kapitalismus* (5th ed., 1922), particularly Vol. I, 1, pp. 334 ff. Besides these, Gustav Schmoller's Introduction to the first volume of *Acta Borussica* must be noted, as well as several of his essays reprinted in *Umrisse, Abhandlungen und Untersuchungen* (1898).

For general bibliography on legislation, see below, Chs. XIV, XVI, and XVII. On the police the literature is not very satisfactory from the standpoint of comparative government. It tends to be somewhat formalistic, following the older European tradition. Raymond B. Fosdick's *European Police Systems* (1915) and *American Police Systems* (1920) are still standard works. In addition, Cmd. 3297 (1929), "Police Powers and Procedure," might be mentioned. The "police state" of the mercantilist-cameralist period is well presented, theoretically speaking, in A. W. Small's *The Cameralists* (1909).

REFERENCES

1. This is the view of Jacob Viner in his recent article cited above (Ch. I, note 6), "Power versus Plenty . . ." (1949), but as my passages show (unaltered since 1937), it is not exactly novel. On the other hand, I sympathize with Viner's desire to make the point emphatically, in the light of such statements as that of Cunningham: "The mercantile system is concerned solely with man as a being who pursues national power." See Section 136, *The Growth of English Industry and Commerce*, by William Cunningham. The entire controversy of the economic (materialistic) interpretation of history clearly is bound up with the few sentences of this paragraph. Suffice it, in lieu of references, to remind the reader that such an interpretation is not peculiar to Karl Marx, as is now often popularly assumed, but is found throughout the later eighteenth and the nineteenth century, and has become very common in the United States.

2. For an exposition of ideas of organic growth, see H. von Treitschke, *Politics* (1916), Vol. I, pp. 15 ff., 45 ff., or Seeley, *Introduction to Political Science* (1896), pp. 43–44 and 53–76, as illus-

trations of what nineteenth-century historians are full of. ⌐Friedrich Ratzel, in his *Politische Geographie* (3d ed., 1923), has given an elaborate exposition of this doctrine, pp. 59 ff. Ratzel's ideas were elaborated by the school of "geopolitics," more especially by General Haushofers and provided a link with the vitalistic superstitions of the Nazis and Fascists. See, besides the works of General Haushofer and his school, analyzed by Andreas Dorpalen, *The World of General Haushofer* (1942), Derwent Whittlesey, *The Earth and the State* (1939)—much better on the earth than on the state. See also Johannes Mattern, *Geopolitik* (1942). Though not explicitly so stated, the conception of an "organic fate" is equally present in Halford J. Mackinder's work. See *Democratic Ideals and Reality* (1919), Ch. II and V. His followers, such as E. M. Earle and Walter Lippmann, show this as clearly as the geopoliticians. The controversy concerning the organic nature of groups is very extended. See Francis W. Coker, *Organismic Theories of the State* (1910), and W. Y. Elliott, *The Pragmatic Revolt in Politics* (1928), particularly Parts IV and V. For John of Salisbury, see John Dickinson, *The Statesman's Book of John of Salisbury* (1927), Introduction, particularly pp. xx–xxi.

3. The observations contained in this paragraph have been a recurrent theme in the writings of monarchists. The French Royalists under Charles Maurras have been particularly emphatic. See his *Enquête sur la Monarchie* (1909). See also Bolingbroke's *The Patriot King* (1749), and Frederick the Great (of Prussia), *Anti-Machiavel* (1741). It should not be forgotten, however, that monarchical society has no monopoly upon furthering the development of culture. Witness Athens, Florence, or Nuremberg.

4. The earlier conceptions here alluded to are reflected in various features of the law of the "police power." Of this, Walton H. Hamilton has poignantly observed that "it is one of two balanced terms (the other being 'due process') which make up a formula for constitutionality." See Ernst Freund, *The Police Power, Public Policy, and Constitutional Rights* (1904), for a searching study of the classical doctrine. For the historical evolution, see for the general ideas of this paragraph G. Schmoller, "Der Deutsche Beamtenstaat vom 16. bis 18. Jahrhundert," *Jahrbuch für Gesetzgebung, Verwaltung und Volkswirtschaft*, Vol. XVIII; and Otto Hintze's article cited above, Ch. II, *Remarks*. See also the author's article, "Some Thoughts on the Politics of Government Control," in *Journal of Social Philosophy*, Vol. I (1936), pp. 122 ff.

5. For the rise of the legislative function, see Charles H. McIlwain, *The High Court of Parliament and Its Supremacy* (1910), especially pp. 46 ff. For Bodin's views and their relation to economics, see R. Chauviré, *Jean Bodin* (1914), particularly Book IV, Ch. III.

6. For the *Ordonnances du Roi*, see Esmein's *Cours Elémentaire d'Histoire du Droit Français* (1903), pp. 774 ff., and the official publication of the *ordonnances* by the Imprimerie Royale. The "progressive" economic policy of Tudor absolutism is treated in all the general works cited at the outset. To these may be added, for documentation, R. H. Tawney and E. E. Power, *Tudor Economic Documents* (1924). It was the economic progressivism of absolutism which aroused the admiration of Schmoller and the historical school and led them to erroneous political inferences. See also G. M. Trevelyan, loc. cit. pp. 190 ff.

7. See Eli Heckscher, *Mercantilism*, Vol. I, Preface, for a lucid discussion of the different views taken and some of the literature. More specific is Philip W. Buck's *The Politics of Mercantilism* (1942), but the last chapter, "Mercantilism and Totalitarianism," is overdrawn. The quotations from Montchrétien and *The British Merchant* are found ibid. Vol. II, p. 187. Note also the interesting recent study by Lawrence A. Harper, *The English Navigation Laws: A 17th Century Experiment in Social Engineering* (1939), giving a good sketch of "The Mercantile Mind" in Ch. II. But why deny *all* connection between mercantilism and planning?

8. The commercial policy of the various countries, of course, has been treated in numerous monographs. Readily accessible sources of reference are Jacob Viner, "English Theories of Foreign Trade before Adam Smith," in *Journal of Political Economy*, Vol. XXXVIII (1930), pp. 249 ff. and 404 ff.; and Charles W. Cole, *French Mercantilist Doctrines before Colbert* (1931). For Colbert, see P. Clement, *Histoire de Colbert* (3d ed., 1892). To these should now be added Walton Hamilton's discussion of the impact of mercantilist thinking upon the makers of the American Constitution, in his and Douglas Adair's *The Power to Govern* (1937). Whether one

must accept the mercantilist view because the Constitutional Convention held it depends upon one's readiness to emphasize the "intention of the framers" as a basis for constitutional interpretation. Hamilton's argument seems more nearly a *reductio ad absurdum*.

9. Among authorities who share the view here taken I note G. M. Trevelyan, who expresses the opinion that the influence of the chartered trading companies on English government and politics was great; op. cit. pp. 201, 215 ff. See E. Levasseur, *Histoire du Commerce de la France* (1911–1912), and the works cited in the *Remarks*. For special companies: William H. Price, *The English Patents of Monopoly* (1906), and Paul Kaeppelin, *La Compagnie des Indes Orientales* (1908), etc.

10. See George L. Beer, *The Old Colonial System, 1660–1754* (1912), and Heckscher, op. cit., who rightly emphasized Adam Smith's position. See *Wealth of Nations*, particularly Book IV. See also Lipson, *Economic History of England*, Vol. II (1934).

11. These problems are the core of Edmund Burke's famous indictment of Warren Hastings in 1788, *Works* (Boston, 1839), Vols. VI–VIII, now skillfully selected from and provided with running commentary by Ross J. S. Hoffman and Paul Levack, *Burke's Politics* (1949), pp. 233–276.

12. For these problems of planning and socialization, see Ch. XXIII, below.

13. Arthur R. Burns, *Money and Monetary Policy in Early Times* (1927); also A. von Luschin und Ebengreuth, *Allgemeine Münzkunde und Geldgeschichte des Mittelalters und der neueren Zeit* (1904).

14. For the quotation, see William Cunningham, *The Growth of English Industry and Commerce* (5th ed., 1910–1912), Vol. II, p. 434.

15. See H. Brougham, *An Inquiry into the Colonial Policy of the European Powers* (1803), and Beer, op. cit.; S. L. Mims, *Colbert's West Indian Policy* (1912); C. G. Haring, *Trade and Navigation between Spain and the Indies in the Time of the Hapsburgs* (1918); Alfred Zimmermann, *Die Kolonialpolitik der Niederländer* (1903); A. Duchêne, *La Politique Coloniale de la France* (1928).

16. See Klaus E. Knorr, *British Colonial Theories, 1570–1850* (1944), especially Part I. The quotes are on p. 126.

17. See, besides Knorr, op. cit., J. S. Furnival, *Colonial Policy and Practice: A Comparative Study of Burma and Netherlands India* (1948), especially Ch. VIII, and the general sketch of imperialism above, Ch. III.

VI · Justice and the Judicial Function

REMARKS

The American literature on the political phase of judicial methods was not very extensive until the Supreme Court fight in 1937. However, Charles Warren's justly famous *The Supreme Court in United States History* (rev. ed. 1937) described the many political issues in which the American high court has been involved. The standard legal histories give little aid in connection with this question, but W. S. Holdsworth, *A History of English Law* (3d ed., 1922), Vol. I, and Frederick Pollock and F. W. Maitland, *History of English Law* (2d ed., 1899), cannot be neglected, nor can the relevant sections in A. Esmein, *Histoire du Droit Français* (8th ed., revue par H. Nézard, 1927–1928), and other continental works, such as Heinrich Brunner, *Deutsche Rechtsgeschichte* (2d ed., 1906 and 1928). To these may be added three recent works of special application: Roscoe Pound, *The Formative Era of American Law* (1939), idem, *Organization of Courts* (1940), and R. M. Jackson, *The Machinery of Justice in England* (1940). See also P. M. Viollet, *Droit Public: Histoire des Institutions Politiques et Administratives de la France* (1890–1903). Literature on recent judicial methods has tended to explore the psychological and sociological implications of judicial techniques. Justice Cardozo's *The Nature of the Judicial Process* (1921) is perhaps the most widely known, but his more recent papers, published under the title *The Growth of the Law* (1924), should be added. See also *Law and Politics: Occasional Papers of Felix Frankfurter, 1913–1938* (ed. MacLeish and Pritchard, 1939). Edward S. Robinson's

Law and the Lawyers (1935), particularly Chs. VIII–XII, gives a thorough analysis of judicial methods in the light of modern psychology. There is also the analysis of German problems in Martin Beradt, *Der Deutsche Richter* (1930), and Friedrich Dessauer, *Recht, Richtertum und Ministerialbüreaukratie* (1928), and the broader comparative treatment by R. C. K. Ensor, *Courts and Judges in France, Germany and England* (1933). See also the bibliography to Ch. XII.

REFERENCES

1. Among recent treatments of "justice" one might mention Roscoe Pound, *Law and Morals* (2d ed., 1926); Max Ascoli, *La Giustizia* (1930); Georges Gurvitch, *L'idee du droit social* (1932); and Gustav Radbruch, *Rechtsphilosophie* (3d ed., 1932), though none agrees with the functionalist position taken here. Much closer is Julius Stone's *The Province and Function of Law: Law as Logic, Justice, and Social Control, A Study in Jurisprudence* (1946), an outstanding contribution.

2. On primitive government, anthropology is producing an increasing literature which is confused in its terminology, unfortunately, because of the failure of political scientists and anthropologists to work together. However, efforts along such lines are being made. The standard sources of information remain: Sir J. G. Frazer, *The Golden Bough* (1890); Robert H. Lowie, *Primitive Society* (1920); and A. M. Hocart, *Kingship* (1927). On the judicial functions of parliament, following the older literature (Thomas Smith, etc.), see Josef Redlich, *The Procedure of the House of Commons* (tr. A. E. Steinthal; 1908); and Charles H. McIlwain, *The High Court of Parliament and Its Supremacy* (1910), where the problem is developed in its ramifications. For the relation of parliament to the courts see William Stubbs, *Constitutional History of England* (1874–1878). For the judicial functions of the French parliament see the recent study by Paul R. Doolin, *The Fronde* (1935), particularly Chs. I and VI.

3. See Charles H. McIlwain, op. cit., particularly Ch. II. For literature on the Roman law phase, see above, Ch. I, note 12. On Bracton, see Holdsworth, op. cit. Vol. II, pp. 230 ff., where the controversial questions of the extent of his "Romanism" are reviewed. See also Max Radin, *A Manual of Roman Law* (1926). For Coke's claim, see Roscoe Pound's *The Spirit of the Common Law* (1921), p. 61.

4. The issue of a "higher law" is crucial in any jurisprudence, as it is the core of the problem of the relation of law and justice. There have been quite a few recent discussions which have been surveyed and analyzed by Charles Grove Haines, *The Revival of Natural Law Concepts* (1930). For a radical criticism of this approach see Hans Kelsen, *General Theory of Law and State* (1945). Much sociological jurisprudence is really looking for a naturalistic higher law. For Sir Thomas Smith, see *English Commonwealth*, II, ii, and II, v–vii.

5. Dr. Bonham's case is found in *Famous State Trials*, or in *Reports*, Vol. VIII. See also the comments in McIlwain, op. cit. pp. 147–148. Regarding the statement of Bacon, see *The Works of Francis Bacon* (1842), Vol. II, p. 235. See also Bacon's whole memorial on codification, ibid. pp. 229 ff. See also S. E. Thorne, "Dr. Bonham's Case," *Law Quarterly Review* (1938), and T. F. T. Plucknett, "Bonham's Case and Judicial Review," *Harvard Law Review* (1926).

6. On the judge's conflict with prerogative, see Francis D. Wormuth, *The Royal Prerogative, 1603–1649* (1939). On Coke, see *Edward Coke, Oracle of the Law*, by Hastings Lyon and Herman Block (1929). For the King's statements see *The Works of Francis Bacon*, Vol. II, pp. 493–494, as well as *Coke on Littleton*, § 97b. Charles Fairman has given us a thorough analysis in his "The Retirement of Federal Judges," *Harvard Law Review*, Vol. LI, No. 3 (1938).

7. Bacon, *Works*, II, 493.

8. See *International Conference on Military Trials, London, 1945* (report by the United States representative, Robert H. Jackson). See also *History of the United Nations War Crimes Commission* (1945).

9. On *stare decisis*, see the brilliant article by Herman Oliphant, "A Return to *Stare Decisis*," in *American Law School Review*, Vol. VI, pp. 215 ff.; and K. N. Llewellyn, *Bramble Bush* (privately printed, 1930), pp. 63 ff. See also the author's "Remarks on Llewellyn's View of Law, Official

Behavior, and Political Science," in *PSQ*, vol. L (1935). Further interesting reflections are found in Edward S. Robinson, *Law and the Lawyers* (1935), p. 257, and in Max Radin, "Case Law and *Stare Decisis*—Concerning Präjudizienrecht in America," 33 *Columbia Law Review*, pp. 199 ff. Cardozo's remark is found in *The Growth of the Law* (1924), p. 62.

10. See Ensor, op. cit., and the able review of it by Wolfgang Kraus in *Harvard Law Review*, Vol. 48, pp. 873 ff. For a rationalistic theory, see A. L. Goodhart, *Precedent in English and Continental Law* (1934), and Roscoe Pound's review of it in *Harvard Law Review*, Vol. 48, pp. 863 ff.

11. The basic issue was discussed with great learning by Charles H. McIlwain, in *Foreign Affairs* (1936), in an article entitled "Government by Law." The as yet unprinted trial records of the "Justices' Case" may be consulted in MS form; note especially the decision itself, however, and the able discussion of the range of problems involved, offered by Charles M. LaFollette, in *Information Bulletin, OMGUS*, Nos. 138–142 June–August, 1948). See also John B. Mason, "The Judicial System of the Nazi Party," *APSR*, Feb. 1944.

12. For this and the following paragraph, see the three striking articles, "Legal Profession and Legal Education," by H. D. Hazeltine, Max Radin, and A. A. Berle, Jr., and the literature cited there. Special mention may be made of Frederick Pollock, *The Origins of the Inns of Court* (1931), and T. F. T. Plucknett, "The Place of the Legal Profession in the History of English Law," in *Law Quarterly Review*, Vol. 48, pp. 328 ff. Concerning the relation of bench and bar, see Charles A. Warren, *A History of the American Bar* (1911), and Thorstein Veblen, *The Theory of Business Enterprise* (1919), Ch. VIII. For the Act of Settlement, see Holdsworth, op. cit. Vol. VI, pp. 230 ff.

13. Concerning the case of the miller, see Rudolf Stammler, *Deutsches Rechtsleben in Alter und Neuer Zeit* (1932), § XXXI, "Der Prozess des Müllers Arnold, 1779–1787," pp. 413 ff.

14. The reforms of Cocceji are treated in Max Springer, *Die Coccejische Justizreform* (1914).

15. The problem of the relationship between courts and classes has been much emphasized by Marxist writers. See, for example, Ernst Fraenkel, *Zur Soziologie der Klassenjustiz* (1927), and the work of Beradt, cited above. It is evident in Stammler's study of the miller's case. In the United States this problem of special prejudice of the judges has been brought forward often in connection with the discussion of the Supreme Court's constitutional review (see below, Ch. XII), and recent attacks have focused renewed attention upon it. A forceful statement of this point of view is Edouard Lambert, *Le Gouvernement des Juges et la Lutte contre la Législation Sociale aux États-Unis* (1921); Charles A. Beard, *The Supreme Court and the Constitution* (1912), F. J. Goodnow, *Social Reform and the Constitution* (1911), and John R. Commons, *The Legal Foundations of Capitalism* (1924), have leaned to similar interpretations, as has Veblen, op. cit.

16. The literature on administrative law is very extensive. See A. V. Dicey, *Law of the Constitution* (8th ed., 1926), particularly Ch. XII. Rejecting the now admittedly untenable position of Dicey, two books are of primary interest: John Dickinson's *Administrative Justice and the Supremacy of Law in the United States* (1927), and William A. Robson, *Justice and Administrative Law* (1928). See also James Hart, *An Introduction to Administrative Law, with Selected Cases* (1940), and J. R. Pennock, *Administration and the Rule of Law* (1941). See the highly authoritative article by Ernst Freund on the subject in the *ESS*, and the literature cited there. See also F. F. Blachly's *Administrative Legislation and Adjudication* (1934), and the pamphlet of the American Bar Association on the subject. The quotation is found in Harold Laski's "Administrative Tribunals" in the *ESS*.

17. For the Conseil d'État, see authorities on French constitutional and administrative law, such as Esmein, Duguit, Hauriou.

18. The quotation is found in Robson, op. cit. pp. 324 f. See also James M. Landis, *The Administrative Process* (1939), and, more recently, Joseph Chamberlain, Noel T. Dowing, and Paul R. Hays, *The Judicial Function in Federal Administrative Agencies* (1942).

VII · *The Making of a Constitution as a Political Process*

REMARKS

As stated in the text, much of the thought of this chapter is derived from the so-called classical constitutionalists of the seventeenth and eighteenth centuries, for they stated several of the most important hypotheses. Herman Finer has a chapter on constitutions, but it is built upon the vague concept of the constitution as "a system of fundamental political institutions." The same is true of most French and German writing, which is essentially legal in nature, and therefore preoccupied with the problems arising from the distinction between ordinary law and constitutional law. This is a distinction of no mean importance; but the political scientists' problem is that of distinguishing between constitutional and unconstitutional government. This problem was more clearly envisaged by the earlier writers than by nineteenth-century thinkers. An outstanding contribution recently published is F. M. Watkins' *The Political Tradition of the West* (1948) which links constitutionalism with the emphasis on law in government as the distinctive feature of Western political life and thought. Mention should be made of W. H. Hamilton and Douglas Adair, *The Power to Govern: the Constitution—Then and Now* (1937), which develops the theme that the American constitution is inadequate for controlling the "unruly economic order." Charles H. McIlwain's *Constitutionalism and the Changing World* (1939) and his *Constitutionalism, Ancient and Modern* (1940) are fundamentalist treatments. Surveys are found in H. M. Clokie, *The Origin and Nature of Constitutional Government* (1936), and John A. Hawgood, *Modern Constitutions Since 1787* (1939). Many important angles of constitutionalism are explored in the collective volume, *The Constitution Reconsidered* (1938), edited for the American Historical Association by Conyers Read.

REFERENCES

1. The textbooks are full of this wearisome discussion about written and unwritten constitutions, or rather of the distinction between constitutions embodied in one document and those in many documents. The most definitive discussion, perhaps, is found in James Bryce, *Constitutions* (1905), but see also the article, "Constitutions," by Howard Lee McBain in the *ESS*, Vol. IV. See also H. W. Horwill, *The Usages of the American Constitution* (1925), and H. L. McBain's *The Living Constitution* (1927).

2. Ideologically speaking, a further development of these issues may be found in the author's *The New Belief in the Common Man* (1942), especially Chs. II and VI.

3. See Charles H. McIlwain, *The High Court of Parliament and Its Supremacy* (1910), particularly pp. 75 ff., 82 ff., 286 ff. The same point was stated earlier but much less satisfactorily by Julius Hatschek, *Englisches Staatsrecht* (1905). See also the survey in D. L. Keir, *The Constitutional History of Modern Britain, 1485–1937* (1938).

4. For the changing pattern of this "personal sphere," see the author's article "Rights, Liberties, Freedoms" in *University of Pennsylvania Law Review*, Vol. 91, p. 312 (1942), as well as Osmond K. Fraenkel's fine study *Our Civil Liberties* (1944). A more specialized but still an important contribution is Louis A. Warsoff's *Equality and the Law* (1938). Note also the contributions of Carl Becker, Max Lerner, and Robert E. Cushman to *Safeguarding Civil Liberty Today* (1945). The American Law Institute's work in this field and its several publications also deserve mention here.

5. In recent years a vast amount of historical research has produced a juster estimate of medieval politics and has brought to light the strictly constitutional nature of much of it. The list of works which may be cited is a long one; perhaps it will suffice to refer to William Stubbs, *English Constitutional History* (1874–1878), which is, of course, outstanding. The general pattern is explored in Otto von Gierke, *Das deutsche Genossenschaftsrecht* (1868), particularly Vols. I and II, which in part has been translated, and has been published with a learned introduction by Ernest Barker, *Natural Law and the Theory of Society* (1934). To these should be added Charles H. McIlwain, *The Growth of Political Thought in the West* (1932), particularly Chs. V,

VI, and VII; R. W. and A. J. Carlyle, *A History of Medieval Political Theory in the West* (1903), particularly Vols. I and III; and Henry O. Taylor, *The Medieval Mind* (1911), passim.

6. The literature on Cromwell is rapidly increasing. This we may owe to the drift toward dictatorship. But Cromwell wanted a constitution; our present dictators do not. See Wilbur C. Abbot's monumental collection of documents, *Writings and Speeches of Oliver Cromwell*, 4 vols. (1937–1947) which contains much penetrating comment and an exhaustive bibliography. See also Wilbur K. Jordan, *The Development of Religious Toleration in England* (1932–1940), especially Vol. III, Ch. II. Very significant also is *Puritanism and Liberty: Being the Army Debates (1647–1649)* . . . (selected and edited by A. S. Woodhouse, 1939).

7. For a contrasting view see R. M. MacIver's "The Philosophical Background of the Constitution" in *Journal of Social Philosophy*, Vol. III (1938), and his broader treatment in *Leviathan and the People* (1939). MacIver retains the state concept. At this point, the discussion in Ch. I should be consulted.

VIII · *The Constituent Power, the Amending Power, and Revolution*

REMARKS

The general problem of constitutional and political change, and of revolution, has received increasing attention in recent years. Aristotle's classic doctrine, however, has not usually served as the point of departure. Nor has a really comprehensive inventory of historical experience, such as probably underlies Aristotle's theory, been attempted. But even partial comparisons have yielded some striking results, like Crane Brinton's *The Anatomy of Revolution* (1938), Pitirim Sorokin's *Sociology of Revolutions* (1925), and Eugen Rosenstock-Hüssy's *Die Europäischen Revolutionen* (1931), presented in a new form in English under the title *Out of Revolution* (1938). R. B. Merriman's strictly historical *Six Contemporaneous Revolutions, 1640–1660* (1938) also is interesting. G. S. Pettee's *The Process of Revolution* (1938) is more specifically concerned with discovering verifiable generalizations. The work of Hegel, Comte, and Marx suggests that modern theories have been inclined to take it for granted that change is change in a certain direction rather than change in any cyclical sense. Besides these, a large body of material regarding revolutions was gathered by writers in the sixteenth and seventeenth centuries who were interested in the "right of revolution." But this material is of little value from the standpoint of modern critical historical scholarship. Nevertheless, it suggests some data not ordinarily covered by modern works. Another body of uncritical dogmatic writings is offered by Socialists and Marxists. These authors attempt to "explain" revolutions in terms of economic changes, a point of view which is also found in certain rather more popular contemporary accounts, such as that of George Soule, *The Coming American Revolution* (1934), Part I, "The Nature of Revolution." Much uncritical use has been made recently of the word *revolution* by popular writers in speaking of the Fascist or Nazi "revolution," which is, correctly speaking, not a revolution, except in the purely governmental sense, but rather a counterrevolution. Concerning this, see the author's "The Nazi Dictatorship in Action" in *Democracy Is Different* (ed. Carl Wittke, 1941).

More recently, further significant contributions have come to the author's attention. Harold Laski, in *Reflections on the Revolution of Our Time* (1943), attempted a re-assessment of the Russian revolution in terms of the Russian, German, and Italian versions of its counterrevolution. Sigmund Neumann, in *Permanent Revolution* (1942), did the same, but from the standpoint of traditional liberalism rather than of socialism. James Burnham, in *The Managerial Revolution* (1941), from still another standpoint, sought to find a synthesis of Sovietism, Fascism, and Nazism, as well as of parallel trends elsewhere in terms of world-wide ascendancy of a new class, the managers whom Arthur Koestler, with poetic license, dramatized as the commissars in *The Yogi and the Commissar* (1945). Lately the idea of a "multiple revolution" has come to the fore; we are in danger of broadening the concept of revolution to include every major change in society.

REFERENCES

1. Internal plebiscites are vitally different from international plebiscites which are employed to determine changes of "sovereignty," to use the language of international law. The international plebiscite always offers the voter a real alternative, when for example it asks him whether he wishes the Saar, for example, to be French or German. See below, Ch. XXV, for references.

2. For the *Instrument*, see Samuel Rawson Gardiner, *Constitutional Documents* (2d ed., 1899), pp. 405 ff. See also Gardiner's summary and comments in the Introduction, pp. liii ff. For Cromwell's speeches, see T. Carlyle, *Oliver Cromwell's Letters and Speeches* (1849). The first quotation is found on pp. 423 f. of Vol. II, the second and third on pp. 424 and 425. The following sentences are from p. 433. See Abbott, op. cit.

3. See Karl Loewenstein, "Opposition and Public Opinion under the Dictatorship of Napoleon the First," *Social Research*, IV (1937). A. Esmein, *Eléments de Droit Constitutionnel Français et Comparé* (8th ed., revue par H. Nézard, 1927–1928), Vol. I, pp. 449 ff.

4. It is very important to keep in mind that the "constituent power" as used here is not identical with the *pouvoir constituant* of French constitutional law, which corresponds to the amending power of American constitutional law. See Esmein, op. cit. Vol. I, pp. 612 ff. However, the legal doctrine is confused, and often includes part of what is here called the constituent power, mingled with the amending power. The expression "constituent power" turns up in the preamble of the official English translation of the German Basic Law of 1949; it is in this case more nearly used in the sense suggested here. That sense is also implicit in the last article of that constitution, which reads: "This Basic Law shall become invalid on the day when a constitution adopted in a free decision by the German people comes into force" (art. 146). Concerning the Swiss constitution, see Ed. His, *Geschichte des neueren schweizerischen Staatsrechts* (1928), pp. 238 ff. and William E. Rappard, *L'Individu et l'État dans l'Évolution Constitutionelle de la Suisse* (1936), and his more recent study, *La Constitution Fédérale de la Suisse, 1848–1948* (1948), passim. The constitutional issue in the American revolution has been emphasized by Charles H. McIlwain, *The American Revolution, a Constitutional Interpretation* (1923).

5. The problem of constitutional change through usage has occupied English and American students for a long time. A convenient summary of some of the prevailing views is found in W. B. Munro, *The Government of the United States* (1919), Ch. V. See also Herbert W. Horwill, *The Usages of the American Constitution* (1925); Karl Loewenstein, *Erscheinungsformen der Verfassungsänderung* (1931) and Oliver P. Field, *The Effect of an Unconstitutional Statute* (1935). Some of the most fundamental aspects of this problem have been stated in the course of the controversy concerning the significance of a written constitution from Burke to Bryce. By far the most careful analysis of the Swiss referendum is offered by Axel Brusewitz' "Folkomröstningsinstitutet i den Schweiziska Demokratien," in *Statens Offentliga Utredningar* (1923). The figures are taken from A. L. Lowell, *Popular Government* (1930), Ch. XII.

6. James Bryce, *Studies in History and Jurisprudence* (1901), Vol. I, pp. 124 ff. The question as to whether an independent amending power existed in Germany was always considered in the extensive discussions on judicial review. See Fritz Morstein Marx, *Variationen über richterliche Zustandigkeit zur Prüfung der Rechtmässigkeit des Gesetzes* (1927), for a general survey.

7. For the background of the enabling act see Arnold Brecht, *Prelude to Silence* (1944), pp. 97 ff., where Brecht coins the intriguing phrase "sliding revolution" for this kind of subversion from within.

8. For a recent program of broad constitutional reform, see W. Y. Elliott, *The Need for Constitutional Reform* (1935). See also the more recent books by Henry Hazlitt, *A New Constitution Now* (1942), and A. Hehmeyer, *Time for Change* (1943).

9. Jane P. Clark, *The Rise of a New Federalism* (1938). See below, pp. 623, 625. The question has recently given rise to extensive constitutional controversy in America. Information on the working of Dutch political institutions is extraordinarily scant. A fair summary is found

in *Jahrbuch des öffentlichen Rechts*, Vol. XVIII (1930), and earlier accounts in Vols. VIII and XII. For England see F. A. Ogg, *English Government and Politics* (1930); for France see Esmein, *Droit Constitutionnel*, pp. 543 ff., and Gordon Wright, *The Reshaping of French Democracy* (1948).

10. The question of possible limitations on the amending power is very controversial. For France the matter is stated with acuteness by most writers on constitutional law. See, for example, Esmein, *Droit Constitutionnel*, Vol. II, pp. 543 ff. A more extended discussion is found in Charles Lefebure, *Études sur les Lois Constitutionnelles de 1875* (1882), pp. 217 ff. The general problem is considered by Egon Zweig, *Die Lehre vom Pouvois Constituant* (1909). The American situation is considered in an article by William Marbury, "The Limitations upon the Amending Power," *Harvard Law Review*, Vol. 33, pp. 323 ff. (1919), where it is argued that such limitations are valid. The opposite view is usually taken by political scientists; see Munro, op. cit. p. 192. Whatever may be the logic of the matter, it is improbable that an amendment to Article V of the Constitution would not be accepted. It is interesting that none other than Alexander Hamilton should have sounded the note of constitutional realism when he wrote: "Wise politicians will be cautious about fettering the government with restrictions that cannot be observed, because they know that every breach of the fundamental laws, though dictated by necessity, impairs that sacred reverence which ought to be maintained in the breast of rulers towards the constitution of a country, and forms a precedent for other breaches where the same plea of necessity does not exist at all, or is less urgent and palpable." (*The Federalist*, No. XXV.)

11. For Cromwell's remarks, see T. Carlyle, op. cit. p. 435; Arthur N. Holcombe, *State Government in the United States* (3d ed., 1931), pp. 129–130.

12. See Leon Trotsky, *Mein Leben* (1930), p. 320. For Rosenstock-Hüssy see the *Remarks* above.

13. See Crane Brinton, *Anatomy of Revolution* (1938), passim. Brinton perhaps overstresses the similarities of the French and Russian revolutions, and minimizes those aspects of the latter which are dealt with by Sigmund Neumann in *Permanent Revolution* (1942).

14. George Pettee, *The Process of Revolution* (1938). The case for interpreting the state as an association is made brilliantly in F. M. Watkins' *The State as a Concept of Political Science* (1936); the association is here described as sovereign. For a brief critical evaluation see *The New Belief in the Common Man* (1942), pp. 52 ff.

15. Walter Lippmann, *The Method of Freedom* (1934).

16. The transition is described by Frederick L. Schuman, *The Nazi Dictatorship* (1935), pp. 214 ff. Of course, all the general works on the Nazi system contain some discussion of this problem. The German constitutional issue is stated by Ulrich Scheuner, "Das Recht der Nationalen Revolution," in *Archiv des öffentlichen Rechts*, Vol. XXIV, particularly pp. 292 ff. Scheuner is silent regarding the exclusion of many deputies; he asserts the "legal" character of the revolution. Otto Köllreuter has outlined the prevailing view in his *Deutsches Verfassungsrecht: ein Grundriss* (1935). That such a controversy could arise suggests the reactionary aspect of this "revolution." For the prerevolutionary difficulties, see Herbert Kraus, *The Crisis of German Democracy* (1932), which gives a good summary. For the statement of Hugh Peters, see Carlyle, op. cit. Vol. I, pp. 353–354. See also Curzio Malaparte, *Coup d'État* (tr. Sylvia Saunders, 1932).

17. For the process of France's negative revolution, see Gordon Wright, *The Reshaping of French Democracy* (1948), and the source book by André Siegfried, Roger Seydoux, and others, *L'Année Politique* (1946). The anonymous publication by the Foundation of Foreign Affairs, *A Constitution for the Fourth Republic* (1947), contains a forthright analysis of the charter itself and a brief sketch of how the third negation, that of the Communists, may be explained; see also Henry W. Ehrmann, "Political Forces in Present-Day France," *Social Research*, vol. xv, pp. 146 ff. (1948). For the background of the Third Republic see D. W. Brogan, *The Development of Modern France* (1940), and Pierre Tissier, *The Government of Vichy* (1942).

18. On the Italian negative revolution see M. Salvadori-Paleotti, "The Patriotic Movement in Italy," *Foreign Affairs*, Vol. XXIV, pp. 539 ff. (1946), and G. A. Almond, "The Resistance and the Political Parties of Western Europe," *PSQ* (1947), Vol. 62, pp. 27 ff. We do not,

however, as yet have a detached study of the Free Italy movement, led by Count Carlo Sforza, and a vital factor in shaping a constituent group for Italy.

19. Among the many books on postwar Germany and the negative revolution of military occupation, mention should be made of: Harold Zink, *American Military Government in Germany* (1946); Hoyt Price and Karl Schorske, *The Problem of Germany* (1946); Russell Hill, *Struggle for Germany* (1947); Marshall Knappen, *And Call It Peace* (1947); and the author's article in *APSR*, Vol. 43, June and August (1949). The constitution itself is contained in an official "agreed Anglo-American" translation which bears no publisher or year, but which appeared in May 1949; it contains some bad errors, like "turnover tax" instead of "sales tax" for *Umsatzsteuer*; what is more, its terminology is apparently politically motivated, as when *Bund* is translated as federation, instead of as Union or Federal Union.

20. Aristotle's discussion occurs in the fifth book of the *Politics*. As modified in Polybius's treatment, Aristotle's theory greatly influenced Machiavelli and his followers.

IX · *The Constitution as a Political Force*

REMARKS

The central theme of this chapter is adumbrated and implied in constitutionalist writings since the English constitutionalists began merging the medieval idea of a fundamental law with the basic pattern of governmental organization. It is carried farther than political realities permit in Charles H. McIlwain's *Constitutionalism and the Changing World* (1938), though the case is most persuasively stated. Any emphasis upon civil liberties or human rights in constitutionalism implies this tendency. Hence the literature on civil liberties is important. This corpus, however, is not so complete as the popular view might lead one to believe. It is only in response to totalitarianism that the issue has recently become a burning one. See Charles Merriam, *The New Democracy and the New Despotism* (1940), for a broadly gauged discussion. Other writings from which the author has particularly profited include W. Y. Elliott's *The Pragmatic Revolt in Politics* (1928), particularly pp. 407 ff. and 470 ff., and Rudolf Smend's *Verfassung und Verfassungsrecht* (1928). The several articles in Part II of *The Constitution Reconsidered* (1938), but especially W. Y. Elliott's "The Constitution as the American Social Myth," are valuable in this connection. The Second World War saw a great crop of books, mostly brief, all dedicated to extolling the virtues of constitutional democracy as contrasted with Fascism. Poets, novelists, historians, and philosophers vied with one another in this task, and thus testified to the constitution as a political force. Archibald MacLeish, Thomas Mann, Charles E. Merriam, John R. Tunis, Carl L. Becker, Avery Craven, A. D. Lindsay, A. P. Davies, to mention only a few, stated again the traditional beliefs. Finally, Charles A. Beard courageously faced the key issues, and published *The Republic, Conversations on Fundamentals* (1943), a running commentary on the key passages of the Constitution, presented to the millions in *Life*.

REFERENCES

1. The citation from Rousseau is found in *Social Contract*, Book II, Ch. XII. Holcombe's phrase is from *State Government in the United States* (3d ed., 1931).

2. The general idea of the bill of rights is discussed in its historical setting by Benjamin F. Wright, Jr., in his *American Interpretations of Natural Law* (1931). In spite of Walton H. Hamilton's brilliant sketch in *The Constitution Reconsidered* (1938), pp. 167–190, we have no adequate treatment of *habeas corpus* nor of the right to bear arms, but the struggle for religious freedom is extensively portrayed in W. K. Jordan, *The Development of Religious Toleration in England* (1932–1940); its general importance was emphasized by Georg Jellinek's *La Déclaration des Droits de l'Homme et du Citoyen* (tr. Georges Fardis, 1902). The freedoms of expression, speech, press, and assembly have received the most extensive treatment. An able survey was presented in "Freedom of Inquiry and Expression," *Annals of the American Academy of Political and Social*

Science (Nov., 1938), ed. by Edward P. Cheyney. Freedom of speech and the lack of it were brilliantly set forth by Zechariah Chafee in his *Freedom of Speech* (1920) of which a new edition appeared in 1941 under the title *Free Speech in the United States*. Along the same lines, the study *A Liberal in Wartime* by Walter Nelles (1940) shows the struggle to maintain freedom during the First World War. The right to work, while not yet crystallized, is implied in some recent works, such as James P. Rowland, *The Legal Protection of the Worker's Job* (1937), Malcolm Sharp and C. O. Gregory, *Social Change and Labor Law* (1939). The interrelationship with other liberties is brought out in R. N. Baldwin and C. B. Randall, *Civil Liberties and Industrial Strife* (1938). See, as well, Georges Gurvitch's *Bill of Social Rights* (1946).

3. A remarkable study of the idea is given in Herschel Baker, *The Dignity of Man* (1947).

4. The point of this paragraph is clearly implied in most writings since the eclipse of the law-of-nature school, but it is often obscured by the squabble about sovereignty. A good statement of the American case can be found in Charles A. Beard's *The American Leviathan* (1930), but it, too, does not make out an argument for the maintenance of "rights" against elements in the community which would destroy them. An interesting analysis is to be found in Karl Loewenstein, *Contrôle Législatif de l'Extrémisme Politique dans les Démocraties Européennes* (1939). The debate and the *British Public Order Act*, November 16, 1936, are reprinted in *International Conciliation*, Jan. 1937.

5. The problem of the abuse of constitutional liberties and what to do about it is still highly controversial. Among the most interesting recent contributions are Robert E. Cushman, "The Repercussions of Foreign Affairs on the American Tradition of Civil Liberties," *Proceedings of the American Philosophical Society* (1948), pp. 92, 257 ff., and David Riesman, "Democracy and Defamation," three articles in *Columbia Law Review* (1942), Vol. XLII, pp. 727 ff., 1085 ff., 1282 ff.

6. The problem of conflicts in written constitutions has vexed lawyers, particularly when reflecting upon judicial review. The problem as a whole is treated comparatively by Charles G. Haines, *The Revival of Natural Law Concepts* (1930). Some historians contest the issue of the Civil War as stated in the text.

7. A suggestive discussion of the implications of a preamble, though from a predominantly legal point of view, occurs in Edward S. Corwin's "We, the People" in *The Doctrine of Judicial Review* (1914), pp. 81 ff. The German preamble is ably discussed in Hugo Preuss, *Reich und Länder* (ed. Gerhard Anschütz, 1928). Duguit's position is stated in his *Traité de Droit Constitutionnel* (2d ed., 1921–1925), Vol. III, Ch. VI, and expanded in Vol. V. The French constitution of 1875 had no preamble; its makers looked upon it as a very provisional charter. Later, however, a school of writers, ably led by M. Leon Duguit, maintained that the *Déclaration des Droits de l'Homme* of 1789 formed an integral part of the French constitution (see *Traité de Droit Constitutionnel* (3d ed., 1928), Vol. II, pp. 182–185). His argument that such bills of right bind the legislator, rejected by other French constitutionalists, is generally accepted in the United States, and is now specifically provided in the German Basic Law, art. 1(3). Insofar as the original bill of rights was individualist rather than socialist, M. Duguit's argument sought to marshal constitutional tradition against socialism. Such a chance was forestalled in the new constitution of 1946 by explicitly stating additional principles, some of which sanction socialization and hence restrict the older right of private property.

8. See the author's *The New Belief in the Common Man* (1942), especially Ch. III; see also A. Lawrence Lowell, *Public Opinion in War and Peace* (1923); Walter Lippmann, *Public Opinion* (1922) and *The Phantom Public* (1925); and the large bibliography given by Lasswell and Casey, *A Bibliography of Public Opinion and Propaganda* (1935). Of Burke's, the most important essay in this connection is *An Appeal from the New to the Old Whigs* (*Works*, Boston, 1839, Vol. III, pp. 333 ff.). Of de Maistre, consult *Considérations sur la France* (3d ed., 1881). Bagehot's view is set forth in his *The English Constitution* (1925; first published 1867), Ch. IX.

9. The Marxist-Communist doctrine of class war is not so much the cause as it is the manifestation of this cleavage in the community. The problem of conflicting loyalties is well

618

put and well investigated in Paul Kosok, *Modern Germany—A Study of Conflicting Loyalties* (1933). For pre-1914 Austria, see Oscar Jaszi, *The Dissolution of the Hapsburg Monarchy* (1929). For Poland, see Raymond L. Buell, *Poland* (1939), and R. Machray, *Poland, 1914–1931* (1932). For Czechoslovakia, see *Czechoslovakia: Twenty Years of Independence* (1940) (R. J. Kerner, ed.). Most important is T. G. Masaryk, *The Making of a State* (1926).

10. See what was said on unification above, pp. 10 f., and the references given there. Sage remarks on the general problem of this paragraph are found in Charles E. Merriam, *The Making of Citizens* (1931), Chs. II and III, and the same author's *Political Power* (1934), passim.

11. See William E. Rappard, *La Constitution Fédérale de la Suisse, 1848–1948* (1948), and *L'Individu et l'État dans l'Évolution Constitutionnelle de la Suisse* (1936); Robert C. Brooks, *Civic Training in Switzerland* (1930). See also Ed. His, *Geschichte des neueren schweizerischen Staatsrechts, Die Zeit der Restauration und der Regeneration, 1814–1848* (1929), and E. Fueter, *Die Schweiz seit 1848* (1928), passim; Burke, op. cit. Vol. III., p. 421.

12. For the debate, see *Verhandlungen der Verfassungsgebenden Deutschen Nationalversammlung*, 1105A, and *Bericht und Protokolle des Achten Ausschusses über den Entwurf einer Verfassung des Deutschen Reichs*, pp. 24–25. For the imperial constitution, see Burt Estes Howard, *The German Empire* (1906), pp. 403 ff. For the controversy about "Reich," see also Gerhard Anschütz, *Die Verfassung des Deutschen Reichs* (14th ed., 1933), Introduction, and pp. 36 ff. Regarding the British Commonwealth, see W. Y. Elliott, *The New British Empire* (1932), pp. 42 ff.

13. The literature on symbols and symbolism is rapidly on the increase. Anthropology and psychology have combined to bring to light the importance of symbols by exploring subrational, emotional elements in human behavior. Thurman Arnold's *Symbols of Government* (1935) popularized the issue, but the series on *The Making of Citizens*, which Charles E. Merriam edited, documents the problem on a wide front. Consult especially Merriam's own *The Making of Citizens* (1931), as well as *The Duk-Duks* (1929) by Elizabeth Weber. See also Max Lerner, "Constitution and Court as Symbols," *Yale Law Journal* (June 1937), Vol. XLVI, No. 8. Merriam's *Power* (1934) suggested *miranda* as a *terminus technicus*. The rapid rise of symbolic logic has further popularized this tendency. See text, Ch. XXV. For the specific issue of nationalism, see Carlton J. H. Hayes, *Essays on Nationalism* (1926), and Lippmann, *Public Opinion* (1922). See also Koppel S. Pinson, *A Bibliographical Introduction to Nationalism* (1935); and H. D. Lasswell and R. D. Casey, *A Bibliography of Public Opinion and Propaganda* (1935).

14. The statements from Burke are found in *Works*, Vol. III, pp. 52, 137. Paine's remark is in *Works* (Patriots Edition, 1925), Vol. VI, p. 20.

15. Mexican War Speech, January 12, 1848, in *Complete Works* (ed. Nicolay and Hay; 2d ed., 1905), Vol. I, pp. 338 f.

X · *The Separation of Powers*

REMARKS

The separation of powers (and the concomitant checks and balances) have been a part of the stock-in-trade of so-called political theory ever since Locke and Montesquieu. Yet after they had served their purpose as platform planks of antimonarchical agitation, they settled back into the dogmatic slumber of an "accepted principle of constitutional law." Hardly any attempt was made to explore the principle as a working hypothesis related to ascertainable matters of fact. (A notable exception is Herman Finer, *Theory and Practice of Modern Government* (1932).) Instead, it was treated as a more or less practicable norm in the particular form which the respective national constitutional law had given it. Practically all the "general" literature is either legal or doctrinal. Today the emergence of governments built upon an almost complete concentration of powers has once more set the stage for scientific reconsideration of the question: under what conditions and in what forms can a separation of powers occur and be maintained? This chapter develops the general position outlined in the introductory chapter. See pp. 25 ff. and references.

REFERENCES

1. Polybius's famous discussion occurs in his *History*, Book VI, Chs. XI ff. Curiously, Mommsen's classic *Abriss des Römischen Staatsrechts* (1893) does not explicitly take up this problem at all. The most elaborate application of the doctrine to English constitutional law occurs in Sir Thomas Smith, *De Republica Anglorum* (1583); see, regarding him, the discussion in J. W. Allen, *A History of Political Thought in the Sixteenth Century* (1928), pp. 262 ff. Its generalized expansion is most extensively set forth by James Harrington in his *Oceana* (1656); the profound influence of his thought upon America is argued by T. W. Dwight in his "James Harrington," *Political Science Quarterly* (1887), Vol. II, pp. 1 ff.

2. The quotations are from *Oceana* (ed. Morley, 1887), pp. 27–37. See also the interesting discussion in Francis D. Wormuth, *The Origins of Modern Constitutionalism* (1949), Ch. XIV.

3. See Locke, *An Essay Concerning the True Origin, Extent and End of Civil Government*, Chs. X–XII. Here Ch. X, dealing with the forms of government, is merely a brief preface to a statement of the doctrine of the separation of powers. For the English development see the literature cited previously; also Ernst Klimowsky, *Die englische Gewaltenteilungslehre bis zu Montesquieu* (1927), and Leopold von Ranke, "Zur Geschichte der Doktrin von den drei Staatsgewalten," in his *Werke*, Vol. XXIV.

4. For the *Instrument*, see Gardiner, *Constitutional Documents*, pp. 405 ff. For Cromwell's speeches, see Carlyle, *Cromwell*, Vol. II, pp. 415 and 464–465.

5. The citation from Blackstone is found in his *Commentaries* (1765) (ed., T. Cooley, 1876), Vol. I, p. 146.

6. The point made in this paragraph has received insufficient attention in the extensive literature on Montesquieu. See Joseph Dedieu, *Montesquieu et la Tradition Politique Anglaise en France* (1909); and H. Jansen, *Montesquieu's Theorie von der Dreitheilung der Gewalten im Staate auf Ihre Quellen Zurückgeführt* (1878). One difficulty has been the purely linguistic one that *power*, *pouvoir*, and *Gewalt* are only roughly comparable.

7. See E. B. Greene, *The Provincial Governor in the English Colonies of North America* (1898); Benjamin F. Wright, Jr., "The Origins of the Separation of Powers in America," in *Economica*, Vol. XIII (1933); and William S. Carpenter, "The Separation of Powers in the Eighteenth Century," in *American Political Science Review*, Vol. XXII (1928). The quotation is from Felix Frankfurter, *The Public and Its Government* (1930), p. 77. Perhaps the ablest and certainly one of the most influential attacks on the separation-of-powers doctrine is J. Allen Smith, *Growth and Decadence of Constitutional Government* (1930).

8. The importance of the two-party system as a constitutional restraint was first clearly stated by Walter Bagehot in his epochal *The English Constitution* (1867 . . . 1928). It was systematically restated by Julius Hatschek, *Englisches Staatsrecht* (1905), Vol. II, pp. 1 ff. The crucial importance of the conventions concerning the parties for restraining the power of the government was made the touchstone of true parliamentary government by Robert Redslob in a brilliant essay, *Die Parlamentarische Regierung in Ihrer Wahren und Ihrer Unechten Form* (1918). The failure to recognize this restraint is an important factor in the destruction of crypto-parliamentary schemes, such as those of Italy and Germany. Those who are disinclined to give adequate weight to this institutional safeguard tend to fall back upon "agreement upon fundamentals" as a substitute. The two are, in a sense, antithetical. See, for example, H. R. G. Greaves, *The British Constitution* (1938).

9. See Benjamin Constant, *Cours de Droit Constitutionnel* (1814); Erich Kaufmann, *Studien zur Staatslehre des Monarchischen Prinzipes* (1906); Esmein-Nézard, *Droit Constitutionnel* (8th ed.), Vol. I; Robert von Mohl, *Staatsrecht, Völkerrecht und Politik* (1860), Vol. I, pp. 3 ff., Vol. II, pp. 4 ff. See also the convenient summary in Conrad Bornhak, *Genealogie der Verfassungen* (1935).

10. See the article, "Legislative Assemblies—Germany," by Otto Köllreuter, in the *ESS*, Vol. IX, and the literature cited there. See also "The Development of the Executive Power in Germany," in *APSR*, Vol. XXVII (1933), by Carl J. Friedrich. The transition to parliamentary

government in France is brilliantly portrayed by Joseph Barthélemy in his *L'Introduction du Régime parlementaire en France sous Louis XVIII et Charles X* (1904). For the city of Strassburg, see Gustav Schmoller, *Deutsches Städtewesen in älterer Zeit* (1922), pp. 214 ff.

11. Regarding Sweden, see "Legislative Assemblies—Scandinavian States and Finland," by Herbert Tingsten, in the *ESS*, Vol. IX; P. E. Fahlbeck, *Die Regierungsform Schwedens* (1911); and Axel Brusewitz, "Maktfördelning och demokrati i den konstitutionella utveck-lingen," in *Statsvenska Tidskrift* (1923), as well as Nils Herlitz, *Grunddragen av det Svenska Statsskickets Historia* (1928), particularly pp. 177 ff.

12. See *Problems of the American Public Service* (ed. Commission of Inquiry into Public Personnel Problems), "Responsible Government Service under the American Constitution," by Carl J. Friedrich, pp. 48 ff.

13. Kant's statement of this analogy occurs in *Anfangsgründe der Rechtslehre*, para. 45. The relevant passage is as follows: "Every state contains three powers, i.e. the general and united will in threefold personification (*trias politica*): the power to rule (sovereignty) in the person of the legislative, the executive power in the person of the governor (in accordance with law) and the law-interpreting power (attributing to each what is his according to law) in the person of the judge (*potestas legislatoria, rectoria et judiciaria*). [....] similar to the three proposi-tions in a practical syllogism: the major premise which contains the law of a will, the minor premise which contains the command to proceed according to that law, i.e. the principle of subsuming [....] under the law, and the consequent which contains the sentence or judicial decision as to what is law in the particular case."

14. R. E. Cushman, "Independent Regulatory Commissions" in Report of the President's Committee on Administrative Management (1937). See also the discussion in "Responsible Government Service under the American Constitution" by the author.

15. See John Dickinson, "Checks and Balances," in the *ESS*, Vol. III. See also W. Hasbach, "Gewaltentrennung, Gewaltenteilung und Gemischte Staatsform," in *Vierteljahrschrift für Sozial- und Wirtschaftsgeschichte* (1916), and the same restatement by Herman Finer, *Theory and Practice of Modern Government* (1932), Vol. I, pp. 153 ff.

16. See, for instance, Woodrow Wilson, *Congressional Government* (1887), pp. 265 ff.; Frank J. Goodnow, *The Principles of the Administrative Law of the United States* (1905), p. 53 and passim. Elliott's *Need for Constitutional Reform* first appeared in 1935.

17. See John Adams, *A Defense of the Constitutions of Government of the United States of America* (1787), pp. 308–309: "All nations, under all governments, must have parties; the great secret is to control them. There are but two ways, either by a monarchy and standing army, or by a balance in the constitution. Where the people have a voice, and there is no balance, there will be everlasting fluctuations, revolutions and horrors...." For Constant, see *Cours de Politique Constitutionnelle* (1872), and the able little sketch by Edwin Mims, Jr., in the *ESS*, Vol. IV. For the prerogative, see the author's article, "Prerogative" in the *ESS*; Dicey's statement is found in his *Law of the Constitution* (8th ed., 1926), p. 420. See also the bibliography cited in the author's article. Laski's view is stated in a pamphlet entitled *The Crisis and the Constitution* (1932), Ch. VI. For the English King's imperial position, see W. Y. Elliott, *The New British Empire* (1932), passim.

18. The idea of guardianship is old. Throughout medieval times, the ecclesiastical author-ities kept "the king's conscience." It is inseparable from the notion of a "fundamental law." For the peculiar features of the French practice, see Antoine Saint Girons, *Droit Public Français: Essai sur la Séparation des Pouvoirs dans l'Ordre Politique, Administratif et Judiciaire* (1881), as well as the leading text, A. Esmein, *Droit Constitutionnel*, Vol. I, Ch. III. On the whole, Ger-man thought was profoundly influenced by French ideas, rather than by American and English notions. See Carl Schmitt, *Der Hüter der Verfassung* (1931). For the general questions of the separation of powers under the Constitution of Weimar, see Rudolf Smend, *Verfassung und Verfassungsrecht* (1928); Hans Bettmann, *Die Gewaltenteilung im demokratischen Rechtsstaate—Eine Untersuchung zum geltenden deutschen Staatsrecht* (1931); and Ernst von Hippel, *Die Lehre Montesquieu's von der Dreiteilung der Gewalten und der Grad ihrer Verwirklichung in den*

Verfassungen des Deutschen Reichs von 1871 und 1919 und den Verfassungen des Preussischen Staates von 1850 und 1920 (1921).

19. See the discussion below, ch. XII, for further detail. The notes give references to the new literature.

20. Out of the considerable literature on the Supreme Court, two volumes may be cited: Charles Warren, *The Supreme Court in United States History* (1922), and Felix Frankfurter and James M. Landis, *The Business of the Supreme Court* (1927). A highly critical estimate is contained in E. S. Corwin's *The Twilight of the Supreme Court* (1934).

XI · *Federalism and the Territorial Division of Power*

REMARKS

The literature on federalism is vast. The rising interest in Britain is testified to by an important comparative survey, *Federal Government* (1946), by K. C. Wheare. But the study is restricted in scope, and fails to place federalism within the framework of constitutionalism. Sobei Mogi has included, in his meritorious survey of *Federalism* (1931), a selected bibliography of twenty-three pages. Much of this literature, unfortunately, revolves around the question of how to combine various doctrines of sovereignty with the constitutional norms of a federal government. A new chapter opened when Hugo Preuss, following Gierke, proposed to eliminate the concept of sovereignty in his *Gemeinde, Staat, Reich als Gebietskörperschaften* (1889), particularly pp. 89 ff. Though Gierke himself disowned Preuss's views (see John D. Lewis, *The Genossenschaft Theory of Otto von Gierke* [1935], p. 100; see also ibid 36, quoting E. Kaufmann), Preuss felt himself to be Gierke's true follower in maintaining that "the entire concept belongs to a set of ideas which is gone together with political institutions (*Staatliche Ercheinungsform*) corresponding to it," and he could point to certain earlier German writers who had attempted to eliminate sovereignty, such as R. von Mohl (see *Enzyklopädie der Staatswissenschaften*, 2d ed., pp. 43, 86). It is not without interest from our point of view that Mohl shares with Preuss a vivid sense of historical reality as contrasted with logical and normative problems. This side of the literature of federalism leaves much to be desired. Siegfried Brie's celebrated *Der Bundesstaat* (1874) is doctrinal, though in the words of R. Emerson's able summary of the whole body of German writings on the subject (cf. Ch. iii, "Federalism," in *State and Sovereignty in Modern Germany* [1928]), Brie's volume "did much to clarify the issues involved in the debate over federalism." Doctrinal, too, are most of the other German writers on the subject. At the same time, historical scholarship began to accumulate an increasing body of data on past federations and federal "states." Swiss, American, and German historians offered materials aplenty on which to base a more realistic view. A synthesis was attempted in a very comprehensive manner by Edward A. Freeman, in his *History of Federal Government in Greece and Italy* (1863), which was to be the first of several volumes dealing with the entire development. Stimulated by him, H. Sidgwick included several chapters (lectures) on federalism, new and old, in his *The Development of European Polity* (1903, and later editions). A striking study showing the importance of the security problem in the development of Swiss federalism is William E. Rappard's *Cinq siècles de Sécurité Collective* (1945). A detailed comparative account of American and German federal structures has recently been given by Herman Finer in his *The Theory and Practice of Modern Government* (1932), Vol. I, Ch. VIII. Robert C. Binkley has made the struggle between unitary and federative polity a main theme of his volume, *Realism and Nationalism, 1852–1871* (1935), expounding the view that the period saw the ultimate defeat of federative plans. A compact survey of the institutional problem is offered by Arthur W. MacMahon in his article, "Federation," in the *ESS*. The notion of an administrative federalism is developed by Arnold Brecht, "Federalism and Business Regulation," in *Social Research*, Vol. II (1935). More recently, the problems of federal-state relations have been dealt with in a thorough manner by Jane P. Clark, *The Rise of a New Federalism* (1938). Important suggestions are contained in George Benson's *The New Centralization: A Study of Intergovernmental Relationships in the United States* (1941).

An interesting discussion of federalism along broad comparative lines is to be found in Erich Hunger, *Zur Idee und Tradition des Föderalismus* (1929), taking up ideas expounded by Constantin Franz, *Der Föderalismus als das leitende Prinzip für die soziale, staatliche und internationale Organisation* (1879). In both, the problem of constitutionalism is in the background. See also Herriot, *The United States of Europe* (tr. R. J. Dingle, 1930), passim, and William E. Rappard, *Uniting Europe* (1930). All this literature contains elements of the views set forth in the text, and there is a great deal of common historical material which is drawn from one or the other. But the particular synthesis of facts and theory set forth here is an attempt to relate federal structures to the general lines of institutional development of modern constitutional government. For the purpose of guiding the Germans charged with framing a federal constitution, OMGUS produced a useful compilation of federal constitutions entitled *Comparative Federal Constitutions* (May 1948), prefaced by a unique topical analysis by Dr. Kurt Glaser.

REFERENCES

1. The significance of objectives (or purposes) was stressed by Heinrich Rosin, following R. von Jhering, *Der Zweck im Recht 1877–1883;* but unhappily Rosin proceeded to make purpose the exclusive criterion. See Emerson, op. cit. pp. 118 ff. For the analogy between federations of governments and those of associations, see MacMahon, op. cit., and H. Preuss, op. cit., particularly Part III, and Gierke, *Das Deutsche Genossenschaftsrecht*, Vol. I, pp. 457 ff. Very valuable also is R. M. MacIver, *Community* (3d ed., 1928), pp. 98 ff., 153 ff., 249 ff., where the problem is discussed in its general setting.

2. For the items on Swiss constitutional development, see W. E. Rappard, *L'Individu et l'État* (1936), particularly pp. 25–30, 36, 63–65, 263–269, 274–280, and his more recent *La Constitution Fédérale de la Suisse—1848–1948* (1948). See also Ed. His, *Geschichte des neueren Schweizerischen Staatsrechts* (1929).

3. No good comparative study of the impact of economic forces exists. W. Sulzbach, *Nationales Gemeinschaftsgefühl und Wirtschafiliches Interesse* (1929), is of some help. The literature on the United States is considerable. For a challenging, though perhaps extreme, position see Charles A. Beard's pathfinding study, *An Economic Interpretation of the Constitution of the United States* (1914). For Germany, the study published by the Friedrich-List-Stiftung concerning the founding of the *Zollverein*, Friedrich Lenz, *Friedrich List, der Mann und das Werk* (1935), is very illuminating on this score. E. Fueter has given much emphasis to this factor in dealing with Swiss history in his *Die Schweiz seit 1848* (1928) as has E. Gagliardi in his *Geschichte der Schweiz von den Anfängen bis auf die Gegenwart* (1927), particularly Vol. III. Most illuminating also are Arnold Wolfers, *Britain and France between Two Wars* (1940), and Nicholas J. Spykman, *America's Strategy in World Politics* (1942). Regarding the League of Nations, Felix Morley's *The Society of Nations* (1932) suggests the essential points. Clarence Streit's *Union Now* (1938) contains a critical appraisal of League difficulties by a friend of the League. The same may be said of the author's *Foreign Policy in the Making* (1938); a competent general appraisal of international organization is given by Clyde Eagleton, *International Government* (rev. ed. 1947), who compares the League and the United Nations. On the balance of power and related problems see also Hans J. Morgenthau, *Politics among Nations* (1948). For the Marshall Plan, see Seymour Harris, *The European Recovery Program* (1949).

4. See Gierke, op. cit. pp. 463 ff. (for the Hanse); ibid. pp. 476 ff. (for the Rhenish League). See also the article by Fritz Rörig in the *ESS* for the former, and the literature cited there and in C. Brinkmann, "The Hanseatic League, a Survey of Recent Literature," in *Journal of Economic and Business History*, Vol. II (1930), pp. 585 ff. For Switzerland, see Gagliardi, op. cit. Vol. I. For the Achaean League, see W. S. Ferguson, *Greek Imperialism* (1913), pp. 238 ff. and passim, as well as the monographs cited there. For the League of Nations, see Felix Morley, op. cit. Ch. X. For the Dutch United Provinces, see D. C. Niyhoff, *Staatkundige Geschiedenis van Nederland* (1893); for Althusius's ideas on federalism, see *Politica Methodica Digesta of Johannes Althusius*, ed. C. J. Friedrich (1932), and the comments of Otto von Gierke, *Johannes*

Althusius, Ch. V. available in translation by Bernard Freyd, under the title *The Development of Political Theory* (1939).

5. See again Morley, op. cit. For other federations, see earlier citations.

6. For literature on second chambers, see below, Ch. XVI, note 5. A very exhaustive recent treatment of the Senate is George H. Haynes, *The Senate of the United States, Its History and Practice* (1938). The unrepresentative quality of the Senate as it affects foreign affairs has recently been the subject of much constitutional analysis. See Royden J. Dangerfield, *In Defense of the Senate* (1933); E. S. Corwin, *The President's Control of Foreign Relations* (1917); Denna F. Fleming, *The Treaty Veto of the American Senate* (1930); Quincy Wright, *The Control of American Foreign Relations* (1922). See also Kurt London, *How Foreign Policy is Made* (1949). The quotation from Elliott is found in his *The Need for Constitutional Reform*, p. 191. The Swiss situation is analyzed in detail in Max Veith, *Der rechtliche Einfluss der Kantone auf die Bundesgewalt* (1902), particularly pp. 78 ff. The statistical figures are taken from *Statistical Abstract of the United States* (1939) and *Statistisches Jahrbuch der Schweiz* (1933). For the "representative" aspect, see below, Ch. XIV, particularly pp. 262 ff. See also Fritz Fleiner, *Schweizerisches Bundesstaatsrecht* (1922), No. 1, pp. 154 ff.

7. A very able analysis of the German problem is offered by Arnold Brecht, *Federalism and Regionalism in Germany* (1945); also valuable is R. E. Dickinson, *The Regions of Germany* (1945), the latter from a geographical viewpoint. The figures in the text are from *Statistisches Jahrbuch für das deutsche Reich* (1927). The data regarding the members of the *Reichsrat* are found in successive editions of the *Handbuch für das deutsche Reich*. See also Josef Held, *Der Reichsrat*, etc. (1926); Gerhard Anschütz, *Die Verfassung des Deutschen Reichs* (14th ed.), pp. 338 ff.; F. Poetzsch-Heffter, "Vom Staatsleben unter der Weimarer Verfassung," *JoR*, Vol. XIII (1927); Herbert Kraus, *The Crisis of German Democracy* (1932), pp. 107 ff.; Johannes Mattern, *Principles of the Constitutional Jurisprudence of the German National Republic* (1928), pp. 402 ff., and the literature cited in these volumes. See also the competent discussion in Finer, op. cit. pp. 369 ff.

8. See Brecht, op. cit.; see also Fritz Hummel, *Preussen und seine Provinzen im Reichsrat* (1928), besides the general commentaries cited in note 7. See also Hugo Preuss, *Reich und Länder* (ed. G. Anschütz [1928]), particularly pp. 24 ff. The memorandum of the Minister of the Interior can be found in the published materials of the *Länderkonferenz Beratungsunterlagen*, pp. 11–12. The statistical tables are found in ibid. on pp. 469 ff.

9. For Austria, the revised standard text by Ludwig Adamovich, *Grundriss des Österreichischen Verfassungsrechts* (4th ed., 1947), is recommended.

10. The question of functions and their distribution is at the core of Jane P. Clark's discussion in op. cit. Much American constitutional law revolves around it, for example, a good part of the extensive literature on the commerce clause. Distribution of functions was also at the center of much of the German juristic writing, particularly in connection with the controversy over *Kompetenz-Kompetenz*, for which compare Emerson, op. cit. See also the general commentaries cited in note 7, but particularly Preuss, note 8, op. cit. pp. 105 ff.

11. For the most vivid portrayal of the transition from federation to federal government in the United States, see *The Federalist*, Nos. 1–10. In Germany the problem of the participation of the *Länder* as units in the amending power was not clearly faced by the Weimar constituent assembly, nor did it receive much attention afterward; it was occasionally adduced as proof that the German constitution did not recognize such a power. The Basic Law, on binding instructions from the Western Allies, still leaves the matter to federal legislation (see art. 79).

12. See the general discussion of executive leadership in Ch. XVIII. The desire to secure effective leadership has, of course, always been recognized as a prime factor in establishing a federalism. For Switzerland, see Fleiner, op. cit. p. 183. For Germany see Kraus, op. cit. pp. 119 f., and Anschütz, op. cit. pp. 111 ff. For the problems of execution see Johannes Mattern, *Bavaria and the Reich* (1923), passim; and F. M. Watkins, *The Failure of Constitutional Emergency Powers under the German Republic* (1939).

13. The literature concerning the judiciary, and more especially the Supreme Court of the United States, is given above, Ch. VI, and below, Ch. XIII. In recent decades the role of the

Court in relation to federalism has declined, as it has tended to give ever wider scope to federal authority. For this constitutional revolution see Edward S. Corwin, *Constitutional Revolution Limited* (1941).

14. Material on Dominion federalism has been increasing. For Canada see the *Report of the Royal Commission on Dominion-Provincial Relations*, Books I and II (1940). The special studies are also valuable. W. P. M. Kennedy, *The Constitution of Canada* (1938), gives a general account of Canadian government. For Australia, the older (1929) *Report of the Royal Commission on the Constitution* is helpful, but should now be read in conjunction with Gordon Greenwood, *The Future of Australian Federalism* (1946). Unfortunately, Greenwood's discussion of federalism neglects the main literature. See also A. P. Canaway, *The Failure of Federalism in Australia* (1930), and W. K. Duncan (ed.), *Trends in Australian Politics* (1935). See also the *Reports of the Commonwealth Grants Commission*.

15. See C. J. Friedrich, *Constitutional Government and Politics*, pp. 202 ff.

16. For this paragraph see A. B. Keith, *The Constitutional Law of the British Dominions* (1933), and Elliott, op. cit. passim, but particularly Chs. I, II, and VIII, and the literature cited there. See also W. Y. Elliott (ed.), *The British Commonwealth at War* (1943); Baron G. E. Elton, *Imperial Commonwealth* (1946); Kenneth C. Wheare, *The Statute of Westminster and Dominion Status* (3d ed., 1947); Arthur B. Keith, *The Dominions as Sovereign States: Their Constitutions and Governments* (1938); Alexander Brady, *Democracy in the Dominions* (1947). Regarding the Imperial Defense Committee, see the discussion by W. I. Jennings in *Cabinet Government* (1938), Ch. X. See also the parliamentary debates (*HCD*) on the subject, March 27, 1928.

17. The speech of the Prime Minister was given in the House of Commons, Nov. 25, 1948.

18. Besides the constitutional text (given as an appendix in Pollock, ed., *Change and Crisis in European Government* (1947, pp. 194 ff.)), consult Jean de la Roche and Jean Gottmann, *La Federation Française* (1945), for background, and the relevant sections in Gordon Wright, *The Reshaping of French Democracy* (1948).

19. The development of the late twenties is well summarized in William E. Rappard, *Uniting Europe* (1930). See also Aristide Briand, *Memorandum on the Organization of a Regime of European Federal Union* (May, 1930). The documentary material of the several conferences, The Hague, Interlaken, and so forth, is relevant and should be consulted. See also the author's "On European Union in Theory and Practice," in *Internationalism and Democracy* (S. G. Brown, ed., 1949).

20. Jane P. Clark, op. cit., and also *Iowa Law Review*, Vol. XXV, No. 3 (March, 1940), offer important material here.

21. The problem of decentralization touches, of course, on the entire literature on local government, to which no appropriate reference can be given here. For this, see the bibliography of the next chapter. The quotation is from W. A. Robson, *The Development of Local Government*, p. 189. The Poor Law Amendment Act may be found in 4 and 5 William IV, c. 76.

22. See E. G. Nourse, J. S. Davis, and J. D. Black, *Three Years of the Agricultural Adjustment Administration* (1937).

XII · *Judicial Review of Legislative Acts*

REMARKS

General literature on this subject is considerable. A veritable avalanche was unloosed in the United States by the "Supreme Court fight" of President Roosevelt in 1937. The case for the proposed reforms has been well stated in Robert Jackson's *The Struggle for Judicial Supremacy* (1940). It rests on the premise that acts of Congress should not be held unconstitutional unless the violation of the Constitution is patent. A similar position was taken by E. S. Corwin in *Court over Constitution* (1938) and by Felix Frankfurter, *Mr. Justice Holmes and Supreme Court* (1938). In the United States, judicial review of legislation has always been considered one of the unique achievements of the country's constitutional scheme. An excellent historical study is that of Benjamin F. Wright, Jr., *The Growth of American Constitutional Law* (1942). A mine of insight and information is contained in the Association of American Law Schools collection in four volumes, *Essays on Constitutional Law* (1938). These deal respectively with (1) The Nature of Judicial Process in Constitutional Cases, (2) Limitations on Governmental Powers, (3) The Nation and the States, (4) Administrative Law, and (5) Taxation. Abroad, judicial review has not found any willing imitators. The literature reflects this cleavage. In recent decades the court's position as guardian of the Constitution has been the subject of violent attacks in the United States, too. The literature is thus divided into writers favoring and writers questioning and opposing the power of the courts to declare acts of the legislature unconstitutional. The related and more detached question, under what conditions can a court function as guardian of a constitution, has received only incidental treatment. Typical examples are Charles Warren's *Congress, the Constitution and the Supreme Court* (1925), and E. S. Corwin, *The Doctrine of Judicial Review* (1914), on the one hand; the discussion in Gerhard Anschütz, *Die Verfassung des Deutschen Reichs* (14th ed., 1933), Vol. I, pp. 369 ff. and elsewhere, or in Esmein-Nézard, *Droit Constitutionnel* (8th ed., 1928), Vol. I, pp. 538 ff., on the other hand. A broad comparative treatment has been offered by Charles G. Haines, "Some Phases of the Theory and Practice of Judicial Review of Legislation in Foreign Countries," in *APSR*, Vol. XXIV, pp. 583 ff. This latter author also wrote a study of the American problem, *The American Doctrine of Judicial Supremacy* (1914), and he later analyzed the underlying philosophical problems in a significant volume, *The Revival of Natural Law Concepts* (1930). The critical social reformist view was expounded before the war by C. A. Beard, *The Supreme Court and the Constitution* (1912), and in a milder form by F. J. Goodnow, *Social Reform and the Constitution* (1911). The English point of view, similarly considered, was set forth by Harold Laski, "Judicial Review of Social Policy in England," in *Harvard Law Review*, Vol. 39, pp. 832 ff. (1925). It may, however, also be stated in terms of conservative preferences, as is shown by the treatment A. V. Dicey gave the subject in *Introduction to the Study of the Law of the Constitution* (8th ed., 1915), Ch. III. That the American tradition is part of an older liberal philosophy of government can be gleaned from such treatments as that given by Robert von Mohl, *Staatsrecht, Völkerrecht und Politik* (1860), Vol. I, pp. 66 ff., "Über die rechtliche Bedeutung verfassungswidriger Gesetze." Mohl was well acquainted with American constitutional doctrine. For interesting aspects of the doctrinal background, see Mario Einaudi, *The Physiocratic Doctrine of Judicial Control* (1939).

REFERENCES

1. The statements of Hamilton on behalf of judicial review (though the doctrine is not found in the Constitution) are given in the *Federalist*, Nos. 78–82.

2. Re literature on Coke, see above, Ch. VI, note 6.

3. Holdsworth's view is found in Vol. IV, pp. 174, 184–185. For McIlwain, see his *The American Revolution* (1924). The study by Robert L. Schuyler, *Parliament and the British Empire: Some Constitutional Controversies Concerning Imperial Legislative Jurisdiction* (1929), while full of interesting material, cannot be said to have undermined McIlwain's central argument, as is sometimes supposed; in fact, Schuyler did not deal with the fundamental constitutional issue at all. See the review by George M. Wrong, APSR, Vol. XXIII, p. 1011. Blackstone's statement is given by him in *Commentaries on the Laws of England* (5th ed., 1773) Introduction, Sections 2 and 3.

4. Adams's views are expounded in *Defense of the Constitutions of Government of the United States of America* (1787). *Marbury v. Madison* is 1 *Cranch* 137 (1903). Concerning this decision and the extensive literature dealing with it, see E. S. Corwin, "Marbury v. Madison and the Doctrine of Judicial Review," in *The Doctrine of Judicial Review* (1914), pp. 1 ff. For the evolution of the idea of "state sovereignty" in Germany, see Rupert Emerson, *State and Sovereignty in Modern Germany* (1928), Ch. I.

5. For Australia, see B. R. Wise, *The Commonwealth of Australia* (1909). The quotation

comes from the article by Felix Frankfurter, "The Supreme Court" in *ESS*. See also Rappard, op. cit. pp. 448–453.

6. Both quotations are from H. F. Pringle, *The Life and Times of William Howard Taft* (1939). The question of constitutional change by interpretation is carefully considered in H. W. Horwill, *Usages of the American Constitution* (1925), and historically traced with a masterful hand by A. C. McLaughlin, *A Constitutional History of the United States* (1935). In terms of the German context, a searching special analysis is given by Karl Loewenstein, *Erscheinungsformen der Verfassungsänderung* (1931).

7. The quotation is from Jackson, op. cit. pp. 312–313.

8. Walton H. Hamilton, "The Path of Due Process of Law," in *The Constitution Reconsidered* (1938). See also R. L. Mott, *Due Process of Law* (1926), and Louis A. Warsoff, *Equality and the Law* (1938), especially Ch. IV.

9. See B. F. Wright, op. cit. pp. 240–241. Holmes' passage is from O. W. Holmes, *The Common Law* (new ed., 1938). For the pocket veto, see 279 U. S. 655, and the comments by R. E. Cushman, APSR, Vol. XXIV, pp. 67 ff.

10. For the commerce problem see E. S. Corwin, *The Commerce Power versus States' Rights* (1936), where restrictive doctrines are attacked, and Felix Frankfurter, *The Commerce Clause under Marshall, Taney and Waite* (1937).

11. See B. F. Wright's comments, op. cit. pp. 192 ff., upon *Schechter Poultry Corp. v. United States*, 295 U. S. 495 (1935). See the literature cited above, Ch. VI, note 9. Also Justice Cardozo, *The Nature of the Judicial Process* (1921), and William A. Robson, *Justice and Administrative Law* (1928), Ch. V.

12. On the subject of scientist and lawyer and the possibilities of a "naturalist" jurisprudence, see Edward S. Robinson, *Law and the Lawyers* (1935), Ch. I. On representation, see the literature below, Ch. XIV.

13. Concerning Siéyès' constitutional jury, see Esmein-Nézard, *Droit Constitutionnel* (8th ed., 1928), Vol. I, pp. 638 ff., where Siéyès' great speech before the Convention is summarized. For this speech, still eminently worth reading, see *Réimpression de l'Ancien Moniteur*, Vol. XXV, pp. 293 ff. See also the study by Trouillard, *Le Sénat Conservateur du Consulat et du Premier Empire* (1912), and the recent study on Siéyès by G. G. van Deusen, *Siéyès; His Life and His Nationalism* (1932), particularly p. 61. A brief comment on the Constitutional Committee is given in Gordon Wright, *The Reshaping of French Democracy* (1948), p. 241.

14. The German Basic Law of 1949 does not clearly recognize the individual litigant, as earlier drafts did. However, the fact that the Basic Rights (arts. 1–19) are declared to be "binding as directly valid law on legislation, administration and judiciary," together with art. 19(4), which gives any person the appeal to a court if his rights are infringed, may well lead to this result. However, similar provisions in state constitutions led to protracted controversies over the implementing legislation. See, for provisions in the Land constitutions, *Constitutions of the German Laender*, CAD, OMGUS (1947). For Austria, see Ludwig Adamovich, *Grundriss des Österreichischen Verfassungsrechts* (1947), pp. 96 ff. and 303 ff. and the same author's *Die Prüfung der Gesetze und Verordnungen* (1924), for the general issues. See also Charles Eisenmann, *La Justice Constitutionnelle et la Haute Cour Constitutionnelle de l'Autriche* (1928).

15. The entire literature bears upon this point. Special mention may be made of Edouard Lambert, *Le Gouvernement des Juges et la Lutte contre la Législation Sociale aux États-Unis* (1921), and the same author's essay (jointly with Halfred C. Brown), *La Lutte Judiciaire du Capital et du Travail Organizés aux États-Unis* (1923). A sharp, if popular, statement is Pearson and Allen's *Nine Old Men* (1936).

16. See, for detailed discussion of the American history, Charles Warren, *The Supreme Court in United States History* (1922), and B. F. Wright, op. cit. One might note the conclusion of Esmein, as set forth in Esmein-Nézard, *Droit Constitutionnel*, Vol. I, p. 636: "Pour attribuer aux tribunaux un rôle si délicat et si important, il faut avant tout que la magistrature possède une bien haute autorité: il faut que le peuple ait une confiance profonde dans sa sagesse et dans sa valeur professionnelle et scientifique."

XIII · Local Self-Government and Grass-Roots Democracy

REMARKS

Far be it from me to attempt in these short bibliographical notes a survey of the extensive literature on local government; this task must be left to books dedicated to this subject. Among the more general titles, the following seem of general value for the student of comparative constitutional government. On the whole, the older studies, such as Rudolf Gneist's justly celebrated *Selfgovernment* [sic], are more helpful for an understanding of the constitutional aspect; more recently it has largely been taken for granted. However, Joseph Redlich's *Englische Lokalverwaltung* (1901, by F. W. First, 1903), especially when read together with his *The Procedure of the House of Commons* (1908), develops this aspect quite fully. An over-all study is Michel Dendias' *Le Gouvernement Local* (1930) with extensive bibliography. On Britain, the monograph by William E. Robson, *The Development of Local Government* (1931, 3d ed., 1947), is the best, unless the reader is tempted to plunge into Sidney and Beatrice Webb's nine volumes, *English Local Government from the Revolution to the Municipal Corporations Act* (1906–1929); see also the texts by John J. Clarke, H. Finer, H. S. Hasluck and J. J. Warren. William Bennett Munro's *The Government of European Cities* (1909), while often outdated, remains valuable. A mine of relevant information is *Handwörterbuch der Kommunalwissenschaften* (1924) in 4 volumes.

On American local government, see the texts by William Anderson, W. B. Graves, C. M. Kneier, A. F. MacDonald, Roy V. Peel, and Harold Zink. For the early history, see Ernest S. Griffith, *History of American City Government—The Colonial Period* (1938), Carl Bridenbaugh, *Cities in the Wilderness* (1938), and Harold A. Stone, Don K. Price, and Kathryn H. Stone, *City Manager Government in the United States* (1940).

REFERENCES

1. The statement is from Granville Hicks' *Small Town* (1946), p. 276, the sentence, from p. 117. Other recent studies pointing in the same direction are Arthur E. Morgan, *The Small Community—Foundation of Democratic Life* (1942), James West, *Plainville USA* (1945), and W. Lloyd Warner et al., *Democracy in Jonesville* (1949), p. 628.

2. See Plato, *Laws*, 738, d, 6–e, 8; also 737 e, 1. Aristotle, *Nicomachean Ethics*, 1170, b, 31; *Politics*, 1326, a, 5–b, 25. See also the remarkable paper of Alexander Rüstow, "Entstehungs— und Lebensbedingungen der Hochkulturen," in *Synopsis—Festgabe für Alfred Weber* (ed. Edgar Salin), (no date—appeared in 1949).

3. For Botero see *Delle Cause della grandezza delle città* (1588, English translation, 1606) in which he shows why cities grow and what prevents such growth from continuing indefinitely. For Bodin and Althusius, see their major works, indicating a declining interest in size of the community, since the sovereign territorial state is their recognized concern. Montesquieu's discussion of the intermediate powers is scattered throughout his work; see especially *De l'Esprit des Lois* (1748), especially Books VIII and XI. Rousseau's discussion occurs in *Contract Social*, Book I, Ch. X, Book II, Ch. IX, Book III, Ch. IV.

4. John Dewey, *The Public and Its Problems* (1927); Walter Lippmann, *Public Opinion* (1922), and *Phantom Public* (1925); A. Lawrence Lowell, *Public Opinion and Popular Government* (new ed., 1926).

5. Bryce, in his *American Commonwealth*, offers an interesting suggestion regarding the relation of corruption to size of cities which has since become commonplace. "City governments begin to be bad when the population begins to exceed 100,000 and includes a large proportion of immigrants." But the retrenchment of Tammany Hall and its eventual defeat by the Fusion group showed that remedial action may eventually be generated even in vast metropolitan communities. For a hopeful view see Guy Greer, *Your City Tomorrow* (1947).

6. In view of Dewey's strident "pragmatism" it is interesting to note that Immanuel Kant, in his *Anthropology pragmatically considered* (1798), showed more realistic insight into man's

propensity toward secretiveness, and into the reasons why this trait is apt to persist in large communities and small ones, than the pragmatist Dewey.

7. For the quaint remark on "dictatorship" of the justice of the peace, see John Ranney and G. Carter, *The Major Foreign Powers* (1949), p. 209. On Gneist see the work quoted above in *Remarks*.

8. The quotation is found in Gneist, op. cit. p. 69. The translation is mine. Passages in brackets are added in order to help the reader follow the argument.

9. For the statement by Sir E. D. Simon, see his admirable *The Smaller Democracies* (1939), p. 89.

10. For a rough and rather outdated survey of this type, see G. D. Harris, *Local Government in Many Lands* (1926, new ed., 1949). Harris calls his a comparative study, but leaves the effort of comparison largely to the reader. Far more comparative insight is to be gathered from W. A. Robson's "Local Government" in *ESS*.

11. See William A. Robson, *The Development of Local Government* (1948), esp. Part I, Ch. I.

12. Herman Finer, *The British Civil Service* (1937). See also Ch. XIX.

13. A somewhat uncritical but comprehensive survey of planning activities is given by Herman Finer in a study entitled "Planning and Nationalization in Great Britain," *International Labour Review*, Vol. LVII. Three official reports should be consulted, the Barlow Report (1940), the Uthwatt Report (1942, Cmd. 6386), and the Scott Report (1942, Cmd. 6378).

14. There are 97 departments (including some overseas): 280 districts, and 3000 cantons, and about 38,000 communes, ranging from Paris to small hamlets (more than half have less than 500 inhabitants). The articles in the new French constitution dealing with local government are 85–89. These are a sad remnant of what was by some hoped would be genuine reform, conferring true self-government upon viable local units.

15. The quotation is from Sir E. D. Simon, *The Smaller Democracies* (1939), pp. 48 and 40. One may also note Lord Bryce's view given in *Modern Democracies*, Vol. II, p. 449, and quoted approvingly by Simon. Swiss attachment to canton and commune is discussed by Robert C. Brooks, certainly the most thorough American student of Swiss government, in *Civic Training in Switzerland* (1930), Ch. XV. For the Swiss official, see Carl J. Friedrich and Taylor Cole, *Responsible Bureaucracy* (1932).

16. As one example of many, consult the *Gemeindeordnung* (1945) and the *Kreisordnung* (1946) of Bavaria, instituted very hastily by military government, and the provisions of the Bavarian constitution, articles 11, 12, and 83, which still await adequate implementation. In article 83, those matters of special local concern are constitutionally defined as follows: the administration of communal property and enterprises; local transportation, including street and road construction and maintenance; water; light; gas; electricity; food; local planning; housing; local police; fire protection; local cultural activities (this refers to theaters, operas, orchestras, museums and the like); elementary and vocational schools and adult education; guardianship and welfare; local health; marriage, motherhood and infant care; physical training of youth; public baths; cemeteries; and monuments and buildings of local historical interest. Clearly, this is a broad pattern, largely comparable to British and American views. See *Constitutions of the German Länder*, containing the German text and official translation, published by CAD–OMGUS (1947).

17. See article 28 of the Basic Law. The official German text is undated.

18. See H. L. McBain, *The Law and the Practice of Municipal Home Rule* (1916). The quotation from Robson is found in his *ESS* article, cited above.

19. See the texts cited above under "Remarks." See also Arthur N. Holcombe, *State Government in the United States* (3d ed., 1931), especially pp. 135 ff., 405 ff., and Ch. XVIII. See also the section in Lord Bryce's *The American Commonwealth* (rev. ed., 1924), Chs. XLVIII–LII (which are still worth consulting). The annual surveys published in the *APSR* and the continuous material presented in *National Municipal Review* should also be considered indispensable.

20. Bryce, op. cit. Vol. I, p. 626.

21. See *The Boston Contest* (1944) published by The Boston University Press and containing

the prize winning programs. The program receiving first prize was submitted by the author, in collaboration with Charles Cherington, Walter F. Bogner, Seymour Harris, Talcott Parsons, and George R. Walker. The discussion in this paragraph follows the approach of our study without going into detail. The governmental and administrative aspects are described in "Planning for the Greater Boston Metropolitan Area" in *PAR*, Vol. V, pp. 113 ff. More recently, Charles R. Cherington has presented the matter anew in *National Municipal Review* (1949). See also Guy Greer's *Your City Tomorrow* (1947), which places this study within a broad context.

22. On the Continent, cities like Berlin and Paris have been effectively unified, whether on the decentralized or centralized pattern. Berlin, under quadripartite "control" has developed, since the War, into a "state"-like entity, with a constitution retaining some federal elements that are more than mere decentralization; unfortunately this constitution was not included in the CAD–OMGUS collection cited above, note 16, probably because it is to be replaced by another.

23. The issue is stated very effectively by William A. Robson in *The Government and Misgovernment of London* (1939), pp. 344 ff. See also J. A. Forshaw and P. Abercrombie, *The County of London Plan* (1943). There is a considerable literature on metropolitan problems. Among the more important, one might mention: *The Government of Metropolitan Areas in the United States* (1930), a report of the National Municipal League, prepared by Paul Studentski; Victor Jones, *Metropolitan Government* (1942); *A Plan for London County* (1942); *Organization for Metropolitan Planning* (1943), a study put out by the American Society of Planning Officials. See also the numerous reports by official bodies in the United States and Britain, such as the Report of the Metropolitan District Commission to the Massachusetts Legislature (1896), the Supplementary Report of the Urbanism Committee to the National Resources Committee (1939), and the numerous parliamentary and royal commission reports, cited by Robson. For Britain, the studies and hearings of the Ministry of Town and Country Planning are also important for the most recent developments. Very valuable is the recent study by Don. J. Bogue, *The Structure of The Metropolitan Community* (1949), based on R. D. McKenzie's previous research in his *The Metropolitan Community* (1933).

24. See the report of the American Society of Planning Officials, quoted in the preceding note, and especially the following: "A start must, of course, be made by a group of citizens who perceive the problems and the need. They would have to agree upon a general plan of what they wanted and why they wanted it." Whether to work through a party or on a nonpartisan basis is a matter of local politics.

25. The Report of the special commission of 1896, quoted above, note 23, already stated this issue quite plainly: "These boards have carried on their work in an admirable manner, but their creation by an act of the Legislature and the appointment of their members by the chief magistrate of the Commonwealth have constituted a wide and serious departure from the political principles upon which this state and nation are founded. . . ."

26. See Robson, op. cit. p. 349.

27. See Robert S. and Helen M. Lynd, *Middletown: A Study in Contemporary American Culture* (1929), and *Middletown in Transition: A Study in Cultural Conflicts* (1937), as well as W. Lloyd Warner (and associates), *Yankee City* (4 vols., 1941, 1942, 1945, 1948).

28. See the interesting experience referred to by David Riesman in his chapter "Criteria for Political Apathy" in *Leadership and Social Action* (1949). Reference should also be made to his article "The Meaning of Opinion" (with Nathan Glazer) in *POQ* (Winter 1948–1949), pp. 633 ff.

29. The illusion of "objectivity" in the sense of "neutrality" is stated at the outset, especially on page 3, where not being "completely objective" is described as a danger. The same point is emphasized by Clark Wissler in his preface. However, he works around to a more pragmatic view at the end, when he expresses the hope that "its perusal should enlighten the conscientious citizen and serve as a suggestion as to what information is needed by those who attempt to direct the affairs of an American town" (p. 7). The view is implied in the discussion of "The Machinery of Government" chapter, as well as in the "Conclusions." The Lynds feel considerable scepticism concerning the workings of traditional democracy in American local com-

munities, for instance, the observation that "... elections are no longer the lively centers of public interest that they were in the nineties." Lynd himself has changed (see *Knowledge for What?* (1939)).

XIV · General Problems of Representation

REMARKS

The literature of political science on representation is rather unsatisfactory. On the one hand, there is the philosophical literature ranging from Hobbes's *Leviathan* through Rousseau's *Contrat Social* to Green and Bosanquet, discoursing in normative and speculative terms. On the other hand, lawyers, or rather jurists, have been splitting hairs over the distinction between representation and delegation. This latter trend, while already seen in Burke's previously cited passages, became particularly popular in postwar Germany, where it produced two voluminous studies of considerable merit. These are Gerhard Leibholz, *Das Wesen der Repräsentation unter besonderer Berücksichtigung des Repräsentativsystems* (1929), and Hans J. Wolff, *Organschaft und Juristische Person*, Vol. II: *Theorie der Vertretung (Stellvertretung, Organschaft und Repräsentation als soziale und juristische Vertretungsformen)* (1934). Besides these, Rudolf Smend must also be mentioned because he has made representation the center of constitutional theory in his magistral *Verfassung und Verfassungsrecht* (1928), emphasizing its value for purposes of integration; see particularly pp. 93 ff. This (learned) insistence upon the difference between representation and delegation, after a long period of interchangeable use, arose out of strictly partisan considerations. Theorists appeared who maintained that "representation" denoted a wholly ideal relationship (this view was also developed by M. Hauriou in his *Leçons sur le Mouvement Social* [1899]), while the humbler *Vertretung* (delegation) was claimed to be a word describing the relationship of a commercial representative or lobbyist to his master. It was then shown that German (and other) parliamentary representatives were mere delegates, and the conclusion readily offered itself that representation had "deteriorated." It was the old trick of so exalting the ideal aspect of an institution as to make its actual operation appear in an unfavorable light. There is a sound and important distinction which has been carefully studied by historians, namely, the distinction between representatives bound by an imperative mandate, legally, and representatives not so bound. The detailed workings of such a system were ably discussed by Alice M. Holden in "The Imperative Mandate in the Spanish Cortes of the Middle Ages," *APSR*, Vol. XXIV (1930), pp. 886 ff. For England, the same material is analyzed in May McKisack, *Parliamentary Representation of the English Boroughs during the Middle Ages* (1932), with which one might supplement the standard work of A. F. Pollard, *The Evolution of Parliament* (2d ed., 1926). To this should be added the convenient and lucid essay by Charles A. Beard on "The Teutonic Origins of Representative Government," in *APSR*, Vol. XXVI (1932), pp. 28 ff., which demolishes the already faded authority of Montesquieu's celebrated claim that representative government originated in "the forests of Germany." A broad comparative and historical view underlies the essay, "Representation," by Francis W. Coker and Carlton C. Rodee in the *ESS*. It is built around a sound generalization resembling the more restricted political definition of representation given by Robert von Mohl in his "Recht und Politik der repräsentativen Monarchie" in *Staatsrecht, Völkerrecht und Politik* (1860), Vol. I, pp. 8 f. In its historical sections it summarizes the profound essay by Otto Hintze, "Weltgeschichtliche Bedingungen der Repräsentativverfassung," in *Historische Zeitschrift*, Vol. CXLIII, pp. 1–47, to which should be added the same author's "Typologie der ständischen Verfassung," ibid. Vol. CXLI, pp. 229 ff. Interesting controversial positions have been advanced by Wundt and Oppenheimer. John T. Salter's books contain a realistic analysis of the relationship between representatives and the people. Besides his *Boss Rule* (1935), see the treatment of "the representative function" in *The Pattern of Politics* (1940). See also E. P. Herring's *The Politics of Democracy* (1940), especially Chapter III. Even the quantitative aspects of representative behavior have in recent years begun to be explored; Stuart Rice has devoted Part V of his interesting volume on *Quantitative Methods in Politics* (1928) to "The Voting Behavior of Representative Groups" (pp. 189–241).

REFERENCES

1. The discussion in J. J. Rousseau here referred to is found in *Contrat Social,* Book III, Ch. XV. A view contrary to that here stated is found in Edwin Mims's able *Majority of the People* (1941). See also my fuller development of this thesis in *The New Belief in the Common Man* (1942), Ch. IV. On the matter of sovereignty, see the discussion in Chapter I and the literature referred to there.

2. Hobbes's view is expounded in *Leviathan*, Book I, Ch. XVI. For Locke's idea of power, see above, Ch. I, note 21; also Ch. XV, note 5.

3. For the estates, see Georg von Below, "System und Bedeutung der landständischen Verfassung," in *Territorium und Stadt* (1900), pp. 163 ff.; Otto von Gierke, *Das Deutsche Genossenschaftsrecht*, Vol. I, § 51 and elsewhere. See also, for a comparative political view, Hugo Preuss, *Verfassungspolitische Entwicklungen in Deutschland und Westeuropa* (1927), § 14. Rudolf Gneist's *Englische Verfassungsgeschichte* (1882), while subject to criticism in many respects, also helps through its discussion of parliamentary institutions as estates, as given in §§ 19–26. For the orthodox view, see William Stubbs, *English Constitutional History* (3d ed., 1887), particularly Ch. XV. The related problem of "charisma" has been dealt with explicitly by Max Weber in *Wirtschaft und Gesellschaft* (1922), Book III, Chs. IX and X. Much of the more recent literature on leadership gives some attention to it. See below, Ch. XVIII, note 3.

4. For Burke's views, see *Works* (Boston, 1839), Vol. II, pp. 12 ff. See also the significant comments by M. Einaudi, *Edmundo Burke e l'Indirizzo Storico Nelle Scienze Politiche* (1930), particularly pp. 78 ff. See also the Introduction to Ross J. S. Hoffman and Paul Levack's splendid selections, *Burke's Politics* (1948).

5. The definition by Robert von Mohl is found in his *Staatsrecht, Völkerrecht und Politik* (1860), Vol. I, pp. 8–9.

6. For literature on the Economic Councils, see below, Ch. XXII, note 8. The subject of restrictive qualifications for the electorate is an unpopular one, but it has to be faced. See the discussion in Edward M. Sait, *American Parties and Elections* (1927), particularly pp. 18 ff. and 38 ff. The abuse made of such methods, however, is a very serious obstacle to any progress along this line.

7. For a fuller development, see the author's *The New Belief in the Common Man* (1942), Ch. V.

8. Professor McIlwain has rightly insisted upon this emphasis on legislation in Bodin. See his *The Growth of Political Thought in the West* (1932), pp. 286 ff. For the identification of parliamentary deliberation and conversation, see Carl Schmitt, *Politische Romantik* (2d ed., 1925), passim, and *Die geistesgeschichtliche Lage des heutigen Parlamentarismus* (1923), pp. 20 ff. For the remainder, see the bibliography below, Ch. XVII. For the problem of "agreement on fundamentals," see above, Ch. IX, and especially "Democracy and Dissent" in *Political Quarterly*, (1939), Vol. X, No. 4.

9. Rousseau's quotation is found in *Contrat Social* (Everyman edition), Book I, Ch. V, pp. 33–34; that of Locke in *Of Civil Government* (Everyman edition), p. 183; that of Richard Hooker, in his *Of the Laws of Ecclesiastical Polity* (Everyman edition), p. 232.

10. The power of the purse is a standpat argument in connection with the development of parliamentary institutions. Hence the literature cited below in Chs. XVI and XVII contains material on the subject.

11. Consult, for this paragraph, the literature on the division of power and federalism, given above, Chs. X and XI.

12. Compare the brief survey of "Medieval Representative Institutions" in H. Sidgwick, *The Development of European Polity* (1903), Ch. XXI. On Simon de Montfort, see Stubbs, op. cit. pp. 96–98. See also the discussion of medieval constitutionalism in Ch. VII, pp. 124 f.

13. These problems are discussed in "Representation and Constitutional Reform in Europe," *The Western Political Quarterly* (1938), Vol. I, pp. 124 ff.

XV · *Electoral Systems in Theory and Practice*

REMARKS

The theory of electoral systems has received less attention than the extensive practice of electoral methods would seem to call for. Only the gradual extension of schemes for proportional representation has stimulated efforts at generalization. There is, of course, the special literature on proportional representation cited below. Walter Bagehot's classical discussion of this question, in his *English Constitution* (2d ed., 1873), Ch. V, and J. S. Mill's in *Representative Government* (1860), Ch. VII, are the main approaches, going beyond the general theory of representation. An important further contribution is James Hogan, *Election and Representation* (1945), which is built around Eire's experience with P. R. The literature on majority rule, to be sure, is relevant in a measure. An important contribution is Edwin Mims's *The Majority of the People* (1941). Wladislaw Konopczynski's able summary in the *ESS*, as well as his *Liberum Veto* (1918), (Fr. tr. by Mme. Korwin-Piotrowska [1930]), contains much genuine scientific theory. Besides these, historical treatments help considerably, such as Otto von Gierke's "Über die Geschichte des Majoritätsprinzips," in *Essays in Legal History*, ed. by Paul Vinogradoff (1913), Ch. XVI; and the recent study by J. G. Heinberg, "History of the Majority Principle," in *APSR*, Vol. XX (1926), pp. 52 ff., and the literature cited there. Of course, a certain amount of generalization is found in the general discussions contained in volumes such as C. E. Merriam and H. F. Gosnell, *The American Party System* (rev. ed., 1929), and E. M. Sait, *American Parties and Elections* (1927), particularly pp. 487 ff. in the latter, but attention is focused upon the workings of particular institutions in specific contexts. H. F. Gosnell's comparative survey, *Why Europe Votes* (1930), is full of significant material. Important further material is to be found in a number of parliamentary reports. For England we have the *Report of the Royal Commission Appointed to Enquire into Electoral Systems* (1910), Cd. 5163, and the *Minutes of Evidence*, Cd. 5162. For France, see *Rapport fait au nom de la Commission de Suffrage universel sur les propositions de loi tendant a établir la représentation proportionnelle;* this report was made by Charles Benoist on April 7, 1904, and is printed in *CD* IX, Annexe No. 160 (1906). For Sweden there is (perhaps the ablest of the three and the most recent) *Proportionsvalssakunnigas Betänkande* (1921).

The comparative analysis of electoral methods underlies F. A. Hermens's magistral study *Democracy or Anarchy?* (1941), in which the electoral experience of all major communities is surveyed. Hermens's treatment represents a considerable advance over George Horwill, *Proportional Representation, Its Dangers and Its Defects* (1925), and Charles Seymour and D. P. Frary, *How the World Votes; the Story of Democratic Development in Elections* (2 vols., 1918). The case for proportional representation is most authoritatively put in G. H. Hallett and C. G. Hoag, *Proportional Representation—the Key to Democracy* (1937). The issue has lately been a very live one in several European countries, notably in France and Germany.

REFERENCES

1. For the problem of qualifications, see the remarks of Bagehot, op. cit. (2d ed., 1873), pp. 209 ff.

2. For the English system, see J. A. Thomas, *The House of Commons* (1939), also W. I. Jennings, *Parliament* (1940), Ch. II. See further the survey in F. A. Ogg, *English Government and Politics* (2d ed., 1936), Ch. XIII, and the literature cited there. For the quotation, see pp. 298–299. The remarks of J. S. Mill are found in op. cit. Ch. X. The quotation from Bagehot is in op. cit. p. 214.

3. The pamphlet by Thomas Hare is entitled *The Machinery of Representation* (2d ed., 1857). The theme is more fully developed in his *Treatise on the Election of Representatives, Parliamentary and Municipal* (1859). Victor de Considérant's scheme is contained in *De la Sincérité du Gouvernement, Lettre á MM. les Membres du Grand Conseil . . . de Genève* (reprinted, 1892). The title of Thomas Gilpin's pamphlet is *On the Representation of Minorities of Electors to Act with the Majority in Elected Assemblies* (1844).

4. Walter Bagehot, *The English Constitution* (1st ed., 1867). Bagehot's studies first were published in the *Fortnightly Review* between the spring of 1865 and 1867. His discussion of p. 2 comes in the sixth article, entitled "The House of Commons," first published on March 15, 1866. The statistics are from Johannes Schauff, *Neues Wahlrecht* (1929), p. 249.

5. John Stuart Mill, *Considerations on Representative Government* (1st ed., 1861). Mill's discussion is contained in Ch. VII entitled "Of true and false democracy; representation of all, and representation of the majority only."

6. Mill, op. cit. p. 137. Italics added.

7. Regarding the apportionment controversy, see E. V. Huntington, "Methods of Apportionment in Congress," in *APSR*, Vol. XXV (1931), pp. 961 ff., and the article on the subject by W. S. Carpenter in the *ESS*. For gerrymandering, see the discussions in Merriam-Gosnell, op. cit., and in Sait, op. cit., as well as in E. C. Griffith, *Rise and Development of the Gerrymander* (1907), and C. O. Sauer, "Geography and the Gerrymander" in *APSR*, Vol. XII, pp. 403 ff.

8. For this and the following paragraphs, see Hermens, *Democracy or Anarchy?* (1941) for a critical view, and Hallett and Hoag for the arguments in favor.

9. Detailed illustrations of the working of these and other systems were given in *Constitutional Government and Politics* (1937), pp. 271 ff.; see also *Constitutional Government and Democracy* (1941), pp. 282 ff. These analyses were superseded by Dr. F. A. Hermens's admirable analysis in op. cit. For his treatment of Belgium, see Ch. XII; of the Scandinavian countries, Ch. XIII.

10. According to recent estimates, the Irish situation is rapidly deteriorating; in accordance with the well-known pattern of coalition government. See the article by James Hogan, "Ireland should Join in the Atlantic Pact," *Sunday Independent*, March 6, 1949. The radicalism of McBride and his followers provides a striking illustration of the ill effects of coalition government.

11. The issue is stated strikingly by Michel Debré in "Du Gouvernement de la Liberté," *Revue du Droit Publique et de la Science Politique en France et a l'Etranger* (1949), especially pp. 44 ff., where the author links the problem to that of "la renouvellement des élites." See also Gordon Wright, *Reshaping of French Democracy* (1948), especially pp. 223, 289. In Germany the issue has been highlighted by the Deutsche Wählergesellschaft led by Alfred Weber and Dolf Sternberger; Sternberger, as editor of *Die Wandlung* has published numerous articles by himself and by others.

XVI · *Parliaments as Representative Assemblies*

REMARKS

The general literature on parliaments is very considerable, as may be gleaned from a perusal of the monographs cited in the section on "Legislative Assemblies" in the *ESS*, Vol. IX, pp. 395–398. Of the general and theoretical studies, Robert Luce's *Legislative Assemblies* (1924) and his *Legislative Procedure* (1922) may be put down together with Herman Finer's *The Theory and Practice of Modern Governments*, Part V (Parliaments), as the broadest comparative treatments of the subject in recent years. Besides these, Roland Young's *This is Congress* (1943) gives an outstanding evaluation of the American representative assembly; more recently, Estes Kefauver and Jack Levin offered a program of reform in *A Twentieth-Century Congress* (1947). For Britain, W. I. Jennings, *Parliament* (1940), should now be placed as the best treatment of the "mother of parliaments." For a more pessimistic estimate, see Harold Laski's *Parliamentary Government in England* (1938). However, in spite of its seemingly special focus, Josef Redlich's *The Procedure of the House of Commons* (a translation of *Recht und Technik des englischen Parlamentarismus* [1905]) is so broadly significant that no student of parliamentary problems can afford to neglect it. For the historical phases of the comparative development, Robert von Mohl's "Recht und Politik der repräsentativen Monarchie," in his *Staatsrecht, Völkerrecht und Politik*, Vol. I, pp. 1 ff., remains valuable. A very broad framework is provided for representative bodies in Charles E. Merriam's *Systematic Politics* (1945), pp. 134 ff., "Conciliar Organs." However, the "organ" theory of continental European constitutional lawyers, like Jellinek, underlying Merriam's systematization, is incompatible with the view here set forth. "An organ," Merriam informs us, "is a persistent cluster of behavior patterns which persists long enough to be identified by the group and recognized as a part of the expectancies of daily life" (p. 118). There are many different kinds of such clusters, only some of which resemble the kind of political institution ordinarily discussed under the head of "organ of the state."

REFERENCES

1. See W. I. Jennings, *Parliament* (1940), especially Ch. X, and pp. 7, 109–110, and 495. Though Finer starts his discussion, op. cit., with the customary proposition that legislatures occupy themselves mainly with lawmaking, control of the executive, and investigations, the body of his discussion tends to support strongly the conclusion that "the procedure of Parliament is directed to influencing the general body of the public rather than its members" (p. 830). For the breakdown of contact between government and citizen in Germany, see Fritz Morstein Marx, *Government in the Third Reich*, pp. 156 f. and passim. Regarding the difficulties encountered by Stresemann, see *Stresemann's Vermächtnis* (ed. Henry Bernhard, 1932), for example, Vol. I, pp. 138 ff. The technique of the United States Chamber of Commerce's referendum is competently described by E. P. Herring, *Group Representation before Congress* (1929), pp. 89 ff. For the problem of America's division before the Second World War, see *The New Belief in the Common Man*, Ch. III and the references.

2. The *schemas* of parliamentary seating arrangements are found in Joseph R. Starr, *Topical Analysis of Comparative European Government* (1934), pp. 30 and 115. Regarding seating arrangements in Congress, see Robert Luce, *Legislative Procedure* (1922), p. 241.

3. For this paragraph, Josef Redlich's masterly analysis in *The Procedure of the House of Commons* (1908), Vol. II, pp. 115 ff., is still important. A valuable recent contribution is J. A. Thomas, *The House of Commons, 1832–1901* (1939). Figures are given by Redlich on p. 125. An interesting comparative table for the year 1924 is given by Herman Finer, op. cit. p. 657. André Tardieu's *La Revolution à Refaire* (1936) (see Ch. XVIII, note 14) contains valuable material. Another interesting contribution is found in Walther Lambach, *Die Herrschaft der Fünfhundert* (1926). The special problems of the German parliament were treated statistically by Viktor Egelhardt, "Die Zusammensetzung des Reichstags nach Alter, Beruf und Religionsbekenntnis," in *Die Arbeit*, Vol. VIII (1931), pp. 31 ff. For the problems of the trade association officials, see these titles, and the interesting though rather controversial account by G. T. Garratt, *The Mugwumps and the Labor Party* (1932). Shaw's statement is quoted by Harold Laski, op. cit. p. 155. Laski comments, "The language is forceful; it is not more forceful than the facts." On Bonn, see Konrad Mommsen, "Bonn—Ein Beamtenparlament," in *Die Wandlung* (1948), Vol. IV, pp. 250 ff. See also the author's article, *APSR*, 1949.

4. For the general development discussed in this chapter, see Redlich, op. cit. Chs. I, II. See also E. Porritt, *The Unreformed House of Commons; Parliamentary Representation before 1832* (3d ed., 1909), for the earlier phase. The quotation from Redlich is found in the English edition of op. cit. Vol. I, p. 207; that from Jennings in op. cit. p. xii.

5. See W. I. Jennings, op. cit. Ch. XI, for the best recent discussion of the whole paragraph; compare the well-balanced discussion in F. A. Ogg, *English Government and Politics* (1929), Chs. XIV and XV, and the literature cited there. On the Senate, see the comprehensive recent treatment by G. H. Haynes, *The Senate of the United States, Its History and Practice* (1938). The general problem of second chambers is discussed by H. W. V. Temperley, *Senates and Upper Chambers* (1910), J. A. R. Marriott, *Second Chambers* (1910 and 1927), and H. B. Lees-Smith, *Second Chambers in Theory and Practice* (1923); it is treated more briefly in Finer, op. cit. Ch. XVII. For a skillful analysis of Labour's position regarding the House of Lords see Dell G. Hitchner, "The Labour Government and the House of Lords," in *The Western Political Quarterly* (1948), Vol. I, pp. 426 ff. The figures are found in Ogg, op. cit. p. 331; the wisecrack was made by Aug. Birrell, a liberal leader. Lord Wemyss's proposal is summarized in Ogg, op. cit. p. 359. The text of the Bryce Committee is reprinted (with omissions) in Howard

L. McBain and L. Rogers, *The New Constitutions of Europe* (1922), pp. 573 ff.; its intellectual value is generally overrated, its proposals were weak and complicated. The quotation is from the Webbs' *A Constitution for a Socialist Commonwealth of Great Britain* (1920), p. 63. The proposal for proportional representation is found in R. Muir, *Peers and Bureaucrats* (1910), pp. 133 ff. The quotation from the *Labour Speakers' Handbook* is given in Ogg, op. cit. p. 356. Bentham's views are set forth lucidly and convincingly by Lewis Rockow, "Bentham on the Theory of Second Chambers," *APSR*, Vol. XXII (1928), pp. 576 ff. They are also succinctly stated in Bentham's *Essay on Political Tactics* (1816–1817), Ch. I, § 5 (followed by a statement of the advantages intended by Bentham, but actually supplied by his editor, Dumont; whether we should question the conclusions of Rockow on this account is doubtful, though Hatschek, *Englisches Staatsrecht*, Vol. I, p. 435, takes it for granted). The problem of second chambers has recently been raised controversially once more in connection with the movement for unicameral legislatures in American states. See Alvin W. Johnson, *The Unicameral Legislature* (1938), Charles W. Shull, *American Experience with Unicameral Legislatures* (1937), Harrison B. Summers, *Unicameralism in Practice: the Nebraska Legislative System* (1937).

6. Cmd. 9038/1918, p. 4.

7. The evaluation of Bentham is shared by Redlich, op. cit. pp. 777 and 784 ff. and by Hatschek, op. cit. pp. 434 ff., though these authors disagree about many other points. See also Élie Halévy's important general study, *The Growth of Philosophic Radicalism* (tr. into English, 1928). The full title of Bentham's work is *An Essay on Political Tactics, or Inquiries Concerning the Discipline and Mode of Proceeding Proper to Be Observed in Political Assemblies: Principally Applied to the Practice of the British Parliament, and to the Constitution and Situation of the National Assembly of France.* This work was first published in French in 1816 by M. Dumont, and translated into German, etc., from this edition. Robert Mohl praised it highly and was himself, as chairman of the Committee on (Procedural) Rules in the National Assembly at Frankfurt, as well as through his active participation in the diets of Württemberg and the new German Empire, instrumental in spreading the gospel. See his comments in *Geschichte und Literatur der Staatswissenschaften* (1855), Vol. I, pp. 310 ff.; in *Württembergisches Staatsrecht* (1836), Vol. III, pp. 627 ff.; and in *Staatsrecht, Völkerrecht und Politik*, Vol. I, pp. 281 and 282, where he commences his noteworthy essay, "Die Geschäftsordnung der Ständeversammlungen," with it (1860). Bentham's ideas are set forth in Bowring's edition (1843) (hereafter referred to), Vol. II, pp. 302 ff. and 310 ff. The quotation is found on p. 313. Hamilton's book is entitled *Parliamentary Logic* (republished in 1927); its editor, Courtney S. Kenny, has offered some shrewd comments in an introduction and notes. Bentham's comments on Hamilton, quite vitriolic to be sure, are found in his *The Book of Fallacies* (ed. cit.), Vol. II, pp. 383 ff. For Redlich's view as stated, see op. cit. pp. 390 ff. Bentham's recognition of parties is suggested in op. cit. p. 361, and the quotation is in ibid. p. 385. Even the fragmentary English edition of Hitler's *Mein Kampf* contains a few passages, pp. 30 ff. (in the original 9th ed., pp. 81 ff.). Hatschek's views are found in op. cit. Vol. I, pp. 426 ff.

8. See Jennings, op. cit. Ch. III. The statement from Bentham is found in op. cit. Vol. II, p. 330. Regarding Speaker Onslow, see Edward Porritt, *The Unreformed House of Commons: Parliamentary Representation before 1832* (1903), pp. 448 ff. See also generally ibid. Chs. XXI–XXII. The reference to Stubbs is found in his *Lectures* (1906), p. 314. For Edward Coke, see Hastings Lyon and H. Block, *Edward Coke: Oracle of the Law* (1929), pp. 60 ff. For the following quotations from Redlich, see op. cit. pp. 422 and 410 ff. The quotation is again from Redlich, op. cit. (in the author's own translation), p. 405. See his entire discussion in the English edition, Vol. II, pp. 131–168.

9. For the American Speakership, the important historical study is M. P. Follett, *The Speaker of the House of Representatives* (1896). For a more recent study of the institution as it exists today, see Robert Luce's *Legislative Procedure* (1922), Chs. XIX–XXII. The quotation from Bryce (whose discussion of the problem is worth considering) is found in *American Commonwealth*, Vol. I, p. 208. The next quotation is from an article by Elwood Mead in the *Independent*, January 8, 1917, which is cited by R. Luce, op. cit. p. 486. Speaker Carlisle's statement

is in ibid. p. 466. This view was reasserted by Speaker Longworth in 1926: "I believe it to be the duty of the Speaker, standing squarely on the platform of his party, to assist in so far as he properly can the enactment of legislation in accordance with the declared principles and policies of his party, and by the same token to resist the enactment of legislation in violation thereof," *Congressional Record*, 69th Congress, 1st Sess., p. 382. The quotation from Reed is given by C. A. Beard, *The American Leviathan*, p. 302, in the course of a very brief but, as usual, perspicacious discussion of the speakership. Luce's criticisms of customary views on the Speaker's powers are found in op. cit. pp. 455 ff. For reform suggestions, see W. Y. Elliott's highly controversial *The Need for Constitutional Reform* (1935), pp. 232 ff. For the relative neutrality of the Speaker in Massachusetts, see Luce, op. cit. p. 456, where this author also criticizes the discussion of the speakership in American state legislatures as found in Arthur Holcombe's *State Government in the United States* (1916), p. 252 (see also later p. 465). Holcombe's views seem to have remained unaltered, however, for he makes the same statements in the third edition (1931), pp. 294 ff.

10. For Bryce's discussion, see *American Commonwealth*, Vol. I, pp. 203 ff. (rev. ed., 1924). For the whips, see Redlich, op. cit. pp. 364 ff.; A. L. Lowell, *Government of England* (1908), Vol. I, pp. 448 ff. Viscount Gladstone's account is found in *APSR*, Vol. XXI (1927), pp. 519 ff. See also M. Ostrogorski, *Democracy and the Organization of Political Parties* (1902), Vol. I, pp. 137 ff. Jennings, op. cit. Ch. III, takes a somewhat more modern view regarding the role of the whips.

11. Lindsay Rogers, *The Senate* (1926), especially Chs. IV and V. Rogers's conclusions were challenged by Robert Luce in *Congress: An Explanation* (1926), as far as the House and its comparison with the Senate were concerned. See also G. R. Brown, *The Leadership of Congress* (1922). The discussion in the House of Commons to which references are made occurred on June 25, ff., 1929. See *HCD*, Vol. CCXXIX, pp. 50 ff.

12. This paragraph's point constitutes the central theme of Redlich's volume. The quotations (in the author's own translation) are found in the original, p. 799. In the English edition this passage occurs in Vol. III, p. 197.

13. See Stuart A. Rice, *Quantitative Methods in Politics* (1928), Ch. XIV.

14. Jennings, op. cit. p. 508.

XVII · *Parliaments as Deliberative Assemblies*

REMARKS

The general literature, of course, is the same as that described in the remarks for Ch. XVI. To these should be added, however, two important American works, Joseph P. Chamberlain, *Legislative Processes, National and State* (1936), and Harvey Walker, *Law Making in the United States* (1934). The first one particularly is full of illustrative material derived from the author's rich practical experience. But neither attempts to define in any general way the social and political conditions of "deliberation." The nearest approach is Robert D. Leigh's discussion in *Group Leadership* (1936). All the works referred to comment upon the problems connected with this central function of parliament, but no studies of this phenomenon as such have come to the author's attention.

REFERENCES

1. The secrecy of parliamentary proceedings is described by Porritt, op. cit. Vol. I, pp. 589–596, and by Th. E. May, *Constitutional History of England* (7th ed., 1882), Vol. II. See also *HCD*, Vol. XI (1808), cited by Redlich, op. cit. p. 291.

2. The central importance of speech is brought out forcefully by Redlich, op. cit. pp. 586 ff. The remarks of the Marquess of Hartington are to be found in *HCD*, Vol. CCLXVII (1882), p. 1327. The problems of parliamentary government in Britain without a majority party are discussed by Ramsay Muir, *How Britain Is Governed* (1930), particularly pp. 145 ff. For the most

recent efforts at "reform," see R. D. Denman, "Procedure in the House of Commons," in *The Nineteenth Century* (1933). On motions, see Bentham, *Political Tactics*, Chs. VIII, IX, and XI; *Works*, Vol. II, pp. 352 ff.

3. For a sketch of this case, see W. I. Jennings, op. cit. pp. 95 f., and compare his discussion (Ch. IV), for the whole paragraph. The interpellations in the French parliament are elaborately analyzed in Finer, op. cit. Vol. II, pp. 869 ff.

4. Closure is one of the most hotly contested issues of modern politics. For the "classical" doctrine of adjournment, see again Bentham, op. cit. Ch. XIII. See also Luce, op. cit. Ch. XII. Speaker Brand's statement is to be found in *HCD*, Vol. CCLVII (1881), pp. 2032–2033. Closure is searchingly discussed by Redlich, op. cit. pp. 198 ff., 201 ff., 219 ff., 598 ff. For Finer's view, see his op. cit. Vol. II, pp. 852 ff. For Speaker Reed's remark, see *Congressional Record*, January 31, 1890 (Vol. XXI, p. 999). It may be observed in passing that Carl Schmitt, if he had familiarized himself with the actual operation of parliamentary bodies instead of with certain theories about them, would not have made all the errors which underlie his "smart" insistence upon the kinship between parliamentarism and the Romantic "everlasting conversation." If he had dug deeper still, he would have discovered that the Romantics in England (where they had some familiarity with parliamentary methods) were the spearhead of antiparliamentary emotionalism. The true kinship is not between parliaments and Romantics, but between Romantics and antiparliamentarism and irrationalism, as opposed to the kinship between parliamentarism, rationalism, utilitarianism, and reform. Lindsay Rogers, *The American Senate* (1926), contains a provocative discussion of the problems of closure; for the particular quotation see pp. 248–250.

5. See Redlich, op. cit. pp. 114 ff., 463 ff., 473 ff.; H. Finer, op. cit. Vol. II, pp. 804 ff. The two quotations are found on pp. 797 and 809, respectively. See *Standing Order 41*. The remarks of Sir Courtenay Ilbert are found in his English edition of Redlich, Vol. III, pp. 215–216. See, especially, W. I. Jennings, *Parliament* (1940), Ch. XI. The quote is from John C. Ranney and Gwendolyn M. Carter, *The Major Foreign Powers* (1948), p. 121.

6. For this paragraph see the thorough discussion in Luce, op. cit. Chs. IV–VIII. For the early beginnings, see R. V. Harlow, *The History of Legislative Methods in the Period before 1825* (1917). Special reference is had to p. 16. The first quotation from Luce is found, op. cit., on p. 100, the second one on p. 151. For a scientifically detailed study of the activities of interest groups before Congress, see E. P. Herring, *Group Representation before Congress* (1929), particularly pp. 249 ff., although he probably overestimates the importance of the caucus, p. 248. See below, note 13. For the figures, see Rogers, op. cit. pp. 186–187. See for England, Muir, op cit. pp. 205–211. On hearings, see Luce, op. cit. pp. 142 ff. See the Supreme Court case, *Jurney* v. *McCracken*, S. Ct. 55 [1935], for the issue of congressional power of investigation. The list of House Standing Committees can be found in the *Congressional Directory*.

7. The history of committee procedure in the French Chamber is sketched by Joseph-Barthélemy, *Essai sur le Travail Parlementaire et le Système des Commissions* (1934), Ch. I. The author does not believe that it is necessary, or indeed desirable, to translate the French term *commission* as commission, inasmuch as that word has acquired a very different connotation in English, particularly in the United States. The fact that the French, who originally also called their standing committees *comités*, changed to *commission* is due to the horror which the committees of the revolutionary tribunals, and more particularly the *Comité du Salut Public*, had left behind. See, for this, Barthélemy, op. cit. pp. 7 and 27. For the party basis of committees, see ibid. pp. 82 ff. (we have omitted reference to the older system of *bureaux* because it is complicated and no longer significant). About committee leadership, see Barthélemy, op. cit. p. 9 and passim. About the reportorial stage, Barthélemy gives examples on pp. 180–181, and he discusses the advisory reports in ibid. p. 197. For the vote without debate, see ibid. pp. 207 ff. As these references show (and many more could be given), no student of the French parliamentary system could afford to neglect Barthélemy's highly informative volume. For the new French situation, see Gordon Wright, *The Reshaping of French Democracy* (1948); for the antecedent situation, see D. Thomson, *Democracy in France* (1946). Robert M. Gooch's recent articles also contribute valuable insights. For Tardieu's criticism, see his op. cit. Vol. II.

8. Jennings, op. cit. p. 334. The problem of financial control is arousing an increasing amount of interest, and rightly so. The mass of public expenditures is ever greater, and some method of supervision seems essential. The literature, however, is quite diffuse; the subject was supposed to be part of public finance and therefore held to be explorable in terms of economics. This is only partially true. In recent years, however, budgetary problems have received careful treatment by a number of scholars, among whom W. F. Willoughby and A. E. Buck stand out. To these might be added Gaston Jèze, the introduction to whose *Allgemeine Theorie des Budgets* (1927) commences with the striking (and probably correct) assertion, "Das Budget ist seinem Wesen nach ein politischer Akt." A. E. Buck's *The Budget in Governments of Today* (1934) is the most comprehensive study of budgetary problems we have. The statement from Ramsay Muir is found in *How Britain Is Governed* (1930), p. 228. Willoughby makes the same point in his *Principles of Public Administration* (1927), p. 481. The reference to the English parliamentary committee is *Reports from the Select Committee on National Expenditures* (1918), p. 115. For the *Budget and Accounting Act* and the methods prevailing since that time, see W. F. Willoughby, *Principles of Public Administration*, Part IV, which gives a broad comparative treatment; for the particular problems of the text, see Ch. XXIII. For the particular technical matters of the audit, see G. C. S. Benson, *Financial Control and Integration*, in *Studies in Systematic Political Science and Comparative Government* (1934), Vol. II. See also Ch. XIX, pp. 404 ff. See also the several contributions in Vol. II of *Public Policy* (1941) devoted to fiscal problems, notably the articles by Rawson, Thompson, and Perloff.

9. The discussion in this paragraph follows Ch. IX of Barthélemy's *Essai* as far as the facts are concerned, though the interpretation varies at times. Specific reference may be made to p. 278, where he discusses the special facilities; to pp. 283 ff., where he discusses the presidents and reporters; to p. 286, where the statement about government and opposition is made. That the *rapporteur* was actually controlling the government is alleged by A. Thibaudet, *La République des Professeurs* (1927), p. 243, as well as by others. Barthélemy's remark about the leftist group is found on p. 354.

10. For this paragraph, see Barthélemy, op. cit. Ch. VI, "Le contrôle parlementaire par les commissions." He also emphasizes the suspicion of the bureaucracy as a central attitude behind the French public's and the parliament's interest in committees as a method of organizing effective control, for example, on pp. 24–25. For the control techniques of Frederick the Great, see W. L. Dorn, "The Prussian Bureaucracy in the Eighteenth Century," *Political Science Quarterly*, Vol. XLVI (1931), pp. 403 ff. The resignations of Briand and Loucheur are described by Barthélemy, op. cit. pp. 233–234. The significance of investigations, politically, is considered by L. Rogers, *The American Senate* (1926), Ch. VI. Joseph P. Chamberlain, op. cit. Ch. VII, also brings out their value for general legislation. Congressional committees have always served another important function, that of surveying a field to which the individual student does not have access. See, for example, the monumental survey of the Temporary National Economic Committee on "Investigation of Concentration of Economic Power," 31 vols., 1940–1941. On the Legislative Reorganization Act, S.2177, see S. Report 1011 and 1400, the Report of the APSA, as well as Joseph P. Harris's able critical article in *PAR*, Vol. VI, pp. 267 ff.

11. See the author's *Foreign Policy in the Making* (1938) for a fuller treatment of these issues. Some of the bibliography is found above, attached to Ch. IV. In the United States, an extensive controversy has issued over the Senate's power in foreign affairs; E. S. Corwin, *The President's Control of Foreign Relations* (1917), and Q. Wright, *The Control of American Foreign Relations* (1922), have treated these problems for the United States, as well as R. J. Dangerfield in his *In Defense of the Senate* (1933). F. R. Flournoy gives an account of British practice in *Parliament and War* (1927), which is critically discussed by A. Ponsonby, *Democracy and Diplomacy* (1915). To these may be added George Young, *Diplomacy Old and New* (1921); P. S. Reinsch, *Secret Diplomacy* (1922); Walter Lippmann, *The Stakes of Diplomacy* (1915); and Aubrey L. Kennedy, *Old Diplomacy and New* (1922), as well as the more recent discussion by Harold Nicolson, called a terminal essay, concluding his trilogy, *Portrait of a Diplomatist* (1930), *Peacemaking, 1919* (1933), and *Curzon: the Last Phase* (1934), and attached to the last volume. All three contain repeated

references to the problem. Finally a broad treatment is undertaken by DeWitt C. Poole, *The Conduct of Foreign Relations under Modern Democratic Conditions* (1924), which blends experience nicely with theory. The French problem has repeatedly been treated by Joseph-Barthélemy, first in his *Démocratie et Politique Étrangère* (1916), then in his *La Conduite de la Politique Extérieure dans les Démocraties* (1930), and finally in Ch. VIII of his *Essai* already cited. The last represents the maturer view. The interpretation of the Dutch situation is based on interviews by the author.

12. Bentham's views on secrecy are set forth in his essay, Ch. II (*Works*, Vol. II, pp. 310 ff.). The point had been made earlier and with broad implications for constitutional government by Immanuel Kant in a number of works; see the author's *Introduction to the Philosophy of Kant* (1949). For Luce's views, see his *Legislative Procedure*, pp. 150–151. For Wilson, see *The New Freedom* (1913), pp. 125–129. The further reference to Bentham is found on pp. 315–316. The problem of secrecy has wide ramifications and awaits scientific study by a sociologically minded political scientist. At present we are groping in the dark as far as answers to the question "Under what conditions do men act secretly?" are concerned. Yet the matter is central to political science.

13. The importance of the caucus is quite controversial among students and observers of American politics. It would seem to the author that Luce's discussion of the matter, op. cit. pp. 506 ff., is rather well balanced, but it should be supplemented by the observations of E. M. Sait, *American Parties and Elections* (rev. ed., 1939, Ch. XII); Charles E. Merriam, *The American Party System* (ed. with H. F. Gosnell, 3d ed., 1940, pp. 53–56). Obviously, the matter is in a state of flux at present.

14. The problem of secrecy continues to trouble representative assemblies. The new French constitution provides (art. 10) that the meetings of the two chambers shall be public, but then withdraws this provision, in effect, by allowing the chambers to convene as a secret committee. The German Basic Law (art. 42) likewise provides that the meetings shall be public, but then provides that the public may be excluded by two-thirds majority, upon motion of either the government or one tenth of the members.

XVIII · *Chief Executives and Cabinet Systems*

REMARKS

The problems of leadership, and more especially those of executive leadership, have received an increasing amount of attention from political scientists, sociologists, and psychologists in recent years. The rise of one-man dictatorship has brought to light facets of the problem which had lain dormant. It is manifestly impossible to survey this entire literature here. Suffice it to mention Chester I. Barnard, *The Functions of the Executive* (1938); T. N. Whitehead, *Leadership in a Free Society* (1936); and Ordway Tead, *The Art of Leadership* (1935). Many texts in social psychology also discuss this problem.

On the specific problems of the chief executive, especially in England and America, a number of important contributions have appeared recently: George F. Milton, *The Use of Presidential Power, 1789–1943* (1944); C. Perry Patterson, *Presidential Government in the United States* (1947); Wilfred C. Binkley, *President and Congress* (1947); along with the prewar studies of Corwin, Herring, Laski, and others. W. I. Jennings, *Cabinet Government* (1936), evaluates the shift toward executive leadership in England; E. P. Herring, *Presidential Leadership* (1940), realistically portrays the president as the prime mover of American politics today; Harold Laski, *The American Presidency* (1940), contrasts American and British Cabinet systems and urges the adoption of British practices; it forms a companion to Laski's *Parliamentary Government in England* (1938). The issue was strikingly high-lighted in a discussion between Harold Laski and Don K. Price in *PAR*, Vol. IV, pp. 347 ff. (1944), Price having the better of the argument. E. S. Corwin, *The President: Office and Powers* (1940), examines the changed constitutional law. Paralleling these, Louis Lipson has offered a new comparative appraisal of *The American*

640

Governor (1939). For a comparative French view see Emile Giraud, *La Crise de la Démocratie et le Renforcement du Pouvoir Exécutif* (1939). An able bibliographical survey of the whole problem is given by Michael Dendias in his *Le Renforcement des Pouvoirs du Chef de L'État dans la Démocratie Moderne* (1932).

An earlier comparative monograph on the cabinet system is W. Hasbach, *Die parlamentarische Kabinettsregierung* (1919), though Herman Finer's part on the executive, in his *The Theory and Practice of Modern Government* (1932) (Part VI, pp. 949 ff.), is as comprehensive and more recent. While somewhat differently focused, Robert Redslob's *Die parlamentarische Regierung* (1918), translated into French as *Le régime parlementaire, Études sur les institutions d'Angleterre, de Belgique, de Hongrie, de France* (1924), advanced the much attacked thesis that the relation between cabinet and parliament in France is such that the system must be called "false" in terms of the older English doctrine. A good deal of important general thought on the subject is digested also in James Bryce's *Modern Democracies*.

REFERENCES

1. For the detailed comparison, see *The Federalist* (ed. H. C. Lodge), pp. 435–6.

2. The doctrines of these writers are found in their individual works. See Thomas Carlyle, *On Heroes, Hero-Worship, and the Heroic in History* (1841), Lecture VI; Charles Maurras, *Enquête sur la Monarchie* (1900; new ed. 1924), especially Book I and Appendix; Friedrich Nietzsche, *The Will to Power* (tr. A. M. Ludovici, 1910), especially Vol. II, Book IV; Jakob Burckhardt, *Weltgeschichtliche Betrachtungen* (1918 ed.), pp. 210 ff.; H. A. Taine, *L'Ancien Régime* (1876), passim; Leopold von Ranke, *Die Grossen Mächte, Meisterwerke* (1914–15 ed.), Vol. X.

3. See the literature on leadership cited in *Remarks*, above.

4. James Burnham, *The Managerial Revolution* (1941), overemphasizes this point. It has occupied a considerable place in recent literature on administrative problems. See the approach in Barnard's study cited above, and in George A. Graham's *Education for Public Administration* (1941).

5. See Harold Lasswell, *World Politics and Personal Insecurity* (1935), for a broad statement.

6. See the author's *The New Belief in the Common Man* (1942), Ch. VII, and his review article of Friedrich A. Hayek's bitter *The Road to Serfdom* (1944), which precipitated Herman Finer's even more vitriolic *Road to Reaction* (1945). The literature on the governmental aspects of planning and its relation to constitutional democracy is growing rapidly. John Jewkes, in *Ordeal by Planning* (1948), has subjected the policy and practice of the British Labour Government to sharp criticism for too much planning; but Paul Sweezey, *Socialism* (1949), insists that there is too little planning to make Britain's a true Socialist government. Laski's writings point in the same direction. Charles E. Merriam has continuously stressed the relation between constitutionalism and planning; See his *Systematic Politics* (1945) and *The New Democracy and the New Despotism* (1939), as well as A. D. Lindsay's *The Modern Democratic State* (1943). See also the literature cited below, Ch. XXIII.

7. F. J. Goodnow, *Politics and Administration* (1900), p. 22.

8. See Ramsay Muir, *How Britain Is Governed* (1930), pp. 81–91, 120–132, which offers a sharply critical account of the decline of parliamentary power over the ministry. Ivor Jennings, in his *Parliament* (1940), takes issue with this view.

9. The problem of this paragraph has been at the heart of many comparative studies, such as Wilson's *Congressional Government* (1885) as well as more recent discussions of constitutional reform, especially W. Y. Elliott, *The Need for Constitutional Reform* (1935), Ch. IX, and Henry Hazlitt, *A New Constitution Now* (1942). But it still remains an open issue.

10. W. I. Jennings, *Cabinet Government* (1936), pp. 139 ff., gives a number of interesting cases illustrating these differences. His analysis underlies the entire discussion.

11. For the significance of that campaign in the evolution of parliamentary and popular influence upon foreign policy, see C. J. Friedrich, *Foreign Policy in the Making* (1938), pp. 92 ff. The quotation from Lowell is found in *The Government of England*, Vol. I, p. 56.

641

12. For Lloyd George's view, see his *War Memoirs*, particularly Vol. III, Ch. I, and passim. For England's wartime government, see *Government of Wartime Europe* (ed. Harold Zink and Taylor Cole, 1941), Chs. I (E. P. Chase) and II (W. H. Wickwar). For Churchill's own view, see his *The Gathering Storm* (1948). Regarding the Imperial Defense Committee, see above, Ch. XI, note 16. For the personnel aspect, see Harold Laski, *The British Cabinet: A Study of Its Personnel, 1801-1924* (1928), and his article on the subject in *APSR*, Vol. XXII (1928), pp. 12 ff.

13. For the Dominions, see the *Report* of the Royal Commission on Dominion-Provincial Relations, Books I and II (1940), Manfred Nathan, *The South African Commonwealth* (1919), and B. R. Wise, *The Commonwealth of Australia* (1909).

14. A significant recent contribution is Gordon Wright's *Raymond Poincaré and the French Presidency* (1942). The workings of the Cabinet system in France have been subjected to an ever-increasing barrage of criticism in recent years. See, for a sharp attack, André Tardieu, *La Révolution à Refaire* (1936), especially Vol. II. For a more detached analysis, see A. Esmein, *Eléments de Droit Constitutionnel*, Vol. II, pp. 4, 230 ff.; David Thomson, *Democracy in France* (1946); and W. L. Middleton, *The French Political System* (1932). Robert de Jouvenel's comments are found in *La République des Camarades* (1914), pp. 93 ff.; the quotation, on p. 115. For the figures, see *Annuaire du Parlement*, Vol. VII, pp. 795-826, Vol. X, pp. 912-923; *Europa Yearbook* (1927), pp. 207-210; and John G. Heinberg, "The Personnel of French Cabinets, 1871-1930," *APSR*, Vol. XXV (1931), pp. 389 ff. The quotation from Barthélemy is found in his *The Government of France* (authorized translation by J. Bayard Morris), pp. 105-106. A realistic insight into the workings of the French Cabinet system can perhaps best be gained by reading D. W. Brogan's *The Development of Modern France* (1940).

15. The ablest analysis of the Weimar system is found in Heinrich Herrfahrdt, *Die Kabinettsbildung nach der Weimarer Verfassung unter dem Einfluss der politischen Praxis* (1927), and in Fritz Poetzsch-Heffter, "Vom Staatsleben unter der Weimarer Verfassung," "I" and "II," in *Jahrbuch des öffentlichen Rechts*, Vol. XIII, pp. 162 ff., and Vol. XVII, pp. 103 ff. As to the points concerning Dr. Brüning, they were contained in lectures given by him before the Lowell Institute and in the Godkin Lectures at Harvard. To these should now be added Otto Braun, *Von Weimar zu Hitler* (1940), a book which sheds much light on the German Republic, and Arnold Brecht, *Prelude to Silence* (1944). See also the account given by Herbert Kraus in his *The Crisis of German Democracy* (1932), and H. J. Heneman's views as set forth in *The Growth of Executive Power in Germany* (1934). For the historical difficulties of Prussia, see Seeley's *Life and Times of Stein* (1879), passim. On the German Basic Law, see the author's "Rebuilding a German Constitution," II, *APSR*, August, 1949.

16. Robert C. Brooks, *Government and Politics of Switzerland* (1918), particularly when supplemented by his *Civic Training in Switzerland* (1930). To this must at least be added the leading constitutional text, Fritz Fleiner's *Schweizerisches Bundesstaatsrecht* (1922-1923), and W. E. Rappard's significant essay in constitutional history, *La Constitution Fédérale de la Suisse, 1848-1948* (1948). The specific references are to pp. 187 and 222 ff. of Fleiner's volume. See also C. J. Friedrich and Taylor Cole, *Responsible Bureaucracy, a Study of the Swiss Civil Service* (1932), particularly pp. 29 ff. The closing quotation is from Brooks, *Government and Politics*, pp. 132-133.

17. See for this the books referred to above in the general remarks. Concerning campaign funds see Louise Overacker, *Money in Elections* (1932).

18. Two monographs trace specially the development of the American cabinet: H. B. Learned, *The President's Cabinet* (1912), and M. L. Hinsdale, *History of the President's Cabinet* (1911). Charles A. Beard, whose Ch. IX on the President in his *The American Leviathan* is admirable, rightly remarks that insight into the substance of Presidential power is to be gained from a careful study of the letters and papers of Theodore Roosevelt and Wilson and their official biographies: J. B. Bishop, *Theodore Roosevelt and His Times* (2 vols., 1920); R. S. Baker, *Life and Letters of Woodrow Wilson* (8 vols., 1927-1939); selections from the correspondence of Theodore Roosevelt and Henry Cabot Lodge; C. Seymour, *The Intimate Papers of Colonel*

House (4 vols., 1926–1928). Carl Sandburg's monumental biography, *Abraham Lincoln, The War Years* (4 vols., 1939) is significant; see also H. F. Pringle, *The Life and Times of William Howard Taft* (1939). To these should now be added at least three major works dealing with the presidency of F. D. Roosevelt: Robert Sherwood, *Roosevelt and Hopkins* (1948), Henry L. Stimson and M. Bundy, *On Active Service in Peace and War* (1948); and Cordell Hull, *The Memoirs of Cordell Hull* (1948). Lord Bryce's citation is from the *American Commonwealth* (1924), Vol. I, p. 85. The quotation from Beard is found on p. 263. The quotation from Laski is on page 257 of *The American Presidency*. See also Herring, op. cit. pp. 92 ff.

19. For a shrewd and balanced estimate of the effects, see A. N. Holcombe, *State Government in the United States* (3d ed., 1931), pp. 326 ff. For the general issues, see Lipson, op. cit.

20. For the Cabinet secretariat see W. I. Jennings, op. cit. Ch. IX. The *Machinery of Government Report* was largely Haldane's work; it is found in 1918 *Reports* (Cmd. 9230). For the Committee of Imperial Defense see the reference given above, Ch. XI, note 16. The American presidential secretariat has not been in existence long enough to make a definitive judgment possible. It is discussed in Herring, op. cit. Ch. V and the other works cited above. See also Fritz Morstein-Marx, *The President and His Staff Advisers* (1947). The Hoover Report is available from the Government Printing Office and from McGraw-Hill under the title *The Hoover Commission Report* (1949).

XIX · *Responsible Government Service*

REMARKS

Problems of responsible government service have received increasing attention, primarily from American students of administration, in recent years. The leading works dealing with principles of administration, more particularly personnel administration, all devote attention to the problem. Among them may be noted Leonard D. White's *Introduction to the Study of Public Administration* (2d ed., 1939), Chs. XXXVI and XXXVII; Lewis Meriam's *Public Personnel Problems* (1938), Ch. XIV; W. E. Mosher and J. D. Kingsley, *Public Personnel Administration* (1936). Besides these, the papers on administration by Luther Gulick, L. Urwick, James Mooney and others, *Papers on the Science of Administration* (1937), contain an interesting contribution. Other valuable discussions may be found in the joint volume, *The Frontiers of Public Administration*, (1936), by J. M. Gaus, L. D. White, and Marshall E. Dimock. Two special studies are "The Experts of Five Federal Commissions," by E. P. Herring, *APSR*, Vol. XXXII, No. 1 (1938), and R. E. Cushman, "The Problem of the Independent Regulatory Commissions," *Report* No. III of the President's Committee on Administrative Management (1937). To these must now be added the very striking volume by Arthur W. MacMahon and John D. Millett, *Federal Administrators* (1939); and Herbert A. Simon, *Administrative Behavior* (1947), a remarkable study of how decisions are arrived at in administrative agencies. The author himself attempted to set the problem in broad perspective in his contribution to *Problems of the American Public Service* (1935), published by the Commission of Inquiry on Public Personnel Problems. However, his views were sharply attacked by Herman Finer in a review entitled "Better Government Personnel—America's Next Frontier," *PSQ*, Vol. LI, No. 4 (1936). Unconvinced, the author reiterated his position in "Public Policy and the Nature of Administrative Responsibility," *Public Policy*, Vol. I (1940), pp. 3 ff. But the problem of responsibility is not limited to governmental organization, as should be clear to all. Chester Barnard's *The Functions of the Executive* (1938) makes an important contribution to a more general view, but the problem has many unexplored ramifications. Two types of organization which particularly deserve further attention are churches and trade unions. It is indicative of the general neglect from which the problem has suffered that the *ESS* does not contain any article on the subject, though "resorts" and "restaurants" are treated. For more recent material, see also the bibliography above, Ch. II.

REFERENCES

1. See Finer, *Theory and Practice of Modern Government* (1932), Vol. II, p. 1168.

2. See op. cit. p. 1167. See also his *The British Civil Service* (1937), and K. B. Smellie, *A Hundred Years of English Government* (1937), chapters on administration.

3. Robert Moses, *The Civil Service of Great Britain* (1914), Ch. II.

4. See J. Donald Kingsley, *Representative Bureaucracy* (1944), and H. R. G. Greaves, *The Civil Service in the Changing State* (1947).

5. See Walter R. Sharp, "Public Personnel Management in France" in *Civil Service Abroad* (1935), as well as the discussion of the Conseil d'État, above, Ch. VI. For the political aspect of the *École Normale* see the interesting, if highly partisan, discussion by Hubert Bourgin, *De Jaurès à Léon Blum* (1938).

6. For a recent evaluation see B. Mirkine-Guetzévitch, "The National School of Administration in France," *APSR* (1949), Vol. XLIII, pp. 1026 ff.

7. See the author's "The Continental Tradition of Training Administrators in Law and Jurisprudence," *The Journal of Modern History*, Vol. XI, No. 2. For a general survey, see Fritz Morstein-Marx, "Civil Service in Germany" in *Civil Service Abroad* (1935).

8. Fritz Morstein-Marx, *Government in the Third Reich* (2d ed., 1937), especially pp. 128 ff. Karl Loewenstein, *Hitler's Germany* (new ed., 1940), pp. 173 f. See also Franz Neumann's magistral *Behemoth* (1944), where the learned author interprets the bureaucracy in terms of a "new ruling class," especially pp. 369 ff. and 378 ff. Here the ministerial bureaucracy is seen as a partner of "industrial capitalism," while in the lower civil service "the key positions are in the hands of the party" and the remainder are terrorized. Military government's efforts at civil service reform remain to be assessed scientifically; the *Reports of the Military Governor*, monthly official documents, carry most of the basic information, as do the corresponding reports of the British MG.

9. For this problem, see the splendid Princeton symposium *The Public Service and University Education* (ed. Joseph E. McLean, 1949), especially the papers by John M. Gaus and Donald C. Stone. The value judgments in the text are supported by the *Hoover Commission Report*, especially Section VI. Its proposals are calculated to promote considerable progress.

10. Besides Leonard White's already cited volume, see the author's "Responsible Government Service under the American Constitution," loc. cit., and the literature cited there, as well as his "The Rise and Decline of the Spoils Tradition" in the *Annals* of the American Academy of Political and Social Science (January, 1937); and E. P. Herring's "The Future of Patronage," *Virginia Quarterly Review* (Winter, 1938). See also Paul H. Appleby, *Big Democracy* (1945).

11. The *Myers Case* is found 272 U. S. 52 (1926); the *Humphreys Case*, correctly cited as Rathbun *v.* United States, 295 U. S. 602 (1935). See the able comment by Cushman, *APSR*, Vol. XXX, pp. 72 ff., concerning this case. The *Myers Case* has also been extensively commented upon; see, for example, W. W. Willoughby, *The American Constitutional System* (2d ed., 1919), Ch. LXXXIV; James Hart, *Tenure of Office under the Constitution* (1930); and E. S. Corwin, *The President's Removal Power under the Constitution* (1927).

12. See here Leonard D. White, *Introduction to the Study of Public Administration* (1926), Ch. XV. For the practice of German disciplinary bodies, see the author's "The German and the Prussian Civil Service," in *The Civil Service in the Modern State* (1930), ed. by L. D. White, and the literature cited there. For a general historical view of discipline, see above, Chapter II. On the judicial function in administrative bodies, see the literature quoted above, Ch. VI, notes 16–18, especially the work by Joseph P. Chamberlain, et al. An interesting recent contribution is Joseph Rosenfarb, *Freedom and the Administrative State* (1948).

13. These trends were discussed at a conference on personnel problems held at the Brookings Institution under the auspices of the Harvard Graduate School of Public Administration, in 1938. See manuscript "Report of a Conference on the Relations of Personnel Problems and Public Relations, February 3, 1938," now at the Littauer Center of Public Administration, Harvard. See also the work by Herbert A. Simon quoted above in *Remarks*.

14. The Commission of Inquiry on Public Personnel Problems published its report, *Better Government Personnel*, in 1935. The statement here quoted is found on pp. 45 ff. For the English situation, see Leonard D. White, "The British Civil Service," in *Civil Service Abroad*, published by the Commission of Inquiry (1935), particularly pp. 17 ff.

The problem of titles relates, sociologically, to prestige and honor. See the able article by Hans Speier, "Honor and Social Structure," in *Social Research*, Vol. II (1935), pp. 74 ff. See also the convincing institutional comments by Arnold Brecht, "Civil Service," in *Social Research*, Vol. III (1936), pp. 202 ff. Regarding morale see above, Ch. II, note 10.

15. For this, see George C. S. Benson, *Financial Control and Integration* (1934), Vol. II, of *Studies in Systematic Political Science and Comparative Government*, ed. by C. J. Friedrich; W. F. Willoughby, *Principles of Public Administration* (1927); W. F. Willoughby, *The Problem of a National Budget* (1918); A. E. Buck, *Public Budgeting* (1929); F. A. Cleveland and A. E. Buck, *Budget and Responsible Government* (1920); R. G. Hawtrey, *The Exchequer and the Control of Expenditure* (1921); and A. C. Saemisch, *Die Kontrolle der staatlichen Finanzwirtschaft* (1931). The advocated reforms are discussed in Benson, op. cit. pp. 30 ff.

16. For the United States Comptroller and related problems, see *Hoover Commission Report*, "Budgeting and Accounting," Part III.

17. The sense of craftsmanship was emphasized by J. M. Gaus, in his contribution, cited above, as *The Frontiers of Public Administration*. It also receives due attention in Barnard's study, p. 146. See the author's restatement of the problem in Ch. VI, "Responsibility and the Sense of Workmanship," in *The New Belief in the Common Man* (1942).

XX · *Political Parties: General Problems*

REMARKS

The problem of parties has received a considerable amount of attention, particularly since the publication of M. Y. Ostrogorski's volumes, *La Démocratie et l'Organisation des Partis Politiques* (1902, tr. by Frederick Clarke as *Democracy and the Organization of Political Parties*). The history of parties in various countries, as well as the general problems which they raise, have been studied by a large number of writers. It stands in the center of such general treatments as James Bryce's *Modern Democracies* (new ed., 1924). Outstanding for America are Merriam, Gosnell, Holcombe, Sait, Herring, and Salter, cited below. To these should be added three notable recent additions: E. E. Schattschneider, *Party Government* (1941), V. O. Key, Jr., *Politics, Parties and Pressure Groups* (1942; new ed., 1947); and Wilfred E. Binkley, *American Political Parties, Their Natural History* (1943). The recognition of the party has undermined the democratic dogma of the unity of the people. Robert Michels, following Max Weber, has analyzed the hierarchical and bureaucratic tendencies of political parties, irrespective of their political faith, in his *Zur Soziologie des Parteiwesens in der modernen Demokratie* (2d ed., 1925). Max Weber's own view is set forth in *Wirtschaft und Gesellschaft* (1922). For a somewhat more popular account, see "Politik als Beruf," in his *Gesammelte Politische Schriften* (1921), pp. 396 ff. For the extensive historical literature, see the items for each country offered in the *ESS*, as well as in the several paragraphs for the next chapter. This entire literature is somewhat askew because of the shift in meaning which the concept of a party has undergone since the war. The rise of Communism and the several forms of Caesarism have been accompanied by the establishment and maintenance of parties of a novel kind: oligarchic factions claiming representative positions on the ground of a fervent faith in their particular creeds. Max Weber went farthest perhaps in recognizing the tendency of parties to claim such universality of appeal and hence representative importance. If such "parties" are not clearly differentiated, the analysis of parties under constitutionalism becomes obscured.

REFERENCES

1. For the change in outlook concerning parties, see John Adams, *Defense of the Constitutions* (1787). For the remarks on Washington, see, for instance, S. E. Morison, *The Oxford History of the United States* (1927), Vol. I, p. 234. See also L. D. White, *The Federalists* (1948), for further detail. Bolingbroke's ideas are set forth in *The Patriot King* (1749). For the whole problem of corruption, see the penetrating study by L. B. Namier, *The Structure of Politics at the Accession of George III* (1929), and the equally revealing monograph by Holden Furber, *Henry Dundas, First Viscount Melville, 1742–1811, Political Manager of Scotland, Statesman Administrator of British India* (1931).

2. For the beginning of this paragraph, see the articles by W. C. Abbott, particularly "The Origin of English Political Parties," in the *American Historical Review*, Vol. XXIV (1918–1919), pp. 578 ff. Consult also M. T. Blauvelt, *The Development of Cabinet Government in England* (1902); G. M. Trevelyan, *The Two-party System in English Political History* (1926); and the work by Namier quoted in the previous paragraph. For the statement from N. Wraxall, see his *Memoirs* (1779), Vol. II, pp. 498 ff. See also the discussion of the cabinet system above, Ch. XVIII.

3. For Sir Erskine May, see *The Constitutional History of England since the Accession of George the Third* (3d ed., 1871), Ch. XVIII. Lord Macaulay's views are stated in his *The History of England* (ed. Firth, 1913), Ch. I. A very able analysis of the emergence of party organization in the course of the Long Parliament is given by J. H. Hexter in *The Reign of King Pym* (1941), especially Chs. III, VIII, and IX, an abstract of which can be found in the volume of abstracts of doctoral dissertations printed by the Harvard University Press each year.

4. For the English development, see Trevelyan, op. cit. For France, see Joseph-Barthélemy, *Introduction du Régime Parlementaire en France* (1904); it deals with the early phase. Georges Weill's *Histoire du Parti Républicain en France, 1814–1870* (1928) is important after that, and following him Gabriel Hanotaux, *Histoire de la France contemporaine 1871–1900* (1903–1908), as well as Roger H. Soltau, *French Parties and Politics, 1871–1921* (new ed., 1930). For Germany, see S. Neumann, *Die Deutschen Parteien* (1932), and Ludwig Bergsträsser, *Geschichte der politischen Parteien in Deutschland* (6th ed., 1932). For the social-democratic party in particular, see Franz Mehring, *Geschichte der deutschen Sozialdemokratie* (12th ed., 1922).

5. The discussion in this paragraph is developed from the views of Max Weber and Robert Michels, but with important modifications. Michels has shown that the "ideal" objectives are often more closely related to power than are the material ones. See also E. P. Herring, *The Politics of Democracy* (1940), Chs. III and VII.

6. See H. F. Gosnell, *Machine Politics: Chicago Model* (1937), and the works of John T. Salter referred to above, Ch. XIV, on *Remarks*. For Holcombe's views, see his *Political Parties of Today* (1924) and *The Middle Classes in American Politics* (1940). To these should be added A. M. Bingham, *Insurgent America; Revolt of the Middle Classes* (1935), and P. H. Odegard and E. A. Helms, *American Politics: A Study in Political Dynamics* (1938 new ed., 1947). A striking account of practical politics in America can be found in Ed Flynn, *You're the Boss* (1947).

7. For Julius Hatschek's theory, see his *Englisches Staatsrecht*, Vol. II (1905), pp. 8 ff. Hume's "Essay on Parties," contained in *Essays and Treatises* (1760), Vol. I, pp. 93 ff., has the quotation on p. 97.

8. See especially John T. Salter's chapter "Of the People" in *The Pattern of Politics* (1940), and C. E. Merriam and H. F. Gosnell, *The American Party System* (4th ed., 1949), Chs. VI and VII. For Michels' views, see op. cit. pp. 400 ff. and passim, and his *Probleme der Sozialphilosophie* (1914). The quotation is found in *Robinson's Diary*, Vol. II, p. 316. There are many other such observations; for example, the terse remarks of Single-Speech Hamilton, cited in the preface to the recent edition of his *Parliamentary Logic* (ed. 1927, by C. S. Kenny). Compare for the general subject, Josef Redlich, *The Procedure of the House of Commons* (1908), Vol. II, pp. 89 ff.

9. Schattschneider's argument is found in *The Struggle for Party Government*, the University of Maryland (1948), which is based upon his earlier book noted above.

10. For this paragraph see the famous historical discussion by M. Ostrogorski, op. cit. Vol. I, pp. 117 ff.

11. A. Lawrence Lowell, *Public Opinion in War and Peace* (1923), Ch. VII. The volume by Friedrich Röhmer is entitled *Lehre von den Politischen Parteien* (1844).

12. André Siegfried's study is contained in the well-known monograph, *Tableau Politique de la France de l'Ouest* (1913). A. Holcombe, in the works previously cited, developed the inter-relation between social class and party development. The entire school of economic and social historians have made numerous contributions. See particularly A. M. Schlesinger, *Political and Social History of the United States* (1925). See, for the German side, the comprehensive *Die Deutschen Parteien; Wesen und Wandel nach dem Kriege* (1932) by Sigmund Neumann. For France as a whole, compare likewise André Siegfried's *Tableau des Partis en France* (1930), translated as *France: A Study in Nationality* (1930), a volume rich in glittering generalities as well as in sound insight. Stuart Rice's findings are set forth in *Farmers and Workers in American Politics* (1924).

XXI · Political Parties: A Panorama of Their Comparative Development in Europe

REFERENCES

1. E. L. Woodward, *Age of Reform* (1938), and R. C. K. Ensor, *England, 1870–1914* (1936). For England, see again Trevelyan, op. cit., and M. H. Woods, *A History of the Tory Party in the Seventeenth and Eighteenth Centuries* (1924) (more particularly the chapter on the party in the nineteenth and twentieth centuries), as well as F. J. C. Hearnshaw, *Conservatism in England* (1933). See also Karl Mannheim, "Das Konservative Denken," *Archiv für Sozialwissenschaft und Sozialpolitik*, Vol. 57, pp. 90 ff. For the growth of liberalism, see Harold Laski, *The Rise of Liberalism* (1931); Hamilton Fyfe, *The British Liberal Party* (1928); J. M. Robertson, *The Meaning of Liberalism* (2d ed., 1925).

2. For this, see the life work of L. T. Hobhouse, especially his *Liberalism* (1911); he realized more clearly than anyone else the issue which socialism posited. In America, a similar importance attaches to the recent writings of Charles Merriam, especially his *The Role of Politics in Social Change* (1936). See Lorenz von Stein, *Geschichte der sozialen Bewegung in Frankreich von 1879 bis auf unsere Tage*, 3 vols. (new ed., 1921). The original of this remarkable book appeared in 1850. There has for a long time been a controversy as to whether Karl Marx took his class doctrine from Lorenz von Stein. Though, on the best evidence, this appears improbable, the resemblance is certainly a striking one. See also Charles Trevelyan, *From Liberalism to Labor* (1921), a revealing personal account. See also Arthur Rosenberg's historical analysis, *Democracy and Socialism* (1939), passim, and Guido de Ruggiero, *The History of European Liberalism* (1927), particularly Parts I, III–IV.

3. For Mirabeau and Siéyès, see G. G. van Deusen, *Siéyès: His Life and His Nationalism* (1932), pp. 74 ff.; and Siéyès, *Qu'est-ce-que le Tiers État?* (1788). Nowhere has the doctrine of integral nationalism of the bourgeois been stated with greater force. For Napoleon, see the study by Hans E. Friedrich, *Napoleon I, Idée und Staat* (1935). For the foreign policy of Louis XVIII, see Frederick B. Artz, *Reaction and Revolution, 1814–1832* (1934), pp. 126 ff., and the literature cited there. The present impact of the French past has been depicted with much skill by C. J. H. Hayes, *France—A Nation of Patriots* (1930), particularly Chs. I–V. For England, see Trevelyan, op. cit. See also Josef Redlich, *The Procedure of the House of Commons* (1908), Vol. I, pp. 127–129, and J. L. Garvin, *The Life of Joseph Chamberlain* (1932–34), Vol. II, Chs. XXX–XXXIII, XXXIX–XLI, XLIV–XLV. See further, R. B. Haldane, *Autobiography* (1929), Ch. VI, and Sir Edward Grey, *Twenty-five Years* (1925), Vol. I, pp. 60 ff. Another source of vital importance is G. E. Buckle and W. F. Monypenny, *The Life of*

Benjamin Disraeli, Lord Beaconsfield (1910–1920), throughout. No individual statesman, however, shows so clearly the kinship between liberalism and imperialism as Lord Palmerston, whose biography by Anthony Ashley (1879) should be added without fail to any reading on this subject.

4. For this and the following paragraph (as for the whole question of liberalism), see the volume by Guido de Ruggiero, op. cit. A really good history of German liberalism has never been written, but Friedrich Meinecke and his school have made important contributions toward such a history. Indeed, Meinecke's *Weltbürgertum und Nationalstaat* (7th ed., 1928) almost constitutes such a history, so far as the problem of the text is concerned. See also Veit Valentin's *Geschichte der Deutschen Revolution 1848–49* (1934), particularly Vol. I, pp. 1 ff. and 297 ff. An abridged English version appeared in 1940 under the title "1848." For Stresemann, see *Stresemann, Ein Vermächtnis* (1932), edited by H. Bernhard in 3 volumes. For Cavour, see W. R. Thayer, *The Life and Times of Cavour* (1911). See also G. M. Trevelyan, *Garibaldi and the Thousand* (1909) and *Garibaldi and the Making of Italy* (1911). For Mazzini, see Gaetano Salvemini, *Mazzini* (4th ed., 1925); a study of this man in the light of problems raised by national socialism would be highly desirable. See also O. Vossler, *Mazzini's politisches Denken und Wollen* (1927).

5. See the work of Mehring cited above, as well as Michels, op. cit. An interesting special study is Eckart Kehr, *Schlachtflottenbau und Parteipolitik, 1894–1901* (1930). See also the materials brought together by Werner Sombart in *Grundlagen und Kritik des Sozialismus* (1919), 2 vols. Concerning Lasalle, see the work of H. Oncken, *Lasalle: Eine politische Biographie* (3d ed., 1920). The Paris Commune has been described by Edward S. Mason, *The Paris Commune* (1930); there is considerable socialist literature on the subject which Mason reviews in the course of his study. Alexandre Zévaès' extensive writings on the history of French socialism and the socialist party are rather diffuse; the most distinctive insight was afforded the author by the collected articles and speeches of Jean Jaurès, published under the title, *Œuvres de Jean Jaurès* (1931). Roger H. Soltau's previously cited volume contains, of course, an account of these developments. Concerning Jules Guesde, see A. Zévaès, *Jules Guesde* (1929), and D. J. Saposs, *The Labor Movement in Post-War France* (1931). Concerning the struggle of Bismarck with the socialists, see Mehring, op. cit., on the socialist side, and Johannes Ziekursch, *Politische Geschichte des neuen deutschen Kaiserreiches* (1927), Vol. II, pp. 323 ff.; and A. Wahl, *Deutsche Geschichte, 1871–1914* (1926), Vol. I, pp. 479 ff., for a more general statement.

For the British Labour Party's background, see Sidney and Beatrice Webb, *The History of Trade Unionism* (1920), as well as the excellent monograph by William P. Maddox, *The British Labour Party in Foreign Affairs* (1934), particularly pp. 24 ff. For the impact of the Midlothian campaign, see the article by Eugene P. Chase, "Parliamentary Control of Foreign Policy in Great Britain," in *APSR*, Vol. XXV (1931), pp. 861 ff. One may refer also to Egon Wertheimer, *Portrait of the Labor Party* (1930), and William Stewart, *J. Keir Hardie: A Biography* (1921). For a proper context, one may compare J. M. Gaus, *Great Britain—A Study in Civic Loyalty* (1929).

6. Concerning this whole subject, see the excellent monograph by Merle Fainsod, *International Socialism and the World War* (1935). Much interesting material is contained in Lloyd George's *War Memoirs, 1917* (1934), Chs. IV and V.

7. For the German "revolution," see Arthur Rosenberg, *The Birth of the German Republic, 1871–1918* (1931), tr. by Ian F. D. Morrow. The blind alley in which German socialist leaders found themselves in 1919 is best seen from two short contemporary analyses: Count U. Brockdorff-Rantzau, *Deutschlands auswärtige Politik* (1919), and Friedrich Lenz, *Staat und Marxismus* (1921). Articles depicting the dissatisfaction of the younger elements among socialists found their expression in the formation of a group known as Young Socialists (*Jungsozialisten*); their magazine, *Der Jungsozialist*, reveals the various aspects of this trouble. For a discussion of Austrian experience, consult J. D. Gregory, *Dollfuss and His Times* (1935).

8. The remark by Asquith is found *HCD*, Vol. CLXIX, p. 860; for the next quotation, see ibid. Vol. CLXXVI, p. 3066. The reference to Baldwin's speech is ibid. Vol. CCXIX,

pp. 62–63. The debate on Unemployment Insurance Bill No. 3 is found *HCD*, Vol. CCLV, July 18–31, 1931.

9. The politics of the Front Populaire have been subjected to much abuse, as journalists and politicians have looked for somebody to blame for the military defeat. See for a juster estimate D. W. Brogan, *The Development of Modern France* (1940), pp. 669 f. See also Alexander Werth, *Which Way France?* and the author's "Paul Reynaud" in *The Atlantic Monthly*, September, 1939. Léon Jouhaux' survey, *C. G. T.* (General Federation of Labor) (1937), is also important.

10. For the problem of Catholic parties, there is a considerable amount of special literature, but no comprehensive treatment at all. For Germany, we have the work of Karl Bachem, *Vorgeschichte, Geschichte und Politik der deutschen Zentrumspartei* (1927–1932). For the papal encyclicals, see *Les Documents Pontificaux sur la Démocratie et la Société Moderne* (with Introduction and Notes by Georges Michon) (1928). For the Action Française group, see the monograph by Madame Charlotte Muret, entitled *French Royalist Doctrines since the Revolution* (1933), and the unprinted thesis by F. M. Watkins, *The Political Theory of the Action Française* (1930) (in the Harvard University Library).

11. For the German side, see Bachem, op. cit., as well as Ludwig Bergsträsser, *Der Politische Katholizismus* (1921–1923). For the German constitutional convention, see Friedrich Meinecke's *Radowitz und die Deutsche Revolution* (1913). On the Vatican problem, see R. de Cesare, *Roma e lo Stato del Papa dal Ritorno di Pio Nono al 20 Settembre* (1907), translated as *The Last Days of Papal Rome, 1850–1870* (1909); J. Bernhart, *The Vatican as a World Power* (1939); and Carl Eckhardt, *The Papacy and World Affairs* (1937). There is also a special monograph by George Shuster, on the problems raised by the advent of Hitler, *Like a Mighty Army, Hitler vs. Established Religion* (1935). On the *Kulturkampf*, see Bachem, op. cit. Vol. III, pp. 193 ff., for the Catholic view; the Protestant view is set forth in most of the Bismarck literature published in Germany; for a sane survey see Robert C. Binkley, *Realism and Nationalism, 1852–1871* (1935), pp. 312 ff. For Swiss Catholicism, see Robert C. Brooks, *Civic Training in Switzerland* (1930), Ch. III, and E. Fueter, *Die Schweiz seit 1848* (1928), pp. 23 ff. For Belgium, see Thomas H. Reed, *Government and Politics of Belgium* (1928), p. 41. For Holland, see A. C. Hoff, and others, *Onze Politieke Partijen* (1918), and the standard history by P. J. Blok. So far as Austria is concerned, consult the literature cited above, note 7.

12. C. J. H. Hayes's *Essays in Nationalism* (1926) portrays the conflict. For the development of National Socialism, the volumes by K. Heiden, *A History of National Socialism* (2d ed., 1936), are the best. Outstanding among German studies are two by Hermann Rauschning, *The Revolution of Nihilism* (1939), and *The Redemption of Democracy* (1941). The literature has been surveyed by Taylor Cole in "Current Appraisals of German National Socialism," *Journal of Politics*, Vol. I, No. 2 (1939); earlier by Hajo Holborn, "National Socialism in Germany: A Short Bibliography," in *International Affairs*, Vol. XIII (1934), pp. 93 ff.

XXII · *Interest Groups and Economic Councils*

REMARKS

The general topic of the relation of the various associations and groups to government is of rather recent interest. The connection of this subject with representation has been stressed by the writers noted above under Ch. XIV. The detailed examination of the actual behavior of different groups has been more particularly an American preoccupation. A government report entitled *Economic Power and Political Pressures* (1942) by Donald C. Blaisdell and Jane Greverus is valuable. E. P. Herring, in his two volumes, *Group Representation before Congress* (1929) and *Public Administration and the Public Interest* (1936), has offered the broadest analysis. To these must now be added his *The Politics of Democracy* (1940). See also V. O. Key, Jr., *Politics, Parties and Pressure Groups* (1947). More special studies have been made by Peter Odegard, *Pressure Politics, the Story of the Anti-saloon League* (1928); H. Childs, *Labor and Capital in National*

Politics (1930); E. E. Schattschneider, *Politics, Pressures and the Tariff* (1935); Belle Zeller, *Pressure Politics in New York* (1937); Kenneth G. Crawford, *The Pressure Boys: the Inside Story of Lobbying in America* (1939), and Wesley McCune, *The Farm Bloc* (1943). For France, Michel Debré's study on *L'Artisanat* (1934) is valuable. Italian sociologists have given some attention to these problems ever since G. Mosca, V. Pareto, and R. Michels, cited earlier, challenged traditional approaches to democracy. However, we do not have concrete studies on particular interest groups of the kind American political scientists have developed. German writers, too, have dwelt more upon the general problems, though E. Tatarin-Tarnheyden's *Die Berufstände* (1922) gives a sketch of the mass of German interest groups. H. Herrfahrdt's *Das Problem der Berufständischen Vertretung von der Französischen Revolution bis zur Gegenwart* (1921) traces the evolution of economic groups from the "estates" at the beginning of the nineteenth century to the situation after the First World War. The estates type of political representation has not been treated with much interest in the United States (and England), since it was regarded as "feudal." Actually, the estates period represents a phase in the evolution of modern constitutionalism, and deserves greater attention in view of the modern interest in functional representation. See the references given by Otto von Gierke in his *Deutsches Genossenschaftsrecht*, Vol. I, pp. 534 ff. and 819 ff., which offers a broad sketch of the legal and institutional characteristics. Gierke also perceived the intimate political and legal relation between these older forms and the modern associational concept and traced it through the study of the *Genossenschaft* concept. See also Gierke's *The Development of Political Theory* (1939) (tr. by Bernard Freyd). For a highly significant analysis of the importance of all groups intermediate between the individual and the "state," see Emil Lederer's *The State of the Masses* (1940), especially Chs. V and VI, where the delusion of a "classless" society in the usual Marxian sense is shown to be the basis for totalitarian despotism. For a discussion and the general literature on "Government Control" see above, Chs. V and XIX, and below, Ch. XXIII.

REFERENCES

1. The quotation is taken from Wilson's *The New Freedom* (1913), p. 125. Bryce's discussion is given in *American Commonwealth*, Vol. I, pp. 691 ff. Regarding Bismarck's council, see Julius Curtius, *Bismarcks Plan eines deutschen Volkswirtschaftsrates* (1919), and the same author's article, "Der preussische Volkswirtschaftsrat, seine Errichtung, seine Tätigkeit, die Ursachen seines Eingehens," in *Wirtschaftliche Nachrichten aus dem Ruhrbezirk* (1921), pp. 593 ff.

2. The story about "One-Speech" Hamilton is told in C. S. Kenny's new edition of his *Parliamentary Logic* (1927). The quotation from Burke is from his "Speech on a motion for a committee to inquire into the State of the Representation of the Commons in Parliament," May 7, 1782, *Works* (1866 ed.), Vol. VII, p. 98. The interrelation between the general interest and the particular interests is set forth in Chs. I and XXIII of Herring's *Public Administration and the Public Interest* (1936). K. C. Cole has for some time been engaged in studying the problem of "interest," and the author has profited from seeing some of his MSS. See his article, "The Role of the Senate in the Confirmation of Judicial Nominations," in *APSR*, Vol. XXVIII (1934), pp. 875 ff.

3. Apart from the studies already mentioned in the general bibliography, attention should be called to the welter of articles and essays cited by Herring in *Group Representation*, particularly pp. 300 ff., and the relevant sections in Lasswell and Casey, *Propaganda and Promotional Activities: an Annotated Bibliography* (1935). The "purposes" of the various organizations are quoted from Herring, op. cit. pp. 22–23. See also Ch. XXIV.

4. There is no realistic study of the Chambers of Commerce or Agriculture. The perversion of these organizations by the Fascists has further confused the situation; much unsound information occasioned the unsound policies of American military occupation in Germany; see below, Ch. XXVI. As for the United States, Gladys Baker has published a good analysis of *The County Agent* (1940). To this should be added John Gaus's collaborative volume (with Leon Wolcott and Verne B. Lewis), *Public Administration and the United States Department of Agriculture*

(1941). The legal information on the chambers of agriculture, commerce, handicraft, etc., is contained in standard treatises on administrative law, such as W. Jellinek, *Verwaltungsrecht* (3d ed., 1931), pp. 180 ff., or M. Hauriou, *Précis de Droit Administratif* (11th ed., 1927), pp. 236 ff. But descriptive accounts of their actual operation are rather unsatisfactory. A. J. Wolfe's studies for the *Special Agents Series* of the Department of Commerce, Bureau of Foreign and Domestic Commerce, Nos. 78, 98, 101, and 102, are of some help. See also Tatarin-Tarnheyden, op. cit. pp. 62 ff.; H. E. Krüger, "Historische und Kritische Untersuchungen über die freien Interessen Vertretungen von Industrie, Handel und Gewerbe in Deutschland," in Schmoller's *Jahrbuch*, Vols. XXXII and XXXIV (1908–1909); Christian Eckert, *Die Stellung der Handelskammern* (1922); and E. P. Herring's study of the French chambers for *APSR*, Vol. XXV (1931), "Chambres de Commerce in France." For the French government's interest in patriotic societies, see C. J. H. Hayes, *France, a Nation of Patriots* (1930), Ch. VIII. For Germany, see Eckart Kehr, *Schlachtflottenbau und Parteipolitik 1894–1901* (1930), particularly pp. 168 ff. The confusion over the various pressure groups in France was causing considerable apprehension. See Daniel Halévy, *La République des Comités* (1934), and Tardieu's work, already referred to.

5. The best study of "The Government and the Bank of France" is that by Karl R. Bopp in *Public Policy*, Vol. II, pp. 3–35. The quotations are from p. 29 of this study. The issue of government spending is ably examined in its broad outlines by Spencer Thompson in "The Investment Budget," *Public Policy*, Vol. II, pp. 63–77. See also A. H. Hansen, *Fiscal Policy and Business Cycles* (1941), Ch. X.

6. See the material cited above, Ch. XXI, note 5. For trade unions, see the comprehensive survey in the *ESS* and the literature cited there for the different countries. Besides these, see Leo Wolman, *The Growth of American Trade Unions, 1880–1923* (1924); Margaret R. Clark and S. Fanny Simon, *The Labor Movement in America* (1938); L. S. Lyon, M. W. Watkins, and Victor Abramson, *Government and Economic Life*, Vol. I (1939); Thomas R. Fisher, *Industrial Disputes and Federal Legislation* (1940).

7. Regarding the situation in prewar Russia see Leon Trotsky, *The History of the Russian Revolution* (tr. Max Eastman, 1932). Concerning the German development, see the literature on the revolution, A. Rosenberg and others, Tatarin-Tarnheyden, op. cit. pp. 144 ff., and Georg Bernhard, *Wirtschaftsparlamente von den Revolutionsräten zum Reichswirtschaftsrat* (1923), pp. 43 ff. See also for further literature C. Hauschild, *Der vorläufige Reichswirtschaftsrat, 1920–1926* (1926), pp. 641 ff. Hugo Preuss's article appeared in *Berliner Tageblatt*, November 14, 1918, and was republished in *Staat, Recht und Freiheit* (1926), pp. 365 ff. Besides the National Economic Council, the bottom layer, the factory councils, were organized by the *Betriebsrätegesetz* of February 4, 1920. Concerning these factory councils, see C. Guillebaud, *The German Works Council* (1928). American military government showed lack of understanding of this tradition when General Clay suspended the works-council law adopted by Hesse and Bremen, evidently deeming them novel developments rather than a return to pre-Nazi democratic trends interrupted by Hitler's government-controlled Labor Front. See below, Ch. XXVI (references), where the relevant military government documents are cited. See John B. Holt, "Corporative Occupational Organization and Democracy in Germany" in *PAR*, Vol. VIII, pp. 34 ff. (1948), an admirably balanced presentation of the problem.

8. For the German National Economic Council, see Dr. Hauschild's collection of materials just cited, and Friedrich Glum's *Der deutsche und der französische Reichswirtschaftsrat* (1929). Neither H. Finer's study, *Representative Government and a Parliament of Industry* (1923), nor a later article by Lindsay Rogers and W. R. Dittmar, "The Reichswirtschaftsrat: De Mortuis," *PSQ*, Vol. L (1935), pp. 481 ff., can be accepted, the former because it is too optimistic, the latter because it is too skeptical regarding its work. A more balanced view is found in Glum's article on the Council in *Handbuch des deutschen Staatsrechts*, Vol. I (1930), pp. 578 ff. Similar balanced discussions of the French and Czechoslovak Councils are given by Edith C. Bramhall, "The French National Economic Council in France," *APSR*, Vol. XX (1926), pp. 623 ff., and E. P. Herring, "The Czechoslovak Advisory Board for Economic Questions," *APSR*, Vol. XXIV

(1930), pp. 439 ff. The latter has a list of countries with councils. For Britain, the development of advisory councils and working parties described in the next chapter is creating a corresponding pattern. Whether an integrated or functional setup is more desirable in the long run is an open question.

9. For the Fascist Corporative State, see two books by Carl T. Schmidt, *The Plough and the Sword: Labor, Land, and Property in Fascist Italy* (1938), and *The Corporate State in Action* (1939); Gaetano Salvemini, *Under the Axe of Fascism* (1936), particularly Part I; and H. Finer, *Mussolini's Italy* (1935), Ch. XVII, pp. 492 ff.

10. For the German *ständische Aufbau*, see Franz Neumann's *Behemoth* (1942) and Guenter Reimann, *The Vampire Economy* (1939). See also Taylor Cole, "The Evolution of the German Labor Front," *Political Science Quarterly*, Vol. LII, No. 4 (Dec. 1937), and Erich Hula, "The Corporative Experiment in Austria," *Social Research*, Vol. VI, No. 1 (Feb. 1939).

11. Literature on the Soviet Union is multiplying very rapidly. Besides older studies, like the Webbs' *Soviet Communism* (1938, 3d ed., 1944), we have many studies, but unfortunately partisanship tends to intrude itself. We note F. L. Schuman, *Soviet Politics at Home and Abroad* (1946), Ch. VII; Michael T. Florinsky, "Russia—The USSR" in Shotwell's *Governments of Continental Europe* (1945), Ch. VI; G. Bienstock, et al. of *Management in Russian Industry and Agriculture* (1944), Alexander Baykov, *The Development of the Soviet Economy* (1946); and Julian Towster, *Political Power in the U.S.S.R. 1917–1947* (1948).

12. See Oliver Garceau, *The Political Life of the American Medical Association* (1941), for a striking case study. See also V. O. Key, Jr., op. cit. passim. See also above, note 3.

13. E. P. Herring, *The Impact of War upon American Government* (1941).

14. See John Gaus, *Public Administration and the U. S. Department of Agriculture*, 1940.

XXIII · Socialization and Planning

REMARKS

The huge literature of socialism and communism is involved in the general topic of this chapter. It is hardly practicable to attempt a selective bibliography of these great movements, beyond what is given above in Chapter XXI.

Descriptive and analytical material on the relation of modern government to economy is also of vast extent, especially if the several modern nations are included in such a survey. Virtually every treatise on general economics deals with this issue at considerable length, and the more specialized studies are legion. For the United States, a good general survey down to the start of the Second World War, from an economist viewpoint, is *Government and Economic Life: Development and Current Issues of American Public Policy* (1939), Leverett S. Lyon, Myron W. Watkins, and Victor Abramson, two volumes. From the standpoint of the student of government, Merle Fainsod and Lincoln Gordon, *Government and the American Economy* (1941), are authoritative. The basic economic issues are associated with the names of J. A. Hobson, A. C. Pigou, Beveridge, and Keynes. The latter's *General Theory of Employment, Interest and Money* (1936) is undoubtedly the most comprehensive statement of the new orthodoxy in economic theory. But since a strictly economic view provides no adequate answer to the insistent governmental and constitutional issues of a free and open society, some economists have made challenging forays into the broader field of politics. Among these, Friedrich Hayek's *The Road to Serfdom* (1944), while mockingly dedicated to the socialists of all parties, actually undertook to saddle socialism with responsibility not only for the totalitarianism of the left but of the right (Fascism) as well. His argument precipitated a number of sharp rebuttals. Besides the author's own review in *The American Political Review*, Vol. XXXIX, pp. 575 ff. (1945), Barbara Wootton's *Freedom under Planning* (1944) deserves special mention, implementing as it does her earlier *Plan or No Plan* (1935). To these criticisms, Hayek replied in *Individualism and the Economic Order* (1948). For a fuller sketch of this economic controversy, Seymour E. Harris' *Economic Planning* (1949), Ch. I, may be consulted. The controversy in Britain is going forward in more specific and concrete terms. John Jewkes' *Ordeal by Planning* (1948) offers a fairly detailed critical analysis of the activities of the Labour government from a conservative standpoint, while Paul Sweezey's *Socialism* (1949) denies the Labour government's claims to socialism from a radical standpoint as not really providing comprehensive planning. Against both, Francis Williams' *Socialist Britain* (1948) offers a readable defense of the official performance against both right and left. Besides these, W. H. Wickwar's two volumes, *Social Services* (rev. ed., 1948) and *Public Services* (rev. ed., 1948), offer a careful survey of developments without excessive partisanship. Ranney and Carter in *The Major Foreign Powers* (1948) have given a good survey; see also the symposium, edited by F. Morstein-Marx, on the formulation of economic programs, in *APSR*, Vol. XLII, pp. 297 ff. (1948).

The general problems of planning in relation to democratic government and, by implication, to constitutionalism have been in the center of the writings of Charles E. Merriam. See especially *The Role of Politics in Social Change* (1936), *The New Democracy and the New Despotism* (1939), pp. 145 ff., *On the Agenda of Democracy* (1941), pp. 72 ff., and *Systematic Politics* (1945). The range of the full employment ("no more poverty") thesis found its classic expression in Lord (William H.) Beveridge's *Full Employment in a Free Society* (American ed., 1945).

REFERENCES

1. For these issues see the writings of R. Niebuhr, A. D. Lindsay, Harold Laski, Karl Mannheim, E. Rosenstock-Hüssy, and Karl Popper, among more recent writers, along with the author's *The New Belief in the Common Man* (1941).

2. See the works by Hayek and Jewkes cited in "Remarks," as well as W. Roepke's *International Economic Disintegration* (1942) and the several contributions to *Ordo—Jahrbuch für die Ordnung von Wirtschaft und Gesellschaft* (1949), especially the brilliant piece by Alexander Rüstow, "Zwischen Kapitalismus und Kommunismus."

3. See especially the writings of Charles Merriam, as cited in "Remarks," Ch. VII, in my *The New Belief in the Common Man* (1941), Arthur Holcombe's *Government in a Planned Democracy* (1935), and Carl Landauer's *Theory of National Economic Planning* (rev. ed., 1947). H. Finer's *Road to Reaction* is marred by an intemperate attitude which belies his protestations of democratic sentiment; surely it is not necessary to denounce a scholar like Hayek as engaged in "lunacy."

4. See the discriminating discussion in Joseph A. Schumpeter, *Capitalism, Socialism, and Democracy* (1942), especially Chs. XIX–XXIII. Harold E. Nourse, in *Controlling Factors in Economic Development* (1949), comes to the conclusion that "a democracy such as ours is inherently incapable of achieving a unified program of government control" (pp. 180 ff.), but that "government regulation is possible without usurpation of vital managerial functions" (pp. 192 ff.).

5. Here the vast literature on socialism is pertinent. See, besides Schumpeter's study, Sidney Hook, *Reason, Social Myth and Democracy* (1940), and the literature discussed there. For Britain, the corpus of the Fabian Society's writings are perhaps the most important source.

6. Seymour Harris, op. cit. p. 17, makes the assertion that "in the USSR, the economic plan has reached its highest state of development," without any awareness, evidently, of the difference between authoritarian and democratic planning. The same view, but in more dogmatic terms, is implied in Paul Sweezey's *Socialism* (1949), especially Chs. 3 and 12.

7. For the United States plans, see Otto Nelson, *National Security and the General Staff* (1946). See also the comments in E. P. Herring, *The Impact of War on American Government* (1941).

8. See Landauer, op. cit. p. 13.

9. See note 6. This is, of course, the reverse of the view of Hayek and others who, neglecting this difference, see all planning as the end of democracy.

10. Walton Hamilton and Douglas Adair, *The Power to Govern* (1937). See also the many significant extracts included by Francis W. Coker in his *Democracy, Liberty, and Property—Readings in the American Political Tradition* (1942), especially Part III.

11. Critics of socialization believe that socialization necessarily narrows the choice of occupation. Thus Jewkes, op. cit. p. 202, writes that the choice of occupation is "inevitably restricted with growing socialization." But he backs these remarks, as do others, by stating that "the big opportunities are to be found as administrators in the State organization." This is no real argument, but a semantic confusion: to lump all state administrations together as "bureaucracy" and call it a "narrow" choice, while not doing the same with "industry" or "business" in the free-market economy is misleading. The real problem is how to maintain freedom of choice between various jobs in this vital field without falling prey to the black-listing of a centralized police setup which builds up elaborate records on each employable person. The only feasible method seems to be much greater care to provide protection for the junior official against being so black-listed by throwing all pertinent records open to his inspection, and allowing him a hearing against unfair comments, as is done in some European countries. See above, Ch. XIX. On the other hand, it has to be admitted that Labour party spokesmen have been admitting the possibility of industrial conscription and related measures which would be unconstitutional under the provisions of the German Basic Law as quoted. For the British views see the Debate on the State of the Nation, on August 6 and 7, 1947, especially the remarks of Attlee and Cripps.

12. See Charles E. Merriam, *On the Agenda of Democracy* (1941), pp. 72 ff. The authoritarian position is stated well (without Fascist or Communist encumbrances) by René deVisme Williamson, *The Politics of Planning in the Oil Industry under the Code* (1936); the quote is found on page 18. See also the discussion in Ch. VII of *The New Belief in the Common Man* (1942).

13. On the whole, it is remarkable how far modern countries, whether listed as capitalist, socialist, or communist, have progressed toward the realization of the "plan" outlined by Marx and Engels. On this, see the shrewd comments by Schumpeter, op. cit. p. 48 f., and elsewhere. See also the able study of the progress of collectivism in Switzerland, William E. Rappard's magistral *L'Individu et l'État dans l'evolution constitutionelle de la Suisse* (no date given), wherein the learned author traces what he believes to be the debilitating effect of these developments upon Swiss constitutional democracy.

14. Preamble of the adopted French constitution; in the rejected constitution, articles 35–36. In the German Basic Law, articles 14–15 and 74 (Nos. 14–17); in the Italian constitution, articles 41–44.

15. See Williams, op. cit. ("Remarks"), pp. 89 ff. Sweezey, op. cit. Ch. III, denies that Britain is getting socialism from the present Labour government.

16. See article by Walton Hamilton, "Property," in *ESS*.

17. See Taylor Cole, and the author's study, *Responsible Bureaucracy* (1932), for a detailed analysis of the trend toward bureaucratization, and one democracy's method of dealing with it. See also "Some Thoughts on the Politics of Government Control" in *Journal of Social Philosophy*, Vol. I, pp. 122 ff. (1936). Schumpeter, op. cit. pp. 205–207, notes that the problem of bureaucratic management is central to a socialist society, but that it is likewise essential to the functioning of democracy in an industrial age, "an inevitable complement," Schumpeter calls it; see also his comments on pages 293–294.

18. Taylor Cole and the author stated the idea of a federative "commonwealth of mutual servants" in the volume cited, p. 88. "Each great service would have its own internal controls, but these would be held together by an individual or a group or by both, controlled in turn by the whole people." It is evident that the British are at present struggling to evolve just such a system. See also Taylor Cole's careful recent analysis of the Canadian public service as a responsible bureaucracy, *The Canadian Bureaucracy* (1949), especially p. 278.

19. See, *contra* the works of Sweezey, Jewkes, cited above. While Jewkes sees an "ordeal of planning," Sweezey insists that no significant innovations have been introduced and that "as far as one can judge from published statements, there has as yet been no 'planning to plan' *in the socialist sense of the term*." (Italics mine.)

20. NEP may be considered by some to be an unfortunate abbreviation, reminiscent as it is of Lenin's "new economic policy" (NEP). Actually, Lenin (in acknowledging the desirability

of a "sector," especially in agriculture, where the free market would continue) presumably thought in terms of the same sort of compromise which the "mixed" socialized economy involves. Francis Williams, *Socialist Britain* (1949), p. 86, distinguishes four main groups of controls. For a general statement see also Sir Oliver Franks' *Central Planning and Control in War and Peace* (1947); Sir Oliver served as the able chairman of the Paris Conference on the Marshall Plan during the summer of 1947. See also Ch. X in Harris, op. cit., on the texts (abbreviated) of some key British plans.

21. See Williams, op. cit. p. 91. The dates of successive nationalizations are given by Wickwar as follows: telegraph, 1868; telephone (trunk), 1892, (local), 1911; electricity (wholesale), 1926, (retail), 1947; radio broadcasting, 1927; London passenger transport, 1933; coal (mineral rights), 1938, (mining), 1946; civil aviation, 1929–1946; central banking, 1946; cables and wireless, 1946; railways, road haulage, canals, and docks, 1947; gas, 1948. See op. cit. p. 133.

22. See "Planning and Socialization in Great Britain" in *International Labour Review*, Vol. LVII (reprint, 1948), p. 13.

23. This is in itself a vast topic, closely related to the problems of local government, for which see above, Ch. XIII. For the bibliography see F. J. Osborn, *A Readers' Guide to Town and Country Planning* (1948). See more especially M. P. Fogarty, *Town and Country Planning* (1948), R. K. Kelsall, *Citizen's Guide to the New Town and Country Planning* (1948), and J. Tyrwhitt, *Planning and the Countryside* (1946); for an American contrast, R. E. Walker, *The Planning Function in Urban Government* (1941); also the *Journal of the American Institute of Planners*. The Barlow Report (Cmd. 6153) is a Royal Commission report on the distribution of industry, rendered in 1940. For later reports see above, note 23, Ch. XIII; likewise on Greater London, above, same note, Ch. XIII. From an economic standpoint, the writings on location of industry are relevant here, beginning with Alfred Weber's *Theory of the Location of Industry* (1909, Engl. tr., 1929); for more recent literature see Edgar M. Hoover, *The Location of Economic Activity* (1948).

24. For Sweden see the shrewd assessment in terms of democratic government by Sir E. D. Simon, *The Smaller Democracies* (1939), Ch. III and IV, where the double budget is briefly discussed. For Swedish literature see Gunnar Myrdal, *Monetary Equilibrium* (1939). For Switzerland's slow evolution toward *étatisme* see W. E. Rappard's *La Constitution Fédérale de la Suisse— 1848–1948* (1948).

25. See Gordon Wright, *The Reshaping of French Democracy* (1948), p. 172. The main official sources for the French situation are the Debates and Documents of the *Assemblée Consultative* (1944–45), of the *Assemblée Nationale Constituante* (1945–6), those of the *Assemblée* and the *Conseil* since that time, and the semi-annual reports of the *Commissariat du Plan*.

26. David Thomson, *Democracy in France—The Third Republic* (1946), pp. 258–259.

27. A skillful abbreviation of the Monnet Plan is given in Harris, op cit. Ch. XVII. See also *Decret* Nr. 47–119 (Jan. 16, 1947). See also ECA's country studies on France.

28. See Edgar Beigel, "France Moves Toward National Planning," *Political Science Quarterly* (1947), pp. 381 ff.; anonymous, "Le Plan Monnet et l'Organization de l'Economie Française," *Droit Social*, Vol. X (1947); Fred W. Riggs, "France: the Fourth Republic on Trial," in *Foreign Policy Reports* (1949); and Henry W. Ehrmann, "France between East and West," *Western Political Science Quarterly*, Vol. II (1949), pp. 74 ff.

29. See *Rapport General sur le Premier Plan*, issued by the Commissariat General du Plan in January 1947, p. 21. The view taken in the text is also argued by Jean Rivero, "Vers un Statut Juridique du Plan Monnet," *Droit Social*, Vol. XII (Jan., 1949).

30. An account of the Italian approach is found in Mario Einaudi's "Extending the Public Sector of the Economy," in *Foreign Governments* (F. Morstein-Marx, ed., 1949), Ch. XIV. The constitutional texts are available in the official documents, of course, but students will find the running commentary, *La Costituzione della Repubblica Italiana* (1948), by three members of the General Secretariat of the House of Deputies, V. Falzone, Filippo Palermo, and Francesco Cosentino, very helpful. The State Department has published a translation in *Documents and State Papers* (April, 1948), but it has proved necessary to deviate from this in a number of places.

The main official sources are, of course, the debates and documents of the Constituent Assembly and especially its Third Subcommission, dealing with economic aspects, and a report on a four-year development program by P. Saraceno, made as a report to the National Economic Council in 1947.

31. Einaudi, loc. cit. pp. 274–275.

32. ECA, *Country Study, Italy* (1949), pp. 44–46.

33. Fred W. Riggs, "Italy's Road Back," *Foreign Policy Report* (1949), and Jacob J. Kaplan, "Economic Stagnation in Italy?" Memorandum No. 32 of Yale Institute of International Studies. Besides the problems of reconstruction and recovery common to all European countries which have suffered from the war, Italy has, along with Germany, the basic problems of lack of resources, both food and raw materials, and "overpopulation."

34. The *Länder* in the British Zone which either have a Social-Democratic leadership, or which co-operate with it, do not have constitutions, and hence the issue here under discussion has only arisen legislatively. The skillfully worded compromise worked out in North-Rhine Westphalia in the summer of 1948 was suspended by British Military Government as premature, since a German constitution was in the making. See *Military Governor's Report*, September, 1948, No. 39, OMGUS. The situation is particularly complex in Berlin where the Social Democratic leadership has clamored for socialization, partly in competition with the Communists. The United States has prevented all moves in that direction from coming into effect.

35. For the Basic Law see above, Ch. VIII, and the literature cited there.

36. See ECA, *Country Study, Germany* (1949), as well as the highly informative *Long Term Program (1952–3) for the United States and United Kingdom Occupied Areas of Germany* (no date, issued in February, 1949, I believe). No attempt is made here to live up to Lilienthal's injunction: "The people must be in on the planning; their existing institutions must be made part of it; self-education of the citizenry is more important than specific projects or physical changes." See *TVA—Democracy on the March* (1944), p. 198.

37. See ECA reports passim; also Seymour Harris, *The European Recovery Program* (1948). A critical evaluation of the obstacles to international planning is given by Lionel Robbins, *Economic Planning and International Order* (1937), but in spite of these criticisms international planning appears on the march; see Lincoln Gordon, "ERP in Operation," in Harvard Business Review (1949), pp. 121 ff., and E. S. Mason, *Economics vs. Politics in International Relations: The European Recovery Program* (May, 1948), published by University of California. Neither mentions the constitutional issues.

38. An official apology by way of a smoke screen is the avowed policy of not "interfering in the internal politics" of member nations under the Plan. I call it a smoke screen because the United States is urging these countries to do more effective planning; if that effectiveness does in fact depend upon democratic methods, it is essential that these aspects be not neglected by all concerned. The Soviet Union's original harping upon the alleged assault upon the sovereignty of Marshall Plan countries has died down, since the Soviets' own interference to prevent countries from joining made the true state of the facts apparent to all.

39. See John Gaus, "The Planning Process in Government," Ch. VII, in *Problems of the Post-War World* (Thomas C. McCormick, ed. 1945) and J. Millet, *The Process and Organization of Government Planning* (1947).

40. Lilienthal, op. cit. Ch. XVIII; C. H. Pritchett, *The Tennessee Valley Authority* (1943), Ch. V; and Philip Selznick, *TVA and the Grass Roots*, 1949.

XXIV · Propaganda and the Control of Communications

REMARKS

There is a rapidly growing body of literature on public opinion, the press, and the radio, but much of it treats these subjects without regard to the political and governmental implications of "public opinion." Studies on the latter, in turn, often fail to consider the institutional channels, and more particularly the press. A comprehensive bibliography has been published by H. D. Lasswell, R. D. Casey, and B. L. Smith, entitled *Propaganda and Promotional Activities* (1935), of which a supplementary volume appeared in 1946, edited by Smith, Lasswell, et al. There are, first of all, the writings of A. Lawrence Lowell, whose *Public Opinion and Popular Government* (1913) and *Public Opinion in War and Peace* (1923) along with Walter Lippmann's *Public Opinion* (1922) and *The Phantom Public* (1925), clearly face the political issues. John Dewey's *The Public and its Problems* (1927), especially Chs. IV–VI, seeks to resolve the issues of mass communication by a revival of the local community, as had Josiah Royce before him. The issue is basically an outgrowth of man's limited rationality and finite mind. The implications of this are sketched in the author's *The New Belief in the Common Man* (1942). Mention may be made here of H. L. Childs, *An Introduction to Public Opinion* (1940), and William Albig, *Public Opinion* (1939). The *Journalism Quarterly* and the *Public Opinion Quarterly* (since 1937) have published many valuable special studies. Dexter M. Keezer's article "Press" for the *ESS* (1934), and R. E. Park's masterly essay, "The Natural History of the Newspaper," in the *American Journal of Sociology*, Vol. XXIX (1923), pp. 273 ff., have been implemented by a more general treatment, A. M. Lee, *The Daily Newspaper in America* (1937). Malcolm M. Willey and Stuart Rice have given a descriptive account of contemporary trends in *Communication Agencies and Social Life* (1933). A suggestive critical analysis is found in Norman Angell's *The Press and the Organization of Society* (1922). The literature on propaganda has been growing very rapidly. A comprehensive inventory of the different approaches of various governments to the problem of how to maintain the loyalty of their citizens was made by Charles E. Merriam in his magistral series of studies on "the making of citizens." Several studies, including Gaus, Schneider, and Brooks, appear elsewhere in this bibliography. The findings of this group of scholars were summarized by Merriam himself in his *The Making of Citizens* (1931). Much of the literature on propaganda, however, is preoccupied with the psychological issues which propaganda raises, implemented by rather general treatment of the governmental aspect. The volume of Leonard Doob, *Public Opinion and Propaganda* (new ed., 1948), is a good example, as is Hadley Cantril's *The Psychology of Social Movements* (1941). The latter's *The Invasion from Mars* (1940) offers a unique analysis of the configuration of mass hysteria. Other works in this field deserving the attention of the student of constitutional government, though none seem aware of constitutional issues, except in the most general terms, are Harold Lasswell, *Democracy through Public Opinion* (1941), Lasswell with Dorothy Blumenstock, *World Revolutionary Propaganda* (1939), F. C. Barlett, *Political Propaganda* (1941), and Jerome S. Bruner, *Mandate from the People* (1944). Two works are especially concerned with "the man in the street": Ellis Freeman, *Conquering the Man in the Street* (1940), and Thomas A. Baley, *The Man in the Street—The Impact of American Public Opinion on Foreign Policy* (1948). On the government's public relations, James C. McCamy's *Government Publicity* (1939) presents a good account of American practice up to the beginning of the Second World War, while Paul A. M. Linebarger deals with wartime activity under *Psychological Warfare* (1948), as does Charles A. H. Thomson, *Overseas Information Services of the U. S. Government* (1948); see also the wartime apologia of Elmer Davis and Myron Price, entitled *War Information and Censorship* (1943). The intricate problems of the interrelationship of various channels were given pioneering attention by Paul C. Lazarsfeld in *Radio and the Printed Page* (1940) and by a group of authors under the editorship of Douglas Waples in *Print, Radio and Film in a Democracy* (1943). These were implemented by the comprehensive work of the "Commission on the Freedom of the Press," published in 1947, more especially the lead volume of the Commission entitled *A Free and Responsible Press; a General Report on Mass Communication: Newspapers, Radio, Motion Pictures, Magazines and Books*, Zechariah Chafee's *Government and Mass Communications* and W. Ernest Hocking, *Freedom of the Press: A Framework of Principle*. The studies by White on radio and Inglis on the movies are cited below where these channels are discussed.

There is a considerable body of literature in French and German on these questions, of which Keezer, op. cit., gives a careful selection. One might mention here Stephane Lauzanne, *Sa Majesté la Presse* (1925), and the work of *Institut de Science de la Presse*, under the able direction of B. Mirkine-Guetzevitch and E. Hamburger, which published *Cahiers de la Presse* until 1940; E. Dovifat, *Die Zeitungen* (1925); Oskar Wettstein, *Über das Verhaltnis zwischen Staat und Presse* (1904); J. Buchhorn, *Politik und Presse* (1920); and Karl Bömer, *Bibliographisches Handbuch der Zeitungswissenschaft* (1929), particularly pp. 192 ff., "Die Zeitung im Staatsleben."

Though there are some interesting psychological studies, the novelty of the radio as an instrument and channel of communication has not yet permitted thorough analysis of its political and governmental aspects. The author's series, *Studies in the Control of Radio* (since 1940), more especially "Congress and the Control of Radiobroadcasting" (1943) and "An Analysis of the Radiobroadcasting Activities of Federal Agencies" (1941) by Jeanette Sayre represent beginnings. Further radio studies by Lazarsfeld, Robinson, Rose, Siepmann, and Grandin are given below. On the BBC, Lincoln Gordon's "The British Broadcasting Corporation," in *The Public Corporation in Great Britain* (1938), Ch. IV, was excellent, but we still lack a first-class study of this central topic.

On the wire communication field, the most authoritative recent study is N. R. Danielian's *A. T. & T., The Story of Industrial Conquest* (1939).

REFERENCES

1. See Charles A. Beard, *The American Leviathan*, p. 257. The view from Lippmann is found in his *Public Opinion*, p. 320. Jefferson's statement is cited by Keezer, op. cit. p. 326, but without reference.

2. See Walter Millis, *The Martial Spirit* (1931), Arnold Brecht, *Prelude to Silence* (1944), and the author's *The New Belief in the Common Man* (1942), especially Ch. III.

3. For the general literature on propaganda see the *Remarks* above. To these may be added several articles: Charles R. Hoffer, "A Sociological Analysis of Propaganda," *Social Forces*, May 1942; Edgar H. Henderson, "Toward a Definition of Propaganda," *Journal of Social Psychology*, August 1943; Francis G. Wilson, "Tradition and Propaganda," *Journal of Politics*, Nov. 1943; W. Hayes Yeager and William E. Utterback, "Communication and Social Action," *Annals*, March 1947; and Louis Wirth, "Consensus and Mass Communication," *American Sociological Review*, Feb., 1948. For the special wartime problems, see below, note 21.

4. For the beginnings, see Bücher, *Die Entstehung der Volkswirtschaft* (1922), Vol. I, pp. 229 ff. and the literature cited there. The quotation from Matthias A. Shaaber is from his *Some Forerunners of the Newspaper in England, 1476–1622* (1929), p. 325. See also F. K. Hunt, *The Fourth Estate* (1850), Chs. IV and V. For the *Gazette* see E. Hatin, *Histoire Politique et Littéraire de la Presse en France* (1859–1861), Vol. I, pp. 28 ff. The later English development is well discussed also by Alexander Andrews, *The History of British Journalism* (1859), and by Stanley Morison, *The English Newspaper* (1932). See also literature cited below, notes 5 and 11.

5. See again Andrews and Hunt, op. cit. Interesting also is Wilhelm Dibelius, *England* (1930), pp. 314 ff. The quotation is from Frederick B. Artz, *Reaction and Revolution, 1814–1832* (1934), p. 286. See also E. L. Woodward, *The Age of Reform* (1938), pp. 28–30, 601.

6. See again Artz, op. cit. pp. 263 ff., and the literature cited there.

7. The most detailed discussion is Lucy M. Salmon, *The Newspaper and Authority* (1923). See also William G. Hale, *Law of the Press* (1923); and for the fundamental issues, Zechariah Chafee, *Freedom of Speech* (1920), new and rev. edition published under the title *Free Speech in the United States* (1941), and Morris L. Ernst and Alexander Lindley, *The Censor Marches On* (1940). See also note 22 below. The publication of the British Foreign Office appeared in 1926 under the title, *The Press Laws of Foreign Countries*, edited by M. Shearman and O. T. Raynor. The figures are taken from Keezer, op. cit., p. 341. Concerning the Zenger case, see C. A. Duniway, *The Development of Freedom of the Press in Massachusetts* (1906), Isaiah Thomas, *The History of Printing in America* (1810), and G. J. Patterson, *Free Speech and a Free Press* (1939). Other significant historical studies are Philip Davidson, *Propaganda and the American Constitution* (1941), Frank L. Mott, *Jefferson and the Press* (1944), and James E. Pollard, *The Presidents and the Press* (1947).

8. The literature on these undertakings is considerable, but not very weighty. For Hearst, mention ought to be made of John Winkler, *Hearst, an American Phenomenon* (1928). An interesting special study was made by R. D. Casey, "Scripps-Howard Papers in the 1928 Presidential Campaign," *Journalism Quarterly* (1930), pp. 210 ff. Walter Millis's *The Martial Spirit* (1931), particularly Chs. I–IV, is valuable for the historical role of Hearst and Pulitzer in bringing about the Spanish-American War. For Northcliffe and Beaverbrook, see the uncritical volumes by Kennedy Jones, *Fleet Street and Downing Street* (1920), and by W. M. Aitken, Baron Beaverbrook, *Politicians and the Press* (1925). For the Hugenberg concern, Ludwig Bernhard's peculiar and in many respects candid study, *Der "Hugenberg Konzern"; Psychologie und Technik einer Grossorganisation der Presse* (1928), is quite informative.

9. Besides the literature cited in the preceding paragraph, consult Keezer, op. cit., for the figures. The broader implications of this development are well stated in R. E. Park's study cited above. See also George L. Bird and Frederick E. Merwin, *The Newspaper and Society* (1942). For France, besides Lauzanne's volume in French, Ch. VI of Carlton J. H. Hayes's *France: A Nation of Patriots* (1930) gives an interesting survey of the press which is supplemented by three Appendices (C, D, and E) containing carefully annotated lists of periodicals and dailies; for both, according to Professor Hayes's preface, we are indebted to Miss Vera Mikol. Besides this chapter, Robert de Jouvenel's spicy comments in *La République des Camarades* (first published in 1914) under the heading, "Le Quatrième Pouvoir," pp. 201 ff., are worth-while. For Germany, see Ludwig Salomon, *Geschichte des deutschen Zeitungswesens*, 3 vols. (1906); F. Bertkau and Karl Bömer, *Der wirtschaftliche Aufbau des deutschen Zeitungsgewerbes* (1932); E. Dovifat, *Die Zeitungen* (1925); and Karl Bömer, *Bibliographisches Handbuch der Zeitungswissenschaft* (1929). The references to particular German papers are found here on pp. 45 ff.

10. An authoritative report on the British press has been offered recently by the so-called Ross Report: *Report of the Royal Commission on the Press*, Cmd. 7700, though the conclusions seem controversial. See also the appropriate section of *Political Handbook of the World; Parliaments, Parties and Press*, an annual publication of the Council on Foreign Relations. A richly illustrated picture may be derived from Stanley Morison's *The English Newspaper* (1932). Kurt von Stutterheim's account, *The Press in England* (tr. W. H. Johnson, 1934), particularly Ch. V, and Wilhelm Dibelius's chapter on the press as previously cited, add insight, as does the more recent discussion offered by Kingsley Martin in an article in the *Political Quarterly*, Vol. I (1930), pp. 428 ff., entitled, "Public Opinion: Rationalization of the Press and Democracy." Much real benefit can also be derived from the biographies of such leading British newsmen as Spender and Steed. Colonel Repington's memoirs also are worth careful attention.

11. For this paragraph, see Park, op. cit.; Allan Nevins, *The Evening Post; a Century of Journalism* (1922); John LaPorte Given, *Making a Newspaper* (1907); O. G. Villard, *Some Newspapers and Newspapermen* (1923), and *The Press To-day* (1930). E. H. Davis, *History of the New York Times* (1921), while quite informative, is not entirely free from a natural partisanship. See also Emil Dovifat, *Der amerikanische Journalismus* (1927). The reference is to p. 311. The quotation from the report of the Interchurch Movement is found in Keezer, op. cit., p. 339; the title of the pamphlet is *Public Opinion and the Steel Strike* (1921), where it appears on p. 147.

12. For this issue see John Bainbridge, *The Little Wonder* (1946). The figures are from the Audit Bureau of Circulations as reported in *The World Almanac* (1949). On the columnists, see Charles Fischer, *The Columnists* (1944).

13. For pertinent material see Oliver Gramling, *AP: The Story of News* (1940). For the competition between radio and news services, see Paul Lazarsfeld, *Radio and the Printed Page* (1940), Chs. V and VI; also the *Hearings* (Summary) of the FCC under order No. 79 (1941).

14. See Thomas Grandin, *The Political Use of Radio* (1939), Arno Huth (ed.), *Radio Today* (1942), and Lincoln Gordon, *The Public Corporation in Great Britain* (1938), p. 166. See also William A. Robson's study of the BBC in the volume he edited, *Public Enterprise* (1937), and H. of C. Debates, Apr. 29, 1936, 311: 955 ff.; July 6, 1936, 314: 865 ff.; Dec. 17, 1936, 318: 272 ff.; 1946: 414–432.

15. See for this issue James R. Angell, *War Propaganda and the Radio* (1940), Harwood L. Childs and John B. Whitton (eds.), *Propaganda by Short Wave* (1942), and the author's "Controlling Radiobroadcasting in Wartime" in *Studies in the Control of Radio* (reprinted from *Public Policy*, Vol. II, 1941). The cold war and peace-time perspectives are ably developed in *Peoples Speaking to Peoples* (1946) by Robert D. Leigh and Llewellyn White.

16. For the statute see 47 *U.S.C.* 606 (c). See also the general references given in the *Remarks*. The basic psychological study is Cantril and Allport, *The Psychology of Radio* (1935). Lazarsfeld, op. cit., also is very important. Much valuable insight can be gained by reading the FCC's "Report of the Committee appointed by the Commission to Supervise the Investigation of Chain Broadcasting (Commission Order No. 37—Docket No. 5060)" (June 12, 1940), and "Digest and Analysis of Evidence Presented in the Hearing on Commission Order No. 37 (Docket 5060) and of the Files of the Commission." But they are, of course, presenting a particular view. See the author's article, "The FCC 'Monopoly' Report: a Critical Appraisal," in *Public Opinion Quarterly*, September, 1940 (Vol. IV, No. 3, pp. 526–532).

17. The Commission's Report is entitled "Public Service Responsibility of Broadcast Licensees" and was published on March 7, 1946. About the same time, Charles Siepmann's *Radio's Second Chance* appeared which took a very similar approach to radiobroadcasting. This led to charges that the report was essentially that of Siepmann, whose former connection with the BBC was duly noted. In fact, the report was written by another specialist in the Commission, owed much to Commissioner C. J. Durr's interest, and had the backing of the Commission. It summed up much earlier criticism, and its educational aspects had been the subject of extensive earlier discussions. For this aspect see "Radiobroadcasting and Higher Education" by C. J. Friedrich, *Studies in the Control of Radio*, No. 4 (1942), and the literature cited there. William S. Paley, the chairman of CBS's board of directors, contributed his criticism in *The Freedom of Radio* (1944), and the whole range of issues was surveyed for the Commission on Freedom of the Press by Llewellyn White in *The American Radio* (1947). See also the numerous articles and studies bearing on these issues in *Radio Research* (1941 and later, edited by Paul F. Lazarsfeld and Frank Stanton, President of CBS). Lazarsfeld also published an interesting study together with Harry Field on the public's reactions to radio, *The People Look at Radio* (1946). See also Lyman Bryson's recent appeal, *Time for Reason about Radio* (1948), which contains a series of discussions on CBS, staged with a view to stating the broadcasters' case to the public.

18. See the FCC *Report* and *Digest* cited previously and "Mutual's White Paper," The Mutual Broadcasting System, Inc. (May 23, 1941), "What the New Radio Rules Mean," Columbia Broadcasting System (May 17, 1941). See also the general studies quoted in the previous paragraph, as well as J. H. Rose, *National Policy for Radiobroadcasting* (1940), and Thomas P. Robinson, *Radio Networks and the Federal Government* (1943).

19. See, besides the general books on Fascism and Nazism, cited elsewhere, Derris Sington and Arthur Weidenfeld, *The Goebbels Experiment* (1943); Harold Ettlinger, *The Axis on the Air* (1943); Ernst Kris, Hans Speier, and associates, *German Radio Propaganda* (1944); Lindley Fraser, *Germany Between Two Wars—A Study of Propaganda and War Guilt* (1945), the last-named perhaps the most striking illustration of egocentric perspective; and finally Ralph F. Bischoff's *Nazi Conquest Through German Culture* (1942). The Chamber of Culture was analyzed by Taylor Cole in "Cooperative Organization of the Third Reich," *Review of Politics*, Oct. 1940. The official point of view is set forth in Karl F. Schrieber, *Das Recht der Reichskulturkammer*, 2 vols. (1935). The quotations are from Marx. The remark about the constructive power is found in Keezer, op. cit. p. 332. So are the circulation figures for *Pravda* and *Izvestia*, p. 333. Concerning Italy, see *Italian Journalism under Fascism*, prepared for the International Press Exhibition (Pressa) at Cologne by Ermanno Amicucci for the National Fascist Union of Journalists. Also Francesco Luigi Ferrari, *Le Régime Fasciste Italien* (1928), pp. 155 ff.; Henry R. Spencer, *Government and Politics of Italy* (1932), Ch. XIII. See also Herman Finer, *Mussolini's Italy*, pp. 234 ff.

20. Concerning press and communications in the Soviet Union, recent research has brought forward much additional information. See Alex Inkeles, "Domestic Broadcasting in the

U.S.S.R.," in *Communications Research* (May 1949). Besides the general treatments in texts like Ranney and Carter, Morstein-Marx, and others, the highly controversial writings on the Soviet Union by authors like Frederick L. Schuman, David J. Dallin, and William Henry Chamberlin all contain general outlines of the way in which the Soviet Union is permeated by propaganda, but the subject awaits more thorough exploration in all its ramifications. There is an older study on the history of the Russian press from Tsarist times to the Soviets: J. Botscharow, *Die Entwicklung der russischen Presse (1621–1928)*. The early revolutionary techniques served Serge Chakotin, *The Rape of the Masses* (1940), for some brilliant generalizations.

21. Besides some of the radio studies cited in note 15, and the works mentioned in *Remarks*, the following studies are relevant: Harold Levine and James Wechsler, *War Propaganda and the United States* (1940); Matthew Gordon, *News Is a Weapon* (1942); Sherman H. Dryer (ed.), *Radio in Wartime* (1942); and, for the First World War, James R. Mock and Cedric Larson, *Words That Won the War* (1939), and *Censorship, 1917*, by James R. Mock (1941), as well as Harold D. Lasswell's pathfinding study, *Propaganda Technique in the World War* (1927). For the Second World War, Frank L. Mott, *Journalism in Wartime* (1944), might be added. The spring, 1943, issue of *The Public Opinion Quarterly* (1943) is entirely devoted to OWI and related issues; it includes an article by the author on "Informational Strategy."

22. Censorship during the Second World War revived the general interest in this subject, and the problem of the "freedom of the press," of which it is a denial. We note the following: Walter W. Jones, *The Law of Journalism* (1940); Newspaper-Radio Committee, *Freedom of the Press* (1942); Frank Thayer, *Legal Control of the Press* (1944); T. F. Koop, *Weapon of Silence* (1946); and, of course, the works by Chafee and the Commission on Freedom of the Press noted above under *Remarks*. The constitutional issues are developed by J. Edward Gerald, *The Press and the Constitution, 1931–1947* (1948).

23. The difficult issues of irresponsible "freedom" are skillfully adumbrated by David Riesman in two articles "Democracy and Defamation: Control of Group Libel" and "Democracy and Defamation: Fair Game and Fair Comment," in *Columbia Law Review*, May and November, 1942.

24. It has not been possible to deal here with the interesting problems of the motion-picture industry. Two studies are especially valuable in this connection: Leo C. Rosten, *Hollywood— The Movie Colony* (1941), and Ruth A. Inglis, *Freedom of the Movies* (1947). See also John E. Harley's *World-Wide Influences of the Cinema: A Study of Official Censorship* (1941).

25. These facts were recently confirmed again in a research study, carried forward under the author's supervision by A. A. Ulin, and published as No. 6 of *Studies in the Control of Radio*, entitled "Small Station Management and the Control of Radiobroadcasting." Compare also the interesting recent study by H. Brucker, *Freedom of Information* (1949).

XXV · *Direct Popular Action*

REMARKS

Direct popular action has been dealt with primarily in connection with the specific issues of the referendum and initiative internally, and the plebiscites externally. A. L. Lowell, to be sure, went into the general phases of the problem both in his *Public Opinion and Popular Government* (1913) and in *Public Opinion in War and Peace* (1923). English writers such as Bagehot usually gave it just passing notice, to discard it in favor of the English representative system. The debates preceding the adoption of the German and Swiss programs are rather interesting sources for an elaborate argument both pro and con direct popular action within the context of a constitutional order. The expression "direct democracy" has often been used in continental Europe; it is rather misleading in view of the implied contention that the introduction of the initiative and referendum changes the whole tenor of the constitutional order. In France, where direct popular action had been widely favored during the revolution (following Rousseau), it has always found a place in general treatises, although its application has been discredited. It is here that the relationship to dictatorial plebiscites has most readily suggested itself, and both topics are treated, for example, in A. Esmein's *Eléments de Droit Constitutionnel Français et Comparé*, particularly Vol. I, pp. 435 ff. From the present writer's standpoint this is the most comprehensive treatment in contemporary literature, although it will be seen that different general views underlie Esmein's discussion. An important treatise appeared in a remote place and has therefore not received the recognition it deserves, Professor Axel Brusewitz' *Folkomröstningsinstitutet i den Schweiziska Demokratien—Dess Förutsättningar, Former och Functioner*, which was published by the Department of Justice of Sweden in 1923, the official reference being *Statens Offentliga Utredningar*, 1923:10. In spite of its specialized title (*The Institution of Popular Votes in the Swiss Democracies—Their Conditions, Forms and Functioning*), the general discussion is carried to an advanced point, the ideological background carefully examined, and a general conclusion reached which is comprehensive and accurate, as far as direct popular action within a constitutional framework is concerned. Unfortunately, the comparative aspects relating referenda to international and dictatorial plebiscites do not find room here. Karl Loewenstein has made several valuable contributions, for which see below. Carl Schmitt, when still a constitutionalist, developed his views on direct democracy in his *Verfassungslehre* (1928), particularly pp. 204 ff. Likewise, Hans Kelsen, from a very different standpoint, has enlarged his views on democracy, as expounded in *Vom Wesen und Wert der Demokratie* (2d ed., 1929), pp. 14 ff., in his magistral *Allgemeine Staatslehre* (1925), particularly pp. 356 ff.

REFERENCES

1. Rousseau's argument against representation is found in *Contrat Social*, Book II, Ch. XV. See also above, Ch. XIV, note 1. For the general will see my *Inevitable Peace* (1948), pp. 169 ff.

2. For Napoleon I, see F. M. Kircheisen, *Napoleon I, sein Leben und seine Zeit* (1911–1932), particularly Vols. V and VII. The figures are found in Vol. V, p. 270, and Vol. VII, pp. 10–12, respectively. See also H. A. L. Fisher, *Napoleon* (1913); J. H. Rose, *The Life of Napoleon I* (8th ed., 1922); and Albert Sorel, *L'Europe et la Révolution Française* (9th ed., 1911), Vols. VI–VIII. None of these works could draw upon a careful study of the Napoleonic plebiscites, for such a study, as Kircheisen remarks, has unfortunately never been made. We have now a study by Karl Loewenstein, "Opposition and Public Opinion under the Dictatorship of Napoleon the First," in *Social Research*, Vol. IV (1937). The need for continuous victories is brought out in H. C. Deutsch, *The Genesis of Napoleonic Imperialism* (1938). For the data concerning Napoleon III, see P. de la Gorce, *Histoire du Second Empire*, Vols. I and VI. The particular data are found in the former on pp. 12–13 and 105, and in the latter in *livre* XXXVIII, particularly pp. 115 ff. What is true of the plebiscites of the first Napoleon is equally true of those of the third. However, there seems to exist an unprinted study of these which is cited by Charles Seignobos, "La Révolution de 1848, le second Empire," in *Histoire de France contemporaine* (ed. Ernest Lavisse), Vol. VI. See also Réné Arnaud, *Le Coup d'État du 2 Décembre* (1926).

3. For this paragraph see Theodore Curti, *Die Resultate des Schweizerischen Referendums* (2d ed., 1911); Simon Deploige, *The Referendum in Switzerland* (tr. C. P. Trevelyan, 1898); Robert C. Brooks, *Civic Training in Switzerland* (1930), pp. 107 ff. The most comprehensive study of the Swiss initiative and referendum, however, has appeared in Sweden: Axel Brusewitz, op. cit. The most recent analysis is given in W. E. Rappard *La Constitution Fédérale de la Suisse—1848-1948* (1948), pp. 328 ff. The quotation is from p. 164 of Brooks, *Government and Politics of Switzerland*. The discussion of the treaty referenda follows F. Fleiner, *Schweizerisches Bundesstaatsrecht* (1932), p. 755. A special study of the social and political aspects of the two treaty referenda held so far would be very desirable.

4. The discussion of this paragraph is based on A. L. Lowell, *Public Opinion and Popular Government* (new ed., 1926), Chs. XI, XIII, and XIV; W. B. Munro, *The Initiative, Referendum and Recall* (1912), Chs. I–XI; and A. N. Holcombe, *State Government in the United States* (3d ed., 1931), Ch. XVI. Another valuable contribution to these problems is W. F. Dodd, *The Revision and Amendment of State Constitutions* (1910). Special reference is made to the figures on p. 268.

The quotations at the end of the paragraph are found in Holcombe, op. cit. pp. 551 and 569. See also Francis Cole, "Votes in New York City on Referenda, 1920–1934 inclusive" (1936), V. O. Key, Jr., and W. W. Crouch, *The Initiative and Referendum in California* (1939), and James K. Pollock, *The Initiative and Referendum in Michigan* (1941).

5. See Lowell, *Public Opinion and Popular Government*, Ch. XV. Carl Schmitt, *Verfassungslehre*, §20, pushes matters to their logical extreme, a method by which he confuses all political problems which involve balance between extremes rather than following out one of them. See also Esmein, *Droit Constitutionnel*, Vol. I, pp. 435 ff.

6. For greater detail see *CGD* (1941), pp. 554–558. Brecht, in *Prelude to Silence* (1944), curiously neglects the referenda.

7. For the division of American public opinion see *The New Belief in the Common Man* (1942), Ch. III. For the most elaborate statement of the provocation thesis, see Charles A. Beard, *President Roosevelt and the Coming of the War* (1947). For the constitutional amendment, proposed by one representative, Ludlow, see the letter by Henry L. Stimson, December 21, 1937, to the *New York Times*, printed in the appendix to C. J. Friedrich, *Foreign Policy in the Making* (1938).

8. For this paragraph, see Sarah Wambaugh, *A Monograph on Plebiscites, with a Collection of Official Documents* (1920), and Johannes Mattern, *The Employment of the Plebiscite in the Determination of Sovereignty* (1921).

9. See Sarah Wambaugh, *Plebiscites since the World War* (1933), and the literature cited there. The two maps in more elaborate form are found there, Vol. I, pp. 87 and 266. The map showing the results of the Schleswig plebiscite is based on "Kort over Afstemnings-Resultaterne i Sønderjylland." That for the plebiscite in Upper Silesia is based on a map published by the British Section, Interallied Administrative and Plebiscite Commission. The Saar plebiscite has been described with detachment, though with sympathy toward the technique, by Sarah Wambaugh, *The Saar Plebiscite* (1940).

10. For the use of the plebiscite under Hitler, see Frederick L. Schuman, *The Nazi Dictatorship* (1935), pp. 256 ff. and 462 ff.; and Otto Köllreuter, *Deutsches Staatsrecht* (1935), who expounds the official Nazi view. For the quotation from him, see p. 146. For the quotation from Schuman, see p. 262. See also Franz L. Neumann, *Behemoth* (1942), pp. 54–55 and 83 ff., and Sigmund Neumann, *Permanent Revolution* (1942), Ch. VII.

11. The plebiscites under Fascism have not been analyzed as carefully as might be desired. The mass of new documents may aid in filling this need. Besides the studies in the previous note, E. B. Ashton's *The Fascist—His State and His Mind* (1937), pp. 71–72, and Herbert Schneider, *Making the Fascist State* (1928), and *Making Fascists* (1928), are helpful, especially the latter. The marching symbol is stressed by Sigmund Neumann, op. cit. p. 228, and is central to G. A. Borgese's *Goliath—The March of Fascism* (1937). Among social psychologists, the problems involved in these plebiscites have received some attention. See especially Hadley Cantril, *The Psychology of Social Movements* (1941), Chs. VIII and IX. There is an interesting chapter on the plebiscitary aspects of "totalitarian voting" in James Hogan, *Election and Representation* (1945).

12. The plebiscitary aspects of Soviet Communism have for long been neglected. The vote on the constitution of 1936 was clearly a totalitarian plebiscite, although differently interpreted by Sidney and Beatrice Webb, *Soviet Communism—A New Civilization?* (1938), especially Ch. VI, against whom some of the remarks in the text are directed. See also the work by Inkeles, cited above, Ch. XIV, note 20. Soviet elections, such as that of 1946, also deserve more detailed study in plebiscitary terms.

13. On the French referenda, see Gordon Wright, *The Reshaping of French Democracy* (1948), especially pp. 79 ff., 176 ff., 224 ff. The statistics are given on p. 260. See also literature given there.

14. On the German problem see the studies by R. G. Neumann, Friedrich, Brecht, and others, cited below, p. 664, "Remarks." See also what was said on the "negative revolutions," above, Ch. VIII, pp. 151 ff.

15. *Considerations on Representative Government* (1873), p. 3

XXVI · *Constitutional Dictatorship and Military Government*

REMARKS

The literature on the subject of this chapter is quite limited, but we have a significant general analysis, Frederick M. Watkins, "The Problem of Constitutional Dictatorship" in *Public Policy*, Vol. I (1940). See also the same author's case study, *The Failure of Constitutional Emergency Powers under the German Republic* (1939). To these has recently been added C. L. Rossiter, *Constitutional Dictatorship* (1948). A considerable amount of controversial writing on this subject appeared in the 'thirties and 'forties of the last century in France; and Karl Marx, who has done more than anyone else to spread the idea of dictatorship in recent times, undoubtedly was influenced by this literature. A number of treatments of contemporary unconstitutional dictatorships contain more or less extensive comments on constitutional dictatorship. Particularly, Alfred Cobban's *Dictatorship: Its History and Theory* (1939) is a valuable general treatment, beside which Carl Schmitt's *Die Diktatur von den Anfängen des modernen Souveränitätsgedankens bis zum proletarischen Klassenkampf* (2d ed., 1928) appears like a partisan tract. See also Hans Kohn, *Revolutions and Dictatorships* (1939). Other works one may mention in this connection are O. Forst de Battaglia, *Prozess der Diktatur* (1930), translated by H. Paterson as *Dictatorship on Trial* (1931); F. Cambo, *Les Dictatures* (1930); and E. Ortega y Gasset, *La Verdad sobre la Dictadura* (1925), digested in H. R. Spencer's article "Dictatorship" in *ESS*. Besides these general treatments, the considerable literature on the several dictatorships should be consulted. On the process of constitutional deterioration through the extensive use of dictatorial powers, Arnold Brecht, *Prelude to Silence* (1944), is particularly illuminating.

Military government has recently been the subject of an increasing number of studies, legal, political, and other. There have not been, however, any comprehensive attempts to integrate the ideas on military government with general principles of government, and the sketch which follows below represents, so far as the author is aware, a first essay in this direction. Besides the special-country studies, cited below, the following general treatments might be mentioned here. Raymond Robin, *Des Occupations militaires en dehors des occupations de guerre* (1913), gives a historical survey. Hajo Holborn, *American Military Government—Its Organization and Policies* (1947), gives the official view and some key documents concerning development during the Second World War. Carl J. Friedrich and Associates, *American Experiences in Military Government in World War II* (1948), gives accounts of actual operations in the several theaters, as well as some general analysis. The January 1950 issue of *The Annals* follows the same pattern. An unpublished dissertation by Robert N. Ginsburgh, *Between War and Peace* (1948), available at Widener Library, gives a broad historical account, as do the two articles by R. H. Gabriel in *APSR*, Vol. XXXVII (1943), pp. 417 ff., and *American Historical Review*, Vol. XLIX (1944), pp. 630 ff.

There is a vast amount of governmental documentation, not only American, but British, French, and other. These documents usually relate to a particular country or zone, like the *Monthly Reports of the Military Governor*, though *The Axis in Defeat*, Dept. State publication (1946) and a few others are of more general scope. The Department of the Army is planning a comprehensive history of military government operations in many volumes. Basic for the U.S. are the two field manuals: *Field Manual 27–5*, "Military Government" (1940), and "Joint Army-Navy Manual of Military Government and Civil Affairs" (1943).

For current information and material see *Military Government Journal*, published since 1948 by the Military Government Association; it contains many valuable articles, for example, Robert H. Slover, "The Goals of Military Government," Vol. II (1949).

REFERENCES

1. The most significant general discussion of constitutional dictatorship is given by J. J. Rousseau, *Contrat Social*, Book IV, Ch. VI.

2. On the royal prerogative in Britain, see Wormuth, cited above, Ch. VI, note 6. The

whole problem is opened up in Otto Hintze's striking essay, "Der Kommissarius und seine Bedeutung in der allgemeinen Verwaltungsgeschichte," in *Festgabe für Karl Zeumer* (1910); Hintze first emphasized the importance of the discussion in Bodin. Bodin's discussion is to be found in Ch. II of Book III of his *De Republica* (Frankfurt ed., 1609), pp. 424 ff. On the intendants, see G. Hanotaux, *Origines de l'institution des intendants* (1884).

3. For the Roman problem, see Theodor Mommsen, *Römisches Staatsrecht* (ed. 1874), Vol. II, 1, pp. 125 ff. See Kurt von Fritz, "Emergency Powers in the Last Centuries of the Roman Republic," *Annual Report, Am. Hist. Association*, Vol. III (1944), pp. 221 ff. On Wallenstein, see the detailed study in Schmitt, op. cit. pp. 79 ff. Concerning Cromwell's dictatorship, see S. R. Gardiner, *History of the Great Civil War* (1893), particularly Vols. II and III. See also the essay by W. C. Abbott, "The Historic Cromwell," in *Adventures in Reputation* (1935).

4. The ruling of the Supreme Court is found in *Ex parte Milligan*, 4 *Wall* 2 (1866). Regarding the statement of Judge Mackintosh, see Charles M. Clode, *The Administration of Justice under Military and Martial Law* (1872), p. 166. For the subject of martial law in the United States, see Charles Fairman, *The Law of Martial Rule* (1930), and the more recent analysis in Robert S. Rankin, *When Civil Law Fails* (1939). Fairman makes clear why martial rule is not always lawful; he also rightly insists that it should be distinguished from military law and military government. The brief discussion in A. V. Dicey, *Introduction to the Study of the Law of the Constitution* (8th ed., 1915), Ch. VII and note 10, is still pertinent. For the rule of law, see what was said above, pp. 103–110.

5. For the state of siege in France, see Esmein-Nézard, *Droit Constitutionnel* (8th ed., 1928), Vol. II, pp. 176 ff. There was an increasing recognition in France of the importance of strong executive leadership. See, for example, Émile Giraud, *La Crise de la Démocratie et le renforcement du Pouvoir Exécutif* (1938). This tendency led to a readier acceptance of the use of emergency powers in the 'thirties. See Otto Kirchheimer, "Decree Powers and Constitutional Law in France under the Third Republic," *The American Political Science Review*, Vol. XXXIV, No. 6 (Dec. 1940). Under the new constitution, the emergency powers remain undefined. Art. 97 merely provides that the parliament shall meet on its own initiative.

6. Concerning the Defense of the Realm Act, see Fairman, op. cit. For American experience, see E. S. Corwin, *The Powers of the President* (1940), and E. P. Herring, *Presidential Leadership* (1940), Appendix I. See also *The Federalist*, Vol. LXXIV, and James Bryce, *The American Commonwealth* (rev. ed., 1924), Vol. I, pp. 55 ff.

7. Concerning Poincaré's "dictatorship," see Esmein-Nézard, op. cit. Vol. II, pp. 112 ff., and the literature cited there. See also the study of Dendias cited below, note 9.

8. F. M. Watkins, "The Problem of Constitutional Dictatorship" in *Public Policy*, Vol. I (1940), p. 353 and C. L. Rossiter, op. cit. A considerable body of highly controversial literature has recently appeared in the United States, and the epithet "dictator" has rather indiscriminately been applied to the American President. In order to forestall the recurrence of such a situation as arose in 1932–1933, constitutional reform has been urged by various writers, among them W. Y. Elliott who, in *The Need for Constitutional Reform* (1935), cast the problem into this framework. See particularly pp. 27 ff. and 73 ff. See also Henry Hazlitt, op. cit. above. Lindsay Rogers interpreted the Wilsonian position during the war as dictatorship; see his "Presidential Dictatorship in the United States," *Quarterly Review* (1919).

9. *Ex parte Merryman* is found in 17 Fed. Cas. 144, the quotation at p. 153. The study by Michael Dendias, *Le Renforcement des Pouvoirs du Chef de l'État dans la Démocratie Parlementaire* (1932), contains much valuable comparative material, but it fails to draw the necessary clear distinction between constitutional and unconstitutional trends.

10. For literature on the emphasis upon legislation, see Ch. XIV, note 8.

11. The comparisons of this paragraph are based upon the extensive literature on totalitarian dictatorship to which reference is made elsewhere in this volume. For a careful assessment of the transition in Germany, see the study by Brecht, quoted in *Remarks*. Concerning the Swiss militia tradition, see the volume by Julian Grande, *A Citizens' Army* (1916). Concerning

Machiavelli, see, for example, *Discourses*, Book III. See also O. Ferrara, *Machiavel* (French ed., 1928), pp. 123 ff., and elsewhere. This point was given central importance in J. L. de Lolme's *The Constitution of England*, etc. (new ed., 1807), particularly Chs. XVII and XVIII. It is also the central theme of Silas Bent McKinley's *Democracy and Military Power* (1934), dedicated to "the man on foot who makes democracies."

12. The numerous critical accounts of political developments under the occupation are replete with illustrative material. See, for instance, George C. S. Benson and Maurice Neufeld, "American Military Government in Italy," and the former's "American Military Government in Austria" in C. J. Friedrich and Associates, op. cit. Other studies in that volume contribute to this point. The issues are quite tellingly presented in an imaginative setting by John Hersey, *A Bell for Adano* (1943). A more sharply critical view is presented by Harold Zink, *American Military Government in Germany* (1947), and, as far as Germany is concerned, by Gustav Stolper, *German Realities* (1948). As a token of the wealth of documentation in the field of military government, the following partial list, relating to Germany, is offered. *Monthly Report of the Military Governor; Official Gazette for the Control Council of Germany; Statistical Annex to the Monthly Report; Monthly Report of the Control Commission for Germany (British Element); Journal Officiel de Gouvernement Militaire de la Zone Française; Information Bulletin*, a monthly published by OMGUS; the Monthly Report for each Land (state) in the American Zone, as well as the Berlin Sector; *Central German Agencies*—a special report of the Military Governor (1946); *Summary of Council of Foreign Ministers' Agreements and Disagreements on Germany* (1947; rev. ed., 1948); *Land and Local Government in the U. S. Zone of Germany* (1947); *The Evolution of Bizonal Organization* (1948); *A Year of Potsdam* (1947); *Economic Data on Potsdam, Germany*—a Special Report of the Military Governor (1947); Monthly Reports of JEIA (Joint Export-Import Agency); and comparable special reports by all the divisions of the Office of Military Government, U. S. (OMGUS), throughout the period 1945–1949. Hence an exhaustive evaluation will be a stupendous undertaking awaiting the future student of this expanding phase of constitutionalism.

13. Re Lieber, see art. 22 of General Order No. 100, U. S. War Department (1863). The Hague Conventions are found in Carnegie Endowment for International Peace, Division of International Law, *Hague Conventions*, pamphlet Nos. 3–20 (1914–1915). See also Merle Fainsod, "The Development of American Military Government Policy during World War II," in C. J. Friedrich and Associates, op. cit.

14. For the Rhineland occupation, consult I. L. Hunt, *American Military Government of Occupied Germany 1918–1920* (mim. 1920, printed 1943), and the evaluation by Ernst Fraenkel, *Military Occupation and the Rule of Law* (1944), with a thorough critical bibliography. See also (General) Henry T. Allen, *The Rhineland Occupation* (1927). The most dramatic critical evaluation from a political standpoint is B. T. Reynolds, *Prelude to Hitler* (1933). Fraenkel was sharply criticized by William F. Sollmann, *APSR*, Vol. XXXVIII, pp. 976 ff., regarding his estimate of the German political situation.

15. Besides the numerous works on democracy cited elsewhere in this bibliography, see the article "Democracy and Education in the Current Crisis," in *Teachers College Record*, Nov. 1940, pp. 99 ff., where sixty aspects of democracy are listed, many of them incompatible with each other, but resulting from inquiries among the faculty and summed up in a *Manifesto*, drafted by Professors Briggs, Childs, and Norton. See also John R. Beery, *Current Conceptions of Democracy* (1943), where the same technique is more broadly applied, and the results of these samplings of general opinion summarized, the areas of agreement indicated, and those of disagreement suggested by a long list of questions. The difficulties of any democratization policy carried out by a large group of Americans thus divided on key issues can be virtually predicted in terms of this analysis.

16. This document is given as Appendix C in Friedrich and Associates, op. cit. pp. 415–416. JCS 1067 and JCS 1067 revised are found ibid. pp. 381 ff. and 402 ff. They are also offered by James K. Pollock and Associates, *Germany under Occupation—Illustrative Materials and Documents* (rev. ed., 1949), pp. 76 ff. and 91 ff. This helpful collection also contains General Clay's

remarkable self-restraining ordinance of June 4, 1947 instructing American military elements to respect the rights of Germans under constitutionalism.

17. See Fraenkel, op. cit. See for the rule-of-law aspect my review in *Harvard Law Review*, 58 (1945), 464 ff. and my paper "Military Government as a Step toward Self-Rule" in *Public Opinion Quarterly*, Vol. VII (1943), 527 ff., as well as "Military Government and Democratization" in Friedrich and Associates, op. cit. pp. 3 ff. See also Ch. VI, above, and references.

18. See Benson, Neufeld, op. cit. See also Mario Einaudi, "Political Change in France and Italy," *APSR*, Vol. XL (1946), pp. 898 ff. See also the Italian constitutional treatises, cited earlier, especially *La Costituzione della Repubblica Italiana* by Falzone, Palermo, and Cosentino, where the constitutional debates are digested. The position of the judiciary is given in commentary on articles 101–113, pp. 185 ff. The Control Council Law is found in Pollock, op. cit. pp. 34–35, whereas its problems are discussed by Karl Loewenstein, "Law and the Legislative Process in Occupied Germany," *Yale Law Review*, Mr.–Ap. 1948. The comparable and highly interesting Japanese situation is the subject of Alfred C. Oppler's "The Reform of Japan's Legal and Judicial System under Allied Occupation," *Washington Law Review*, Vol. 24 (1949), 290 ff. For the workings of military government courts proper, see E. E. Nobleman, "Military Government Courts: Law and Justice in the American Zone of Germany," *American Bar Association Journal* (1947).

19. For the situation in Japan, see *Prospects of Japan* (1946), Douglas C. Haring, editor, especially the papers by Fainsod, Watkins, and Friedrich as far as the governmental side is concerned. See also the paper by Arthur D. Bouterse and Arthur A. Maass, "American Military Government Experience in Japan," in Friedrich and Associates, op. cit., and the several papers in *The Annals*, Jan. 1949, dealing with Japan.

20. The quotation is from Merle Fainsod, "The Development of American Military Government Policy during World War II," in Friedrich and Associates, op. cit. p. 51. The future of military government will be shaped to a considerable extent by what conventions, if any, may become feasible in the years to come to replace the outmoded Hague Convention on the subject. An interesting contribution to the legal aspects is R. E. Elder, "Quadripartite Military Government Organization and Operations in Germany," *Am. Journal of International Law* (1947). Naturally, German lawyers have given a good deal of attention to these questions, for instance, Erich Kaufmann, *Deutschlands Rechtslage unter der Besatzung* (1948), and Wilhelm Grewe, *Ein Besatzungsstatut für Deutschland* (1948). For the general problems of the occupation statute—the text of which is given by Pollock, op. cit. pp. 294 ff. though erroneously designated as "West" German occupation statute—see the author's article in *APSR*, cited above, p. 617, note 19.

Index

This index covers both the text and the bibliography. References to the former are indicated by page numbers. References to the "Remarks" section of the bibliography are indicated by the page numbers alone, as above. Numbered footnotes in the bibliography are indicated thus: "611–7" refers to "page 611, footnote 7". "611–7, 8" refers to "page 611, footnotes 7 and 8"; "611, 611–7, 8" refers to "page 611, 'Remarks,' footnote 7, and footnote 8."